W9-CFB-853

McGRAW-HILL
SHARE
the
Music

- **Outstanding Songs, Listenings, and All-New Recordings**
- **Culturally Authentic Music**
- **Sequenced Learning Process**
- **Integrated Curriculum with Related Arts**
- **A Teacher's Edition Organized for both Music Specialists and Classroom Teachers**

COORDINATING AUTHORS
Judy Bond, Marilyn Copeland Davidson,
Mary Goetze, Vincent P. Lawrence,
Susan Snyder

AUTHORS
René Boyer-White, Margaret Campbelle-
duGard, Robert de Frece, Doug Goodkin,
Betsy M. Henderson, Michael Jothen,
Carol King, Nancy L. T. Miller, Ivy Rawlins

McGraw-Hill School Division
A Division of The McGraw-Hill Companies

Copyright © 1998, 1995 McGraw-Hill School Division, a Division of the
Educational and Professional Publishing Group of The McGraw-Hill
Companies, Inc.

McGraw-Hill School Division
1221 Avenue of the Americas
New York, New York 10020

Printed in the United States of America

ISBN 0-02-295284-5 / 6

1 2 3 4 5 6 7 8 9 073 99 98 97

**McGraw-Hill
School Division**

New York   Farmington

*C*ONTENTS

*U*NIT PLANNER

Quick reference to multicultural perspectives, integrated curriculum, assessment, concepts, skills, and technology opportunities.

*A*CROSS THE CURRICULUM

Two-page section following each Core lesson for connections to other curriculum areas, including related arts.

Meet THE MUSICIAN

Recorded Interviews—a "career motivator." Includes Linda Ronstadt, Wynton Marsalis, Midori, Bobby McFerrin, Marvin Hamlisch, Debbie Allen, Gregory Hines, and more.

Encore

Music connections to related arts, history, culture, literature, and technology in optional lessons following each unit.

TECHNOLOGY

- **Music with *MIDI*,** correlated to Grades 1–8, allows students to create and revise music with the MIDI sequencer.

- ***SHARE THE MUSIC* Videos,** for K–8, make music come alive through movement, signing, and performances.

- **Music Ace™** software, Grades 3–6, reinforces musical concepts in a lively, interactive environment.

- **MusicTime™** notational software develops music literacy through activities correlated to lessons in Grades 3–8.

All are available separately.

CELEBRATIONS

Cross-referenced section of patriotic, seasonal, and holiday songs that allows flexibility in planning your instruction.

MUSIC LIBRARY

Alternate songs and listening selections in cross-referenced *Reading, Song, Choral* (Grades 5 and 6), and *Listening* anthologies, plus *Musicals.*

OUR AUTHORS

SHARING A UNITY OF PURPOSE AND A DIVERSITY OF TALENTS

JUDY BOND
COORDINATING AUTHOR

Judy is Coordinator of Music Education at the University of Wisconsin Stevens Point. Her teaching experience includes elementary and middle school general music and high school choral music. She is a past president of the American Orff-Schulwerk Association, and has presented workshops nationally and abroad.

MARILYN COPELAND DAVIDSON
COORDINATING AUTHOR

Marilyn is a celebrated author, arranger, and composer. Her teaching experience spans over thirty years, and ranges from kindergarten through graduate courses. Marilyn has presented teacher-training sessions and workshops on the national and international level. She is a past president of the American Orff-Schulwerk Association and was a principal author of the *Music and You* series (Grades K–6).

DR. RENÉ BOYER-WHITE

René is Professor of Music Education at the University of Cincinnati's College Conservatory of Music and is widely known for her work in multi-cultural music and international presentations. A well-known national clinician, René is also president of the National Black Music Caucus of MENC and the Coordinator and Director of the Orff-Schulwerk Certification Program at the University of Cincinnati.

DR. ROBERT DE FRECE

Robert is a Professor of Music and Music Education at the University of Alberta in Edmonton, Alberta, Canada. He is director of the University of Alberta Mixed Chorus the Faculty of Education Handbell Ringers, and Edmonton's Greenwood Singers, a chamber choir which he founded in 1980. Despite his busy schedule, he finds time to teach several kindergarten music classes each week.

MARGARET CAMPBELLE-DUGARD

Margaret has been a music specialist in the Nashville, Tennessee, public schools for 13 years. She is widely known for her national and state presentations in the United States and Canada, and for her university-level Orff-Schulwerk training courses. Margaret was a contributing composer to the *Music and You* series, and she has published numerous original songs.

DR. MARY GOETZE
COORDINATING AUTHOR

Mary is an internationally known clinician, composer, arranger, and guest conductor. She has published many choral pieces and written numerous articles about children's singing and children's choirs. Mary is currently an Associate Professor of Music at the Indiana University School of Music, where she teaches music education and directs a children's choir program.

DOUG GOODKIN

Doug is a music specialist at The San Francisco School in California, where he has taught preschool through middle school since 1975. He has presented workshops and teacher-training courses in Orff-Schulwerk throughout the United States, Canada, Europe, and Australia. Doug has published numerous articles on music education, and is a founding member of the Orff performing group *Xephyr*.

DR. VINCENT P. LAWRENCE
COORDINATING AUTHOR

Vincent is a sought-after clinician and consultant in music education. He was formerly Professor of Music at Towson State University in Maryland, where he directed the University Chorale. At the same time, he was actively involved in teaching general music in the middle school. Vincent is an author of *Music and You* and of the high school text *Music! Its Role and Importance in Our Lives.*

BETSY M. HENDERSON

Betsy is the Elementary Fine Arts Coordinator for the Garland Independent School District in Texas. She is a church organist, children's choir director, workshop/festival clinician, and a director of children's musicals. Betsy has served as Elementary Chairperson for both the Texas Choral Directors Association and the Texas Music Educators Association.

NANCY L. T. MILLER

Nancy is a performing arts specialist at The College School of Webster Groves, Missouri, and also teaches the Orff certification courses at the University of Kentucky, Webster University, and St. Thomas University. In her teaching she has developed approaches that integrate music, dance, literature, and theater, and has written and produced over 25 musical plays.

DR. MICHAEL JOTHEN

Michael is an Associate Professor of Music and Coordinator of the Graduate Program in Music Education at Towson State University in Maryland. He is a nationally known music educator, choral clinician, and conductor. Michael has received many commissions for choral compositions, and has been recognized by ASCAP for his contributions as a composer. He is an author of *Music and You.*

IVY RAWLINS

Ivy lives in Indiana, where she is currently pursuing doctoral studies. Prior to this she taught methodology and supervised student teachers in the Kodály certification program of the Hartt College of Music, University of Hartford. She has also taught at Holy Names College; in Budapest, Hungary; and while serving with the Peace Corps, in Uganda, East Africa.

CAROL KING

Carol is currently an elementary school Orff specialist in the Memphis City Schools, where she also served as acting supervisor for three years. Over the years she presented numerous sessions at state and national music conferences in the United States and Canada. Carol has also published books for recorder and for Orff instruments and has coauthored many curriculum guides.

DR. SUSAN SNYDER
COORDINATING AUTHOR

Sue has taught elementary music for over twenty years, and is a prominent consultant in general music, curriculum development, early childhood, integrated language arts, multicultural education, and cooperative learning. Currently, Sue teaches at Hunter College, New York City. She is an author of the *Music and You* series.

A **P**HILOSOPHY

SHARING YOUR COMMITMENT TO SUCCESSFUL LEARNING

SHARE THE MUSIC is a child-centered program that involves students of all learning styles. Sequenced and thematic activities develop the cognitive, affective, and psychomotor domains of learners.

SHARE THE MUSIC helps you address the issues of today and tomorrow. Here's how!

OUTSTANDING SONGS, LISTENINGS, AND ALL-NEW RECORDINGS

- Present the highest-quality, age-appropriate materials in a variety of musical styles.
- Highlight the natural sound of children's voices recorded with artistic and captivating accompaniments.

CULTURALLY AUTHENTIC MUSIC

- Celebrates cultural diversity and similarities through developmentally appropriate multicultural materials and recordings.
- Broadens the students' experiences with diverse vocal techniques used in songs around the world, while consistently building vocal skills.

SEQUENCED LEARNING PROCESS

- Teaches concepts and skills through a proven learning sequence—experience, imitate and explore, describe, identify and label, practice, reinforce, read or interpret visual representation, create, and maintain.
- Integrates Kodály, Orff, Dalcroze, and traditional music approaches.
- Provides a sequenced movement curriculum as an integral part of music learning.
- Builds music literacy and understanding through singing, listening, moving, creating, music reading, critical thinking, and meaningful assessment.

 INTEGRATED CURRICULUM WITH RELATED ARTS

- Provides an *Across the Curriculum* activity section after each CORE lesson for connections to other curriculum areas and themes.
- Provides activities in related arts—art, drama, theater, dance, and literature—to develop students' awareness of the varied aspects of a culture's artistic expression.
- Connects to today's music technology through software, videos, and MIDI sequencer lessons.

ORGANIZED FOR MUSIC SPECIALISTS AND CLASSROOM TEACHERS

- Provides sequenced and thematic lesson instruction for specialists.
- Provides a **Basic Program** and curriculum-related activities for classroom teachers with minimal music experience.

AN RGANIZATION

DEDICATED TO MEETING DIVERSE TEACHING NEEDS

- **LESSONS ORGANIZED FOR 9- OR 12-MONTH SCHOOLS**

- **INSTRUCTION FOR MUSIC SPECIALISTS AND CLASSROOM TEACHERS**

- **6TH-GRADE FLEXIBLE FORMAT FOR ELEMENTARY AND MIDDLE SCHOOL CURRICULUM**

- **RELATED ARTS INTEGRATED THROUGHOUT**

GRADES K–5 ORGANIZATION

6 SEQUENCED UNITS

- **Core Lessons 1, 2, 4, 5**
  Introduce and use new concepts and skills.

- **NEW** **Across the Curriculum**

- **Non-Core Lessons 3, 6, 7, 8**
  Reinforce concepts and skills.

- **Unit Review and Assessment—Lesson 9**

NEW SPECIAL SECTIONS K–6

- **Encore**

- **Celebrations**

- **Music Library**
  Reading Anthology
  Song Anthology
  Choral Anthology (Grades 5–6)
  Listening Anthology
  Musicals

NEW GRADE 6 ORGANIZATION

UNIT 1 *The Music Makers*

- **Core Lessons 1–8**
  Introduce, use, and reinforce concepts and skills. (Can be used for a 9-week course.)

- **Across the Curriculum**

- **Unit Review and Assessment—Lesson 9**

UNITS 2–5
Musical Adventures
The Keyboard Connection
Our Musical Heritage
On Stage

- **Core Lessons 1, 2, 4, 5**
  Introduce and use new concepts and skills.

- **Across the Curriculum**

- **Non-Core Lessons 3, 6, 7, 8**
  Reinforce concepts and skills.

- **Unit Review and Assessment—Lesson 9**

UNIT 6 *From Rag to Rap*

- **Playalongs**

- **Eras of American music history**

NEW **Basic Program** activities for classroom teachers can be taught with a minimum background in music and are indicated by a ▶.

The **Grade 6** organization provides options for Elementary and Middle School curriculum differences. For more detail on this and other schedules, see Options for Scheduling in the back of the Teacher's Edition.

THE LESSON PLAN DESIGNED FOR

SHARE THE MUSIC builds on our tradition of sequential teaching from lesson to lesson and unit to unit.

Related Arts indicator shows presence of movement, theater, and visual arts content within lesson suggestions.

Song Range, Tonal Center, and Tone Se[...]

CORE LESSONS 1, 2, 4, and 5 introduce and use new concepts and skills.

NON-CORE LESSONS 3, 6, 7, and 8 reinforce and extend concepts and skills taught in CORE lessons.

LESSON PLANNER
A quick outline of the lesson.

NEW **CD NUMBER AND TRACK**
Quick reference at the point of use.

BASIC PROGRAM
Activities for **classroom teachers** can be taught with a minimum background in music and are indicated by a ▶.

MEETING INDIVIDUAL NEEDS
Optional resources for alternate strategies, extension, higher-level activities, special learner strategies, critical thinking, background information, and pronunciation guides.

Approximate lesson length:
Grades K–1, 25 minutes
Grades 2–5, 30 minutes
Grade 6, 35 or 50 minutes

UNIT FIVE
LESSON 3

RELATED ARTS MOVEMENT THEATER VISUAL ARTS

LESSON PLANNER

FOCUS Rhythm

OBJECTIVE
OBJECTIVE 1 Clap a syncopated rhythm pattern with a song

MATERIALS
Recordings
Comedy Tonight CD4:36
One CD4:37
Won't You Charleston with Me? CD4:35
Recorded Lesson: Interview with
  Marvin Hamlisch CD4:38

▶ = BASIC PROGRAM

INTERMISSION

Marvin Hamlisch wrote the musical *A Chorus Line* in 1975. In the story, a group of dancers are trying out for parts in a Broadway musical. As each performer appears, the audience learns about the sacrifices and frustrations of professional Broadway dancers. At the end of *A Chorus Line*, the dancers who have been chosen for the parts perform in the new musical, which features the song "One."

ONE

Music by Marvin Ham[...]
Words by Edward K[...]

One sin-gu-lar sen-sa-tion, ev'-ry lit-tle step she takes,—

One thrill-ing com-bi-na-tion, ev'-ry move that she mak[...]

One smile and sud-den-ly no-bod-y else will do.

You know you'll nev-er be lone-ly with you know wh[...]

200

MEETING **INDIVIDUAL** NEEDS

BACKGROUND: *A Chorus Line*  THEATER

None of its orginators expected to make any money from *A Chorus Line*. It was to be a small Off-Broadway show of innovative musical theater; Hamlisch was originally paid only $900 for the score. The show is set in the backstage of a theater sometime in 1975 where an unseen director is auditioning a group of dancers for a Broadway show. Critics loved the funny and original story, as well as the music, and within a few months *A Chorus Line* had moved to a large theater on Broadway, where it ran for more than 10 years to become one of the longest-running productions in Broad-

way history. It received a Pulitzer Prize in drama and Tony awards, and the original cast recording received a gold record.

MOVEMENT: *"One"* MOVEMENT

Basic Step (chorus-line kick): In twos, students stan[...] by side and hold hands. With the weight on the L foo[...] slightly bend their knees (1 beat) and then kick the R [...] as high as they can, straightening L knee (1 beat). Th[...] peat on the other side. When students are comfortable [...] this and the height of their kicks match, they begin to [...]

200 Lesson 3 INTERMISSION

x

CREATIVE INSTRUCTION AND MANAGEABILITY

Ooh! Sigh! Give her your at-ten-tion, Do I

One mo-ment in her pres-ence and you can for-get the rest,—

For the girl is sec-ond best— to none, son,

real-ly have to men-tion She's the one?—

RHYTHMS FROM BROADWAY

re are some dotted rhythm patterns heard in two songs from
sicals. This rhythm comes from "One."

s rhythm from "Won't You Charleston with Me?" comes from
dance, the Charleston.

AP the melodic rhythm of "Old vo-de-o-do," also from
on't You Charleston With Me?"

first three notes shown are a "short-long-short" combina-
. This is one kind of syncopated rhythm pattern. Syncopation
urs when stressed sounds are heard in unexpected places,
n as between beats.

Unit 5 On Stage **201**

---

1 GET SET

"Let's begin by singing 'Comedy Tonight.'
Keep the beat in your own way as you sing."
Have students:

▶ • Sing "Comedy Tonight" CD4:36 (page 198).

• Decide if there are beats in the melody with
no new sound on them. (yes)

"In this lesson, you're going to learn more
about a rhythm that you just sang in "Comedy
Tonight" and review a rhythm you already
know."

2 DEVELOP

1. Introduce "One" CD4:37. **Pat dotted
rhythm pattern.** Have students:

▶ • Listen to the recording and identify the vocal
category. (unchanged)

• Follow you in patting the rhythm of the introduction with alternating hands. (The rhythm
is the first dotted rhythm pattern on page 201.
A varied version is found in the coda of the
recording.)

• Recognize the ♫ pattern. (See Unit 3, Lesson 4, pages 106–109.)

• Find sections in "One" with syncopation.
(mm. 2, 3, 6, 10, 14, 18, 19, 20, 25, 27)

▶ • Read page 200, then sing "One."

**2. Review "Won't You Charleston with
Me?"** CD4:35 **(p. 197). Introduce syncopation.**
Have students:

▶ • Sing "Won't You Charleston with Me?"

• Look at the two rhythms from "Won't You
Charleston with Me?" on page 201.

• Try patting the first rhythm as they sing the
song (on *Won't you* and *Charles-ton*).

• Clap the rhythm of *Old vo-de-o-do*.

---

1 GET SET
Supports *Objectives* and relates to prior
learning and students' lives, to actively
engage and motivate them.

2 DEVELOP
Sequenced lesson steps.

---

ge their body facing to the left on the R-foot kick and
right when on the L-foot kick. They can also try this
ng each other's waists or with arms over shoulders.

ation 1: Instead of raising the whole leg as in Step 1,
nee is raised.

ation 2: Bend both knees, raise R knee, bend knees,
R leg to left. Repeat with L leg to right.

ation 3 (jump-hop step): Jump on both feet, hop on
ot and kick right (at same time), jump on both feet,
ight and kick left.

Final Form: Have four pairs work together in a "chorus
line" to put the steps together (in groupings of two, four, or
eight of the same step). For an ending, they can try the
"domino" or "wave effect" by lunging forward and/or pretending to take their hats off one after another.

Unit 5 ON STAGE **201**

Related Arts strategies in "Meeting Individual
Needs" are highlighted by logos:

MOVEMENT   THEATER   VISUAL ARTS

Piano Accompaniments conveniently bound
in a separate booklet for each grade.

THE *L*ESSON PLAN (continued)

RECORDED LESSON
Two- to five-minute Recorded Lessons that introduce, model, and reinforce parts of the lesson. The bracket indicates where the Recorded Lesson appears in the lesson.

3 APPLY
Lesson steps that present materials for application and synthesis of concepts.

UNIT FIVE LESSON 3

continued from previous page

3. Meet the composer of "One." Have students:

▶ • Read about Marvin Hamlisch.

Recorded Lesson CD4:38

▶ • Listen to "Interview with Marvin Hamlisch" and hear about his musical training and career as a composer.

▶ • Sing "One" again.

3 APPLY

Review "Comedy Tonight." Identify and clap the syncopated rhythm. Have students:

▶ • Sing "Comedy Tonight," keeping the beat.

• Find places with a "short-long-short" syncopated pattern. (There are 26 in all. Each time the words *Something* or *Nothing* are sung, these two notes and the note following them create the syncopated pattern, quarter note-half note-quarter note in ⅜ meter. The pattern also appears seven more times with different words: *Bring on the; li-ars, and; Old sit-u-; new com-pli-; Weight-y af-, just have to; No re-ci-.*)

OBJECTIVE 1 Informal Assessment
• Sing the song again, clapping this ostinato:

Meet MARVIN HAMLISCH

When Marvin Hamlisch (b. 1944) was very young, his parents noticed his musical talent. At the age of six, he began taking piano lessons at The Juilliard School of Music in New York City. Hamlisch loved to listen to musicals and rock 'n' roll. At age 7 he began to write his own songs. By the time he reached the sixth grade, Hamlisch could play songs on the piano after hearing them a few times on the radio. Later on, Hamlisch realized how much he loved to write songs and decided to become a composer.

Marvin Hamlisch has written the music for three musicals: A Chorus Line, They're Playing Our Song, and The Goodbye Girl. He has also composed music for more than forty movies. He has won three Academy Awards, or Oscars, for his film music.

202 INTERMISSION

MEETING **INDIVIDUAL** NEEDS

ALTERNATE TEACHING STRATEGY

OBJECTIVE 1 Notate the syncopated rhythm pattern for "Comedy Tonight" on the board. Have half the class step with the beat as the other half claps the rhythm. Then switch. Play the recording and have them try this twice, first without singing, then while singing along. Finally, have everyone clap the rhythm as they sing.

CAREERS: *Songwriter*

Use the interview with Marvin Hamlisch to introduce students to the career of songwriter. A songwriter may write the lyrics, melody, or both. Songwriters work in different ways. Some write the music first, then try to find appropriate lyrics. Others write the lyrics first, then try to compose the perfect tune. Some compose at the same time every while others wait until an idea strikes them. Once the s is finished, the songwriter must market it. She or he loo for a music publisher or recording act. Usually the song writer makes a demonstration cassette to play for mana performers, or publishers. The demo should be profess and show off the tune to its best advantage.

202 Lesson 3 INTERMISSION

TEACH TOWARD CAREERS

Help students discover career opportunities in:

• PUPIL EDITION sections such as *Encore*, *Meet* (recorded interviews), *Spotlight On*, and instrument-playing activities.

• TEACHER EDITION sections such as *Meeting Individual Needs* (biographies and careers).

• *MUSIC WITH MIDI, Music Ace*™, and *MusicTime*™ through hands-on experiences in music making.

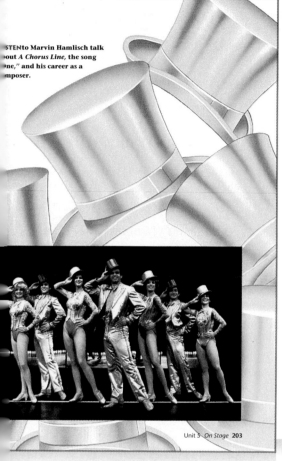

STENto Marvin Hamlisch talk
out *A Chorus Line,* the song
ne," and his career as a
mposer.

4 CLOSE

"What kind of rhythm did you learn in this lesson?" (syncopated rhythm)

"Clap some syncopated patterns with me."
(Choose two or three rhythm patterns to clap.)

Have students:
▶ • Sing "Comedy Tonight" again.

LESSON SUMMARY

Informal Assessment In this lesson,
students:

OBJECTIVE 1 Clapped a syncopated
rhythm pattern with "Comedy Tonight."

MORE MUSIC: Reinforcement
"Old Ark's A-Moverin'," page 332 (syncopation)
"Every Morning When I Wake Up," page 334
(syncopation)
"Follow the Drinkin' Gourd," page 370 (syncopation)

Unit 5 On Stage **203**

ROVISATION: *Syncopated Interludes*

students review the syncopated rhythm pattern they
ed with "Comedy Tonight" and use it in improvisa-
either as an ostinato or as an interlude between repe-
of other songs.

ENRICHMENT: *More Practice with Syncopation*

Have students try walking the beat while clapping the
melodic rhythm of "Comedy Tonight." Students might also
try making up their own syncopated patterns to clap with
the song.

Unit 5 ON STAGE **203**

---

4 CLOSE
A creative summary that provides teachers
with a check for student understanding.

LESSON SUMMARY
Indicates how each *Objective* was
accomplished.

MORE MUSIC: Reinforcement
Alternate songs and listenings in *Encore,
Celebrations,* and *Music Library* —as
well as the *Songs to Sing and Read*
component—for reinforcement and extension.

LESSON ASSESSMENT steps:
- **Informal Assessment** activities
  (Lessons 1–8) correlate to *Objectives*
  and *Alternate Strategies.*
- **Lesson Summary** indicates how each
  objective was accomplished.

UNIT ASSESSMENT steps:
- Review and Assessment (Lesson 9)
  provides a recap of unit song materials
  and measures objectives taught in
  CORE lessons.
- Recorded Assessments provide two
  options for quick informal assessment in
  the pupil edition or for formal written
  responses using the Resource Masters.

OTHER OPTIONS:
- Portfolio Options for music and related
  arts are given in each *Unit Planner.*
- Music Journal opportunities are listed
  in each *Unit Planner.*

NEW RECORDINGS

OUTSTANDING SOUNDS AND INNOVATIVE CHOICES

SONG RECORDINGS

- Children's voices that provide motivating vocal models.

- Rich, contemporary instrumental arrangements that inspire participation.

- The warm sound of analog recordings mixed and mastered with state-of-the-art digital technology.

- **Divided Tracks** allow students to hear the vocal and instrumental tracks separately.

- **Divided Vocal Parts** in part songs allow students to hear one vocal part at a time over a stereo accompaniment.

- **Performance Mixes** provide a stereo accompaniment without vocals for musicals and other selected songs.

- **Vocal performing groups** were chosen from a variety of regions, including California, Florida, Georgia, Maryland, New Jersey, Texas, Indiana, Virginia, and Utah.

RECORDED LESSONS present concepts, skills, guided listening, pronunciation for non-English songs, and movement instructions in a lively, interactive format.

RECORDED INTERVIEWS bring the voices and music of famous choreographers, actors, and musicians—Linda Ronstadt, Jean Ritchie, Midori, Wynton Marsalis, Bobby McFerrin, and others—into the classroom to help motivate students toward lifelong musical involvement.

RECORDED UNIT ASSESSMENTS use familiar and new material for pre and post-testing, and informal and formal assessment.

MUSIC ACROSS CULTURES

- Authentic song recordings from many American cultures that open a new world of understanding to your students.

- Pronunciation guides by native speakers for every non-English song.

- Variety of ethnic instruments.

- Native singers, speakers, and instrumentalists provide authentic regional music and cultural background.

INTEGRATED ARTS

VISUAL ARTS • DANCE • THEATER • MUSIC

Motivating materials invite students to explore connections among the visual arts, dance, theater, and music.

Related arts strategies in *Share the Music* are found:

- Integrated within lessons throughout Student Book and Teacher Editions.

- In "Meeting Individual Needs." These are highlighted by logos:

   THEATER   VISUAL ARTS   MOVEMENT

- On "Across the Curriculum" pages in Teacher Editions.

- Throughout *Share the Music* videos.

ENCORE Carmina

Do you remember some of the first song-and-dance games you played? Perhaps you danced to "Skip to My Lou" or played "London Bridge Is Falling Down." These songs and dances are part of a long folk tradition.

Folk songs and dances grew out of daily activities and rituals. At one time, important events, such as a birth or marriage, were celebrated with dances. Other songs refer to historical events or natural disasters. For example, the line "Ashes, ashes, all fall down" in "Ring Around the Rosy" may refer to the devastating effect of the plague over 600 years ago. Today, the original meaning of many dances is lost. Most folk dances that still exist today are performed for recreation.

THE BREVIARY OF QUEEN ISABELLA OF CASTILE
This miniature painting from about 1495 comes from an illustrated prayer book once owned by Queen Isabella of Castile (employer of Christopher Columbus). Illustrated books such as this were prepared with special colors and decorations that made the paintings glow.

Yagi Bushi
LISTENING
Japanese Folk Song

The Yagi Bushi is performed in the summer at the Bon Odori festival, a three-day celebration honoring one's ancestors. At that time, people gather at the local temple, where they build a high platform. The musicians perform from the top of the platform while the people dance and join in the chorus.

LISTEN to the song. Create your own dance steps. Then learn the traditional dance. Are any of the steps you created actually in the dance?

Encore 185

THE STORY CONTINUES...

Starlight Express
by Richard Stilgoe and Andrew Lloyd Webber

The underdog in the cross country race is Rusty, an old fashioned steam locomotive. In the first stage of the race, Rusty loses because Greaseball has used dirty tricks. Discouraged, Rusty decides not to enter the next stage. Rusty's love interest, the young railroad car named Pearl, doesn't understand the real reason why he lost and deserts him. Poppa, an old steam engine, tells Rusty about the Starlight Express, a mysterious force that can help him win. Rusty is inspired to re-enter the race.

WRITE down some words that describe Rusty's vocal tone color.

Rusty

Unit 5 • On Stage 207

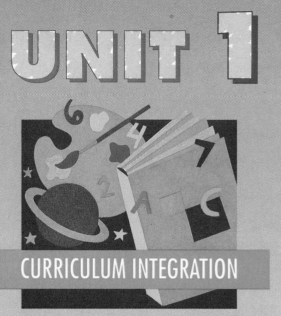

UNIT 1

MULTICULTURAL PERSPECTIVES

Through exposure to diverse materials, students develop an awareness of how people from many cultures create and participate in music. This unit includes:

African/African American and Caribbean

Asian/Asian American

European/European American

Hispanic/Hispanic American and Brazilian

For a complete listing of materials by culture throughout the book, see the Classified Index.

CURRICULUM INTEGRATION

Activities in this unit that promote the integration of music with other curriculum areas include:

Art

Math

Reading/Language Arts

Science

Social Studies

PLANNER

ASSESSMENT OPTIONS

Informal Performance Assessments

Informal Assessments correlated to Objectives are provided in every lesson with Alternate Strategies for reteaching. Frequent informal assessment allows for ongoing progress checks throughout the course of the unit.

Formal Assessment

An assessment form is provided on pupil page 40 and Resource Master 1•10. The questions assess student understanding of the following main unit objectives:

- Distinguish between band and orchestra
- Identify the four families of the orchestra
- Identify letter names of some pitches on the treble staff
- Read notation for eighth notes, quarter notes, and quarter rests

Music Journal

Encourage students to enter thoughts about selections, projects, performances, and personal progress. Some journal opportunities include:

- Cricital Thinking: Compare and Contrast, TE 9
- *Think It Through*, 16, 36
- Critical Thinking: Making Decisions, TE 37

Portfolio Opportunities

Update student portfolios with outcome-based materials, including written work, audiotapes, videotapes, and/or photos that represent their best work for each unit. Some portfolio opportunities in this unit include:

- Enrichment: The Music Makers Chart, TE 1
- Movement: Creative Movement, TE 4 (videotape)
- Playing Instruments: Samba Playalong, TE 11 (audiotape)
- Perform instrumental ostinatos with a song, TE 15 (audiotape)
- Read and perform pitched instrument playalong, 19 (audiotape)
- Create countermelody for "Fung Yang Song," 25 (audiotape)
- Improvisation: "Fung Yang Song," TE 25 (audiotape)
- Play I and V chords with song, TE 31 (audiotape)
- Movement: Choreographing "A Zing-a Za," TE 34 (audiotape)
- Check It Out; formal assessment (Resource Master 1•10), 40
- Portfolio Assessment (Resource Masters TA•1–5), 40
- Create, 41 (audio/videotape)
- Write, 41

UNIT 1 CONCEPT

			LESSON 1 CORE p.1G	LESSON 2 CORE p.8	LESSON 3 CORE p.14
FOCUS			Tone color/Form	Form	Rhythm
SELECTIONS			We Are the Music Makers (poem) Dancin' on the Rooftop Accentuate the Positive	Dancin' on the Rooftop Muss i denn (listening) A Zing-a Za National Emblem (listening)	Rock Around the Clock A Zing-a Za

MUSICAL ELEMENTS	CONCEPTS	UNIT OBJECTIVES Bold = Tested	LESSON 1 CORE	LESSON 2 CORE	LESSON 3 CORE
EXPRESSIVE QUALITIES	Dynamics		• Hear and sing *p, mp, mf, f, ff*, and diminuendo	• Hear and sing *p, mp, mf, f, ff*, and diminuendo	
	Tempo		• Hear allegro	• Hear allegro	• Hear allegro
	Articulation		• Hear marcato articulation	• Hear staccato and marcato articulation	
TONE COLOR	Vocal/ Instrumental Tone Color	• **Identify brass, woodwind, string, and percussion families** • **Distinguish between band and orchestra**	• **Hear and recognize woodwind, brass, string, and percussion families (E/D/I/P)** • **Distinguish band from orchestra (E/D/I/P)** • Identify tone color	• **Hear, learn about, and name Brazilian percussion (Rf)** • **Hear German brass band (Rf)** • **Compare bands (Rf)** • **Identify instrument families in band (Rf)**	• **Play unpitched percussion (Rf)** • **Hear rock accompaniment (Rf)**
DURATION	Beat/Meter		• *Move to emphasize beat* • Hear and sing ¾	• Move to beat • Hear and sing ¾ and ⁴⁄₄	• Hear ¾ and sing ¾ and ⁴⁄₄
	Rhythm	• **Read and perform ♪ ♪ ♩ ♩ and 𝄾**	• Clap rhythmic ostinatos (E/I)	• *Play unpitched percussion ostinatos (E)* • *Play drum patterns to show sections (E)*	• Review rhythmic notation and move to show values (D/L/P) • **Perform rhythmic ostinatos using ♪ ♪ ♩ ♩ and 𝄾 (Rf)** • **Identify song from its rhythm (Rf)**
PITCH	Melody	• **Identify some pitch letter names in treble staff** • Recognize melodic contour	• *Compare melodies of contrasting sections*		
	Harmony	• **Distinguish I and V chords**		• Notice harmony part	
	Tonality major/minor		• Hear major	• Hear major	• Hear major
DESIGN	Texture			• Hear two-part song	• Perform rhythmic ostinatos with song
	Form/ Structure	• **Recognize repeating and contrasting sections** • **Recognize A B form** • **Recognize march form** • **Recognize verse-refrain form**	• Show contrasting and repeated sections • Recognize rondo form • Understand *D.S. al Coda* and Coda	• Show form • Learn march form, intro-duction, trio, A B form • Learn and use verse-refrain form	• Review verse-refrain form • *Make up movement to show sections*
CULTURAL CONTEXT	Style/ Background		• *Poet: Arthur O'Shaughnessy* • *Composer: Teresa Jennings*	• Learn about Brazil, samba, and samba bateria • *Learn about the march* • *Composer: E. E. Bagley*	• *Learn about "Rock Around the Clock"*

Learning Sequence: E = Explore, D = Describe, I = Identify, P = Practice, Rf = Reinforce, Rd = Read, C = Create   See also *Program Scope and Sequence,* page 432.

OVERVIEW

Italic = Meeting Individual Needs

LESSON 4 CORE p.18	LESSON 5 CORE p.22	LESSON 6 CORE p.26	LESSON 7 CORE p.30	LESSON 8 CORE p.34
Pitch	Pitch	Texture/Tone color	Pitch/Harmony	Tone color
A Zing-a Za Dancin' on the Rooftop Fung Yang Song	A Zing-a Za I Shall Sing Fung Yang Song	I Shall Sing You Sing for Me Capriccio espagnol (listening)	I Shall Sing Walk Together Children Day-O	Music for the World Dancin' on the Rooftop A Zing-a Za Rock Around the Clock
		• Hear *ppp* through *f*, cresc., dim.		• Hear and sing *mf*, *f*, *ff*
• Hear and sing andante	• Hear and sing allegro and andante	• Hear allegretto, allegro, presto, accelerando	• Hear and sing allegretto, andante	• Hear and sing allegro
	• Sing accent	• Hear staccato, accent, legato, marcato • Sing accent	• Hear accent	
• **Listen for percussion instruments in accompaniment (Rf)**		• **Hear and recognize stringed instruments (P/Rf)** • **Recognize families of orchestra (P/Rf)** • **Compare band and orchestra (Rf)**	• **Learn about and hear steel band (Rf)**	• **Recognize instruments and families (Rf)** • **Learn about and create arrangement (Rf/C)** • *List favorite songs and their instruments (Rf)*
• Hear and sing ⅔ and ¼	• Hear and sing ⅔ and ¼	• Hear ⅝ and ⅔	• Hear and sing ⅔	• *Devise movement using 4-beat ostinatos*
• **Recognize and clap note values in playalong (Rd)** • **Speak song rhythm (Rd)**	• **Play countermelody using rhythmic ostinatos (Rd)** • *Play melody using song rhythm (Rd)*		• *Create and notate rhythmic ostinatos (C)*	• **Choose rhythmic ostinato to play with song (Rf/Rd)**
• **Show melodic contour of treble staff pitches (E/D)** • **List song pitches from low to high (I)** • **Sing pitch letter names (P/Rf)**	• **Play and sing from nota- tion with pitch letter names, pitch syllables, hand signs (Rd)** • **Read notes of melody on staff from low to high with letter names (Rd)** • **Learn about ledger lines (Rd)** • **Create melodies (C)**			• **Read pitch letter names (Rd)**
• Sing melody and countermelody	• Learn about counter- melody and sing with song		• Learn about, recognize, sing, and play I and V chords in C major • *Play guitar to accompany song*	
• Hear major	• Hear major	• Hear major and minor	• Review C major scale	• Hear major
• Sing melody and counter- melody	• Sing melody and counter- melody	• Discuss effect of adding countermelody to song • Learn about texture • Distinguish texture changes		• Learn about arranging songs • *List favorite songs and use of texture* • Make up and compare song arrangements
	• Recognize verse-refrain form	• Recognize verse-refrain form		• *Make up movement to show verse-refrain form*
• *Learn about "Fung Yang Song" and traveling Chinese musicians*	• *Composer: Van Morrison*	• *Learn about Nicolai Rimsky-Korsakov*	• Learn about steel band • *Learn about spirituals*	• Learn about the career of arranger

UNIT 1

SKILLS

SKILLS		LESSON 1 CORE p.2	LESSON 2 CORE p.8	LESSON 3 CORE p.14
CREATION AND PERFORMANCE	Singing	• *Practice good posture and breathing for singing* • Sing *p*, *mp*, *mf*, *f*, *ff*, and diminuendo • *Sing in scat style* • *Expand the vocal range*	• Sing *p*, *mp*, *mf*, *f*, *ff*, and diminuendo	• Echo speech rhythms
	Playing	• Clap rhythmic ostinatos with song	• *Create unpitched percussion ostinatos for song* • *Create drum patterns for sections of listening*	• Perform unpitched percussion ostinatos with song
	Moving	• Move to identify same and different sections of song • *Move to emphasize beat* • *Create movement for song sections*	• Create movement variations to show form of song • *Individually lead class in movement to show form*	• *Create movement to reflect song form and words* • Perform song rhythm with body percussion • *Move to represent different note values*
	Improvising/ Creating	• *Create movement for song sections*	• Create movement variations to show form of song • *Create unpitched percussion ostinatos for song* • *Create drum patterns for sections of listening*	• *Create movement to reflect song form and words* • *Create and notate one-measure rhythm patterns*
NOTATION	Reading		• Notice parts in two-part song	• Review rhythmic notation • Read rhythmic ostinatos and song rhythm • *Move to show rhythmic notation*
	Writing		• Show form with letters and words	• *Create and notate one-measure rhythm patterns*
PERCEPTION AND ANALYSIS	Listening/ Describing/ Analyzing	• Describe contrast and repetition in a song	• *Compare and contrast two bands*	• Identify song from its rhythm

 **TECHNOLOGY**

SHARE THE MUSIC VIDEOS

Use videos to reinforce, extend, and enrich learning.
• **Lesson 1, pp. 2–5:** Making a Music Video (popular music, ideas to videotape); Musical Expression (big band)
• **Lesson 2, p. 10:** Sounds of Percussion (samba bateria)
• **Lesson 4, p. 21A:** Making a Music Video (music and images)
• **Lesson 5, p. 24:** Making a Music Video (ideas to videotape)
• **Lesson 6, pp. 28–29:** Musical Expression (Rimsky-Korsakov)
• **Lesson 7, p. 32:** Sounds of Percussion (steel drum band)
• **Lesson 8, pp. 36–37:** Creating Musical Moods (arranging)

MUSIC WITH *MIDI*

MIDI technology allows students to manipulate musical elements and make musical decisions with this song:
• **Lesson 7, p. 30:** Walk Together Children

MUSICTIME™

This notational software develops students' music reading and writing skills through activities correlated to these lessons:
• **Lesson 3, Project 1** (review and notate basic rhythm patterns)
• **Lesson 7 Project 2** (create rhythmic ostinatos)
• **Lesson 9, Project 3** (create an accompaniment for a song)

OVERVIEW

Italic = Meeting Individual Needs

LESSON 4 CORE p.18	LESSON 5 CORE p.22	LESSON 6 CORE p.26	LESSON 7 CORE p.30	LESSON 8 CORE p.34
• Speak rhythm of song • *Learn about and practice singing in two parts*	• Sing accents	• Sing accents	• Sing chord roots	• Sing *mf, f, ff*
• Create and play pitched accompaniment to song	• Play melodic fragments from notation and identify songs • Create and play counter-melody for song • *Improvise section of song*	• Play I and V chords to accompany song • *Play arpeggiated chords* • *Play tremolo I and V chords with songs*	• *Play rhythmic ostinatos for a song*	• Choose rhythmic ostinato to play with song
• *Move to show melodic contour of song* • *Create dance to accompany song*	• *Perform song with hand signs*	• Perform square dance with a song • *Stand when they hear an assigned instrument or section*	• *Create pantomime movement to fit words of song*	• *Create movement for song to show verse-refrain form using movement ostinatos*
• Create pitched accompaniment to song • *Create dance to accompany song*	• Create counter-melody for song • *Improvise pentatonic section for song using song rhythm*		• Create body percussion patterns to signal chord changes • *Create pantomime movement to fit words of a song*	• *Create movement for song to show verse-refrain form* • Create song arrangement
• Trace melodic contour of song • Read pitch letter names of and perform playalong • Identify same melodic contour • Identify and clap note values • Speak notated song rhythm	• Play and sing melodic fragments from notation and identify songs with letter names • Learn about ledger lines	• Learn about ties		
• Trace melodic contour of song measures in the air • List song pitches from low to high • *Show melodic contour of song with handprints*	• Write notes of melody on staff from low to high with letter names • *Write pitches of melody on staff with letter names* • *List song pitches*		• *Play and notate rhythmic ostinatos for song*	
		• Describe effect of adding counter-melody to song • Describe texture changes		• Describe how arrangement expresses song words • Compare arrangments of song

MUSIC ACE™

Music Ace reinforces musical concepts and provides ear-training opportunities for students.
Lesson 4, p. 18: Lesson 1 (pitch names); Lesson 17 (song pitches); Lesson 24 (ascending and descending pitches)
Lesson 8, p. 34: Lesson 9 (pitch identification)

UNIT ONE
LESSON 1

RELATED ARTS | MOVEMENT | THEATER | VISUAL ARTS |

UNIT 1
MUSIC

LESSON PLANNER

FOCUS Tone color/Form

OBJECTIVES
OBJECTIVE 1 Signal to show recognition of brass, woodwind, and percussion instruments in a recording (tested)

OBJECTIVE 2 Show the repeating and contrasting sections of a song by performing two different ostinatos

OBJECTIVE 3 Signal to indicate whether a song is played by a band or an orchestra (tested)

MATERIALS
Recordings
Dancin' on the Rooftop   CD1:1
Accentuate the Positive   CD1:2

Resources
Resource Master 1 • 1 (practice)
Resource Master 1 • 2 (practice)
Resource Master 1 • 3 (background)
Musical Instruments Masters—saxophone, trombone, trumpet

VOCABULARY
tone color, coda, big band, band, orchestra

▶ = **BASIC PROGRAM**

MEETING **INDIVIDUAL** NEEDS

VOCAL DEVELOPMENT: *Posture and Breathing*

Posture: Good posture is necessary to breathe correctly for singing. If standing, have students place their feet slightly apart with the weight evenly balanced on both feet. Have them raise their arms up over their heads and bring them down. This will put the shoulders back and down, the correct position for singing. If sitting, have the students sit tall, with their shoulders relaxed, back and down. Teach students that this is the "singing position."

Breathing: Breathing for singing needs to be deeper than normal breathing to get the energy (breath) needed to

support the singing tone. Have students assume the "singing position," then put one hand on their abdomens with the other on their sides at the waist. Have them pretend they are slowly sipping juice through a straw, inhaling to the count of three and exhaling on *s-s-s* to the count of five. Explain that they should feel their abdominal and waist muscles expand. Repeat this step, inhaling to the count of four and exhaling to the count of five. (Explain that they must control the exhalation of air to have enough to sing musical phrases in one breath.) Finally, have students "sip in" air and sing the first phrase of "The Star-Spangled Banner" in one breath.

MAKERS

FROM

WE ARE THE MUSIC MAKERS

We are the music makers
We are the dreamers of dreams
We are the movers and shakers
of the world, forever, it seems.

—*Arthur O'Shaughnessy*

"No matter who they are or where they live, most people enjoy making music. Many people find it's even more fun when they have someone to share the music with." Have students:

▶ • Read "We Are the Music Makers" and share something about "music makers" they know of who work in groups. (As students talk, write the names and kinds of the musical groups they mention on the board.)

"As we learn about music makers this year, you will hear many different groups. You will meet some of them in this lesson. Through singing, moving, and playing instruments, you too will have a chance to be music makers."

BIOGRAPHY: *Arthur William Edgar O'Shaughnessy*

Arthur O'Shaughnessy (1844–1881) was an English poet of many talents—he was also a scientist, a translator, a writer. As a scientist, he studied reptiles and amphibians and published several papers, even though he had received no formal training. He was also an expert translator of French to English. As a poet, he published four books of short poems. He also wrote a book of children's stories with his wife. Sadly though, O'Shaughnessy had a short life that was marked by tragedy. Although he lived to be only 37, both his wife and two children died before him.

ENRICHMENT: *The Music Makers Chart*

Have students begin a chart of music groups that can become a year-long project. As students hear recordings or go to concerts, they can add the names of the groups to the chart, listing comments about the kinds of ensembles heard, the number of musicians used, the types of instruments played, and so on. Newspaper and magazine clippings about musical groups could also be added to their notebooks or displayed on a bulletin board. (Optional: Use **Resource Master 1 • 1.**)

UNIT ONE
LESSON 1

continued from previous page

2 DEVELOP

1. Introduce "Dancin' on the Rooftop"
CD1:1. **Move to identify same and different sections of a song.** Have students:

• Follow you as you move. (Play "Dancin' on the Rooftop" without revealing the title. See *Movement* below.)

• Describe how parts of the movement sequence show contrast and repetition. (Forward/backward walk contrasts with grapevine-like walk to the side and moving in place; the A and B sections repeat.)

• Say what the form is. (Students may recognize: intro A B A C A B A coda—rondo form.)

Let's get together, movers and shakers!

MOVE along with the sections of this song. Show the contrast and repetition in the form of the song with contrasting and repeated movements.

D minor

Dancin' on the Rooftop

Words and Music by
Teresa Jennings

I'm danc-in' on the roof-top, roof-top, roof-top.
Danc-in' in my sneak-ers, heel and toe. I'm swing-in' on a tree-top,
tree-top, tree-top. Hang-in' by my shoe-strings. Watch me go! The
weath-er's fine on ol' Cloud Nine. All the birds are danc-in',
too. But I won't come down to the ground till I find my par-a-

2

MEETING **INDIVIDUAL** NEEDS

BIOGRAPHY: *Teresa Jennings*

American composer Teresa Jennings (b. 1956) says music has always been important in her life. One of Jennings's earliest memories is of sitting under a grand piano, listening as her father, Donald Riggio, conducted rehearsals for everything from operas to Broadway musicals. Her mother, Suzanne, was a well-known horn player. Jennings became a virtuoso oboist who also plays many other instruments. Her primary focus is composing, particularly music for children to sing. Her work with jazz and rock has helped develop her unique style.

MOVEMENT: *"Dancin' on the Rooftop"*   MOVEMENT

Introduction: Knee bounces in place, arms moving to the beat.

A section: (Each step or snap takes one beat.)
(Verbal Cue—*step, snap*) Step forward, then snap. (8 times—16 beats)
Step backward, then snap. (8 times—16 beats)

B section: 7 grapevine-like steps to one side and clap on 8: *side, back, side, front, side, back, side, clap.* Repeat same t the opposite side.

A section: Repeat A section.

2. Sing "Dancin' on the Rooftop" with movement. Have students:

▶ • Sing "Dancin' on the Rooftop." (The style of singing in section C is called *scat singing*. Scat singing uses nonsense syllables to imitate the sounds of instruments. When students sing *Wa wa wa wa*, the curved lines leading to the notes mean that they should start slightly below the written pitch and slide up to it.)

• Practice the movement, then perform it with the song.

Dance Break—Touch R foot on R side, step R (in place), then touch L foot on L side and step L. Repeat sequence once, then do one more step on R foot. (4½ measures— count to 9.)

Do a low turn for remaining 3½ measures.

C section: Movement in place

Scat Singing—In place, echo rhythms of scat singing, using varied body percussion.

A section: Repeat A section.

B section: Repeat B section.

A section: Repeat A section.

Coda: Continue A-section-style movement, responding to changes in dynamics by changing range of movement.

MOVEMENT: *Walk to the Beat*

Play "Dancin'" again as students improvise their own walk around the room, emphasizing the beat. You may give signals for changes in direction (walking backward or forward), body facing (turning to 3 o'clock, 6 o'clock), level (walking short or tall), and range (large or small steps).

UNIT ONE
LESSON 1

continued from previous page

3. Identify instruments and their families in the big band accompaniment to "Dancin' on the Rooftop." Have students:

▶ • Read the definition of tone color on page 5. Identify the instruments they heard in the recording of "Dancin' on the Rooftop" and the instrument families to which they belong. (brass—trumpets and trombones; woodwind—saxophones; percussion—piano and drums; string—string bass)

▶ • Read about *D.S. al Coda* and coda.

OBJECTIVE 1 Informal Assessment

▶ • Listen to the recording, signaling when an instrument family is clearly heard: hand open for brass, hand closed for woodwinds, and two hands clasped for percussion.

The famous big band,
The Sweethearts of Rhythm

4

MEETING **INDIVIDUAL** NEEDS

ALTERNATE TEACHING STRATEGY

OBJECTIVE 1 Play the recording again, stopping just after a solo instrument or instrument family has played. Ask students to describe and name the instrument(s). Repeat until they have successfully identified all the featured instruments. Then ask them to compare the similarities and differences between these instruments. (Optional: Use **Resource Master 1 • 2** to review the four instrument families.)

ENRICHMENT: *Student Performance Videotape*

A series of performance tapings (video or audio) could be made during the year, including a choral work, instrumental playalong, folk dance, original choreography, dramatic reading, choral reading of a poem, song with instrumental accompaniment and dance, and even some solo or small group performances. This project could represent the best performances of the class and culminate in a viewing by parents or other classes.

4. Identify big band instruments. Have students:

▶ • Look at the picture of a 1940s big band on pages 4–5 and read about big bands and the difference between a band and an orchestra.

▶ • Name the instruments in the picture and their families. (saxophones—woodwind; trombones, trumpets—brass; drum set, piano—percussion; guitar, string bass—string)

Tone color refers to the special sound of each musical instrument. What instruments did you hear in "Dancin' on the Rooftop"? To which family does each of these instruments belong?

The marking *D.S. al Coda* tells you to go back to the sign (𝄋) at the beginning of the song. When you see this sign, ⊕, jump ahead to the section marked *Coda*. A **coda** is a short section of music that brings the song to a definite close.

This group includes the same instruments used in "Dancin' on the Rooftop." It is called a **big band**. Groups like this were popular in the 1930s and 1940s. These years were known as the "Big Band Era." The group is a **band** because it features the woodwind, brass, and percussion families. If the group also featured strings, it wouldn't be a band. It would be an **orchestra**.

NAME as many of the instruments as you can.

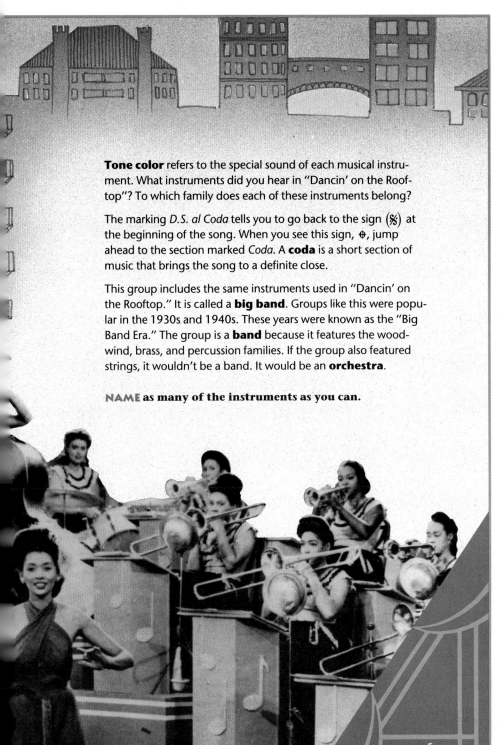

5

 MOVEMENT: *Creative Movement*

Divide the class into small groups to choreograph each section of "Dancin' on the Rooftop": A B C coda. Groups can choreograph either the entire song or just one section. Encourage students to move with the beat and to show contrast and repetition in their movements. They can include locomotion, body and arm movements, and/or body percussion. Students needing a starting point could begin with the movement introduced in *Develop 1* and create group spatial variations (forward/backward, right/left, high/low, circle/line). Students doing the C section may wish to pantomime instrument-playing during the scat singing.

 MOVEMENT: *Assessment Guidelines*

Help students develop their capabilities for meaningful assessment of movement by providing opportunities for them to critique each other's work. Encourage them to say what they liked as well as making suggestions for changes. The following terms will help them describe what they see.

Movement: locomotion, body design, spatial formations, pathways, facings, range

Choreography: theme, variations, unity, contrast

Performance: beginning—middle—end; unison, style, energy, relation to partner/group/audience

UNIT ONE
LESSON 1

continued from previous page

5. Introduce "Accentuate the Positive"
CD1:2. Notice contrast and repetition in the form. Have students:

▶ • Listen to the song and follow as you perform two different ostinatos, joining in as they are able. (Each rest or clap takes one beat.)

A section: *rest-clap, rest-clap*
B section: *rest-clap, clap-rest*

OBJECTIVE 2 Informal Assessment

▶ • Form two groups, one group singing the song along with the recording, the other performing the two ostinatos above as accompaniment to the A and B sections. Switch groups and repeat.

3 APPLY

Distinguish a band from an orchestra in the recording of "Accentuate the Positive."
Have students:

▶ • Review the difference between a band and an orchestra. (See page 5.)

OBJECTIVE 3 Informal Assessment

▶ • Listen to the recording, and hold thumbs-up if this musical group is a band, or make an *O* if it is an orchestra. (band)

This song was written in the 1940s during World War II. Why do you suppose a song about being positive was so popular at that time?

LISTEN for the instruments that accompany the singer.

ACCENTUATE THE POSITIVE

With a Swing

Music by Harold Arlen
Words by Johnny Mercer

You've got to ac - cen - tu - ate the pos - i - tive,

E - lim - i - nate the neg - a - tive,—

Latch on to the af - firm - a - tive,

Don't mess with Mis- ter In - be - tween.— You've got to spread joy

F major

6 MUSIC MOVES

MEETING **INDIVIDUAL** NEEDS

ALTERNATE TEACHING STRATEGIES

OBJECTIVE 2 Help students clearly identify the A section. Sing it for them and ask them to sing it for you as they look at the notation. Then ask them to find the beginnings of the other two A sections. The B section is very different, both rhythmically and melodically, from the A section. If students still don't change ostinatos at the correct time, the body percussion may be the problem. Change the ostinato so that they pat instead of resting.

OBJECTIVE 3 Ask students what instrument families form a band. (woodwinds, brass, percussion) Then ask which

instrument family is prominent in an orchestra, but not in a band. (strings) Have students notice that "Accentuate" features woodwind, brass, and percussion (including piano); so the group performing is a band.

SPECIAL LEARNERS: *Accentuating the Positive*

Children with disabilities should have opportunities to develop friendships with nondisabled peers early in the school year. Small group activities (no more than one disabled student per group) provide ideal opportunities for social and musical development. Have groups make decisions

"Today you sang two new songs. What were they and what did you discover about their form?" ("Dancin' on the Rooftop" and "Accentuate the Positive." Each had contrast and repetition, yet were put together in different ways. "Dancin' on the Rooftop" has a rondo form, "Accentuate the Positive" is A A B A.) Have students:

▶ • Listen for the instruments and form as they sing "Accentuate the Positive" with the recording. (Optional: Have students complete **Resource Master 1 • 3** to learn more about songwriters Johnny Mercer and Harold Arlen.)

LESSON SUMMARY

Informal Assessment In this lesson, students:

OBJECTIVE 1 Signaled to show recognition of brass, woodwind, and percussion instruments in the recording of "Dancin' on the Rooftop."

OBJECTIVE 2 Showed the repeating and contrasting sections of "Accentuate the Positive" (A A B A) by performing two different ostinatos.

OBJECTIVE 3 Signaled to indicate whether "Accentuate the Positive" was played by a band or an orchestra.

MORE MUSIC: Reinforcement

"O Canada," page 290 (band instruments)
Symphony No. 5 in C Minor, Op. 67, First Movement, page 413C (orchestra)
"Ride of the Valkyries," page 413E (contrasting/repeating sections, brass family)
"Seventeen Come Sunday," page 413G (contrasting/repeating sections, band instruments, *D.S.*, coda)

---

regarding which instruments were heard, which families, and so on. Emphasize that groups should encourage all members to participate in the decision and *Accentuate the positive* regarding contributions.

VOCAL DEVELOPMENT: *Vocal Range*

The following vocalise develops students' higher singing range so that they can sing higher pitches in "Accentuate the Positive" with a free and unstrained vocal quality.

Continue up by half steps to E' or F. Say breathe *on Beat 3 so that students breathe on Beat 4.*

Oo,   oo———   (breathe)   Oo,   oo———   (breathe)

Demonstrate the vocalise. Have students assume the correct posture for singing and breathe deeply. (See page 1G, *Vocal Development.*) Then ask them to breathe and feel the beginning of a yawn in the back of their throats as they sing the *oo* (lips rounded, but not tight). Tell them to think the pitch and raise their hands and imagine touching the pitch above their heads. Finally, have students move one hand upward as they sing to help avoid flatting the pitch.

ACROSS the

LANGUAGE ARTS / ART

MURAL

"We Are the Music Makers"

GROUP   **15–30 MIN**

MATERIALS: mural paper, paints, brushes, used magazines, tape, scissors, reference books

Have the class prepare a mural celebrating "Music Makers" of today and the past. Each student lists favorite performers, composers, and other music makers. They share lists and form groups based on common interests. Within each group, students prepare biographies, paint portraits, or bring in magazine pictures to represent the musicians they choose.

Each group contributes its work to the class mural. Help students organize the mural by categories or time periods. Once the mural is started, students can add to it throughout the year.

Students can include images of themselves as music makers in the mural—pictures of themselves playing instruments, singing, whistling, or just tapping rhythms.

COMPREHENSION STRATEGY: Organizing and displaying information

SOCIAL STUDIES / ART

NEIGHBORHOOD MAP

"Dancin' on the Rooftop"

PAIR   **15–30 MIN**

MATERIALS: drawing paper, rulers, colored pencils, markers

Have students imagine they could have a bird's-eye view of their neighborhoods' rooftops. Working in pairs, have them draw maps of their neighborhoods—as if they were able to look down over the houses, buildings, roads, and streets.

Partners should draw the streets and roads and then brainstorm to identify all the buildings whose rooftops they will add to their maps. They should be careful to represent direction as accurately as they can. Have them draw a directional rosette in the lower right-hand corner as a guide.

COMPREHENSION STRATEGY: Exploring spatial relationships

CURRICULUM

SCIENCE

PARACHUTE MODEL

"Dancin' on the Rooftop"

INDIVIDUAL   **15–30 MIN**

MATERIALS: paper napkin (large square), yarn (30-cm pieces), number cube (or piece of cork), pencil

The song mentions a parachute. Students can build a parachute model to explore air resistance.

They start by poking eight tiny, pencil-point holes in a paper napkin—one in each corner, and one midway between corners (along each edge). They tie one end of a piece of yarn to each hole. (All pieces must be the same length.) Finally, they tape the free ends of the pieces of yarn to the number cube, distributing the ends evenly around the sides of the cube. They hold their parachutes by "pinching" them at the center of the napkin, lifting them so that the cube dangles, and letting them fall.

Students can refine their models—by using different lengths of yarn, lifting to different heights, and cutting the napkin to smaller areas.

COMPREHENSION STRATEGIES: Using models, revising

MATHEMATICS

COORDINATE GAME

"Accentuate the Positive"

PAIR   **15 MIN OR LESS**

MATERIALS: graph paper, number cube, math counter, colored pencils (different for each player), ruler

Preparation: Mark the counter with crayon, X on one side and Y on the other. Draw a horizontal line across the middle of the graph paper. Draw a vertical line down the center.

To play: One player starts by placing a pencil point where the two lines meet. That player will move the pencil based on flipping the counter and tossing the number cube:

- X—the player moves left or right;
- Y—the player moves up or down.

The player moves along a line by the number of squares indicated by the number cube. The other partner decides the direction by announcing *positive* (X—right; Y—up) or *negative* (X—left; Y—down). The pencil should not extend past the edge of the paper. Players alternate. Each player moves three times. The player who has moved farther from the starting point wins. (Players use the ruler to measure distances.)

COMPREHENSION STRATEGIES: Following directions, exploring spatial relationships

UNIT ONE
LESSON 2

RELATED ARTS MOVEMENT | THEATER | VISUAL ARTS

LESSON PLANNER

FOCUS Form

OBJECTIVES
OBJECTIVE 1 Signal recognition of A B form in a song
OBJECTIVE 2 Identify march form in a recording by sequencing form cards

MATERIALS
Recordings
Dancin' on the Rooftop   CD1:1
Listening: Muss i denn   CD1:3
A Zing-a Za   CD1:4
Listening: National Emblem by
  E. E. Bagley   CD1:5

Other Optional—index cards

Resources
Resource Master 1 • 4 (practice)
Listening Map Transparency T • 1
  (Muss i denn)
Musical Instruments Masters—brass
  family, flute/piccolo, percussion family,
  woodwind family

VOCABULARY
march form, introduction, trio, verse-refrain form

▶ = **BASIC PROGRAM**

Step to the Music

Here's a marching band. This group is from Bavaria, in southern Germany. What families of instruments are shown below?
brass and percussion

Most music in **march form** goes something like this:

Introduction	AA	BB	Trio Trio

An **introduction** lets us hear the style, key, and tempo before the main part of the piece starts. The **trio** of a march contrasts with the sections that come before it. Trios were once played by only three instruments.

MEETING **INDIVIDUAL** NEEDS

BUILDING SELF-ESTEEM: *Follow the Dancer* ᴹᴼⱽᴱᴹᴱᴺᵀ

Give volunteers an opportunity to lead the class in the movement they have developed for one of the sections of "Dancin' on the Rooftop." Have a different student lead each section. In all, seven students would take turns leading during one listening. You could further challenge them by saying that each leader must do movement that does not repeat any movement in the preceding section. Leading a group is challenging because of the fear of making a "mistake" in front of one's peers. Facing this fear and going beyond it can help students grow in self-confidence.

BACKGROUND: *The March*

Marching music began as a way to keep soldiers moving together in formation. The music gave courage to the soldiers, and sometimes the tight, disciplined formations alone were enough to scare off the enemy. To keep marchers in step, the march had a strong rhythm, usually a regular, repeated drum rhythm. During the 1600s, the march stepped off the battlefield and into operas and ballets. From there it moved into weddings and funerals. For example, the wedding march (often called "Here Comes the Bride") is from *Lohengrin*, an 1848 opera by German composer Richard Wagner.

Muss i denn German March
LISTENING

The melody of a popular German folk song is heard in the trio of this march.

LISTENING MAP Listen for the form and follow the map as you hear this Bavarian band.

Introduction

: A :|

|: B :|

Trio 1

Trio 2

Unit 1 *Music Makers* 9

"See how well you remember the movement we did for each of the three sections of 'Dancin' on the Rooftop.'" Have students:

• Recall the movement. (walked forward/backward on A, walked sideways on B, echoed rhythms in place during C—See *Movement* on pages 2–3.)

• Listen and move using new movement variations (see *Movement* below), singing along as much as possible CD1:1.

• Tell the form of the song and what kind of musical ensemble accompanied it. (A B A C A B A; big band)

"Today you are going to hear more musical forms and other musical groups."

2 DEVELOP

1. Introduce "Muss i denn" CD1:3. **Learn about march form.** Have students:

▶ • Look at the photo of the Bavarian band in their books and tell what instruments they see. (trombones, tubas, bass drum, snare drum)

▶ • Compare the instrument families in the photo with those in the photo of the big band on pages 4–5. (The Bavarian band pictured has no woodwinds or strings.)

▶ • Read about march form, introduction, and trio.

▶ • Follow the listening map as they listen to "Muss i denn" (mʊs i dɛn). (Optional: Use **Listening Map Transparency T • 1.**)

▶ • Identify the form. (intro A A B B trio 1 trio 2)

Today, processional marches, especially Edward Elgar's *Pomp and Circumstance Number 1,* are also heard at school ceremonies. The title of "March King," however, belongs to John Philip Sousa, an American band leader who wrote many famous marches, including *Stars and Stripes Forever.*

MOVEMENT: *"Dancin' on the Rooftop" Variations* MOVEMENT

A section: Do a jazzy walk around the room.

B section: Add high-level movement to the sideways walks. (High-level movement includes raising arms, standing taller, stretching, jumping, leaping, or hopping.)

C section: While echoing rhythms, stay close to the floor or on the floor itself.

CRITICAL THINKING: *Compare and Contrast*

Initiate a discussion about why the Bavarian band and the one that played "Dancin' on the Rooftop" are both classified as bands. Students might begin by listing characteristics that are the same and those that are different. Do they agree with the classification?

UNIT ONE
LESSON 2

These performers belong to a group called a **samba bateria.** The music they are performing is samba. Samba was invented in Brazil and was influenced by African music. It is especially popular at carnival time, in February or March. Which family of instruments is pictured here?

10 STEP TO THE MUSIC

continued from previous page

2. Introduce "A Zing-a Za" CD1:4. **Listen to a samba bateria.** Have students:

▶ • Read about the samba bateria (**sam** bə ba te **ri** a) and answer the question about the family of instruments pictured. (percussion, the only family in a traditional samba bateria, which usually includes drums of various sizes and shapes, tambourines, agogo bells, scrapers, and shakers)

▶ • Listen to the first verse and refrain of "A Zing-a Za" (a **zing** a **za**), paying attention to the accompaniment.

▶ • Try to name the instruments in the accompaniment (the percussion instruments of the samba bateria plus a guitar) and compare them with the instruments in the other two bands they have heard. (This one has mostly percussion instruments, no brass or woodwinds.)

MEETING **INDIVIDUAL** NEEDS

ALTERNATE TEACHING STRATEGY

OBJECTIVE 1 Ask students to sing only the section with the words *A zing-a za, O le, O la.* Ask them what section of the song they were singing. (B) Then ask what the other sections were. (A)

MULTICULTURAL PERSPECTIVES: *Samba*

MOVEMENT

The samba (**sam** bə) is a Brazilian dance music that has its roots in African rhythms. Traditional samba is performed by a solo dancer in the middle of a circle of dancers. A ballroom dance version of the samba spread to many other countries during the 1930s and 1940s. This dance is done by partners who tilt backward on the forward steps and forward on the backward steps.

BACKGROUND: *Brazil*

Brazil produced varied musical styles—the samba in the 1940s, the bossa nova (a cross between the samba and jazz) in the early 1960s, and Tropicalismo (a mixture of peasant music, samba, and rock 'n' roll) in the 1980s. Brazil has the world's largest tropical rain forest, thousands of miles of beautiful coastline, mountains, and dry plains. The places mentioned in "A Zing-a Za" refer to states (or their capital

A Zing-a Za

Brazilian Rural Samba
Arranged by Mary Goetze

C major

Verse

1. Ma - ri - a from old Ba - hi - a, Though
2. Ma - ri - a from Per - nam - bu - co, I'll
3. Ma - ri - a from ole São Paul - o Who
4. Ma - ri - a from Ri -o de Ja - nei - ro, With
5. Ma - ri - a, Ma - ri-a, Ma - ri - a, From

Verses 4 and 5 only

I long for Ri - o de Ja - nei - ro,

we nev - er can a - gree - a; Don't
fol - low where - ev - er you go; I'll
cares if you shriek or growl - o Or
cab - bage leaves in your hair - o; Don't
you I can nev-er be free - a, From

I long for Ri - o de Ja - nei - ro,

mat - ter at all to me - a,
stick to you just like glue - o,
yo - del or yell or yowl - o,
wor - ry 'bout what you wear - o,
now to e - ter - ni - ty - a,

I long for Ri - o de Ja - nei - ro,

Unit 1 *Music Makers* 11

---

3. Identify the form of "A Zing-a Za" as A B. Have students:

▶ • Notice that the notation is written for two different groups singing at the same time and that the second staff is shaded. (Explain that in this lesson they will sing only the unshaded melody.)

▶ • Listen to the first verse and refrain of "A Zing-a Za," tell how many sections were heard, and identify the form. (A B)

OBJECTIVE 1 Informal Assessment

▶ • Sing the entire song and show recognition of the section changes by raising a hand while singing the A section and putting it down during the B section.

---

cities) located along the east coast, where most of the population lives: the northeast state of Bahia (bɑ hi ə)—whose capital is Salvador (sæl və dor); Pernambuco (per nəm bu ko)—a state to the north of Bahia; São Paulo (saʊ paʊ lu)—the name of a state as well as of its capital; Rio de Janeiro (ri o de ʒɑ nɛ ro)—again, the name of a state and its capital city, about a thousand miles south of Bahia.

PLAYING INSTRUMENTS: *Samba Playalong*

Divide the class into groups of three to create unpitched percussion ostinatos to perform with "A Zing-a Za." Challenge students to create one ostinato for each instrument in their group. Each ostinato should be based on a phrase taken from the song and last for either one or two measures. Examples:

Bongos: Words: Old Ba - hi - a

Tambourine: Words: la A zing - a za, O le, O

Unit 1 **MUSIC MAKERS** **11**

continued from previous page

4. Use "A Zing-a Za" to introduce verse-refrain form. Have students:

▶ • Answer the question about the words of the verse and refrain on page 12. (five sets of words; one set of words)

▶ • Learn what makes verse-refrain form. (The words to the A section are different each time it is sung; the words to the B section remain the same.)

3 APPLY

Introduce "National Emblem" CD1:5. **Describe its march form.** Have students:

▶ • Look at the photo of the marching band on page 13, notice the instruments, and read about the band.

▶ • Compare the instruments shown here with instruments in the samba bateria. (Marching band has woodwinds, brass, and percussion. Bateria has only percussion.)

▶ • Listen to "National Emblem."

OBJECTIVE 2 Informal Assessment

▶ • Using index cards (or pieces of paper), make "form cards" on which they write one letter or word: intro, A, A, A, B, B, B, trio, trio, trio. Listen to "National Emblem" again, sequencing the appropriate cards to show march form. (Circulate to look for: intro A A B B trio trio.)

▶ • Answer the question about "Muss i denn" and "National Emblem" on page 13.

As long as you sing a song with A zing-a za! O le, O

Ri - o, It is for me - o! A zing - a - zing - a - zing - ay!

la! A zing-a za! O le, O la! A zing-a za! O le, O

Zing-a-zing-a!___ Zing-a-zing-ay! Zing-a-zing-a!___ Zing-a-zing-ay!

la! A zing-a za! O le, O la! la! O le!

Zing - a - zing - a!___ Zing - a - zing - ay!__ O le, O la! la! O le!

Describe the form of this song using letters of the alphabet. How many sets of words are there in the section marked verse? In the refrain? A song that has more than one set of words for one section and only one set of words for another section is in **verse-refrain form.**

12 STEP TO THE MUSIC

MEETING **INDIVIDUAL** NEEDS

ALTERNATE TEACHING STRATEGY

OBJECTIVE 2 Ask students to explain what they learned from reading the text on march form. (A march usually has: intro A A B B trio trio. An introduction happens before the main part of the piece. A trio is a contrasting section.) Then play one section of the march at a time, asking after each one what the students thought the section was and why. Accept all answers for which students can give a reason. Then play the march again and have the students arrange their form cards in sequence.

You've seen marching bands in parades and during halftime at football games. Drum majors, baton twirlers, and elaborate movements add to the excitement of marching band performances. Which family of instruments is missing in this band? **strings**

LISTENING

National Emblem

by E. E. Bagley

How is the form of this march the same as or different from the form of "Muss i denn?" **Both marches have the form Intro AA BB Trio Trio. "National Emblem" has one trio that repeats; "Muss i denn" has two different trios.**

Unit 1 *Music Makers* **13**

4 CLOSE

"In each of the four band performances you have heard today, the basic elements of form were present: repetition and contrast. The way these elements were arranged determined what the form was." Have students:

▶ • Identify the two pieces that had a similar form. (Both marches had: intro A A B B trio trio.)

▶ • Recall the form of "A Zing-a Za." (verse-refrain)

▶ • Sing "A Zing-a Za" again.

LESSON SUMMARY

Informal Assessment In this lesson, students:

OBJECTIVE 1 Signaled to show recognition of A B form in "A Zing-a Za."

OBJECTIVE 2 Identified march form in "National Emblem" by sequencing form cards.

MORE MUSIC: Reinforcement

"Bashana Haba'ah," page 318 (A B form)

"Ecce gratum" listening map, page 44 (listening map)

The Drum, page 86 (percussion)

Frame Drums, page 86 (percussion)

"Meet Glen Velez," page 89 (percussion)

"De Lanterna na Mão", page 344 (percussion; Brazil)

"*John B.* Sails", page 347 (verse-refrain)

"Bound for the Promised Land," *Songs to Sing and Read,* page 11 (verse-refrain)

"Camptown Races," *Songs to Sing and Read,* page 15 (verse-refrain)

"Hold On!," *Songs to Sing and Read,* page 48 (verse-refrain)

BIOGRAPHY: *E. E. Bagley*

Edwin Eugene Bagley (1857–1922) was an American band musician and composer. The eighth of ten children, Bagley began his career as a traveling boy singer and comedian. He never took a lesson on any musical instrument in his life, but became a cornetist and performed with many bands. He later played trombone with the Boston Symphony Orchestra. Bagley was also a talented artist who specialized in drawing caricatures of people. "National Emblem" was written in 1905. Although Bagley wrote other compositions, he is remembered mainly for this march.

PLAYING INSTRUMENTS: *Drum Along*

After reviewing the march form of "National Emblem," students can create drumming patterns to go with each section, using two drumsticks, pencils, or hands. Those who can sustain a clear pattern for a reasonable time can lead the class. Make certain that patterns for the trios are simpler and have a lighter attack than those for other sections. (Optional: Have students play the rhythms on **Resource Master 1 · 4.**)

ACROSS the

MATHEMATICS

ARRANGEMENTS

"Muss i denn"

PAIR   **15 MIN OR LESS**

MATERIALS: 4 index cards

Preparation: Each pair of students labels four cards (one of each of these labels per card):

- INTRODUCTION
- A A
- B B
- TRIO 1 / TRIO 2

Each pair starts by arranging the cards to show the march form of "Muss i denn," the only arrangement that makes sense musically. However, as a mathematical challenge, ask students to find how many other arrangements they can make by varying the order of the cards.

Have students work out a method for rearranging the cards to show all the possibilities. They should record each arrangement to avoid duplications. (24 arrangements; method—start with any one card and vary the order of the remaining three; repeat, using another card as the first card)

COMPREHENSION STRATEGY: Sequencing

LANGUAGE ARTS

MUSICAL MEANING

"Muss i denn"

INDIVIDUAL   **15–30 MIN**

To many German Americans who immigrated by boat to the United States during the twentieth century, the tune of "Muss i denn" has special meaning. It was often the melody that was played as the ocean liner left their home port—a musical symbol of their country.

Have students consider what songs they would choose as musical representations of the United States, their state, their hometown, their school, and their own favorite song. For each category, have the student explain why a given song was selected.

COMPREHENSION STRATEGY: Expressing point of view

MULTICULTURAL PERSPECTIVES

CURRICULUM

SOCIAL STUDIES

MAPS

"A Zing-a Za"

PAIR   **15 MIN OR LESS**

MATERIALS: map of Brazil (available in encyclopedias), string or tape measure

Brazil is made up of over 20 states. Have students, working in pairs, use a map of Brazil to find the four states named in the song—*Pernambuco, Bahia, São Paulo, Rio de Janeiro.* Have them name, locate, and record the capital city of each of the four states.

Suppose they were to travel from one capital city to another. Which pair are the closest to each other? Which are the farthest apart? Have students list all possible pairs of the four state capitals—six in all—in order from closest to farthest apart. They can use string or a tape measure to estimate relative distances between cities.

(Capitals: Pernambuco—Recife; Bahia—Salvador; São Paolo—São Paulo; Rio de Janeiro—Rio de Janeiro. Distances, closest to farthest: São Paolo to Rio de Janeiro; Recife to Salvador; Salvador to Rio de Janeiro; Salvador to São Paolo; Recife to Rio de Janeiro; Recife to São Paolo)

COMPREHENSION STRATEGY: Estimating

LANGUAGE ARTS

NEW WORDS

"A Zing-a Za"

GROUP   **15 MIN OR LESS**

Have students work in groups to substitute words and phrases that fit the rhythm of the original words and phrases of the song: Examples:

- *A zing-a za!*—I never knew
- *Rio de Janeiro*—Salt Lake City, Utah
- *Maria*—Sylvester

Using these simple substitutions as a start, students should write new phrases for as much of the original as they can to produce a new version of the song that tells a funny story. Groups should write out, practice, and perform the new words.

COMPREHENSION STRATEGY: Expressing main ideas

UNIT ONE
LESSON 3

RELATED ARTS | MOVEMENT | THEATER | VISUAL ARTS |

LESSON PLANNER

FOCUS Rhythm

OBJECTIVES

OBJECTIVE 1 Play a rhythmic ostinato with a song using half, quarter, and eighth notes and quarter rests (tested)

OBJECTIVE 2 Perform quarter, eighth, and sixteenth notes in the countermelody of a song (tested)

MATERIALS
Recordings
Recorded Lesson: Echoing Rhythms	CD1:6
Rock Around the Clock	CD1:7
A Zing-a Za	CD1:4

Instruments unpitched percussion instruments

Resources
Resource Master 1 • 5 (practice)
Recorder Master R • 1 (pitches A B)
Playing the Guitar G • 8 (eighth-note rhythms)

▶ = **BASIC PROGRAM**

GOTTA GET Rhythm

Think about the kinds of musical groups you've seen so far and take a look at the lyrics of "Rock Around the Clock." What kind of group might play and sing this song? Which instruments do you think they would play?

PLAY percussion instruments along with this song as you sing.

14

MEETING **INDIVIDUAL** NEEDS

ALTERNATE TEACHING STRATEGY

OBJECTIVE 1 Rehearse only one ostinato at a time with all students playing it but none singing. Have students try each ostinato alone before trying two of them together. After students are comfortable combining two ostinatos, they should combine all three. Repeat the recorded lesson, "Echoing Rhythms," so that they can hear all three rhythms together.

BACKGROUND: *"Rock Around the Clock"*

"Rock Around the Clock" has come to symbolize the beginning of the era of rock 'n' roll, bobby socks, saddle shoes, and Elvis Presley. First recorded by Bill Haley and the Comets in the early 1950s, it became a success when it was chosen as the theme song for the 1955 movie *Blackboard Jungle*. The movie was about tensions at a tough city high school, and the song came to stand for the restlessness of young people and the energy of the rock 'n' roll life. The song shot to the top of the charts and sold 22 million copies in 1955, making Bill Haley a worldwide star.

Rock Around the Clock

Words and Music by Max Freedman
and Jimmy De Knight

One, two, three o'clock, four o'clock, rock.
Five, six, seven o'clock, eight o'clock, rock.
Nine, ten, eleven o'clock, twelve o'clock, rock.
We're gonna rock around the clock tonight.

1. Well, get your glad rags on, join me hon,' we're gonna
   have some fun when the clock strikes one,
   We're gonna rock around the clock tonight, we're gonna
   rock, rock, rock 'til the broad daylight,
   We're gonna rock, gonna rock around the clock tonight.

2. When the clock strikes two, three and four, and the band
   slows down we'll yell for more,
   We're gonna rock around the clock tonight, we're gonna
   rock, rock, rock 'til the broad daylight,
   We're gonna rock, gonna rock around the clock tonight.

3. When the chimes ring five, six, and seven, we'll be rockin'
   up' in seventh heaven
   We're gonna rock around the clock tonight, we're gonna
   rock, rock, rock 'til the broad daylight,
   We're gonna rock, gonna rock around the clock tonight.

4. When it's eight, nine, ten, eleven too, I'll be going strong
   and so will you,
   We're gonna rock around the clock tonight, we're gonna
   rock, rock, rock 'til the broad daylight,
   We're gonna rock, gonna rock around the clock tonight.

5. When the clock strikes twelve we'll cool off, then, start
   a-rockin' 'round the clock again,
   We're gonna rock around the clock tonight, we're gonna
   rock, rock, rock 'til the broad daylight,
   We're gonna rock, gonna rock around the clock tonight.

Unit 1 *Music Makers* 15

1 GET SET

"Today you're going to be the music makers. Stand and echo these rhythm patterns." Have students:

Recorded Lesson CD1:6

▶ • Listen to "Echoing Rhythms" and echo and combine speech patterns. (The speech patterns are shown for your reference.)

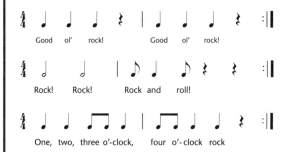

Good ol' rock! Good ol' rock!

Rock! Rock! Rock and roll!

One, two, three o'-clock, four o'-clock rock

2 DEVELOP

1. **Introduce "Rock Around the Clock"** CD1:7. **Develop accompaniment from speech ostinatos.** Have students:

▶ • Answer the questions about who would play and sing the song. (Rock 'n' roll band; electric guitars, bass, keyboards, drums)

• In three groups, perform one ostinato each from *Get Set*. (Have students whisper the words while clapping the rhythm.)

• Perform all three ostinatos together, and then with the recording.

• Select unpitched percussion instruments on which to play assigned ostinatos.

OBJECTIVE 1 Informal Assessment
• Practice and perform instrumental ostinatos with the song. (Half of each ostinato group can sing along with the recording as the other half plays. Then switch parts and perform again.)

PLAYING INSTRUMENTS: *More Ostinatos*

If students can easily handle the three ostinatos for "Rock Around the Clock," teach them these as a challenge.

Got - ta dance! Got - ta dance!

snare drum, drumsticks on a hard surface, or hand drum

Keep on rock - in' with the rock and roll. (Gon-na)

conga or bongo drums

MOVEMENT: *"Rock Around the Clock"*

Have students work in groups to use the steps learned for "Dancin' on the Rooftop" to create new sequences for "Rock Around the Clock." Suggest that the choreography fall into three different types of movement: the introduction, the first two phrases of each verse, and the last part of each verse. Let the words suggest the movement. The groups should choreograph a different movement for the first two phrases of each verse. The movement for the last part of each verse (*We're gonna rock*) should be the same each time. (It is almost like a refrain.)

UNIT ONE
LESSON 3

continued from previous page

2. Review and label relative note values; imitate simple rhythms. Have students:

• Look at the chart on page 16, briefly review the relative length of each kind of note, and read or clap it with your help. (Optional: Use **Resource Master 1 • 5.**)

• Review the three patterns from *Get Set*, page 15. (notes only, no words)

• Use the recorded lesson "Echoing Rhythms" again, or echo you in reading the patterns.

• Match the notation on page 16 with the speech patterns.

3 APPLY

Review "A Zing-a Za" CD1:4 (pp. 11–12). **Identify and clap note values in the countermelody**. Have students:

▶• Sing the melody and recall that it is in verse-refrain form (page 12).

OBJECTIVE 2 Informal Assessment
• Look at the countermelody for the verse only and sing it with the recording. Then clap the rhythm of measures that have quarter and eighth notes and pat, with alternating hands, measures that are all sixteenth notes. (Quarter and eighth notes are in Measures 1, 3, and 5 and sixteenth notes are in Measures 2, 4, 6, and 7.)

All music has one thing in common—that all-important element, **rhythm**. Rhythm is created by organizing sounds and silences of different lengths. Composers write rhythm using notes and rests. People who can read and write rhythm know how much time one note or rest takes in relation to other notes or rests. Look at the chart below and see if you can figure out why there is only one whole note but 16 sixteenth notes. It takes 16 sixteenth notes to equal the duration of one whole note.

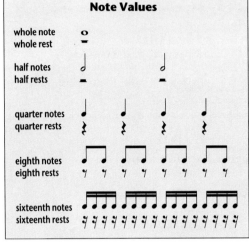

THINK IT THROUGH
Imagine that you are in a band. How would you use an understanding of note values?

READ and clap these rhythms.

"Good Ol' Rock"

"One, two, three o'clock, four o'clock rock"

"Rock! Rock! Rock and roll!"

Bill Haley (right) and the Comets recorded "Rock Around the Clock" in 1954.

16 GOTTA GET RHYTHM

MEETING **INDIVIDUAL** NEEDS

ALTERNATE TEACHING STRATEGY

OBJECTIVE 2 Ask students to look at the beams on the notes in the countermelody of "A Zing-a Za" and compare them to similar notes in the note-value chart. Then put the notation for Measures 1 and 2 on the board and ask a volunteer to clap just the sixteenth notes. If the class agrees with the volunteer, have them all clap the measure. Then have them look at the notation and point out all the measures with sixteenth notes. Repeat the process for the measures with quarter and eighth notes.

ENRICHMENT: *Student Rhythm Patterns*

Sit in a circle and have students create their own one-measure patterns using eighth, quarter, half notes, and rests as you play the beat on a drum. They should take turns clapping, patting, and snapping their patterns, playing each pattern twice before the next pattern is played. Challenge them to keep the patterns coming without a break. Then have students write the notation for their patterns large enough to be seen from a distance and put the notation on the floor in front of them. After one round, all stand up, rotate one chair to the left, and begin the rhythm circle again using a neighbor's pattern.

"Let's review what you've done with rhythm in this lesson. First, listen to the rhythm of a song you know and see if you recognize it." Have students:

▶ • Listen as you clap the verse of one of the songs in this lesson and guess the name of the song.

• Tell what they did with rhythm in this lesson. (echoed, named, moved to, and played rhythm patterns containing sixteenth, eighth, quarter, and half notes and quarter rests)

▶ • Sing the song you clapped.

LESSON SUMMARY

Informal Assessment In this lesson, students:

OBJECTIVE 1 Played a rhythmic ostinato with "Rock Around the Clock" using half, quarter, and eighth notes and quarter rests.

OBJECTIVE 2 Performed quarter, eighth, and sixteenth notes in the counter-melody for "A Zing-a Za."

MORE MUSIC: Reinforcement
"Dona nobis pacem," page 338 (reading rhythms)
"De allacito carnavalito," page 342 (reading sixteenth rhythms)
"Follow the Drinkin' Gourd," page 370 (reading rhythms)
"Crawdad Song," *Songs to Sing and Read,* page 22 (reading rhythms)
"Minka," *Songs to Sing and Read,* page 66 (reading rhythms)
"Tallis Canon," *Songs to Sing and Read,* page 101 (reading rhythms)
"The Wabash Cannon Ball," *Songs to Sing and Read,* page 105 (reading rhythms)

MOVEMENT: *The Moveable Note-Value Chart* MOVEMENT

Have students form groups of five, one for each note value on the chart. The student representing the quarter note sets the tempo, patting the beat. When that beat is well established, the eighth note starts clapping, followed by the sixteenth, either clapping or snapping. The half note, then the whole note enter, making certain to fill the time of their note value with movement. Once the clapping is well established, this activity can be transfered to walking and clapping. (The student performing the sixteenth-note rhythm will probably clap only, since walking with such a fast step would be difficult.)

ACROSS the

MATHEMATICS

ADDING UNITS OF TIME

"Rock Around the Clock"

PAIR   **15–30 MIN**

MATERIALS: paper plate with two pencils (one shorter than the other—to use as hour and minute hands), number cube

Preparation: One partner draws a clock face on the inside of a paper plate. The same student uses two pencils as clock hands to show a time on the clock.

The other student tosses the number cube three times to get an amount of time: the first number stands for hours, the last two stand for minutes—for example, 6, 4, and 2 would mean 6 hours 42 minutes.

Both students race to find what the new time on the clock would be if the amount of time shown by tossing the cube passed. The first student to answer correctly wins the round. Partners switch roles and repeat as often as they wish.

COMPREHENSION STRATEGIES: Using a model, sequencing

ELAPSED TIME

"Rock Around the Clock"

INDIVIDUAL   **15–30 MIN**

Have students write an outline of a typical 24-hour day, starting with waking up, and ending with waking up the next day. The outline should be in the form of a list of activities, with an approximate time for each activity, and the amount of time that elapses until the next activity:

- 6:30 A.M. Wake up,
  45 minutes to shower and dress;
- 7:15 A.M. Breakfast,
  30 minutes to eat;
- 7:45 A.M. Start for school,
  and so on.

COMPREHENSION STRATEGY: Sequencing

CURRICULUM

SCIENCE

TIME ZONES

"Rock Around the Clock"

GROUP   **15 MIN OR LESS**

MATERIALS: globe or world map (with longitude in intervals of 15°) or encyclopedia article on "time zones," drawing paper, markers, pencil

Starting at 0° (prime meridian), every 15° interval of longitude represents an hour of time. With some differences due to political considerations, each 15° interval is a time zone—with a total of 24 time zones (24 hours) around the globe. A simple rule applies at any point in time:

- the time in any time zone is one hour earlier than in the zone to its east and one hour later than in the zone to its west

Across the continental United States, there are four time zones—east to west: Eastern, Central, Mountain, Pacific (corresponding roughly to 75°W, 90°W, 105°W, 120°W). Have students work in groups to draw an outline of the United States and show the boundaries of the four time zones. Have them label several cities in each zone. One group member gives a time for any city. Then the other group members tell the time in each of the other cities on their map.

COMPREHENSION STRATEGIES: Sequencing, displaying information

LANGUAGE ARTS

PERSONAL NARRATIVE

"Rock Around the Clock"

INDIVIDUAL   **15–30 MIN**

Have students think about the most eventful day they can remember—either in their own lives or in events taking place anywhere in the world. Based on the theme of "A Day I'll Never Forget," have students write a composition describing the events that took place on that important day and explaining why the events were so meaningful to them.

Before they write the composition, have students outline the paragraphs they intend to write—to make sure each contains a main idea with supporting details.

COMPREHENSION STRATEGY: Expressing main ideas and supporting details

UNIT ONE
LESSON 4

RELATED ARTS | MOVEMENT | THEATER | VISUAL ARTS |

LESSON PLANNER

FOCUS Pitch

OBJECTIVES
OBJECTIVE 1 Trace in the air the melodic contour of two phrases in a song
OBJECTIVE 2 Sing part of a song with pitch letter names (tested)

MATERIALS
Recordings
A Zing-a Za   CD1:4
Dancin' on the Rooftop   CD1:1
Fung Yang Song   CD1:8
Recorded Lesson: Pronunciation
    for "Fung Yang Song"   CD1:9

Instruments pitched instruments (for resonator bells, use D E F F♯ A B)

Resources
Resource Master 1 • 6 (practice)
Recorder Master R • 2 (pitches A B)

VOCABULARY
pitch, melodic contour

      ▶ = **BASIC PROGRAM**

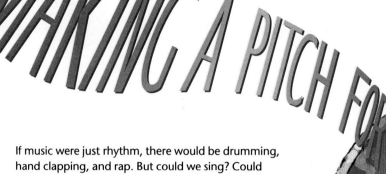

If music were just rhythm, there would be drumming, hand clapping, and rap. But could we sing? Could trumpets play melodies? For these we need **pitch.**

Pitch is the highness or lowness of a tone in relation to other tones. When you string pitches together, you can make a melody.

In melodies, pitches can:

- move by step, up or down.

- skip pitches going up or down.

- take long leaps up or down.

- stay the same as the previous pitch.

When you talk about pitches moving, you are talking about the shape of melody— its direction, or **melodic contour.**

18

MEETING **INDIVIDUAL** NEEDS

ALTERNATE TEACHING STRATEGY

OBJECTIVE 1 Have students trace the melodic contour of the measures directly in their books and notice whether their finger goes up, down, or stays at the same level. Then they can trace them in the air. Ask students to repeat both of these steps while singing the measures.

MOVEMENT: *Steppin' Out the Measure*

Put a large staff on the floor with masking tape and let students choose a measure of "Dancin' on the Rooftop" to step out, using their footsteps as the notes. They can walk for stepwise progression and leap for skips and leaps.

PLAY the music below with the first three sections (ABA) of "Dancin' on the Rooftop." The example below can remind you of the pitch name of each line and each space of the staff.

treble clef

C D E F G A B C' D' E' F'

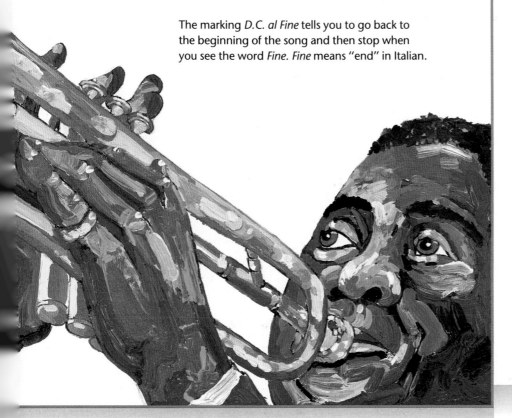

playalong Ⓐ

Fine

Ⓑ

D.C. al Fine

The marking *D.C. al Fine* tells you to go back to the beginning of the song and then stop when you see the word *Fine. Fine* means "end" in Italian.

1 GET SET

"Today you're going to look at pitch." Have students:

▶ • Listen to the introduction of "A Zing-a Za" CD1:4 and tell how they can recognize it. (shape of melody; rhythm)

▶ • Sing "A Zing-a Za." (pp. 11–12)

"Reading pitches will help you recognize any melody you see."

2 DEVELOP

1. Review "Dancin' on the Rooftop" CD1:1 **(pp. 2–4). Introduce pitch letter names.** Have students:

▶ • Read about pitch and melodic contour.

OBJECTIVE 1 Informal Assessment

• Trace in the air the melodic contours of the tinted measures, 12–13 and 16–17, and discuss them. (Both patterns move down, then up.)

• List the pitches of Measures 12–13 and 16–17 from lowest to highest. (D E F G A) (See example on page 19 for the pitch letter names on the treble staff. Optional: Use **Resource Master 1 • 6** for more practice reading pitches from notation.)

• Sing these measures with letter names.

2. Learn a playalong for "Dancin' on the Rooftop." Have students:

• Identify the note values in the playalong (quarter, half, and whole notes) and note the treble clef. Then identify the pitches as they perform the playalong on pitched instruments.

• Sing the playalong with pitch letter names, clapping the rhythm at the same time.

• Play the pitches with the first three sections of "Dancin' on the Rooftop." Start on Measure 2.

ENRICHMENT: *Handprint Melodic Contours*

Have the class print giant melodic contours of "Dancin' on the Rooftop" on long sheets of shelf or wrapping paper by dipping one hand in paint or chalk dust and printing the notes with their hands. Each student can be responsible for printing one measure of the song. The students should know the placement of their measures and be able to explain where each hand note goes before printing it. If the class is large, it may be necessary either to have two different groups do this activity or to assign each student only one note to print.

ART CONNECTION: *Using Color* VISUAL ARTS

Ask students which elements of the artwork on pages 18–19 are realistic (man and trumpet). "What is *not* realistic?" (color) Tell students that before 1800 most artists used color in a naturalistic way. During the 1800s they began to use colors more freely to express mood or feeling. The use of color in this artwork is in the style of the Fauves, a group of artists working in the early 1900s. The Fauves used bold strokes of vivid color to create lively, bold statements. "Describe how color was used in this picture." (bold, unblended strokes; bright, contrasting colors)

UNIT ONE
LESSON 4

continued from previous page

3. Introduce "Fung Yang Song" CD1:8. Review rhythms and identify percussion instruments. Have students:

▶ • Read about the song, then listen to it.

Recorded Lesson CD1:9

▶ • Listen to "Pronunciation for 'Fung Yang Song.' "

▶ • Sing the song with the recording.

▶ • Look at the first four measures of the song and speak the rhythm.

▶ • Listen to the recording for the percussion instruments named in the song.

• Listen to the countermelody of "Fung Yang Song" and sing it separately. (On the recording, the countermelody is heard alone after the English verse and refrain. When students are secure singing the melody and countermelody separately, have them sing both parts together.)

3 APPLY

Describe melodic contour and name pitches in "Fung Yang Song." Have students:

• Listen to the song again, tracing the melodic contour in the air.

• Tell which measures have exactly the same contour. (Measures 3–4 are the same as 7–8.)

• List the pitches of Measures 1–4 from lowest to highest. (D E F♯ A B D')

OBJECTIVE 2 Informal Assessment

• Sing Measures 1–4 with pitch letter names.

Here is a new song to read and sing. It is part of a very old tradition of street performances in China. The music is called "Fung Yang Song" because it comes from Fung Yang, a district in northern China. Since about 1700, songs like this have been popular all over China.

LISTEN for the rhythm and melodic contour of this song.

20 MAKING A PITCH FOR PITCH

MEETING **INDIVIDUAL** NEEDS

ALTERNATE TEACHING STRATEGY

OBJECTIVE 2 Have students trace the melodic contour in the air as they sing it on *loo*. Put a pentatonic scale on the board, then have students sing pitch letter names as you point out the melody pitches on the scale. Finally, have students sing the pitches while looking at the notation.

VOCAL DEVELOPMENT: *Countermelody*

Students who are uncertain singers may get confused when they hear the countermelody in "Fung Yang Song." When teaching a harmony part, begin by having the majority of the class, including the uncertain singers, sing the melody, while you and a few students (including one uncertain singer) stand off to the side singing the countermelody.

BACKGROUND: *"Fung Yang Song"*

This song comes from the late 1300s, during the time of the first ruler of the Ming dynasty, when there was a period of drought in China. The crops failed and many people went hungry. Because the people were so poor, they had to travel around from place to place—singing songs such as this as they begged for food and money.

4 CLOSE

"Today you worked with pitch. Use your skills to join the Chinese music makers and accompany 'Fung Yang Song.'" Have students:

• Play any two pitches from Measures 1–4 with the recording. (They should play on Beat 1 of each measure.)

LESSON SUMMARY

Informal Assessment In this lesson, students:

OBJECTIVE 1 Traced in the air the melodic contour of two phrases from "Dancin' on the Rooftop."

OBJECTIVE 2 Sang Measures 1–4 of "Fung Yang Song" with pitch letter names.

MORE MUSIC: Reinforcement

"The Star-Spangled Banner," page 292 (melodic contour)
"Haji Firuz," page 317 (melodic contour)
"Where'er You Walk," page 362 (melodic contour)

MOVEMENT: *Ribbon Dance for "Fung Yang Song"*

A truly beautiful spectacle in China is the ribbon dance, in which the dancers trace designs in the air with very long ribbons attached to hand-held wands. Wands can be made by attaching 1½-inch-wide ribbon to the end of a rhythm stick or dowel that is about 12 inches long.

To get ideas for choreography, have students experiment drawing pathways in the air with their wands overhead, in front, to the sides, changing hands, figure eights, and other designs. Have students try turning, walking, mirroring a partner, and following the leader with the ribbons.

Then have groups of four choreograph a dance. Suggested guidelines:

—effective beginning and ending group formation
—repetition and contrast in overall dance form, and in body facing, level, and direction and speed of movement
—some unison movement; some individual movement

PRONUNCIATION: *"Fung Yang Song"*

a father	e chaotic	ɛ pet	i bee	o obey
ɔ paw	u moon	ʌ up	ə ago	

ACROSS the

ART — PAINTING

"Dancin' on the Rooftop"

INDIVIDUAL　　　　　　　　**15–30 MIN**

MATERIALS: paints, brushes; optional shoe-laces, leaves

This song is rich in images:

- *dancin' on the rooftop*
- *hangin' by my shoestrings*
- *swingin' on a treetop*

Have students paint images from this song, using themselves as the subject. They can paint a portrait of themselves in any single image or may combine the many images of the song in one composed piece of artwork. They might like to paste shoelaces and leaves to images showing themselves hanging by shoestrings or swinging on treetops.

COMPREHENSION STRATEGY: Visualizing

SCIENCE — WEATHER WATCH

"Dancin' on the Rooftop"

PAIR　　　　　　　　**30 MIN OR LONGER**

MATERIALS: optional—weather thermometer, barometer

To check if *The weather's fine,* have students make a weather log for each day of a month. They should record:

- cloud cover: clear, partly cloudy, partly sunny, overcast
- present weather: drizzle, rain, snow, sleet, shower, thunderstorm, haze, fog
- daily high and low temperatures and air pressures: available from broadcast weather reports or by use of instruments—thermometers and barometers
- wind speed (calm, slight-moderate-strong breeze, gusts, heavy winds) and direction from which wind is approaching

Students can try to find relationships based on their records. What conditions precede a thunderstorm? Does pressure rise or fall when storms approach?

COMPREHENSION STRATEGIES: Recording information, drawing conclusions

CURRICULUM

LANGUAGE ARTS

DESCRIPTIVE WRITING

"Fung Yang Song"

INDIVIDUAL　　　　　　**15–30 MIN**

Songs like the "Fung Yang Song" were often sung by traveling groups of people, families, or individuals, performing on the streets for food and money.

Have students imagine that they were traveling the country today with their families, performing for a living. What would it be like? Where would they travel to and from?

Ask them to write a day's entry into a diary or journal describing what performing for a living for one day might be like. Be sure they include the names of people who would be with them, the names of the songs they would sing, and where they were traveling from and to on that day.

COMPREHENSION STRATEGY: Expressing main ideas and supporting details

SOCIAL STUDIES

MAPS

"Fung Yang Song"

PAIR　　　　　　**15–30 MIN**

MATERIALS: map of China (available in encyclopedias)

Have students imagine they are part of a traveling group of performers going throughout China singing songs like "Fung Yang Song." Have them work in pairs to plan a journey throughout China.

Have students use maps to plan their itinerary. They should begin with a list of cities they intend to visit in the order they will visit them—starting perhaps at the national capital, Beijing. Their plans should indicate the rivers, mountains, and hills they will cross as well as the names of the provinces they will pass through from city to city.

Students can write out their travel plans as well as present them to the class on a map.

COMPREHENSION STRATEGIES: Sequencing, organizing information

UNIT ONE
LESSON 5

LESSON PLANNER

FOCUS Pitch

OBJECTIVES

OBJECTIVE 1 Identify familiar songs by playing and singing notated melodic fragments (tested)

OBJECTIVE 2 Read pitches in a counter-melody of a song (tested)

OBJECTIVE 3 Identify verse-refrain form of a song

MATERIALS

Recordings
A Zing-a Za   CD1:4
I Shall Sing   CD1:10
Fung Yang Song   CD1:8

Instruments
resonator bells or other pitched instruments

Resources
Resource Master 1 • 7 (practice)
Resource Master—staff paper
Orff Orchestration O • 1 (I Shall Sing)
Recorder Master R • 3 (pitches G A B)

VOCABULARY
countermelody, ledger lines

▶ = **BASIC PROGRAM**

BREAK THE CODES

Now that you've learned something about rhythm and pitch, it's time to do a bit of song sleuthing. The mystery is . . . What song does the measure below come from? *"A Zing-a Za"*

Here are some clues that could help you break both the rhythm and pitch codes.

- The measure is from a song you know.
- The rhythm and the melody of the measure appear more than once in the song.

How did you arrive at your answer? by looking at the rhythm, the leaps and steps of the pitches
Here's an even more challenging mystery. On the next page are four song fragments. Your assignment is to identify one of the songs.

FOLLOW the steps below as you work with others to break the codes. Use a pitched instrument to help you.

- Describe the melodic contour.
- Name the pitches.
- Play the fragment on an instrument.
- Sing it with pitch letter names.
- Identify the song (but don't tell the other groups).

PLAY and sing your fragment for the other groups. See if they can identify it.

22

MEETING **INDIVIDUAL** NEEDS

ALTERNATE TEACHING STRATEGY

OBJECTIVE 1 If students are unable to identify their assigned song from the melodic fragment, have them trace the melodic contour once more, then look in their books for songs in this unit with this same contour. They can then compare the rhythm and specific pitch notation to see if it is identical.

ENRICHMENT: *More Musical Detective Work*

Have students practice their melodic reading skills with other fragments from the four songs used in *Develop 2*.

Secretly assign each small group one of the songs from which they will choose a new fragment not more than two measures long. Have them copy this fragment from the book onto a staff and, at your signal, pass the song fragment to the next group to read. You may wish to use staff paper (available on the last page of the *Resource Master* booklet). Each group must then name the pitches, or sing or play the fragment for the entire class to guess.

Mystery Melody 1 "Accentuate the Positive"

Mystery Melody 2 "Dancin' on the Rooftop"

Mystery Melody 3 "Fung Yang Song"

Mystery Melody 4 "Rock Around the Clock"

23

1 GET SET

"Here is one measure of a song you know. Can you name it?" Have students:

• Look at the melodic fragment on page 22.

• Try to sing the fragment after hearing a starting pitch, then name the song. ("A Zing-a Za")

"You have just done a bit of musical detective work. What did you see in the melodic fragment that gave you the answer?" (the rhythm and the leaps and steps of the pitches) "Today you will get a chance to apply your observation skills to other musical mysteries."

2 DEVELOP

1. Review "A Zing-a Za" CD1:4 **(pp. 11–12). Sing in two parts.** Have students:

• Sing the song with its countermelody from the notation. (On the recording, the countermelody is heard after Verse 3 and its refrain.)

2. Read song fragments. Have students:

• In groups of three, study an assigned song fragment, following the directions on page 22. (at least one group per fragment)

OBJECTIVE 1 Informal Assessment

• Tell the name of the song to other members of their own group. (Circulate to hear their reasoning.)

• Listen as one representative from each group plays for the class their assigned song fragment on a pitched instrument. (Using resonator bells with letter names will aid students in this task.)

• Identify each song by hearing the fragment.

UNIT ONE
LESSON 5

continued from previous page

3. Introduce "I Shall Sing" CD1:10. **Learn countermelody.** Have students:

▶ • Listen to the melody for Verses 1–2, following the notation.

▶ • Listen to the highlighted countermelody alone.

• With a partner, list the pitches of the countermelody from low to high (C D E), writing notes and letter names on a staff. (Optional— Use Resource Master staff paper.) (Have students read about ledger lines on page 25.)

OBJECTIVE 2   Informal Assessment
• Sing the countermelody with pitch names.

▶ • Sing the countermelody with the words.

4. Sing "I Shall Sing" and identify its form. Have students:

▶ • Sing the melody of the song, then the countermelody with the recording. (When students are secure singing melody and countermelody separately, have them sing both parts together.)

OBJECTIVE 3   Informal Assessment
▶ • Identify the form by silently closing the book at the end of the song if it is verse-refrain, or leaving it open if it is not. (verse-refrain)

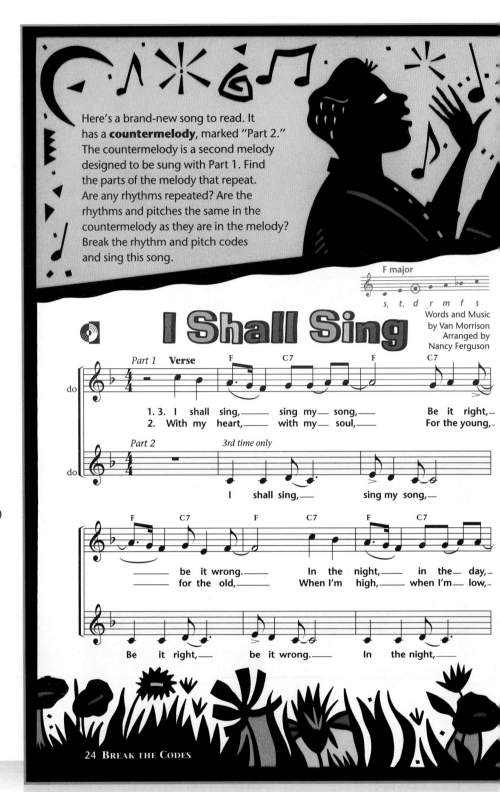

24 BREAK THE CODES

MEETING **INDIVIDUAL** NEEDS

ALTERNATE TEACHING STRATEGIES

OBJECTIVE 2   Ask students to copy the entire countermelody on their own staff and name each pitch below it. Then they should be able to sing with the correct pitch letters.

OBJECTIVE 3   Ask for a volunteer to define *refrain*. (a section of a song that repeats, always with the same words and music) Ask students to look at "I Shall Sing" and tell if there is such a section and whether it is repeated. (Yes, the section with only *la* for words; it repeats between Verses 1, 2, and 3.) Finally, ask them if "I Shall Sing" is verse-refrain. (yes)

BIOGRAPHY: *Van Morrison*

Irish singer and songwriter Van Morrison (b. 1945) grew up listening to his father's blues records. He has since mastered many musical styles—his music can sound like jazz, soul, or folk, as well as the blues. Some of his songs touch on his Irish roots, and he has played with Celtic bands. He plays guitar, saxophone, drums, and harmonica. Morrison's many hits include "Brown Eyed Girl" and "Moon Dance."

ORFF: *"I Shall Sing"*
See **O · 1** in *Orchestrations for Orff Instruments.*

Review "Fung Yang Song" CD1:8 (p. 20).
Create a new countermelody. Have students:

• Assign a pitch to each note for one of the rhythmic ostinatos on page 25, choosing from only D E F♯ and A.

• Arrange the pitches in any sequence.

• Practice their pattern with another student who chose the other rhythm pattern.

• Play or sing the melodic ostinato they create as a countermelody to the song.

4 CLOSE

"In learning to read music, you have to break the code. What part of the music-reading code did you work on today?" (pitch) "Practice your code-breaking by singing 'Fung Yang Song' again, looking at the notation."

Fine

An - y - how,_____ an - y - way,_____ I_____ shall sing:
When I'm fast,_____ when I'm slow,_____ I_____ shall sing:

in the day,_____ An - y - how,_____ an - y - way._____

Refrain
F   C7   F   C7   F   C7   F   C7

La la la la la la la la,   la la la la la la la.   (clap)

D.C. (last time al Fine)

F   C7   F C7 F   C7   F   C7

La la la la la la la la,   la la la la la la la.___ la la la.___ la.

The notation of the countermelody of this song uses **ledger lines**. Ledger lines are short pieces of staff lines that help you read the notes that are too high or low to fit on the regular staff. In this countermelody, a ledger line is needed for the note C.

What is the form of this song? **verse-refrain**

CREATE your own countermelody for "Fung Yang Song." Use one of these rhythm patterns with the pitches D, E, F♯, and A:

LESSON SUMMARY

Informal Assessment In this lesson, students:

OBJECTIVE 1 Identified familiar songs by playing and singing notated melodic fragments.
OBJECTIVE 2 Read pitches in the countermelody of "I Shall Sing."
OBJECTIVE 3 Identified the verse-refrain form of "I Shall Sing."

MORE MUSIC: Reinforcement
"Battle Hymn of the Republic," page 295 (verse-refrain, countermelody)
"Gypsy Rover," page 346 (verse-refrain, ledger lines, pitch letter names)

PITCH SYLLABLES: *"I Shall Sing"*

Ask students to list the pitches of the verse melody, writing the pitches on a staff, then add any pitches from the countermelody. (C B♭ A G F E; D C) Tell them that F is *do* and let each group write in the syllable for each pitch. (*so fa mi re do ti, la, so,*) (Optional: For more practice with *ti,* have students complete **Resource Master 1 • 7.**) Have them sing the countermelody, then the melody with syllables. Then add hand signs.

do   re   mi   fa   so   la   ti

IMPROVISATION: *"Fung Yang Song"*

Set all barred instruments and resonator bells in D pentatonic scale (D E F♯ A B D'). Have students clap the rhythm of the words of the song, then play the rhythm of the words on D, using only their fingernails. Have them use the mallets to play the rhythm of the words on all notes of the D pentatonic scale, playing a different bar for each syllable. Incorporate this as a B section to the song.

Across the

LANGUAGE ARTS

EDITORIAL

"I Shall Sing"

INDIVIDUAL   **15–30 MIN**

In "I Shall Sing," the words mention singing *for the old.* Have students think about senior citizens whom they may know—family members, neighbors, people in the community. Ask students to write an essay on the theme of "Getting Older." Have them respond to these questions:

- What special needs may people have as they get older?
- What do older people have to share with younger people?

In their essays, have students describe how they might share part of their day with older people—volunteering time to do chores for people, sharing friendships, learning from the skills and talents that older people have acquired, and so on.

COMPREHENSION STRATEGY: Expressing point of view

MATHEMATICS

RATES

"I Shall Sing"

PAIR   **15–30 MIN**
MATERIALS: index cards

The words of "I Shall Sing," *When I'm fast, when I'm slow,* suggest a rate game. Working in pairs, one student labels 4 *distance* cards: 10 miles, 10 miles, 20 miles, 20 miles. The partner labels 4 *time* cards: 30 min, 1 hour, 2 hours, 4 hours.

Players shuffle the cards and place one distance card with each time card. They determine which pair of distance-time cards is "fastest" (greatest distance covered per unit of time) and which is "slowest" (least distance per unit), and order all four pairs from fastest to slowest.

(The strategy is to determine the distance covered in an equal time period—an hour—for each pair. Thus, 10 miles/30 min represents a speed of 20 miles/hour, while 10 miles/2 hours represents 5 miles/hour.)

COMPREHENSION STRATEGY: Compare and contrast

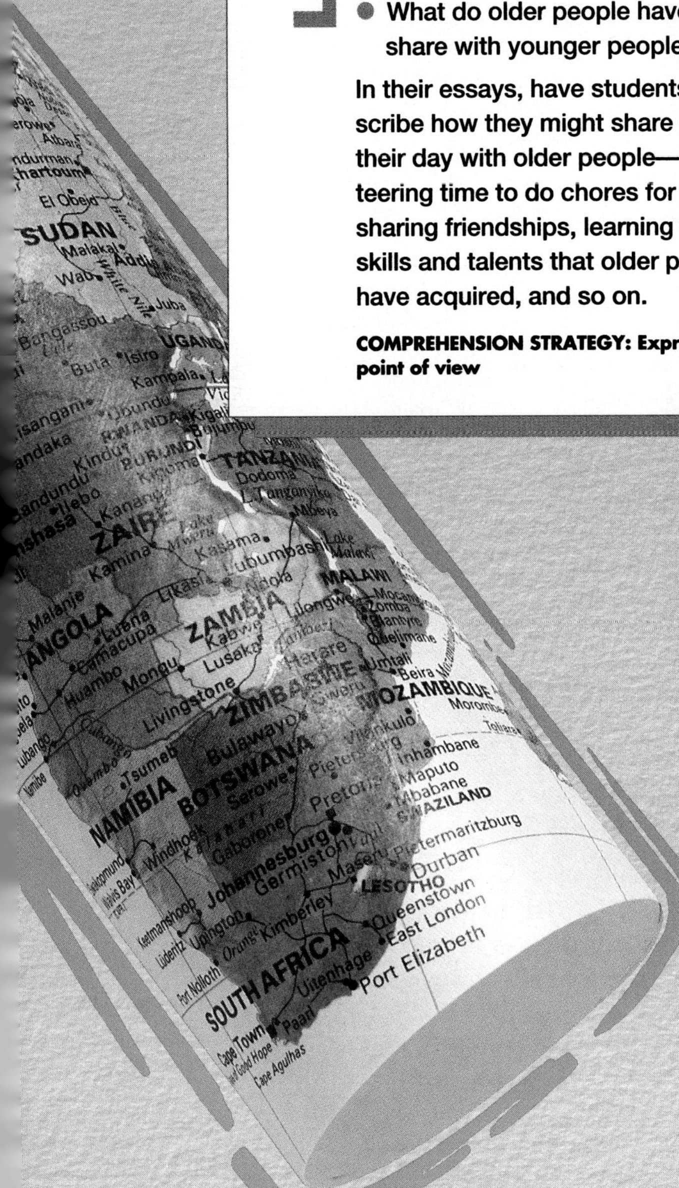

CURRICULUM

SCIENCE

NIGHT AND DAY

"I Shall Sing"

WHOLE CLASS   **15–30 MIN**

MATERIALS: globe, flashlight, reference texts on the planets, poster board, crayons or markers; optional—baseballs, basketballs

"I Shall Sing" refers to singing *in the night, in the day.* Have students model day/night on Earth:

- hold a flashlight about two feet away from a globe, aimed at the center of one side—hemisphere;
- with dimmed room lights, spin the globe slowly counterclockwise.

Students can summarize and apply what they see—half the globe is in (day)light and half in darkness at any given time. With one complete spin (rotation), places on Earth go through one day/night cycle.

The day/night cycle (rotation period) on Earth is just under 24 hours. How long does each of the other planets of the solar system take to rotate once—how long is the day/night cycle? Have students research this information and mount it on a solar system bulletin board display. Students can use baseballs and basketballs to model the rotations of the other planets.

COMPREHENSION STRATEGIES: Using a model, drawing conclusions

LANGUAGE ARTS

SONG CONTEST

"I Shall Sing"

GROUP   **30 MIN OR LONGER**

MATERIALS: optional—record magazines listing current hit songs

The students work in groups to list songs that they enjoy singing—from old favorites, folk songs, current popular tunes, Broadway musical tunes, and so on. Each group categorizes the songs into groups:

- Songs That I Sing When I'm Happy;
- Songs That I Sing When I'm Blue, or any other groups they prefer.

For each category, group members rate the songs from 1 (low) to 10 (high) and list the songs in order of their ratings. Group members should give written descriptions of why they rated songs either above or below a 5.

Groups can then offer their lists to the class for comparison. They might hold a class vote for favorites in each category.

COMPREHENSION STRATEGIES: Compare and contrast, classifying

UNIT ONE
LESSON 6

RELATED ARTS | MOVEMENT | THEATER | VISUAL ARTS

LESSON PLANNER

FOCUS Texture/Tone color

OBJECTIVE

OBJECTIVE 1 Signal to identify strings as the instrumental family not featured in a band (tested)

MATERIALS
Recordings
I Shall Sing — CD1:10
You Sing for Me — CD1:11
You Sing for Me (performance mix) — CD1:12
Listening: Capriccio espagnol (excerpt) by N. Rimsky-Korsakov — CD1:13

Resources
Resource Master 1 • 8 (practice)
Resource Master 1 • 9 (listening map)
Listening Map Transparency T • 2 (Capriccio espagnol)
Musical Instruments Masters—banjo, dulcimer (Appalachian), guitar, string bass, string family
Playing the Guitar G • 1 (I and V chords)
Playing the Guitar G • 2 (I and V chords)
Playing the Guitar G • 3 (I and V chords)
Recorder Master R • 4 (pitches G A B)

VOCABULARY
texture, ties

▶ = **BASIC PROGRAM**

MUSIC ON A String

Listen for the instruments in this country string group. They are: fiddle, string bass, dulcimer, guitar, and banjo. How many voice parts are in this song? one part in verse, refrain has a countermelody

YOU SING FOR ME

Words and Music by Raymond K. McLain

Verse

G major

1. I've come through storm-y weath-er, I'm sure you've seen it too.
2. I'll nev-er be more read-y to sing a-long with you.

But now we're here to-geth-er and it's good to be with you.
To keep each oth-er stead-y,— well, this is what to do.

Well, here I am and there you are with noth-ing much to say.
You lis-ten to the rhy-thm, then start mov-in' to the beat.

Sure-ly there's some bet-ter way to cel-e-brate to-day.
Come on, sweet mu-sic mak-er,— let's give our-selves a treat.

26

MEETING **INDIVIDUAL** NEEDS

ENRICHMENT: *"You Sing for Me" Countermelody*

To learn the entire countermelody, ask students to look at the first eight measures of the refrain, noting that most notes are repeated several times. Sing the opening section. Then ask students to look at the rest of the countermelody for other repeated notes. Sing the entire countermelody in unison. When students are secure singing the melody and countermelody separately, have them sing both parts together.

MOVEMENT: *"You Sing for Me"*
MOVEMENT

Preparation:
A section: Students walk with the music, changing direction, at first every eight counts, then every four counts. With a partner, try this going toward and away from each other.

B section: Clap the following rhythm:

Try the same rhythm with the feet, alternating feet with each step: R, L, R; L, R, L

You sing for me,_____ I'll sing for you._____ We need each

You sing for me, I'll sing for you. We need each

oth - er, yes we do._____ It takes sweet mu - sic

oth - er, yes we yes we do. It takes sweet mu - sic

ev' - ry day to keep those lone - some blues___ a - way.

ev' - ry day to keep those lone - some blues a - way.

Doot doot doo-dle-oo doot doot doot, doot doot doot doot doo-dle-oo doot.

Doot doot doo-dle-oo doot doot doot, doot doot doot doot doo-dle-oo doot.

"What songs have we sung that have a countermelody?" ("A Zing-a Za," "I Shall Sing") Have students:

- Review both parts of "I Shall Sing" CD1:10 (pp. 24–25), then sing in two parts.
- Name the two parts. (melody/countermelody)

"How does adding a countermelody change the way 'I Shall Sing' sounds?" (It makes the sound more complicated.) "Today you will hear a new song with a countermelody."

2 DEVELOP

1. Introduce "You Sing for Me" CD1:11. **Identify tone color of stringed instruments.** Have students:

▶ • Listen to the song with books closed and try to identify the instruments in the accompaniment, then read about the instruments used in the recording.

▶ • Tell how this song is like "I Shall Sing." (Both have verse-refrain form.)

▶ • Sing the melody from notation. (To hear melody only, shift balance to the left.)

2. Learn about texture and add the countermelody to "You Sing for Me." Have students:

▶ • Answer the question about the voice parts on page 26, then turn to page 28 and read about textures and ties. (Optional: For review of musical symbols, see **Resource Master 1 · 8**.)

- Learn the first eight measures of the highlighted countermelody, then divide into two groups and take turns singing both parts.

- Sing the entire song, with only the first eight measures of the countermelody.

Final Form:

Formation: couples, side by side, square formation (See *Glossary*.)

A section: Verse

Measures 1–4: Head couples move 4 steps forward, 4 steps backward.

Measures 5–8: Side couples move 4 steps forward, 4 steps backward.

Measures 9–12: Head couples move 8 steps forward to exchange places.

Measures 13–16: Side couples move 8 steps forward to exchange places.

B section: Refrain

All partners face each other and do the following steps:

Measures 1–2:

right close right   left close left

Measures 3–4: 4 steps to change places with partner

Measures 5–8: Repeat first four measures.

Measures 9–16: "Promenade Home"—walk side by side clockwise with partner until back at starting point, finishing out the music with elbow or two-hand swing. (See *Glossary* for hand position.)

UNIT ONE
LESSON 6

continued from previous page

3 APPLY

Introduce "Capriccio espagnol" CD1:13.
Identify families of the orchestra. Have
students:

▶ • Read about the orchestra and about texture
in "Capriccio espagnol" (ka **pri** chyo
es pa **nyol**).

OBJECTIVE 1 Informal Assessment

▶ • Signal what family of instruments they hear
in this piece of music that is not featured in a
band by making the first letter of that family's
name with their hands, or by tracing the letter
in the air. (*S* for strings)

▶ • Listen again and be able to describe how the
composer varied the texture. (alternated between solo instruments, small groups, and the
full orchestra) (Optional: Have students follow
the listening map on **Resource Master 1 • 9** or
Listening Map Transparency T • 2.)

▶ • Tell which families of instruments are featured most prominently in the piece. (woodwind, string)

When you described the number of voice parts in "You Sing for
Me," you were talking about **texture**. Musicians use the term
texture to describe the number of sounds going on at one time
and how these sounds relate to each other.

At the beginning of the refrain, each group sings a phrase while
the other holds a pitch. In the notation of the refrain melody,
curved lines called **ties** tell the singers to hold the note.

STRINGS AND MORE STRINGS

In a symphony orchestra, the string section is the heart of the
sound. An orchestra might have 65 string players, 16 woodwind
players, 15 brass players, and two percussionists. With a full symphony orchestra, you can hear the contrast between many instruments playing at once and only one or two instruments at a time.

28 MUSIC ON A STRING

MEETING **INDIVIDUAL** NEEDS

ALTERNATE TEACHING STRATEGY

OBJECTIVE 1 Have students recall the instrument families
that played in "Muss i denn" (page 9—brass, percussion)
and in "National Emblem" (page 13—brass, woodwinds,
percussion). Ask which specific instruments were missing
in those bands. (Answers will vary, but some members of
the string family will be mentioned.) Ask students which
instrument family was missing from both of these bands.
(strings) (Students may have heard some bands that include
strings. Point out that a typical band does not feature
strings.)

BIOGRAPHY: *Nicolai Rimsky-Korsakov*

Although he didn't plan to become a musician, Nicolai
Rimsky-Korsakov (ni ko laɪ **rim** ski **kɔr** sa kɔf),
1844–1908, took piano lessons as a child in Russia. When
he was 12 years old, he left the countryside and went to St.
Petersburg, where he entered naval school. He continued to
study piano, this time with a professional musician. His
teacher introduced him to a few composers, with whom
Rimsky-Korsakov kept in touch. He started composing,
even while he was on a $2\frac{1}{2}$ year voyage with the Navy, becoming so skillful as a composer that in 1871 he was made
a professor at the St. Petersburg Conservatory.

Capriccio espagnol (excerpt)
by Nicolai Rimsky-Korsakov

Listen for the thick and thin textures in this 1887 orchestral piece. Sometimes only one instrument is played. At other times, you will hear the entire orchestra. Notice when instruments are played by themselves or with just one or two others. Which families of instruments (brass, woodwinds, percussion, strings) are featured most prominently?

strings

4 CLOSE

"Texture variations are just as important in instrumental music as in vocal music. How did the changes in texture in the music we heard in today's lesson affect your listening?" (Discuss the families of instruments and how they were grouped in the music.)

"Listen once again to 'Capriccio espagnol.' See which of the instruments you can recognize, and listen for thick and thin texture."

LESSON SUMMARY

Informal Assessment In this lesson, students:

OBJECTIVE 1 Signaled to identify strings as the instrumental family not featured in a band.

MORE MUSIC: Reinforcement
"Bo Hai Huan Ten," page 313 (Chinese orchestra)
"Oh, How Lovely Is the Evening," page 336 (string family)
"Oh, Sinner Man," page 339 (country strings)
You're Invited, page 410 (instrument families in orchestra)
Concerto for Orchestra, Second movement ("Game of Pairs"), page 413I (texture, instrument families in orchestra)

Eventually he left the Navy to become a full-time composer. The boy who didn't plan to be a musician went on to write 15 operas and several symphonies.

ENRICHMENT: *Active Listening*

Have students sit in a circle and name either a solo instrument or an orchestral section that they will represent. Then have them write the instrument's or section's name on paper large enough for all to see. Make certain that all instruments and sections are included. (The instruments are given on **Resource Master 1 • 9**.) Then, as students listen to "Capriccio espagnol," have them stand with the name of their instrument in view each time they hear that instrument. Encourage students to comment on thick and thin texture; which students (instruments) stood alone; if there was a time during which all students were standing; and what instruments they did not hear.

ACROSS the

SCIENCE

STORM SAFETY

"You Sing for Me"

GROUPS   **30 MIN OR LONGER**

MATERIALS: reference texts (encyclopedias) or information from U.S. National Weather Service; optional—poster board, markers

"You Sing for Me" refers to *stormy weather*. Three severe storms affect the United States, each with hazards:

- thunderstorms—high winds, lightning, torrential rains;
- hurricanes—high winds, severe waves and flooding along shores;
- tornadoes—extremely high winds, sudden, not always predictable.

Have groups of students prepare "radio alert" presentations describing the approach of a severe storm and suggesting precautions. Students should research their presentations to include what parts of the country the radio program might be from. Groups might also prepare storm-safety bulletin boards, with safety tips on how to avoid the hazards of each storm.

(thunderstorms—get out of water, avoid open areas; hurricanes—listen to radios for possible evacuation to high ground; tornadoes—seek shelter in strong buildings or storm cellars; and so on)

COMPREHENSION STRATEGY: Organizing and presenting information

SCIENCE

WIND SPEEDS

"You Sing for Me"

PAIR   **30 MIN OR LONGER**

One way to estimate wind speed is to use the Beaufort scale. This scale lists wind speeds (in knots—knot is about 1.15 miles or 1,852 meters per hour) that produce certain effects.

Have students classify wind each day over a month—or longer. They might try to relate wind speed to other weather factors. (See page 21A.)

COMPREHENSION STRATEGY: Compare and contrast

BEAUFORT WIND SCALE

Effect	Type of Wind	Speed (knots)
Smoke rises vertically.	Calm	0–1
Smoke drifts slowly.	Light air	1–3
Leaves rustle; vanes move.	Light breeze	4–6
Twigs move; flag is full.	Gentle breeze	7–10
Small branches move.	Moderate breeze	11–16
Small trees sway.	Fresh breeze	17–21
Large branches sway.	Strong breeze	22–27
Trees bend; hard to walk.	Moderate gale	28–33
Twigs break off trees.	Fresh gale	34–40
Shingles blow off roofs.	Strong gale	41–47
Trees are uprooted.	Whole gale	48–55
Widespread damage occurs.	Storm	56–63
Violent destruction occurs.	Hurricane	64–71

CURRICULUM

LANGUAGE ARTS

WRITING A SCRIPT

"You Sing for Me"

GROUP   **15–30 MIN**

"You Sing for Me" describes two people, one of whom has *nothing much to say.* Have students work in groups to write a short script about two people who meet for the first time and one (if not both) has little to say. In the script, students should clarify why the character is so quiet— is the character shy or upset? Also, the script should describe how the quiet character finally opens up. The script might include other characters as well.

After an initial review, allow group members to revise, practice, and perform their scripts.

COMPREHENSION STRATEGIES: Expressing main ideas, revising

SOCIAL STUDIES

GREAT CIRCLE ROUTES

"Capriccio espagnol"

PAIR   **15 MIN OR LESS**
MATERIALS: globe, string

Have students work in groups to find routes to Spain from different parts of the world. First, have group members use a globe to find and list four cities or areas from different hemispheres. Then have them use a string to find the shortest possible flight route from each place to Spain. Have them hold one end of the string at a given starting point and extend the string to Spain, trying different directions— over the North Pole, the South Pole, around a latitude line, and so forth.

When they decide on the shortest route, have them record the places— countries, bodies of water, land features—that they pass, in order, from the starting point en route to Spain.

COMPREHENSION STRATEGIES: Sequencing, compare and contrast

LESSON PLANNER

FOCUS Pitch/Harmony

OBJECTIVES
OBJECTIVE 1 Name the pitches in I and V chords in C major and show their location on the staff
OBJECTIVE 2 Play I and V chords as accompaniment to a song in C major
OBJECTIVE 3 Use body percussion to show recognition of I and V chords in a song

MATERIALS
Recordings
I Shall Sing	CD1:10
Walk Together Children	CD1:14
Walk Together Children (performance mix)	CD1:15
Recorded Lesson: Chords and Chord Changes	CD1:16
Day-O	CD1:17

Instruments pitched instruments

Resources
Orff Orchestration O • 2 (Walk Together Children)
Playing the Guitar G • 4 (chord roots)
Recorder Master R • 5 (pitches E G A B)

Technology Music with MIDI: Walk Together Children

VOCABULARY
chord, root, triad

▶ = **BASIC PROGRAM**

MAKING HARMONY

Harmony is often provided by **chords**, groups of three or more pitches that sound at the same time. Listen for the organ accompaniment in order to hear the chords in this recording of "Walk Together Children."

WALK TOGETHER CHILDREN

African American Spiritual
Arranged by René Boyer-White

Refrain

Solo

1. Oh, walk
2. Oh, clap } to-geth-er chil-dren, don't___ you get___wear-y,
3. Oh, sing

Walk
Clap } to-geth-er chil-dren, don't___ you get___ wear-y,
Sing

Walk
Clap } to-geth-er chil-dren, don't___ you get___ wear-y, There's a
Sing

great camp meet-ing in the prom-ised land.

30

MEETING **INDIVIDUAL** NEEDS

ALTERNATE TEACHING STRATEGIES

OBJECTIVE 1 Put a treble staff on the board with a scale from C to G'. Add pitch letter names. Have volunteers form I and V chords above C and second line G. (C E G and G B D) Ask others to label these pitches. Erase everything and repeat the activity without the scale.

OBJECTIVE 2 Have students write the words to the refrain on the board and ask class members to circle any words that are sung on the V chords. Have them sing with the recording, listening to the bass line of the organ and checking whether or not they circled the correct words.

MULTICULTURAL PERSPECTIVES: *Spirituals*

Spirituals such as "Walk Together Children" date from the 1800s, when southern Christians began holding "revivals" to renew their faith. Revivals are exciting, emotional meetings. Traditional hymns were adapted, and new songs were written to express that emotion through rhythm and colorful language. Most spirituals are based on stories and characters from the Bible. Created mainly by African Americans, the songs express the enslaved people's suffering and yearning for a better life in heaven. Some spirituals communicated escape routes to the northern states and freedom.

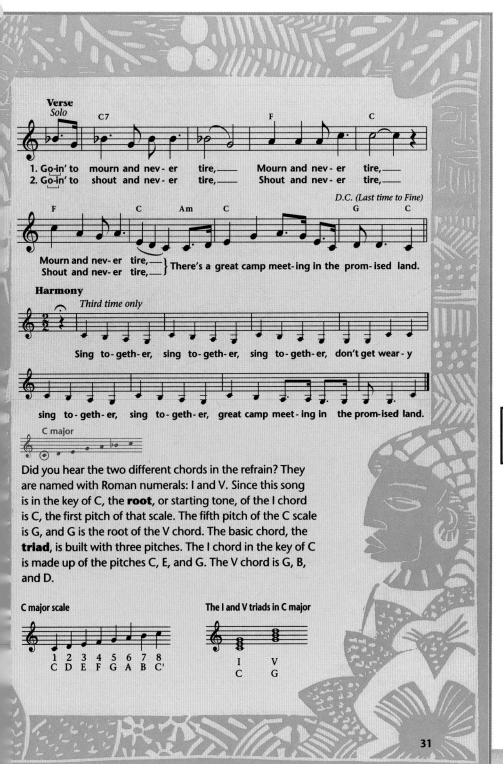

Verse
Solo

C7

1. Go-in' to mourn and nev-er tire,—— Mourn and nev-er tire,——
2. Go-in' to shout and nev-er tire,—— Shout and nev-er tire,——

F   C   Am   C   D.C. *(Last time to Fine)*   G   C

Mourn and nev-er tire,—— There's a great camp meet-ing in the prom-ised land.
Shout and nev-er tire,——

Harmony
Third time only

Sing to-geth-er, sing to-geth-er, sing to-geth-er, don't get wear-y

sing to-geth-er, sing to-geth-er, great camp meet-ing in the prom-ised land.

C major

Did you hear the two different chords in the refrain? They are named with Roman numerals: I and V. Since this song is in the key of C, the **root**, or starting tone, of the I chord is C, the first pitch of that scale. The fifth pitch of the C scale is G, and G is the root of the V chord. The basic chord, the **triad**, is built with three pitches. The I chord in the key of C is made up of the pitches C, E, and G. The V chord is G, B, and D.

C major scale

1 2 3 4 5 6 7 8
C D E F G A B C'

The I and V triads in C major

I   V
C   G

1 GET SET

"The songs we have been singing have instrumental accompaniment, which adds tone color and texture to the song. An accompaniment usually adds harmony as well." Have students:

▶ • Read about chords, then listen to "I Shall Sing" CD1:10 (pp. 24–25), and tell how many different chords they heard. (2)

"These kinds of chords are used all the time in music. Today you're going to learn more about them."

2 DEVELOP

1. Introduce "Walk Together Children" CD1:14. **Introduce I and V chords.** Have students:

▶ • Listen to the refrain, following the chords over the notation and paying attention to when they change.

▶ • Read about I and V chords.

Recorded Lesson CD1:16
▶ • Listen to "Chords and Chord Changes," and echo the roots and pitch letter names of the I and V chords in C major.

OBJECTIVE 1 Informal Assessment
• Say the pitch letter names of the I and V chords while pointing to the lines on the staff on page 31.

▶ • Sing the melody, then try the countermelody. (When ready, have students try singing both parts together.)

2. Play a I–V accompaniment with "Walk Together Children." Have students:

• In groups of three, name the pitches in the I and V chords in C major. Practice playing the chords on pitched instruments.

OBJECTIVE 2 Informal Assessment
• Play the chords to accompany the refrain. (One student may play either an entire chord or one tone.)

31

ENRICHMENT: *Arpeggiated Chords*

Playing arpeggiated chords is a good way to reinforce pitch names. Have students build C and G chords with pitched instruments and practice playing one note after the other: C E G E and G B D B. When they can do this, have them sing pitch letter names as they play the arpeggios. Then ask them to sing each arpeggiated chord without instruments.

ORFF: *"Walk Together Children"*

See **O · 2** in *Orchestrations for Orff Instruments*.

ENRICHMENT: *Singing I–V Roots*

Once students can hear the chord changes in a well-known song harmonized with I–V, have one group sing the chord roots as another group sings the song. Songs might include "Run, Joe, Run," "Simple Gifts," "I Shall Sing," "Day-O," "A Zing-a Za" (refrain). As an additional activity, a group of students can accompany the rest on resonator bells with tremolo I and V chords.

UNIT ONE
LESSON 7

continued from previous page

3 APPLY

Introduce "Day-O" CD1:17. Practice identifying chord changes. Have students:

▶ • Listen to "Day-O" and signal when they hear a chord change, thumbs up for I, five fingers up for V.

▶ • Read about steel-drum bands.

▶ • Sing "Day-O," following the notation.

OBJECTIVE 3 Informal Assessment
• Create two different body percussion patterns: clap to signal for the I chord and pat to signal the V chord. Listen a third time with books closed, signaling chord changes when they hear the phrase *Daylight come and me wan' go home* (starting at the end of line 3—the phrase starts on I each time).

STEEL DRUMS— RECYCLING AT ITS BEST

Here's another music-making group. It's a steel drum band and has only percussion instruments, all of them made from oil barrels. Steel drums come in four sizes that produce pitches from high to low. These drums originated in Trinidad, where they're considered the national instrument.

DAY-O

Words and Music by
Irving Burgie and
William Attaway

Day-o,   day-o,—   Day-light come and me wan' go home.—

Day,   me say day, me say day, me say day, me say day, me say

2nd time to Verse 2
3rd time Fine

day - o.   Day-light come— and me wan' go home.

32

MEETING **INDIVIDUAL** NEEDS

ALTERNATE TEACHING STRATEGY

OBJECTIVE 3 Have students work in pairs. One student holds a card with a "I" written on it and the other holds a card with a "V" written on it. They should listen for the phrase *Daylight come and me wan' go home* in the song, standing up when they hear their assigned chord, and sitting when they don't hear it. After that, reintroduce the idea of using body percussion to signal each chord. Have students start with just one chord, as they did with the cards. When this is successful, they can do the body percussion to signal both chords.

BACKGROUND: *The Steel Drum*

Necessity was truly the mother of this musical invention—in the 1940s, islanders on Trinidad did not have the money to buy instruments, so they made their own out of old oil drums. With a lot of hammering to raise different-sized areas on the drum top, different pitches could be sounded. Steel drums come in four sizes; the smaller the drum, the higher the pitch.

GUITAR: *"Day-O"*

Have students accompany this song with the chords: D A A7.

Work all night— un - til we're done.— Day-light come— and me
wan' go home. Stack ba-nan - a 'til de morn-ing come.——
Day - light come— and me wan' go home. Come, Mis-ter tal-ly man,
tal - ly me ba-nan - a. Day-light come— and me wan' go home.

1.
2.
wan' go home. 1. Lift six hand sev-en hand eight hand bunch.
2. Beau-ti - ful bunch— of ripe ba-nan-a.

Day - light come— and me wan' go home. Six hand sev-en hand
Day - light come— and me wan' go home. Hide the dead - ly

eight hand bunch. Day-light come— and me wan' go home.
black ta - ran - t'la. Day-light come— and me wan' go home.

Unit 1 *Music Makers* **33**

4 CLOSE

"The three songs you sang today came from very different kinds of music-making groups and were distinct from each other in style and sound. Yet they did have a basic musical element in common. What was it?" (I–V accompaniment) "What were the main instruments in 'Walk Together Children' and in 'Day-O'?" (organ; steel band) Have students:

▶ • Sing "Day-O" again (with partners) and add their own body percussion during the phrase *Daylight come and me wan' go home* to signal the I–V chord changes.

LESSON SUMMARY

Informal Assessment In this lesson, students:

OBJECTIVE 1 Named the pitches in I and V chords in C major and showed their location on the staff.
OBJECTIVE 2 Played I and V chords as accompaniment to "Walk Together Children."
OBJECTIVE 3 Used body percussion to show recognition of I and V chords in "Day-O."

MORE MUSIC: Reinforcement
Introduce "Ecce gratum," page 44 ("Day-O")
"The Boatman," page 332 (I and V in G)

PLAYING INSTRUMENTS: *Rhythm Ostinatos*

Students can create four- or eight-beat rhythm ostinatos to be played with "Day-O," using quarter, eighth, and half notes and rests. They may write out the patterns and then develop the body percussion, or write down the rhythm based on the body percussion they make up. Transfer the ostinatos to unpitched Latin-style percussion instruments.

MOVEMENT: *"Day-O"*

Preparation: Have students form small "work parties," with a tally man and a few workers to create a pantomime.

Each "worker" decides how he/she feels, as this has an impact on their movement. Partners choreograph cooperative work movements, such as lifting heavy bunches and moving crates, for the verses. The whole group choreographs rhythmic movement with mm. 1–10, pantomiming talk with the tally man and showing how tired they are.

Final Form: *Verses*—Partners, unmetered pantomime of loading the boat, stretching, yawning, and so on, in place.

Refrain mm. 1–10—Rhythmic group movement, moving through space, talking with the tally man and showing how glad they are to go home.

Unit 1 MUSIC MAKERS **33**

ACROSS the

LANGUAGE ARTS

WRITING NEW WORDS

"Walk Together Children"

PAIR   15–30 MIN

Have students work in pairs to write a new version of the line *There's a great camp meeting in the promised land.* The new words should fit the same rhythm and the same spirit of hope, for example:

● *There are great things coming in the days to come.*

Have students substitute their new line for the original each time it appears in the refrain and verses. Have them look for other repeating phrases (*Walk together children, don't you get weary*) and try writing their own substitutions for them.

Students can focus their new words on specific expectations—holidays that are coming, family gatherings, and other celebrations—future events that are meaningful to them.

COMPREHENSION STRATEGY: Expressing main ideas

SOCIAL STUDIES

MAP COORDINATE GAME

"Day-O"

PAIR   15 MIN OR LESS

MATERIALS: globe, index cards (or slips of paper)

Have students, working in pairs, locate the island of Trinidad on a globe at approximately 10°N latitude and 61°W longitude.

Then have them play a coordinate-jumble game. They change the coordinate directions to get three more locations:

● 10°N and 61°E
● 10°S and 61°W
● 10°S and 61°E

Have them search the globe to discover what is located at each new set of coordinates. They can extend the game even further by jumbling latitudes with longitudes:

● 10°W and 61°N, and so on.

COMPREHENSION STRATEGIES: Compare and contrast, following directions

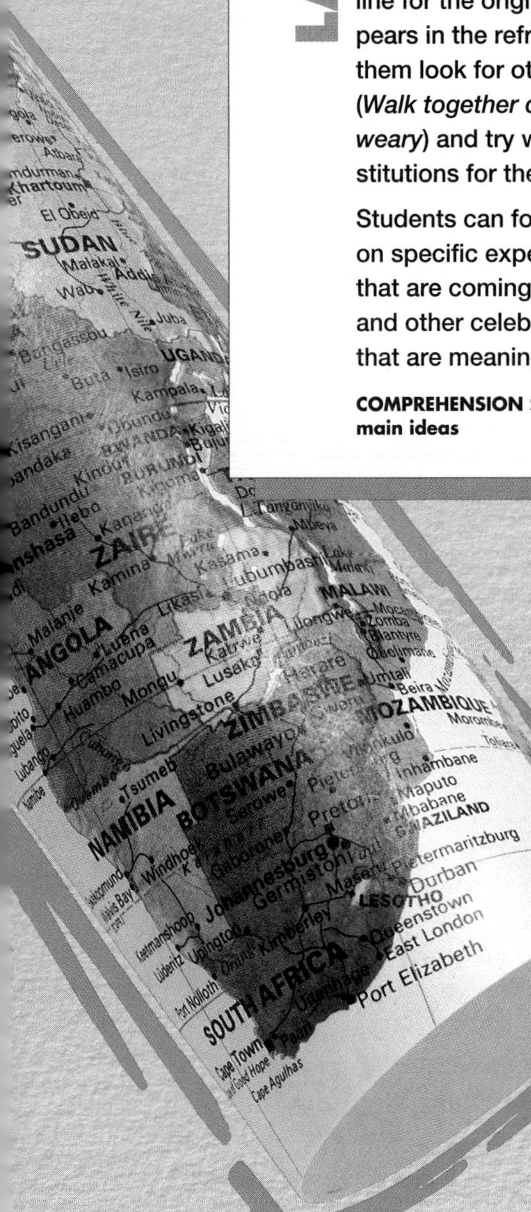

CURRICULUM

MATHEMATICS

HOURS IN THE DAY

"Day-O"

PAIR   **15 MIN OR LESS**

MATERIALS: optional—model clock made from paper plate with pencils used as clock hands

The farther away any location is from the equator, the greater the number of hours of daylight (and night) vary from summer to winter—although one day/night cycle is always 24 hours. So the phrase *work all night* can represent different amounts of time at various places, depending on the seasons.

Have students find the sunrise times from the following information. (The "hours of night" include twilight.)

Sunset	Hours of Night	Sunrise
6:20 P.M.	11 hours 30 min	
8:30 P.M.	8 hours 40 min	
5:10 P.M.	14 hours 10 min	

Have them extend the activity by telling how many hours of daylight follow each sunrise if the sunset time is about the same for the following day.

(Sunrises in order: 5:50 A.M.; 5:10 A.M.; 7:20 A.M.. Following days: 12 hours 30 min; 15 hours 20 min; 9 hours 50 min)

COMPREHENSION STRATEGY: Compare and contrast

LANGUAGE ARTS

PERSONAL NARRATIVE

"Day-O"

INDIVIDUAL   **15–30 MIN**

The song describes long hours of physical work. Based on this idea, ask students to think about the hardest job they have ever tackled. The job could be a chore they had to do at home, a school assignment, or perhaps a hobby or sport that took long hours of practice. The job could have been tough because of physical effort, or maybe because it involved difficult decisions.

Have students write a composition based on the theme of "The Toughest Job I've Ever Had to Do." Have them describe the tough job and explain what made the job so hard to do. Have them conclude by explaining the outcome of performing the job— what was accomplished.

COMPREHENSION STRATEGIES: Expressing main ideas, cause and effect

UNIT ONE
LESSON 8

RELATED ARTS [MOVEMENT] [THEATER] [VISUAL ARTS]

LESSON PLANNER

FOCUS Tone color

OBJECTIVES
OBJECTIVE 1 Identify pitches in the countermelody of a song (tested)
OBJECTIVE 2 Perform a rhythmic ostinato while singing a song (tested)
OBJECTIVE 3 Make arrangement suggestions for a song

MATERIALS
Recordings
Music for the World (piano accompaniment)   CD1:18
Dancin' on the Rooftop   CD1:1
A Zing-a Za   CD1:4
Rock Around the Clock   CD1:7
Music for the World (orchestral accompaniment)   CD1:19

Resources Recorder Master R • 6 (pitches D E G A)

VOCABULARY
arranger, instrumentation

▶ = BASIC PROGRAM

C major

Here's one more musical group to hear.
What performers do you hear in this recording?

chorus and piano

Music for the World

Words and Music by
Gene Grier and Richard Derwingson

Bright Rock

1. Mel - o - dy mak - ers all join in___ and sing out with a smile!___
2. Strike up the band___ and start to play___ a song for all to share.___

Har - mo - ny shap - ers, let's be - gin___ to sing it with some style!___
Or - ches - tra lead - ers, show the way.___ Let mu - sic fill the air!___

Rhy - thm and tem - po set the pace.___ So ev' - ry - one can fly.___
Play it with feel - ing, show our class,___ no mat - ter what the style.___

So - pra - no and al - to, ten - or, bass,___ let's give it our best try.___
Wood - winds, per - cus - sion, strings and brass,___ to - geth - er with a smile!___

Refrain

We're sing - ing }
(2.) We're play - ing } mu - sic for the world,___ so ev' - ry - one can hear.___

34

MEETING **INDIVIDUAL** NEEDS

ALTERNATE TEACHING STRATEGY

OBJECTIVE 1 Have students look at a C major scale on the board, as you point to each note and ask whether that note is in Measures 1–2 of the countermelody. Then point to each pitch in the C major scale and have students give the pitch letter names. Finally, have students name the pitches in Measures 1–2. As further reinforcement, call out pitch letter names in the C major scale and have students take turns playing the pitches on pitched instruments.

ENRICHMENT: *Arrangements of Popular Songs*

Have students add to the chart of popular performers that they have been keeping. Have them choose songs by groups that are favorites with many students. List for each one the instrumentation, use of lead singer and back-up groups, and other texture variations, such as clapping rhythms or sound effects.

MOVEMENT: *Choreographing "A Zing-a Za"*

Students can choreograph movement that will show the verse/refrain form of this song. This will give them an

We're spread-ing love through-out the world,___ O___ yeah!___ So

sing it loud and clear.___ We're shar-ing mu-sic with our friends___

___ from sea to shin-ing sea.___ We're mak-ing mu-sic for the world,___

___ O___ yeah!___ It starts with you and me.

To Coda ⊕   *1.*

2. Does-n't mat-ter who you are___ or where you make your home.___

D.S. al Coda

All you have to do___ is sing this song___ and you won't be___ a-lone.___

Coda ⊕   *cresc. poco a poco*

___ you and me. Yes, mu-sic for the

ff

world be-gins with you and me.___

1 GET SET

"What are some music-making groups?"
(brass band, big band, steel band, samba
bateria, orchestra, chorus with organ, country
string group) Have students:

▶ • Listen to "Music for the World" CD1:18 (piano
accompaniment), following the notation.

▶ • Answer the question about the performers on
the recording.

"Someone called an arranger, decided what
voices and accompaniment to use in this
recording. Today you'll get a chance to be an
arranger yourself."

2 DEVELOP

1. Review "Dancin' on the Rooftop" CD1:1.
Review instrument families. Have students:

▶ • Sing "Dancin' on the Rooftop" (pp. 2–4).

▶ • Tell what instrument families they heard on
the recording. (brass, woodwind, percussion,
string)

▶ • Briefly list the instruments in another piece
of music they have studied. (Possible answers:
"A Zing-a Za" has mostly percussion; "Capriccio espagnol" has all the families.)

2. Review "A Zing-a Za" CD1:4. **Review
countermelody and pitch letter names.** Have
students:

• Sing "A Zing-a Za" in two parts (pp. 11–12).

OBJECTIVE 1 Informal Assessment

• Listen as a volunteer gives the pitch letter
name of each note in Measures 1–2 of the
countermelody (C D E F G A) and raise hands
if they agree.

• Tell whether the countermelody was part of
the original song. (No, both the words and
melody were created by the arranger.)

opportunity to see the texture of a song reflected in movement. Divide the class into four groups, each to choreograph a different section of the song: Group 1—verse
melody, Group 2—refrain melody, Group 3—verse countermelody, and Group 4—refrain countermelody.

Preparation:

All groups develop:

—a beginning and ending group formation

—a 2-measure movement ostinato (four beats) that can be
repeated for the length of their section

Each group has a different movement focus: Group 1—
partner movement, Group 2—stamps and footwork, Group
3—running, and Group 4—twists and turns.

Final Form:

Verse: Group 1 performs its movement.

Refrain: Group 2 performs its movement.

Verse countermelody: Group 3 performs its movement.

Refrain countermelody: Group 4 performs its movement.

Verse with its countermelody: Groups 1 and 3 together.

Refrain with its countermelody: Groups 2 and 4 together.

UNIT ONE
LESSON 8

continued from previous page

3. Review "Rock Around the Clock" CD1:7
(p. 15). Review rhythmic ostinatos. Have students:

▶ • Echo you as you clap the rhythmic ostinatos from Lesson 3, *Get Set*, page 15.

▶ • Name the song in which these ostinatos were used. ("Rock Around the Clock")

▶ • As a class, choose an ostinato to play and in what part of the song to use it.

OBJECTIVE 2 Informal Assessment

▶ • Sing the song with the recording, accompanying themselves with the ostinato.

▶ • Tell how they acted as arrangers. (They chose an ostinato to go with the song and decided when it would be played.)

3 APPLY

Create an arrangement for "Music for the World." Have students:

▶ • Read about song arranging on page 36.

OBJECTIVE 3 Informal Assessment

▶ • Divide into small cooperative learning groups to create an arrangement of "Music for the World" by reading about instrumentation and answering the questions on page 37.

▶ • Listen to "Music for the World" (orchestral accompaniment CD1:19) and compare the professional arrangement to their group decisions.

Many people behind the scenes help to create the sound of your favorite recordings. For example, Quincy Jones worked on some of Michael Jackson's greatest hits. Jones arranged the music to get that Jackson sound. Many popular music stars, past and present, from big bands to the Beatles, have used arrangers to get the sound they want from their instrumentalists and singers.

SPOTLIGHT ON
QUINCY JONES

Quincy Jones is an American who is active in many areas of music. He is a pianist, trumpeter, bandleader, composer, arranger, and producer. As a jazz musician, he played with Lionel Hampton and Dizzy Gillespie. He has worked with musicians in many styles, including jazz, pop, and rap.

What does an **arranger** do? An arranger makes choices that determine how a musical performance will sound. These choices might include the style of the accompaniment, the rhythms and pitches in the accompaniment parts, the number of singers and players, the instruments and the parts they play, and the texture.

"MUSIC FOR THE WORLD" (AS YOU LIKE IT)

This is your chance to be an arranger. The song is "Music for the World." The choices are:

What style of accompaniment do I want? Big band, orchestra, country string band, samba bateria, pop-style band?

What instruments should I use? Woodwinds, brass, percussion, strings? Clarinets? Violins? You are choosing the **instrumentation** of the song.

36   ARRANGE IT!

MEETING **INDIVIDUAL** NEEDS

ALTERNATE TEACHING STRATEGIES

OBJECTIVE 2 Have students sing the song several times. If possible, have them memorize just Verse 1 and do their ostinato with only that much of the song. Additional rehearsal of the ostinato without singing will also help.

OBJECTIVE 3 Give each group only part of the song to arrange, either the verse or the refrain. Let them decide on only one or two elements, for example: instrumentation and when various instruments will play; or whether or not there will be two-part singing and when. Then the class can pool their ideas for one arrangement.

COOPERATIVE LEARNING: *Arranging a Song*

As a class, students can choose to arrange a simple song that they all know. Have them work in small groups of three to four students to make decisions about the instrumentation, vocals, texture, and special effects. Set a time limit and assign roles within each group such as recorder, reporter, and time keeper. Have the class make a decision about a final arrangement based on their combined ideas.

Should part of the arrangement feature an instrument or section of instruments? Drum solo, electronic keyboard interlude, rhythm pattern for tambourine? When in the music should it happen?

The texture—thick, thin, or both? Soloist with back-up singers, two-part chorus, melody with countermelody? The texture could change partway into the song. What change would sound best?

THINK IT THROUGH
How can these choices help express the meaning of the words?

4 CLOSE

"All music makers use arranging skills." Have students:
▶ • Listen to both recordings of "Music for the World" and compare them.

LESSON SUMMARY

Informal Assessment In this lesson, students:

OBJECTIVE 1 Identified pitches in the countermelody of "A Zing-a Za."
OBJECTIVE 2 Performed a rhythmic ostinato while singing "Rock Around the Clock."
OBJECTIVE 3 Made arrangement suggestions for "Music for the World."

MORE MUSIC: Reinforcement
"Ghost Ship," page 296 (pitch letter names, arrangements, reading rhythm; Halloween)
"Old Abram Brown," page 299 (pitch letter names, arrangement; Halloween)

CAREERS: *Arranger*
Use the different arrangements of "Music for the World" to introduce students to the career of arranger. An arranger adapts a composition to a new style. To be an arranger, you must study musical theory and notation. If possible, provide students with additional experiences hearing varied arrangements of the same song. Jazz music is an ideal source for arrangements of popular songs. Songs called standards have been used many times as the basis for arrangements and improvisations. For example, "The Sunny Side of the Street" has been recorded by vocalists Billie Holiday and Ella Fitzgerald, pianist/singer Nat King Cole, and pianist Art Tatum. Lionel Hampton recorded it on vibraphone and Bruce Forman on guitar. Recently, Harry Connick, Jr. did another rendition.

CRITICAL THINKING: *Making Decisions*
Students can try out their arranger's decision-making on a song they already know, including current songs. After they have written out and shared their ideas with the class, have them bring in the original recording so they can analyze what the professional arrangers have done and compare it with their own ideas.

ACROSS the

SOCIAL STUDIES

GLOBE GAME

"Music for the World"

GROUP   **15–30 MIN**

MATERIALS: globe, index cards (or sheets of paper), watch or clock

Students work in groups of four—two teams of two students. The starting team has five minutes to locate a place anywhere on the globe and list five facts about it: the hemisphere it is in, the continent it is on, surrounding countries and landforms, and so on.

That team challenges the other team to name the place by telling each of the facts one at a time. The challenged team may use the globe and gets 2 points for identifying the place. If the challenged team does not guess correctly after hearing all the facts, it is told the identity—but can still score 1 point by using the globe to tell other facts that would have helped to identify the place.

Teams alternate and play as many rounds as they wish.

COMPREHENSION STRATEGIES: Using maps and globes, finding main ideas

SCIENCE

SOUND

"Music for the World"

PAIR   **15 MIN OR LESS**

MATERIALS: book, stereo, aluminum foil, meter stick

How does *music fill the air* as the song describes? Have students explore how sound travels through air. Two students stand about a meter apart. One holds a sheet of aluminum foil. The other waves a large book up and down in the direction of the foil. Have the students observe and describe what happens to the foil.

Repeat the activity, this time with a stereo instead of a book. Have the student holding the foil describe what he or she feels as the stereo is played in front of it.

Have students relate the two activities by explaining how they think sound travels. (Sound starts as a vibration. The vibration sets air—matter—in motion. Molecules in the air move up and down as the energy of the vibration passes through and eventually reaches the foil, causing the foil to shake.)

COMPREHENSION STRATEGIES: Cause and effect, drawing conclusions

CURRICULUM

MATHEMATICS

CIRCLES

"Music for the World"

PAIR	15–30 MIN

MATERIALS: construction paper, scissors, tape, ruler, globe

Have students cut long narrow bands out of construction paper. Make sure the bands have parallel, straight edges by having students draw parallel lines across the construction paper before cutting.

Have the students wrap one band around the "world"—a globe or large ball—at the equator. (They may need to tape two small bands together to reach.) Have them tape the ends together. Repeat at two higher latitudes—at about 40°N and 60°N. They will have produced three circular bands.

Have students explore their three "circles" by telling how they are different—and measuring or calculating the differences. (They have different circumferences, diameters, radii, and areas. They can find the circumferences by measuring the length of each band. The greatest distance across a circle is the diameter—half of which is the radius. The area can be found by the formula: $A = \frac{1}{2} \times C \times r$ or $\pi \times r^2$.)

COMPREHENSION STRATEGY: Compare and contrast

SOCIAL STUDIES

MAP PROJECTION

"Music for the World"

PAIR	15 MIN OR LESS

MATERIALS: globe, plastic wrap (or balloon cut on one side), markers

Have students wrap a globe with a single piece of plastic wrap, stretching the wrap to reach smoothly around the equator and crinkling together edges near the poles. (For large globes, they can cover just the Western or Eastern Hemisphere—stretching the sheet to reach from North Pole to South Pole, crinkling up the ends at the poles.)

Have them use a marker to trace outlines of continents onto the wrap. Then they remove the wrap, stretching out the edges. Some of the outlines will become fragmented. Have them trace over the broken outlines and compare the continent shapes with the way the continents appear on the globe. (The distortion is greater at greater distance from the equator.)

COMPREHENSION STRATEGIES: Cause and effect, compare and contrast

UNIT ONE
LESSON 9

LESSON PLANNER

OBJECTIVES
To review songs, skills, and concepts learned in Unit 1 and to test students' ability to:
1. Distinguish between band and orchestra
2. Identify the four families of the orchestra
3. Identify letter names of some pitches on the treble staff
4. Read notation for ♫ ♩ and 𝄽

MATERIALS
Recordings

Dancin' on the Rooftop	CD1:1
Accentuate the Positive	CD1:2
A Zing-a Za	CD1:4
Fung Yang Song	CD1:8
I Shall Sing	CD1:10
You Sing for Me	CD1:11
Walk Together Children	CD1:14
Unit 1 Assessment A	CD1:20–23
Unit 1 Assessment B	CD1:24–27

Resources
Resource Master 1 • 10 (assessment)
Resource Master TA • 1 (assessment)
Resource Master—staff paper

▶ = BASIC PROGRAM

REVIEW

MAKING YOUR OWN MUSIC

Music-making groups come in many shapes and sizes. Listen to and sing "Dancin' on the Rooftop" and discuss the instruments that you hear. Now do the same for "Accentuate the Positive." How are the instrumental groups accompanying these two songs similar? Both are bands; They have the same instrument families.

Both "Dancin' on the Rooftop" and "Accentuate the Positive" come from the United States. But music-makers come from all over the world. "A Zing-a Za" is accompanied by the sound of a Brazilian band. Listen for the Chinese music-makers in "Fung Yang Song." Which instrument families are heard in both recordings? percussion, strings, woodwinds

Music-makers create harmony by adding a countermelody to a song. Sing "I Shall Sing," with its countermelody. What other songs in this unit had countermelodies? "You Sing for Me," "Walk Together, Children"

38

MEETING **INDIVIDUAL** NEEDS

PROGRAM IDEA: *Music Makers Contest*

This review can be enjoyed in the classroom or presented as a simple program. Additional materials from Unit 1, *Celebrations,* or the *Music Library* may be added as well as original work from the students.

Have students take part in a "Music Makers Contest," complete with an announcer who sets the scene and introduces each group, including information about that type of group. Have different groups of students represent different musical groups (in costume if possible) competing for title of

"Best Music Makers in the World." Students can sing along with the recording, with the vocal track turned off or with the performance mix (if available).

At the end, have the audience (or class) vote for the best group. Discuss and set up criteria for how they will assess each group beforehand. For example: How well prepared was the group? How appropriate and effective were their costumes? What level of skill did they display? Which performance had the best over-all effect?

REVIEW

1. Review instrumental groups with "Dancin' on the Rooftop" CD1:1 **(pp. 2–4) and "Accentuate the Positive"** CD1:2 **(pp. 6–7).** Have students:

▶ • Listen to "Dancin' on the Rooftop" and "Accentuate the Positive," and discuss the instruments they hear.

▶ • Answer the questions about the two groups. ("Accentuate the Positive" has a Broadway band with fewer instruments than the big band accompanying "Dancin' on the Rooftop.")

2. Review percussion and string families with "A Zing-a Za" CD1:4 **(pp. 11–12) and "Fung Yang Song"** CD1:8 **(pp. 20–21).** Have students:

▶ • Listen to "A Zing-a Za" and "Fung Yang Song" and tell what instrument families they hear in both recordings.

3. Review countermelody with "I Shall Sing" CD1:10 **(pp. 24–25).** Have students:

▶ • Sing "I Shall Sing" and discuss the effect of adding a countermelody to a melody. (thicker texture, more complicated)

• Name other songs with countermelodies. ("You Sing for Me" CD1:11, pp. 26–27; "Walk Together Children" CD1:14, pp. 30–31)

4. Reinforce unit theme by describing music-making groups. Have students:

▶ • Name as many music-making groups as they can. Describe how each group sounds and name its instrument families. (Optional: Perform the songs in a "Music Makers Contest" as described in the *Program Idea* on the bottom of page 38.)

DRAMA CONNECTION: *Storytellers*

Just as music-makers make their unique music, storytellers create their own special dramas. Have students create an observation chart of several favorite television shows (or plays or movies). Beside the name of each show, list the number of main characters and the situations represented on each show (family, group of friends, co-workers). Then name the cultural groups represented on each show. Finally, ask students which shows tell one main story per episode and which tell more than one. Use the chart as a basis for a discussion about variety and quality in the television medium.

ASSESSMENTS A AND B CD1:20–27

Different recorded examples for Assessments A and B allow for two uses of the same set of questions. When appropriate, recorded examples for Assessment A use familiar musical examples with which students have worked, for the given concept. The recorded examples for Assessment B use musical selections the students have not previously worked with for the concept, encouraging the application of knowledge to new material.

The pupil page is intended for those who wish to assess quickly, with the whole class or in small groups. Each assessment may be used as a pretest or as a final review before presenting the written test (**Resource Master 1 • 10**).

ANSWERS

	ASSESSMENT A	ASSESSMENT B
1.	a	c
2.	a	b
3.	c	d
4.	c	d

CHECK IT OUT

1. Which instruments do you hear?
   - a. brass and percussion
   - c. strings
   - b. woodwinds and brass
   - d. percussion

2. Which type of musical group do you hear?
   - a. band
   - b. orchestra
   - c. something else

3. Which rhythm pattern do you hear?

4. Which example shows the pitches you hear?

40

MEETING **INDIVIDUAL** NEEDS

PORTFOLIO ASSESSMENT

To evaluate students' portfolios, use the Portfolio Assessment form on **Resource Master TA • 1**. See page 1B for a summary of Portfolio Opportunities in this unit.

ENRICHMENT: *Creating Assessment Guidelines*

Discuss the following to help children create their own assessment guidelines for compositions and performances.

Facts and feelings: What musical elements did the composition or performance contain? Name three things you liked about the performance. Why? Name one thing you might change. Why?

Group processing: How did your group work successfully together to complete this task?

Use these guidelines throughout the school year whenever children create and perform for each other.

CREATE

Play Your Own Accompaniment

Work in groups. First choose a song in Unit 1 to accompany.

- Develop a rhythm for your accompaniment patterns using half, quarter, and eighth notes. The patterns should be either four or eight beats long. Write your rhythm patterns down using music notation.
- Choose instruments for each pattern. If you choose pitched instruments, select any pitches on the treble staff.
- Organize your patterns to fit the form of the song. For each section of the song, change the rhythm pattern or the instrumentation.

PRACTICE your accompaniment with the song. Make any changes or improvements you see fit.

PERFORM your arrangement for the class.

CREATE movement to the song if you wish. If the song is in more than one section, there should be a change of movement or number of people in each section.

Write

Write a paragraph about a music-making group you have heard. Where does this group perform? Who might be listening to their music? Discuss what instruments were in the group and to what families they belong.

Unit 1 *Music Makers* **41**

CREATE AND WRITE

1. Create an accompaniment and movements for a song. Have students:

- Follow the instructions on page 41 to create and play their own accompaniment patterns with a song of their choice from Unit 1. (If students choose pitched instruments, they may figure out which pitches go with the song, or you may wish to limit them to the pitches of the song's key or the appropriate pentatonic scale.) (Optional: Have students notate their accompaniments on staff paper, available in the *Resource Master* booklet.)
- Create movement for the song, showing changes in sections through changes in the choreography. (They might change body facing, level, number of people dancing, and so on.)

2. Write about a music-making group. Have students:

▶ • Write a paragraph about a music-making group, answering the questions in the book.

▶ • Read their paragraphs to the class, or post as part of a bulletin board display.

LANGUAGE ARTS CONNECTION: *Editing*

Have students exchange paragraphs and edit their partner's paragraph. They should correct punctuation, incorrectly spelled words, and so on. They should also look for incomplete sentences, verb/subject agreement, and other grammatical errors. The main idea should be stated clearly, and each sentence should follow in a sequence that makes sense to the reader.

MOVEMENT: *Dance from "Create" Section*

Ask students to critique their choreography and performances based on the assessment terms given in *Movement*, page 5.

ʈarmina

RELATED ARTS MOVEMENT THEATER VISUAL ARTS

LESSONLINKS

Introduce "Ecce gratum" *(10 min)*

OBJECTIVE Compare Carl Orff's "Ecce gratum" to "Day-O" and learn about the historical background of *Carmina Burana*, a collection of songs and poems

Reinforcement Day-O, *page 33*

MATERIALS
Recordings
Ecce gratum (excerpt) from
  Carmina Burana by C. Orff
  (listening)   CD1:28
Day-O   CD1:17

"Ecce gratum" Listening Map *(20 min)*

OBJECTIVE Follow the "Ecce gratum" listening map and create movements for the piece

Reinforcement listening map, *page 13*

MATERIALS
Recording Ecce gratum (excerpt)
  from *Carmina Burana* by
  C. Orff (listening)   CD1:28

Resources Listening Map Transparency
  T • 3

THE BREVIARY OF QUEEN ISABELLA OF CASTILE
This miniature painting from about 1495 comes from an illustrated prayer book once owned by Queen Isabella of Castile (employer of Christopher Columbus). Illustrated books such as this were prepared with special colors and decorations that made the paintings glow.

MEETING **INDIVIDUAL** NEEDS

BACKGROUND: *Carmina Burana*

Carmina Burana is a collection, consisting mainly of love songs, that dates to the 1200s. In 1936, composer Carl Orff took some of the songs and created a "dramatic cantata" for solo singers, chorus, and orchestra using the music and mimed action. His cantata arrangement has 25 movements and is based on 24 of the Latin poems.

BIOGRAPHY: *Carl Orff*

Carl Orff (kärl ôrf), 1895–1982, was a German composer who wanted to revive old musical forms with a new sound. This music was often based on folktales or other ancient stories. He also developed an approach to music education that allows children to learn about music through speech, singing, moving, and playing instruments. An important aspect of the approach is to encourage improvisation. Orff developed special children's instruments to use along with more traditional instruments. These include xylophones, glockenspiels, and metallophones of various registers.

Burana

Have you ever hunted through an old trunk in your attic or basement and come upon a long-lost treasure? Paintings, manuscripts of musical works, and books often remain in storage for centuries, forgotten by the outside world. This is what happened to a collection of poems and songs dating from the 1200s.

During that time, groups of students and young monks wandered about the countryside, entertaining themselves, and anyone who cared to listen, with amusing songs. The songs were sung in Latin, French, and German.

Many of these songs were not written down but were passed from one group of singers to another through the oral tradition. About 700 years ago, someone assembled manuscripts for a number of these works and placed the collection in the Library of the Benedictine Monastery at Beuren, in Germany, for safekeeping. The manuscript contained words to the songs, with some medieval musical notation.

In the mid-1800s, a scholar discovered the manuscript and published it under the title "Carmina Burana," which means "Songs of Beuren." In 1936, the German composer Carl Orff took the texts for some of these songs and composed a new musical version of "Carmina Burana" for chorus and orchestra. Through the popularity of Orff's work, these ancient Latin poems have become familiar to people all over the world.

Carl Orff

Encore 43

Introduce "Ecce gratum" CD1:28

1. Compare "Day-O" to "Ecce gratum." Have students:

• Sing "Day-O" CD1:17 (page 32).

• Sing the first two measures of "Day-O" and think of a motion to do each time this phrase is heard. (For example, beginning with both hands to one side, move hands over head to the other side on each *Day-o*.)

• Listen to "Ecce gratum," noting how the opening motive is similar to that of "Day-O." (Both openings are dramatic and sound somewhat similar in the pitches used, then are followed by sections that are lower in pitch and less dramatic.)

• Tell how many times they heard this motive in "Ecce gratum." (It occurs three times, beginning each of the three recurring sections.)

• Listen to "Ecce gratum" again, doing the motion they chose for "Day-O" each time it occurs in the music.

2. Learn about the historical background of *Carmina Burana*. Have students:

• Read pages 42–43, then summarize what *Carmina Burana* (kɑɾ **mi** nɑ bu **ɾɑ** nɑ) is and how it was discovered.

• Tell how the songs were first used. (For entertainment; they were passed on through the oral tradition.)

• Think of ways they learn songs (from recordings, from radio or television, from friends, at camp, or at school) and how music is "stored" today. (in music books or recordings)

SOCIAL STUDIES CONNECTION: *Medieval Period*
Have students research life in the Medieval Period or Middle Ages, a period from 400–1450. Students can report on the system of feudalism that developed over that time. Students might work together to create a mural showing life in the 1200s, when the songs from *Carmina Burana* were popular. They might include medieval architecture, knights and noblewomen, farmers, and craftspeople.

ART CONNECTION: *Illuminated Manuscripts* VISUAL ARTS
Have students look at the decorated capital letters and borders that illustrate pages 42–45. Point out that this lettering is done in the style of books called illuminated manuscripts. Before the printing press was invented, monks and nuns copied and decorated books by hand. Flower and animal motifs were often incorporated into the lettering. Miniature paintings, such as the one reproduced on page 42, were included as well. Invite students to choose a favorite poem or quotation to copy and decorate in the style of an illuminated manuscript.

ENCORE

continued from previous page

"Ecce gratum" Listening Map

1. Listen to Carl Orff's interpretation of "Ecce gratum" from *Carmina Burana*. Have students:

• Read the words in English aloud, summarizing their meaning. (They tell about the coming of spring and summer.)

• Name things they associate with spring and summer.

• Listen to the music, paying attention to sounds that show the contrast of the seasons or particular images in the lyrics, such as flowers or the sun.

2. Follow the listening map. Have students:

• Preview the map. Find the three sections and relate them to the words, then find repeat signs. (Each section represents a stanza of the song. Optional: Use **Listening Map Transparency T • 3**.)

• Tell what the different rows of illustrations on the map might suggest about the song. (They show loudness, accented parts, and sections that are smoother and flowing.)

• Follow the listening map as they listen to "Ecce gratum," noting such things as tempo changes, contrasts of tone color, and contrasts of dynamics.

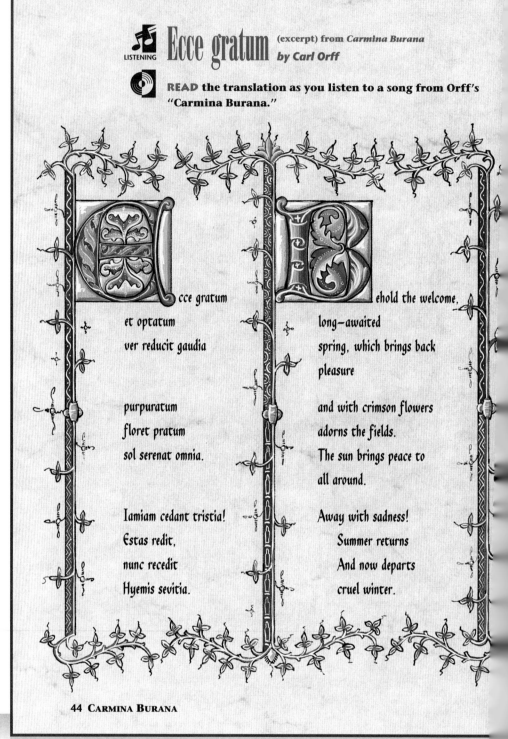

Ecce gratum (excerpt) from *Carmina Burana* **by Carl Orff**

READ the translation as you listen to a song from Orff's "Carmina Burana."

Ecce gratum
et optatum
ver reducit gaudia

purpuratum
floret pratum
sol serenat omnia.

Iamiam cedant tristia!
Estas redit,
nunc recedit
Hyemis sevitia.

Behold the welcome,
long-awaited
spring, which brings back
pleasure

and with crimson flowers
adorns the fields.
The sun brings peace to
all around.

Away with sadness!
Summer returns
And now departs
cruel winter.

44 CARMINA BURANA

MEETING **INDIVIDUAL** NEEDS

BACKGROUND: *"Ecce gratum"*

"Ecce gratum" (**ɛt** chɛ **grɑ** tum) is one of the songs from *Carmina Burana*. It is sung by the full chorus early in the cantata in a section appropriately called "In Springtime." *Ecce gratum* is Latin for "Behold the welcome." The song welcomes spring by praising the pleasure it brings.

LANGUAGE ARTS CONNECTION: *Poetry*

Have students write poetry about spring. Start them out by discussing the fact that poetry often uses imagery that appeals to the senses. In "Ecce gratum," for example, the twelfth-century poet used "and with crimson flowers adorns the fields" to create a visual sense of spring. Students should use their own imagery for spring in their poems.

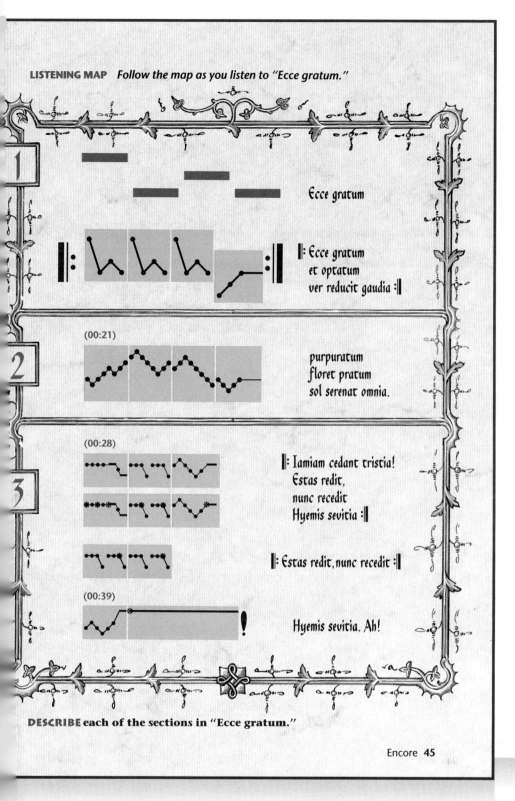

1

Ecce gratum

‖: Ecce gratum
et optatum
ver reducit gaudia :‖

2

(00:21)

purpuratum
floret pratum
sol serenat omnia.

3

(00:28)

‖: Iamiam cedant tristia!
Estas redit,
nunc recedit
Hyemis sevitia :‖

‖: Estas redit, nunc recedit :‖

(00:39)

Hyemis sevitia. Ah!

DESCRIBE each of the sections in "Ecce gratum."

3. Create movement for "Ecce gratum."
Have students:

• Suggest adjectives that describe each of the rows in the map of "Ecce gratum," for example:

Section 1 Row 1—sustained, swinging; Row 2—punchy, accented

Section 2 Row 3—smooth, connected

Section 3 Row 4—excited, explosive; Row 5—sharp, short; Row 6—short, abrupt; Row 7—sustained, long

• Divide into seven groups, each group creating movements that reflect the adjectives for one row of illustration. The movement should include locomotor (moving through space) and nonlocomotor movement. Include different levels of movement (jump high, crouch low, raise arms over head, and so on).

• Listen again, taking turns moving to their assigned rows. (Students should arrange themselves in the order in which their parts will be played on the recording.)

MOVEMENT: *"Ecce gratum"*

After all seven groups have performed their movement, have students analyze what they saw using the terms given in *Movement,* page 5. Based on their observations of unity and contrast, ask them to change the movements in such a way that all seven parts can work together as a coherent sequence of choreography. Ask them to make performance suggestions as well.

MUSICAL ADVENTURES

MULTICULTURAL PERSPECTIVES

Through exposure to diverse materials, students develop an awareness of how people from many cultures create and participate in music. This unit includes:

African/African American
- **Kokoleoko,** Liberian folk song, 57
- **Joshua Fit the Battle of Jericho,** American spiritual, 58, 76

European/European American
- **One Moment in Time,** song by Americans Albert Hammond and John Bettis, 49
- **Canon,** instrumental piece by British composer Henry Purcell, 52
- **Tune in a CAGe,** recorder playalong by American Norm Sands, 53
- **I Believe in Music,** by American composer Mac Davis, 54
- **Cancan,** orchestral music by French composer Jacques Offenbach, 56
- *At the Moulin Rouge: The Dance,* by French painter Henri de Toulouse-Lautrec, 56
- **Alla turca,** movement for piano by Austrian composer W. A. Mozart, 60
- **Tortoises,** orchestra piece by French composer Camille Saint-Saëns, 63
- **Flying Free,** by American Don Besig, 64
- **Anitra's Dance,** orchestra piece by Norwegian composer Edvard Grieg, 79

Asian/Asian American (Middle Eastern)
- **Tumbai,** Israeli folk song, 66
- **Üsküdar,** Turkish folk song, 73

For a complete listing of materials by culture throughout the book, see the Classified Index.

CURRICULUM INTEGRATION

Activities in this unit that promote the integration of music with other curriculum areas include:

Art
- Draw world of today and/or tomorrow, 53A
- Research and draw reptiles, 65B
- Use patterns to decorate sashes, 69B
- Make a textured vase, 76

Math
- Compute how old in days one is, 53B
- Determine elapsed time, 57B
- Write and solve rate problems, 65A
- Design paper airplanes, then measure and graph flight lengths, 65A
- Write and solve "frequent flier" problems, 69A

Reading/Language Arts
- Write a letter of introduction, 53B
- Explore the theme of a "universal language," 57A
- Write a rondo-form poem, 61
- Write a description of a special place, 65B
- Write song lyrics, 69B
- Create a one-act movie, 84

Science
- Describe healthful daily routines, 57B
- Research and draw reptiles, 65B

Social Studies
- Find locations on a map, 53A
- Create a "Time Capsule" to show life in hometown, 57A
- Play a latitude-longitude game, 69A

PLANNER

ASSESSMENT OPTIONS

Informal Performance Assessments

Informal Assessments correlated to Objectives are provided in every lesson with Alternate Strategies for reteaching. Frequent informal assessment allows for ongoing progress checks throughout the course of the unit.

Formal Assessment

An assessment form is provided on pupil page 84 and Resource Master 2•5. The questions assess student understanding of the following main unit objectives:

- Read and play ♫♫ and ♫♫
- Identify a major scale
- Identify A B A form

Music Journal

Encourage students to enter thoughts about selections, projects, performances, and personal progress. Some journal opportunities include:

Discuss music of other times and places, TE 63

Think It Through, 63, 67

Portfolio Opportunities

Update student portfolios with outcome-based materials, including written work, audiotapes, videotapes, and/or photos that represent their best work for each unit. Some portfolio opportunities in this unit include:

- Purcell "Canon" playalong, page 52 (audiotape)
- "Tune in a CAGe" playalong, 53 (audiotape)
- "Kokoleoko" playalong, 57 (audiotape)
- Movement: "Joshua Fit the Battle of Jericho," TE 59 (videotape)
- Perform "Alla turca" rhythm, 60
- Move to show A B A form of "Tumbai," 68 (videotape)
- Sing and move with "Tumbai" in canon, 71 (videotape)
- Perform "Üsküdar" with ostinato, TE 72
- Perform "Joshua Fit the Battle of Jericho" with ostinatos, 59, TE 73
- Perform "Üsküdar" with accompaniment, TE 75 (audiotape)
- Create B section for "Kokoleoko," 80 (audiotape)
- Playing Instruments: Keyboard, TE 80 (audiotape)
- Check It Out, 84
- Create, 85 (audiotape)
- Write, 85
- Portfolio Assessment (Resource Masters TA•1–5), TE 84

MY MUSIC NOTEBOOK

			LESSON 1 CORE p.46	LESSON 2 CORE p.54	LESSON 3 p.58
		FOCUS	Pitch	Rhythm	Form
		SELECTIONS	Your World (poem) One Moment in Time Canon (listening) Tune in a CAGe (listening)	I Believe in Music Cancan from *Gaité parisienne* (listening) Kokoleoko	Joshua Fit the Battle of Jericho Alla turca from Piano Sonata in A Major (listening)
MUSICAL ELEMENTS	**CONCEPTS**	**UNIT OBJECTIVES** **Bold = Tested**			
EXPRESSIVE QUALITIES	Dynamics				• Hear *p*, *mf*, *f*, cresc., dim.
	Tempo		• Hear and sing andante	• Hear and sing allegro, andante	• Hear allegro • Sing andante
	Articulation		• Hear and sing legato	• Hear marcato	• Hear staccato, legato, accent
TONE COLOR	Vocal/ Instrumental Tone Color		• Hear orchestra • Perform recorder playalongs	• Hear orchestra • Play pitched and unpitched instruments • *Accompany song on guitar*	• Play percussion • Hear piano
DURATION	Beat/Meter		• Hear ⅜ and ¼	• Snap on beats 2 and 4 of song • Move to beat • Recognize beats with ♪	• Tap beat • Recognize 4 sounds per beat as ♫♫
	Rhythm	• **Read and play ♫♫♫ and ♫♫**		• **Echo-clap, describe, and identify ♪ patterns (E/D/I)** • **Perform rhythm patterns with ♫♫♫ ♫♫ ♩ (P)** • Snap pattern with ♩ and ♪	• **Recognize 4 sounds per beat as ♫♫ (Rf)** • **Play rhythmic accompaniment with ♫♫ (Rd)**
PITCH	Melody	• Aurally recognize whole and half steps • Locate half steps in melody	• Discuss melodic contour of scale • Aurally recognize whole and half steps • Trace melodic contour • Learn about sharps and flats, intervals	• Note stepwise motion in song	
	Harmony			• *Accompany song with guitar chords*	
	Tonality major/minor	• **Identify major scale** • Play major scale	• **Play, sing, and learn about major scale (E/D/I)** • **Recognize whole and half steps in major scale (E/D/I)** • Learn about tonal center	• Play G major scale (P)	
DESIGN	Texture	• Sing in 3-part canon • Understand monophony, homophony, polyphony	• Play C major scale accompaniment		
	Form/ Structure	• **Identify A B A form** • Show same and different sections • Sing in 3-part canon • Show rondo form	• Learn about canon	• Recognize A B or verse-refrain form	• Locate verse, refrain, coda • Show same and different sections • Learn about and show rondo form • Find coda in map • *Compose rondo-form poem*
CULTURAL CONTEXT	Style/ Background		• Learn about new music technology • Career: pop singer Whitney Houston • *Poet: Georgia Douglas Johnson*	• *Composers: Mac Davis, Jacques Offenbach* • *Artist: Henri de Toulouse-Lautrec* • *Learn about Liberia*	• *Composer: Wolfgang Amadeus Mozart* • *Learn about "Alla turca"*

Learning Sequence: E = Explore, D = Describe, I = Identify, P = Practice, Rf = Reinforce
Rd = Read, C = Create   See also *Program Scope and Sequence*, page 432.

Italic = Meeting Individual Needs

LESSON 4 CORE p.62	LESSON 5 CORE p.66	LESSON 6 p.70	LESSON 7 p.74	LESSON 8 p.78
Pitch	Form/Rhythm	Pitch/Texture	Texture	Form/Pitch
Cancan from *Gaité parisienne* One Moment in Time Tortoises from *The Carnival of the Animals* (listening) Flying Free	Flying Free Tumbai	Tumbai Üsküdar Joshua Fit the Battle of Jericho	I Believe in Music Tumbai Üsküdar Joshua Fit the Battle of Jericho	Anitra's Dance from *Peer Gynt Suite No. 1* (listening) Joshua Fit the Battle of Jericho Kokoleoko
• Hear *mf* through *ff*, *cresc.*		• Sing *crescendo* and *ff*		• Sing *crescendo* and *ff* • Hear *pp* through *f*
• Hear allegro, vivo, accelerando	• Sing andante and allegro	• Sing andante	• Sing andante, allegro	• Hear allegretto
• Hear staccato, accent	• Sing accent	• Sing accent	• Sing accent	• Hear staccato, legato
• Hear orchestra • Play pitched instruments	• Hear Israeli folk ensemble	• Hear Turkish lute • Play pitched instruments	• Hear piano accompaniment	• Hear orchestra
	• Tap beat with song rhythms	• Tap beat to song • Identify number of beats in rhythm pattern	• *Compose 8-beat ostinatos for song*	• Learn about ⅜ meter • Distinguish ⅜ meter in listening
	• **Read and clap rhythms using ♫♫♫ ♫♫ ♫♫ (Rf/Rd)** • **Pat song rhythm from notation (Rf)**	• **Read and perform ostinatos with ♪ (Rd)** • Perform ♫ ostinato with song	• **Perform rhythm of melody in canon (Rd)** • **Add rhythmic accompaniment to song (Rd)**	• **Review ♪ rhythms (Rf)** • **Read and create a rhythm pattern with ♪ (C)**
• Name pitches in melody • Locate half steps in melody • Sing melody with pitch syllables and hand signs	• Locate half steps in melody	• *Create pentatonic melody*		• Create melody in pentatonic scale
		• Hear three-part harmony	• Accompany song with chord roots • *Accompany song with guitar chords*	
• **Recognize, play, sing, read major scale (Rf/Rd)** • **Learn pitch syllables in major scale (Rf)** • **Locate half steps in major scale (Rf)**	• Hear minor	• Learn about, play, identify minor scale • Locate half steps in minor • Recognize tonal center • Tell key signature and tonal center of minor song		• **Review half step locations in major (Rf)** • **Sing major and minor scales (Rf)** • Name songs in major and minor • Identify minor
		• Sing in 3-part canon • Sing melody with rhythmic ostinatos	• Describe texture changes • Sing in unison and canon • Build homophonic texture for song • Add accompaniments • Identify textures	• Perform rhythmic ostinatos with song
• Identify A A B A form	• **Show sections of A B A form (I)** • **Play A B A form (P)** • Review A A B A form	• Move to show canon • Sing in 3-part canon • Add introduction and coda to song • *Improvise section of song*	• *Make up dance for song to show phrases* • Perform rhythm of melody in canon	• **Recognize and create A B A form (Rf/Rd/C)** • Recognize verse-refrain form with introduction and coda • *Compose rondo form for song*
• *Composers: Camille Saint-Saëns, Don Besig* • *Learn about "The Tortoise" by Ogden Nash*	• *Learn about Israel and "Tumbai"*	• *Learn about Turkey and "Üsküdar"* • *Learn about the saz (Turkish folk lute)*	• *Learn about spirituals*	• *Learn about Edvard Grieg and "Anitra's Dance"*

UNIT 2

SKILLS

SKILLS		LESSON 1 CORE p.48	LESSON 2 CORE p.54	LESSON 3 p.58
CREATION AND PERFORMANCE	Singing	• *Sing upward leaps* • Hear and sing legato	• Read and speak rhythm pattern of listening	
	Playing	• Play C major scale • *Play scalewise passages on recorder* • Play C major scale accompaniment • Play recorder melody	• Snap on beats 2 and 4 of song • Echo-clap patterns with sixteenth notes • *Accompany song on guitar* • Play G major scale • Echo-clap song rhythm • Perform rhythmic playalong	• Tap to beat with song • Play rhythm pattern with listening
	Moving	• Trace melodic contour in the air	• Move to the beat with listening	• Move to show same and different sections of song
	Improvising/ Creating	• *Create rhythm patterns for simultaneous ascending and descending C major scales*	• *Create new words for song*	• Create movement to show song sections • *Create rondo-form poem*
NOTATION	Reading	• Read and play C major scale as accompaniment • Read and play 3-note accompaniment	• Read rhythm pattern • *Read and play guitar chords* • Read and speak rhythm pattern	• *Find song sections from notation* • Play rhythm pattern of listening from notation
	Writing	• Trace melodic contour		
PERCEPTION AND ANALYSIS	Listening/ Describing/ Analyzing	• Describe melodic contour of scale	• Identify major scale in listening	• Identify sections in rondo listening

 **TECHNOLOGY**

SHARE THE MUSIC VIDEOS

Use videos to reinforce, extend, and enrich learning.
· Lesson 3, p. 60: Musical Expression (classical music)
· Lesson 4, p. 64: Making a Music Video (popular music)
· Encore, pp. 86–89: Sounds of Percussion (drumming along, Glen Velez)

MUSIC WITH MIDI

MIDI technology allows students to manipulate musical elements and make musical decisions with these songs:
· Lesson 3, p. 58: Joshua Fit the Battle of Jericho

MUSICTIME™

This notational software develops students' music reading and writing skills through activities correlated to these lessons:
· Lesson 1, Project 1 (create a melody)
· Lesson 5, Project 2 (create an ostinato for Tumbai)
· Lesson 9, Project 3 (compose a piece in ABA form)

OVERVIEW

LESSON 4 CORE p.62	LESSON 5 CORE p.66	LESSON 6 p.70	LESSON 7 p.74	LESSON 8 p.78
	• Sing accent • *Learn about breathing from the diaphragm*	• Sing in 3-part canon • Sing crescendo and *ff* • Sing melody with rhythmic ostinatos • *Learn how to sing several "l" sounds in succession*	• Speak rhythm of melody in canon	• Speak and sing rhythmic ostinatos • Sing crescendo and *ff*
• Play C major scale with listening	• Clap rhythms using quarter, eighth, sixteenth notes • *Play B section of A B A form*	• *Improvise B section for song*	• Perform rhythm of melody in canon • Perform pitched and unpitched accompaniments • *Accompany song with guitar chords* • *Create and play ostinatos*	• Play B section for A B A form • *Create and play sections of rondo*
• *Perform dance with listening*	• Move to show sections of A B A form	• Move in three-part canon	• *Create dance for song*	
	• Create movement for B section in A B A form	• *Improvise B section for song*	• *Create ostinatos for song* • *Create dance for song*	• Create B section for A B A form • *Create rondo form for song*
• Locate half steps in notated melody	• Read rhythms using quarter, eighth, sixteenth notes • Pat song rhythm from notation	• Tell key signature and tonal center of song from notation	• Accompany song with notated chord roots	• Review sixteenth-note rhythms in song
			• *Create and notate ostinatos for song*	
• Describe ways to remember location of half steps in major scale • Identify major scale in listening			• Describe texture changes • Identify texture of listenings	• Identify A B A form in listening

MUSIC ACE™

Music Ace reinforces musical concepts and provides ear-training opportunities for students.

Lesson 1, p. 48: Lesson 20 (whole steps and half steps)
Lesson 4, p. 62: Lesson 20 (half steps); Lesson 24 (intervals in major scales)
Lesson 9, p. 82: Lesson 24 (major scales)

UNIT TWO
LESSON 1

RELATED ARTS `MOVEMENT` `THEATER` `VISUAL ARTS`

LESSON PLANNER

FOCUS Pitch

OBJECTIVES

OBJECTIVE 1 Perform an accompaniment with a recording in C major (tested)

OBJECTIVE 2 Aurally identify whole and half steps (tested)

MATERIALS

Recordings

One Moment in Time	CD1:29
Listening: Canon by H. Purcell	CD1:30
Listening: Tune in a CAGe by N. Sands	CD1:31
Recorded Lesson: Stepping Up the Scale	CD1:32

Instruments
keyboard, resonator bells, recorder

Resources
Resource Master 2 • 1 (practice)
Resource Master 2 • 2 (practice)
Resource Master 2 • 3 (practice)
Musical Instruments Master—recorders
Recorder Master R • 7 (D E G A B C')
Signing Master S • 6 • 1 (One Moment in Time)

VOCABULARY
scale, major scale, half step, whole step, interval, canon, tonal center, sharp, flat

▶ = **BASIC PROGRAM**

UNIT 2

46

MEETING **INDIVIDUAL** NEEDS

BIOGRAPHY: *Georgia Douglas Johnson* THEATER

American poet and playwright Georgia Douglas Johnson (1886–1966) was an important figure of the Harlem Renaissance. The Harlem Renaissance was a burst of creative expression from African American artists of every kind in the 1920s. The movement's center was in New York City. Some of the more famous contributors included writers Langston Hughes and Zora Neale Hurston. Although Johnson lived in Washington, D.C., she hosted regular meetings with Harlem Renaissance writers and other artists. Her poetry deals with the two causes to which she devoted much of her time—rights for women and minorities. She never saw her plays staged because producers felt her subject matter—violence against African Americans—was too controversial.

YOUR WORLD

Your world is as big as you make it.
I know, for I used to abide
In the narrowest nest in a corner,
My wings pressing close to my side.

But I sighted the distant horizon
Where the skyline encircled the sea.
And I throbbed with a burning desire
To travel this immensity.

I battered the cordons around me
And cradled my wings on the breeze
Then soared to the uttermost reaches
With rapture, with power, with ease!

—Georgia Douglas Johnson

47

1 GET SET

"Most everyone loves adventure! Adventure can involve taking some risks and exploring the unknown. Get ready for adventures in music." Have students:

▶ • Read the poem "Your World."

▶ • Discuss how the narrator of the poem feels about adventure and exploration.

"Exploring music can be as exciting as a good adventure book or movie. In this unit, you will get a chance to create your own musical adventures."

continued from previous page

2 DEVELOP

1. Discuss how music enriches life. Have students:

▶ • Read page 48 and discuss how music introduces us to other places and times.

▶ • Discuss how technological developments have influenced music. (Students might discuss how the way music is passed along has changed from live performances to records to tapes and compact discs. They might also mention instruments such as the electric guitar, or electronic instruments such as the synthesizer.

Technology has also influenced music indirectly. For example, the introduction of fast travel by plane has helped to make the spread of musical styles quicker and easier because performers can appear more often and in more diverse places.

General developments in computer technology have had a great influence on many areas of music. Computers are used today to make music notation easier, to create and/or alter musical sounds, to coordinate performances, and to assist in the recording process. The ever-increasing access to powerful personal computers has allowed more people than ever before to produce professional-quality music at home or in school.)

Do you ever feel as though your world is just too small, too limiting, and you want to be off to other places or other times? Music is a way you can travel with your ears. It can take you to far-away places, introduce you to other ways of life, and teach you different languages. Music can show you what people have in common, no matter where they are.

Just as planes and spaceships have changed how we travel and the kinds of adventures that are possible, the invention of CDs, tapes, and videos allows us to travel through music more often, more easily, and to more distant places.

48

MEETING **INDIVIDUAL** NEEDS

VOCAL DEVELOPMENT: *Upward Leaps*

The melody of "One Moment in Time" moves primarily by step, but there are several places where the music leaps upward. Singing upward leaps correctly requires more breath support. Review the breathing exercise (Unit 1, page 1, *Vocal Development*) and the vocalise for expanding the vocal range (Unit 1, page 7, *Vocal Development*). Then, as students sing the following vocalise, have them bend their knees as they "touch" the high pitch. This promotes "going into the body" for breath support for the top pitch, rather than straining for it from below.

Continue up by half steps to A.

Ah   ah   *(breathe)*   Ah   ah   *(breathe)*   Ah   ah   *(breathe)*

Tell students to use the same technique with "One Moment in Time."

▶ • Listen to the song, tracing the melodic contour in the air with their hands.

▶ • Sing "One Moment in Time."

ONE MOMENT IN TIME

Words and Music by Albert Hammond and John Bettis

Each day I live I want to be a day to give the best of me.
I'm only one, but not alone. My finest day is yet unknown.
I broke my heart for ev'ry gain. To taste the sweet, I faced
the pain.
I rise and fall, yet through it all this much remains:

I want one moment in time when I'm more than I thought
I could be,
when all of my dreams are a heartbeat away
and the answers are all up to me.
Give me one moment in time when I'm racing with destiny.
Then, in that one moment in time, I will feel, I will feel eternity.

I've lived to be the very best. I want it all, no time for less.
I've laid the plans, now lay the chance here in my hands.

I want one moment in time when I'm more than I thought
I could be,
when all of my dreams are a heartbeat away
and the answers are all up to me.
Give me one moment in time when I'm racing with destiny.
Then, in that one moment in time, I will feel, I will feel eternity.

You're a winner for a lifetime if you seize that one moment in time,
make it shine.

Give me one moment in time when I'm more than I thought
I could be,
when all of my dreams are a heartbeat away
and the answers are all up to me.
Give me one moment in time when I'm racing with destiny.
Then, in that one moment in time,
I will be, I will be, I will be free. I will be free.

Unit 2 *Musical Adventures* **49**

SIGNING: *"One Moment in Time"*
Signing Master S · 6 · 1 has sign language for this song.

UNIT TWO
LESSON 1

continued from previous page

3. Discuss the work of a famous performer.
Have students:

▶ • Read about Whitney Houston.

▶ • Discuss the performer and the songs she has sung.

▶ • Tell some of the activities involved in the career of a professional pop singer like Whitney Houston. (learning songs, rehearsing with other musicians, recording in a studio, traveling to locations of live performances, performing in live concerts, promotional appearances)

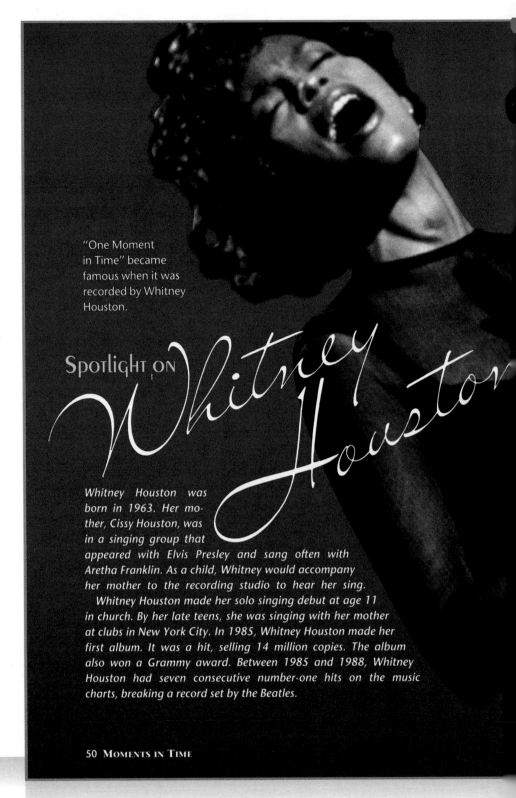

"One Moment in Time" became famous when it was recorded by Whitney Houston.

Spotlight on Whitney Houston

Whitney Houston was born in 1963. Her mother, Cissy Houston, was in a singing group that appeared with Elvis Presley and sang often with Aretha Franklin. As a child, Whitney would accompany her mother to the recording studio to hear her sing.

Whitney Houston made her solo singing debut at age 11 in church. By her late teens, she was singing with her mother at clubs in New York City. In 1985, Whitney Houston made her first album. It was a hit, selling 14 million copies. The album also won a Grammy award. Between 1985 and 1988, Whitney Houston had seven consecutive number-one hits on the music charts, breaking a record set by the Beatles.

50 MOMENTS IN TIME

MEETING **INDIVIDUAL** NEEDS

RECORDER: *Scalewise Passages*

Have students echo and improvise scalewise passages on recorder on G A B C'. They can combine scalewise motives to create a melody.

Students can also practice identifying whole and half steps within D E and G A B C': you, or a volunteer, play two pitches a step apart from each other. The class echoes, then identifies the interval as a whole or half step.

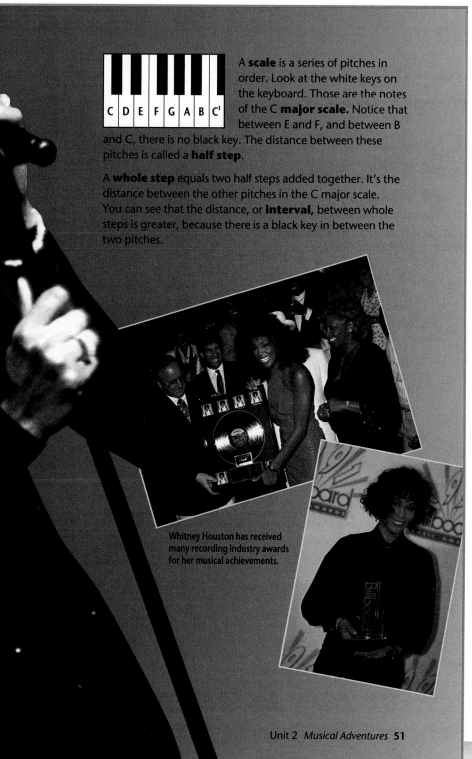

A **scale** is a series of pitches in order. Look at the white keys on the keyboard. Those are the notes of the C **major scale**. Notice that between E and F, and between B and C, there is no black key. The distance between these pitches is called a **half step**.

A **whole step** equals two half steps added together. It's the distance between the other pitches in the C major scale. You can see that the distance, or **interval**, between whole steps is greater, because there is a black key in between the two pitches.

Whitney Houston has received many recording industry awards for her musical achievements.

Unit 2 *Musical Adventures* **51**

4. Introduce the major scale and whole and half steps. Have students:

▶ • Listen as one or more volunteers echo you in playing the pitches C D E F G A B C' (as an experiential step, without labeling it as a scale).

▶ • Describe the melodic motion of what was just played. (stepwise, no skips, pitches in order from lowest to highest)

▶ • Read about the scale, the C major scale, whole and half steps, and the definition of an interval on page 51.

UNIT TWO
LESSON 1

continued from previous page

5. Introduce Purcell's Canon CD1:30. **Play a melodic accompaniment.** Have students:

• Learn to play the melodic accompaniment for Canon by Henry Purcell (**pər səl**) on page 52 (without the recording).

▶ • Read the definition of canon.

OBJECTIVE 1 Informal Assessment
• Play the melodic accompaniment with the recording. (Optional—For more instrument parts, use **Resource Masters 2 • 1** and **2 • 2.**)

6. Introduce "Tune in a CAGe" CD1:31. **Play a recorder part.** Have students:

• Look at the notation and answer the question.

• Play "Tune in a CAGe" on recorders or other pitched instruments.

3 APPLY

1. Play a C major scale. Have students:

▶ • Play a C major scale. (C D E F G A B C') (Optional: For more practice with the C major scale, use **Resource Master 2 • 3.**)

▶ • Read about tonal center, sharps, and flats.

THE C SCALE IN HISTORY

LISTENING **Canon** *by Henry Purcell*

A **canon** *is a melody that is imitated exactly in one or more parts. The English composer Henry Purcell wrote this canon in the late 1600s.*

PLAY this with the Purcell Canon, first alone and then with the recording. It uses every pitch in the C major scale.

PLAY a C major scale on bells, keyboard, piano, or on another pitched instrument.

The **tonal center**, or starting and ending point, of the C major scale is C. But what if you wanted to play a major scale starting on another pitch, such as D? Could you just start on D and play only white keys?
No, the half and whole steps would be out of order.
A **sharp** (♯) before a note raises it a half step. A **flat** (♭) lowers it a half step. You can see on the keyboard that each black key has both a sharp name and a flat name.

By using sharps and flats, you can make the half and whole steps fall in the right places, no matter what major scale you are playing.

52 MOMEMTS IN TIME

MEETING **INDIVIDUAL** NEEDS

ALTERNATE TEACHING STRATEGIES

OBJECTIVE 1 Have students play the melodic accompaniment to Purcell's Canon—without the recording—while singing the pitch letter names. Then have them "play" along with the recording, using their fingers to identify pitches while looking at resonator bells or other pitched instruments (or charts of bells or keyboard), and singing the letter names. Finally, have them play with the mallets along with the recording.

OBJECTIVE 2 Have the class close their eyes to hear the difference between the whole step and the half step. Play a

major scale. Tell students that if the interval sounds like that at the beginning of the scale (between Steps 1 and 2), then it is a whole step. If the interval sounds like that at the end of the scale (between Steps 7 and 8), then it is a half step.

SPECIAL LEARNERS: *Playing a Pitched Instrument*

Even students with severe intellectual disabilities who have difficulty with the concepts of whole and half steps should enjoy playing along with the Canon recording. Provide adaptations and prompts as needed. Adaptations might include playing all dotted half notes instead of repeated quarter notes. In some cases, a student might play only the first

Tune in a CAGe *by Norm Sands*

Practice reading these notes by playing "Tune in a CAGe" on the recorder. You've seen them before. What notes are they? CAG

---

2. Identify visually whole and half steps.

Have students:

- Identify visually whole and half steps on the keyboard and/or resonator bells.

OBJECTIVE 2 Informal Assessment
Recorded Lesson CD1:32

▶ • Listen to "Stepping Up the Scale," which contains examples of whole and half steps played one note at a time, and signal a "W" with their fingers if they hear a whole step or two fingers pointing to the side (palm toward the body) to show a sign-language "H" if they hear a half step.

4 CLOSE

"Scales are one of music's basic materials. In this lesson, you worked with a scale that gives you the basis for understanding other scales. What was it?" (C major) Have students:

▶ • Tell where the half steps are found in the C major scale. (between E and F and between B and C)

"'One Moment in Time' is in C major. Let's sing it again to close the lesson."

LESSON SUMMARY

Informal Assessment In this lesson, students:

OBJECTIVE 1 Played the instrumental accompaniment as they listened to Purcell's Canon.

OBJECTIVE 2 Signaled as to whether they were hearing whole or half steps in the recorded lesson, "Stepping Up the Scale."

MORE MUSIC: Reinforcement
"Orion," page 350 (C major scale)
"Merry Minstrels," *Songs to Sing and Read,* page 64 (Purcell Canon, C major scale)

C in the first measure of the part when cued by another student or with physical assistance from a nondisabled peer. Code or underline notes as necessary. To deemphasize adaptations, assign some nondisabled students to any part that you modify for students with disabilities.

IMPROVISATION: *Purcell's Canon*

Set barred instruments in a C scale. Have some students play the scale, using the following rhythm patterns.

Alto instruments (going up the scale):

Soprano instruments: Go down the scale in steady dotted half notes from C' to C.

Have other students play the bass pattern (line 4) on **Resource Master 2 • 1** at the same time.

Then have students create their own rhythms for playing up and down the scale simultaneously. These rhythms must complement one another and sound well with the canon.

ACROSS the

MAPS

"Your World"

WHOLE CLASS   **15–30 MIN**

MATERIALS: world map or classroom globe; optional—stick-on dots or bits of clay (or modeling compound)

Have students explore this theme: "Your world may stretch far beyond your hometown." Ask them:

● Where have you traveled outside of your hometown?

● Do they have family roots in other parts of the country or the world?

Have students compile lists of their "links" to other parts of the country and the world, and point out these locations on a map. Students can organize a class presentation: "The World of Our Class." They can use stick-on dots to mark all the worldwide locations to which they are linked. Students can give oral presentations of accounts of their trips or of their family members in other locations. They might like to display snapshots they took or have received from family members.

COMPREHENSION STRATEGY: Displaying information

DRAWINGS

"Your World"

INDIVIDUAL   **30 MIN OR LONGER**

MATERIALS: drawing paper, pencils, erasers, oil pastels; optional—examples of art by Marc Chagall, such as *Paris Through My Window* or *I and the Village*, for display

The theme of this poem offers students a chance to draw their "world." Ask students to make a mental list of the people, places, and things that make up their world today, as well as their hopes and dreams for the future. This list can form the main idea and supporting details of their drawing.

Students might choose to draw their world today or their vision of tomorrow, or somehow to combine the two. As an initial idea, students might make pencil sketches of their profiles, leaving room inside the sketch to draw images, shapes, and objects that represent their world. They can use oil pastels in vivid colors to add details and finishing touches to their pictures.

COMPREHENSION STRATEGIES: Visualizing, exploring spatial relationships, expressing main ideas

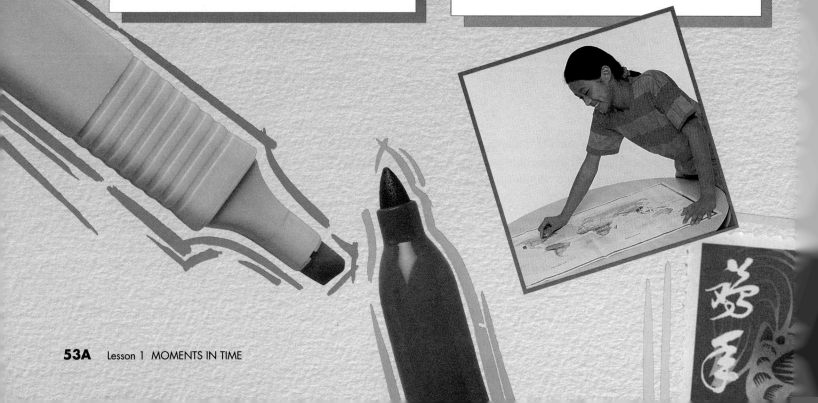

CURRICULUM

MATHEMATICS

ELAPSED TIME

"One Moment in Time"

PAIR   **15 MIN OR LESS**

MATERIALS: optional—calculator

The words *Each day I live* suggests a challenge: "How many *days* old am I?" Have students work in pairs to outline a method for solving this problem. One quick method—to multiply one's age in years by 365 days—does not account for the number of days since the most recent birthday.

(Suggestion—Subtract, using numbers for months (1–12) and days (1–31):

	Year	Month	Day
Today's Date	199_	___	___
−Birth Date	___	___	___
Difference	___	___	___

Multiply the difference in years by 365. Add a day for each leap year between the two years. (A leap year is a year divisible by 4—1992.) Multiply the difference in months by 31—an estimate since most, but not all, months have 31 days. Add the two values above to the number of days in the difference.)

COMPREHENSION STRATEGY: Deciding upon steps in a process

LANGUAGE ARTS

WRITING A LETTER

"One Moment in Time"

INDIVIDUAL   **15–30 MIN**

Have students list the five things that they value the most, at this moment in time. Then have them list the five things they like the most about themselves. Based on the lists, have them write a letter of introduction—to a new friend or a maybe a distant family member whom they never met. For example:

Dear Uncle Mike:

I thought I'd give you a chance to know me better.

As part of their letter, they might describe a vision of themselves in the future—ten years from today—including what they hope to be doing, and what they might have already accomplished by that point in time.

COMPREHENSION STRATEGY: Expressing point of view

75th Anniversary of Rotary International

HEALTH, HUNGER & HUMANITY

HAPPY NEW YEAR!

USA

UNIT TWO
LESSON 2

RELATED ARTS MOVEMENT | THEATER | VISUAL ARTS

LESSON PLANNER

FOCUS Rhythm

OBJECTIVE
OBJECTIVE 1 Read and play the rhythm of a playalong pattern that contains quarter, eighth, and sixteenth notes (tested)

MATERIALS
Recordings
Recorded Lesson: Echoing
  Sixteenth Notes   CD1:33
I Believe in Music   CD1:34
Listening: Cancan from *Gaité
  parisienne* (excerpt) by J.
  Offenbach   CD1:35
Kokoleoko   CD2:1

Instruments
drum and resonator bells or xylophones

Resources
Orff Orchestration O • 3 (Kokoleoko)
Recorder Master R • 8 (pitches G A B C'
  D')

▶ = **BASIC PROGRAM**

RHYTHM OF TIME

This song was written in the 1970s. It expresses the appeal of music as a universal language. Music can be a bridge, spanning distances between people and ideas.

SNAP this rhythm with "I Believe in Music":

I Believe in Music

For guitar, transpose to key of D.

Eb major

Words and Music by Mac Davis
Words adapted by Marilyn Davidson

Verse
Eb(D)

1. Well   I could just sit a-round mak - in' mu -   sic
2. Mu - sic is love,   love is mu - sic if you
3. Mu - sic is the u -   ni - ver - sal lan - guage and

Ab(G)   Bb(A)

all   day long.____   Long as   I'm   mak - in' mu-
know what I mean.____   Peo - ple who be - lieve in   mu-
love is the key,____   To peace,____   love,   and

54

MEETING **INDIVIDUAL** NEEDS

BUILDING SELF-ESTEEM: *"I Believe In Music"*

Discuss what songwriter Mac Davis expresses in "I Believe in Music." (that music and love are the key to peaceful, harmonious living) Point out that some may agree with Davis, while others may have different ideas. Ask students what they believe contributes to understanding and peace among people, encouraging everyone to give their ideas without comment from others in the class. Write all ideas on the board under the heading "I Believe in . . . ."

Then work as a class to write a new refrain, replacing the words *music* and *love* with students' own ideas, for example: "I believe in justice, I believe in peace . . . ." Finish the activity by singing the new refrain.

GUITAR: *"I Believe in Music"*

Have students accompany the song with the guitar in the key of D, following the chords on the notation.

- sic I know I can't do no-bod-y wrong.____ And
- sic are the hap-pi-est peo-ple I've ev-er seen.____ So
un-der-stand-ing,____ to liv-in' in har-mo-ny.____ So

who knows, may-be some-day I'll come up with a song,____
clap your hands, stomp your feet,____ shake your tam-bou-rine.
take your neigh-bor by the hand and sing a-long with me.

that makes peo-ple wan-na stop their fuss-
Lift your voic-es to
And find out what it real-

- in' and fight-in', just long e-nough to sing a-long.
____the sky and tell____ us what you mean. Ev-'ry-bod-y sing
- ly means to be young____ and____ rich and free.

Refrain

I be-lieve in mu-sic. I____ be-lieve in

love. Sing it to me chil-dren, I I be-lieve in mu-sic.

I be-lieve in love.____

"Your musical adventure continues today as you travel to other continents. Even though the places you will go may be new to you, some of the rhythms will be familiar." Have students:

Recorded Lesson CD1:33

▶ • Listen to "Echoing Sixteenth Notes" and echo-clap various rhythms containing sixteenth notes, including the first four measures of "Kokoleoko" (ko ko le **o** ko).

"Today you're going to have a chance to play some of these rhythms on different instruments."

2 DEVELOP

1. Introduce "I Believe in Music" CD1:34. **Review quarter notes and rests, and stepwise melodic contour.** Have students:

▶ • Listen to the song, snapping on the second and fourth quarter notes in each measure.

• Identify the rhythm of the pattern as quarter notes and quarter rests.

▶ • Briefly discuss the song's meaning.

▶ • Identify the form of the song. (Verse-Refrain or A B)

• Note stepwise motion in the refrain.

▶ • Sing the song.

SPECIAL LEARNERS: *Clapping Rhythm Patterns*

Students with coordination problems, who have trouble meeting hands at midline (clapping), will probably have trouble clapping rhythm patterns with eighth and sixteenth notes. They may be more successful with small up-and-down movements. Have students keep the heel of their dominant hand on their desk or thigh and move only the fingers to tap the rhythms. Demonstrate how this same movement—fingers tapping together—is used to play the tambourine and hand drum. Have several students use this tapping movement to play the rhythms on percussion instruments.

BIOGRAPHY: *Mac Davis*

Mac Davis (b. 1942) is an American singer and songwriter. Born in Texas, Davis has made up songs since he was a child, although he never learned to read music. At fifteen, Davis left home and traveled to Atlanta, where he formed a rock-and-roll band and tried to sell his songs. At first, he wrote rock songs. When he started to write more personal songs, they "came out country," he says. After Elvis Presley recorded a couple of his songs, Davis became in demand as a songwriter. Over 150 artists—including Davis—have recorded his songs.

UNIT TWO
LESSON 2

continued from previous page

2. Introduce Offenbach's "Cancan" CD1:35.
Review quarter, eighth, and sixteenth notes.
Have students:

▶ • Look at the rhythm of the theme and read it according to the directions.

▶ • Learn to do a "dance" with "hand-feet" to the main theme. (See *Movement* below.)

3. Play a G major scale, then listen for the descending scale in "Cancan." Have students:

• Learn to play a descending G major scale on pitched instruments.

• Listen to "Cancan," patting with the beat to the opening section with alternating hands, doing the "hand-feet" dance when they hear the main theme, and "freezing" when they hear a descending scale.

3 APPLY

1. Introduce "Kokoleoko" CD2:1. **Echo-clap the rhythm.** Have students:

▶ • Listen to "Kokoleoko," then sing the song.

• Echo as you clap the rhythm of the song's first four measures.

Music can let us travel back in time.

LISTENING **Cancan** *from Gaîté parisienne* (excerpt)
by Jacques Offenbach

The dance pictured below is the cancan, which has a lot of high kicks. Offenbach composed his "Cancan" in 1866. Listen for a major scale at the end of the dance theme.

LISTEN to "Cancan."

READ the rhythm of the theme, saying:

■ *I'm for* ♩   ■ *dancing for* ♫   ■ *here in Paris for* ♬

AT THE MOULIN ROUGE: THE DANCE
Henri de Toulouse-Lautrec painted scenes of life in Paris in the late 1800s. He is famous for his paintings of cafés and theaters. Toulouse-Lautrec made this theater scene in 1890.

Philadelphia Museum of Art; The Henry P. McIlenny Collection in memory of Frances P. McIlenny.

56 RHYTHM OF TIME

MEETING **INDIVIDUAL** NEEDS

ALTERNATE TEACHING STRATEGY

OBJECTIVE 1 Have students find the measures in the playalong with the same rhythm. (first three) Then have them perform the playalong slowly as you play a drum on the beat. Gradually increase speed.

MOVEMENT: *Hand-feet Dance for "Cancan"*

MOVEMENT

Beat 1: Pat with both hands.
Beat 2: "Kick" R hand forward and pat with L hand.
Beat 3: Pat with both hands.
Beat 4: "Kick" L hand forward and pat with R hand.

BIOGRAPHY: *Jacques Offenbach*

Jacques Offenbach (ʒak ɔ fɛn **bak**), 1819–1880, was France's favorite musical theater composer during the late 1800s. Born in Germany, he performed as a cellist before writing his first stage works. His bright, witty music soon made him popular in Paris, where he even had his own theater. Today, he is remembered more for his only dramatic work, *The Tales of Hoffmann,* than for his operettas. In 1938, some of his music, including "Cancan," was arranged by Manuel Rosenthal as the score for Massine's ballet *Gaîté parisienne* (gɛ **te** pa ɾi **zyē**) (*Parisian Gaiety*).

"Kokoleoko" is a folk song from Liberia, in western Africa. Though "Kokoleoko" and "Cancan" originated miles away from each other, the two pieces are alike in some ways, too. Look for groups of four sixteenth notes in "Kokoleoko." They were in "Cancan," too.

KOKOLEOKO

Liberian Folk Song

Verse

1. Ko - ko - le - o - ko, ma - ma, ko - ko - le - o - ko.
2. Let me sleep some more, ma - ma, let me sleep some more.

Ko - ko - le - o - ko, chick - en crow - ing for day.
Let me sleep some more, chick - en crow - ing for day.

Refrain

A - by,— ma - ma, a - by,— a - by,— chick- en crow- ing for day.

PLAY this rhythm on a drum.

Unit 2 *Musical Adventures* 57

Have students:

• Listen to the song and show recognition of beats on which there are four sounds by patting the sixteenth notes with alternating hands. (Beat 1 of Measures 1, 2, and 3)

OBJECTIVE 1 Informal Assessment

• Play the rhythm of the playalong on a drum.

• Take turns performing the playalong on resonator bells or xylophones with the song. (Play only D, alternating right-hand and left-hand mallets.)

4 CLOSE

"What countries did you 'visit' today?" (U.S., France, and Liberia) "What rhythm notation was featured?" (half, quarter, eighth, and sixteenth notes)

"Now let's end today's musical adventure by singing 'I Believe in Music' one more time."

LESSON SUMMARY

Informal Assessment In this lesson, students:

OBJECTIVE 1 Read and played the rhythm of a playalong pattern that contains quarter, eighth, and sixteenth notes.

MORE MUSIC: Reinforcement

"Oh, Sinner Man," page 339 (reading sixteenth notes)

BIOGRAPHY: *Henri de Toulouse-Lautrec* VISUAL ARTS

French artist Henri de Toulouse-Lautrec (ã **ɾi** də tu **luz o trɛk**), 1864–1901, was born into a rich and eccentric family. As a child, he suffered from a bone disease. He only grew to be four-and-a-half feet tall, with a normal upper body and short, deformed legs. Toulouse-Lautrec loved to paint and sketch singers, dancers, and friends in the popular music halls and cabarets of Paris. His colorful posters of high-kicking cancan dancers are so lively, they almost dance off the cardboard. By the time of his death at age 36, his posters and paintings had made him a well-known artist.

BACKGROUND: *"Kokoleoko"*

Liberia was founded in 1822 by the descendants of enslaved Africans from the United States. "Kokoleoko" is a well-known song in Liberia. A version by Liberian female vocalist Miata Fahnbulleh (mi **a** ta fɑn bu **le**) became a hit record. The word *kokoleoko* imitates the sound of a rooster's crow. *Aby* (a **bɑɪ**) means "good-bye."

ORFF: *"Kokoleoko"*

See **O • 3** in *Orchestrations for Orff Instruments.*

ACROSS the

LANGUAGE ARTS

COMMUNICATION

"I Believe in Music"

GROUP   **15–30 MIN**
MATERIALS: optional—drawing paper

This song describes music as *the universal language*. Have students work in groups to tell what else might belong to a universal language. Have them imagine non-English speaking people visiting their hometown from a foreign nation. What would the vistors be able to understand? How would they be able to communicate?

Have students list words, objects, symbols, and so on, that would be readily understood:

- traffic or parking signs
- danger signs
- no-smoking signs

Sign language, pantomime, body language, and some brand names might be understood around the world. Based on the group findings, have students create a classroom display of "UNIVERSAL LANGUAGE."

COMPREHENSION STRATEGIES: Visualizing, understanding points of view

SOCIAL STUDIES

TIME CAPSULE

"Cancan"

GROUP   **15–30 MIN**
MATERIALS: optional—students' selection of common objects

Explain to students that the cancan is a stylish, high-kicking dance that originated in Paris in the nineteenth century. Although rarely done today, it has become a symbol of Parisian life.

Ask students to come up with symbols of modern-day life in their hometown. Working in groups, have them list objects, customs, dances, music, and so on, that would best summarize their hometown. Group members can represent their special interests in the list.

Members from each group can then form a "Time Capsule" committee to summarize lists from all the groups and organize a display of drawings, photos, and so on, to show life in their hometown.

COMPREHENSION STRATEGIES: Organizing information, finding main ideas

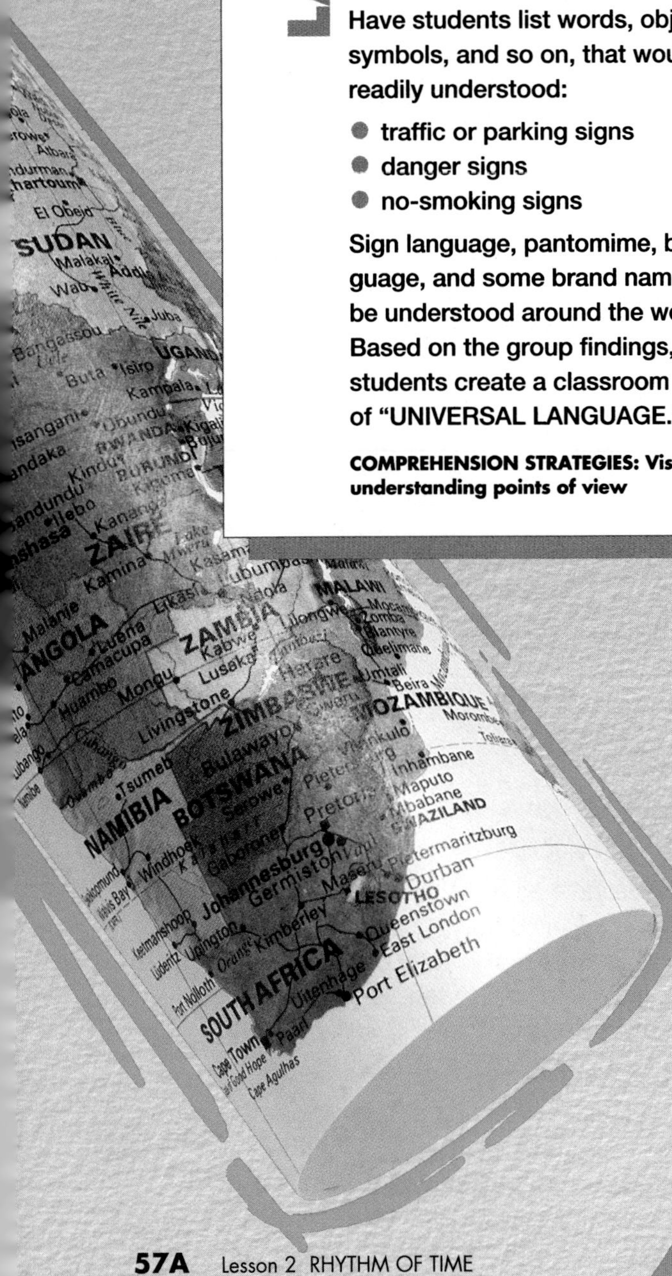

CURRICULUM

SCIENCE

HEALTH

"Kokoleoko"

INDIVIDUAL   **15–30 MIN**

The character in the song may not be getting enough sleep. Have students write an essay that describes their daily routines for staying healthy.

- How much sleep do they get a day? (eight hours recommended)
- What kind of physical exercise do they do? How often? How much?
- How many servings from the basic food groups do they get a day?

Recommended Daily Servings (for children)

- **Bread Group:** bread, cereal, rice, pasta—9
- **Fruit/Vegetable Groups:** Fruit Group—3; Vegetable Group—4
- **Dairy Group:** milk, cheese, yogurt—2–3
- **Meat Group:** meat, chicken, fish, dried peas and beans, eggs, nuts—2, totaling 6 oz.

Students can include a paragraph on what they can do to improve their daily routines for staying healthy.

COMPREHENSION STRATEGIES: Making decisions, compare and contrast, summarizing

MATHEMATICS

ELAPSED TIME

"Kokoleoko"

PAIR   **15 MIN OR LESS**
MATERIALS: 11 index cards

Players work in pairs to determine the elapsed time between a given bed-time and a given wake-up time.

Setup: One student writes 6 to 11 on cards, one number per card, to represent clock times in hours. The other student writes 10, 20, 30, 40, 50 on cards to represent minutes.

Play: Each set of cards is shuffled separately. One student picks two "hour" cards and decides that one represents P.M. and the other A.M. The other student picks two "minutes" cards and places each next to an "hour" card.

Students race to determine how much time elapsed in hours and minutes between the P.M. "bedtime" and the A.M. "wake-up time." To replay, cards are returned to their respective piles and reshuffled.

COMPREHENSION STRATEGIES: Making decisions, determining steps in a process

UNIT TWO
LESSON 3

LESSON PLANNER

FOCUS Form

OBJECTIVES
OBJECTIVE 1 Perform original movements to show same and different sections of a song

OBJECTIVE 2 Show awareness of rondo form by performing a rhythm pattern with the A sections of a recording

MATERIALS
Recordings
Joshua Fit the Battle of Jericho   CD2:2
Listening: Alla turca from Piano
  Sonata in A Major, K. 331, by
  W. A. Mozart   CD2:3

Instruments
drum sticks, rhythm sticks, or other sound sources playable with two hands

Resources
Listening Map Transparency T • 4 (Alla turca)
Orff Orchestration O • 4 (Joshua Fit the Battle of Jericho)
Playing the Guitar G • 6 (spirituals)

Technology Music with MIDI (Joshua Fit the Battle of Jericho)

▶ = **BASIC PROGRAM**

Into the Past

Through musical adventures we can revisit great events in history. The Battle of Jericho was fought in southwestern Asia between 1400 and 1200 B.C. Today the city of Jericho is in Jordan. In this song, how many times is the refrain section sung? The verse section? four; three

Joshua Fit the Battle of Jericho

African American Spiritual
Additional Words by MMH

58

MEETING **INDIVIDUAL** NEEDS

ALTERNATE TEACHING STRATEGY

OBJECTIVE 1 Have small groups of students look at the refrain and verse sections of "Joshua" as labeled in their books. Have students identify where the coda begins. (labeled, after the double bar) Tell them that their verse movement should stop at this point. They should note the words at the beginning of sections, then listen for them as they perform the movements.

SPECIAL LEARNERS: *Group Activities*

Make partner or small group assignments carefully so that the disabled student will have opportunities to offer ideas and participate to the fullest extent possible. Look for nondisabled students who show kindness, reciprocity, and the potential for continuing friendship with their disabled peer. If a disabled student will be more successful with a special friend, divide the class into a mix of pairs (including the disabled student and friend) and small groups.

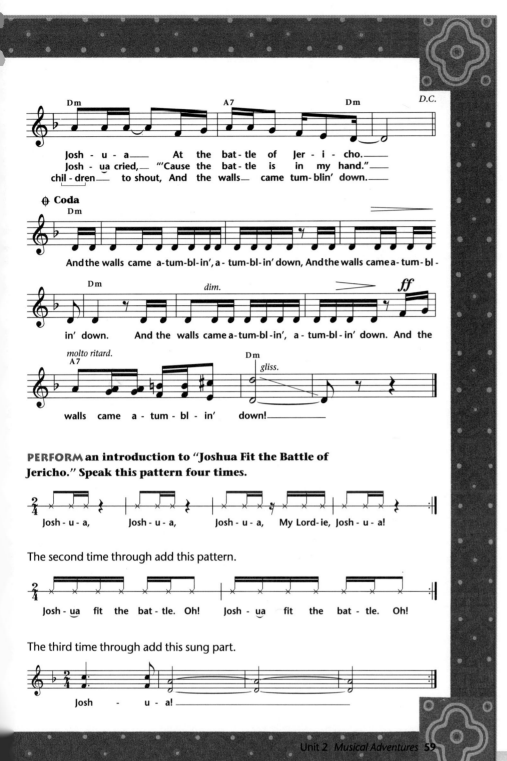

Josh - u - a____ At the bat - tle of Jer - i - cho.____
Josh - ua cried,____ "'Cause the bat - tle is in my hand."
chil - dren____ to shout, And the walls____ came tum-blin' down.____

Coda

And the walls came a-tum-bl-in', a - tum-bl-in' down, And the walls came a-tum-bl -

in' down. And the walls came a-tum-bl-in', a - tum-bl - in' down. And the

walls came a - tum - bl - in' down!____

PERFORM an introduction to "Joshua Fit the Battle of Jericho." Speak this pattern four times.

Josh - u - a, Josh - u - a, Josh - u - a, My Lord - ie, Josh - u - a!

The second time through add this pattern.

Josh - ua fit the bat - tle. Oh! Josh - ua fit the bat - tle. Oh!

The third time through add this sung part.

Josh - u - a!____

"Look around the room for repeated patterns." Have students:

▶ • Note repeated patterns in the classroom. (rows of books, striped shirts, etc.)

"Today, you're going to work with repeated sections in music, and with their opposite—contrasting sections. Knowing about form in music can give you a better understanding of compositions you hear and perform."

2 DEVELOP

1. Introduce "Joshua Fit the Battle of Jericho" CD2:2. **Identify same-different sections.** Have students:

▶ • Read about Jericho and listen to "Joshua Fit the Battle of Jericho."

▶ • Review coda (p. 5). Locate the coda.

▶ • Find the two main sections of the song (refrain and verse), note that they are different from one another, and answer the questions on page 58.

▶ • Sing the refrain and verse with the recording while tapping with the beat. (The introduction and coda are taught in Lesson 6.)

• Tell how many notes fit into one beat at the words *Josh-ua fit the . . .* (4) Identify these as four sixteenth notes.

2. Use movement to show the form of "Joshua Fit the Battle of Jericho." Have students:

▶ • In small groups, create contrasting movements for the refrain and verse. (See *Movement* below.)

OBJECTIVE 1 Informal Assessment

▶ • Demonstrate same-different sections of this verse-refrain song by performing contrasting original movements for each main section as the class sings the song.

MOVEMENT: *"Joshua Fit the Battle of Jericho"*

Here are some suggestions for creating movement:
Contrasting movements—sustained movements during the verse and sharp, percussive movements during the refrain.

Body facing—facing partner during verse and away from partner during the refrain.

Body percussion—clap/snapping during refrain, and clapping partner's hands during verse.

ORFF: *"Joshua Fit the Battle of Jericho"*

See **O • 4** in *Orchestrations for Orff Instruments.*

BACKGROUND: *"Joshua Fit the Battle of Jericho"*

When performing spirituals it is common to "swing" the rhythms. The rhythms are performed more freely than written in order to produce a livelier sound. Students may notice that the sixteenth notes in the recording of this song are "swung," or performed slightly unequally.

UNIT TWO
LESSON 3

continued from previous page

3 APPLY

Introduce "Alla turca" CD2:3. **Identify rondo form.** Have students:

• With drumsticks, rhythm sticks, or other sound sources, read and play the rhythm pattern on page 60. (Pat alternating hands on sixteenth notes.)

▶ • Read about the composition and rondo form.

▶ • Listen to "Alla turca" (**al la tur** ka), following the listening map and pointing in their books to show that they're keeping up with the progress of the piece. (Optional: Use **Listening Map Transparency T • 4.**)

OBJECTIVE 2 Informal Assessment
• Listen again, performing the rhythm pattern from page 60 with the recording each time the A section occurs.

▶ • Find the coda on the map. (bottom)

The celebrated composer Wolfgang Amadeus Mozart was a child prodigy who started playing keyboard instruments at age three and wrote large pieces for orchestra by age nine. Here Mozart, aged thirteen, is seated at the keyboard, perhaps working on a new composition. The year is about 1770. Later he composed the rondo "Alla turca" ("in Turkish style") that you're about to hear. Mozart wanted to give his European audiences a sense of the fascinating sounds of Turkey.

LISTENING
Alla turca
from Piano Sonata in A Major, K. 331
by Wolfgang Amadeus Mozart

READ this rhythm from the rondo and play it. Use drumsticks or another sound source.

Say: ■ *March* for ♩   ■ *Everybody* for ♫♫

Rondo form is usually ABACA or a simple variation of that idea. But Mozart really varied the form for the rondo "Alla turca." One way to describe it is:
ABA C DED C ABA C Coda.

60 INTO THE PAST

MEETING **INDIVIDUAL** NEEDS

ALTERNATE TEACHING STRATEGY

OBJECTIVE 2 In order to help students recognize the different sections, play each theme separately, using the indexing on the CD or the following timings: Section B begins at 00:15, Section C at 00:44, Section D at 00:58, Section E at 1:13, Coda at 2:40.

BIOGRAPHY: *Wolfgang Amadeus Mozart*

Austrian composer Wolfgang Amadeus Mozart (**volf** gang a ma **de** us **mo** tsart), 1756–1791, was one of the great composers of Western music. Although he died at 35, he wrote a tremendous amount of music, including 18 operas and 41 symphonies. The son of a musician, he began playing harpsichord at age three and by six was touring Europe with his sister, playing for kings and queens. At nine he wrote his first symphony. By the time he was 25, he had tired of traveling, so he settled down to compose and give concerts and lessons. But he was often poor and in debt. He wrote an opera for Emperor Joseph II, but when the emperor died, Mozart was never paid. His last opera, *The Magic Flute,* made a fortune for the theater manager with whom he worked, although Mozart received only a little money. That same year, Mozart died.

LISTENING MAP *Listen for the repetitions of the A, or rondo, theme as you follow the map of the rondo "Alla turca."*

‖: A :‖   ‖: B   A' :‖   ‖: C :‖

‖: D :‖   ‖: E   D' :‖   ‖: C :‖

‖: A :‖   ‖: B   A' :‖   ‖: C' :‖

Coda

Listening Map Concept by Barb Stevanson

4 CLOSE

"Today we explored form in music." Have students:

▶ • Name some ways they used repetition and contrast in music in the lesson. (showed verse-refrain form of "Joshua Fit the Battle of Jericho" through movement, followed repeating and contrasting themes in the "Alla turca" listening map.)

"Form is important in music and is part of what makes it interesting. Keep listening for it! Now let's play the rhythm pattern with the rondo 'Alla turca' again for fun."

LESSON SUMMARY

Informal Assessment In this lesson, students:

OBJECTIVE 1 Performed original movements to show same and different sections of "Joshua Fit the Battle of Jericho."

OBJECTIVE 2 Showed awareness of rondo form in "Alla turca" by performing a rhythm pattern with the A sections.

MORE MUSIC: Reinforcement

"Bamboo," page 340 (verse-refrain)
"Soon Ah Will Be Done," page 354 (verse-refrain)
"Old Joe Clark," page 396 (verse-refrain)

MULTICULTURAL PERSPECTIVES: *"Alla turca"*

During Mozart's time, the Turks were invading Eastern Europe and the Austrian Empire was right in the midst of it. This resulted in a Viennese fascination for "things Turkish." Turkey was considered exotic, a place of adventure. Mozart and several other composers used Turkish-sounding elements in some of their music. The name of this particular rondo means "in Turkish style," and it has become known to English-speaking people as the "Turkish Rondo."

LANGUAGE ARTS CONNECTION: *Rondo Poem*

In poetry, a rondeau is a poem of 13 lines in which some of the words are repeated. Discuss with students the connection between the rondeau in poetry and the rondo in music. (The Italian word *rondo* comes from a French word, *rondeau* (ran **do**), which in turn comes from the Latin word for "circular.") Then have students work in small groups using A B A C A or A B A C A B A to write a rondo-form poem. The letters can be lines, pairs of lines, or verses.

UNIT TWO
LESSON 4

RELATED ARTS MOVEMENT THEATER VISUAL ARTS

LESSON PLANNER

FOCUS Pitch

OBJECTIVES
OBJECTIVE 1 Signal to indicate the location of half steps in major scale (tested)
OBJECTIVE 2 Identify the location of half steps in notation of a melody in C major (tested)

MATERIALS
Recordings
Listening: Cancan from *Gaité parisienne* (excerpt) by
J. Offenbach   CD1:35
One Moment in Time   CD1:29
Listening: Tortoises from *The Carnival of the Animals* by
C. Saint-Saëns   CD2:4
Flying Free   CD2:5
Flying Free (performance mix)   CD2:6

Instruments resonator bells or other pitched instruments

Resources
Resource Master 2 • 4 (practice)
Recorder Master R • 9 (pitches D E G A B C' D')

▶ = **BASIC PROGRAM**

Tortoise Tale

Here's what the C major scale looks like on the staff. Can you tell by looking at the pitches where the half steps are?

PLAY and sing the C major scale.

Each note in the major scale also has a pitch syllable name.

Which pitch syllables are a half step apart? *mi* and *fa; ti* and *do'*

C	D	E	F	G	A	B	C'
do	*re*	*mi*	*fa*	*so*	*la*	*ti*	*do'*

PLAY and sing these pitches. Perform the bell part below with the refrain of "One Moment in Time."

62

MEETING **INDIVIDUAL** NEEDS

ALTERNATE TEACHING STRATEGY

OBJECTIVE 1 If students are having difficulty remembering the pitch syllables between which a half step occurs, have them play a C scale on a keyboard, playing the first four notes with the fingers of their left hand, and the last four with the fingers of their right hand (no thumbs). They should discover that the half step comes between the third and fourth fingers used on both hands. It may be helpful if you sing or play each pair of notes as you say their names.

BIOGRAPHY: *Camille Saint-Saëns*

French composer Camille Saint-Saëns (ka **mi** yə sã **sɔn**), 1835–1921, began playing piano when he was five and composing at age six. He went on to write 169 works of music, including *The Carnival of the Animals,* a collection of pieces about different animals. Many of the sections contain musical in-jokes. For example, "Cuckoo in the Woods" contains a two-note bird call, played by clarinet (a wood instrument). It is said that Saint-Saëns had various friends in mind as he wrote *Carnival*. He didn't allow the piece to be published in his lifetime.

LISTENING

Tortoises
from *The Carnival of the Animals*
by *Camille Saint-Saëns*

How would you describe the tempo, or speed of the beat, of "Cancan"? fast

Let's visit Paris, France, in the late 1800s to hear "Cancan" performed again. Listen especially for the tempo this time.

The "Cancan" melody was there, but how was it changed? much slower tempo

Saint-Saëns borrowed the "Cancan" melody for a new piece, which he called "Tortoises."

SING the beginning of "Tortoises" with pitch syllables.

do   re fa mi re   so so so la mi fa   re re re fa mi re   do do' ti la so fa mi re   do

THINK IT THROUGH

Why do you think this piece is considered a musical joke?
Would someone who had not heard "Cancan" get the joke?

Unit 2 *Musical Adventures* **63**

1 GET SET

"Suppose you could travel to any time or place—where would you go? What would you do? What sort of music do you think you'd hear?" Have students:

▶ • Discuss some of their ideas.

"Today, you will again travel through time, using your new skill with pitches to add new touches to the music you hear. Let's begin by traveling back to the 1800s. Perform the hand-feet dance to 'Cancan' again." CD1:35 (See Lesson 2, page 56, *Movement.*)

2 DEVELOP

1. Review "One Moment in Time" CD1:29 **(p. 49). Introduce major scale on the staff and identify half steps in a major scale.** Have students:

• Name the pitches in the resonator bell part on page 62. Watch as you put the notes on a staff from lowest to highest, and describe what they see. (a C major scale)

▶ • Read about the pitch syllables in the C major scale. (Note that a knowledge of the keyboard helps in identifying whole and half steps.)

• Play the bell part with the song.

OBJECTIVE 1 Informal Assessment
• Listen as you name each interval in the scale (*do* to *re* and so on) and raise a hand to indicate where the half steps occur (*mi* to *fa, ti* to *do'*).

2. Introduce "Tortoises" CD2:4. **Sing theme with pitch syllables.** Have students:

▶ • Listen to "Tortoises" and answer the question about its melody.

• Divide into two groups. One group plays measures 4–5 on page 63 with the recording and sings the pitch syllables for the descending scale. The other group does the "hand-feet" dance in slow motion.

• Sing the theme with pitch syllables.

▶ • Discuss the *Think It Through* questions.

ENRICHMENT: *"The Tortoise"*

American poet Ogden Nash wrote a series of poems to go with *The Carnival of the Animals*. Like "Tortoises," this poem has an 'inside' joke. Read it to students and discuss the joke. (Based on the fable "The Tortoise and the Hare," the narrator figured a tortoise could outrun a hare. When the tortoise lost, the narrator lost the bet—and a lot of money.)

Come crown my brow with leaves of myrtle/I know the tortoise is a turtle./Come carve my name in stone immortal,/I know the turtoise is a tortle./I know to my profound

despair/I bet on one to beat a hare./I also know I'm now a pauper/Because of its tortley turtley torpor.

MOVEMENT: *"Cancan"* MOVEMENT

For fun, have students transfer the hand-feet movement to the feet and do the cancan. (Jump, kick R, jump, kick L.)

PITCH SYLLABLES: *Theme to "Tortoises"*

Have students add hand signs as they sing the beginning of "Tortoises" with pitch syllables.

continued from previous page

3 APPLY

Introduce "Flying Free" CD2:5. Identify A A B A form and find half steps. Have students:

▶ • Listen to "Flying Free" as they follow the notation, then discuss its meaning.

▶ • Answer the questions on page 65 about the form of the song. (Lines 1–2, 3–4, 7–8 are similar; Lines 5–6 are different; A A B A)

▶ • Sing the song (without the descant). (The descant is taught in Lesson 5.)

OBJECTIVE 2 Informal Assessment
• Find half steps in the first two lines.
  Measure 1—*is a*: E-F
  Measures 2–3—*my own*: B-C
  Measure 4—*where I*: E-F
  Measure 6—*by the*: F-E

Music can take you to wherever you want to be, even . . .

Flying Free

Words and Music by Don Besig

Descant on 3rd verse only

1. There is a place I call my own_____ where I can
2. But life is not a dis-tant sky_____ with-out a
3. So life's a song that I must sing,_____ a gift of

So life's a song, a gift of

stand_____ by the sea,_____
cloud,_____ with - out rain,_____
love_____ I must share._____

love_____ I must share._____

And look be - yond the things I've known,_____ and dream that
And I can nev - er hope that I_____ can trav - el
And when I see the joy it brings,_____ my spir - its

And when I see, my spir - its

64 TORTOISE TALES

MEETING **INDIVIDUAL** NEEDS

ALTERNATE TEACHING STRATEGY

OBJECTIVE 2 Put the C major scale on the board. As a class, have students tell where the half steps are. Then have them use the scale for a reference as they look at the notation of "Flying Free" and identify the half steps.

EXTRA HELP: *Form in "Flying Free"*

If students are having difficulty identifying the A sections of "Flying Free," be sure that they understand that sections need only be similar, not identical, in order to be considered A sections—starting the same way and remaining basically the same throughout most of the phrase.

**LOOK for similar and different parts of the song.
Describe the form with letters. AABA**

"Today, you read and played the C major scale from the staff. How can you remember where the half steps occur in the major scale?" (Encourage students to suggest different strategies, such as practicing the C major scale on a keyboard.) Have students:

▶ • Sing "Flying Free," listening for the half steps as they sing.

LESSON SUMMARY

Informal Assessment In this lesson, students:

OBJECTIVE 1 Signaled to indicate the location of half steps in the major scale.

OBJECTIVE 2 Identified the location of half steps in the first phrase of "Flying Free."

MORE MUSIC: Reinforcement
"Jubilate Deo," page 336 (C major scale)
"The Singing School," *Songs to Sing and Read,* page 90 (C major scale)

BIOGRAPHY: *Don Besig*

American composer Don Besig (b. 1936) taught vocal music in public schools for 25 years before leaving to compose full-time. Most of his works are for chorus. He often collaborates with Nancy Price (b. 1958), a high school choral director in upstate New York. Besig also loves musical theater, where he has worked as a director, choreographer, and designer.

ENRICHMENT: *Breaking a Musical Code*

For more practice reading pitches from the C major scale, have students complete **Resource Master 2 • 4.**

MATHEMATICS

RATES

"Flying Free"

GROUP   **15–30 MIN**

MATERIALS: map of the state or United States, tape measures or rulers, calculator

Some birds can fly up to 100 miles (160 kilometers) per hour. Have students work in groups to write and challenge each other to solve "imaginary bird flight" problems.

Each group decides upon a "flight speed"—anything up to 100 mph (160 kph). Have members of the group pick two locations on a map. Then, as a problem, they write out the flight speed and the two locations, asking how long it would take to fly from one location to the other.

Students may add "imaginary" details to their problems: If the bird is flying against a prevailing wind, it may need to add an extra 15 minutes to every hour of flying time.

Have groups exchange their problems and try to solve them. (They will need to use a ruler and map scale bar to determine the distance between two locations.)

COMPREHENSION STRATEGIES: Distinguishing between fact and fantasy, using formulas

MATHEMATICS

MEASUREMENT

"Flying Free"

PAIR   **30 MIN OR LONGER**

MATERIALS: paper, chalk, tape measures, graph paper

Have students work in pairs to design their own paper airplanes. When the planes are complete, have students go outside and fly their planes. They can make a chalk line for the starting line and use a tape measure to measure the distance from the starting line to the plane's landing position.

Have each pair of students do ten trial flights and record the distance of each flight. Then the students can plot the distances on a bar or line graph. Suggest that students display their airplanes and graphs and compare results.

Based on comparisons with other pairs' results, students may wish to revise their airplane designs and repeat the activity to see if they can improve their distances.

COMPREHENSION STRATEGIES: Making decisions, compare and contrast

CURRICULUM

LANGUAGE ARTS

PERSONAL NARRATIVE

"Flying Free"

INDIVIDUAL   **15–30 MIN**

Have students think of a place described in the song, *There is a place I call my own*, a place where a student can dream *I might be free*. Ask them to describe a place that they feel is "their own." It need not be a place where they are alone. Here are some ideas:

● a room
● a place outdoors
● a friend's house

The place may even be an imaginary place—somewhere they would like to be, where they could feel free. Ask students to write about this special place. They should describe the place, why they like to go there (or would like to), when was the last time they were there (if ever), and when they hope to go back.

COMPREHENSION STRATEGIES: Expressing point of view, expressing main ideas

SCIENCE / ART

FANTASY MURALS

"Tortoises"

GROUP   **30 MIN OR LONGER**

MATERIALS: white mural paper (4 ft to 5 ft lengths), paints or markers, decorative materials, reference books with pictures of reptiles

As students listen to "Tortoises," have them imagine reptiles in a chorus line. Have them name and describe the reptiles in the chorus line. Their descriptions might use real facts. Reptiles are vertebrates (backboned animals) that have scales and breathe by means of lungs, are cold-blooded, and reproduce by laying eggs. Also:

● turtles (water dwelling; limbs are flippers used for swimming)
● tortoise (land dwelling; short, heavy limbs, with clawed feet)
● crocodiles (triangular head with pointed snout; teeth stick out when mouth is closed)
● alligators (blunt, rounded snout; teeth tuck into its closed mouth)
● snakes (no limbs, ear openings, or eyelids)

Have groups illustrate sections of a "reptile" chorus line on sheets of paper. The drawings can be combined into a long chorus line mural.

COMPREHENSION STRATEGIES: Distinguishing fact from fantasy, visualizing

75th Anniversary of Rotary International

HEALTH, HUNGER & HUMANITY

APPY NEW EAR!

USA

UNIT TWO
LESSON 5

RELATED ARTS MOVEMENT | THEATER | VISUAL ARTS

LESSON PLANNER

FOCUS Form/Rhythm

OBJECTIVES

OBJECTIVE 1 Pat the rhythm of a song from notation including quarter, eighth, and sixteenth notes (tested)

OBJECTIVE 2 Perform movements to show different sections of an A B A song (tested)

MATERIALS
Recordings
Flying Free   CD2:5
Tumbai (unison)   CD2:7

Resources
Orff Orchestration O • 5 (Tumbai)
Playing the Guitar G • 12 (Tumbai)
Recorder Master R • 10 (pitches D E G A B C')

VOCABULARY
unison

▶ = **BASIC PROGRAM**

Israel is a land of rugged hills, fertile valleys, and olive and orange groves. Why do you think Israel is called the "land of milk and honey"?

SING the melody of this folk song all together, in unison.

MEETING **INDIVIDUAL** NEEDS

ALTERNATE TEACHING STRATEGY

OBJECTIVE 1 Help students understand the eighth note: two sixteenth notes relationship by reviewing the one-to-two relationship of quarter:two eighths. Then, review the rhythm chart on page 67.

VOCAL DEVELOPMENT: *Breathing*

These exercises help students breath from the diaphragm, as well as strengthening the abdominal muscles, so that they can sustain musical phrases in one breath. Have students assume the posture for singing and imagine they are

locomotives releasing steam with the sound *ch–ch–ch–*. They should put their hands on their abdomens to feel the impulses from their abdominal muscles. Then they should inhale "down" to the area where they felt the impulses as if they were filling up a large balloon inside themselves. Next, inhale to the count of three and exhale on *s-s-s* to the count of five as they pull a string from an imaginary ball of yarn. Repeat, each time extending the release of air. This gradually increases breath control. Have them pull out a string from the imaginary ball of yarn for each phrase of "Flying Free," making certain to sing each phrase on one breath.

READ and clap these note values. Some of them can be found in the rhythms of "Tumbai."

READ the same rhythms from the notation of "Tumbai." Work in groups to practice these rhythms.

THINK IT THROUGH
How are the rhythms in the chart like the rhythms in the song? Could rhythms from the chart be played at the same time as those from the song? Why or why not?

Unit 2 *Musical Adventures* **67**

"As you sing this song, notice the rests." Have students:

▶ • Sing "Flying Free" **CD2:5** on pages 64–65.

▶ • Recall that this song has four sections and is in A A B A form.

"Rhythm, including rests, can help you discover the form of a song. Today you will sing a song that contains an interesting rhythm pattern."

2 DEVELOP

1. Learn the descant of "Flying Free." Have students:

• Sing the highlighted descant.

• Split into two groups, one group singing the descant as the other sings the melody.

2. Introduce "Tumbai" (CD2:7 unison). Read ♫ Have students:

▶ • Read about Israel and sing "Tumbai."

• Clap each line of the chart on page 67.

• Form two groups. One group taps with the beat as the other pats the rhythm of the first two lines of "Tumbai" from notation with alternating hands.

• Tell how many of each note value they patted to one beat. (1 quarter, two eighths, or four sixteenth notes to a beat)

• Work in pairs to figure out how to pat Line 3 with alternating hands.

OBJECTIVE 1 Informal Assessment
• Pat the rhythm of Line 3 all together. Then, pat the rhythm of the entire song reading from notation.

• Discuss the *Think It Through* questions.

BACKGROUND: *"Tumbai"*

Many "tumba" songs were brought to Israel by Eastern European settlers. The words themselves are nonsense.

PRONUNCIATION: *"Tumbai"*

ɑ f**a**ther   ɪ **i**t   u m**oo**n

ORFF: *"Tumbai"*

See **O • 5** in *Orchestrations for Orff Instruments.*

A bit one sided here (

MULTICULTURAL PERSPECTIVES: *Israel*

Israel is a small nation on the eastern shore of the Mediterranean Sea. Throughout the early 1900s, many Jews fled their countries to escape religious persecution, and in 1948 they founded the republic of Israel on the land of ancient Palestine, their ancestral home. It was planned as a nation where both Muslims and Jews could live in peace, but the Palestinians and other Arabs resented the Jews moving into their lands. Israel has often been at war with its Arab neighbors. Today Israel is the most technologically advanced country in the Middle East.

UNIT TWO
LESSON 5

continued from previous page

3 APPLY

Show the form of "Tumbai" through movement. Have students:

▶ • Discover the number of phrases in "Tumbai" (3), then sing the song.

▶ • Show the phrases by moving as directed on page 68, then do group movement.

▶ • Listen to the entire recording and read about the A B A form.

▶ • Read about, then create their own movement for the instrumental B section. (See *Movement* on the bottom of page 69.)

OBJECTIVE 2 Informal Assessment

▶ • Show that they can identify the form of "Tumbai" by performing, to the recording, the circle dance with the A sections and the partner movement with the instrumental B section. (Remind students to stand next to their partners in the circle dance so they are ready for the partner movement.)

LET'S MOVE!

LEARN this dance step.

1 step right

2 cross back

3 step right

4 hop right

MOVE to show each phrase of "Tumbai."

- Phrase 1: walk right 4 counts, walk left 4 counts.
- Phrase 2: right, back, right, hop; left, back, left, hop as shown above.
- Phrase 3: move forward 3 steps and clap, back 3 steps and clap.

Now try this movement as a circle dance.

68 LAND OF MILK AND HONEY

MEETING **INDIVIDUAL** NEEDS

ALTERNATE TEACHING STRATEGY

OBJECTIVE 2 Explain to students that the instrumental section of "Tumbai" is the B section. Then have them mirror you in movements that illustrate the form. For example, the A section could be side steps, with arms outstretched or in motion; and the B section could be forward and backward steps, with arms at side.

COOPERATIVE LEARNING: *Creating Movement*

MOVEMENT

Have students create their own movements to the B section of "Tumbai" in cooperative groups of four (two pairs of partners). Then have them find a way to write down each dance instruction in words or a picture. Assign one student in each group to be the recorder. The recorder is responsible for writing down the group's movement instructions. Give the written instructions to another group to see if they can interpret them. Point out to students that writing clear instructions is difficult, especially for movement, and that the other group's interpretation may not be exactly what they intended.

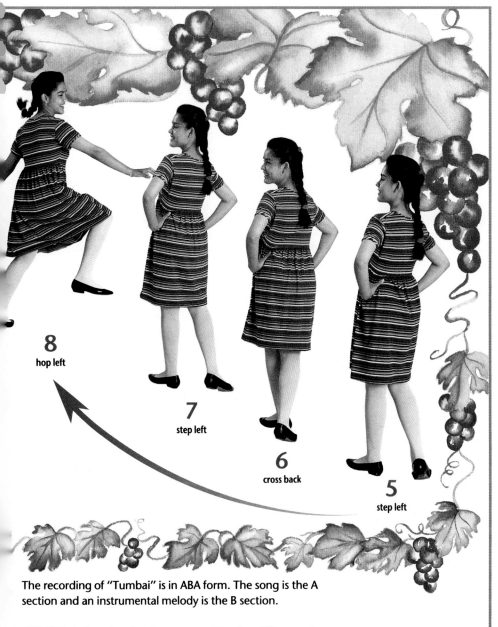

8
hop left

7
step left

6
cross back

5
step left

The recording of "Tumbai" is in ABA form. The song is the A section and an instrumental melody is the B section.

CREATE sixteen beats of movement to do with a partner during the B section.

Now dance the big ABA form.
- Do the circle dance with the A section.
- Do your own partner movement with the B section.

Unit 2 *Musical Adventures* **69**

"You started today's lesson by singing 'Flying Free.' Then you sang 'Tumbai.' How would you compare the rhythm of these two songs?" (gentle rhythm in "Flying Free," stronger rhythmic character in "Tumbai")

"Which song had the new rhythm that we learned?" ("Tumbai"—♫)

LESSON SUMMARY

Informal Assessment In this lesson, students:

OBJECTIVE 1 Patted the rhythm of "Tumbai" from notation including quarter, eighth, and sixteenth notes.

OBJECTIVE 2 Performed movements to show different sections of an A B A song, "Tumbai."

MORE MUSIC: Reinforcement

"Old Ark's A-Moverin'," page 332 (A B A form)

"Where E'er You Walk," page 362 (A B A form; quarter, eighth, sixteenth notes)

"Soft Shoe Song," page 383 (A B A form)

MOVEMENT: *"Tumbai" (B Section)*

Have students create sixteen beats of movement with a partner. They should choose a body facing with their partner, then step with the quarter notes in an 8-beat sequence. The movement for the second 8-beat sequence should be the opposite of the movement for the first 8-beat sequence. For example, students might swing their partner in one direction for eight beats, then in the other direction for eight beats. Because the tempo is fast and the movement might involve some elevation (hop, jump, leap, skip), have students warm up with knee bends, ankle extensions, and walking before beginning to choreograph.

RECORDER: *"Tumbai" (B section)*

Have students who know the fingerings for E G A B C' play along with the instrumental B section.

ACROSS the

MATHEMATICS

PROBLEM SOLVING

"Flying Free"

PAIR   **15–30 MIN**

MATERIALS: national map

Apply the idea of "flying free" to the "frequent flier" policies of many airline companies. Have students work in pairs to create problem-solving situations based on:

- "Imaginary Airlines" Frequent-Flier Policy—For every 1,000 miles you fly, get 100 miles free.

Each pair of students picks a destination in the nation where someone might want to fly for free from your nearest airport. Two pairs exchange their destinations. Each pair must plan trips that they must pay for in order to get a free trip to the designated destination.

The trips should be national to avoid distortion of relative distances over wide areas. Have maps available for students to measure the distances to their locations.

COMPREHENSION STRATEGY: Compare and contrast

SOCIAL STUDIES

MAPS/GLOBES

"Flying Free"

PAIR   **15–30 MIN**

MATERIALS: index cards or slips of paper, classroom globe or world map

The words of the song, *where I can stand by the sea*, can provide the theme for a latitude/longitude game. Each pair of players locates on a globe a place along an ocean coast. They write down the latitude and longitude of the place on a card; on the back of the card they write the location's name. Then two pairs exchange cards (name-side down) and search for each other's "place by the sea." The first pair to locate the place wins the round.

Each pair can turn the card over to confirm their answer or to double check that the latitude and longitude are actually correct. Players can repeat the round as often as they wish to try to become the locator-champion team.

COMPREHENSION STRATEGY: Estimating

CURRICULUM

ART

SASHES

"Tumbai"

INDIVIDUAL   **15 MIN OR LESS**

MATERIALS: sashes (felt or shopping-bag paper cut into 4-in. wide strips), crayons, markers, paints, decorations (beads, fabric scraps, sequins, ribbon, yarn), glue, scissors, reference books showing Middle Eastern clothing

Give each student a felt or paper sash. Their goal is to decorate them. Have them create patterns that reflect the rhythm they hear as they listen to "Tumbai," or show them pictures of Middle Eastern clothing for ideas about color and patterns.

Encourage students to write a description of their sashes based on what they heard or saw that led them to create a particular design or pattern.

COMPREHENSION STRATEGIES: Visualizing, finding patterns

LANGUAGE ARTS

WRITING WORDS

"Tumbai"

PAIR   **15–30 MIN**

Have students compose their own words to sing to the melody of "Tumbai." Have them base their new words around the main idea of "a happy event" or "the time of day I enjoy the most."

Their words should give a description of what the event or time of day is and why it is "happy." Like the pattern of the song itself, the students' words can include repetition.

Students' words should match the rhythm of the song as closely as possible. If they need to use more than one syllable per note of "Tumbai," the syllables should be easy to pronounce quickly. Have pairs perform their new words in song and dance.

COMPREHENSION STRATEGY: Expressing main ideas

LESSON 6

LESSON PLANNER

FOCUS Pitch/Texture

OBJECTIVES
OBJECTIVE 1 Sing a song in three-part canon with movement
OBJECTIVE 2 Perform a rhythmic ostinato containing ♫ with a song
OBJECTIVE 3 Perform pitch and rhythmic ostinatos containing sixteenth notes as an introduction to a song

MATERIALS
Recordings
Tumbai (unison)	CD2:7
Tumbai (canon)	CD2:8
Üsküdar	CD2:9
Recorded Lesson: Pronunciation for "Üsküdar"	CD2:10
Recorded Lesson: Major or Minor?	CD2:11
Joshua Fit the Battle of Jericho	CD2:2

Instruments piano or resonator bells

Resources
Playing the Guitar G • 7 (minor)
Playing the Guitar G • 14 (minor)

VOCABULARY
key signature, minor scale

▶ = **BASIC PROGRAM**

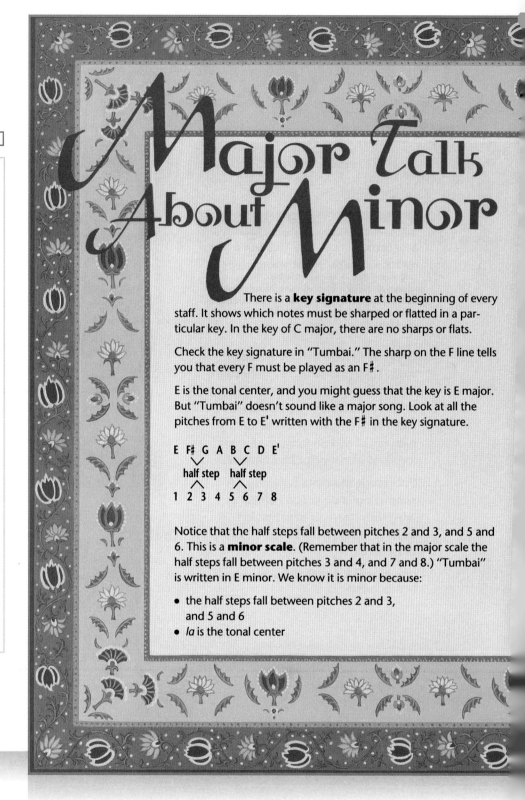

Major Talk About Minor

There is a **key signature** at the beginning of every staff. It shows which notes must be sharped or flatted in a particular key. In the key of C major, there are no sharps or flats.

Check the key signature in "Tumbai." The sharp on the F line tells you that every F must be played as an F♯.

E is the tonal center, and you might guess that the key is E major. But "Tumbai" doesn't sound like a major song. Look at all the pitches from E to E¹ written with the F♯ in the key signature.

E F♯ G A B C D E¹
half step half step
1 2 3 4 5 6 7 8

Notice that the half steps fall between pitches 2 and 3, and 5 and 6. This is a **minor scale**. (Remember that in the major scale the half steps fall between pitches 3 and 4, and 7 and 8.) "Tumbai" is written in E minor. We know it is minor because:

• the half steps fall between pitches 2 and 3, and 5 and 6
• *la* is the tonal center

MEETING **INDIVIDUAL** NEEDS

ALTERNATE TEACHING STRATEGY

OBJECTIVE 1 Have students sing "Tumbai" in unison and two-part canon. Then, have them sing with the recording, or with you as the third part. Try a challenge in which two or three students sing each part face-to-face with one another. Sometimes the additional challenge helps!

VOCAL DEVELOPMENT: *The "tra-la's" in "Tumbai"*
Often when "l's" are sung in rapid succession, the tendency is to "chew" them, thus distorting the vowels sounds that follow. This diction exercise will prepare students to sing

the *tra-la's* in "Tumbai" correctly. Have students practice singing the following measures:

Continue up by half steps to C and down by half steps to F.

la - la   la   la - la - la - la la   la - la   la - la   la - la

As students sing the *la's*, the jaw should remain open, relaxed, and down. Each time the "l" is articulated, the tip of the tongue should flip down from the upper gum quickly and vigorously. As they sing the *tra-la's* in "Tumbai," remind them to sing the "l's" as they did in the exercise.

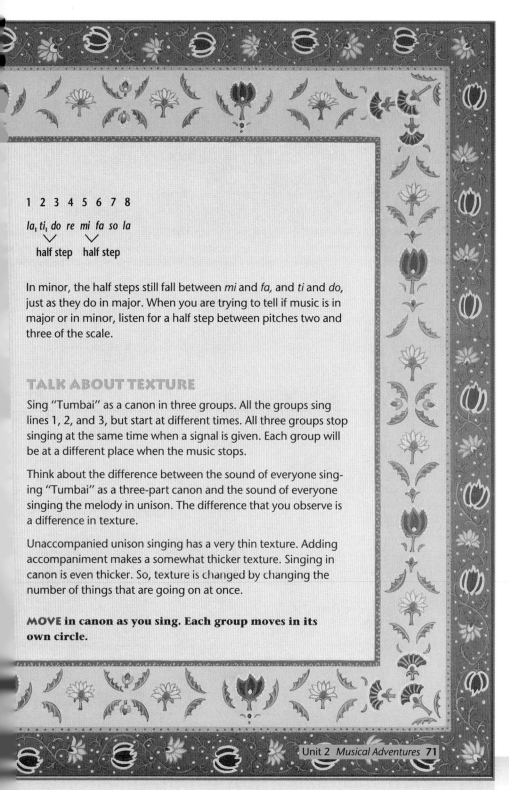

1 2 3 4 5 6 7 8

la, ti, do re mi fa so la
‿ ‿
half step   half step

In minor, the half steps still fall between *mi* and *fa*, and *ti* and *do*, just as they do in major. When you are trying to tell if music is in major or in minor, listen for a half step between pitches two and three of the scale.

TALK ABOUT TEXTURE

Sing "Tumbai" as a canon in three groups. All the groups sing lines 1, 2, and 3, but start at different times. All three groups stop singing at the same time when a signal is given. Each group will be at a different place when the music stops.

Think about the difference between the sound of everyone singing "Tumbai" as a three-part canon and the sound of everyone singing the melody in unison. The difference that you observe is a difference in texture.

Unaccompanied unison singing has a very thin texture. Adding accompaniment makes a somewhat thicker texture. Singing in canon is even thicker. So, texture is changed by changing the number of things that are going on at once.

MOVE in canon as you sing. Each group moves in its own circle.

1 GET SET

"So far, you've learned about half and whole steps in the key of C major. Now, try to listen for where the half steps are in 'Tumbai' as we sing it." (CD2:7) Have students:

• Try to find the half steps in the song (between B–C and F♯–G).

• Recognize that it must be in a scale other than C, since there is an F♯.

"Today you're going to learn about this scale and why the black keys on the piano are important."

2 DEVELOP

1. Introduce minor scale and sing "Tumbai" in canon CD2:8. Have students:

▶• Sing "Tumbai" in unison again.

▶• Read about key signature and the tonal center of the song.

• Put an E minor scale on the board and bracket the half steps (B–C and F♯–G). Put numbers under each pitch.

▶• Read about the minor scale.

• Play the scale on piano, resonator bells, or pantomime playing it on the keyboard on page 53.

• Read about singing in canon.

OBJECTIVE 1 Informal Assessment

• Sing the song with movement, as a three-part canon. (See *Movement* below.)

MOVEMENT: *"Tumbai" in Three-Part Canon*

Have students do the circle dance from Lesson 5 (pages 68–69) in three different circles, corresponding to the three different entries of the canon. Tell students to start dancing when they start singing.

An alternate way to perform the song in three-part canon is to have six groups—three of singers and three of dancers. The first group of dancers begins dancing when the first group of singers begins singing. (This eliminates the difficulties some students have with singing while dancing.)

Another possibility is trying an alternate spatial formation: three concentric circles, with the innermost circle being the smallest and the other two increasing in size. Students can decide which circle should begin the canon first.

After viewing the dance with both formations (three separate circles, three concentric circles), students can discuss what they liked about each formation and how they might go from one to the other to make a longer, more varied dance.

UNIT TWO
LESSON 6

continued from previous page

2. Introduce "Üsküdar" CD2:9. **Identify minor. Add a ♪♪ ostinato.** Have students:

• Listen to "Üsküdar," decide if it is major or minor by the sound and the tonal center (minor; E), and recognize that it is in the same key as "Tumbai."

▶ • Read about the rhythms in "Üsküdar" and "Tumbai" and listen to "Üsküdar" while tapping with the beat. Determine how many beats the new rhythm combination gets. (one)

• Tap the ♪♪ rhythm while listening to the song.

Recorded Lesson CD2:10
▶ • Listen to "Pronunciation for 'Üsküdar.'"
▶ • Sing the song.

OBJECTIVE 2 Informal Assessment
• Sing the song as some play or clap the rhythmic ostinato.

3 APPLY

1. Review "Joshua Fit the Battle of Jericho" (pp. 58–59). Identify minor. Have students:

Recorded Lesson CD2:11
▶ • Listen to "Major or Minor?" and signal whether the song is in major or minor.

• Turn back to pages 58–59 and describe the key signature. (one flat) Remember the function of a flat and the function of one flat in the key signature. (lowers all B's to B♭) Recognize the tonal center. (D)

72 MAJOR TALK ABOUT MINOR

MEETING **INDIVIDUAL** NEEDS

ALTERNATE TEACHING STRATEGIES

OBJECTIVE 2 Have students follow these steps without pausing.

Step 1: Clap the rhythm ostinato while saying *travel.*
Step 2: Clap the rhythm ostinato, whispering *travel.*
Step 3: Clap the rhythm ostinato, mouthing *travel* silently.
Step 4: Clap the rhythm ostinato, thinking *travel* as they hear the song.
Step 5: Clap the rhythm ostinato, singing the song.

OBJECTIVE 3 Have each group of students stand in its own circle to perform the patterns in the introduction to "Joshua Fit the Battle of Jericho," so that they can hear one another. Practice with the recording.

BACKGROUND: *"Üsküdar"*

A popular song in the Middle Eastern nation of Turkey, especially the cities, "Üsküdar" was written in the early 1900s by an unknown composer. It was first recorded in the United States in both Turkish and English by Edie Gormé. A version called "Uska Dara" became a hit song for Eartha Kitt in 1953.

This song mentions Üsküdar, the city in Turkey pictured at left.

SING this song.

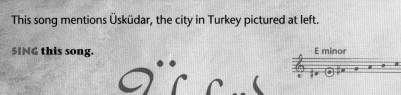

Üsküdar

Popular Turkish Song
English Version by MMH

E minor

Turkish: Üs - kü - dar' a gi - der— i ken al - di - da bir yağ mur,
Pronunciation: üs kü dar a gi der i ken al di da bir ya mur
English: Üs - kü - dar, a dis - tant— cit - y. I walk a- long the road.

Ka - ti - bi - min se - tre - si u - zun e - te - gi - ça -
ka ti bi min sε trε si u zun ε te gi ja
On a rain - y morn - ing there— I— met— my

mur. e - te - gi - ça - mur.
mur ε tε gi ja mur
friend. there— I— met— my friend.

Do you hear something familiar about this song? In what way does it sound like "Tumbai"? It's also in minor.

Many of the rhythm patterns in "Üsküdar" and "Tumbai" are the same.

- Identify the rhythms in "Üsküdar" that you recognize from "Tumbai." two eighths, eighth and two sixteenths, four sixteenths
- What is the rhythm pattern that is not found in "Tumbai"? dotted eighth-sixteenth
- Another way to write ♩♪ is ♫♫ How many beats does it take to play this rhythm? This rhythm occurs in the song on the word Üsküdar. 1

TAP this rhythm while listening to the song.

---

2. Identify sixteenth-note patterns in "Joshua Fit the Battle of Jericho" CD2:2. Have students:

▶ • Sing the song as in Lesson 3 (no introduction), then add the coda.

• Notice and then say the rhythm patterns in the introduction. Divide into groups, each to practice one pattern.

OBJECTIVE 3 **Informal Assessment**
• Perform the ostinatos as an introduction to the whole song.

4 CLOSE

"Today you studied a new scale, a new rhythm, and texture." Have students:

▶ • Recall what they learned about the minor scale and the ♩♪ pattern.

• Recall the different textures they used— canon and melodies with rhythmic ostinatos.

"Let's sing 'Joshua Fit the Battle of Jericho.'"

LESSON SUMMARY

Informal Assessment In this lesson, students:

OBJECTIVE 1 Sang "Tumbai" in three-part canon with movement.
OBJECTIVE 2 Performed a rhythmic ostinato containing ♩♪ with "Üsküdar".
OBJECTIVE 3 Performed pitch and rhythmic ostinatos containing sixteenth notes as an introduction to "Joshua Fit the Battle of Jericho."

MORE MUSIC: Reinforcement
"Carol from an Irish Cabin," page 307 (minor; Christmas)
"Hotaru Koi," page 333 (minor)
"Oh, How Lovely Is the Evening," page 336 (canon)
"I Got a Letter," page 341 (minor)

MULTICULTURAL PERSPECTIVES: *The Saz*

The stringed instrument heard in "Üsküdar" is a Turkish folk lute, or *saz*. The saz is a wooden instrument with eight to ten metal strings. Like the guitar, the strings are tuned by pegs at the outer end of the neck. Frets, made of gut, are tied around the neck at various points. A *fret* is a way to shorten the vibrating length of a string and control its pitch. The shorter the string, the higher the pitch. When the saz player places a finger on a string between two frets, the lower fret stops the string's vibration past that point to give the desired pitch.

RECORDER: *Creating a B Section for "Üsküdar"*

Have students create a B section for "Üsküdar" by improvising on E G A B. Then review high C and D and add these pitches to the improvisation.

PRONUNCIATION: *"Üsküdar"*

α f**a**ther	ε p**e**t	i b**ee**	u m**oo**n
ɾ flipped r	ü lips form [u] and say [i]		

RELATED ARTS MOVEMENT | THEATER | VISUAL ARTS

LESSON PLANNER

FOCUS Texture

OBJECTIVES
OBJECTIVE 1 Perform the rhythm of a melody in canon
OBJECTIVE 2 Identify texture in two versions of a song

MATERIALS
Recordings
I Believe in Music	CD1:34
Tumbai (canon)	CD2:8
Üsküdar	CD2:9
Joshua Fit the Battle of Jericho	CD2:2
Listening: Joshua Fit the Battle of Jericho (version 1: V. Green)	CD2:12
Listening: Joshua Fit the Battle of Jericho (version 2: F. Quivar)	CD2:13

Instruments pitched instruments

▶ = **BASIC PROGRAM**

Through THICK & THIN

Anything you study—math, meteorology, medicine—has its own vocabulary. Music is no exception. You already know and understand many of these specialized terms.

DESCRIBE **what you know about the term** *texture* **as it's used in music, using the pictures below.**

Here are the three words describing texture: *monophony, homophony, polyphony. Mono-* means alone or single in Greek. *Homo-* means the same. *Poly-* means many.

74

MEETING **INDIVIDUAL** NEEDS

ALTERNATE TEACHING STRATEGY

OBJECTIVE 1 Have students say the words as they perform the body percussion in unison. Then perform as a two-part canon, continuing to speak the words. Next, perform as a three-part canon. Finally, try the three-part canon, singing the words.

COOPERATIVE LEARNING: *Eight-Beat Patterns*

Form the class into small groups of three or four and assign each member a role, such as recorder (records group ideas), timekeeper (keeps the group on time and on track), idea-

tester (tries out patterns suggested by group members), and instrument player (plays the group's pattern for the class). Each group is to create an eight-beat accompaniment pattern from the one-beat rhythm combinations in the chart on page 67. However, they may not *duplicate* the rhythm of the melody on any beat of any line. A possible pattern is:

Each group then decides on an instrument for their pattern, and helps the instrument player learn to play it with

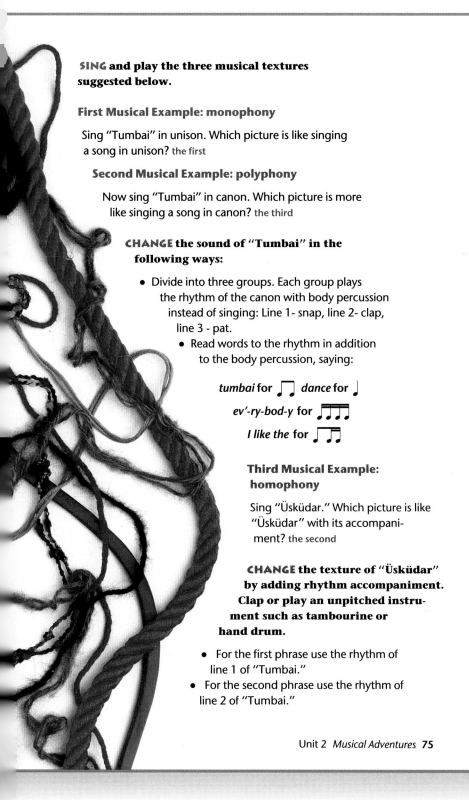

SING and play the three musical textures suggested below.

First Musical Example: monophony

Sing "Tumbai" in unison. Which picture is like singing a song in unison? the first

Second Musical Example: polyphony

Now sing "Tumbai" in canon. Which picture is more like singing a song in canon? the third

CHANGE the sound of "Tumbai" in the following ways:

- Divide into three groups. Each group plays the rhythm of the canon with body percussion instead of singing: Line 1- snap, line 2- clap, line 3 - pat.
  - Read words to the rhythm in addition to the body percussion, saying:

  tumbai for ♫ *dance* for ♩

  ev'-ry-bod-y for ♬

  I like the for ♩♫

Third Musical Example: homophony

Sing "Üsküdar." Which picture is like "Üsküdar" with its accompaniment? the second

CHANGE the texture of "Üsküdar" by adding rhythm accompaniment. Clap or play an unpitched instrument such as tambourine or hand drum.

- For the first phrase use the rhythm of line 1 of "Tumbai."
- For the second phrase use the rhythm of line 2 of "Tumbai."

Unit 2 *Musical Adventures* 75

---

1 GET SET

"Let's sing 'I Believe in Music,' with just a few people on the verses and everybody on the refrain." Have students:

▶ • Sing "I Believe in Music" CD1:34 (pages 54–55) as described. Discuss how the sound, or texture, changed when the whole class sang.

"Today, you will be musical arrangers by changing the sound of some familiar songs."

2 DEVELOP

1. Review "Tumbai" (CD2:8 canon) (pp. 66–67). Identify texture of a canon and practice the rhythm of "Tumbai." Have students:

▶ • Sing the song in unison and in canon.

▶ • Read about different musical textures. Tell whether unison or canon had thicker texture. (canon)

• Change the sound of "Tumbai" according to the directions on page 75.

OBJECTIVE 1 Informal Assessment

• Perform the rhythm of the melody in canon with the body percussion, thinking the words. (first as a two-part canon with you as "Group 1"; then, three-part canon with three groups)

2. Review "Üsküdar" CD2:9 (p. 73). Describe texture. Have students:

▶ • Sing "Üsküdar."

• Build an accompaniment, using pitched instruments alternating between E/E', A/A', and B/B'. Play them with a soft tremolo, changing from one to the other on a signal from you. (Follow the chord roots on the notation.)

• Sing the song again to decide on the texture. (melody with accompaniment)

• Change the texture of "Üsküdar" according to the directions.

"Tumbai" or "Flying Free." The instrument player then plays it for the rest of the class. Combine one or more patterns with the song and discuss the changes in texture.

GUITAR: *"Üsküdar"*

Have students accompany "Üsküdar" with guitar, following the chords on the notation.

MOVEMENT: *"Üsküdar"*

Have students create their own dance, using the steps suggested as a basis. They can change direction or facing on every new phrase.

Suggested steps:

A section:

$\frac{2}{4}$ ♩　　♩　　｜♩♩　♩　｜｜

　　R　　L　　　R　L　R

Formation: Holding hands and circling with a partner

B section:

$\frac{2}{4}$ ♫　♫　｜♫　♫　｜♩　♩　｜♩　𝄽　｜｜

　R L　R L　　R L　R L　　R　　L　　R

Formation: Holding hands in a group and circling

continued from previous page

3. Review texture. Have students:

• Summarize what they learned about the texture of "Tumbai" and "Üsküdar."

4. Review "Joshua Fit the Battle of Jericho" CD2:2 **(pp. 58–59). Practice patterns in introduction.** Have students:

• Practice each part of the song's introduction separately, then together.

• Recognize that texture was changed in the introduction when the different parts were combined.

• Form groups and sing the song with the introduction.

3 APPLY

Identify textures in two versions of "Joshua Fit the Battle of Jericho." Have students:

▶ • Read about spirituals on page 76.

▶ • Listen to the selections and identify the texture of each version. (CD2:12 version 1: unison refrain and solo verse—monophonic; CD2:13 version 2: Florence Quivar/thick, melody with chordal accompaniment—homophonic)

OBJECTIVE 2 Informal Assessment

▶ • Identify texture in the two versions by holding up one or two fingers to signal the answers to the questions on page 76.

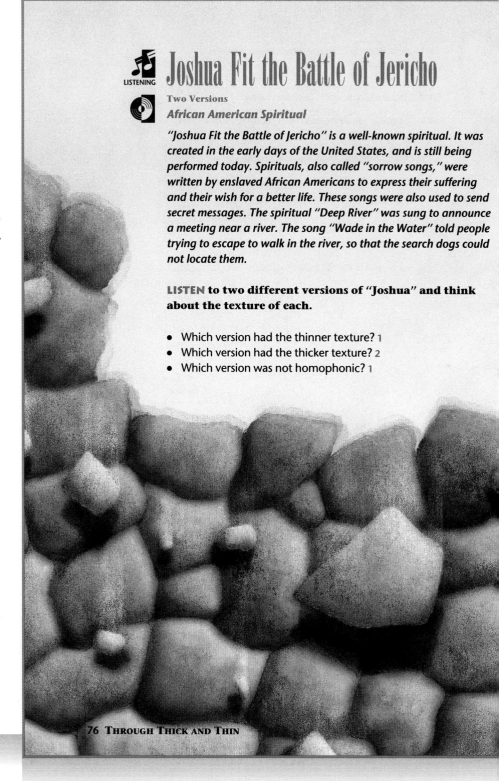

🎵 Joshua Fit the Battle of Jericho

LISTENING

Two Versions
African American Spiritual

"Joshua Fit the Battle of Jericho" is a well-known spiritual. It was created in the early days of the United States, and is still being performed today. Spirituals, also called "sorrow songs," were written by enslaved African Americans to express their suffering and their wish for a better life. These songs were also used to send secret messages. The spiritual "Deep River" was sung to announce a meeting near a river. The song "Wade in the Water" told people trying to escape to walk in the river, so that the search dogs could not locate them.

LISTEN to two different versions of "Joshua" and think about the texture of each.

• Which version had the thinner texture? 1
• Which version had the thicker texture? 2
• Which version was not homophonic? 1

76 THROUGH THICK AND THIN

MEETING **INDIVIDUAL** NEEDS

ALTERNATE TEACHING STRATEGY

OBJECTIVE 2 Listen to Versions 1 and 2 of "Two Versions of 'Joshua Fit the Battle of Jericho'." Ask students which version had performers singing or playing the same thing. (Version 1—monophony) Which version had performers singing or playing different things? (In Version 2 the singer has the melody and the pianist plays a chordal accompaniment, making the texture homophony.)

ART CONNECTION: *Texture*

VISUAL ARTS

Have students brainstorm words for textures that we can feel, such as smooth, rough, grainy, fuzzy, and bumpy. Then provide students with clay and various materials such as pencils, sponges, leaves, plastic knives, and cloth scraps. Have each person experiment with creating textures on the clay. Ideas might include poking holes in the clay with a pencil, smoothing it with a wet sponge, or pressing leaves or scraps of cloth into the clay. Discuss what kind of

Opera singer Florence Quivar
and pianist Armen Guzelimian

Vonetta Green, vocalist

"You used and heard several different textures today. How many can you name?" Have students:

▶ • Name ways the texture was changed in the lesson materials. (Sang "Tumbai" in unison and canon; sang "Üsküdar" in unison, with accompaniment and added rhythm patterns; added the introduction to "Joshua," which uses thick texture; heard different textures in "Two Versions of 'Joshua.'")

"Let's finish by singing one of the songs from the lesson again, as you think about its texture. From now on, try to think about texture in the music you hear and perform."

LESSON SUMMARY

Informal Assessment In this lesson, students:

OBJECTIVE 1 Performed, in canon, the melodic rhythm of "Tumbai."

OBJECTIVE 2 Signaled to identify texture in "Two Versions of 'Joshua Fit the Battle of Jericho.'"

MORE MUSIC: Reinforcement

"Ocho Kandelikas," page 303 (monophony/homophony; Hanukkah)
"Si me dan pasteles," page 304 (texture; Christmas)
"Silent Night," page 306 (homophony; Christmas)
"Siyahamba," page 309 (texture; Kwanzaa)
"Fortune," page 342 (monophony/polyphony)
"Michael, Row the Boat Ashore," *Songs to Sing and Read,* page 65 (spiritual)
"Train Is A-Comin'," *Songs to Sing and Read,* page 103 (spiritual)

textures they have created, then have each student form a piece of clay into a small vase or pot with texture(s) of his/her choice. Encourage students to consider how texture adds interest to the vase.

LESSON PLANNER

FOCUS Form/Pitch

OBJECTIVE
OBJECTIVE 1 Create an A B A form by developing an original B section to a familiar song, using sixteenth notes

MATERIALS
Recordings
Listening: Anitra's Dance from *Peer Gynt Suite* No. 1 by E. Grieg — CD2:14
Joshua Fit the Battle of Jericho — CD2:2
Kokoleoko — CD2:1

Instruments
unpitched instruments and resonator bells, xylophones, or keyboards

Resources
Listening Map Transparency
  T • 5 (Anitra's Dance)
Playing the Guitar G • 5 ($\frac{2}{4}$ meter)

▶ = **BASIC PROGRAM**

One Last Adventure

Almost all of the music you've encountered on your musical adventures so far used only two different meter signatures: $\frac{2}{4}$ and $\frac{4}{4}$. This music moved in groups of twos rather than threes.

In the meter signature $\frac{3}{4}$, the 3 means that there are three beats to a measure, and the 4 means that each beat has a quarter-note value.

How would you like to meet a troll king in a mountain cave, a chieftain in a desert tent, become fabulously wealthy, and then lose it all? This is what happens to Peer Gynt, the main character in an 1867 play by the Norwegian playwright Henrik Ibsen. The background music for the play was written in 1874 by Ibsen's fellow countryman, Edvard Grieg.

Peer Gynt's adventures take him to northern Africa. It is the late 1800s. A chieftain's tent is spread with a lavish feast. Musicians are entertaining assembled guests. The music is in a minor key, but there is something different about the meter.

IDENTIFY the meter of this music. How can you tell? $\frac{3}{4}$; the music moves in threes.

78

MEETING **INDIVIDUAL** NEEDS

BIOGRAPHY: *Edvard Grieg*

Norwegian composer Edvard Grieg (**ɛd** vɑrt **grig**) (1843–1907) began studying piano with his mother, from whom he learned many of Norway's folk songs. As a young adult, he studied music in Denmark and Germany, and his early work was greatly influenced by German composers. Returning to Norway to teach and conduct, he founded the Norwegian Academy of Music in 1867. At that time Norway was ruled by Sweden, but the people of Norway wanted to be independent. To show Norway's pride in

its culture and traditions, Grieg collected many Norwegian folk tunes and used them in his compositions.

Grieg's background music for Ibsen's play *Peer Gynt* (per gɪnt)—the two Peer Gynt suites—contains some of his most famous music. (A suite is a group of related pieces.) "Anitra's Dance," "In the Hall of the Mountain King," and "Aase's (ɑ zəz) Death" are known all over the world.

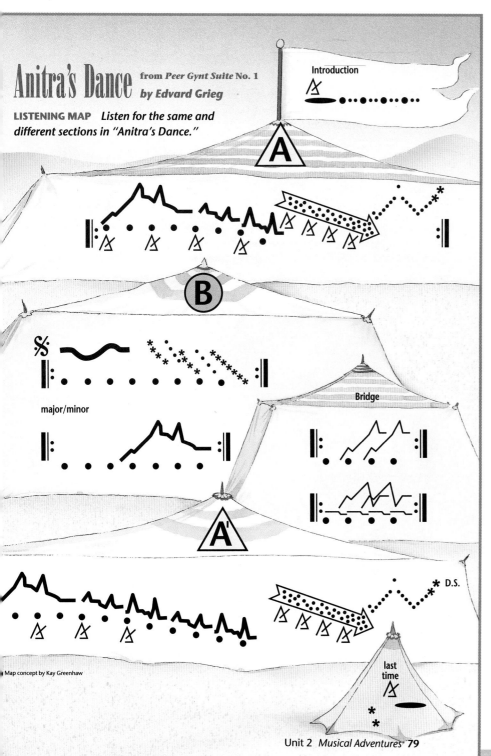

Anitra's Dance
from Peer Gynt Suite No. 1
by Edvard Grieg

LISTENING MAP *Listen for the same and different sections in "Anitra's Dance."*

Introduction

A

B

%

major/minor

A'

Bridge

last time

D.S.

Map concept by Kay Greenhaw

Unit 2 *Musical Adventures* **79**

"In this unit, you've worked with form and songs in minor or major. What are some examples?" Have students:

▶ • Name a song and its form. ("Tumbai" in the unison version is A B A form.)

▶ • Name songs in minor ("Üsküdar," "Tumbai," "Joshua Fit the Battle of Jericho") and in major ("One Moment in Time," "Kokoleoko," "Flying Free," "I Believe in Music").

"Today you'll use what you've learned about music to create a new section for a song."

2 DEVELOP

1. Introduce "Anitra's Dance" CD2:14. **Show meter and identify form.** Have students:

▶ • Read about ¾ meter and "Anitra's (ə **nl** traz) Dance."

▶ • Listen to the first section, patting with the strong beat and counting the weak beats in between, to show its meter. Decide if it is major or minor. (¾; minor)

▶ • Use the listening map to count the number of main sections. (3, with a bridge between the second and third sections)

▶ • Follow the listening map as they listen to the music (Stop the recording at the end of the A' section, before the D.S.). (Optional: Use **Listening Map Transparency T · 5.** Each group of three dots represents one three-beat measure.)

▶ • After listening, discuss the form with a partner. Then, raise a hand to signal which combination of letters describes the form: A A A, A B B, or A B A. (A B A) (Continue playing the recording to the end, pointing out that Grieg extended the form by repeating Sections 2 and 3.)

continued from previous page

2. Review "Joshua Fit the Battle of Jericho" CD2:2 (pp. 58–59). Sing major and minor scales and describe form. Have students:

▶ • Perform the song with the introduction.

• Review the sixteenth-note rhythms used in the song.

• Recall the placement of half steps in the minor scale (2–3, 6–7) and the major scale (3–4, 7–8). Listen as someone plays a D major scale and a D minor scale on a pitched instrument, then sing each scale.

▶ • Describe the form. (verse-refrain form with introduction and coda)

3 APPLY

Review "Kokoleoko" CD2:1 (p. 57). Create an eight-beat rhythm pattern. Have students:

▶ • Sing "Kokoleoko."

• Read about creating a B section for the song, then create an eight-beat rhythm pattern containing at least one beat of sixteenth notes or combination of eighth and sixteenth notes, as in the chart on page 67.

• Play the pattern on unpitched instruments.

• Transfer the pattern to pitched instruments, using the pitches C D E G A.

OBJECTIVE 1 Informal Assessment
• Sing "Kokoleoko," with their pattern (played twice) as a B section for an A B A form. Perform it as: A A B B A A (Verse 1 Verse 2, B B, Verse 1 Verse 2).

Now, take some time to compose some music of your own. Working with a partner, use what you have learned in this unit about rhythm, pitch, and form.

CREATE a B section for an ABA form with "Kokoleoko" as the A section.

• Make up an eight-beat rhythm pattern.
• Use sixteenth notes in at least one of those beats.

80 ONE LAST ADVENTURE

MEETING **INDIVIDUAL** NEEDS

ALTERNATE TEACHING STRATEGY

OBJECTIVE 1 If students are having difficulty playing the sixteenth notes, have them change the sixteenth notes to eighth notes until they are comfortable playing the pattern at tempo. Then have them replace the eighth notes with the original sixteenth notes.

PLAYING INSTRUMENTS: *"Kokoleoko"*

Appoint an accompaniment group to develop a four-beat accompaniment pattern on unpitched instruments for "Kokoleoko."

PLAYING INSTRUMENTS: *Keyboard*

Have students create a rondo form by creating a second eight-beat pattern and performing it on a keyboard or other pitched instrument, as a C section with "Kokoleoko," as follows: A A B B A A C C A A.

You might also have small groups or individuals create their own eight-beat patterns, then combine two of them for an A B A form.

PLAY YOUR RHYTHM PATTERN

- Choose instruments or other sound sources that make short sounds.
- Combine your pattern with the pattern of another pair of students who have an instrument that is different from yours. Play the patterns one after the other, or both at the same time. The choice is yours.
- Practice until the combined patterns are easy to play.

PLAY your pattern on a pitched instrument such as bells, xylophone, or keyboard.

- Choose three to five pitches from the C major scale.
- Transfer the rhythm pattern you created to the pitched instrument, using the pitches you have chosen. Hint: make your phrase sound like C major by ending it on C, E, or G.
- Play your pattern with another pair of students who have instruments with contrasting tone colors.
- Make any changes you and your partners think would make your patterns sound better.

Here it is! The final production!

A Sing "Kokoleoko" twice.

B Play your pitched pattern twice.

A Sing "Kokoleoko" twice more.

This art is based on a batik cloth design from the Ivory Coast.

4 CLOSE

"In this lesson, you used a musical form in a way that challenged your creativity." Have students:

▶ • Identify the forms used in the lesson. (verse-refrain with introduction and coda; A B A)

- Tell how they changed the form of "Kokoleoko." (added a B section, sang the A section again at the end to give the song A B A form)

"A B A form gives us unity, with the repetition of the A section—and variety, with the contrast of the B section. Let's end the lesson with a different kind of variety—let's take a vote to choose a favorite song that you haven't sung for a while to finish today."

LESSON SUMMARY

Informal Assessment In this lesson, students:

OBJECTIVE 1 Created an A B A form by developing an original B section for "Kokoleoko," using sixteenth notes.

MORE MUSIC: Reinforcement

"Holiday Sing-Along," page 301 (major/minor, $\frac{3}{4}$; Christmas)

"Winter Poem," page 302 (winter; sixteenth notes)

"Dona nobis pacem," page 338 ($\frac{3}{4}$)

"Spring Rain," page 345 ($\frac{3}{4}$, minor)

"Orion," page 350 ($\frac{4}{4}$ vs. $\frac{3}{4}$)

"Las mañanitas," page 353 ($\frac{3}{4}$)

"El zapatero," page 404 (sixteenth notes)

"Acres of Clams," *Songs to Sing and Read*, page 2 ($\frac{3}{4}$ meter)

"Zandunga," *Songs to Sing and Read*, page 108 ($\frac{3}{4}$ meter)

GUITAR: *"Kokoleoko"*

Students can accompany the song using the chords in the notation on page 57.

ART CONNECTION: *Resist* VISUAL ARTS

The figures on this page are based on a *batik* from the Ivory Coast. Batik is an art form that involves a technique called "resist." Artists paint wax patterns onto cloth and then dye the cloth. The places painted with wax "resist" the dye. Students can try a similar resist technique by drawing designs on paper with a wax crayon and applying watercolor. The wax design will resist the watercolor.

ENRICHMENT: *Recording the Performance*

When students have created and practiced their rhythm patterns, have a group rehearsal with the recording. Then have some students play instruments while others sing. Make an audio- or videotape of this performance so that students can hear themselves. This can be part of a tape library of their performances, which they can hear from time to time to mark their musical growth.

UNIT TWO
LESSON 9

RELATED ARTS MOVEMENT THEATER VISUAL ARTS

LESSON PLANNER

OBJECTIVES
To review songs, skills, and concepts learned in Unit 2 and to test students' ability to:
1. Read and play ♫♫♫ and ♫♫
2. Identify a major scale
3. Identify A B A form

MATERIALS
Recordings

One Moment in Time	CD1:29
Kokoleoko	CD2:1
Flying Free	CD2:5
Tumbai	CD2:7
I Believe in Music	CD1:34
Unit 2 Assessment A	CD2:15–20
Unit 2 Assessment B	CD2:21–26

Instruments pitched instruments

Resources
Resource Master 2 • 5 (assessment)
Resource Master TA • 1 (assessment)
Resource Master—staff paper

▶ = BASIC PROGRAM

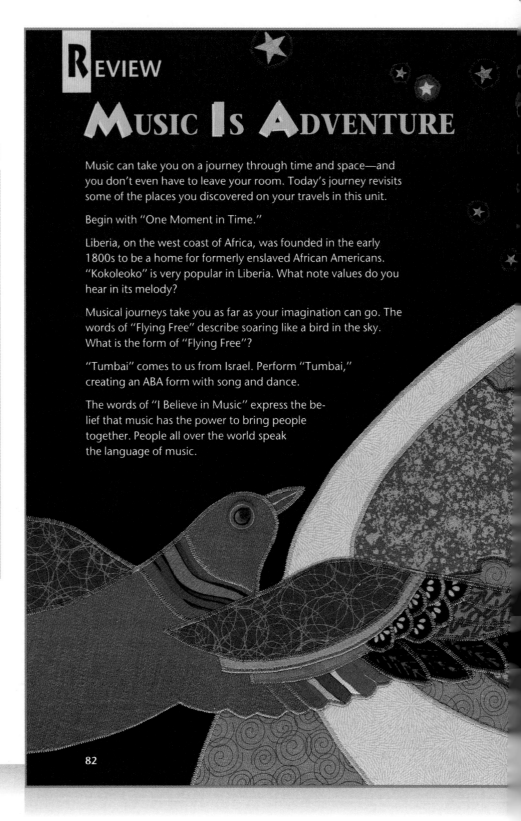

REVIEW
MUSIC IS ADVENTURE

Music can take you on a journey through time and space—and you don't even have to leave your room. Today's journey revisits some of the places you discovered on your travels in this unit.

Begin with "One Moment in Time."

Liberia, on the west coast of Africa, was founded in the early 1800s to be a home for formerly enslaved African Americans. "Kokoleoko" is very popular in Liberia. What note values do you hear in its melody?

Musical journeys take you as far as your imagination can go. The words of "Flying Free" describe soaring like a bird in the sky. What is the form of "Flying Free"?

"Tumbai" comes to us from Israel. Perform "Tumbai," creating an ABA form with song and dance.

The words of "I Believe in Music" express the belief that music has the power to bring people together. People all over the world speak the language of music.

82

MEETING INDIVIDUAL NEEDS

PROGRAM IDEA: *A Trip Around the World*

This review can be enjoyed in the classroom or presented as a simple program. Additional materials from Unit 2, *Celebrations,* or the *Music Library* may be added as well as original work from the students.

Have students take a "A Trip Around the World" with stops to sing the music from the different countries in Unit 2. Begin by listing the songs they have learned in this unit, and work together to decide which songs would be best for opening and closing the program. Then choose an order for

the songs in the middle. Point out that students need not use every song learned.

Discuss with students how they would like to link the songs. One idea is to write a brief travelogue for each stop that would also serve to introduce the song for that country. Whatever linking idea students choose, assign small groups to work on each stop. They should decide how to present the music, including whether or not to add a dance, costumes, or instrumental accompaniment. Each group should present their idea to the class. All groups then practice and prepare for the final performance.

REVIEW

1. Review melodic contour with "One Moment in Time" CD1:29 **(p. 49).** Have students:

▶ • Sing "One Moment in Time," tracing the melodic contour in the air with their hand.

2. Review sixteenth-note rhythms with "Kokoleoko" CD2:1 **(p. 57).** Have students:

• Sing "Kokoleoko," and tell what note values they hear in its melody.

• Find note values from "Kokoleoko" in the chart on page 67 and pat each rhythm four times without stopping. (♩ ; ♬♬ ; ♫♪)

• Sing the song again with the above rhythm sequence as an accompaniment, choosing one of the rhythms to repeat four times at the end to make eight bars altogether.

3. Review form and major scale with "Flying Free" CD2:5 **(pp. 64–65).** Have students:

▶ • Sing "Flying Free" and describe its form.

• List all the pitches in the first phrase of the melody (up to *by the sea*) from lowest to highest. (C D E F G A B C' D') Then tell which scale these notes belong to and where the half steps are in this scale. (C major; E-F and B-C or Steps 3–4 and 7–8)

• Find half steps in Lines 1–2. (*is a* —E-F; *my own*—B-C; *where I*—E-F; *by the*—F-E)

4. Review sixteenth notes and form with "Tumbai" CD2:7 **(p. 66).** Have students:

• Find the patterns with sixteenth notes from the chart on page 67 that are also found in "Tumbai." (♬♪ ; ♫♪)

▶ • Recall the form of "Tumbai" and how the form is created. Perform "Tumbai," singing and dancing the A B A form. (See Lesson 5, pages 68–69.)

5. Reinforce unit theme with "I Believe in Music" CD1:34 **(pp. 54–55).** Have students:

▶ • Sing "I Believe in Music" and talk about the unit theme of musical adventures.

Unit 2 *Musical Adventures* **83**

DRAMA CONNECTION: *Production Values*
THEATER

The *Program Idea* on page 82, "A Trip Around the World," is an opportunity to introduce production values in performance. Have small groups discuss, research, and plan a production design (costumes, lighting, settings) that supports the intent of the music for each "stop." Guide each group in creating performances that support the class effort. Help the class design beginnings, endings, and transitions (or links) between songs. Explain that these parts must be "choreographed," even if only to plan how students will enter and exit the stage or performance area.

Encourage each group to watch the other groups during rehearsal to observe the production choices that the other groups made. Have students note effective elements and offer suggestions for improvement.

UNIT TWO
LESSON 9

ASSESSMENTS A AND B CD2:15-26

Different recorded examples for Assesments A and B allow for two uses of the same set of questions. When appropriate, recorded examples for Assessment A use familiar musical examples with which students have worked for the given concept. The recorded examples for Assessment B use musical selections the students have not previously worked with for the concept, encouraging the application of knowledge to new material.

The pupil page is intended for those who wish to assess quickly with the whole class or in small groups. Each assessment may be used as a pretest or as a final review before presenting the written test (**Resource Master 2 • 5**).

ANSWERS		
	ASSESSMENT A	**ASSESSMENT B**
1.	c	b
2.	d	b
3.	a	b
4.	b	a
5.	b	a
6.	a	b

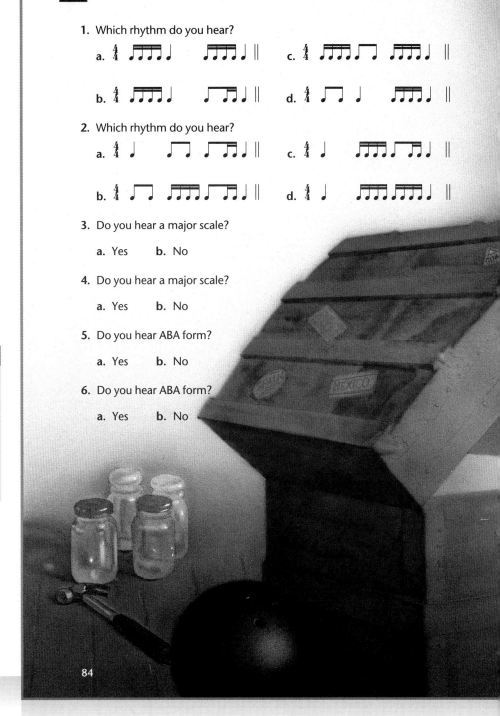

CHECK IT OUT

1. Which rhythm do you hear?

2. Which rhythm do you hear?

3. Do you hear a major scale?

   a. Yes   **b.** No

4. Do you hear a major scale?

   a. Yes   **b.** No

5. Do you hear ABA form?

   a. Yes   **b.** No

6. Do you hear ABA form?

   a. Yes   **b.** No

84

MEETING **INDIVIDUAL** NEEDS

PORTFOLIO ASSESSMENT

To evaluate students' portfolios, use the Portfolio Assessment form on **Resource Master TA • 1**. See page 46B for a summary of Portfolio Opportunities in this unit.

EXTRA HELP: *Writing Dialogue*

To help students write realistic dialogue, have them listen to or tape informal conversations. They might also stage an improvised dialogue in the classroom. Have them note that in real life people often use contractions, incomplete sentences, and idiomatic expressions.

LANGUAGE ARTS CONNECTION: *Mystery Movie*

Have students work in groups of four to expand the ideas developed as a class into a short "movie." The movie should be in the form of a one-act play with a clear beginning, middle, and end. Students should edit and add dialogue and music as needed. If a videocamera is available, you might tape each student's initial work, then the group movie to show them how their ideas evolved.

CREATE

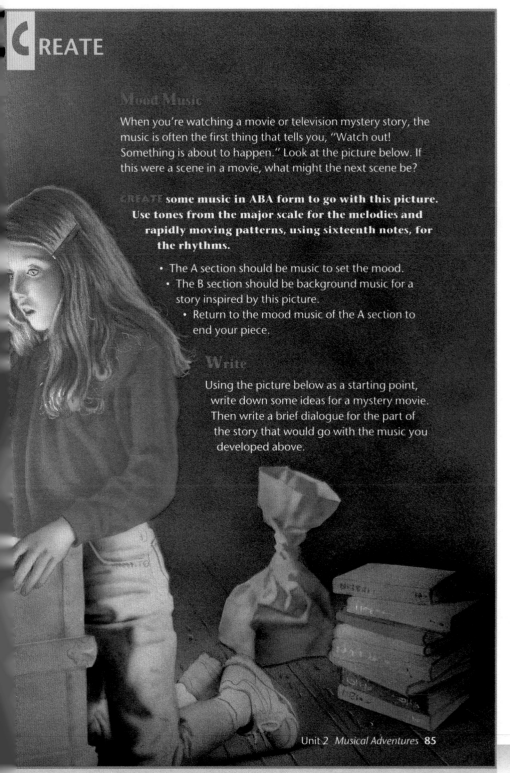

Mood Music

When you're watching a movie or television mystery story, the music is often the first thing that tells you, "Watch out! Something is about to happen." Look at the picture below. If this were a scene in a movie, what might the next scene be?

CREATE **some music in ABA form to go with this picture. Use tones from the major scale for the melodies and rapidly moving patterns, using sixteenth notes, for the rhythms.**

- The A section should be music to set the mood.
- The B section should be background music for a story inspired by this picture.
  - Return to the mood music of the A section to end your piece.

Write

Using the picture below as a starting point, write down some ideas for a mystery movie. Then write a brief dialogue for the part of the story that would go with the music you developed above.

Unit 2 *Musical Adventures* 85

CREATE AND WRITE

1. Compose and play music in A B A form. Have students:

- Follow the directions on page 85 to compose music in A B A form. (Optional: Have students notate their music on staff paper, available in the Resource Master booklet.)
- Play the composition on a pitched instrument and revise as desired.

2. Write and perform dialogue for a mystery movie. Have students:

▶ • Follow the instructions to invent a plot for a mystery movie. (The class might work together to brainstorm ideas. To get them started, ask leading questions such as: What is the setting for the scene? What is the approximate year? What kind of day is it? Who's in trouble? Who's the hero/heroine/villain? Does the mystery involve a ghost? A detective?)

- Using one of the ideas as the basic plot, write a brief dialogue for a mystery-movie scene to go with the music they composed.

- Choose classmates to read each part and help play their music as needed, then perform for the class.

DRAMA CONNECTION: *Images*

THEATER

Movies and videos communicate primarily through the language of images. Have students view movie segments with the sound turned off. Ask them to observe and describe the different ways filmmakers use images to tell stories. "How close is the camera?" (close-up, midrange, or long shot) "Is the camera still or does it move across a scene? If it does move, how quickly does it move? What is the point of view of the camera?" (like an audience, like a character, like a hidden observer) "Notice how the shots are edited together." (faded, abrupt) Discuss why the filmmaker chose each kind of element to tell the story.

LESSONLINKS

The Drum: A Percussion Instrument *(15 min)*

OBJECTIVE Develop a definition of percussion instruments and learn ways they are played

Reinforcement percussion family, *page 13*

MATERIALS
Instruments Optional—classroom drums

Resources Musical Instruments Master—drum

Frame Drums *(15 min)*

OBJECTIVE Learn about different kinds of frame drums

Reinforcement percussion family, *page 13*

MATERIALS
Instrument Optional—tambourine

Resources Musical Instruments Master—tambourine

Meet Glen Velez *(20 min)*

OBJECTIVE Listen to Glen Velez tell about his career as a drummer

Reinforcement percussion family, *page 13*

MATERIALS
Recording Recorded Lesson: Interview with Glen Velez   CD2:27

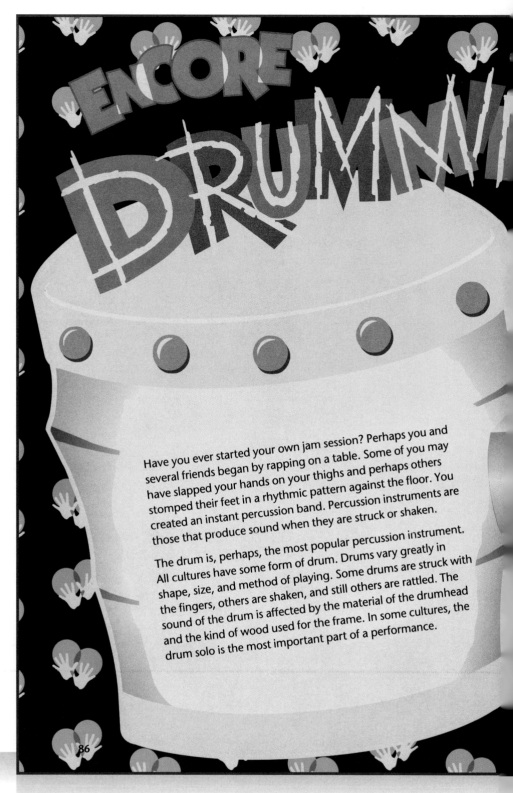

Have you ever started your own jam session? Perhaps you and several friends began by rapping on a table. Some of you may have slapped your hands on your thighs and perhaps others stomped their feet in a rhythmic pattern against the floor. You created an instant percussion band. Percussion instruments are those that produce sound when they are struck or shaken.

The drum is, perhaps, the most popular percussion instrument. All cultures have some form of drum. Drums vary greatly in shape, size, and method of playing. Some drums are struck with the fingers, others are shaken, and still others are rattled. The sound of the drum is affected by the material of the drumhead and the kind of wood used for the frame. In some cultures, the drum solo is the most important part of a performance.

86

MEETING **INDIVIDUAL** NEEDS

BACKGROUND: *The History of Drums*

Drums may well be the earliest instruments. Their development began when early people first tapped together sticks, stones, and bones to produce rhythms. The first drums may have been made from hollowed-out tree trunks that were covered at one or both ends with animal skins. These early drums were used to send messages or for ceremonial, religious, or military purposes. Today drums are still popular all over the world, often as an accompaniment to singing and dancing. Drums have been heard in Western orchestras since the 1700s.

Indian tablas

African talking drum

Korean changko

Middle-Eastern dumbek

The Drum: A Percussion Instrument

1. Develop a definition of percussion instruments. Have students:

• Read page 86, then give a definition of a percussion instrument. (an instrument producing sound when struck, shaken, or rattled)

• Look at the drums on page 87, then name instruments that belong to the percussion family and explain how they are played.

• Listen as a few volunteers tell about their experiences playing percussion instruments.

2. Learn how a drum is played. Have students:

• Practice drumming sounds by lightly tapping their desktops or classroom drums with their fingers.

• Name other ways drums can be played besides having the head struck with the hand or a mallet or stick. (They can be shaken, rattled, rubbed, and so on.)

• Give reasons why drumming might be important in some cultures. (See *Background* on the bottom of page 86.)

ENRICHMENT: *Making Percussion Instruments* VISUAL ARTS

Have students use barrels, cake tins, cardboard cylinders, or other recycled containers to create percussion instruments. Encourage students to consider how percussion instruments can be sounded (struck, shaken, rattled) as they experiment in creating their instruments. They can enclose rice or other grains in the instruments to make a rattling sound. They should try different striking tools as well; striking a drum with a spoon will make a different sound than striking it with a stick. They might also vary the shape to alter the sound; a cylindrical drum sounds different from an hourglass drum.

ENCORE

MULTICULTURAL PERSPECTIVES

continued from previous page

Frame Drums

Learn about different kinds of frame drums. Have students:

• Read page 88, then define what a frame drum is. (a portable, circular instrument held in one hand and struck with the other)

• Tell about experiences hearing or using a tambourine, and listen to a volunteer shake a tambourine, if available.

• Describe the similarities of the tambourine, riq (rĭk), and bodhran (bɔ rɔn). (circular frames)

• Describe the differences among the three frame drums. (size differs; tambourine has jingles and is shaken as well as struck; pitch can be adjusted on the riq; bodhran is played with a double-headed stick)

Frame drums are portable instruments with circular frames. They are small enough to be held in one hand and struck with the other.

The tambourine, which originated in Southwest Asia, is a very simple and versatile instrument. It is one of the more popular frame drums. In addition to a drum head, the tambourine has jingles on it that ring when the instrument is struck.

The riq, a drum from Egypt, resembles the tambourine. It is used in dance music, concert music, and religious music. The pitch of this drum can be raised or lowered.

Popular for more than a hundred years, the bodhran is a frame drum from Ireland. It has a low, deep sound, but brighter, ringing sounds can be drawn from it as well. Traditionally, this drum is played with a double-headed stick and is used in Irish folk music.

88 DRUMMING ALONG

MEETING **INDIVIDUAL** NEEDS

BACKGROUND: *Frame Drums*

Frame drums originated in the Middle East and are still popular there. Drums of this type consist of one or two membranes stretched over a simple, narrow frame. Most frames are circular but other shapes exist, such as square or oval. Like the tambourine, many frame drums have metal jingles attached to the rim.

PLAYING INSTRUMENTS: *Percussion*

Have students play rhythmic patterns on classroom percussion instruments or on the instruments they made. (See *Enrichment* at the bottom of page 86.) You may want to use the following ostinatos, which can be played together:

Meet GLEN VELEZ

Glen Velez, who first started studying the drums with his uncle at the age of eight, is an internationally known drummer, composer, scholar, and teacher. He has combined his background in Western percussion with the study of tambourine performance styles from around the world. For 15 years, Velez performed with the Steve Reich ensemble. He has been the percussionist with the Paul Winter Consort since 1983.

LISTEN to Glen Velez talk about his career and demonstrate some of the drums he has collected from around the world.

Encore **89**

Meet Glen Velez

Listen to Glen Velez tell about his career as a drummer. Have students:

• Read about Glen Velez on page 89.

Recorded Interview CD2:27

• Listen to "Interview with Glen Velez" to hear the drummer talk about his career and demonstrate drums from his collection, including a tambourine, riq, and bodhran.

• Discuss how tone colors of the drums varied.

• Tell which drumming technique they found especially interesting, giving reasons why.

THE KEYBOARD CONNECTION

MULTICULTURAL PERSPECTIVES

Through exposure to diverse materials, students develop an awareness of how people from many cultures create and participate in music. This unit includes:

African/African American

European/European American

Middle Eastern

For a complete listing of materials by culture throughout the book, see the Classified Index.

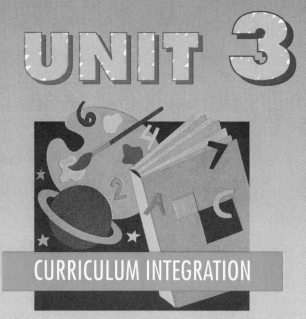

UNIT 3

CURRICULUM INTEGRATION

Activities in this unit that promote the integration of music with other curriculum areas include:

Art

Math

Reading/Language Arts

Science

Social Studies

OVERVIEW

LESSON 4 CORE p.106	LESSON 5 CORE p.110	LESSON 6 p.114	LESSON 7 p.120	LESSON 8 p.124
Rhythm	Rhythm/Tone color	Tone color	Tone color	Rhythm
Harmony Tee galop pour Mamou Mazurka (folk dance) (listening) Chopin: Mazurka (listening) Heart and Soul (listening)	Player Piano (poem) The Old Piano Roll Blues Trio No. 39 (listening)	This Can't Be Love (listening) Said I Wasn't Gonn' Tell Nobody Sonata in G Minor (listening)	Said I Wasn't Gonn' Tell Nobody Kakokolo (listening) Kakokolo (song) Three Dances (listening)	Rhythm-a-ning (listening) Lean on Me
	• Hear *p, mp, mf, f, ff,* dim.	• Hear *p, mp, mf, f, ff,* cresc.		
• Hear and sing allegro	• Hear and sing allegro • Hear presto	• Hear moderato		• Hear andante
• Learn about accents	• Hear staccato	• Sing glissando and grace notes		
	• **Review sound of organ, harpsichord, piano and how sounds are produced (Rf)** • Learn about player piano • Hear chamber music ensemble and identify fortepiano	• **Hear jazz piano (Rf)** • **Recognize organ, piano** • **Recognize harpsichord (Rf)** • **Compare harpsichord, piano, organ (Rf)** • Learn about sound envelope • *Play electronic keyboards*	• **Recognize electric organ** • **Compare prepared and unprepared piano (Rf)** • Hear mbira (thumb piano) • Hear prepared piano • Prepare piano • *Improvise piece for prepared instrument*	• **Hear duo-pianists (Rf)** • **Play piano with song (Rf)**
• Review meaning of ¾ • Recognize three beats in measure • Recognize beat with ♫ • *Compose patterns in ¾*			• *Improvise ostinatos in ¼*	• Compose melody in ¾ • *Accompany melody in ¼*
• **Distinguish equal and unequal sounds (E/D)** • **Identify, clap, and play ♩ ♪ and ♫ (I/P)** • *Create ♫ patterns (C)*	• **Clap and say ♫ pattern (Rf)** • **Clap, speak, and play ♩ ♪ and ♫ (Rf/Rd)** • *Create movement with ♫ (C)*		• **Move to ♩ ♪ pattern (Rf/Rd)** • *Improvise rhythmic ostinatos (C)*	• **Create melody using ♩ ♫ ♫ (C)**
• *Sing melody with pitch syllables and hand signs* • *Compose pentatonic patterns*			• *Compose piece with pitched ostinatos*	• Show melodic contour • Sing melody with pitch letter names
				• Play chords to accompany song
	• Hear major and minor			• Tell key from signature
• Add rhythmic ostinato accompaniments	• Add rhythmic ostinato accompaniment	• Recognize texture of fugue as polyphony	• *Accompany song with ostinatos*	• Listen for melody and accompaniment
	• Show rondo form • *Recognize rondo form*	• Sing call and response • Learn about, hear, perform, recognize fugue • *Learn about the sonata*		
• Learn about mazurka and accordion • Composer: Frédéric Chopin • Painter: Eugène Delacroix • *Learn about Cajun music*	• Composer: F. J. Haydn • Learn about chamber music • *Poet: John Updike* • *Style: Ragtime*	• Performer: Ellis Marsalis • Composer: Domenico Scarlatti • *Styles: Jazz, gospel* • *Songwriters: Richard Rodgers and Lorenz Hart*	• *Learn about African folktale* • *Style: minimalism*	• *Composer/performer: Thelonius Monk* • *Learn history of bass clef*

UNIT 3 PLANNER

SKILLS		LESSON 1 CORE p.90	LESSON 2 CORE p.98	LESSON 3 p.102
CREATION AND PERFORMANCE	Singing	• Hear and sing *mf*, *f*, cresc. • Sing moderato	• Sing in canon • Sing andante • Sing harmony part • *Sing open vowel sounds*	• Sing *p*, *mp*, *mf*, *f*, *ff*, cresc. • Sing allegro • Sing ritardando • Sing minor scale with scale numbers • *Practice matching pitch*
	Playing	• Pantomine playing bass line on keyboard	• Play F major scale • *Play 5-note keyboard melodies*	• *Add pitched playalong to song*
	Moving	• Move to show melodic contour	• *Move in unison and in canon*	• *Add gospel-choir step to song*
	Improvising/ Creating	• Create movement to show melodic contour		
NOTATION	Reading		• Identify *do* from key signature	• Identify key from signature • *Read playalong*
	Writing			
PERCEPTION AND ANALYSIS	Listening/ Describing/ Analyzing	• Tell meaning of harmony • Describe difference between song with and without harmonic accompaniment • Describe sound of pipe organ, harpsichord, piano • *Tell why piano can substitute for orchestra*	• *Discuss why organ is often used to accompany church music*	• Compare major and minor

 TECHNOLOGY

SHARE THE MUSIC VIDEOS

Use videos to reinforce, extend, and enrich learning.
· **Lesson 1, pp. 92–97:** Making a Music Video (part songs); Signing, Grades 3–6 (Harmony); Sounds of Percussion (piano)
· **Lesson 3, pp. 104–105:** Creating Musical Moods (synthesizers)
· **Lesson 4, p. 107:** Blending Musical Styles (cajun)
· **Lesson 5, p. 113:** Musical Expression (classical music)
· **Lesson 6, pp. 114–115:** Musical Expression (jazz)
· **Lesson 7, p. 120:** Sounds of Percussion (mbira)
· **Encore, pp. 132–135:** Musical Expression (jazz); Blending Musical Styles (blues)

MUSIC WITH *MIDI*

MIDI technology allows students to manipulate musical elements and make musical decisions with this song:
· **Lesson 2, p. 98:** Alleluia

Italic = Meeting Individual Needs

LESSON 4 CORE p.106	LESSON 5 CORE p.110	LESSON 6 p.114	LESSON 7 p.120	LESSON 8 p.124
• Sing allegro	• Sing allegro	• Sing in call-and-response style • *Hear and imitate good vocal models*		• Sing melody with pitch letter names
• Clap and play dotted-rhythm accompaniments • *Play recorder accompaniment* • *Play patterns on pitched or unpitched instruments*	• Clap and say dotted rhythm pattern • Play pattern to show rondo form	• Play sounds to hear envelopes • *Play electronic keyboards*	• Prepare an instrument and demonstrate sound • *Play percussion ostinatos with song* • *Improvise piece for prepared instrument* • *Make and tune thumb piano* • *Play piece with pitched and rhythmic ostinatos*	• Play chords to accompany song • Play melody with accompaniment
• *Step with beat* • *Dance mazurka*	• *Create movement with dotted rhythms*		• Move to dotted rhythm pattern	
• *Create rhythm and pitch patterns*	• *Create dance for song*		• Create movement for song with dotted rhythm • *Improvise rhythmic ostinatos* • *Improvise piece for prepared instrument* • *Make and tune thumb piano* • *Create piece with pitched and rhythmic ostinatos*	• Create group melody and method of notation
• Read and clap dotted rhythm • Find dotted rhythm in notation • Review meaning of ¾ time signature • *Read melody with pitch syllables and hand signs*	• Read notated dotted rhythms	• Read and sing glissando and grace notes	• Move to notated rhythm	• Learn about and name pitches in treble and bass clefs, grand staff • Tell key and melodic contour from notation • Read pitches with letter names
	• Outline rondo form		• *Notate melody they create*	• Notate group melody
	• Describe sound of fortepiano • Signal and play to show rondo form • *Listen for themes in rondo form*	• Listen for and describe different sound envelopes • Identify keyboard instruments • *Compare sounds of harpsichord, piano, organ*	• Compare sound of prepared piano to that of other instruments • *Compare prepared and unprepared piano*	• Describe roles of left and right hands on keyboard • Listen for melody and accompaniment and sound effects • Describe melodic contour

UNIT 3 PLANNER

MUSICTIME™

This notational software develops students' music reading and writing skills through activities correlated to these lessons:
Lesson 3, Project 1 (create an accompaniment)
Lesson 8, Project 2 (create a melody in ¾ with accompaniment)
Lesson 9, Project 3 (compose a melody in ¾ using C D E F G)

MUSIC ACE™

Music Ace reinforces musical concepts and provides ear-training opportunities for students.
· **Lesson 2, p. 98: Lesson 24 (major scale intervals)**
· **Lesson 3, p. 102: Listening Selection 1 (Prelude in A Minor)**

UNIT THREE
LESSON 1

RELATED ARTS MOVEMENT | THEATER | VISUAL ARTS

LESSON PLANNER

FOCUS Tone color

OBJECTIVES

OBJECTIVE 1 Show recognition of the sounds of harpsichord, pipe organ, and piano (tested)

OBJECTIVE 2 Show understanding of how sound is produced on three keyboard instruments (tested)

MATERIALS

Recordings

Harmony	CD2:28
Harmony (performance mix)	CD2:29
Listening: Heart and Soul by H. Carmichael	CD2:30
Listening: Rondeau by E. C. Jacquet de la Guerre	CD2:31
Recorded Lesson: The World of Keyboards	CD2:32

Resources

Musical Instruments Masters— harpsichord, piano

Recorder Master R • 11 (pitches D E F♯ G A B)

Signing Master S • 6 • 2 (Harmony)

VOCABULARY

organ, harpsichord, piano

▶ = **BASIC PROGRAM**

U N I T 3

The Keyboard Connection

TO CATALINA

Love thy piano, Oh girl,
It will give you back
Note for note
The harmonies of your soul.
It will sing back to you
The high songs of your heart.
It will give
As well as take . . .

—Frank Horne

90

MEETING **INDIVIDUAL** NEEDS

BIOGRAPHY: *Frank Horne*

American poet Frank Horne (1899–1974) began his working life as an optometrist, went on to become a teacher, and finally went to work for the government to provide better housing for African Americans. Throughout his life, he wrote poems as well. He often wrote about death and illness, perhaps because he suffered from a painful disease that made it difficult for him to walk. He also wrote about African American life in the United States, in poems that teach children to be proud of their heritage or that poke fun at those who discriminate against people based on their skin color. His most famous work, *Letters Found Near a Suicide* (1925), contains 11 poems (including the selection) dedicated to people who had an effect on the narrator's life.

Jeunes filles au piano (detail)
by Pierre August Renoir

91

"Keyboard instruments can produce some of the most moving and exciting music written." Have students:

▶ • Read and discuss the poem "To Catalina."

▶ • Discuss experiences they have had playing or hearing keyboard instruments. (As a starter idea, ask them to name some songs or pieces of classical music that they may have heard played on a piano or other keyboard instruments.)

"In this unit, you'll find out why some keyboard instruments sound as they do and learn more about how to play them."

ART CONNECTION: *The Impressionists* VISUAL ARTS

The painting above was done by Pierre August Renoir, an important Impressionist artist. The Impressionists, who worked in the late 1800s, often tried to capture a moment in time. They did this by using light, color, and line to create a sense of atmosphere. "Do you think this shows the girls in a moment of activity or are they posing?" (active) "Describe the lines in the painting." (blurred, soft) "From which direction is the light shining? How can you tell?" (from above and behind girls; brighter, lighter areas fall on left side of painting)

ENRICHMENT: *Piano*

Students may have heard (or played) piano transcriptions of music written for other instruments or orchestra. Any student who has been to a community theater may have heard the piano take on the job of a full orchestra. Ask students why a piano can substitute for an orchestra. (It has a wide range of pitches, a rich tone color, and several pitches can be played at one time.)

UNIT THREE
LESSON 1

continued from previous page

2 DEVELOP

1. Introduce "Harmony" CD2:28. **Identify the instrument in the accompaniment as a piano.** Have students:

▶ • Read about keyboards.

▶ • Listen to the song and identify the instrument in the accompaniment. (piano)

▶ • Discuss the meaning of the song and the different meanings of the word "harmony." (Harmony in the sense used in the song refers to peaceful, friendly relationships between people. Harmony in music refers to different pitches that sound pleasing when played together.)

What do the piano, organ, and harpsichord have in common? They all have keyboards. Keyboard instruments are popular because you can play harmony on them, accompanying yourself. What keyboard instrument is used in "Harmony"? piano

Harmony

Words and Music by
Artie Kaplan and
Norman J. Simon

1. The time has come, let us be-gin— With all our voic-es join-ing in,— To sing of love and broth-er-hood,— And peo-ple do-ing what they should to Help us shape a bet-ter day.— Ah— make this world a

2. Like the shep-herd guards the sheep,— Watch your child-ren as they sleep,— And like the pot-ter turns the clay,— And peo-ple do-ing what they should to Help us shape a bet-ter day.— Let us sing a

92

MEETING **INDIVIDUAL** NEEDS

BIOGRAPHY: *Artie Kaplan*

American musician Artie Kaplan (b. 1935) is a native of Brooklyn, New York. Listening to jazz greats Stan Kenton, Dizzy Gillespie, and Charlie Parker inspired him to study music and go on to a career as a professional saxophone player. Kaplan's first jobs were with dance bands that traveled around the country. He also spent time in the recording studio, performing on hit records by famous singers such as Neil Diamond, Carole King, and Barry Manilow.

In the 1970s, he began to write music as well, composing for the children's television show *Wonderama*. Since then, Kaplan has made writing music for young people his specialty. For the original recording of "Harmony," he both wrote the music and sang the vocals. "Harmony" was a hit record in Europe and has been re-recorded many times by artists all over the world.

SIGNING: *"Harmony"*

Signing Master S • 6 • 2 has sign language for this song.

2. Sing "Harmony" without and with accompaniment. Have students:

▶ • Sing the melody alone.

▶ • Sing the song with accompaniment and discuss the difference. (Students may say that the accompaniment helps them stay on pitch while singing, or that the piano accompaniment enhances the overall mood and style of the piece.)

▶ • Listen to the recording, noting the two different vocal lines. (One is the melody, the other is a harmony line. Students will learn the harmony part in Lesson 2, *Develop 3,* page 100.)

CAREERS: *Piano Tuner-Technician*

Introduce students to the career of piano tuner-technician. A piano tuner's main job is to adjust the 220 or so piano strings so that they will be in proper pitch. After muting the strings on either side so their sound will not interfere with the tuning, the piano tuner uses a tuning hammer to tighten or loosen the string being tested, until its frequency matches that of a tuning fork. Other strings are tuned in relation to the starting string. A tuner usually begins by working as an apprentice to an experienced tuner. A good sense of pitch is essential. Piano tuners also make minor repairs, such as replacing worn hammers.

Have students learn more about frequency by researching the terms *frequency* and *pitch* from science texts.

continued from previous page

3. Introduce "Heart and Soul" CD2:30.
**Pretend to play the bass line with the
recording.** Have students:

• Say the pitch letter names of the notes in
the part.

• Pretend to play the bass line on the keyboard in their books with the recording.
(one pitch per quarter-note beat)

har- mo- ny,— And sing a- way— the hurt and fear,— A

har- mo- ny,— And sing a- way— the hurt and fear,— A

great new day will soon be here.

great new day will soon— be— here.—

Heart and Soul *by Hoagy Carmichael*

*This song was written in 1938. Many beginning pianists learn to
play it and its accompaniment as a duet.*

FOLLOW this keyboard to play the bass line for "Heart
and Soul." Touch one key on each beat. Play these notes
in sequence: C E A₁ C D F G₁ B₁

G₁ A₁ B₁ C D E F

start here

94 THE KEY TO KEYBOARDS

MEETING **INDIVIDUAL** NEEDS

SPECIAL LEARNERS: *Keyboard Accompaniments*

For "Heart and Soul," create less complex accompaniment
patterns (for example—in half notes: C A D G). Use an appropriate fingering pattern in the left hand if possible (1, 3,
1, 5). Have disabled and nondisabled students sit as partners at the keyboard and play either the same accompaniment pattern in different octaves, or different patterns, as
the class sings the song.

Throughout this unit, help students work toward independent playing of single-note keyboard accompaniments for
familiar songs from pitch letter names and simple melodies
such as "Row, Row, Row Your Boat" or "Jingle Bells."

BACKGROUND: *The Pipe Organ*

The history of the pipe organ can be traced back more than
2,000 years. Many pipe organs are so large that they must
be built as part of the building—church, concert hall, or
theater—where they are to be used. An organist creates
music by combining the sounds of different rows of individual pipes. A large pipe organ can have over 5,000 pipes
and as many as six keyboards.

4. Move to show the pitches of the bass line for "Heart and Soul." Have students:

▶ • Practice an 8-beat movement to "play" the pitch sequence of the bass-line ostinato with their feet:

> (Have students pretend to step the pitches on a keyboard.)
> Cross L foot over R foot (C).
> Step out to right with the R foot (E).
> Open to the left with the L foot (A₁).
> Step R foot back to beginning position (C).
> Cross L foot over to the right (D).
> Step R foot to the right (F).
> Take a large step out to the left with the L foot (G₁).
> Step R foot to the right (B₁).

▶ • Perform the movements with the recording.

▶ • Read about the pipe organ.

THE GIANT OF KEYBOARDS: THE PIPE ORGAN

Keyboard instruments have developed over hundreds of years. One of the oldest is the organ.

Pipe **organs** are the largest of all musical instruments. When organ keys are pressed, air is forced through pipes shaped like long tubes. The air vibrates in the tubes, creating sound. Organists play two or more keyboards, called *manuals,* as well as large, wooden foot pedals. Different tone qualities are produced by devices called *stops.* Stops control which pipes are used. Imagine playing an organ in a cathedral. By controlling hundreds of different-sized organ pipes, you can produce a great number of sounds.

Unit 3 *The Keyboard Connection* 95

BIOGRAPHY: *Hoagy Carmichael*

Songwriter Hoagy Carmichael (1899–1981) was also a singer, pianist, and bandleader. His mother was a pianist in a movie theater, but Carmichael taught himself to play by ear while still a child. He put himself through college playing piano at dances, then worked as a lawyer for a time. In 1927, he wrote what is believed to be the most recorded song in history—"Stardust." Although not very successful at first, "Stardust" became a hit song when a 1935 recording by Artie Shaw sold more than two million copies. The song has been recorded more than 500 times. In the 1940s,

Carmichael began yet another career—that of an actor—when he appeared as a pianist in the movie *To Have and Have Not.* He went on to be a frequent performer in movies and on radio and television.

MOVEMENT: *Stepping with the Bass Line*

Students can work in groups or with partners to choreograph body-facing variations of this pattern. For example: side by side facing the same way, or side by side with opposite facings; front to front or front to back; or changing facings (such as beginning front to front, then changing to side by side).

UNIT THREE
LESSON 1

continued from previous page

3 APPLY

Introduce Jacquet de la Guerre's Rondeau CD2:31. Recognize the sounds of keyboard instruments. Have students:

▶ • Read about the harpsichord and Rondeau (*ran* do), then listen to the composition.

▶ • Read about the piano.

Recorded Lesson CD2:32

▶ • Listen to "The World of Keyboards," which illustrates the tone colors of the pipe organ, the harpsichord, and the piano.

OBJECTIVE 1 Informal Assessment

▶ • Show recognition of the sounds of the harpsichord, organ, and piano by holding up 1 finger for harpsichord, 2 fingers for piano, and 3 fingers for pipe organ. (You may wish to write the name and number of each instrument on the board for reference.)

OBJECTIVE 2 Informal Assessment

▶ • Show understanding of how sound is produced on each instrument by holding up 1 finger for harpsichord, 2 fingers for piano, and 3 fingers for pipe organ in response to the following statements:

—The sound is produced by plucking a string. (1: harpsichord)
—The sound is produced by air vibrating within a tube. (3: pipe organ)
—The sound is produced by a hammer hitting against a string. (2: piano)

AN ANCESTOR OF THE PIANO: THE HARPSICHORD

If you had attended a party at George Washington's home, you might have danced to the sounds of the **harpsichord.** The harpsichord is similar to the piano in shape, but it is smaller and much lighter. When the keys are pressed, metal strings inside the instrument are plucked, much like the strings of a harp.

  Rondeau

LISTENING

by Elizabeth-Claude Jacquet de la Guerre

This composition is from a 1707 collection of harpsichord pieces dedicated to King Louis XIV of France. De la Guerre (1664–1729) was a child prodigy who often performed for the king.

96 THE KEY TO KEYBOARDS

MEETING **INDIVIDUAL** NEEDS

ALTERNATE TEACHING STRATEGIES

OBJECTIVE 1 If students experience difficulty recognizing the sounds of the three keyboard instruments in the lesson, have them discuss which of the instruments are familiar and which are not and where they have heard each instrument. (organs—at the ballpark, church, skating rink; pianos—in school, at home, at a concert; harpsichord—may not have heard) Encourage them to use these experiences to help them classify the instruments.

OBJECTIVE 2 If students experience difficulty recognizing how sound is produced on the three keyboard instruments, conduct a classroom demonstration to show how the sound is produced. For an organ, you might blow through a pipe or across the open top of a bottle. For the piano and harpsichord, tie several guitar strings to drawer handles and let students hit them with a small wooden mallet, then pluck them. If available, allow students to look inside the school piano. A local musician or music technician could be brought in to further discuss and demonstrate the instruments.

THE AMAZING PIANO

The **piano** was invented in the 1700s, and within a hundred years or so it had replaced the harpsichord as the most popular keyboard instrument. *Piano* is short for *pianoforte,* which means "soft-loud" in Italian. The piano was the first keyboard instrument to be able to play a range of volume from soft to loud. When one of its eighty-eight keys is struck, small padded hammers hit strings inside the instrument. The strings vibrate and produce sound. The harder the key is struck, the louder the sound. As soon as the key is released, a felt pad, called a *damper,* touches the strings and stops the sound.

Unit 3 *The Keyboard Connection* **97**

"How do you play a keyboard instrument?" (by pressing keys) "Then why don't all keyboard instruments sound alike?" Have students:

▶ • Recall keyboard instruments in the lesson. (piano, harpsichord, and pipe organ)

▶ • Tell how sound is produced on each of these instruments.

▶ • Describe how the instruments sound.

"Let's close by singing 'Harmony' once again. Listen for the piano accompaniment as you sing."

LESSON SUMMARY

Informal Assessment In this lesson, students:

OBJECTIVE 1 Showed recognition of the sounds of harpsichord, pipe organ, and piano.

OBJECTIVE 2 Showed understanding of how sound is produced on three keyboard instruments.

MORE MUSIC: Reinforcement

"O Canada," page 290 (piano)
"Bo Hai Huan Ten," page 313 (Chinese New Year)
"Diwali Song," page 315 (harmonium; New Year)
"Bashana Haba'ah," page 318 (vocal harmony)

BIOGRAPHY: *Elisabeth-Claude Jacquet de la Guerre*

French composer Elisabeth-Claude Jacquet de la Guerre (e **li** za bɛt **klod** ʒa **kɛt** də la **gɛɾ**), 1664–1729, was a member of a family of professional musicians and instrument-makers who recognized her talent at a very early age. She came to the attention of King Louis XIV after she amazed his court with her improvising, sight-reading, and performing on the harpsichord. At that time, a good deal of the music written in France was composed and played for the king. He supported the musicians, so it was important for a musician to impress the court.

Jacquet de la Guerre went on to write a great variety of music, including an opera, a ballet, and music for keyboard and violin. These musical accomplishments, unusual for women in her time, helped open the way for other professional women musicians and made Jacquet de la Guerre rich and famous. The changing attitudes toward women lived on after her. Five years after Jacquet de la Guerre's death, a woman was appointed as the king's official harpsichordist for the first time.

ACROSS the

LANGUAGE ARTS

WRITING POETRY

"To Catalina"

INDIVIDUAL   **15 MIN OR LESS**

In the poem the author talks about his love for his piano. Have students think of their most precious possessions—these might be objects or emotions, such as the love of family or a close friendship. Have them write poems to explain why they cherish these possessions.

Ask students what it means when the poem says *it will give as well as take*. Have them explain how their precious objects *give* and *take*.

COMPREHENSION STRATEGY: Expressing point of view

SOCIAL STUDIES

COMMUNITY

"Harmony"

GROUP   **30 MIN OR LONGER**

Explain to students that they can help maintain harmony in their community. On the board make a chart with two headings: community and country. Then have the class brainstorm what they would like to change in each of these areas. Remind students that these proposed changes would have to benefit the community.

Divide the class into groups. Each group proposes a goal from the list. Have them make a plan telling how they might achieve this goal. Have them discuss the problems they may encounter along the way, and how to overcome these obstacles. Groups can share plans. Have the class vote on whether or not it wants to take on one of these projects.

COMPREHENSION STRATEGIES: Making decisions, drawing conclusions, cause and effect

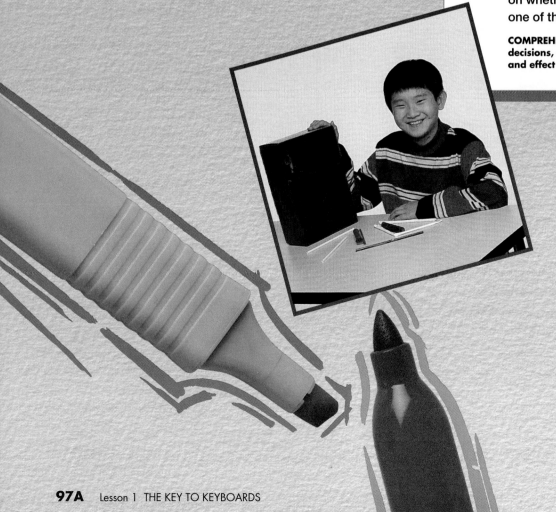

CURRICULUM

HEART MODEL

"Heart and Soul"

PAIR   **30 MIN OR LONGER**

MATERIALS: shoe box, scissors, straws, paper, two balloons, tape, felt, markers

Have students work in pairs to make a model that shows the path of blood circulation in and out of the heart. The model should show these facts:

● The heart is made up of four "rooms," two on the left and two on the right—an upper room (*atrium*) and a lower room (*ventricle*) on each side.

● The two sides of the heart (left and right) are separated by a thick muscular wall. Blood from one side never flows directly into the other side.

● On each side (left, right), blood from the body enters the upper room. The blood enters flowing through a *vein*, a relatively thin-walled blood vessel.

● On each side, blood is pumped out of the heart from the lower room through an *artery*, a thick-walled blood vessel.

● The right side collects blood that has traveled through the body. This blood is low in oxygen.

● The right side pumps blood to the lungs, where it collects oxygen.

● The left side collects oxygen-rich blood coming from the lungs.

● The left side pumps oxygen-rich blood through an artery called the *aorta*. The aorta branches out throughout the body.

● A muscular wall keeps blood on either side from mixing.

● On each side, blood from the upper room flows through a valve into the lower room.

One simple model that can show these facts uses an open shoe box, with strips cut from the lid to divide the box into four rooms. Also:

● Straws can be used for veins.

● Paper tubes can be arteries.

● Balloons can be lungs.

Students can use a marker to draw arrows to show the path of blood.

COMPREHENSION STRATEGIES: Sequencing, exploring spatial relationships

UNIT THREE
LESSON 2

RELATED ARTS MOVEMENT | THEATER | VISUAL ARTS

LESSON PLANNER

FOCUS Pitch

OBJECTIVES
OBJECTIVE 1 Identify B as the pitch that must be flatted in the F major scale
OBJECTIVE 2 Identify the pitch that is *do* in the key of E♭

MATERIALS
Recordings
Alleluia   CD2:33
Harmony   CD2:28

Instruments resonator bells or any available keyboard instruments

Resources Recorder Master R • 12 (pitches D E F♯ G A B)

Technology
Music with MIDI: Alleluia

▶ = **BASIC PROGRAM**

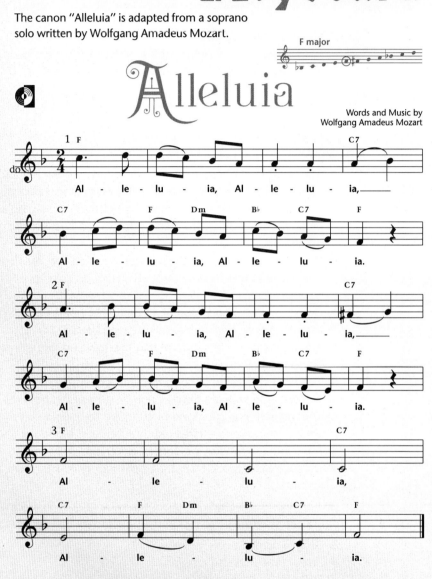

Genius at the Keyboard

The canon "Alleluia" is adapted from a soprano solo written by Wolfgang Amadeus Mozart.

Alleluia

Words and Music by
Wolfgang Amadeus Mozart

98

MEETING **INDIVIDUAL** NEEDS

VOCAL DEVELOPMENT: *Shaping Vowel Sounds*

The following vocalise helps to shape the vowels, aiding in clear diction and a good tone quality.

Continue up by half steps to D, then back down to A.

Ah - eh - ee - oh - oo (breathe)   Ah - eh - ee - oh - oo (breathe)

Remind students of correct posture and breathing for singing. Then have students listen as you demonstrate the vocalise. Model an open, relaxed jaw with the tongue

forward and its tip resting against the gum just below the bottom teeth. As you change from vowel to vowel, the mouth stays open and only closes slightly on the *oh* and *oo*. Have students sing the vocalise as demonstrated.

Latin contains several open vowels—*ah, eh,* and *oo.* As students sing "Alleluia," remind them to keep the same open quality as for the vocalise.

PRONUNCIATION: *"Alleluia"*

In this song, the word *Alleluia* is pronounced ɑl lɛ **lu** yɑ.

     ɑ f<u>a</u>ther   ɛ p<u>e</u>t   u m<u>oo</u>n

Spotlight on

Wolfgang Amadeus Mozart

This portrait of Wolfgang, his sister Maria Anna, and their father, Leopold, was painted when Wolfgang was 7 or 8 years old.

When Wolfgang Amadeus Mozart (1756–1791) was only three years old, he was writing music for the harpsichord and violin. His father recognized his son's great talent and started giving him lessons on the harpsichord. Soon afterwards, his father began taking Mozart and his older sister to play concerts throughout Europe.

There are many stories about Mozart's musical genius. One is about an extraordinary feat he accomplished when he was fourteen. Mozart visited the Sistine Chapel in Rome. He heard a long composition for solo voices. The Pope had ruled that this piece could only be performed in the Sistine Chapel. He carefully guarded the music. After the performance, Mozart returned to his hotel room and wrote out the entire piece from memory. When the Pope learned of this accomplishment, he was not angry. Instead, he awarded Mozart a medal.

When Mozart was grown, he worked as an organist, pianist, music director, and composer. Although Mozart died at the early age of 35, he wrote a large number of compositions during his life, including several operas and many symphonies.

Unit 3 *The Keyboard Connection* **99**

"Think about the instruments that you studied in the last lesson." Have students:

▶ • Name the instruments from Lesson 1. (piano, organ, harpsichord)

▶ • Name something that they have in common. (a keyboard)

"In this lesson, you will learn more about the arrangement of the keys in keyboard instruments. This will help you learn to play melodies on these instruments."

2 DEVELOP

1. Introduce Mozart's "Alleluia" CD2:33.
Sing in unison and canon. Have students:

▶ • Listen to "Alleluia" as they follow the music on page 98 and identify the keyboard instrument that accompanies it. (organ)

▶ • Read about "Alleluia" and Mozart.

▶ • Sing the song in unison.

• Sing the song in canon.

MOVEMENT: *"Alleluia" (Canon)* MOVEMENT

Preparation: *Measures 1–8*—Walk forward four measures, then back four measures stepping this pattern:

Repeat, slowly raising arms while stepping the first four measures, then lowering them for the next four measures. *Measures 9–16*—Walk anywhere in the room stepping the same pattern, but return to the starting place by the end of the eight measures. *Measures 17–24*—Slowly raise arms (four measures), then slowly lower them (four measures).

Final Form: six groups, three to sing and three to dance

Formation: three straight lines or three concentric circles

Have the three groups dance in unison one time through while the class sings. Then dance in three-part canon.

BACKGROUND: *"Alleluia"*

W. A. Mozart wrote "Alleluia" in 1773 as part of *Exsultate, Jubilate* (ɛg sul **ta** tɛ yu bi **la** tɛ), a brilliant piece for solo singer and orchestra. The piece in its original form requires a high voice, typically soprano.

Unit 3 THE KEYBOARD CONNECTION **99**

continued from previous page

2. Review the flat symbol and introduce the F major scale. Have students:

• Review the pitches in the C major scale, indicating where the half steps occur:

C D E F G A B C'
W W H W W W H

• Listen as a volunteer plays a scale from F to F', without using any black keys, and decide if it sounds correct. (no)

OBJECTIVE 1 Informal Assessment

• Figure out the major scale pattern beginning on F and indicate which pitch must be lowered by showing the correct number of fingers. (fourth pitch of the scale—B)

• Play an F major scale on resonator bells or keyboard. (F G A B♭ C D E F') Read about F major, then find the key signature of "Alleluia."

• Read about flat key signatures.

3. Review "Harmony" CD2:28 **(pp. 92–93). Practice singing in two parts.** Have students:

▶ • Sing the melody.

• Practice the harmony part. (When students are secure singing the harmony part, have them sing the two parts together.)

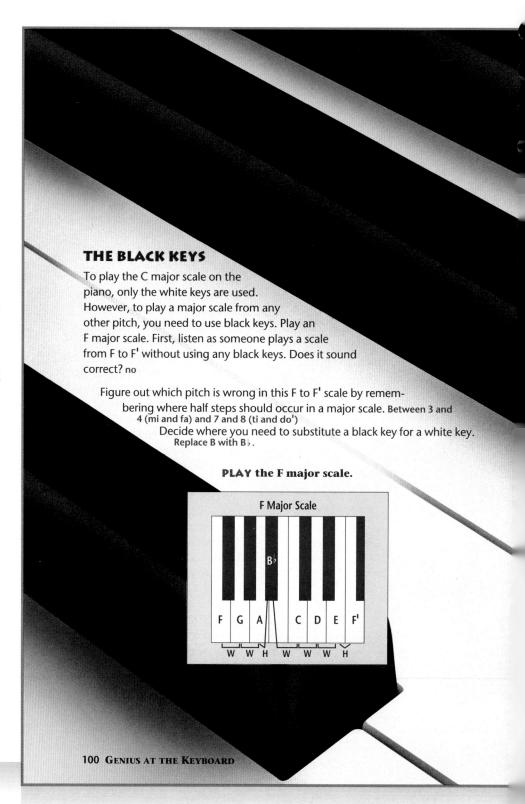

THE BLACK KEYS

To play the C major scale on the piano, only the white keys are used. However, to play a major scale from any other pitch, you need to use black keys. Play an F major scale. First, listen as someone plays a scale from F to F' without using any black keys. Does it sound correct? no

Figure out which pitch is wrong in this F to F' scale by remembering where half steps should occur in a major scale. Between 3 and 4 (mi and fa) and 7 and 8 (ti and do')

Decide where you need to substitute a black key for a white key. Replace B with B♭.

PLAY the F major scale.

F Major Scale

B♭

F G A   C D E F'
W W H W W W H

MEETING **INDIVIDUAL** NEEDS

ALTERNATE TEACHING STRATEGIES

OBJECTIVE 1 Have students review again the sequence of whole and half steps in the major scale. Then play "Alleluia" for them with B♮ so that they can hear the necessity for the flatted note.

OBJECTIVE 2 Have students review the information on key signatures with flats on page 101. Have them find a few other songs in flat keys and identify *do*—for example, "Said I Wasn't Gonn' Tell Nobody" (page 116). Students may also benefit from an alternative way of finding *do*. In key signatures with more than one flat, *do* is always the second to the last flat. For example, in a key with three flats, the second to the last is E♭, so E♭ is *do*.

SPECIAL LEARNERS: *More Keyboard Practice*

Have all students practice the first five notes of the C major scale, using Fingers 1, 2, 3, 4, 5 for the right hand or 5, 4, 3, 2, 1 for the left hand on imaginary keyboards on their desks. Playing each of the five notes with Fingers 1–5 will position the hand for playing the first phrases of many simple songs such as "Are You Sleeping?" "Three Blind Mice," and the beginning phrases for "Lean on Me" (Lesson 8, pages 126–127).

Find *do* in E♭ major. Have students:

• Discover the number of flats in the key signature for "Harmony." (3)

• Recall how to find *do* in flat keys.

OBJECTIVE 2 Informal Assessment

• Decide what *do* is in this key. Raise their hands to show the answer they agree with as you say these possibilities aloud: B♭, E♭ and A♭. (E♭)

4 CLOSE

"What were the two keys you studied in the two songs today?" (F major—"Alleluia" and E♭ major—"Harmony") "Understanding key signatures will help you feel comfortable reading music. Now let's close by singing 'Harmony.'"

The key signature for F major has one flat: B♭.

B♭

What is the key signature of "Alleluia?" F major—one flat

In key signatures that have one or more flats, the flats always appear in the same order. What word do the first four flats spell? BEAD

B E A D

You can find *do* in any flat key. Here's how. The last flat in any flat key is *fa* (or 4) of the scale. To find *do,* just count down three places on the staff from the last flat. If the only flat is B♭, that's the last flat. Count down three and you've found *do* (F).

FIGURE OUT what *do* is in "Harmony." E♭

Unit 3 *The Keyboard Connection* 101

LESSON SUMMARY

Informal Assessment In this lesson, students:

OBJECTIVE 1 Identified B as the pitch that must be flatted in the F major scale.

OBJECTIVE 2 Identified the pitch that is *do* in the key of E♭ in "Harmony."

MORE MUSIC: Reinforcement

"America," page 287 (flat key signature)

"Haji Firuz," page 317 (flat key signature; Iranian New Year)

"Auld Lang Syne," p. 319 (flat key signature; Scottish New Year)

"Come, Follow Me!" page 337 (flat key signature)

"Shenando'," page 352 (flat key signature)

"Hill an' Gully," *Songs to Sing and Read,* page 46 (flat key signature)

When the C major scale is reviewed, pair disabled students with nondisabled students to play the first five notes at the piano. Have students play with left or right hands in different octaves. Prompt students or position their hands as necessary. Some students may be able to play phrases of familiar songs by ear.

CRITICAL THINKING: *Drawing Conclusions*

Discuss the fact that the organ is often used to accompany religious music like "Alleluia." Ask students why the instrument is especially well-suited to accompany music per-

formed in churches and cathedrals. (Possible answer: These are large buildings and an instrument capable of great dynamic power is needed in order to be heard.) Encourage them to suggest other instruments that might work well in cathedrals and to explain their reasoning. (Students should conclude that any powerful instrument will do, such as the trumpet, tuba, or any amplified electronic instrument.)

ACROSS the

LANGUAGE ARTS

IMAGERY

> *"Harmony"*

PAIR   **15–30 MIN**

Have students work in pairs to play a verb-image game. The game is based on the use of images with verbs in the song lyrics:

- *Like the shepherd guards his sheep* is an image for *watch* *(Watch your children)*
- *Like a potter turns the clay* is an image for *shape (Help us shape a better day)*

The game is in two parts.

Part 1: Each member lists five verbs—specifically, action words. Members exchange lists. For each word on the list a player receives, the player must write a descriptive image, starting with *Like:*

- Verb: *skate*
- Image: *Like a child gliding on ice*

Players exchange answers and get a chance to revise and discuss them.

Part 2: Two pairs of students play as teams. Each team reads out loud a descriptive image and allows the other team to guess the verb. For each incorrect try at the verb, the team gets a point. The team with fewer points wins.

COMPREHENSION STRATEGIES: Visualizing, building vocabulary

SOCIAL STUDIES

WRITING LETTERS

> *"Alleluia"*

INDIVIDUAL   **15–30 MIN**

At the age of 31, Mozart was already very famous. He was visited by the 17-year-old Ludwig van Beethoven, who had come to Vienna from Germany to see his musical hero. After meeting Beethoven and listening to him play, Mozart told friends that Beethoven was a musician with a great future.

Ask students to think of people alive today whom they admire and would choose to be their mentors. Explain that a mentor is someone who functions as a teacher or guide, someone whose life the student may want to emulate.

Then have students write letters to their choices, expressing why they admire him or her, and what they would like to learn.

Encourage students to identify ways they can nurture and challenge themselves to develop attributes they admire in others.

COMPREHENSION STRATEGIES: Expressing main ideas and supporting details, making decisions

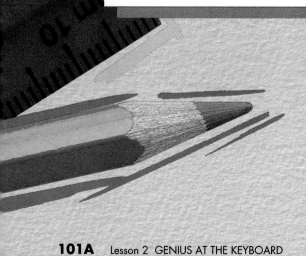

CURRICULUM

LANGUAGE ARTS

PERSONAL NARRATIVE

"Alleluia"

INDIVIDUAL **30 MIN OR LONGER**

Mozart came from a musical family, as did Bach, Beethoven, and a number of other famous musicians. Family members spent a great deal of time practicing and playing music, often together. They taught and learned from one another.

Have students write personal narratives describing something they have learned from family members. Guide students to identify clearly what gets taught and who did the teaching. Ask them to explain how the teaching affected them. Did they use the taught material in their lives? If so, how?

Encourage students to write about their feelings and to add the most important and meaningful parts of their recollections to their personal stories.

COMPREHENSION STRATEGIES: Distinguishing between important and unimportant information, expressing main ideas

ART

DRAWING

"Alleluia"

INDIVIDUAL **30 MIN OR LONGER**

MATERIALS: art paper, crayons, paints, pencils; optional—biographies and pictures of Mozart

Have students look at the picture of Mozart on page 99 and talk about his life story. Ask students to imagine what Mozart would look like if he were alive today. What kind of clothing would he wear? What instruments might he play? What kind of music might he create? What type of band or orchestra might accompany him?

Have students create a modern-day portrait of Mozart. Students share their portraits and talk about what made them show Mozart as they did.

COMPREHENSION STRATEGY: Visualizing

UNIT THREE
LESSON 3

LESSON PLANNER

FOCUS Pitch

OBJECTIVES
OBJECTIVE 1 Identify the location of half steps in the minor scale
OBJECTIVE 2 Identify a song as being in major

MATERIALS
Recordings
Alleluia   CD2:33
Listening: Prelude in A Minor by
  J. S. Bach   CD2:34
Hymn to Freedom   CD2:35

Instruments pitched instruments such as resonator bells

Resources
Resource Master 3 • 1 (practice)
Resource Master 3 • 2 (practice)
Musical Instruments Master—
  synthesizers

VOCABULARY
pedal point, relative minor, synthesizer

▶ = **BASIC PROGRAM**

The Pipes Speak

🎵 **Prelude in A Minor**
LISTENING

by Johann Sebastian Bach

Bach wrote the Prelude in A Minor for pipe organ. The music begins with sixteenth-note patterns played on the manuals. Soon you will hear six or eight notes to a beat, tumbling over one another like a waterfall. Then the low pedals play a **pedal point**—*a single pitch held for a long time under changing chords and fast scales. Later there are more pedal points.*

Bach was famous throughout Germany for his skill as an organist.

102

MEETING **INDIVIDUAL** NEEDS

ALTERNATE TEACHING STRATEGY

OBJECTIVE 1 Help students discover that the half steps in the minor scale are between the same pitch syllables as in the major scale (*mi* and *fa, ti* and *do*). Only the tonal center—*la*—is different. Use the picture of the keyboard on page 103 to review where whole and half steps occur in the A minor scale and let students hear the scale. Build another major scale and its relative minor (for example, F major and D minor).

VOCAL DEVELOPMENT: *Matching Pitch*

Students who are unable to match pitch may need practice singing individual pitches or short melodic patterns correctly before being asked to sing songs with a wider range. As students sing the C major scale, stand next to a student who is having difficulty with pitch. Take the student's hands, and as you both sing the scale, move your hands up together. Often this physical gesture, plus your encouragement, contributes to the student's ability to match pitch.

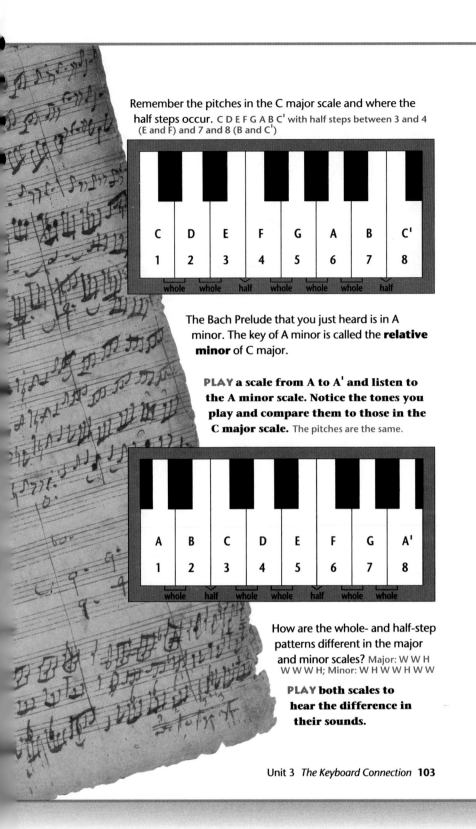

Remember the pitches in the C major scale and where the half steps occur. C D E F G A B C' with half steps between 3 and 4 (E and F) and 7 and 8 (B and C')

C	D	E	F	G	A	B	C'
1	2	3	4	5	6	7	8
whole	whole	half	whole	whole	whole	half	

The Bach Prelude that you just heard is in A minor. The key of A minor is called the **relative minor** of C major.

PLAY a scale from A to A' and listen to the A minor scale. Notice the tones you play and compare them to those in the C major scale. The pitches are the same.

A	B	C	D	E	F	G	A'
1	2	3	4	5	6	7	8
whole	half	whole	whole	half	whole	whole	

How are the whole- and half-step patterns different in the major and minor scales? Major: W W H W W W H; Minor: W H W W H W W

PLAY both scales to hear the difference in their sounds.

Unit 3 *The Keyboard Connection* **103**

1 GET SET

"Let's begin by turning to page 98 to look at 'Alleluia.'" CD2:33 Have students:

- Tell what key "Alleluia" is in. (one flat, B♭: key of F major)
- ▶ Sing it in unison (if able, in canon) with the recording. (Students might do the movement. See Lesson 2, page 99, *Movement*.)
- ▶ Name the instrument that accompanies "Alleluia" on the recording. (organ)

"Today you will hear the organ used in a different style."

2 DEVELOP

1. Introduce Prelude in A Minor CD2:34. **Listen to a pipe organ solo.** Have students:

- ▶ Recall how sound is produced in the pipe organ. (See page 95.)
- ▶ Read about, then listen to Prelude in A Minor.
- ▶ Compare the way the organ is used in this composition with the way it is used in "Alleluia." (solo instrument in Prelude, accompanying instrument in "Alleluia")

2. Contrast C major with its relative minor, A minor. Have students:

- Sing a C major scale with pitch letter names, or play it on a pitched instrument.
- Work through the exercises on page 103 to compare the C major and A minor scales.
- Listen and sing along, with books closed, singing scale numbers as you or a volunteer slowly play the A minor scale.

OBJECTIVE 1 Informal Assessment
- Listen with eyes closed as you sing each interval in the minor scale with scale numbers (sing *1–2* [pause], *2–3* [pause], and so on) and raise hands when you sing numbers of the scale steps between which half steps occur. (2–3; 5–6)

BIOGRAPHY: *Johann Sebastian Bach*

German composer Johann Sebastian Bach (**yo** han sə **bas** tyən **box**), 1685–1750, is considered one of the world's great composers. Bach was born into a family that had produced musicians for many generations. In fact, almost every town in his province had a Bach as a town musician, church organist, or choirleader. An excellent organist himself, Bach wrote much of his finest music for organ and clavier (kla **vir**). (Clavier means "keyboard.")

Much of this music is still played by pianists today. Many of Bach's children continued the family tradition, and three became well-known composers.

MATHEMATICS CONNECTION: *Tempered Tuning*

Most keyboard instruments use tempered tuning, which makes all scales sound in tune. Have students explore the math behind tempered tuning by completing **Resource Master 3 • 1.**

UNIT THREE
LESSON 3

continued from previous page

3 APPLY

Introduce "Hymn to Freedom" CD2:35.
Identify major. Have students:

▶ • Listen to the song and its synthesizer accompaniment.

▶ • Read about the synthesizer and Oscar Peterson.

▶ • Sing "Hymn to Freedom."

OBJECTIVE 2 Informal Assessment

• Listen as you play the first phrase of the melody as written, then in the key of C minor (with B♭ E♭ A♭ in place of B E A). Raise hands if they agree that the actual melody is in major. (yes)

• Look at the song to identify the tonal center. (no sharps or flats: C)

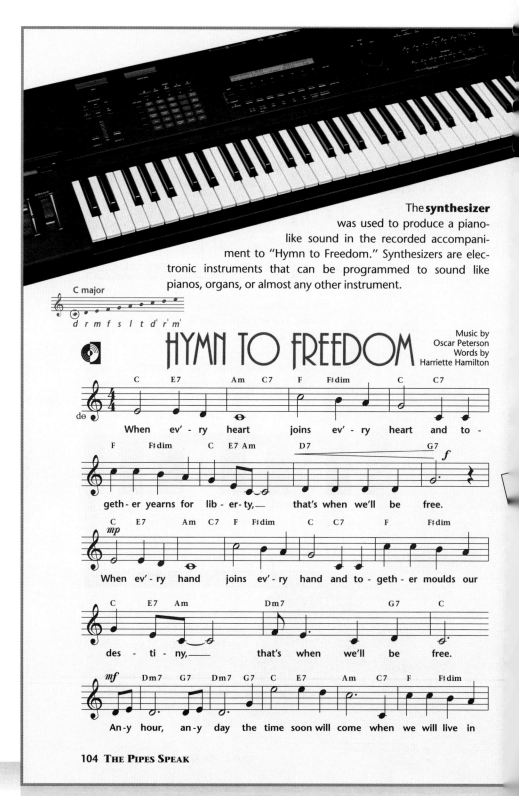

The synthesizer was used to produce a piano-like sound in the recorded accompaniment to "Hymn to Freedom." Synthesizers are electronic instruments that can be programmed to sound like pianos, organs, or almost any other instrument.

HYMN TO FREEDOM

Music by
Oscar Peterson
Words by
Harriette Hamilton

When ev'-ry heart joins ev'-ry heart and to-

geth-er yearns for lib-er-ty,— that's when we'll be free.

When ev'-ry hand joins ev'-ry hand and to-geth-er moulds our

des-ti-ny,— that's when we'll be free.

An-y hour, an-y day the time soon will come when we will live in

104 THE PIPES SPEAK

MEETING **INDIVIDUAL** NEEDS

ALTERNATE TEACHING STRATEGY

OBJECTIVE 2 Play a simple melody such as "Three Blind Mice" in major and then in minor to give students further experience in hearing the difference.

PLAYING INSTRUMENTS: *"Hymn to Freedom"*

Have students learn the playalong for "Hymn to Freedom" on **Resource Master 3 · 2.**

MOVEMENT: *"Hymn to Freedom"*

Have students add a traditional gospel-choir step to this song. (Verbal cue: *step, clap, touch, clap*)

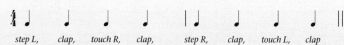

step L, clap, touch R, clap, step R, clap, touch L, clap

dig - ni - ty,— that's when we'll be free. When ev' - ry one

joins in our song, and to - geth - er sing - ing

har - mo - ny,— that's when we'll be free.

that's when we'll be free.— We'll be free.

Spotlight on Oscar Peterson

Oscar Peterson, composer of "Hymn to Freedom," was born in Montreal, Canada, in 1925. His parents came to Canada from the West Indies. His father led a family band in church. Oscar began playing the trumpet, but soon switched to the piano. Oscar Peterson is known throughout the world for the speed and rhythmic drive of his playing as well as for his compositions. He has been called one of the outstanding jazz personalities of the century.

Unit 3 *The Keyboard Connection* **105**

4 CLOSE

"Today you heard two keyboard instruments and two related scales. What were they?" (organ, synthesizer; C major, A minor) Have students:

• Name the scale numbers in the major scale between which half steps occur. (3 and 4, 7 and 8)

• Name the scale numbers in the minor scale between which half steps occur. (2 and 3, 5 and 6)

"Let's end today's lesson in a major key by singing 'Hymn to Freedom' again."

LESSON SUMMARY

Informal Assessment In this lesson, students:

OBJECTIVE 1 Identified the location of half steps in the minor scale.

OBJECTIVE 2 Identified "Hymn to Freedom" as being in major.

MORE MUSIC: Reinforcement
"Bo Hai Huan Ten," page 313 (Chinese New Year)
"De allacito carnavalito," page 342 (A minor)
"De Lanterna na Mão," page 344 (A minor)

TECHNOLOGY IN MUSIC: *Synthesizer*

The synthesizer was invented by Robert A. Moog, an American physicist, in 1964. The sounds are played on a keyboard. The many controls determine how the music sounds. Players can create just about any sound by adjusting the controls for loudness, pitch, tone color, and attack, decay, sustain, and release. The synthesizer then plays the signal the player has set with the controls. The mixers in a synthesizer combine several electronically created signals. By joining two or more signals, a synthesizer can sound like a group of instruments, even a large orchestra. From the mixer, the signal goes to an amplifier and loudspeaker, or it can be recorded directly on tape. Sampling synthesizers contain a store of pre-recorded, or "sampled," instrumental or vocal sounds.

Even the smallest synthesizer has a computer that controls its operation. More advanced synthesizers can be hooked up to outside computers. This greatly expands their capabilities. For instance, a composer can enter a melody into the computer. The computer can add chords and rhythm and then direct the synthesizer to play the whole song. The computer can even print out the complete score.

UNIT THREE
LESSON 4

RELATED ARTS MOVEMENT | THEATER | VISUAL ARTS

A DOT MAKES A Difference

LESSON PLANNER

FOCUS Rhythm

OBJECTIVES
OBJECTIVE 1 Play an accompaniment with a dotted quarter-eighth pattern (tested)
OBJECTIVE 2 Pat, with alternating hands, a rhythm with a ♫ pattern (tested)
OBJECTIVE 3 Aurally differentiate between ♫ ♩ ♩ and ♫ ♩ ♩ (tested)

MATERIALS
Recordings
Harmony   CD2:28
Tee galop pour Mamou   CD2:36
Recorded Lesson: Pronunciation
  for "Tee galop pour Mamou"   CD2:37
Listening: Mazurka (folk dance)
  (excerpt)   CD2:38
Listening: Mazurka, Op. 68,
  No. 3 by F. Chopin   CD2:39
Listening: Heart and Soul by H.
  Carmichael   CD2:30

Instruments rhythm instruments

Resources
Resource Master 3 • 3 (practice)
Recorder Master R • 13 (D F♯ G A B C' D')

VOCABULARY
dotted note, mazurka, accent, accordion

▶ = **BASIC PROGRAM**

SAY the following rhythm patterns, and you'll see what a difference a dot makes.

First try this pattern, made up of equal sounds.

Sing   my   song

Now try the same pattern, with the second beat divided equally into two parts.

Sing   me   a   song

Sometimes, rhythm patterns with unequal sounds are needed. Dots after notes lengthen their value. Try the example below. This time, instead of saying "me" out loud, just think it.

Sing—— (me) a   song

Try clapping or playing this pattern with the recording of "Harmony."

A **dotted** note is lengthened by half its value. Here's some musical math for you:

♩ = ♪ ♪   (A quarter note is as long as two eighth notes.)

♩. = ♪ ♪ ♪   (A dotted quarter note is as long as three eighth notes.)

106

MEETING **INDIVIDUAL** NEEDS

ALTERNATE TEACHING STRATEGY

OBJECTIVE 1 Have half the class step or pat with the beat as the other half plays the ostinato (*Sing a song*) on instruments. Switch and repeat, then have students try adding the ostinato to "Harmony" again.

PITCH SYLLABLES: *"Tee galop pour Mamou"*

Have students read "Tee galop pour Mamou" with pitch syllables and hand signs.

MULTICULTURAL PERSPECTIVES: *Cajun Music*

The term *Cajun* comes from "Acadian." The Acadians were French people from the easternmost part of Canada who were driven out by the British during a land dispute. Many Acadians migrated to New Orleans, where a sizable French population already lived. In time, they spread into the rural areas of southern Louisiana and east Texas. Cajun music often uses the fiddle, the accordion (from German roots), and the *tee fer,* a triangle made from the tine of a hay rake. "Tee galop pour Mamou" was written just after the Depression, when luxuries such as candy and coffee were scarce.

A KEYBOARD INSTRUMENT IN FOLK MUSIC—THE ACCORDION

Cajuns are French-speaking residents of Louisiana. This Cajun song describes going by horse and buggy to get supplies from Mamou, a small town that specialized in rice and crawfish.

Tee galop pour Mamou

Gallop On to Mamou

Cajun Folk Dance
English Version by MMH

French:	Tee ga-lop, tee ga-lop pour Ma-mou!___ J'ai ven-du mon tee mu-
Pronunciation:	ti ga lo ti ga lo puɾ ma mu ʒe vã dü mɔ̃ ti mü
English:	Gal-lop on, gal-lop on to Ma-mou!___ Sold my mule for on-ly

	let pour quinze sous.___ J'ai ache-té du can-di rouge pour les tee,___
	le puɾ kãz su ʒe ash te dü kã di ɾuʒ puɾ le ti
	fif-teen pen-nies.___ Bought red can-dy for the lit-tle chil-dren,

	___ du su-cre et du ca-fé pour les vieux.
	dü sü kɾə e dü ka fe puɾ le vyo
	sug-ar and some cof-fee for the old folks.

Three-tone

d   r   m

You know that: ♩. = ♪ ♪ ♪
So, it stands to reason that: ♪ = ♪ ♪ ♪

Look for dotted notes in this song.
Is the pattern ♩. ♪ or ♫. ?

Unit 3 *The Keyboard Connection* **107**

---

1 GET SET

"You have been studying the basic rhythmic note values—whole notes, half notes, and so on." Have students:

▶ • Sing "Harmony" CD2:28 on pages 92–93.

• Listen as you clap a dotted quarter-eighth pattern a few times, then tell whether they heard equal or unequal sounds. (unequal)

"In this lesson, you'll learn two rhythm patterns with unequal sounds. The first is a pattern often heard in rock music."

2 DEVELOP

1. Introduce dotted rhythms and add an ostinato to "Harmony." Have students:

• Echo or imitate you in reading the rhythm patterns on page 106.

OBJECTIVE 1 Informal Assessment

• Form two groups. Group 1 sings the verse of "Harmony" while Group 2 plays the ostinato (*Sing a song*) on selected rhythm instruments. (Stop the ostinato on the refrain.) Switch and repeat for the second verse.

• Read about dotted notes.

2. Introduce "Tee galop pour Mamou" CD2:36. **Learn about ♫. pattern.** Have students:

• Read about, then listen to, "Tee galop pour Mamou."

▶ • Read about ♫ and find the rhythm in the notation. (Measures 2, 4, 6, 8)

Recorded Lesson CD2:37

▶ • Listen to "Pronunciation for 'Tee galop pour Mamou.'"

▶ • Sing the song.

PLAYING INSTRUMENTS: *Rhythm Instruments*

Have students say and then play ostinatos with "Harmony."

Har - mo - ny, let's sing some

Fill this land with song.

RECORDER: *"Tee galop pour Mamou"*

Have students play this accompaniment on recorder.

PRONUNCIATION: *"Tee galop pour Mamou"*

α father	e chaotic	i bee	o obey	ɔ paw
u moon	ə ago	ö lips form [o] and say [e];		
ɾ flipped r	ü lips form [u] and say [i]		ʒ pleasure	
~ nasalized vowel				

UNIT THREE
LESSON 4

continued from previous page

3. Introduce Mazurka (Polish-Israeli Folk Dance) CD2:38. **Introduce ¾ meter, ♩♪ rhythms, and the accordion.** Have students:

• Listen to part of the mazurka and tell how many beats they feel in each measure. (3)

▶ • Read about the mazurka (ma **zor** ka), ¾, accents, and the accordion.

• Listen as you speak and clap this pattern. Tell when the dotted note occurs (Beat 1):

Danc - ing to the mus - ic!

OBJECTIVE 2 Informal Assessment

• With alternating hands, pat the above pattern as an ostinato, while listening to the mazurka.

3 APPLY

1. Introduce Chopin's Mazurka, Op. 68, No. 3 CD2:39. **Review** ♫ Have students:

▶ • Read about Chopin (**fre** de ɾik **sho** pɛ̃).

• Echo-clap the rhythm below, deciding which beat the dotted rhythm is heard on. (Beat 1) Listen for the rhythm sequence in Mazurka.

• Clap the rhythm sequence with Mazurka during the first A section.

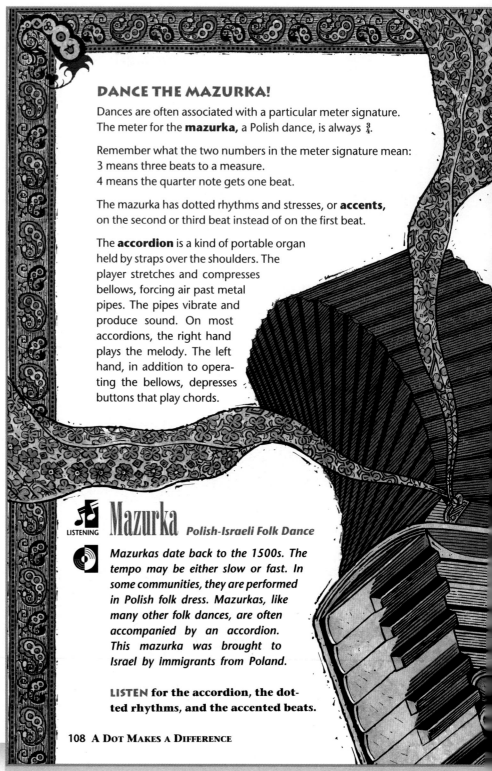

DANCE THE MAZURKA!

Dances are often associated with a particular meter signature. The meter for the **mazurka,** a Polish dance, is always ¾.

Remember what the two numbers in the meter signature mean:
3 means three beats to a measure.
4 means the quarter note gets one beat.

The mazurka has dotted rhythms and stresses, or **accents,** on the second or third beat instead of on the first beat.

The **accordion** is a kind of portable organ held by straps over the shoulders. The player stretches and compresses bellows, forcing air past metal pipes. The pipes vibrate and produce sound. On most accordions, the right hand plays the melody. The left hand, in addition to operating the bellows, depresses buttons that play chords.

🎵 **Mazurka** *Polish-Israeli Folk Dance*
LISTENING

Mazurkas date back to the 1500s. The tempo may be either slow or fast. In some communities, they are performed in Polish folk dress. Mazurkas, like many other folk dances, are often accompanied by an accordion. This mazurka was brought to Israel by immigrants from Poland.

LISTEN for the accordion, the dotted rhythms, and the accented beats.

108 A DOT MAKES A DIFFERENCE

MEETING **INDIVIDUAL** NEEDS

ALTERNATE TEACHING STRATEGIES

OBJECTIVE 2 Notate the *Danc-ing to the music* pattern on the board. Have students practice the rhythm without the recording while stepping with the beat. Then try doing it with the recording of the mazurka again.

OBJECTIVE 3 Notate Patterns 1 and 2 on the board and have students look for the dot in the dotted pattern. Then clap the rhythms again and have them tell where the rhythms are different. (the first beat)

BACKGROUND: *Mazurka, Op. 68, No. 3*

This is one of Chopin's 51 mazurkas. In playing Chopin's music, performers use what is called *tempo rubato* for a freer, more expressive feeling. "Tempo rubato" (ɾu **ba** to) literally means "stolen time," but the time is really only "borrowed." Music played with rubato often slows slightly from a steady beat, then rushes a bit to catch up. The performer must feel the underlying steady beat even as the music pulls back and pushes forward.

SPOTLIGHT ON Frédéric Chopin

Frédéric Chopin (1810–1849) was born in Warsaw, Poland. Like Mozart, he showed great musical talent at an early age. When he was eight, he gave his first public performance on the piano. Chopin left Warsaw and settled in Paris, France.

Almost all of Chopin's compositions are for solo piano. They explore a wide expressive range—from the quiet and dreamlike to the very bold and dramatic. For this reason, Chopin is called the "Poet of the Piano."

FRÉDÉRIC CHOPIN
This portrait by Eugène Delacroix (1798–1863) contrasts light and shadow to focus attention on the composer's face.

 LISTENING

Mazurka, Op. 68, No. 3
by Frédéric Chopin

During the 1800s the mazurka became so popular that it was danced throughout Europe. Chopin's mazurkas were intended for listening.

IDENTIFY the beat with the dotted rhythm. What is the form of this mazurka? first beat; ABA

Unit 3 *The Keyboard Connection* **109**

• Review the bass line for "Heart and Soul" on page 94, changing each ♩ to 🎵 then to 🎵 and say which is dotted. (first rhythm: 🎵)

OBJECTIVE 3 Informal Assessment
• Listen as you clap the following and raise hands for the dotted rhythm pattern.

4 CLOSE

"Today, you learned about two new rhythm patterns, two types of folk music, and two keyboard instruments." Have students:

• Clap the two new rhythm patterns.

"Let's finish by playing along again during the A sections of Chopin's 'Mazurka.'"

LESSON SUMMARY

Informal Assessment In this lesson, students:

OBJECTIVE 1 Played an accompaniment to "Harmony" that included a dotted quarter-eighth pattern.
OBJECTIVE 2 Patted a rhythm with an 🎵 pattern in "Mazurka" (Folk Dance).
OBJECTIVE 3 Listened as you clapped two rhythm patterns and raised hands to indicate which contained a dotted rhythm.

MORE MUSIC: Reinforcement
"I Have a Dream," page 320 (dotted rhythms— ♩. ♪ ; Martin Luther King, Jr.)
"Soft Shoe Song," page 383 (♩. ♪ and 🎵)

MOVEMENT: *Mazurka (Polish/Israeli Folk Dance)* MOVEMENT

The mazurka is one of Poland's national dances. The basic step is similar to that of a waltz, a dance that is also in ¾ time. (Optional: Use **Resource Master 3 · 3** to teach a complete mazurka.)

Mazurka Step (Verbal cue: *right, left, right*)
Beat 1 Step on right foot.
Beat 2 Step on ball of left foot behind right heel.
Beat 3 Step on right foot in place.

Reverse the footwork on alternate measures. For example, the next measure would go: left, right, left.

PLAYING INSTRUMENTS: *Creating Rhythm Patterns*

Have students create their own four-measure rhythm patterns, using each of the two patterns in *Apply 2* at least once. They can play their patterns on unpitched or pitched instruments. If using resonator bells, set them up in pentatonic (for example, C D E G A) to avoid minor-2nd dissonances between *mi fa* and *ti do*. Possible rhythm pattern:

MATHEMATICS

BUY-SELL GAME

"Tee galop pour Mamou"

PAIR   **15 MIN OR LESS**

MATERIALS: 10 cards or slips of paper, note pads; optional—calculator

In each verse of the song, something is sold and the money is used to buy things. Have pairs of students play a buy-sell game.

Setup: On five cards, each player writes the name of an object for sale. On the other side of each card, players write the selling price:

- three items range from $20–$30
- two items range from $30–$40

To play: Both players lay out their cards in a row, item-side up. Then each player turns over two of the partner's cards. The total amount shown is the partner's cash for buying. Players record the amounts.

Then each player takes one item from the partner's remaining item cards. The player uses his/her cash to buy the item. Each player subtracts from his/her total amount of cash the amount used for the sale and adds the amount gained by selling an item to the partner.

Then each player decides whether to try to make one more purchase or to stop. (If a player does not have enough cash to make a purchase, that player simply returns the item card unpurchased—but can still sell an item.) Each player finds his/her new total amount of cash. The one who has the higher amount of cash wins.

COMPREHENSION STRATEGY: Making decisions

CURRICULUM

WRITING WORDS

"Tee galop pour Mamou"

PAIR   **15–30 MIN**

Have students work in pairs to write their own words to this song. Both members agree on different means of traveling than *Gallop on*. They must choose a means that takes three syllables to replace *Gallop on*:

● Skating on   ● Pedal on

The partners brainstorm for words related to their replacement:

● ice, blades, snow, rust
● bicycle, tires, brakes

Then together they compose verses about traveling on to Mamou and events that happen along the way or when they arrive. Their new versions of the song should use some of the words from their lists.

Have students perform their new versions. Prizes go to the most original, the most far-out, the most detailed verses, and so on.

COMPREHENSION STRATEGY: Brainstorming

MAPS

Chopin's Mazurka

GROUP   **15–30 MIN**

MATERIALS: map of Europe (world map or atlas), tape measure

Ask students to assume that Chopin made a trip from Warsaw to Paris by coach. Have students use maps and work in groups to decide upon possible coach routes between the two cities, with stops or connections at three cities along the way. Although the routes would not be straight lines (due to natural barriers), students might use straight lines as a means of estimating the distances.

Have students track the four lengths of the journey—from city to city—and use the map scale to measure these distances. Then have them make charts of their routes stage by stage, with a total distance for each route.

Have students compare their results. Which route is the longest? The shortest? Which passes the most scenic parts of Europe? Which routes seem least likely due to natural barriers (mountains)?

COMPREHENSION STRATEGIES: Determining sequence of events, compare and contrast

UNIT THREE
LESSON 5

LESSON PLANNER

FOCUS Rhythm/Tone color

OBJECTIVE

OBJECTIVE 1 Perform an accompaniment from notation containing ♩ ♪ and ♫ rhythm patterns with a recording (tested)

MATERIALS
Recordings
The Old Piano Roll Blues   CD2:40
Listening: Trio No. 39 Finale
  (Gypsy Rondo) by F. J. Haydn   CD2:41

Instruments unpitched instruments

Resources Recorder Master R • 14 (pitches E F♯ G A B C' D')

VOCABULARY
player piano, chamber music, fortepiano

▶ = **BASIC PROGRAM**

A Piano that Plays Itself

Player pianos were very fashionable during the late 1800s and early 1900s. A player piano uses a roll of paper with patterns of holes that correspond to the different pitches in a piece of music. The roll moves over a cylinder, which also has small holes. Air is sucked through the matching holes in the moving roll and the cylinder. The air causes the piano's hammers to move and strike the strings, producing musical sounds. With a player piano, listeners could be entertained by their favorite piano music without having to play the instrument themselves.

PLAYER PIANO

My stick fingers click with a snicker
As, chuckling, they knuckle the keys,
Light-footed, my steel feelers flicker
And pluck from the keys melodies.

My paper can caper, abandon
Is broadcast by dint of my din,
And no man or band has a hand in
The tones I turn on from within.

At times I'm a jumble of rumbles,
At others I'm light like the moon,
But never my numb plunker fumbles,
Misstrums me, or tries a new tune.
　　　　　　　　　—John Updike

110

MEETING **INDIVIDUAL** NEEDS

BIOGRAPHY: *John Updike*

John Updike (b. 1932) writes novels, short stories, poems, and essays with equal success. Born to a relatively poor family in Pennsylvania, he won a scholarship to Harvard, where he studied literature and worked on the *Harvard Lampoon,* a magazine well-known for satirical humor. *The Carpentered Hen,* from which the poem was taken, was Updike's first book. His books often deal with ordinary, working-class people. His most famous works comprise the prize-winning series about Harry "Rabbit" Angstrom, four books that examine the American dream of success.

MULTICULTURAL PERSPECTIVES: *Ragtime*

The ragtime craze swept the United States, and later Europe, between the 1890s and World War I. Ragtime's syncopated melodies probably originated in traveling African American minstrel shows. Musicians called it playing in "ragged time" or "broken time" because of the music's dotted rhythms, the effect of the strict "oom-pah" in the pianist's left hand against the syncopation in the right. The music was soon called "rag" or "ragtime."

Today, when people think of ragtime, they usually think of Scott Joplin (1868–1917), who wrote "The Entertainer,"

Player pianos in the old days often played popular songs in a style called "ragtime." This style often used the dotted-rhythm pattern ♫

LISTEN for this dotted rhythm in "The Old Piano Roll Blues." Then sing the song.

The Old Piano Roll Blues

Words and Music by Cy Coben

I wanna hear it again, I wanna hear it again,
The Old Piano Roll Blues.
We're sittin' at an upright, my buddy and me,
Pushin' on the pedals, makin' sweet harmony,
When we hear rinkity tink, and we hear plinkity plink,
The music's better it seems.
And while we sing, sing, sing away all our cares,
The player piano's playin' razzamatazz,
I wanna hear it again, I wanna hear it again,
The Old Piano Roll Blues.

Unit 3 *The Keyboard Connection* **111**

"How many keyboard instruments can you name?" (Encourage students to list as many as possible. "Here's a keyboard instrument many people don't know." Have students:

▶ • Read about player pianos.

▶ • Read and discuss the poem "Player Piano."

"The player piano never misses a note—and it doesn't even know how to read music! But people aren't machines, so to play an instrument, it helps to be able to read notes. Today you are going to work on your rhythm-reading skills. Reading rhythms will help you to play any instrument."

2 DEVELOP

1. Introduce "The Old Piano Roll Blues" CD2:40. **Aurally identify the ♫ rhythm pattern.** Have students:

▶ • Read about the rhythm in this song.

▶ • Listen to the song, paying attention to the sound of the piano.

▶ • Sing the song.

• Clap the rhythm of *hear it again* in Measures 1–2 to hear the uneven effect of the dotted eighth-sixteenth note pattern.

• Find other parts of the song that seem to contain the ♫ pattern and say these words in rhythm. (Examples: *sittin' at an upright, pushin' on the pedals, makin' sweet harmony, rinkity tink, plinkity plink*)

"Maple Leaf Rag," and a ragtime opera. Like popular music today, most ragtime was meant to be danced to, and the composer might print dance directions right above the notation. In time, ragtime gave way to jazz, but the music never really went away. In the 1970s, a renewed interest created by the music in the movie *The Sting* made Joplin more famous than he'd ever been while he was alive.

MOVEMENT: *"The Old Piano Roll Blues"*

Have students work in pairs to make up two movements using side-crossing steps. One movement should have feet moving to a long phrase from "The Old Piano Roll Blues," either *sittin' at an upright* or *pushin' on the pedals*. The other movement should have feet moving to a short phrase, either *hear it again* or *rinkity tink*.

Example of a movement for a short phrase:

step right,	cross left back, step right,	cross left front
♪.	♪ ♪.	♪
hear	it a	gain

Have them try the movements side by side and facing each other. They can use their two movement-fragments to create a dance for the entire piece.

UNIT THREE LESSON 5

continued from previous page

2. Review how sound is produced on keyboard instruments. Have students:

▶ • Review differences between the sounds of the organ, the harpsichord, and the piano, and tell how sound is produced on each.

3 APPLY

Introduce Trio No. 39 Finale ("Gypsy Rondo") CD2:41. **Clap or play dotted rhythms.** Have students:

▶ • Read about Franz Joseph Haydn (frɑnts yo zɛf haɪ dən), chamber music, and his piano trio.

▶ • Listen to the piece and describe the sound of the fortepiano.

▶ • Listen again, signaling when they hear the A section return.

• Outline the rondo form. (A B A C A Coda) (To review rondo form, see Unit 2, Lesson 3, pages 60–61.)

• Practice the playalong rhythm and remember where they used it. (to accompany "Harmony," Lesson 4, page 106)

OBJECTIVE 1 Informal Assessment
• Listen to the rondo and, on each return of the A section, clap or play the playalong on unpitched instruments.

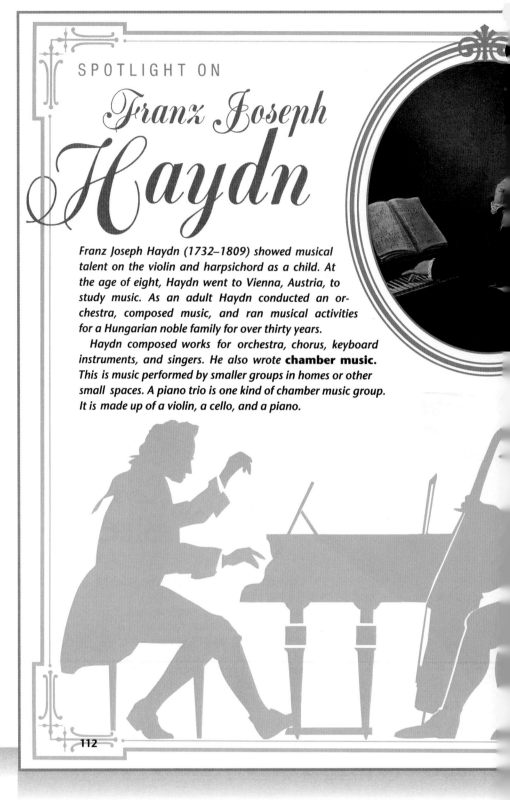

SPOTLIGHT ON
Franz Joseph
Haydn

Franz Joseph Haydn (1732–1809) showed musical talent on the violin and harpsichord as a child. At the age of eight, Haydn went to Vienna, Austria, to study music. As an adult Haydn conducted an orchestra, composed music, and ran musical activities for a Hungarian noble family for over thirty years.

Haydn composed works for orchestra, chorus, keyboard instruments, and singers. He also wrote **chamber music.** This is music performed by smaller groups in homes or other small spaces. A piano trio is one kind of chamber music group. It is made up of a violin, a cello, and a piano.

112

MEETING **INDIVIDUAL** NEEDS

ALTERNATE TEACHING STRATEGY

OBJECTIVE 1 Remind students of the three-to-one relationship of dotted notes. Put the rhythms on the board. For the dotted quarter-eighth pattern, show them where each half beat occurs by placing numbers and symbols under the notation: 1 & 2 & 3 & 4 &. For the dotted eighth-sixteenth pattern, show them where each quarter beat occurs using: 1 e & a, 2 e & a, and so on.

BACKGROUND: *Trio No. 39 Finale*

Each section of Trio No. 39 Finale ("Gypsy Rondo") contains several thematic ideas. The following diagram shows the overall form, the different thematic ideas contained within each section (in lowercase letters), and the number of measures (in $\frac{2}{4}$ meter) that they occupy.

Section:	A	B	A	C	A	Coda
Part:	a a ba ba	cc dd ee ff	a ba	gg hh	a ba	
No. Measures:	8 8 18 18	16 16 16 12	8 18	16 24	8 18	17

Trio No. 39 Finale (Gypsy Rondo)
by Franz Joseph Haydn

LISTENING

Listen to a piano trio by Franz Joseph Haydn. The piano you hear was made in 1797 and is called a **fortepiano**. It is smaller and quieter than modern pianos. This movement is called the "Gypsy Rondo." Perform the rhythm below whenever you hear the A section of the rondo. Where have you played the rhythm of the first two measures before? It was used to accompany "Harmony."

A fortepiano built in
Vienna, Austria, around 1790

113

4 **CLOSE**

"Think about the keyboard instruments you heard today." Have students:

▶ • Name the keyboard instruments in the lesson. (player piano and fortepiano)

"By this time you have heard many types of keyboards, each known for specific styles of music. Let's close by singing in one of those styles with 'The Old Piano Roll Blues.'"

LESSON SUMMARY

Informal Assessment In this lesson, students:

OBJECTIVE 1 Performed an accompaniment from notation containing ♩. ♪ and ♫ rhythm patterns with Trio, No. 39 Finale ("Gypsy Rondo").

MORE MUSIC: Reinforcement
"Battle Hymn of the Republic," page 295 (♩. ♪ and ♫)
"The Boatman," page 332 (♩. ♪ and ♫)
"Hotaru Koi," page 333 (♫)
"Come, Follow Me!" page 337 (♩. ♪)
"Shady Grove," page 367 (♫)
"Shall I Dream a Dream?" page 380 (♩. ♪)

BIOGRAPHY: Franz Joseph Haydn

Austrian composer Franz Joseph Haydn (1732–1809) began life as a peasant, the son of a wagon-repairer and a cook. Both his parents loved music; his father played the organ and his mother sang in the village choir. From his parents, Haydn learned Austrian, Hungarian, and Croatian folk songs. He often used folk or Gypsy melodies in his compositions, as in the listening example. (Gypsies are a nomadic people believed to have come originally from India or Egypt.)

Haydn is also known for having refined and improved the symphony. One important improvement was "thematic elaboration," in which the second theme in a movement "grows" out of the first. The whole movement develops from a single melody that has been broken down and put back together in creative ways. The music of Haydn's student, Ludwig van Beethoven, shows the influence of this technique.

LANGUAGE ARTS

WRITING POETRY

"Player Piano"

INDIVIDUAL   **15–30 MIN**

Updike uses poetic devices to make the player piano come alive:

- onomatopoeia—words that imitate sounds: *click, pluck, flicker*
- personification—qualities of a living being given to the piano: *My stick fingers . . . knuckle the keys; my steel feelers flicker*
- alliteration—repetition of the first letter or consonant sound in series of words: *dint of my din, The tones I turn*
- rhyming words within a line—*click with a snicker, My paper can caper*
- simile—a visual comparison using the word *like* or *as*: *I'm light like the moon*
- metaphor—a comparison without using *like* or *as*: *My stick fingers, I'm a jumble of rumbles*

Have students pick instruments or any inanimate objects that they might like to "bring to life" in a poem. Have them use some of these devices to write poems about their own inanimate object "come to life."

COMPREHENSION STRATEGIES: Extending vocabulary, visualizing

MATHEMATICS

TREE DIAGRAM

Trio, No. 39

PAIR   **15–30 MIN**

MATERIALS: drawing paper, markers

Ask students to suppose they were arranging the three instruments of Trio, No. 39—violin, cello, and piano—on a stage—left, middle, and right. Have them work in pairs to draw tree diagrams to show the different possible arrangements they could make with the three instruments. As an extension, have them arrange the instruments of a quartet.

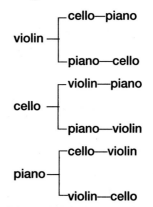

violin
- cello—piano
- piano—cello

cello
- violin—piano
- piano—violin

piano
- cello—violin
- violin—cello

COMPREHENSION STRATEGIES: Using a diagram, sequencing

CURRICULUM

SOCIAL STUDIES

TIME LINE

Trio, No. 39

GROUP   **15–30 MIN**

MATERIALS: poster board (or mural paper), ruler or meter stick; optional—reference materials

Have students create a time line to show world events during the lives of:

- Franz Joseph Haydn (1732–1809)
- Wolfgang Amadeus Mozart (1756–1791)
- Frédéric Chopin (1810–1849)

Have them begin by tracing a line across the length of a poster board. The line should be across the center, leaving space for writing above and below. They need to label the ends of the line "1700" (left) and "1900" (right), and the midpoint "1800." Then they mark off decades within each century by drawing nine equally-spaced vertical lines along each half of the line and labeling them "1710," "1720," and so on.

Above the time line, have them use markers to draw (and label) horizontal bars showing the span of each composer's life. Then they can plot events along the line, such as:

- *1725* Industrial Revolution begins
- *1756* French and Indian War begins
- *1762* Catherine the Great becomes Empress of Russia
- *1770* Boston massacre
- *1776* North American colonies declare independence from Great Britain
- *1789* French Revolution begins; Washington becomes first President of United States
- *1803* United States makes the Louisiana Purchase
- *1804* Napoleon crowns himself Emperor of Europe
- *1820* African slave trade abolished by most countries by this date
- *1821* Central America becomes Independent from Spain
- *1848–1849* California Gold Rush

Students may add to the time line as they find dates throughout the year.

COMPREHENSION STRATEGY: Sequencing

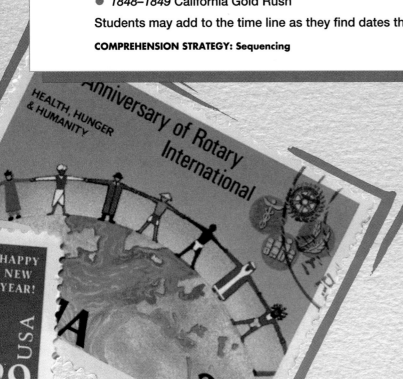

UNIT THREE
LESSON 6

RELATED ARTS   MOVEMENT   THEATER   VISUAL ARTS

LESSON PLANNER

FOCUS Tone color

OBJECTIVE
OBJECTIVE 1 Signal to show aural identification of harpsichord

MATERIALS
Recordings
Recorded Lesson: Interview with
  Ellis Marsalis   CD2:42
Listening: This Can't Be Love by
  L. Hart and R. Rodgers   CD3:1
Said I Wasn't Gonn' Tell Nobody   CD3:2
Listening: Sonata in G Minor
  (The Cat's Fugue) by
  D. Scarlatti   CD3:3

Instruments pitched instruments

Resources
Resource Master 3 • 4 (listening map)
Listening Map Transparency T • 6 (Sonata
  in G Minor, sections)
Listening Map Transparency T • 7 (Sonata
  in G Minor, comprehensive)
Musical Instruments Master—
  synthesizers

VOCABULARY
envelope, fugue, stretto, subject,
countersubject, episode

▶ = **BASIC PROGRAM**

The Envelope, Please

meet
Ellis Marsalis

Ellis Marsalis, born in 1934, is a pianist, composer, and music teacher from New Orleans, Louisiana. While he was studying to be a music teacher, Marsalis played jazz in clubs around New Orleans. Later, he played with jazz greats Ornette Coleman, Don Cherry, and others. Since the 1970s, Ellis Marsalis has been very successful as a teacher, helping many young jazz musicians to develop their talents. Among Ellis's students are his sons Wynton and Branford, and the singer-pianist Harry Connick, Jr. All have become famous jazz musicians.

114

MEETING **INDIVIDUAL** NEEDS

MULTICULTURAL PERSPECTIVES: *Jazz*

Jazz originated in the early 1900s with African American musicians in and around New Orleans. In this music the performer is also a composer. Jazz musicians improvise and experiment with the music they play so that no two performances sound alike. New Orleans was settled by French-speaking people, and the word *jazz* may have come from the French *jaser* (ʒɑ **ze**), which means to chatter or gossip. The music itself, however, developed from African American call-and-response songs and the African tradition of

musical improvisation. Living in a seaport, New Orleans' musicians were also influenced by many other peoples, especially those from the Caribbean and Europe.

Like ragtime, from which it took syncopated rhythms, jazz quickly spread across the world, and it remains popular to this day. Over the years, many different styles of jazz have evolved. Jazz is also one of the roots of rock and other popular music.

This Can't Be Love

by Lorenz Hart and Richard Rodgers

Listen to Ellis Marsalis and his band perform this song from the 1938 musical **The Boys from Syracuse.** *Jason Marsalis, the youngest son of Ellis Marsalis, is playing drums in this recording.*

THE SHAPE OF SOUND

Every sound we hear has the same parts. It has a beginning, a middle, and an end. These parts are called *attack, decay, sustain,* and *release.*

DEMONSTRATE **these stages by playing tones on a resonator bell. The picture below represents four stages of any sound.**

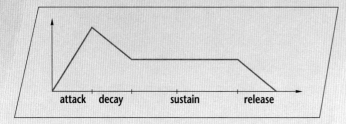

Attack: The pitch begins with the sharp sound of the mallet hitting the bell.
Decay: The sound fades a bit.
Sustain: As the pitch sounds, it rings and sustains.
Release: The sound gradually fades away.

Attack, decay, sustain, and release help give all instruments and voices their own unique character. The combination of these four stages is called an **envelope**. The same pitch played on a piano, an organ, and a harpsichord will have a completely different envelope.

Unit 3 *The Keyboard Connection* 115

1 GET SET

"By now you should be familiar with how keyboard instruments sound." Have students:

▶ • Name the keyboard instruments they have studied and compare their sounds. (piano, organ, harpsichord, accordion, fortepiano) "Today, you'll learn more about why each of these instruments has its own special sound. But first you're going to 'meet' a jazz musician who has started many people on musical careers."

2 DEVELOP

1. Introduce "This Can't Be Love" CD3:1. **Learn about a jazz musician.** Have students:

▶ • Read about Ellis Marsalis (mɑr **sæl** ɪs).

Recorded Lesson CD2:42

▶ • Listen to "Interview with Ellis Marsalis," in which Marsalis talks about teaching and his career in music.

▶ • Read about "This Can't Be Love" and listen to the recording.

2. Identify four stages of a sound. Have students:

▶ • Read about the four stages of sound.

▶ • Listen to the sound of a resonator bell or other pitched instrument (played by a volunteer) and compare it to the graph in the book.

▶ • Play sounds on pitched instruments with different tone colors and made of different materials (such as piano, xylophone, guitar, and recorder), and discuss the attack, decay, sustain, and release of each.

BIOGRAPHIES: *Richard Rodgers & Lorenz Hart*

American songwriters Richard Rodgers (1902–1979) and Lorenz Hart (1895–1943) began working together when Rodgers was only 17. Rodgers wrote the music and Hart wrote the lyrics. Through good luck, their very first song "Any Old Place with You" was used in a Broadway musical. Unfortunately, after that almost no one showed interest in their songs for the next five years. The two kept trying, writing songs for amateur theater shows. Their big break

came when they wrote the songs for a musical revue. The revue had been planned to run for one Sunday only, but sold so many tickets that it ended up running for six months. After that, the two wrote many hit musicals, including *Pal Joey* and *The Boys from Syracuse,* an adaptation of Shakespeare's *The Comedy of Errors.* After Hart died, Rodgers went on to work with Oscar Hammerstein II (*Oklahoma!, South Pacific, The Sound of Music*) and on his own (*No Strings*).

UNIT THREE
LESSON 6

continued from previous page

3. Introduce "Said I Wasn't Gonn' Tell Nobody" CD3:2. **Hear electric organ.** Have students:

▶ • Read about gospel music and call-and-response songs.

▶ • Listen to "Said I Wasn't Gonn' Tell Nobody" and try to identify the keyboard instruments in the accompaniment. (electric organ)

This song brings a message of good news. It is in a style known as *gospel*. Gospel music is often accompanied by both piano and electric organ. Gospel may be sung in a call-and-response style. In this vocal style, each phrase is sung by a soloist, then answered by a chorus. "Said I Wasn't Gonn' Tell Nobody" is in call-and-response style.

116 THE ENVELOPE, PLEASE

MEETING **INDIVIDUAL** NEEDS

VOCAL DEVELOPMENT: *Vocal Models*

Singing in tune and with good tone quality requires that students' attention and energy be focused on that challenge. One of the most effective motivational strategies is to have them listen to examples of fine children's singing voices. This can be done through recordings or by having students in the class serve as vocal models. Ask two or three students who know the call of "Said I Wasn't Gonn' Tell Nobody" to be the "callers." Choose those students who

demonstrate the singing skills and tone quality you wish others to imitate (for example: use of breath support; relaxed, open jaw; and unforced singing). Ask the other students to imitate the "callers."

116 Lesson 6 THE ENVELOPE, PLEASE

Said I Wasn't Gonn' Tell Nobody

African American Gospel Song
Arranged by René Boyer-White

Said I wasn't gonn' tell no-bod-y but I___ Oh___
could-n't keep it to my-self,___
Oh_____ ah
could-n't keep it to my-self,___ could-n't keep it to my-self.___
Said I___ wasn't gonn' tell no-bod-y but I___ just what the
could-n't keep it to my-self.___
Lord has done for me.
Lord has done for me.

4. Sing "Said I Wasn't Gonn' Tell Nobody" in call-and-response style. Have students:

▶ • Identify the style in which the performers are singing as call and response.

▶ • Form two groups, Group 1 to sing the call and Group 2 the response. Reverse roles and repeat. (You may wish to ask volunteers to act as lead singers.)

BACKGROUND: *Electric Organ*

An electric organ is similar to the pipe organ, but its sound is amplified electronically. Since it has no pipes, it is much smaller than the pipe organ, although the console (which holds the keyboard and stops) may be a similar size. Its small size makes the electric organ popular for homes. The stops are labeled in a way similar to those on a pipe organ. Various sound effects and rhythms are available, depending on the brand of organ used.

UNIT THREE
LESSON 6

continued from previous page

3 APPLY

Introduce Sonata in G Minor ("The Cat's Fugue") CD3:3. Review harpsichord sound.
Have students:

▶ • Read about the fugue. Listen as four students read aloud about the fugue in "fugal style" as directed. (See *Extra Help* on the bottom of page 119 for tips on reading in the fugal style.)

• Decide if a fugue is monophonic, homophonic, or polyphonic. (polyphonic)

▶ • Read about Domenico Scarlatti (do **me** ni ko skaɾ **la** ti).

▶ • Listen to the sonata, as they follow the listening map, and point to the appropriate picture on the map as each section (subject-countersubject and episode) is heard. (Optional: Use **Listening Map Transparency T • 6** to identify sections. Use **Listening Map Transparency T • 7** or **Resource Master 3 • 4,** which is a comprehensive map of the sonata.)

OBJECTIVE 1 Informal Assessment

▶ • With eyes closed, indicate which instrument they heard by holding up one finger for piano, two fingers for harpsichord, or three for organ. (two—harpsichord)

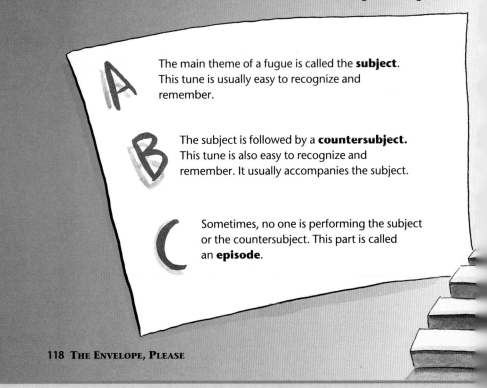

FLIGHTS OF FANCY

The **fugue** is a musical form used by Bach and other composers. The word *fugue* means "flight." In a fugue, the parts seem to be trying to get away from each other. Parts of a fugue sound like a canon, because the different voices enter one at a time and imitate one another. To create a fugue, a composer must follow a set of rules of musical form.

PERFORM this four-part spoken fugue from the chart below.

1. At a signal, each person reads parts **A**, **B**, and **C** all the way through. Reader 1 begins alone. When each reader reaches **B**, the next reader begins. When the readers finish **C**, they repeat it until everyone is reading **C** together.

2. At a signal, the readers perform step 1 again.

3. At a signal, the readers perform a **stretto**. To do this, Reader 1 begins **A** alone. Every few seconds another reader begins **A**. The readers repeat **A** until a signal is given to say, all together, "the end." The stretto makes the end of a fugue exciting.

A The main theme of a fugue is called the **subject**. This tune is usually easy to recognize and remember.

B The subject is followed by a **countersubject.** This tune is also easy to recognize and remember. It usually accompanies the subject.

C Sometimes, no one is performing the subject or the countersubject. This part is called an **episode**.

118 THE ENVELOPE, PLEASE

MEETING **INDIVIDUAL** NEEDS

ALTERNATE TEACHING STRATEGY

OBJECTIVE 1 Play portions of "Harmony," Rondeau, and Prelude in A Minor, and ask students to identify the instruments. (piano, harpsichord, pipe organ) (Alternatively, play the recorded lesson "World of Keyboards" again.) Then play part of Sonata in G Minor again and have them compare its sound to the instruments they just heard. (Possible answer: Harpsichord sound does not sustain, sounds plucked.)

SPECIAL LEARNERS: *Electronic Keyboards*

When introducing sounds produced and synthesized electronically, allow students to experiment with an inexpensive electronic keyboard. Electronic keyboards provide ways for disabled students to make independent choices (timbres, rhythms, and so on). After students are comfortable with the keyboards, have them play harmonic accompaniments from previous lessons and make changes in tone color.

Sonata in G Minor (The Cat's Fugue)
by Domenico Scarlatti

Domenico Scarlatti was born in 1685, the same year as J. S. Bach. Scarlatti was Italian, but lived and worked much of his life at the Spanish royal court in Madrid. He wrote over 500 short pieces for the harpsichord. This is his only fugue. It is called "The Cat's Fugue" because the subject sounds like a cat walking across the keyboard.

LISTENING MAP *Point to either "subject-countersubject" or to "episode" in the map when you hear those parts of "The Cat's Fugue." Which keyboard instrument do you hear?* harpsichord

subject-countersubject

episode

"What keyboard instruments did you hear today?" Have students:

▶ • Name the instruments they heard today. (piano, electric organ, harpsichord)

"Let's close by singing 'Said I Wasn't Gonn' Tell Nobody,' accompanied by electric organ."

LESSON SUMMARY

Informal Assessment In this lesson, students:

OBJECTIVE 1 Signaled to show aural identification of harpsichord sound in Sonata in G Minor ("The Cat's Fugue").

MORE MUSIC: Reinforcement
"Brilliant Corners," page 134 (piano, jazz)
"Montage of Performance Styles," page 135 (piano, jazz)
"Battle Hymn of the Republic," (listening) page 294 (piano, jazz)
"Follow the Drinkin' Gourd," page 370 (call-response, spiritual)

EXTRA HELP: *Performing in Fugal Style*

Assign numbers to the four readers. Designate a leader who will indicate when each person is to begin reading by signaling the assigned numbers in order. *Step 1:* Reader 1 reads A on page 118. The others begin when the person before her/him starts reading B. *Step 2:* After all four have completed Step 1, the leader signals Reader 1 to read A again. All repeat Step 1. *Step 3:* On a pre-arranged signal (such as leader raising both hands), all perform a stretto of A, beginning one at a time and continuing until all have read A at least once. Then, on the leader's cue, all say "the end" together.

BACKGROUND: *The Sonata*

A sonata is an instrumental form that usually consists of three or four complete movements (pieces that fit into a larger whole) in contrasting tempos. The word *sonata* has meant different things over the years, but it was first used to distinguish instrumental from vocal music. For instance, Scarlatti's sonatas for harpsichord are each only one movement long. Today the word means a work for one or two performers. Sonatas for three instruments are called trios; those for four are called quartets. A symphony is a sonata for orchestra.

RELATED ARTS MOVEMENT | THEATER | VISUAL ARTS

LESSON PLANNER

FOCUS Tone color

OBJECTIVES
OBJECTIVE 1 Create and dance an original movement pattern that includes the rhythm $\frac{4}{4}$ 𝅗𝅥. ♪ ♩ ♩ 𝄽 ‖

OBJECTIVE 2 Demonstrate their creation of a "prepared" pitched instrument

MATERIALS
Recordings

Said I Wasn't Gonn' Tell Nobody	CD3:2
Listening: Kakokolo by Samite	CD3:4
Recorded Lesson: Pronunciation for "Kakokolo"	CD3:5
Kakokolo	CD3:6
Listening: Three Dances for Two Amplified Prepared Pianos (excerpt) by J. Cage	CD3:7

Instruments
resonator bells, piano, or other pitched instruments

Other
paper, coins, spoons, erasers, and other classroom materials

Resources Resource Master 3 • 5 (practice)

VOCABULARY
mbira (thumb piano), prepared piano

▶ = BASIC PROGRAM

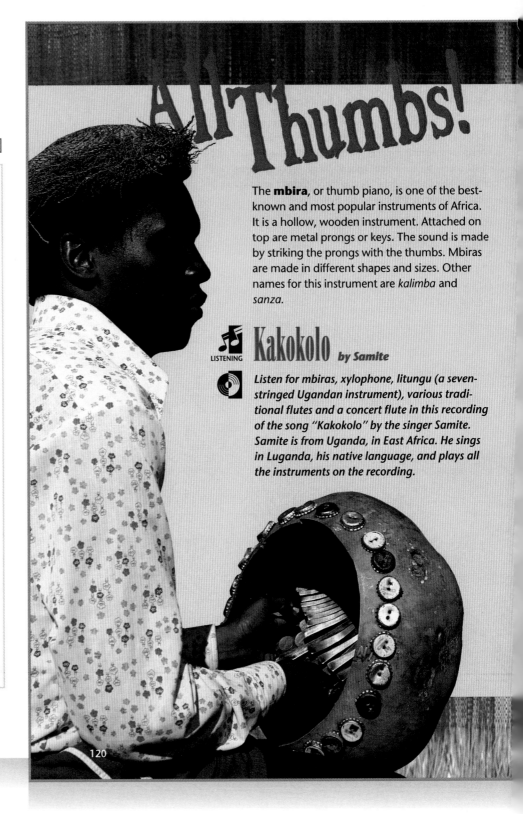

All Thumbs!

The **mbira**, or thumb piano, is one of the best-known and most popular instruments of Africa. It is a hollow, wooden instrument. Attached on top are metal prongs or keys. The sound is made by striking the prongs with the thumbs. Mbiras are made in different shapes and sizes. Other names for this instrument are *kalimba* and *sanza*.

LISTENING **Kakokolo** *by Samite*

Listen for mbiras, xylophone, litungu (a seven-stringed Ugandan instrument), various traditional flutes and a concert flute in this recording of the song "Kakokolo" by the singer Samite. Samite is from Uganda, in East Africa. He sings in Luganda, his native language, and plays all the instruments on the recording.

120

MEETING **INDIVIDUAL** NEEDS

ALTERNATE TEACHING STRATEGY

OBJECTIVE 1 If students need more structure to help them create a dance to "Kakokolo," suggest they use a form with which they are familiar, for example: A B or A B A.

BACKGROUND: *"Kakokolo"*

Samite based "Kakokolo" on an African folktale that teaches that strangers may not be what they seem. A forest creature turns itself into a traveling musician who intentionally "forgets" his instrument. A child calls after the

"musician" to come back for his guitar. The musician tries to lure the child to bring the guitar to him.

MOVEMENT: *"Kakokolo"*

Creating the step: Have small groups create a step using the dotted quarter-eighth pattern, for example:

$\frac{4}{4}$ 𝅗𝅥.　　♪ ♩ 𝄽 ｜ 𝅗𝅥.　　♪ ♩ 𝄽 ‖
　R　　 L R (clap)　 L 　 R L (clap)

Choosing a formation: Have groups choose a formation to go with the step. Ugandan dances use many formations—line

Kakokolo

Words and Music by Samite

Luganda: Ka - ko - ko - lo gwe ka - ko - ko - lo,_____
Pronunciation: ka ko ko lo gwe ka ko ko lo
English: Ka - ko - ko - lo, Hey! ka - ko - ko - lo,_____

ka - ko - ko - lo kwa - ta en-ton-go-li yo._____
ka ko ko lo kwa tan ton go li yo
Ka - ko - ko - lo Oh____ Take up your gui - tar!

N - de-ter-a, maa-ma, nde-ter-a. Agen-da-no___ mu-lun-gi ta - la-ga.
n de te ra ma ma nde te ra gen da no mu lun gi ta la ga
Bring it to me, ma-ma, play a song. Don't tell me___ you are go-ing a-way.

Kyi maa-ma kyi nya-bo___ jang-ue-no nga o-yim-ba.
chi ma ma chi nya bo yang we no ngo yim ba
Hey, ma-ma, pret-ty one,___ Come a-way, sing a song.

Kyi maa-ma kyi nya-bo___ jang-ue-no nga o-yim-ba.
chi ma ma chi nya bo yang we no ngo yim ba
Hey ma-ma, pret-ty one,___ Come a-way, sing a song.

CREATE and perform a dance for "Kakokolo." Step to the rhythm pattern you used for "Harmony" and the "Gypsy Rondo."

C major

l, t, d r m f s l t d'

1 GET SET

"Keyboards are very versatile instruments that can be used for many different styles of music. Let's focus on the style of a song you know." Have students:

▶ • Sing "Said I Wasn't Gonn' Tell Nobody" **CD3:2**. (See pages 116–117.)

▶ • Recall its style. (gospel)

▶ • Recall that the song is accompanied by electric organ.

"You may be familiar with the electric organ. In today's lesson, you will hear keyboards that may not be so familiar to you. You will also create and play your own pieces."

2 DEVELOP

1. Introduce "Kakokolo." Listen to the sound of a mbira and create a dance using dotted rhythms. Have students:

▶ • Read about the thumb piano (also called mbira (**mbi** ra), kalimba (ka **lum** ba), or sanza (**san** za).

▶ • Read about and listen to "Kakokolo" (listening, **CD3:4**) by Samite (**sa** mi te).

Recorded Lesson CD3:5

▶ • Listen to "Pronunciation for 'Kakokolo.'"

▶ • Sing "Kakokolo" (song, **CD3:6**).

OBJECTIVE 1 Informal Assessment

• Create and perform a dance step for the rhythm of the 4/4 ♩. ♪ ♩ 𝄽 ‖ pattern they used with "Harmony" in Lesson 4 (page 106) and Trio, No. 39 ("Gypsy Rondo") (page 113). (See *Movement* on the bottom of page 120.)

• Do the step as a dance to "Kakokolo."

(both shoulder to shoulder and front to back like a parade), circle, snake-like, and zigzag. They might change from one formation to another at a given point.

PRONUNCIATION: *"Kakokolo"*

a f<u>a</u>ther   e ch<u>a</u>otic   i b<u>ee</u>   o <u>o</u>bey
u m<u>oo</u>n   ŋ n sounded as syllable   ɾ flipped r

IMPROVISATION: *"Kakokolo" Ostinatos*

Have the class create six 2-measure ostinatos in 4/4 meter to play on unpitched instruments. Combine patterns to accompany the dance and/or the song. Possible patterns:

Have several students learn each instrument pattern. Then have six students perform the patterns in additive style. Pattern 1 plays alone, then repeats as Pattern 2 enters, and so on through Pattern 6. All instruments then play together until the end of the song.

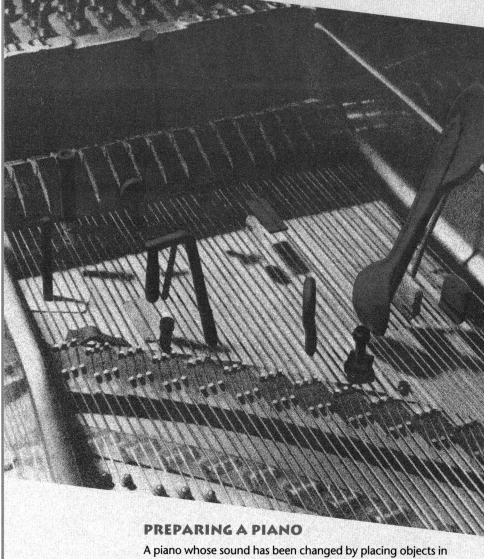

PREPARING A PIANO

A piano whose sound has been changed by placing objects in contact with the strings is called a **prepared piano.** Items such as pieces of paper, coins, spoons, or erasers are placed on or between the piano's strings. This causes the instrument to produce sounds that are completely different from those a piano usually makes. In addition to striking the keys, the performers hit wooden parts of the piano and reach inside the instrument to pluck, strum, or tap the strings.

The idea of the prepared piano was introduced by American composer John Cage in the early 1940s.

122 ALL THUMBS!

continued on next page

2. Introduce "Three Dances for Two Amplified Prepared Pianos" (excerpt) CD3:7. Listen to the sound of a prepared piano. Have students:

▶ • Listen to the excerpt from "Three Dances" with books closed and try to identify the instrument they hear.

▶ • Read pages 122–123.

▶ • Answer the *Think It Through* question. (Students may notice the similarity in sound of the prepared piano to the mbira, but encourage them to come up with a variety of ideas.)

3 APPLY

Prepare a piano and create a piece for the prepared piano using the ♩ ♪ or ♫ rhythm. Have students:

▶ • In small groups, decide on one way to prepare a piano, autoharp, or other pitched instrument, using paper, pencils, and other materials found in the classroom, then prepare the instrument.

OBJECTIVE 2 Informal Assessment

▶ • In their groups, demonstrate the sounds produced by their prepared instruments.

MEETING **INDIVIDUAL** NEEDS

ALTERNATE TEACHING STRATEGY

OBJECTIVE 2 To illustrate how different an instrument can sound when it is "prepared," play part of "Alla Turca" (Unit 2, Lesson 3, page 60) and then "Three Dances." Ask students to compare the sounds. Then ask them to try to make that great a difference in sound between the unprepared and prepared sounds of their instruments.

SCIENCE CONNECTION: *A Thumb Piano*

Have students use the directions on **Resource Master 3 · 5** to explore making and tuning a thumb piano.

IMPROVISATION: *Prepared Instruments*

Have students create an informally improvised composition on the prepared instrument that uses one or both dotted rhythms studied: ♩ ♪ or ♫ (Suggest the composition be about 30 seconds.)

Spotlight on

John Cage

John Cage (1912–1992) was the son of an inventor. As a young man he studied composition. Like his father, he saw new ways to use old materials. In addition to the prepared piano, he developed what is called chance music. The performer is given the task of making major decisions about the music. A player might choose some of the pitches, or decide the order in which to perform the parts of a composition.

John Cage had many other innovative ideas. Sometimes he invited the audience to join in on the performance. Once, he asked them to go out and get garbage cans because they were needed for percussion sounds.

🎵 **LISTENING** 💿

Three Dances for Two Amplified Prepared Pianos (excerpt) *by John Cage*

Cage used the sounds of Asian music in this piece, which he wrote in the mid-1940s.

THINK IT THROUGH

What musical instruments or other sounds do you think the prepared pianos sound like?

Unit 3 *The Keyboard Connection* **123**

"Describe the instruments in today's lesson and how they were played." Have students:

▶ • Listen as volunteers describe the mbira and the prepared piano, and the effect of the sounds created.

▶ • Sing "Kakokolo."

LESSON SUMMARY

Informal Assessment In this lesson, students:

OBJECTIVE 1 Created and danced original movement patterns for "Kakokolo" using a ♩ ♪ rhythm pattern.

OBJECTIVE 2 Demonstrated their creation of "prepared" pitched instruments.

MORE MUSIC: Reinforcement
"Chíu, chíu, chíu," page 360 (♩. ♪)
"Lobster Quadrille," page 390 (♩. ♪)

COOPERATIVE LEARNING: *Minimalist Music*

Some people have called John Cage a minimalist. In this style, a small number of pitches, harmonies, and rhythms are used in gradually changing ostinatos. A minimalist composer might create and repeat an ostinato of a few pitch syllables, for example, *do re mi re*. Gradually pitches are added to the pattern, and the rhythm may also change. The result may sound hypnotic or relaxing.

Ask students to work in groups of three to compose their own minimalist compositions on resonator bells, other pitched instruments, or their prepared instruments. Have

them follow the techniques described above. The compositions should be about one minute long. Help students achieve the goal by assigning these roles:

Facilitator—makes sure everyone takes turns giving ideas until about one minute of music has been created

Player—plays proposed phrases on the bells; makes sure everyone has a chance to play the melody after it has been decided upon

Recorder—records the melody using pitch syllables, pitch letter names, or any other method the group chooses

KEYS FOR TWO

LESSON PLANNER

FOCUS Rhythm

OBJECTIVES
OBJECTIVE 1 Play a melody on the piano, electronic keyboard, or other keyboard instrument
OBJECTIVE 2 Participate in creating an original melody containing a ♩♪ rhythm combination

MATERIALS
Recordings
Listening: Rhythm-a-ning by T. Monk — CD3:8
Lean on Me — CD3:9

Instrument any keyboard instrument

Resources
Resource Master 3 • 6 (practice)
Musical Instruments Master—piano

VOCABULARY
bass clef, grand staff, duo-pianists

▶ = BASIC PROGRAM

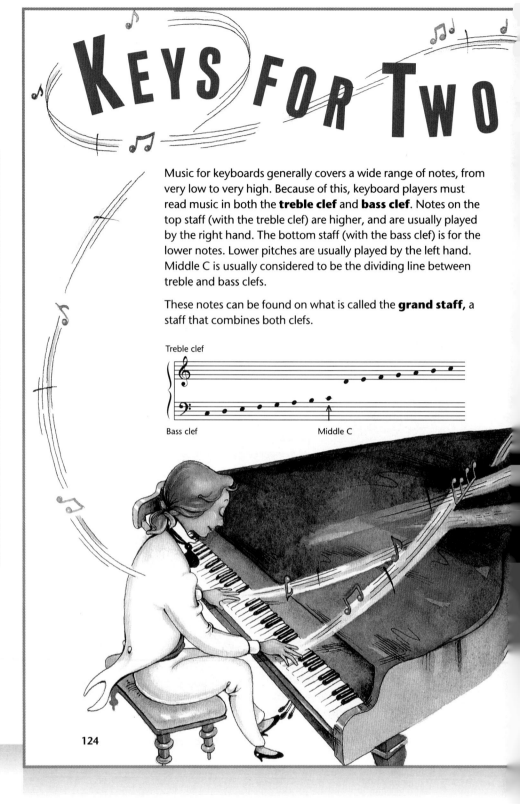

Music for keyboards generally covers a wide range of notes, from very low to very high. Because of this, keyboard players must read music in both the **treble clef** and **bass clef**. Notes on the top staff (with the treble clef) are higher, and are usually played by the right hand. The bottom staff (with the bass clef) is for the lower notes. Lower pitches are usually played by the left hand. Middle C is usually considered to be the dividing line between treble and bass clefs.

These notes can be found on what is called the **grand staff,** a staff that combines both clefs.

Treble clef

Bass clef   Middle C

124

MEETING **INDIVIDUAL** NEEDS

BIOGRAPHY: *Thelonious Monk*

Thelonious Monk (thɛ **lo** ni əs **mʌnk** 1920–1982, was one of the great composers of jazz music. Monk grew up in New York City and started playing piano when he was 11 years old. In the early 1940s, Monk was one of the musical innovators who developed the jazz style that became known as bebop. Bebop is usually performed in small groups of three or four players, and centers on improvised solos. Along with other jazz greats like trumpeter Dizzy Gillespie and saxophonist Charlie Parker, Monk pioneered the new, more complicated harmonies and rhythms heard in bebop.

At first Monk did not get a lot of attention for his compositions and his piano-playing, but by the late 1950s, he had developed a large and devoted following. Art Blakey, a famous jazz drummer, once said, "Monk is the one who started it all."

BACKGROUND: *The Bass Clef*

The bass clef, used to notate low pitches, has been around since the Middle Ages. The word *clef* means "key" in French, and a clef is a key to reading notation. The bass clef points to the note F by surrounding the F line with two

SPOTLIGHT ON

Katia & Marielle Labèque

Katia and Marielle Labèque are French sisters who play together as **duo-pianists.** Using two pianos, they get a thick, full sound. One pianist plays melody parts with both hands. The other plays accompaniment parts with both hands. Sometimes, the pianos exchange melody and accompaniment roles.

LISTENING

Rhythm-a-ning *by Thelonious Monk*

Listen to the Labèque sisters play "Rhythm-a-ning," a composition by the great jazz pianist Thelonious Monk. The title sounds like the word **lightning.** Listen for lightning-and-thunder effects in the music. Try to follow the higher pitches of the melody and the lower pitches of the accompaniment.

Unit 3 *The Keyboard Connection* **125**

"You've heard and read about many types of keyboards." Have students:

▶ • Take turns naming the instruments studied and telling a fact about each. (pipe organ, harpsichord, piano, electric organ, mbira, synthesizer, player piano, accordion)

"Today you're going to become both a keyboard composer and performer."

2 DEVELOP

1. Introduce "Rhythm-a-ning" CD3:8**. Introduce accompaniment and melody roles on the piano.** Have students:

• Read about the treble clef, the bass clef, and
▶ the grand staff.

• Working from middle C, try to name the pitches notated in the treble and bass clefs.

• Describe the usual roles of the left and right
▶ hands when playing keyboard. (right—melody; left—accompaniment)

• Read page 125, then describe how Katia and
▶ Marielle Labèque (**ka** ti a, ma ʀyɛl la **bɛk**) play as duo-pianists.

• Listen to "Rhythm-a-ning," with attention to
▶ the melody and accompaniment, and to the thunder-and-lightning effects.

---

dots. Originally the bass clef looked like the letter F, but it gradually changed in appearance over many centuries. The two other clefs, the G or treble clef, and the C or alto clef, also originally looked like the letter names of the notes to which they point. Today most music for low voices is written with the bass clef. It is also used for keyboard instruments and the bassoon, the cello, and the trombone.

ENRICHMENT: *Partners*

The Labèques represent an artistic partnership. Have students think of tasks they have carried out together with partners. Have them describe in writing, or orally, how the partnership worked. Did working together with a partner make the end result a greater or lesser achievement than if each person had worked alone?

UNIT THREE
LESSON 8

continued from previous page

2. Introduce "Lean on Me" CD3:9. **Play melody on a keyboard.** Have students:

• Listen to "Lean on Me" while following the notation. Notice the scalewise movement of the notes in the first eight measures. Name the key. (C major—no sharps or flats)

▶ • Sing the song with the words.

• Sing the first eight measures of the melody, using pitch letter names.

• Learn how to play the first chord (E, G, C: a triad in first inversion) on the keyboard with the right-hand thumb, index, and little finger. Then a few students take turns playing the first eight measures of "Lean on Me," with the little finger playing the melody and the thumb and index finger playing the other two chord tones. (Keep hand in same position; play triads in first inversion under each melody note: D, F, B,; E, G, C; F, A, D; G, B, E; A, C F)

OBJECTIVE 1 Informal Assessment
• Take turns playing the melody of the first eight measures with the chords on a keyboard instrument. (By using different octaves, three can play together at a piano at the same time.)

3 APPLY

1. Create a short melody as a group project. Have students:

OBJECTIVE 2 Informal Assessment
• Take turns suggesting individual pitches and rhythms to create a short melody (eight measures of $\frac{2}{4}$) with these pitches: A, C D E G A.

PLAY the melody of this song on a keyboard with a chordal accompaniment underneath it.

LEAN ON ME

C major

s, l, t, d r m f

Words and Music by Bill Withers

Some-times in our lives ___ we all have pain ___ we all have sor-row. ___ But if we are wise ___ we know that there's ___ al-ways to-mor - row. ___ Lean on me when you're not strong ___ and I'll be your friend ___ I'll help you car - ry — on ___ for it won't be long ___ 'til I'm gon-na need ___ some-bod-y to lean on. Please ___ swal-low your pride ___ if I have things ___ you need to bor - row ___ for no one can fill

126 KEYS FOR TWO

MEETING **INDIVIDUAL** NEEDS

ALTERNATE TEACHING STRATEGIES

OBJECTIVE 1 Review the names of the lines and spaces of the treble clef, the pitches used in the first eight measures of "Lean on Me," and where they are found on the keyboard. Have students form pairs and help each other to learn the melody on the practice keyboard on page 94. When they are successful at playing the melody alone, have them add the chords.

OBJECTIVE 2 Review pitch names on the treble staff and rhythm note values. Then work as a class to revise the group melody where necessary.

CRITICAL THINKING: *Notating the Group Melody*

Have students create several ways to notate the group melody. (Encourage them to explore ways other than staff notation.) Ask each student to choose which notation works best and then write a paragraph explaining the notation and the reason for her or his choice.

COOPERATIVE LEARNING: *A Group Melody*

Have students work in groups of four to create the group melody in *Apply*. Assign these roles:

those of your needs ___ that you won't let ___ show. ___ You just

call on me, broth- er, when you need a hand, ___ we all need some-bod- y to lean ___

___ on. ___ I just might have a prob-lem that you'll un- der-stand. ___ We all

need some-bod- y to lean ___ on. ___ 1.Lean on me when you're not strong
2. If there is a load ___

___ and I'll be your friend, ___ I'll help you car - ry ___ on
you have to bear ___ that you can't ___ car - ry,

for it won't be long _____ 'til I'm gon - na need ___ some-bod- y to lean ___
I'm right up the road. _____ I'll share your load ___

on. You just ___ if you just call ___ me.

(The melody should begin and end on C and use at least one dotted eighth-sixteenth combination. Each pitch must equal one beat: for example; ♩ ♫ or ♫ Optional: Have students record the melody on **Resource Master 3 • 6.**)

2. Perform the group melody with accompaniment. Have students:

▶ • Listen as one student plays the resulting original melody from *Apply 1*, and another plays the first four notes of the "Heart and Soul" bass line (C E A' C, page 94) twice through as an accompaniment.

4 CLOSE

"In today's lesson you focused on melody and accompaniment." Have students:

• Tell what they studied in this lesson. (grand staff, the role of duo-pianists, that the left hand usually plays the accompaniment, the right the melody)

"Now let's play the class melody one more time. When you go home today, try singing or playing the melody for someone else."

LESSON SUMMARY

Informal Assessment In this lesson, students:

OBJECTIVE 1 Played the first eight measures of the melody to "Lean on Me" on the piano, electronic keyboard, or other keyboard instrument.

OBJECTIVE 2 Participated in creating an original melody containing a ♫ rhythm combination.

MORE MUSIC: Reinforcement
"Soon Ah Will Be Done," page 354 (♫)

Facilitator—makes sure everyone has a chance to give ideas until eight measures of ²⁄₄ have been created

Echo—restates each idea suggested, checking for clarity and understanding

Player—plays proposed measures on keyboard or other pitched instrument and, after the melody has been decided upon, makes sure that everyone has a chance to play the melody

Recorder—records the melody using notation or any other method students choose to help them remember

---

PLAYING INSTRUMENTS: *Keyboard*

On the board write out the bass line for "Heart and Soul" in the bass clef. Each pitch takes one-quarter note beat. The whole pattern takes two measures in ⁴⁄₄. Put the letter names of the pitches underneath each pitch (C E A, C D F G, B,). Have students practice the bass line on any keyboard instrument and then combine it with the first eight measures of the melody of "Lean on Me." They should perform the bass line four times, the last time changing the last two quarter-note beats (G, B,) to a half note on E.

UNIT THREE LESSON 9

RELATED ARTS MOVEMENT THEATER VISUAL ARTS

LESSON PLANNER

OBJECTIVES
To review songs, skills, and concepts learned in Unit 3 and to test students' ability to:
1. Identify the difference in sound between the pipe organ and the piano
2. Identify how sound is produced on pipe organ, harpsichord, and piano
3. Recognize dotted patterns

MATERIALS
Recordings
Listening: Heart and Soul by H. Carmichael	CD2:30
Harmony	CD2:28
Alleluia	CD2:33
Tee galop pour Mamou (Gallop on to Mamou)	CD2:36
The Old Piano Roll Blues	CD2:40
Unit 3 Assessment A	CD3:10–13
Unit 3 Assessment B	CD3:14–17

Instrument keyboard

Resources
Resource Master 3 • 7 (assessment)
Resource Master TA • 1 (assessment)
Resource Master—staff paper

▶ = **BASIC PROGRAM**

KEYBOARD COLLECTION

Press a key and what sound comes out? Depending on whether it's a piano, organ, harpsichord, accordion, or synthesizer, the sound might be very different indeed.

The heart and soul of the organ, harpsichord, and piano are their keyboards. Listen to "Heart and Soul" and perform the bass line with it.

With keyboard instruments you can play several pitches at the same time, creating harmony. Make some harmony by singing "Harmony" in two parts.

Some keyboard instruments, such as the organ, have been around for several centuries. "Alleluia," a song more than two centuries old, was written by Mozart. Listen for the organ accompanying the song on the recording.

The accordion is also a keyboard instrument, but it is much more portable than the piano or organ! "Tee galop pour Mamou" comes from the southern part of Louisiana, where French is spoken. In this area the accordion is a favorite instrument.

For the player piano, you don't need to press down a key at all. Player pianos became popular at the beginning of the twentieth century because they played all by themselves. Sing "The Old Piano Roll Blues" and imagine that a player piano is playing it.

128

MEETING **INDIVIDUAL** NEEDS

PROGRAM IDEA: *Keyboard Demonstration* THEATER

This review can be enjoyed in the classroom or presented as a simple program. Additional materials from Unit 3, *Celebrations,* or the *Music Library* may be added as well as original work from the students.

Have students demonstrate keyboard instruments, using some of the statements on page 128 as a script. Some students could perform the bass line with "Heart and Soul" while a group "dances" the bass line as in Lesson 1, page 95, *Movement.* Some could sing "Harmony." All could sing

"Alleluia" with the recording, pointing out the pipe organ accompaniment. Some could sing "Tee galop pour Mamou" with the recording (or have someone bring in a real accordion, if possible). Finish by having everybody sing "The Old Piano Roll Blues."

If presenting this idea as a performance, have some students create scenery, perhaps a backdrop of a giant keyboard.

1. Review pitches on the keyboard and dotted rhythms with "Heart and Soul" CD2:30 **(p. 94).** Have students:

• Say the pitch letter names of the notes in the bass line to "Heart and Soul" as they pretend to play them on the keyboard.

• Perform the bass line with the dotted rhythms (changing each ♩ to ♪ as in Lesson 4, page 109, *Apply 2*) along with "Heart and Soul." (Optional: Have students perform the bass-line ostinato movement in Lesson 1, page 95, *Develop 4*.)

2. Review sound of keyboard instruments with "Harmony" CD2:28 **(pp. 92–94), and "Alleluia"** CD2:33 **(p. 98).** Have students:

▶• Identify the piano as the keyboard instrument heard in the recording of "Harmony," then sing the song in two parts.

▶• Sing "Alleluia" with the recording and tell what keyboard instrument is accompanying it. (pipe organ)

▶• Compare the sound of the piano accompanying "Harmony" with the sound of the pipe organ accompanying "Alleluia." (Students should describe the tone color of the two instruments in their own words. Optional: Students can demonstrate keyboard instruments as in the *Program Idea* on the bottom of page 128.)

3. Review dotted rhythm patterns with "Tee galop pour Mamou" CD2:36 **(p. 107), and "The Old Piano Roll Blues"** CD2:40 **(p. 111).** Have students:

• Find the dotted rhythm pattern ♪ in "Tee Galop pour Mamou" (Measures 2, 4, 6, 8), and then sing the song.

• Listen to "The Old Piano Roll Blues" and find the ♪ rhythm pattern. (See Lesson 5, page 111, *Develop 1*.)

Unit 3 *The Keyboard Connection* **129**

UNIT THREE
LESSON 9

ASSESSMENTS A AND B CD3:10–17

Different recorded examples for Assessments A and B allow for two uses of the same set of questions. When appropriate, recorded examples for Assessment A use familiar musical examples with which students have worked for the given concept. The recorded examples for Assessment B use musical selections the students have not previously worked with for the concept, encouraging the application of knowledge to new material.

The pupil page is intended for those who wish to assess quickly with the whole class or in small groups. Each assessment may be used as a pretest or as a final review before presenting the written test (**Resource Master 3 · 7**).

ANSWERS

	ASSESSMENT A	ASSESSMENT B
1.	c	a
2.	b	d
3.	b	a
4.	a	b

CHECK IT OUT

1. Which rhythm do you hear?

2. Which rhythm do you hear?

3. Which keyboard instrument do you hear?

   a. piano   **b.** pipe organ   **c.** harpsichord

4. How is this keyboard sound produced?

   a. A hammer hits a string.

   b. Air vibrates in a tube.

   c. A string is plucked.

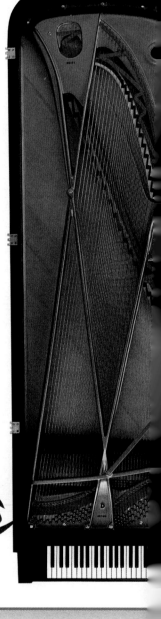

130

MEETING **INDIVIDUAL** NEEDS

PORTFOLIO ASSESSMENT

To evaluate students' portfolios, use the Portfolio Assessment form on **Resource Master TA · 1**. See page 90B for a summary of Portfolio Opportunities in this unit.

CREATE

Write a Tune in ¾ Time

CREATE your own melody in ¾ meter.
Follow these suggestions.

- The melody must be eight measures long.
- Use only the pitches C, D, E, F, and G.
- The last note of the fourth measure must be G.
- The last note of the piece must be C.
- Write your melody in notation.

How to do it? Read the rhyme below to find out.
Do you recognize this rhythm? *mazurka*

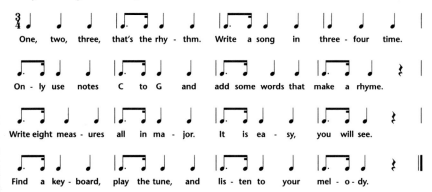

One, two, three, that's the rhy - thm. Write a song in three - four time.

On - ly use notes C to G and add some words that make a rhyme.

Write eight meas - ures all in ma - jor. It is ea - sy, you will see.

Find a key - board, play the tune, and lis - ten to your mel - o - dy.

Write

Write a paragraph comparing two different keyboard instruments that you have heard, either live or on recordings. What was the same or different about the way the two instruments sounded?

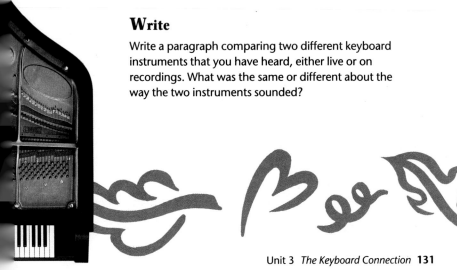

CREATE AND WRITE

1. Compose an eight-measure melody. Have students:

- Review the dotted rhythms learned in this unit, and if necessary, review ¾ meter, and the half and whole step sequence in the first five steps of the major scale.

- Clap the rhythms of the rhyme and then say the words in rhythm.

- Follow the guidelines on page 131 to compose and write an eight-measure melody in notation. (Optional: Have students notate the melody on staff paper, available in the Resource Master Booklet.)

- Play the melody on a keyboard, and revise as desired.

2. Write a paragraph comparing two keyboard instruments. Have students:

▶ • List different keyboard instruments they have heard and choose two to compare. (You may wish to have them write the comparison as an imaginary dialogue between the two instruments.)

▶ • Write a paragraph as described on page 131.

ART CONNECTION: *Keyboard Instruments* VISUAL ARTS

Illustration: Have students illustrate their comparison of keyboard instruments with a labeled drawing of each keyboard instrument. The labels can be used to point out same and different parts of the two instruments.

Tone Color Drawings: Have students create abstract drawings which project the effect of the tone colors of one of the keyboard instruments. Assemble their drawings on a bulletin board around a picture of that instrument.

ENRICHMENT: *Keyboard Compositions*

Have students work on electric keyboards to find appropriate chords to add to their melodies. They should also choose tone colors and accompaniment patterns.

LESSON LINKS

A Blues Montage (25 min)

OBJECTIVE Learn about three jazz artists, then compare and contrast three jazz/blues selections

Reinforcement blues style, *page 245*

MATERIALS
Recordings
Recorded Lesson: Interview
with Dorothy Donegan   CD3:18
A Blues Montage (listening)   CD3:19

Brilliant Corners (15 min)

OBJECTIVE Learn about Max Roach and listen to him perform "Brilliant Corners"

Reinforcement piano, jazz style, *page 119*
1980s jazz style, *page 273*

MATERIALS
Recording Brilliant Corners by
T. Monk (listening)   CD3:20

Montage of Performance Styles (25 min)

OBJECTIVE Learn about Keith Jarrett and listen to him play in four distinct styles

Reinforcement improvisation, piano, jazz style, *page 119*

MATERIALS
Recordings
Recorded Lesson: Interview with
Keith Jarrett   CD3:21
Montage of Performance Styles
(listening)   CD3:22

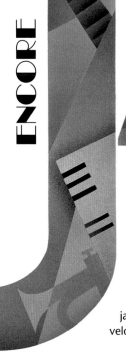

ENCORE JAZZ

Jazz is a musical style that grew out of African rhythms, European harmony, and melodies from folk songs and other popular sources. Jazz focuses on individual interpretations. Within this freedom of expression, the jazz musician varies the beat, rhythm, melody, and volume as desired. This technique, known as improvisation, is a main ingredient of jazz.

As jazz became popular, it developed new forms. The variety of styles includes Dixieland, swing, big band, bebop, and jazz-rock. Meet a few of the jazz musicians who helped to develop some of these styles.

SPOTLIGHT ON *Jazz Artists*

MEMPHIS MINNIE

Memphis Minnie, a blues singer and guitarist, was born in Algiers, Louisiana. At the age of eight, she arrived in Memphis, Tennessee, where she worked as a street musician. In 1928 she moved with her husband to Chicago. Together they made many successful recordings. Memphis Minnie continued to make popular recordings with other artists for many years. She is best known for the forceful style of her guitar playing and the strong quality of her voice.

132

MEETING **INDIVIDUAL** NEEDS

MULTICULTURAL PERSPECTIVES: *Twelve-Bar Blues*

The term *blues* refers to a melancholy state of mind. The blues may have originated in "hollers," which were improvised work songs that enslaved African Americans in the southern United States sang while they worked in the fields. Blues songs often use pitches not in the major or minor scales. These are called *blue notes*. In particular, the third above the tonal center often sounds somewhere between a minor and major third.

The twelve-bar blues that developed usually consists of this typical chord progression: I I I I IV IV I I V V (or IV) I I. Individual performers vary the rhythm, melody, and harmony to create their own blues styles. (See also Unit 6, Lesson 2, pages 242–243.)

MARY LOU WILLIAMS

The musical style of Mary Lou Williams, a jazz pianist and arranger-composer, strongly influenced modern jazz musicians. During the 1930s, she played with Andy Kirk's band, whose style was a result of Mary Lou Williams's solo performances and compositions. She also wrote arrangements for many popular swing bands of the era, including Benny Goodman's.

meet DOROTHY DONEGAN

Dorothy Donegan, a jazz pianist for nearly fifty years, was recently elected to the Jazz Hall of Fame. Praised for her piano technique, Donegan plays a mixture of different jazz styles.

LISTEN to Dorothy Donegan talk about her playing style.

A Blues Montage CD3:19

1. Learn about jazz artists Memphis Minnie, Mary Lou Williams, and Dorothy Donegan. Have students:

• Tell what improvisation is and why it is so important to jazz. (Improvisation happens when musicians vary musical elements, such as melody or rhythm. This allows musicians to express their individuality and creativity by making up music on the spot. Improvisation is a central feature of jazz.)

• Summarize the musical abilities of each of the jazz artists of "A Blues Montage." (Memphis Minnie is a blues singer and guitarist, Mary Lou Williams is a jazz pianist and arranger-composer, and Dorothy Donegan is a jazz pianist.)

Recorded Lesson CD3:18

• Listen to "Interview with Dorothy Donegan," to hear the jazz pianist's description of her playing style.

ART CONNECTION: *Montage*

VISUAL ARTS

Have students study the treatment of the performers' photographs on pages 132–133. "How has the illustrator added meaning to these photos?" (by combining each photo with images of the musician's instrument) Explain that a picture made of several overlapping images is called a *montage*. Have students create their own portrait montages. Each student should draw one or more objects that they are especially identified with (for example, a musical instrument, a football) and glue a photocopy of their school picture on top of their drawings. Display the montages and discuss the variety of ideas used.

CRITICAL THINKING: *The Roots of Blues*

Ask students to think about the connection between the origin of blues in the United States and the life of enslaved African Americans at the time. Lead students to consider how blues gave people a chance for personal expression. What was this musical form saying about the lives of the people who sang or played it? Students might also share situations in which music has reflected their moods.

ENCORE
MULTICULTURAL PERSPECTIVES

continued from previous page

2. Listen to three blues selections and compare and contrast them. Have students:

• Read about "A Blues Montage."

• Divide into small groups to listen to the montage. (Explain to students that as they listen, they will become "listening detectives," discovering what the three pieces have in common and what is different about them. Each group writes down everything that is the same or similiar and everything that is different. Ask them to be as specific as possible, using musical terminology if they can.)

• Share their finding, recording the information in two columns on the board. (similarities—all 12-bar blues, all use some form of boogie-woogie bass [a melodic, steady-beat bass line]; differences—instrumentation, tempos, melodies, lengths)

Brilliant Corners CD3:20

Learn about Max Roach and listen to him perform "Brilliant Corners." Have students:

• Read about Max Roach and jazz drumming, then listen to "Brilliant Corners," telling how many instruments of the trap set can be heard.

• Choose one instrumental part and play along with body percussion.

• Listen again, singing along with the melody as they are able. (This may take several listenings.)

• Try to follow the drum solo by singing the melody to themselves and lightly patting the beat. (This may be challenging, but encourage students to do the best they can.)

  A Blues Montage

LISTENING

Listen to examples of the twelve-bar blues. Memphis Minnie plays "When the Levee Breaks," Mary Lou Williams plays "Boogie Misterioso," and Dorothy Donegan plays "St. Louis Blues." In this style, popular in the 1930s, the bass plays a variety of patterns. The style became popular again during the early years of rock and roll. How are these selections alike? How are they different?

MAX ROACH

Max Roach, a famous jazz drummer, played an important role in the development of modern jazz. He performed in the 1940s and 1950s with world-famous musicians such as saxophonist Charlie Parker and trumpeter Dizzy Gillespie. During these years, Roach helped create a new style of drumming for bebop jazz. For nearly 40 years, he has continued to play in this tradition.

 Brilliant Corners *by Thelonious Monk*

LISTENING

LISTEN to Max Roach perform in "Brilliant Corners."

The trap set, or drum set, is an important part of a jazz ensemble. The main part of the rhythmic background is carried by the cymbals. Snare drum and tom-toms fill in the background. Occasionally the bass drum plays strong accents. The solo passages usually feature the snare drums.

134 JAZZ

MEETING **INDIVIDUAL** NEEDS

BACKGROUND: *"Brilliant Corners"*

Thelonious Monk once said that when he struck two notes together he was trying to get at the note in between. "Brilliant Corners" shows Monk's attempts at creating new harmonies. When "Brilliant Corners" was recorded, the musicians improvised and pushed their limits, creating a rendition that gives the song its own life. Because Monk pushed, those who played with him did, too. Jazz artist Miles Davis once said that Monk's major contribution was to give musicians "more freedom."

LANGUAGE ARTS CONNECTION: *Music in Life*

Have students write a short essay that responds to the following statement by Keith Jarrett: "Music is a part of life. It is not a separate, controlled event where a musician presents something to a passive audience. It is in the blood."

How many parts of the trap set can you hear the drummer play at the beginning of the piece? Notice how he waits for the saxophone player to pause, then fills in the space with drumming. Now listen to his solo.

 meet
KEITH
JARRETT

Keith Jarrett is best known as a modern jazz pianist. Many of his concerts are on-the-spot improvisations at the piano. He is also skilled at many other kinds of music. In addition to performing and recording classical piano music, he plays soprano saxophone, guitar, recorders, and several different kinds of percussion instruments.

LISTEN to this famous jazz pianist talk about his career and his recording techniques.

 LISTENING **Montage of Performance Styles**

LISTEN to Keith Jarrett play in four different styles.

Keith Jarrett plays the jazz standard "I Hear a Rhapsody," two pieces he composed—"Improvisation: Part 2A," and "Spirits: No. 5," and "Prelude No. 1 in C Major" by J. S. Bach. What is different about the playing styles he uses for each selection?

Encore **135**

Montage of Performance Styles CD3:22

Listen to Keith Jarrett talk about his career and play in four distinct styles.
Have students:

• Read page 135.

Recorded Interview CD3:21

• Listen to "Interview with Keith Jarrett" to hear Jarrett tell about playing the piano and his involvement with different styles of playing.

• Listen to "Montage of Performance Styles" and think about the different styles in each piece. ("I Hear a Rhapsody"—jazz; "Improvisation: Part 2A"—pop/jazz improvisation; "Spirits: No. 5"—Jarrett plays recorders and drums in the style of South American folk music; "Prelude No. 1 in C Major" from *The Well-Tempered Clavier*—music from the 1700s.)

• Write sentences describing each one, then listen as volunteers share their descriptions with the class.

ART CONNECTION: *Color Families* VISUAL ARTS

Have students compare the artwork on these pages with the previous two pages (similar images and design, different colors). "What colors are used on pages 132–133?" (blue green, blue, blue violet, red violet—cool colors) Have students list things in nature that are in cool colors. (ice, sky, water) "What colors are used on pages 134–135?" (red violet, red, red orange, yellow—warm colors) Have students

list things in nature that are in warm colors. (sun, fire, clay, fall leaves) "Why might the artist have chosen to use cool and warm colors to illustrate a lesson on jazz?" (Jazz music expresses many different moods.)

OUR MUSICAL HERITAGE

MULTICULTURAL PERSPECTIVES

Through exposure to diverse materials, students develop an awareness of how people from many cultures create and participate in music. This unit includes:

African/African American
- **Yonder Come Day,** American folk song, 154

Asian/Asian American
- **Tsing Chun U Chü (Youth Dance Song),** Taiwanese folk song, 156
- **Hoe Ana,** Tahitian folk song, 164

European/European American
- **Love Letter to America,** poem by American student Mattie Catherine Johnson, 137
- **Liberty Fanfare,** by American John Williams, 139
- **Away to America,** by Linda Williams, 140
- **El Capitán,** by John Philip Sousa, 145
- **Trav'ler,** by M. Wilson and J. F. Knox, 147
- **Dance for the Nations,** by John Krumm, 150
- **American Dream,** by American Ed Harris, 151
- **Greensleeves,** English folk song, 158
- **Fantasia on Greensleeves,** by British composer Ralph Vaughan Williams, 160
- **Movin' On,** by Raymond R. Hannisian, 174
- **An American Hymn,** song by Americans Lee Holdridge and Molly-Ann Leikin, 178

Hispanic/Hispanic American
- **El tambor,** Panamanian folk song, 142

Native American
- **Taos Round Dance,** Taos Pueblo song, 166
- **Navajo Courtship Song,** 167
- **Whip Man,** poem by Nez Perce Phil George, 168
- **Tekanionton'néha',** Iroquois dance song, 170

For a complete listing of materials by culture throughout the book, see the Classified Index.

UNIT 4

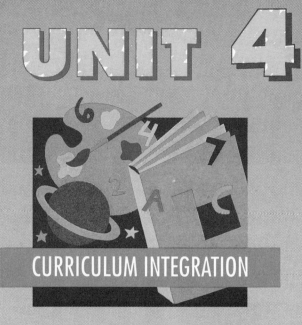

CURRICULUM INTEGRATION

Activities in this unit that promote the integration of music with other curriculum areas include:

Art
- Create a poster of the neighborhood, 153A
- Explore harmony in color and design, 175

Math
- Make a circle graph, 145A
- Find the area of the shaded portion of a circle, 153B
- Classify a triangle, 165A

Reading/Language Arts
- Write a letter describing an imaginary journey, 145A
- Write about one's future self, 153B
- Stage a scene from *Romeo and Juliet,* 161A
- Rewrite lyrics to ''Greensleeves,'' 161B
- Write about a day in a Pacific Ocean journey, 165B

Science
- Identify areas along the Tropic of Cancer, 161A
- Plot active volcanoes on a map, then look for clusters, 165B

Social Studies
- Tell latitude and longitude of three locations; estimate distances, 145B
- Plan and compare two ocean voyages, 145B
- Plan and describe a railroad journey, 153A
- Make a time line of events in sixteenth-century England, 161B
- Plot Pacific islands on a grid, 165A
- Prepare an oral history of music, 169
- Make a family tree, 182

PLANNER

ASSESSMENT OPTIONS

Informal Performance Assessments

Informal Assessments correlated to Objectives are provided in every lesson with Alternate Strategies for reteaching. Frequent informal assessment allows for ongoing progress checks throughout the course of the unit.

Formal Assessment

An assessment form is provided on pupil page 182 and Resource Master 4•6. The questions assess student understanding of the following main unit objectives:

*   Read and perform rhythms in $\frac{6}{8}$ meter
*   Recognize the first five steps of a minor scale

Music Journal

Encourage students to enter thoughts about selections, projects, performances, and personal progress. Some journal opportunities include:

*   Critical Thinking: Composer's Purpose, TE 153
*   Critical Thinking: To Meter or Not to Meter, TE 167
*   *Think It Through,* 169
*   Discuss music that is special to your family, 176

Portfolio Opportunities

Update student portfolios with outcome-based materials, including written work, audiotapes, videotapes, and/or photos that represent their best work for each unit. Some portfolio opportunities in this unit include:

*   Create accompaniments for "Away to America" and "El tambor," 141 (audiotape)
*   Perform "El Capitán" playalong and create patterns, 145 (audiotape)
*   Perform "Tsing Chun U Chü" ostinatos, TE 156, 159 (audiotape)
*   Perform playalong for "Greensleeves," 159 (audiotape)
*   Play I and V chord roots and rhythm patterns with "El tambor," 162–163 (audiotape)
*   Perform accompaniments to "Hoe Ana," 165 (audiotape)
*   Perform Alligator Dance, TE 170–171 (videotape)
*   Play chordal accompaniment to "Movin' On," 174, 177 (audiotape)
*   Play melodic bass line with "An American Hymn," 178 (audiotape)
*   Check It Out, 182 (Resource Master 4•6)
*   Portfolio Assessment (Resource Masters TA•1–5), 182
*   Create, 183
*   Write, 183

			LESSON 1 CORE p.136	LESSON 2 CORE p.146	LESSON 3 p.154
FOCUS			Rhythm	Pitch	Rhythm
SELECTIONS			Love Letter to America (poem) Liberty Fanfare (listening) Away to America El tambor El Capitán (listening)	Travel (poem) Trav'ler Dance for the Nations Tsing Chun U Chü American Dream	Üsküdar Yonder Come Day Tsing Chun U Chü
MUSICAL ELEMENTS	**CONCEPTS**	**UNIT OBJECTIVES** Bold = Tested			
EXPRESSIVE QUALITIES	Dynamics		• Hear *p, mp, mf, f, ff,* and *cresc.*		• Hear and sing *mp*
	Tempo		• Hear allegro • Hear and sing moderato	• Hear and sing moderato and allegro	• Hear and sing andante and allegro • Hear and sing ritardando and fermata
	Articulation		• Hear staccato and legato	• Hear and sing legato	
TONE COLOR	Vocal/Instrumental Tone Color		• Hear solo and group singing • *Accompany poem with instruments*		• Play unpitched percussion
DURATION	Beat/Meter	• **Read and perform rhythms in 6/8 meter** • Read and perform rhythms in 2/4 meter	• **Pat-clap to beat (E)** • **Identify and perform beat divisions in twos and threes (E/D)** • **Create 6/8 and 2/4 rhythmic accompaniments (Rf/Rd/C)**	• Clap-snap to beat	• Perform rhythm patterns in 2/4
	Rhythm		• Create rhythmic accompaniments • Echo 6/8 patterns (I/P/Rd)		• Learn about and clap syncopated rhythms • Pat and play rhythmic accompaniment • Aurally recognize song rhythms • Find ♫ and ties
PITCH	Melody		• *Compose pentatonic accompaniment*	• Sing pitch letter names in bass clef • Learn about melodic motive and recognize in song	
	Harmony	• Play roots of I and V chords • Play I, IV, and V chords • Play bass line		• Sing harmony part	
	Tonality major/minor	• **Recognize first 5 steps of minor scale** • Recognize first 5 steps of major scale • Locate half steps in minor scale		• **Discuss and recognize songs in major and minor (Rf)** • **Locate half steps in first 5 pitches of major and minor scales (Rf)** • **Devise questions to test knowledge of major and minor (Rf)** • Learn about sharp key signatures • Learn D major scale	
DESIGN	Texture		• Add ostinatos to songs	• Sing and move in unison and canon	• Add percussion ostinatos to song
	Form/Structure		• *Make up movement "poem"* • Recognize sections	• Recognize sections in major and minor	• Play ostinatos to show sections
CULTURAL CONTEXT	Style/Background	• Perform Native American dance	• Learn about Panama • *Learn about ancestors' musical traditions* • *Composers: John Williams, Linda Williams, John Philip Sousa*	• *Poet: Edna St. Vincent Millay* • *Songwriters: Jane Foster Knox and Mark Wilson*	• *Learn about Georgia Sea Islands and their singing style* • *Learn about "Tsing Chun U Chü"*

Learning Sequence: E = Explore, D = Describe, I = Identify, P = Practice, Rf = Reinforce, Rd = Read, C = Create   See also *Program Scope and Sequence,* page 432.

OVERVIEW

Italic = Meeting Individual Needs

LESSON 4 CORE p.158	LESSON 5 CORE p.162	LESSON 6 p.166	LESSON 7 p.172	LESSON 8 p.176
Rhythm, § meter	Pitch/Harmony	Style	Harmony	Harmony
El tambor Tsing Chun U Chü Greensleeves Fantasia on Greensleeves (listening)	Greensleeves El tambor Hoe Ana	Taos Round Dance (listening) Navajo Courtship Song (listening) Whip Man (poem) Tekanionton'néha' (Alligator Dance) (listening)	Taos Round Dance (listening) Hoe Ana Yonder Come Day Movin' On	Away to America Movin' On An American Hymn
			• Sing *diminuendo*	• Sing *diminuendo, crescendo*
• Hear and sing andante, moderato	• Hear and sing andante, moderato		• Hear and sing andante, moderato, allegro	• Hear and sing moderato, allegro
• Hear legato, staccato				• Hear and sing ritardando and fermata
• Perform percussion and pitched instrument playalongs	• Play pitched and unpitched instrumental ostinatos • Recognize, learn about, and play ukulele	• Hear and imitate Navajo vocal tone color	• Play chords on pitched instruments • *Play recorder and handbell accompaniment*	• Play pitched instruments with song
• **Recognize ⁴₄, ³₄, and §₈ meters (Rf/Rd)** • **Distinguish beat divisions (Rf)** • **Create §₈ ostinatos (C)**	• **Play §₈ ostinatos (Rf/Rd)** • *Move to §₈ beat (Rf)* • *Play chords to beat*	• Discover meter in Native American songs • Pat to beat	• Step to beat	• Play one pitch per measure in ²₄
• Recognize song from rhythm • Recognize ♫♫♫ and ♫♫ • Perform rhythmic playalong • Clap rhythms including ♪♫	• Play rhythmic ostinatos • *Pat-clap rhythm patterns*		• Speak song rhythms	
• Perform melodic playalong	• Sing pitch letter names in bass clef • *Aurally recognize whole and half steps*			• Play melodic bass line • Sing pitch letter names of melody
	• Perform I and V chord roots with songs • *Play I and V chord roots in C, F, G, D* • *Play chords with song*		• Discuss presence or absence of harmony in songs • Perform chord roots with song • Play I, IV, and V chords	• Learn about and play chord inversions • Play I, IV, V chords • Play melodic bass line
	• **Aurally recognize minor (Rf)** • **Recognize location of half and whole steps in major and minor scales (Rf)**	• Try to identify tonality in Native American song	• ***Create section in minor for song (C)***	• Recognize major scale
• Add playalong to song	• Add pitched and unpitched playalongs	• Recognize texture • Recognize solo and group singing	• Compare song textures • Add ostinatos to song	• Add playalong to song
• Identify A B A form • *Create ostinatos to show form*		• Recognize solo and group sections and sing responses	• *Compose section for song*	• Play repeating phrases with song
• *Composer: Ralph Vaughan Williams* • *Learn about Renaissance music*	• *Learn about Tahiti and "Hoe Ana"*	• Learn Navajo singing style • Learn Iroquois dance • *Learn about Navajo nation* • *Poet: Phil George* • *Learn about poem "Whip Man" and oral history* • *Learn about Iroquois*	• *Learn about gospel choir step* • *Learn about harmony in art*	• Discuss music special to their family

SKILLS

SKILLS		LESSON 1 CORE p.136	LESSON 2 CORE p.146	LESSON 3 p.154
CREATION AND PERFORMANCE	Singing	• Sing moderato • *Practice singing in tune*	• Sing in unison and canon • Sing moderato and allegro • Sing legato	• Sing *mp* • Sing andante and allegro • Sing ritardando and fermata • *Learn breathing for chest voice*
	Playing	• Pat-clap to beat • Perform beat divisions in twos and threes • Play along with listening • *Accompany poem with instruments*	• *Play bell accompaniment* • *Play whole and half steps on keyboard*	• Clap song rhythm • Pat and play percussion accompaniment
	Moving	• *Create movement for poem* • *Move to song*	• Move in unison and canon	• *Move to song*
	Improvising/ Creating	• Create rhythmic accompaniments • *Create movement and pentatonic accompaniment for poem* • *Create movement for song*	• Create phrases to remember order of sharps • Create questions to test knowledge of major and minor	• *Create movement for song*
NOTATION	Reading	• Read and perform rhythmic accompaniments	• Tell key from signature • Read pitch letter names in bass clef • Create phrases to remember order of sharps • Identify major and minor from notated pitches	• Read rhythmic accompaniment • Find ♫ and ties in notation
	Writing	• Create rhythmic patterns and organize notation to match them • Discuss notation for listening		• Organize notation to match song
PERCEPTION AND ANALYSIS	Listening/ Describing/ Analyzing	• Identify division of beat into threes	• Describe difference between major and minor • Identify motive in song • Identify major and minor • Create questions to test knowledge of major and minor	• Aurally identify song rhythms

 **TECHNOLOGY**

SHARE THE MUSIC VIDEOS

Use videos to reinforce, extend, and enrich learning.
• **Lesson 1, pp. 138–142: Creating Musical Moods (movie composer); The Mariachi Tradition (Mexican folk music)**
• **Lesson 2, pp. 151–153: Signing, Grades 3–6 (American Dream)**
• **Lesson 7, pp. 172–175: Making a Music Video (harmony)**

MUSIC WITH *MIDI*

MIDI technology allows students to manipulate musical elements and make musical decisions with these songs:
• **Lesson 4, p. 158: Greensleeves**

MUSICTIME™

This notational software develops students' music reading and writing skills through activities correlated to these lessons:
• **Lesson 1, Project 1 (create an accompaniment for El tambor)**
• **Lesson 5, Project 2 (add a I–V accompaniment to a song)**
• **Lesson 7, Project 3 (add a I–IV–V accompaniment to a song)**
• **Lesson 9, Project 4 (compose a melody for a poem)**

OVERVIEW

LESSON 4 CORE p.158	LESSON 5 CORE p.162	LESSON 6 p.166	LESSON 7 p.172	LESSON 8 p.176
• Sing andante, moderato • *Expand vocal range*	• Sing andante, moderato • Sing pitch letter names in bass clef	• Imitate Native American singing styles	• Sing *diminuendo* • Sing andante, moderato, allegro	• Sing *diminuendo, crescendo* • Sing moderato, allegro • Sing ritardando and fermata
• Pat-clap beat and beat divisions • Perform percussion and pitched instrument playalongs	• Play pitched and unpitched instrumental ostinatos • *Play ukulele chords*		• Play chords on pitched instruments • *Improvise on barred instruments* • *Play recorder, handbell, and guitar accompaniments*	• Play pitched instrument chords and bass line with songs
	• *Play cup game* • *Move to song*	• Perform Iroquois dance	• *Move to song*	• *Move to song*
• *Create ostinatos for listening*		• *Create notation for Native American music*	• *Create section for song*	
• Read melodic and rhythmic playalongs • Find ♫♫ and ♫♪ in notation • Read rhythms with ♫	• Read melodic and rhythmic playalongs • Tell key from signature • Tell tonality from notated pitches • Read bass clef			• Read chord notation • Read pitched playalong • Read pitch letter names of melody
		• *Find ways to notate Native American music*		
• Aurally identify meter • Identify A B A form	• Aurally identify minor • *Aurally identify whole and half steps*	• Hear and analyze Native American rhythm and pitch • Identify texture • Listen for soloist and sing response	• Describe presence or absence of harmony in songs	

UNIT 4 PLANNER

MUSIC ACE™

Music Ace reinforces musical concepts and provides ear-training opportunities for students.
- **Lesson 2, p. 146: Lesson 24 (major scale intervals)**
- **Lesson 8, p. 176: Lesson 10 (ledger lines); Lesson 24 (major scale)**

UNIT FOUR
LESSON 1

RELATED ARTS | MOVEMENT | THEATER | VISUAL ARTS |

LESSON PLANNER

FOCUS Rhythm

OBJECTIVE

OBJECTIVE 1 Read and perform patterns in ⅜ and ²⁄₄ to accompany a recording (tested)

MATERIALS

Recordings
Listening: Liberty Fanfare (excerpt) by J. Williams	CD3:23
Away to America	CD3:24
Recorded Lesson: ⅜ Rhythm Patterns	CD3:25
El tambor (The Drum)	CD3:26
Recorded Lesson: Pronunciation for "El tambor"	CD3:27
Listening: El Capitán by J.P. Sousa	CD3:28

Instruments
drumsticks and/or unpitched percussion instruments

Resources
Resource Master 4 • 1 (practice)
Resource Master 4 • 2 (practice)
Musical Instruments Master—
  sousaphone
Orff Orchestration O • 6 (El tambor)
Playing the Guitar G • 13 (⅜ meter)
Recorder Master R • 15 (pitches D F G A
  B C' D')

▶ = **BASIC PROGRAM**

UNIT 4 OUR MUS

136

MEETING **INDIVIDUAL** NEEDS

BUILDING SELF-ESTEEM: *Cultural Contributions*

This unit offers a good opportunity to emphasize that many cultures have contributed to the music of the United States. Every student can feel proud of his or her ancestors' contributions both here and in their native lands. To further build self-esteem, have students research various musical traditions at the library and through interviews. Then have them learn a song or two from each tradition and present the songs in a musical extravaganza with student-written narration. The narration could explain what the song means to people in this country and in its country of origin.

PLAYING INSTRUMENTS: *"Love Letter to America"*

Have students set up resonator bells in the key of A minor pentatonic (remove Bs and Fs). Then use pitched and un-pitched instruments to create a "sound carpet" to accompany "Love Letter to America." (Tell students to choose sounds that will highlight the meaning of the words.) This can be a group assignment. Divide the poem into three sections and have each of the three groups create the sound carpet for their section.

CAL HERITAGE

Love Letter to AMERICA

Dear America
    I love 10 things about you:
Your combination of cultures,
Your beautiful oceans,
Your mystical forests,
Your majestic mountains,
Your big cities,
Your small towns,
The way you open your arms
To anyone who cares to enter,
Your lovely snowflakes in the winter,
Your warm sunshine in the summer,
Your gentle breezes,
Your windy gales,
    I love you, America.
                Forever yours,

—*Mattie Catherine Johnson*

"Do you know anyone who immigrated to this country?" Have students:

▶ • Discuss why any immigrants they know moved to the United States. (Students whose family histories originated in other countries may wish to share what they know about their roots.)

▶ • Read "Love Letter to America" and briefly discuss the feelings expressed in the poem.

"In this unit, you'll be singing songs that are now heard in the United States but came from many different cultures."

MOVEMENT: *"Love Letter to America"*

Have students take individual words from the poem that seem to have either a specific movement or design image and work with those words to form a movement "poem." One group can perform the movement as the rest of the class performs the "sound carpet" described in *Playing Instruments* at the bottom of page 136.

Following the performance, have students discuss how each participant felt as he or she worked cooperatively on the choreography, performed for peers, and then watched the

work of others. Encourage students to be honest in their sharing, and assure them that there are no "right" answers. Help them become aware of the expressive nature of the experience and ways that it might benefit other aspects of their lives, for example, their emotional well-being.

UNIT FOUR
LESSON 1

continued from previous page

2 DEVELOP

1. Introduce "Liberty Fanfare" CD3:23. Feel the beat. Have students:

▶ • Read pages 138–139 and listen to "Liberty Fanfare," maintaining the steady beat with a pat-clap pattern.

▶ • Briefly discuss the contributions of different immigrants to this country.

Coming to

"Love Letter to America" was written by Mattie Johnson, a seventh-grade student in Northfield, Minnesota. How does Mattie's letter compare with your feelings about the United States?

MEETING **INDIVIDUAL** NEEDS

BIOGRAPHY: *John Williams*

American composer John Williams (b. 1932) has written many hit movie soundtracks, including *Jaws* (1975) and *Superman* (1979). In 1977 he composed the music for both *Star Wars* and *Close Encounters of the Third Kind*. When both scores were nominated for an Academy Award (Best Original Score), Williams was forced to compete against himself! *Star Wars* won, giving him one of the four Oscars he has taken home over the years. A well-known conductor as well, in 1980 Williams succeeded Arthur Fiedler as conductor of the Boston Pops.

BACKGROUND: *The Statue of Liberty*

VISUAL ARTS

France gave the 151-foot-high statue, named *Liberty Enlightening the World*, to the United States in 1884 as an expression of friendship and as a monument to U.S. independence. Liberty was portrayed by French sculptor Frédéric-Auguste Bartholdi (**fre** de ɾik o **gŭst bar tol** di) as a proud woman carrying a torch. The statue was placed on Bedloe's Island (now called Liberty Island) in New York Harbor. Over the years, it has become a symbol of the United States. Millions of immigrants first saw the weathered copper statue as they entered the United

America

People have come to the United States from many parts of the world. With them, they have brought art, literature, and music. Imagine what music from Panama, Taiwan, England, and Tahiti might sound like. Think of the music of Native Americans, whose ancestors came to North America long before the Europeans.

LISTENING

Liberty Fanfare (excerpt)
by John Williams

In this piece, an American composer celebrates freedom. As you listen, notice that each beat can be divided into smaller parts. The chart below shows beats divided into twos and threes.

PERFORM these beat divisions.

The United States of America has been called the Nation of Immigrants. It has welcomed more newcomers than any other country. Some come to avoid poverty or starvation, some to escape being treated unjustly, and some because war made it impossible to live in their native country. Others come to find adventure or to join family members.

In the late 1800s, many newcomers to our country came from the British Isles, Germany, and Scandinavia. They traveled to America by ship, and entered the country through New York Harbor.

2. Divide beats into twos and threes. Have students:

• Perform the beat-division exercise. (Form two groups. Group 1 will pat with the beat, shown by the thin, light blue rectangles. Group 2, shown by the dark blue rectangles or squares, will clap, dividing the beat, first into two equal parts and then into three equal parts. Repeat the pattern shown four times.)

States at nearby Ellis Island, an immigration station until 1954. To them, the statue was a symbol of freedom and the better life they hoped to find in this country. Both the Statue of Liberty and Ellis Island are now national monuments run by the National Park Service.

UNIT FOUR
LESSON 1

continued from previous page

3. Introduce "Away to America" CD3:24.
Feel the divisions of the beat in 6/8 meter.
Have students:

▶ • Clap with the accented beat and snap the unaccented beats as they listen to the recording.
(As they listen, ask them to try to discover
how many divisions they hear within each
beat.)

▶ • Tell how many divisions they hear within
each beat. (3)

▶ • Sing "Away to America." (The refrain countermelody is included below. When students
are secure singing melody and countermelody
separately, have them sing both parts together.)

▶ • Listen as volunteers tell the story of "Away
to America" in their own words.

Words and Music by Linda Williams

140 COMING TO AMERICA

MEETING **INDIVIDUAL** NEEDS

VOCAL DEVELOPMENT: *Singing in Tune*

One of the most important components in the process of
singing in tune is for students to *listen*. Sometimes they
sing with such enthusiasm that they do not listen to themselves or others around them. One way to correct this is to
put a student who is having pitch problems between two
very strong, on-pitch singers. Tell the middle student to
"listen as loudly as you sing." Often, singing more softly
and listening to others singing on pitch helps a student sing
the correct pitch. Use this procedure as students sing
"Away to America."

SPECIAL LEARNERS: *Rhythm Accompaniments*

Have all students practice tapping the ♩ 𝄽 and ♩ 𝄽 patterns
with "Away to America" and "El tambor" (p. 142) before
creating rhythmic accompaniments or performing the different patterns in 6/8 or 2/4 meter. Since these patterns sound
identical when clapped without the music, students need
only clap on the first beat in either meter to perform successfully. Tell students that they may change to the "beat-
rest" pattern at any time while reading the rhythm patterns
or clapping a rhythmic accompaniment. Select students
who are able to clap the beat-rest patterns to play percussion instruments.

Recorded Lesson CD3:25

▶ • Listen to "⅜ Rhythm Patterns" and echo each one-beat pattern on page 141, using body percussion.

• As a class, create a four-measure rhythmic accompaniment to "Away to America," using the two-beat building blocks on page 141. (Optional: Students can cut up and organize the rhythmic building blocks on **Resource Master 4 • 1**.)

• Take turns performing the rhythmic accompaniment as the rest of the class sings the song.

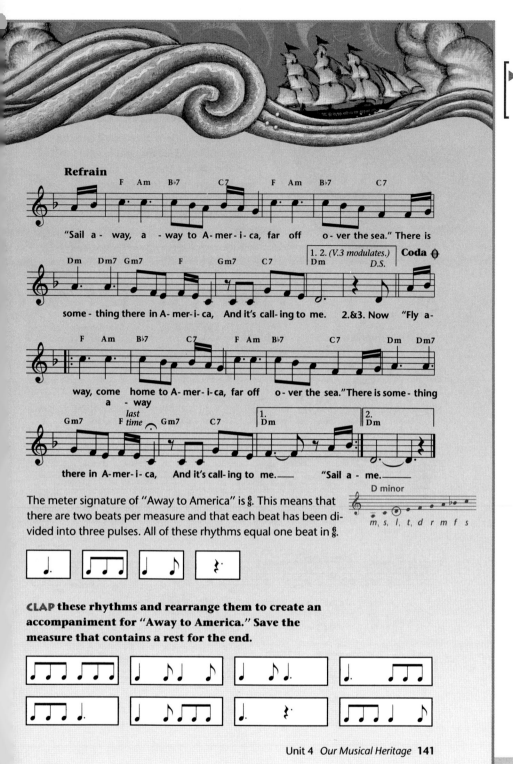

Refrain

"Sail a - way, a - way to A - mer - i - ca, far off o - ver the sea." There is some - thing there in A - mer - i - ca, And it's call - ing to me. 2.&3. Now "Fly a - way, come home to A - mer - i - ca, far off o - ver the sea." There is some - thing a - way there in A - mer - i - ca, And it's call - ing to me.— "Sail a - me.—

The meter signature of "Away to America" is ⅜. This means that there are two beats per measure and that each beat has been divided into three pulses. All of these rhythms equal one beat in ⅜.

D minor
m, s, l, t, d r m f s

CLAP these rhythms and rearrange them to create an accompaniment for "Away to America." Save the measure that contains a rest for the end.

Unit 4 *Our Musical Heritage* 141

BIOGRAPHY: *Linda Williams*

American composer Linda Williams (b. 1931) is well known for her children's songs and other compositions. She studied music at Brigham Young University, winning a national contest for a set of piano pieces she composed while still a student. She has since written all kinds of music, from theater music to sonatas. Her advice to young composers? Listen to the music of great composers while studying the score. This is one of the best ways to learn about composition and how to write for different instruments.

"Away to America" was written about Linda Williams's grandfather, John Evans, who came to America from Wales in the late 1800s when he was 12 years old. John Evans's family settled in Colorado, where he later married a woman who was the daughter of English immigrants. (Ms. Williams is not related to John Williams, the composer of "Liberty Fanfare.")

UNIT FOUR
LESSON 1

continued from previous page

5. Introduce "El tambor" CD3:26. **Feel the beat in ²⁄₄ meter.** Have students:

▶ • Clap with the accented beat and snap with the unaccented beat as they listen to the recording.

Recorded Lesson CD3:27
▶ • Listen to "Pronunciation for 'El tambor.'"

▶ • Sing the song.

MUSIC ENRICHES US

The contributions of different cultures have enriched life for people who live in the United States. "El tambor" was brought north from Panama. Clap the strong beat and snap the weak beat as you listen to this song.

EL TAMBOR
THE DRUM

Panamanian Folk Song

Refrain

Spanish: El tam-bor, el tam-bor, el tam-bor de a-le-grí-a. Yo
Pronunciation: el tam bor el tam bor el tam bor ðe a le gri a yo
English: El tam-bor, el tam-bor, el tam-bor the drum of glad-ness, I

Fine **Verse** *Solo*

quie-ro que tú me lle-ves el tam-bor de a-le-grí-a. O Jua-
kye ro ke tu me ye ßes el tam bor ðe a le gri a o xwa
want you to give me the— drum, el tam-bor the drum of glad-ness. Oh Jua-

ni-ta o Jua-ni-ta, Jua-ni-ta a-mi-ga mí-a
ni ta o xwa ni ta xwa ni ta a mi ga mi a
ni-ta, oh Jua-ni-ta, Jua-ni-ta my friend, a-mi-ga

Group *D.C. al Fine*

Yo quie-ro que tú me lle-ves el tam-bor de a-le-grí-a.
yo kye ro ke tu me ye ßes el tam bor ðe a le gri a
I want you to give me the—— drum, el tam-bor the drum of glad-ness.

142 COMING TO AMERICA

MEETING **INDIVIDUAL** NEEDS

MULTICULTURAL PERSPECTIVES: *"El tambor"*

This lively piece from Panama accompanies the tamborito (tɑm bo ɾi to), a popular two-step dance from that country. The tamborito is traditionally danced by couples in colorful costumes. The word *tambor* in the dance can refer either to a drum or to the name of the dance.

ORFF: *"El tambor"*

See **O·6** in *Orchestrations for Orff Instruments.*

PRONUNCIATION: *"El tambor"*

ɑ father	e chaotic i bee o obey
u moon	ß b without lips touching ð the
ɾ flipped r	x slightly guttural h, *Spanish* bajo

MOVEMENT: *"El tambor"*

Have students create their own dances.

Preparation: Students individually explore how to do a step-close-step movement (the basic two-step). They can move forward and backward, side to side, in place,

Let's review some of the rhythms you already know. Clap each of the following rhythmic building blocks.

ORGANIZE the building blocks in your own order to accompany "El tambor." Use the block that contains a quarter rest as the last measure to give the accompaniment the feeling of an ending.

This art is based on Panamanian pottery designs.

6. Read and perform rhythm patterns in $\frac{2}{4}$ to "El tambor." Have students:

• Read and clap the $\frac{2}{4}$ rhythmic building blocks on page 143.

• As a class, create a four-measure rhythmic accompaniment to "El tambor," using the rhythmic building blocks on page 143. (Optional: Students can cut up and organize the rhythmic building blocks on **Resource Master 4 · 2**.)

• Take turns performing the rhythmic accompaniment as the rest of the class sings the song.

---

traveling through space, and turning, but the feet should always move like this:

step close step

Then, using the same step, they should explore possible variations with a partner. Have them try holding hands and not holding hands, facing one another, standing side by side with the same body facing or opposite body facings, and moving away from partner and coming back toward partner.

Final form:

Refrain (8 measures)—Create dance with partner, using the guidelines in the Preparation.

Verse (8 measures)—Leave partner and do own step, returning to partner in time for the refrain.

Advanced version: Do the first refrain with partner and the first verse by oneself. Then, on the next refrain, improvise with whomever is close by at the end of the first verse. Repeat refrain-verse-refrain pattern.

UNIT FOUR
LESSON 1

continued from previous page

3 APPLY

1. Introduce "El Capitán" CD3:28. **Aurally distinguish between § and ⅔.** Have students:

▶ • Listen to "El Capitán" (ɛl ka pi **tan**), showing the steady beat and meter by performing a pat-clap pattern.

• Identify the section of the piece that has the beat divided into twos and the section that has the beat divided into threes.

• Without the recording, read and clap the rhythmic accompaniment to the march (each box is one beat, white boxes are rests), stressing the beats marked with an accent mark (>). (Optional: Use drum sticks or other unpitched percussion instruments.)

• Perform the playalong with "El Capitán."

• Discuss how the red section, which is in §, should be notated. (dotted quarter notes and dotted quarter rests for each beat)

2. Create and play a rhythmic accompaniment to "El Capitán." Have students:

• Use the rhythmic patterns for "Away to America" and "El tambor" to create and write down a rhythmic accompaniment to each section of the march. (Optional: Students can cut up and organize the rhythmic building blocks on **Resource Masters 4 • 1** and **4 • 2**.)

OBJECTIVE 1 Informal Assessment
• Read and perform their rhythmic accompaniment to the recording with drumsticks or unpitched percussion instruments.

Spotlight on *John Philip* SOUSA

The Granger Collection

John Philip Sousa (1854–1932) was an American bandmaster and composer who gave concerts all over the United States and Canada. His marches became so famous that he became known throughout the world as the "March King." Sousa wrote many popular marches, including "The Stars and Stripes Forever" and "The Liberty Bell." Sousa had the idea for a tuba with a circular shape that could be carried over the player's shoulder in a marching band. This instrument is now called the sousaphone.

144

MEETING **INDIVIDUAL** NEEDS

ALTERNATE TEACHING STRATEGY

OBJECTIVE 1 Clap some § rhythm patterns for students once through. Then have them echo-clap the patterns after you. Repeat with ⅔. Finally, lead students in performing the rhythm patterns or choose students who have mastered the patterns to lead the group.

You might also have students perform their accompaniments at a slower tempo without the recording. Gradually have them increase tempo until they are ready to perform their accompaniment parts with the recording.

BIOGRAPHY: *John Philip Sousa*

John Philip Sousa (1854–1932) was an American bandmaster and composer. Today, he is remembered for the marches and operettas he composed. As a child, Sousa played the violin in a dance band. Later, he led the U.S. Marine Corps Band. Sousa expected his players to work hard, and under his leadership, the band became one of the best in the country. Later, Sousa formed his own band, and they traveled throughout the world, playing his marches as well as the music of other composers.

El Capitán *by John Philip Sousa*

LISTENING

This march comes from Sousa's operetta El Capitán, composed in 1896. An operetta is a musical play with singing and spoken words.

PERFORM a playalong with this well-known march. **Which part of the piece has beats divided into threes? Twos?** red; blue

Play three times

Unit 4 *Our Musical Heritage* **145**

4 CLOSE

"Today, we performed rhythm patterns in ⅛ and ¾." Have students:

▶ • Identify the division of the beat in each of these meter signatures. (⅛ has division of the beat into threes; ¾ has division of the beat into twos.)

"Throughout this unit, you will continue to work with these different divisions of the beat to accompany some of the different music that has come together in the United States."

LESSON SUMMARY

Informal Assessment In this lesson, students:

OBJECTIVE 1 Read and performed ⅛ and ¾ patterns to accompany "El Capitán."

MORE MUSIC: Reinforcement

"Haiku Calendar," page 284 (accompany poem)
"Jarabe tapatío," page 328 (⅛; Mexican immigrants)
"De colores," page 328 (⅛; Mexican immigrants)
"Down in the Valley," *Songs to Sing and Read,* page 31 (⅛)
"Git Along, Little Dogies," *Songs to Sing and Read,* page 38 (⅛)
"Haul Away, Joe," *Songs to Sing and Read,* page 44 (⅛)
"List to the Bells," *Songs to Sing and Read,* page 60 (⅛)

COOPERATIVE LEARNING: *"El Capitán"*

Have students work in groups of three or four to create an unpitched percussion accompaniment to show changes in the ⅛ and ¾ sections of "El Capitán." Set a time limit of 10 minutes. Then work as a class to choose a class pattern for each section. Everyone should play the final accompaniment, using drumsticks, unpitched instruments, or substitute percussion such as pens or spoons. Possible roles are:

Facilitator—makes sure everyone gives ideas until each accompaniment has been created.

Echo—replays each idea suggested by patting on knees or table.

Player—plays proposed rhythms on an unpitched instrument, leads the group in the final accompaniment.

Checker—keeps the beat and makes sure the correct rhythm is being played for each section.

ACROSS the

MATHEMATICS

CIRCLE GRAPHS

"Love Letter to America"

GROUP   **15–30 MIN**

MATERIALS: compass, drawing paper, scissors, crayons, tape

Students work in groups of four to brainstorm a list of 10 favorite places in the United States—places they have visited or places they hope to visit.

From that list, each student picks his or her favorite. They show the results of their decisions on a circle graph. To do so, they use a compass to draw a large circle. They cut out the circle and fold it in half, twice, to make four equal sections. Each student labels one section with her or his favorite place. If more than one student picks the same place, they should label adjoining sections.

Students can color the sections to show decisions, a different color for each place. They can tape the circle to drawing paper and label sections clearly along the outside.

COMPREHENSION STRATEGIES: Compare and contrast, displaying information

LANGUAGE ARTS

WRITING A LETTER

"Away to America"

INDIVIDUAL   **15–30 MIN**

Have students imagine that they are the Grandfather in the song (or some other person making the trip to America on a long ocean voyage).

Have them write letters back home to describe their journeys across the Atlantic Ocean and their trips by railroad to Denver. They should include their reactions to the difficult journey and to their new land. They may also include in the letter a reason why they made the journey and why they feel the journey will be worthwhile.

COMPREHENSION STRATEGY: Expressing main ideas

CURRICULUM

DISTANCES

"Away to America"

PAIR 15–30 MIN

MATERIALS: globe, tape measure

Have students locate "Grandfather's" route on a globe. Working in pairs, have them find Bristol. Assume that "Grandfather" landed in New York City and took the railroad to Denver, Colorado. Have students find these other locations.

Then have them sum up the route by giving the latitude and longitude of each of the three locations. Then have them use a tape measure (or string) to compare the distances of the two lengths of the journey: Bristol to New York and New York to Denver. (Simplify by assuming straight-line routes.) Have them estimate what fraction or whole number could be used to show the relationship of the two distances. (Bristol to New York is twice the distance of New York to Denver, or, New York to Denver is about half the distance of Bristol to New York.)

COMPREHENSION STRATEGY: Compare and contrast

SOCIAL STUDIES

PANAMA CANAL

"El tambor"

PAIR 15–30 MIN

MATERIALS: globe, tape measure

Have students work in pairs to make an imaginary ocean voyage from Bristol, England, to San Francisco. Have them plan two voyages: one that assumes the Panama Canal was not built and the other that takes them through the Panama Canal.

For both voyages, have them write a description of the directions in which they are going, including names of the places they are sailing past (that is, to the west of South America, and so on).

Then have them use string to compare the lengths of the two trips. What fraction or whole number can show the relationship between the two lengths? (Answers may vary. The Canal cuts the distance roughly in half.)

COMPREHENSION STRATEGY: Compare and contrast

ACROSS THE CURRICULUM

UNIT FOUR
LESSON 2

RELATED ARTS MOVEMENT | THEATER | VISUAL ARTS

LESSON PLANNER

FOCUS Pitch

OBJECTIVES

OBJECTIVE 1 Signal to identify minor and major (tested)

OBJECTIVE 2 Signal to identify whole and half steps in the major and minor scales (tested)

MATERIALS
Recordings

Recorded Lesson: Two Versions of "America"	CD3:29
Trav'ler	CD3:30
Trav'ler (performance mix)	CD3:31
Dance for the Nations	CD3:32
Tsing Chun U Chü (Youth Dance Song)	CD3:33
American Dream	CD4:1
American Dream (performance mix)	CD4:2
Recorded Lesson: Major and Minor Scales	CD4:3

Instruments keyboard or resonator bells

Resources
Recorder Master R •16 (pitches D E F G A D')
Signing Master S • 6 • 3 (American Dream)

VOCABULARY
motive

▶ = **BASIC PROGRAM**

TRAVELING ON

Travel

The railroad track is miles away,
And the day is loud with voices speaking,
Yet there isn't a train goes by all day
But I hear its whistles shrieking.

All night there isn't a train goes by,
Though the night is still for sleep and dreaming
But I see its cinders red on the sky
And hear its engine steaming.

My heart is warm with the friends I make,
And better friends I'll not be knowing,
Yet there isn't a train I wouldn't take,
No matter where it's going.

—Edna St. Vincent Millay

146

MEETING **INDIVIDUAL** NEEDS

BIOGRAPHY: *Edna St. Vincent Millay*

American poet Edna St. Vincent Millay (1892–1950) grew up in Maine in a family that encouraged her to write. Her widowed mother could not afford to send her to college, but when she was 19, Millay wrote "Renascence," a poem that was selected for a poetry anthology. The poem attracted the attention of other writers, and a family friend offered to send Millay to college. She graduated from Vassar in 1917, the same year her first book of poems was published.

After graduation, Millay went to live in Greenwich Village in New York City, where she was one of a group of free-thinking actors, artists, and writers called Bohemians. She wrote and acted in plays while continuing to write poems. She also got involved in social and political causes and was once arrested during a protest. Her talent and independence soon made the poet famous, and she became a symbol of the bold 1920s woman. In 1923 Millay won the Pulitzer Prize for her third book of poems. The same year, she got married and moved to upstate New York, where she lived for the rest of her life, writing poems in a shack near her house.

TRAV'LER

Music by Mark Wilson
Words by Jane Foster Knox

1. Would you like to be a trav'-ler sail-ing far____ a-cross the
2. We will sure-ly find en-chant-ment, in a land____ so far a-

sea?   I can take you on a jour-ney, to a place where you have longed to
way.   But we fail to see the splen-dor that sur-rounds us ev'-ry

Part 1

be,   For oth-er lands seem so much more ex-ci-ting!____ Our spir-its
day.   For beau-ty blooms where it is plan-ted!____ It

Part 2

soar with ev'-ry pass-ing mile;   and won- d'rous beau- ty
shines in cor-ners we ig- nore,   and waits for us to

calls to us, "Come pause____ and rest a-while." } So close   your
slow our step; to pause____ and to ex- plore. }

So close your

So close your

"We are going to listen to two versions of a song you already know." Have students:

Recorded Lesson CD3:29

▶ • Listen to "Two Versions of 'America,'" in which they hear the song played in major and minor and describe the difference they notice between the two versions. (First is major; second is minor. Students may say that the two versions actually have different melodies; some may know and use the terms *minor* and *major*.)

"The two versions of the melody were constructed using two different scales. Today you're going to find out why these scales are important when creating melodies."

2 DEVELOP

1. Introduce "Travel" and "Trav'ler" CD3:30. **Compare text of "Trav'ler" to "Away to America."** Have students:

▶ • Read and discuss the meaning of the poem "Travel."

▶ • Read the text of "Trav'ler" and discuss how the message of this song relates to the text of "Away to America" (pp. 140–141). (Both songs tell of someone heading to a far-off land in search of adventure.)

▶ • Listen to the recording of "Trav'ler."

▶ • Sing the melody.

BIOGRAPHIES: *Jane Foster Knox and Mark Wilson*

Jane Foster Knox (b. 1926) is an American lyricist and musician in Lincoln, Nebraska. Her career as a lyricist began when she sent a poem and a holiday cake to her friends. One of the friends was a composer who set the poem to music and published it as a song entitled "A Christmas Reflection." Knox met Mark Wilson in 1977, and the two have since collaborated on more than 50 choral works. For most of their songs, including "Trav'ler," Wilson first composes a melody. Knox listens to it, hears where the music leads her imagination, and then writes words that fit the melody.

American composer Mark Wilson (b. 1952) began to study piano at an early age. He soon began improvising his own music, often recording his improvisations so he could remember what they sounded like. While in college, Wilson attended a summer music workshop, where he turned an improvised song into his first written composition. The song was accepted for publication right away, and Wilson has been composing ever since. Like most of his music, "Trav'ler" began as an improvisation. Along with composing, Wilson teaches music and serves as music director at a church in Maryland.

UNIT FOUR
LESSON 2

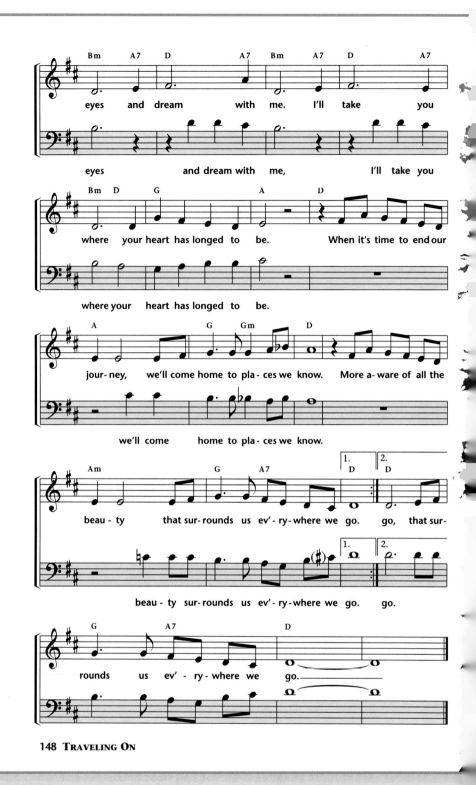

148 TRAVELING ON

continued from previous page

2. Note the key signature of "Trav'ler" and identify pitches of D major scale. Have students:

• Recall what a sharp does to a pitch. (raises it a half step)

▶ • Read about the key signature of "Trav'ler" and about key signatures with sharps.

• Learn the order of the sharps.

• Find the pitches of the D major scale on the keyboard in their books.

3. Explore pitch letter names in the bass clef and sing "Trav'ler" in two parts. Have students:

• Tell what the bass clef is used for. (To notate low pitches; see pages 124–125.) Look at Part 2 and notice that it is written in the bass clef, then try reading the pitch letter names of notes in the first three lines of Part 2 on page 147. (G, A, B, C♯, D E)

• Sing Part 2 (for cambiata voices). (When students are secure singing both parts separately, have them sing both parts together.)

MEETING **INDIVIDUAL** NEEDS

PLAYING INSTRUMENTS: *"Trav'ler" Bell Part*

Have students add this resonator-bell part written by Mark Wilson to "Trav'ler." The bells always enter on the word *close* of the phrase *So close your eyes and dream with me.*

Introduction
(not in Pupil book)

A MAJOR JOURNEY

The melody of "Trav'ler" is in D major. Notice that the key signature has two sharps.

In major keys with sharps in their key signatures, the last sharp is *ti*. A half step up from this sharp is the pitch that gives the key its name. The last sharp in this key signature is C♯; this tells you that the name of the key is D major.

The sharps in a key signature always fall in the same order. Remember the order of sharps by saying:

Father **C**harles **G**oes **D**own **A**nd **E**nds **B**attle

What is the sequence of the whole and half steps in the D major scale? W W H W W W H

4. Review whole and half steps in the major scale. Have students:

• Answer the question about half steps and whole steps. (Remind students that a half step on the keyboard is the distance between two keys that have no other key between them. A whole step is the distance between two keys that are separated by one other key.)

ENRICHMENT: *The Order of Sharps*

Have students make up their own phrases, using the order of the sharps (F C G D A E B) instead of "Father Charles Goes Down And Ends Battle."

UNIT FOUR
LESSON 2

continued from previous page

5. Introduce the meaning of a melodic motive and count the number of times a motive is heard in "Trav'ler." Have students:

▶ • Read about the musical meaning of the word *motive*.

• Listen as you or a volunteer plays the melodic motive at the top of the page on resonator bells or keyboard.

• Listen to the recording of "Trav'ler" and count the number of times they hear the melodic motive it contains. (8)

6. Introduce "Dance for the Nations" CD3:32. Compare the first five steps of the minor scale to the first five steps of the major scale. Have students:

▶ • Clap to the accented beat and snap to the unaccented beat as they listen to the recording.

▶ • Sing "Dance for the Nations" in unison, then as a three-part canon.

• Compare the sequence of whole and half steps in the first five tones of the D minor and D major scale. (You might compare each to the opening measures of "Dance for the Nations"—minor; and "Trav'ler"—major.)

• Identify the tone that is different in each scale sequence and that gives the feeling of major or minor. (the third step)

▶ • Learn the movement. (See *Movement* below.)

A **motive** is a short fragment of a melody or a rhythm that can be easily recognized. How many times is this melodic motive used in the melody of "Trav'ler"? 8

A MINOR DIVERSION

The melody of "Dance for the Nations" uses the D minor scale. Compare the sequence of whole and half steps in the first five pitches of this scale to that in the D major scale of "Trav'ler." Which scale step is different? W H W W; W W H W; the third

DANCE FOR THE NATIONS

Words and Music by John Krumm

'Round and 'round we go! We hold—— each oth-er's hands and

weave our-selves in a cir - cle. The

time is gone, the dance goes—— on!——

150 TRAVELING ON

MEETING **INDIVIDUAL** NEEDS

ALTERNATE TEACHING STRATEGY

OBJECTIVE 1 Slowly play examples of the first five tones of various major and minor scales for students, telling them to listen for the third step of the scale which gives the characteristic sound of major and minor.

SOCIAL STUDIES CONNECTION: *Flags*

Have students try to identify the flags on pages 150–151 and the continents they represent. (India, Canada, Brazil, Thailand, Sweden, Kenya, U.S.A.; all continents except Australia and Antarctica)

MOVEMENT: *"Dance for the Nations"*

Formation: three concentric circles, students facing inward

Dance Steps:

Measures 1–2—Each person turns to their own right in place, making a complete circle (4 steps).

Measure 3—Join hands with neighbors and raise arms.

Measure 4—Lower arms.

Measures 5–8—Still holding hands, the circle faces left and takes seven steps counterclockwise. Pivot to reverse body facing on Beat 8.

"American Dream" expresses the composer's vision of this country's future. It has one section in B♭ major and one section in G minor.

B♭ major   G minor

Is the first phrase of the A section major or minor? The first phrase of the B section? *minor; major*

AMERICAN DREAM

Words and Music by Ed Harris

Part 1
Gm

1. For A- mer- i - ca,——————   for A-
2. For our dig- ni- ty,——————   and e -

Part 2

1. For A - mer - i - ca,——————
2. And our li - ber- ty,——————

Gm   E♭   Cm   D   Gm

mer-i-ca,—— for A- mer-i-ca—— I dream.   In my mind I have a
qual-i-ty,—— This and more I dare— to dream.   No more dan-ger or sus-

for A - mer - i - ca—— I dream.
This and more I dare—— to dream.

Part 1 only
F   Gm   Gm   F   E♭

vi - sion of what A - mer - i - ca can be,   and we're faced with a de-
pi - cion, and no more fight- ing, no more pain,   no more self - ish con-dem-

B♭ major

1. Introduce "Tsing Chun U Chü" (Youth Dance Song) CD3:33 **and "American Dream"** CD4:1**. Identify major and minor.** Have students:

• Listen to "Tsing Chun U Chü," holding palms up if they hear major and palms down if they hear minor. (minor) (The notation for "Tsing Chun U Chü" is on pages 156–157.)

OBJECTIVE 1 Informal Assessment
• Listen to "American Dream," holding palms up when they hear major and palms down when they hear minor. (Section A is minor; Section B is major; Form is A B A B.)

• Read page 151 and answer the question about major and minor.

▶ • Sing the melody of "American Dream." (When students are secure singing the melody, have those with cambiata voices learn Part 2. Then have the class try singing both parts together.)

Measures 9–10—Take three steps forward in a clockwise direction. (3 beats) Reverse body facing on Beat 4.

Measures 11–12—Take three steps backward, still going clockwise (3 beats). On Beat 4, face center and drop hands.

Structure of Dance:

Unison—Do the dance one time through in unison.

Canon—Each circle does the dance two times through in canon. The canon begins with the outside circle starting line 1 (Measures 1–4) while the two other circles remain still. When the outside circle comes to line 2 (Measures

5–8), the next circle begins line 1. The innermost circle begins line 1 when the second circle begins line 2.

Coda—When Group 1 finishes for the second time, they do the steps for line 1 three more times. When Group 2 finishes, they do line 1 two more times; Group 3 does line 1 once more. On the very last time through, everyone holds arms raised after Measure 3.

continued from previous page

2. Identify whole and half steps between the first five pitches of major and minor scales in "American Dream." Have students:

• Compare the whole and half steps between the first five pitches of the scales that are used to construct the melodies of the A section (G minor) and the B section (B♭ major). (minor— W H W W; major—W W H W)

Recorded Lesson CD4:3

OBJECTIVE 2 Informal Assessment

▶ • Listen to "Major and Minor Scales," in which they hear an analysis of the first five pitches of major and minor scales and signal when they hear whole steps by holding up three fingers ("W") and half steps by pointing two fingers to the side (sign language "H"; palm is facing the body).

4 CLOSE

"Today, we compared the way the first five tones of the major and minor scales are constructed. Pretend that you're giving a test on major and minor. What questions would you ask?" Have students:

• Work in pairs to make up one or two questions on how the major and minor scales are constructed, then test another pair (or you). (Sample questions: Between what steps are half steps found in each type of scale? Which scale has a lowered third?)

152 TRAVELING ON

MEETING **INDIVIDUAL** NEEDS

ALTERNATE TEACHING STRATEGY

OBJECTIVE 2 Have students work in pairs or small groups at the keyboard, playing whole and half steps for each other to identify. Remind them that a half step is formed by any two keys on the keyboard that touch with no other key in between; a whole step is formed by two keys with one other key in between.

SIGNING: *"American Dream"*

Signing Master S • 6 • 3 has sign language for this song.

SPECIAL LEARNERS: *American Sign Language*

Adding sign language to a song provides opportunities to talk about American Sign Language (ASL). Students may know that sign language is used by many people with impaired hearing as well as by hearing individuals. Tell them that American Sign Language is a complete language with its own grammar and syntax. To become very skilled takes years of study; the language cannot be learned only from pictures in a book. If a student knows ASL, discuss the expressive qualities of movement in the language.

choice. Dream—— the A-mer-i-can dream with me, dream—— from sea to

choice. Dream, dream with me, from sea to

shin-ing sea. Share—— the A-mer-i-can dream with me, come dream of what can

shin-ing sea. Share the dream, come dream of what can

be. dream with me, come dream of what can be. Come a-

be. dream with me, come dream of what can be. Come a-

long, come a-long, dream a dream with me.———

long, come a-long, dream a dream with me.———

MORE MUSIC: Reinforcement

"O musique," page 343 (minor)
"The Kettle Valley Line," page 368 (minor)
"Voice from a Dream," page 375 (minor/major)
"Symphony No. 5 in C Minor," page 413C (motive)
"Shalom Chaverim" (Shalom, Good Friends), *Songs to Sing and Read*, page 88 (minor)
"Vine and Fig Tree," *Songs to Sing and Read*, page 104 (minor)
"When Johnny Comes Marching Home," *Songs to Sing and Read*, page 106 (minor)

CRITICAL THINKING: *Composer's Purpose*

Have students work in pairs to decide how a minor key "feels" and how a major key "feels." They should come up with several words describing each. For example, a minor key might feel sad, blue, mysterious, or religious. Then ask each pair to speculate about why Ed Harris used minor and major at various points in "American Dream." If they had been the composer, would they have done it any differently? After a few minutes of discussion time, ask volunteers to present their ideas to the class.

ACROSS the

MAPS

"Travel"

PAIR · **15 MIN OR LESS**

MATERIALS: maps of continental United States, tape measure; optional—reference books

Have students plan a family railroad trip across the continental United States. Traveling by rail, they can stop off along the way to their destination, and see the sights.

Have them assume they can travel by railroad between large cities. Using a map of the United States, have them select several major cities as points on the trip and plot a route that allows them to see major sights, such as the Great Lakes or the Rocky Mountains.

Then have them use a tape measure to find the length of the trip. They can use the map scale to determine how many miles or kilometers the rail trip might cover.

Finally, have them describe the trip in writing, citing the route, places they plan to see, and the distance they will cover.

COMPREHENSION STRATEGIES: Sequencing, summarizing

ART

POSTERS

"Trav'ler"

GROUP · **30 MIN OR LONGER**

MATERIALS: drawing paper, poster board, markers, paints, crayons

Have students work in groups to organize posters depicting the beauty found in their own neighborhoods. Members of each group should think of what makes their neighborhood special to them—including places they like to visit and people who live there.

All members should sketch their drawings and contribute them to those who will organize and complete the final posters. Group members should write messages for their posters. The messages should summarize the special feelings that the images in the posters evoke.

COMPREHENSION STRATEGIES: Visualizing, expressing main ideas

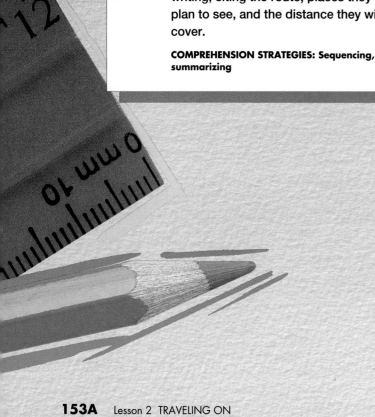

CURRICULUM

MATHEMATICS

CIRCLES

"Dance for the Nations"

PAIR   **15–30 MIN**

MATERIALS: drawing paper, compass, marker, pencil, scissors, ruler, calculator

Have each partner use a compass to draw a large circle (radius = 6 cm). Then have them adjust the compasses to draw small circles (radius = 1, 2 and/or 3 cm) inside the large one—making sure the circles do not overlap. Then each partner uses the side of a pencil to shade the area of the large circle that is not inside any of the smaller circles.

Partners exchange drawings. Their goal is to be the first to determine how to find the area of the shaded portion of the large circle.

(Students find the area of the large circle. Then they find the areas of the smaller circles and add them. They subtract the sum from the area of the larger circle.)

COMPREHENSION STRATEGY: Compare and contrast

LANGUAGE ARTS

AUTOBIOGRAPHY

"American Dream"

INDIVIDUAL   **30 MIN OR LONGER**

Ask students what the future might be like if their dreams for themselves and the country were to come true. Have students pick a year—five years, ten years, or more—from the present.

Have students write about a day in their lives at that future time. Have them describe where they are living, what their personal goals are, what they do on a typical day, and so on.

Students might have a chance to tape-record or videotape each other presenting their visions of the future.

COMPREHENSION STRATEGY: Expressing main ideas and supporting details

UNIT FOUR
LESSON 3

RELATED ARTS MOVEMENT THEATER VISUAL ARTS

LESSON PLANNER

FOCUS Rhythm

OBJECTIVES
OBJECTIVE 1 Read rhythmic patterns in ²/₄ meter
OBJECTIVE 2 Perform rhythmic patterns in ²/₄ meter to accompany a song

MATERIALS
Recordings
Üsküdar   CD2:9
Yonder Come Day   CD4:4
Tsing Chun U Chü (Youth
    Dance Song)   CD3:33
Recorded Lesson: Pronunciation
    for "Tsing Chun U Chü"   CD4:5

Resources
Resource Master 4 • 3 (practice)
Playing the Guitar G • 20 (syncopation)

VOCABULARY
syncopation

▶ = BASIC PROGRAM

Rhythmic Explorations

"Yonder Come Day" is an African American folk song from the Georgia Sea Islands off the Georgia coast. When tied notes appear in the music, you hear **syncopation**. Syncopation results from placing stresses on weak beats or parts of beats that are normally unstressed.

YONDER COME DAY

Georgia Sea Islands Folk Song
Additional Words and Arrangement
by Judith Cook Tucker
Arrangement Adapted by Michael Jothen

154

MEETING **INDIVIDUAL** NEEDS

VOCAL DEVELOPMENT: *Breathing for Chest Voice*

The low pitches in "Yonder Come Day" are in heavy or chest-voice range. When pitches are low and close to the speaking voice, students often forget to breathe properly for singing. Remind them that even though the pitches are low, they need to breathe deeply to support the tone for singing. For further practice, use this exercise.

Step 1 Ask students to imagine they have an inner tube around their waists and to put their hands at the waist. Then tell them to blow the "old" air out and to inhale as you count to three. They should feel their waists expanding.

Step 2 Point your index finger at them to "puncture" the inner tube to the count of five. As the air escapes, they should make a hissing sound and expand their hands out to the side. This prevents them from collapsing as the air is released.

Step 3 Repeat Steps 1 and 2, but inhale to the count of four and exhale to the count of six.

MULTICULTURAL PERSPECTIVES: *Georgia Sea Islands*

"Yonder Come Day" is from the Georgia Sea Islands, a group of islands off the southern coast of the United States that were worked as plantations by African Americans

1 GET SET

"Some time ago, we sang a song from Turkey. What was its name?" ("Üsküdar," page 73) Have students:

▶ • Sing "Üsküdar" **CD2:9**. (Optional: Listen to the song again and put the measures of rhythmic notation on **Resource Master 4 • 3** in correct order to match the song.)

"This song, popular in Turkey, is now part of America's musical heritage as well because Americans of Turkish descent sing it. In this lesson, you will practice reading rhythms in other songs that represent our American musical heritage."

2 DEVELOP

1. Introduce "Yonder Come Day" CD4:4. Review rhythm patterns. Have students:

• Read about the rhythm of the song on page 154. (Explain that ties do not always indicate syncopation, but they do in this song; and distinguish between the ties and slurs—curved lines connecting different pitches sung on one syllable—mm. 1–3 in Part 3, for example.)

▶ • Listen to "Yonder Come Day" while following the rhythm of Part 1.

• Clap the rhythm of Part 1.

▶ • Sing Part 1.

during and after the time of slavery. Because the people were isolated from the mainland United States until quite recently, they created a distinct culture, much of it remembered from their ancestors in West Central Africa. They developed an English dialect known as Gullah (**gʌ** lə), based on West African speech patterns. In 1992, a movie called *Daughters of the Dust* was made about the Gullah people, their music, and their culture.

MULTICULTURAL PERSPECTIVES: *Accompaniment*

"Yonder Come Day" is traditionally sung a cappella or accompanied only by body percussion or rhythm instruments.

This tradition comes from the time when enslaved African Americans were not allowed to play instruments. Instead, they thought of ways to imitate the drums of Africa through body percussion. They noted that a snap sounds different from a slap, a cupped-hand slap sounds different from an open-hand slap, and a slap on the thigh sounds different from a slap on the belly. Each had its place in their rhythm accompaniments, along with foot stamping. Note that the claps in the song are on the weak beats, as is typical in traditional African American songs. (Movement for "Yonder Come Day" is found in Lesson 7, page 172.)

continued from previous page

2. Read and pat rhythmic patterns. Have students:

• Read and pat (with alternating hands) the rhythms of the first two boxes shaded purple on page 157. (These two boxes contain most of the rhythmic elements found in the other four-measure rhythm patterns that will be assigned for group work.)

• Divide into three groups.

OBJECTIVE 1 Informal Assessment
• Read and pat (with alternating hands) the rhythm assigned to their group. (Group 1—blue; Group 2—yellow; Group 3—orange)

3 APPLY

Review "Tsing Chun U Chü" (Youth Dance Song) CD3:33 (p. 151). Perform rhythmic patterns to accompany the song. Have students:

• Listen to "Tsing Chun U Chü" and identify rhythms in the first four measures (without looking at the music in the book).

Recorded Lesson CD4:5
▶ • Listen to "Pronunciation for 'Tsing Chun U Chü.'"

▶ • Sing "Tsing Chun U Chü."

OBJECTIVE 2 Informal Assessment
• Perform the rhythmic patterns on page 157 to accompany the recording. (See the top of page 157 for form.)

RHYTHMS FROM TAIWAN

Taiwan is a large island off the east coast of the Chinese mainland. The Republic of China is governed from this island. Residents of Taiwan include native Taiwanese and immigrants from China and their descendants. In the past thirty years, many people have come to the United States from Taiwan.

Tsing Chun U Chü

D minor

YOUTH DANCE SONG

Taiwanese Folk Song
Collected and Transcribed
by Kathy B. Sorensen

Chinese: 太 陽 下 山 明 朝 依 舊 爬 上 來
Pronunciation: tai yang sia shan ming jau yi jiu pa shang lai
English: Though the sun has dis-ap-peared in-to the___ west,

花 兒 謝 了 明 年 還 是 一 樣 的 開
hua ər siɛ liau ming niɛn hai shi yi yang di kai
still the sun will rise a-gain each morn-ing at dawn.

美 麗 小 鳥 一 去 無 踪 影 我 的 青 春 小 鳥 一 樣
me li shiau niau yi tsü wu ying jung wɔ di tsingchun shiau niau yi yang
Though the flow-ers wilt and___ die in-fall, there will be new blos-soms when the

156 RHYTHMIC EXPLORATIONS

MEETING **INDIVIDUAL** NEEDS

ALTERNATE TEACHING STRATEGIES

OBJECTIVE 1 Have students choose just one of the rhythms, following along and patting the rhythm they have chosen when it occurs. Switch rhythms each time, until they can perform the entire rhythmic accompaniment.

OBJECTIVE 2 Have students practice performing their rhythms in the correct order without the recording.

PLAYING INSTRUMENTS: *Unpitched Instruments*

Have students transfer the rhythmic accompaniment for "Tsing Chun U Chü" to unpitched instruments.

PRONUNCIATION: *"Tsing Chun U Chü"*

a f<u>a</u>ther	e ch<u>a</u>otic	ɛ p<u>e</u>t	i b<u>ee</u>	o <u>o</u>bey
ɔ p<u>a</u>w	u m<u>oo</u>n	ə <u>a</u>go	ü lips form [u] and say [i]

不 回 來 我 的 青 春 小 鳥 一 樣 不 回 來
bu hue lai wɔ di tsing chun shiau niau yi yang bu hue lai
spring comes_ on. There will be new blos-soms when the spring comes_ on.

別 的 那 呀 喲　　　　別 的 那 呀 喲
bie di na ya yo　　　　bie di na ya yo
But the bird that flies_____　ne - ver will re - turn.

我 的 青 春 小 鳥 一 樣 不 回 來
wɔ di tsing chun shiau niau yi yang bu hue lai
So it is when youth has flown a - way it is gone.

READ and pat these rhythms.

Interlude

Verse

SING the verse, then pat these rhythms to accompany the interlude and the repeat of the verse.

PLAY the rhythms on unpitched percussion instruments.

Form

Introduction; Verse 1: All sing; Interlude: All three groups—purple; Verse 1: Group 1—blue, then Group 2—yellow, then all three groups—purple, then Group 3—orange

4 CLOSE

"Today, you used your skill at reading rhythms. Now use them one more time with 'Yonder Come Day.'" Have students:

• Find measures that contain dotted eighth-sixteenth patterns and clap the rhythm of one measure.

• Find measures containing ties and clap the rhythm of one measure.

▶ • Sing Part 1 of "Yonder Come Day" again.

LESSON SUMMARY

Informal Assessment In this lesson, students:

OBJECTIVE 1 Read rhythmic patterns in $\frac{2}{4}$ meter to accompany "Tsing Chun U Chü."

OBJECTIVE 2 Performed rhythmic patterns in $\frac{2}{4}$ meter to accompany "Tsing Chun U Chü."

MORE MUSIC: Reinforcement

"Qué bonita bandera," page 289 (syncopation; patriotic, Puerto Rican immigrants)
"Bo Hai Huan Ten," page 313 (Chinese music, Chinese immigrants)
"Nobody Knows the Trouble I've Seen," page 334 (syncopation; African American)
"Island in the Sun," page 364 (syncopation; Caribbean immigrants)
"Garifalia," page 372 (meter; Greek immigrants)
"El robalo," page 374 ($\frac{2}{4}$ meter; Venezuelan immigrants)

MULTICULTURAL PERSPECTIVES: *"Tsing Chun U Chü"*

"Tsing Chun U Chü" was brought to Taiwan from the People's Republic of China over 40 years ago. The song is believed to have originated with the Uigur (**wi** gər), a Turkic people in northwestern China known for their love of music and dancing. The Uigur were powerful in Mongolia and eastern Turkestan between the eighth and twelfth centuries A.D. The Turkic influence helps to explain the song's lively style. Today "Tsing Chun U Chü" is sung as a tender goodbye to youth by grade school students and teenagers.

MOVEMENT: *"Tsing Chun U Chü"*

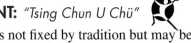

This dance is not fixed by tradition but may be improvised in Chinese style. Provide students with these guidelines.

—Use arms and hands to show meaning of the words. For example, raise and lower arms to show the sun rising and setting. The head can follow the direction of the arms.

—Create a short step moving forward, then back (not side to side), for example: Step R foot forward, close L foot next to R foot, step R foot backward, close L foot.

—Hold relatively still at the hips and waist.

UNIT FOUR
LESSON 4

RELATED ARTS [MOVEMENT] [THEATER] [VISUAL ARTS]

LESSON PLANNER

FOCUS Rhythm, § meter

OBJECTIVES
OBJECTIVE 1 Aurally identify § meter in a song (tested)
OBJECTIVE 2 Read and perform § rhythm patterns to accompany a song (tested)

MATERIALS
Recordings
El tambor — CD3:26
Tsing Chun U Chü (Youth Dance Song) — CD3:33
Recorded Lesson: Pronunciation for "Tsing Chun U Chü" — CD4:5
Greensleeves — CD4:6
Listening: *Fantasia on Greensleeves* by R. Vaughan Williams — CD4:7

Instruments
unpitched percussion instruments and recorder, keyboard, or resonator bells

Resources
Listening Map Transparencies T • 8, T • 9 (*Fantasia on Greensleeves*)
Playing the Guitar G • 7 (Greensleeves)
Recorder Master R • 17 (pitches C D E F G A B C' D')

Technology Music with MIDI: Greensleeves

▶ = **BASIC PROGRAM**

Meter Matters

"Greensleeves" was written in Renaissance England. Early American colonists knew and sang this song.

PAT-CLAP as you listen to the song and decide if the beats are divided into twos ($\frac{2}{4}$) or threes ($\frac{6}{8}$). $\frac{6}{8}$

GREENSLEEVES

16th Century English Song

A-las, my love— you do me wrong— to cast me off dis-
cour-teous-ly; And I have loved———— you so long,— de-
light-ing in— your com-pa-ny. Green-sleeves— was
all my joy,—— Green-sleeves— was my de-light. Green-sleeves was my
heart of gold,—— and who but my la-dy Green-sleeves.

E minor

158

MEETING **INDIVIDUAL** NEEDS

ALTERNATE TEACHING STRATEGIES

OBJECTIVE 1 Have students divide into two groups and listen to the recording of "Greensleeves," one group clapping with the beat, the other patting the underlying beat division. Hearing the triple division of the beat in this way will help students to identify the meter as §.

OBJECTIVE 2 Have students divide into eight groups to work on the accompaniment for "Greensleeves," each group rehearsing and perfecting one measure of the melodic accompaniment for the A section and one measure of the melodic accompaniment for the B section (measure

9). Have the groups take turns playing their measures. Trade parts several times to give students the opportunity to perfect more than two measures of the accompaniment.

VOCAL DEVELOPMENT: *Expanding Vocal Range*

Instructing students to "place" the voice often results in a forced, constricted tone. Instead, the goal is to achieve a relaxed and open tone. The following humming vocalise is effective in developing a free and resonant tone production. Remind students to use correct posture and breathing.

1 GET SET

"Some songs have a distinct rhythm." Have students:

- Listen as you tap the rhythm of "El tambor" CD3:26 (p. 142). Identify the song.
- ▶ Sing "El tambor."

"Rhythm is such a basic part of music that you can often identify a song by hearing only the rhythm of the melody."

2 DEVELOP

1. Review "Tsing Chun U Chü" (Youth Dance Song) CD3:33. Identify meter and perform the playalong. Have students:

- ▶ Listen to "Tsing Chun U Chü" as they follow the notation on pages 156–157.

Recorded Lesson CD4:5
- ▶ Listen to "Pronunciation for 'Tsing Chun U Chü.'"
- ▶ Sing "Tsing Chun U Chü."
- Look at the music and identify the meter ($\frac{2}{4}$) and the ♫♫♫ and ♫♫ patterns.
- Practice, then perform the playalong on page 157 with unpitched instruments.

2. Introduce "Greensleeves" CD4:6. Aurally identify meter, then read and play rhythms in $\frac{6}{8}$ meter. Have students:

- Perform a pat-clap pattern with the beat to "Greensleeves."

OBJECTIVE 1 Informal Assessment
- Identify the meter by holding up 2 fingers for $\frac{2}{4}$ or 3 fingers for $\frac{6}{8}$ meter. ($\frac{6}{8}$)
- ▶ Sing "Greensleeves."
- Clap the rhythm of the playalong. (Focus on ♫♫ Rehearse each measure using pitched instruments, extending until they can play the entire accompaniment.)

OBJECTIVE 2 Informal Assessment
- Play the accompaniment with the song.

PLAY this melodic accompaniment for "Greensleeves" on recorder, keyboard, or bells.

Unit 4 *Our Musical Heritage* **159**

Go down by half steps to G.

N-n-n-oo - n-n *(breathe)* N-n-n-oo - n-n *(breathe)* N-n-n-oo - n-n *(breathe)*

Step 1 Have students hum the letter "n" on G with their lips and teeth slightly apart and the tip of the tongue resting lightly against the bottom teeth. Now have them imitate the whine of a mosquito, still humming "n."

Step 2 Have them hum the vocalise. As they lower the jaw for the "oo" in the vocalise, tell them to feel the openness in the back of the throat as in the beginning of a yawn.

Step 3 Sing the following vocalise which will expand the vocal range.

Go up by half steps to E.

N-n - noo_____ *(breathe)* N-n - noo_____ *(breathe)*

As the students sing "Greensleeves," instruct them to sing with the same forward tone quality as they did in the vocalise.

UNIT FOUR
LESSON 4

continued from previous page

3 APPLY

Introduce *Fantasia on Greensleeves* CD4:7.
Aurally identify meter in the A and B sections. Have students:

▶ • Listen to the recording while following the listening map. (Students should follow the windows in the castle to count the beats in each measure.) (Optional: Use **Listening Map Transparencies T • 8 and T • 9.**)

• Identify the form as A B A.

• Identify the meter in the A and B sections. ($\frac{6}{8}$; $\frac{4}{4}$)

4 CLOSE

"In this lesson, you read and performed rhythms in different meters with songs that people have been singing for a long time." Have students:

• Tell what rhythms and meters they used.

• Identify the beat division in $\frac{2}{4}$ and $\frac{6}{8}$ meter. (2; 3)

▶ • Sing "Greensleeves."

Fantasia on Greensleeves
by Ralph Vaughan Williams

In 1934, the British composer Ralph Vaughan Williams used "Greensleeves" and another Renaissance tune called "Lovely Joan" to create his **Fantasia on Greensleeves.**

LISTENING MAP *Listen for the form of this piece as you follow the map. What meter do you hear in the A section? In the B section?* ABA; $\frac{6}{8}$; $\frac{4}{4}$

Introduction: Violin and Harp

a
a'
b
b'

Fine

160 **METER MATTERS**

MEETING **INDIVIDUAL** NEEDS

BIOGRAPHY: *Ralph Vaughan Williams*

British composer Ralph Vaughan Williams (1872–1958) was very interested in native British music, as can be seen by his use of folk songs in *Fantasia on Greensleeves.* A member of the English Folk Song Society, he often worked folk songs, hymns, and street tunes into his music. He even incorporated the chimes of Big Ben, the famous London clock tower, into a composition. His love for the music of Great Britain was part of his love for his country; he took time out from composing to serve as an officer in the

British Army during World War I. After the war he became a professor at the Royal College of Music in London. He continued to compose music all his life, completing his ninth symphony at the age of 85.

PLAYING INSTRUMENTS: *Creating Ostinatos*

Have students create their own four-beat patterns of $\frac{6}{8}$ rhythm and perform their patterns on unpitched percussion instruments with the A section of *Fantasia on Greensleeves.*

three times

c

d

Interlude: Violin and Harp

D. S. al Fine

Listening Map concept by Rebecca Grusendorf

MULTICULTURAL PERSPECTIVES: *The Renaissance*

The music used by Vaughan Williams to compose *Fantasia on Greensleeves* is from the Renaissance. Renaissance music was the music of Europe from around 1450–1600. The French word *renaissance* (rə ne **säs**) means "rebirth." During this period, scholars and artists were interested in rediscovering the ancient Latin and Greek writings that had been largely lost to Europe during medieval times (although kept in circulation in the Arab world). It was also a period of new discoveries in science, art, and exploration. Music played an important part in this life. It was heard in the cathedrals and courts of Europe. It was also heard at home, often accompanied by the lute, the most popular home instrument at this time. The people sang love songs, story songs, and party songs. Music written for instruments only also became popular. The spread of all this music was due to an important invention—the printing press. Printed books of religious music date from 1476, and the first book of secular songs was printed in 1501.

ACROSS the

SOLSTICES

"Tsing Chun U Chü"

PAIR   **15–30 MIN**

MATERIALS: globe, flashlight

Have students work in pairs to locate Taiwan at about 23°N, 120°E. This island is on the Tropic of Cancer, 23½°N. In late June each year, on the summer solstice (the beginning of summer in the Northern Hemisphere), this latitude gets the most direct sunlight on Earth.

Have one student hold a flashlight about 30 cm from the globe and tilt the globe slightly, with the North Pole leaning toward the flashlight, so that a direct beam hits the Tropic of Cancer. Without changing the tilt, the partner rotates the globe slowly counterclockwise. Starting at Taiwan, have the two students identify land and water areas—in sequence—that they find along the Tropic of Cancer.

(They can repeat the activity for the Tropic of Capricorn, 23½°S, which gets the most direct sunlight on the winter solstice in December. They hold the globe at the same tilt, but with the flashlight on the opposite side of the globe so that the South Pole is tilted toward the light.)

COMPREHENSION STRATEGIES: Sequencing, compare and contrast

SCENE STUDY

"Greensleeves"

GROUP   **30 MIN OR LONGER**

MATERIALS: annotated copy of Shakespeare's *Romeo and Juliet;* optional— reference books

Explain to students that if they were to go to a theater in England in the late 1500s, they probably would be going to see a play by William Shakespeare, whose great works are still performed today.

Have them work in groups to stage the balcony scene from *Romeo and Juliet,* Act 2, Scene 2. Explain that the scene depicts a meeting of a young man and woman who are in love but whose families are fighting each other. Different groups of students can be actors, directors, and stage managers, set designers, and costume designers. You might wish students to write their own dialogue based on the original—dialogue they might memorize—or to perform the original, using scripts.

Set and costume designers might research the staging and dress of the time or use modern settings if the directors choose.

COMPREHENSION STRATEGY: Expressing main ideas

CURRICULUM

LANGUAGE ARTS

FAMILIAR LANGUAGE

"Greensleeves"

INDIVIDUAL　　　　　　**15–30 MIN**

Have students imagine that they are in England 400 years ago hearing "Greensleeves" sung. Ask which phrases and words in the song sound different from English as spoken today in the United States.

Have students rewrite the words of "Greensleeves" using more familiar words and expressions. The new words need not fit the rhythm of the song but should express the original meaning of the words.

What are some expressions the students use today that people of England 400 years ago might not understand? Have students write some informal expressions they use and then rewrite them in language that people of 400 years ago might understand.

COMPREHENSION STRATEGIES: Expressing main ideas, compare and contrast

SOCIAL STUDIES

TIME LINE

"Greensleeves"

GROUP　　　　　　**30 MIN OR LONGER**

MATERIALS: mural paper, rulers or tape measures, markers, reference books

Have students make a time line showing the succession of rulers in sixteenth-century England. They draw a horizontal line across mural paper. They plot a large dot at the left end of the line, and equally space ten more dots along the line to divide it into ten decades—labeled 1500, 1510, and so on to 1600.

Have them plot these major events:

- 1509—Henry VIII becomes king
- 1547—Edward VI becomes king
- 1553—Mary I becomes queen
- 1558—Elizabeth I becomes queen

Students can work in groups to research the lives of these rulers. Each group can focus on one ruler and can add details to the time line based on their research.

COMPREHENSION STRATEGIES: Sequencing, organizing and displaying information

ACROSS THE CURRICULUM

75th Anniversary of Rotary International

HEALTH, HUNGER & HUMANITY

HAPPY NEW YEAR!

USA

UNIT FOUR
LESSON 5

RELATED ARTS | MOVEMENT | THEATER | VISUAL ARTS |

LESSON PLANNER

FOCUS Pitch/Harmony

OBJECTIVES
OBJECTIVE 1 Identify the sequence of whole and half steps in the minor scale and major scale while singing the scales (tested)
OBJECTIVE 2 Play roots of I and V chords in D major to accompany a song

MATERIALS
Recordings
Greensleeves CD4:6
El tambor CD3:26
Hoe Ana CD4:8
Hoe Ana (performance mix) CD4:9
Recorded Lesson: Pronunciation
for "Hoe Ana" CD4:10

Instruments
recorders, keyboard, or resonator bells, and conga drum, bongos, or other un-pitched percussion instruments

Resources
Resource Master 4 • 4 (practice)
Playing the Guitar G • 10 (I and V chords)
Recorder Master R • 18 (pitches C D E F F♯)

VOCABULARY
ukulele

► = BASIC PROGRAM

ROOTS and RHYTHM

Rhythmic and harmonic accompaniments add color and excitement to music. Accompany "El tambor" with chord roots based on the first and fifth steps of the scale (*do* and *so*) . In accompaniments, the fifth step often is used as a low pitch as well as a high pitch.

do	re	mi	fa	so	so,	do
1	2	3	4	5	5	1

SING the lower version of the fifth step for this accompaniment.

1   1   1   5   5   5   5   1

- Transfer the accompaniment to keyboard, bells, or recorder.
- Stamp this rhythm with your feet and then transfer it to a conga drum.

- Pat the rhythm below. Pat down-stemmed notes on your left leg and up-stemmed notes on your right leg. Notice the syncopated rhythm (♪♪♪) in the second measure. Once you have learned the pattern, transfer it to bongos.

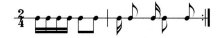

162

MEETING **INDIVIDUAL** NEEDS

ALTERNATE TEACHING STRATEGY

OBJECTIVE 1 Have students listen as you play individual examples of half and whole steps and sing them. Have them take turns playing whole or half steps for others to sing and then identify.

SPECIAL LEARNERS: *Roots of I and V Chords*
Since students played the first five notes of the C scale on the keyboard in Unit 3, Lesson 2, begin by having students play these notes on the keyboard. Have them count to identify the first and fifth notes, then write the pitch letter names next to the roman numerals on the board. With imaginary keyboards, have students position their hands and "play" C and G as you point to the letters. Have students "accompany" as you sing familiar songs in the key of C. Then select pairs to play the accompaniment on the keyboard in different octaves as the class sings. Students should then be able to transfer this skill to other keys such as F, G, and D that do not use black keys for either of the chord roots.

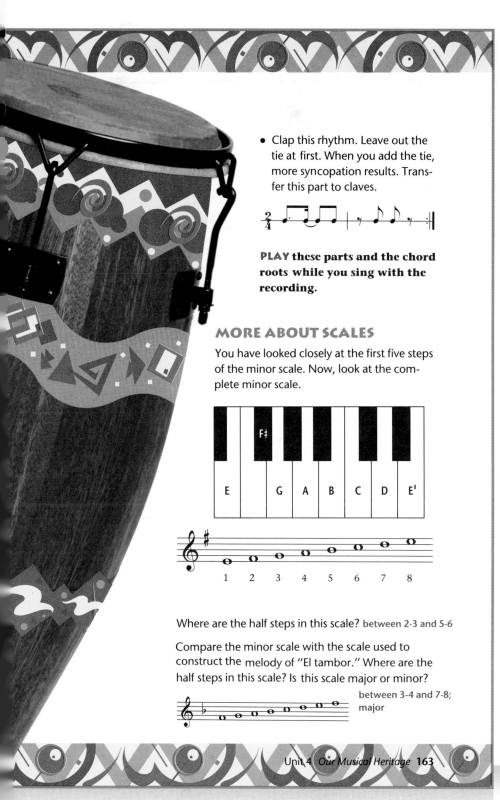

• Clap this rhythm. Leave out the tie at first. When you add the tie, more syncopation results. Transfer this part to claves.

PLAY these parts and the chord roots while you sing with the recording.

MORE ABOUT SCALES

You have looked closely at the first five steps of the minor scale. Now, look at the complete minor scale.

Where are the half steps in this scale? between 2-3 and 5-6

Compare the minor scale with the scale used to construct the melody of "El tambor." Where are the half steps in this scale? Is this scale major or minor?

between 3-4 and 7-8; major

Unit 4 Our Musical Heritage **163**

1 GET SET

"Identify the meter of this music. Tell if it's major or minor." Have students:

• Listen to the four-measure instrumental introduction to "Greensleeves" CD4:6. (§ ; minor)

▶ • Sing the song. (See page 158.)

"Today you will carry your understanding of music one step further by adding harmonic accompaniments to melodies."

2 DEVELOP

1. Review "El tambor" CD3:26 **(p. 142). Play roots of I and V chords, then perform a rhythmic accompaniment.** Have students:

▶ • Sing "El tambor."

• Listen as you play I and V chords in F, and recall that the lowest pitch is known as the root. Tell the pitch syllable name of each root. (I = *do*; V = *so*)

• Read page 162. Then sing the chord roots (singing "one" and "five") with "El tambor."

• Play the chord root accompaniment on pitched instruments with the recording.

• Pat and clap the rhythmic playalongs (alternate hands on one leg for sixteenth notes), then transfer to bongos and claves.

• Perform the chord root and rhythmic playalong parts with "El tambor."

2. Identify sequence of whole and half steps in minor and major scales. Have students:

• Look at the notation of the minor scale on page 163 and answer the questions.

OBJECTIVE 1 Informal Assessment
• Sing the major and then the minor scale using numbers (1–2, 2–3, . . .), identifying the size of each scale step by showing 3 fingers ("W") for whole step and 2 fingers extended sideways, palm inward, ("H") for half step.

ENRICHMENT: *Game for "El tambor"*

Play this game with the recording of "El tambor." Be sure to start the first movement on the downbeat.

Formation: sitting in a circle (Each student has a sturdy plastic cup.)

Game: Begin with the cup upside down in front of the L knee.

Grab-move: Grab bottom of cup with R hand and move cup from in front of L knee to in front of the person to the right on Beat 7.

UNIT FOUR
LESSON 5

continued from previous page

3 APPLY

1. Introduce "Hoe Ana" CD4:8. Identify major and play roots of I and V chords to accompany the song. Have students:

▶ • Listen to the recording (with books closed) and try to identify the accompanying instruments. (ukulele, guitar, percussion) Then read about the ukulele on page 165.

• Look at the scale upon which the melody of "Hoe Ana" is constructed. Identify the sequence of whole and half steps in the scale and tell whether it is major or minor. (major)

• Sing the roots of the I and V chords to accompany "Hoe Ana."

OBJECTIVE 2 Informal Assessment
• Play the roots of the I and V chords to accompany the song.

2. Sing "Hoe Ana," then play accompaniment parts with the song. Have students:

• Read and perform the § rhythm patterns to accompany the song.

Recorded Lesson CD4:10
▶ • Listen to "Pronunciation for 'Hoe Ana.'"

▶ • Sing the melody of "Hoe Ana."

• Add rhythmic and chord root accompaniment parts to the song.

A SONG FROM THE SOUTH PACIFIC

LISTEN for the instrument that accompanies the singing in "Hoe Ana," a folk song from Tahiti. Then sing the song.

Hoe Ana

Tahitian Folk Song
Collected and Transcribed
by Kathy B. Sorensen
Cambiata Part by Robert J. de Frece

164 ROOTS AND RHYTHM

MEETING **INDIVIDUAL** NEEDS

ALTERNATE TEACHING STRATEGY

OBJECTIVE 2 Have students divide into two groups. One group plays the root of the I chord and the other plays the root of the V chord as you play the complete chords. Repeat and switch roles. Some students will prefer to play the same root for each performance.

PRONUNCIATION: *"Hoe Ana"*

ɑ f<u>a</u>ther	e ch<u>a</u>otic	ɛ p<u>e</u>t	i b<u>ee</u>
o <u>o</u>bey	ɾ flipped r		

MULTICULTURAL PERSPECTIVES: *"Hoe Ana"*

MOVEMENT

This folk song tells of the long-ago migration to Tahiti from the legendary homeland, *Havaiki* (hɑ **vɑɪ** ki). Some people think Havaiki is really Hawaii, and some think it may be the Cook Islands. *Hoe ana* means "Let's paddle," and *vaka* means "canoe." Loosely translated, it means, "Let's paddle. Let our canoes take us to land." Like most Tahitian folk music, the motions are as much a part of "Hoe Ana" as the words; the song is always performed with its motions. Songs such as these are still popular in Tahiti and are sung and danced by people of all ages at schools, parties, and weddings.

The **ukulele** played the accompaniment to "Hoe Ana." It is a four-stringed instrument that originated in Hawaii. The ukulele is widely used to accompany songs in the South Pacific islands. It developed from two other instruments, the ukeke and the bragha. The ukeke is a native Hawaiian stringed instrument. The Portuguese brought the bragha, a small guitar, to Hawaii in the 1870s.

The melody of "Hoe Ana" uses pitches from this scale.

Look at the key signature and figure out the name of the key. Where are the half steps in this scale? Is it a major or minor scale? D major; between 3-4 and 7-8; major

SING the roots of the I and V chords to accompany "Hoe Ana." Use this chart. Each shell represents one ♩ beat. Sing D for I and A for V. Then play the roots on keyboard or bells.

ADD these rhythmic patterns. First pat them, then transfer them to unpitched percussion instruments.

Pattern 1

Pattern 2

Unit 4 *Our Musical Heritage* **165**

---

3. Read pitch letter names in bass clef and sing "Hoe Ana" in parts. Have students:

• Look at the cambiata part and notice that it is in bass clef. Read the pitch letter names of the notes in the part. (A, D)

• Sing the part with pitch letter names.

• Sing the descant part. (When students are secure singing each part separately, have them sing the parts together.)

4 CLOSE

"Today, you combined harmony and rhythm to play accompaniments." Have students:

• Recall which songs in the lesson are minor and which are major. ("Greensleeves"—minor; "El tambor"—major; "Hoe Ana"—major)

▶ • Give a final performance of "Hoe Ana."

LESSON SUMMARY

Informal Assessment In this lesson, students:

OBJECTIVE 1 Identified the sequence of whole and half steps in the minor scale and major scale while singing the scales.

OBJECTIVE 2 Played roots of the I and V chords in D major to accompany "Hoe Ana."

MORE MUSIC: Reinforcement

"Diwali Song," page 315 (§ ; Indian immigrants)
"Haji Firuz," page 317 (§ ; Iranian immigrants)
"Autumn Canon," page 343 (minor)
"Drill, Ye Tarriers," page 363 (minor/major; Irish immigrants)
"Scarborough Fair," page 366 (minor; British immigrants)

MOVEMENT: *"Hoe Ana"*

Formation: lines of 6–8 students, in rows of "canoes," either standing or sitting back on the haunches with feet tucked beneath buttocks

Words	Motions (done on the ♩ beat)
Hoe ana	Paddle "canoe" twice on the right.
Hoe ana	Paddle twice on the left.
Hoe a te vaka	Paddle once on right, once on left.
Te vaka nei	Paddle once on right, once on left.
Haere mai na	With L hand on hip, wave R hand above head toward body twice (as if beckoning).
Haere mai na	With R hand on hip, beckon with L hand twice.
Haere mai e ine mae	Extend arms out to sides, bring around forward and in to tap chest, then straight out front with palms down. Wave hands.

PLAYING INSTRUMENTS: *Ukulele*

Have students play D and A7 chords on the ukulele to accompany "Hoe Ana." Strum on the ♩ beat. (If unavailable, use an autoharp or keyboard with chord buttons.) See **Resource Master 4 • 4**.

ACROSS the

SOCIAL STUDIES

PACIFIC ISLAND POSTER

"Hoe Ana"

PAIR　　　　　　　　　**15–30 MIN**

MATERIALS: globe or map of the Pacific Ocean (Pacific Islands), poster board, rulers, markers

Have students draw a graph grid on poster board (horizontally—the longer side along the bottom):

- 14 vertical lines, equally spaced—labeled from left to right in 10° units (120°E to 180° and to 110°W).
- 9 horizontal lines, equally spaced—labeled from bottom to top in 10° units (50°S to 0° [equator] to 30°N).

Students should make all lines in the same direction parallel. The lines should fill the area of the poster.

Have them refer to a map or globe to locate the Pacific Islands and plot them on their grids, including: American Samoa, Western Samoa, Cook Islands, Easter Island (plot at 110°W), Fiji, French Polynesia (which includes Tahiti), Guam, the Hawaiian Islands, Marshall Islands, Solomon Islands, and New Caledonia. The larger the poster board, the clearer the relationships of these islands can be visualized.

COMPREHENSION STRATEGIES: Exploring spatial relationships, visualizing

MATHEMATICS

TRIANGLES

"Hoe Ana"

PAIR　　　　　　　　　**15–30 MIN**

MATERIALS: plastic wrap, wax (china) markers, tape, map of Pacific Islands (available in most encyclopedias), rulers, protractors

The song tells of an ancient migration to Tahiti from a homeland that may have been Hawaii or the Cook Islands. Have students find these three locations on a map of the Pacific. Have them place a flattened piece of plastic wrap over the map and plot the three points. (They can plot a central point for the Cook Islands.) They connect the points to draw a triangle.

Have students measure the sides and angles of their triangles and try to classify the triangles based on their measures: equilateral, isosceles, scalene, obtuse, acute, or right.

(Answers will vary depending on the map projection used and on the point at which students plot the Cook Islands. In general, the triangle is obtuse—the angle with Tahiti as the vertex is greater than 90°—and scalene—no sides are equal.)

COMPREHENSION STRATEGY: Classifying

CURRICULUM

SCIENCE

VOLCANOES

"Hoe Ana"

GROUP   **30 MIN OR LONGER**
MATERIALS: world map, clay; optional—
reference texts

Tahiti and many other islands of the Pacific are volcanic. Have students locate active volcanoes on a map and plot them with dots of clay.

> Arat 39°N, 44°E; Azores 38°N, 30°W; Cape Verde 16°N, 24°W; Cotopaxi 0.4°S, 78°W; Damavand 35°N, 52°E; Dempo 4°S, 103°E; Etna 37°N, 15°E; Galapagos 0.3°S, 90°W; Hekla 64°N, 19°W; Katmai 58°N, 155°W; Krakatoa 6°S, 105°E; Lassen 40°N, 121°W; Mauna Loa 19°N, 155°W; Misti 16°S, 71°W; Mount St. Helens 46°N, 122°W; O'Sima 42°N, 140°E; Osorno 40°S, 73°W; Paricutín 19°N, 102°W; Pelée 15°N, 61°W; Poas 2°N, 76°W; Purace 10°N, 84°W; Stromboli 38°N, 15°E; Taal 14°N, 121°E, Vesuvius 40°N, 14°E; Vulcano 38°N, 15°E

Have them describe any clustering or patterns. What do some locations have in common? (They are along continental edges of the Pacific Ocean and in a line extending through the Mediterranean into Asia. There are volcanic chains in the Pacific.)

COMPREHENSION STRATEGIES: Compare and contrast, generalizing

LANGUAGE ARTS

TELLING A STORY

"Hoe Ana"

INDIVIDUAL   **15-30 MIN**
MATERIALS: map of Pacific Islands; optional—
Kon-Tiki by Thor Heyerdahl

In 1947, Thor Heyerdahl and several colleagues sailed on rafts from Peru in South America to the Tuamotu Archipelago, a group of islands in French Polynesia. He was testing his idea that ancient South Americans could also have made this voyage to Polynesia. Heyerdahl reached Tahiti.

Have students locate Peru, Tahiti, and Tuamotu on a map—to sense the distance. Have them write about what a day of the voyage might have been like—the weather, how they got food, and so on.

Students can compare their writings with Heyerdahl's book *Kon-Tiki*.

COMPREHENSION STRATEGY: Expressing main ideas

RELATED ARTS | MOVEMENT | THEATER | VISUAL ARTS |

LESSON PLANNER

FOCUS Style

OBJECTIVE
OBJECTIVE 1 Perform a traditional Native American dance

MATERIALS
Recordings
Listening: Taos Round Dance   CD4:11
Recorded Lesson: Interview
  with Freddy Wheeler   CD4:12
Listening: Navajo Courtship
  Song   CD4:13
Recorded Lesson: Interview
  with Mohawk Singers   CD4:14
Listening: Tekanionton'néha'
  (Alligator Dance)   CD4:15

Instruments
hand drum or conga drum, rattle or shaker

▶ = **BASIC PROGRAM**

The Original American Music

You have learned that music from many parts of the world has contributed to the rich heritage of American music. But before all of this music arrived, the music of American Indians was already here.

There are still hundreds of different Indian nations living in the United States today. They represent many different cultures and languages.

LISTENING

Taos Round Dance

The music of the Native Americans has been passed down through the generations by oral tradition. Children have learned songs from their parents and grandparents.

LISTEN to a dancing song from the Taos nation of New Mexico. Does the song sound major or minor? Do you hear a meter? major

The Taos people do not think of their music as being major or minor, or having meter. It is important to remember that the same ideas do not always apply to the music of all cultures.

166

MEETING **INDIVIDUAL** NEEDS

MULTICULTURAL PERSPECTIVES: *The Navajo Nation*

The Navajo (**na va ho**) probably arrived in the Southwest sometime before the 1500s. They traditionally hunted and gathered what they needed in order to survive. Later, they became sheepherders. Using the wool from their sheep, they learned to make beautiful rugs and other cloth. The Navajo are also known for their silver jewelry, some of which uses the blue gemstone, turquoise.

Today the Navajo are one of the largest of the Native American groups. About 165,000 people live on the 16-million-acre reservation, which includes parts of Arizona, New Mexico, and Utah. The reservation is rich in oil, coal, and uranium. Their schools teach the Navajo language and customs and are a model for other American Indian educators. Singers like Freddy Wheeler are also vital to keeping Navajo legends and songs alive, passing them on orally, just as their ancestors did in this and other Native American cultures.

LISTENING

Navajo Courtship Song

Sung by Freddy Wheeler

This song comes to us from another Southwest Indian nation, the Navajo. Listen to Freddy Wheeler talk about the importance of music to the Navajo and describe the "Navajo Courtship Song." Find a quiet way to keep the beat as you listen to the song.

Freddy Wheeler

Unit 4 *Our Musical Heritage* **167**

"In this unit, you've been seeing how music from various parts of the world has come together to create our American musical heritage. But long before any of this music came to the Western Hemisphere, Native American music could be heard." Have students:

▶ • Read about "Taos Round Dance" CD4:11, then listen to it, echoing and singing along as they are able.

• Answer the questions on page 166 about the sound and meter. (Major; students may not hear a meter. See *Critical Thinking* below.)

• Tell what texture they hear. (solo and group—monophony)

"Today, you're going to explore the musical heritage of some of the Native American nations."

2 DEVELOP

1. Introduce "Navajo Courtship Song" CD4:13. **Discuss stylistic elements.** Have students:

▶ • Read about "Navajo Courtship Song."

Recorded Lesson CD4:12
▶ • Listen to "Interview with Freddy Wheeler" and hear the artist talk about how he learned "Navajo Courtship Song."

▶ • Listen to "Navajo Courtship Song," patting with the beat.

• Discuss the meter and how it is not clear in this music what the meter is. ($\frac{2}{4}$; some may hear the beat divided in threes. See *Critical Thinking* below.)

▶ • Notice the singer's use of "pulsation" (a rapid alteration of pitch or volume on held notes), which is a common practice among Southwestern and Plains Indian nations.

▶ • Sing along as they are able, trying to match the singer's vocal timbre.

CRITICAL THINKING: *To Meter or Not to Meter*

Have students discuss the meters of "Taos Round Dance" and "Navajo Courtship Song," noticing that the meters may not be easily determined. Tell students that much Native American music does not fit the Western European concept of meter—a regular grouping of equally spaced beats. (Even when the music sounds to us as if it had a meter, it was not created with meter in mind.) Then have them ex-plore ways of notating Native American rhythm and pitch. What parts of the standard notational system, if any, would they keep? What parts would they have to invent?

continued from previous page

2. Introduce "Whip Man." Discuss the poem. Have students:

▶ • Read the poem and discuss its mood and character.

▶ • Identify the main idea of the poem. (Possible answer: the importance of taking care of the past)

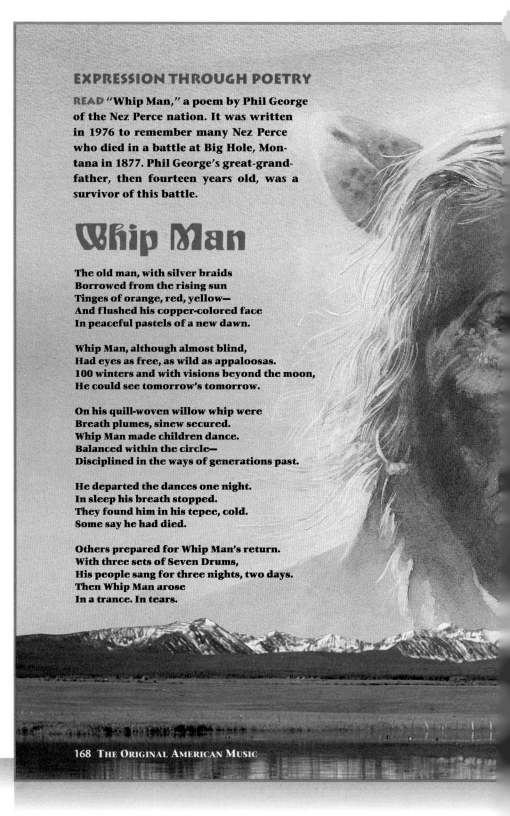

EXPRESSION THROUGH POETRY

READ "Whip Man," a poem by Phil George of the Nez Perce nation. It was written in 1976 to remember many Nez Perce who died in a battle at Big Hole, Montana in 1877. Phil George's great-grandfather, then fourteen years old, was a survivor of this battle.

Whip Man

The old man, with silver braids
Borrowed from the rising sun
Tinges of orange, red, yellow—
And flushed his copper-colored face
In peaceful pastels of a new dawn.

Whip Man, although almost blind,
Had eyes as free, as wild as appaloosas.
100 winters and with visions beyond the moon,
He could see tomorrow's tomorrow.

On his quill-woven willow whip were
Breath plumes, sinew secured.
Whip Man made children dance.
Balanced within the circle—
Disciplined in the ways of generations past.

He departed the dances one night.
In sleep his breath stopped.
They found him in his tepee, cold.
Some say he had died.

Others prepared for Whip Man's return.
With three sets of Seven Drums,
His people sang for three nights, two days.
Then Whip Man arose
In a trance. In tears.

168 THE ORIGINAL AMERICAN MUSIC

MEETING **INDIVIDUAL** NEEDS

BIOGRAPHY: *Phil George*

Poet Phil George (b. 1946) is a member of the Nez Perce nation. He wrote "Whip Man" for the National Park Service as part of the 1977 memorial of the Big Hole Battle of 1877 that occurred in Montana during the Nez Perce War. George's great-grandfather, then 14 years old, survived the battle, in which many Nez Perce were killed, including children. George wrote the poem in honor of the children who survived the battle. The Park Service displayed it at the battlefield site.

MULTICULTURAL PERSPECTIVES: *"Whip Man"*

Years ago, in some Native American communities, certain individuals were designated to carry out discipline because parents did not believe in punishing their own children. The designated person, called the "Whip Man," would go from community to community to discipline children using a willow stick. The children were not harmed, but they learned not to misbehave. George's poem is about an imaginary Whip Man who is encouraging Native Americans today to honor and preserve their heritage.

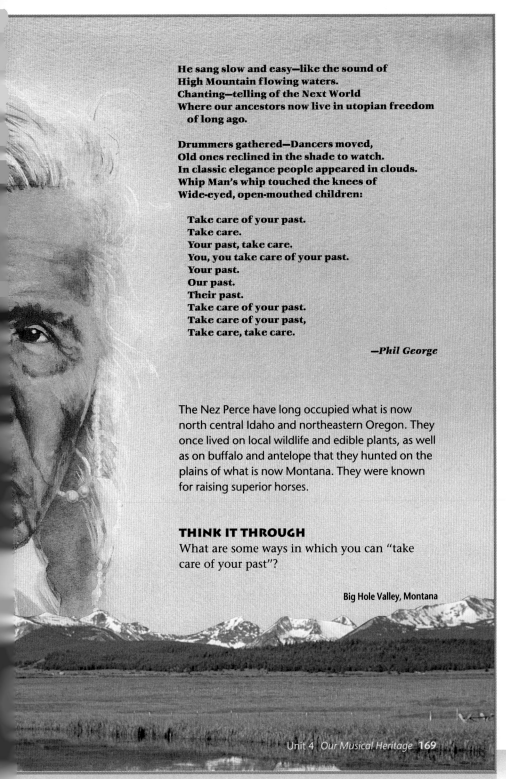

He sang slow and easy—like the sound of
High Mountain flowing waters.
Chanting—telling of the Next World
Where our ancestors now live in utopian freedom
   of long ago.

Drummers gathered—Dancers moved,
Old ones reclined in the shade to watch.
In classic elegance people appeared in clouds.
Whip Man's whip touched the knees of
Wide-eyed, open-mouthed children:

   Take care of your past.
   Take care.
   Your past, take care.
   You, you take care of your past.
   Your past.
   Our past.
   Their past.
   Take care of your past.
   Take care of your past,
   Take care, take care.

               —Phil George

The Nez Perce have long occupied what is now
north central Idaho and northeastern Oregon. They
once lived on local wildlife and edible plants, as well
as on buffalo and antelope that they hunted on the
plains of what is now Montana. They were known
for raising superior horses.

THINK IT THROUGH

What are some ways in which you can "take
care of your past"?

Big Hole Valley, Montana

3. Learn about the Nez Perce nation. Have
students:

▶ • Read about the Nez Perce (nɛz pərs) people.

▶ • Discuss the *Think It Through* question. (Students may suggest talking with older people,
reading history, studying artifacts, and recording current events by such means as writing,
photos, or videos.)

SOCIAL STUDIES CONNECTION: *Oral History*

Native American culture is traditionally passed on orally
from generation to generation. Ask each student to choose a
family member or community figure to interview about the
music that was popular when she or he was growing up.
Students should prepare by making a list of questions to
ask. During the interview, they should take notes or use a
tape recorder. They can then present the results in an oral
report. Challenge several interested students to pool what
they learned to produce a history of popular music over the
past 50 years or so.

continued from previous page

3 APPLY

Introduce "Tekanionton'néha' (Alligator Dance)" CD4:15. **Perform the traditional dance.** Have students:

▶ • Read about the Iroquois Confederacy and "Tekanionton'néha' " (de ga **nyü** dū **ne** ha).

Recorded Lesson CD4:14
▶ • Listen to "Interview with Mohawk Singers" and hear the singers tell the history of the "Alligator Dance."

▶ • Listen to "Tekanionton'néha'," paying close attention to the places where the group responds to the soloist. Sing the responses as directed on page 171. (The responses are *vocables*, syllables that are not words.)

▶ • Learn the basic step of the "Alligator Dance." (See *Movement* on the bottom of page 171.)

OBJECTIVE 1 Informal Assessment
▶ • Perform the "Alligator Dance" and sing the responses. (See *Movement* on the bottom of page 171.)

170

MEETING **INDIVIDUAL** NEEDS

ALTERNATE TEACHING STRATEGY

OBJECTIVE 1 Point out to students that the basic step is a relaxed shuffle. Remind them to keep their knees loose and relaxed. On the 4-beat turn, the boy should be sure to turn *in place* so that the girl may easily dance in a circle around him.

MULTICULTURAL PERSPECTIVES: *Iroquois Dance*

"Tekanionton'néha'" is a simple Iroquois couples dance, performed by members of the Mohawk nation. The instruments heard on the recording are a small water drum and cow-horn rattles. The Mohawk nation is one of the six Indian nations that make up the Iroquois Confederacy, one of the world's first democratic systems of government. "Tekanionton'néha'" came to the Iroquois as part of their peace-making process. The confederacy would send out messengers to other tribes to invite them to "sit under the Tree of Peace." When an agreement was reached, the two nations would teach each other a song or a dance. This would serve as a record that they had established friendship and peace with one another and would support each other during bad times.

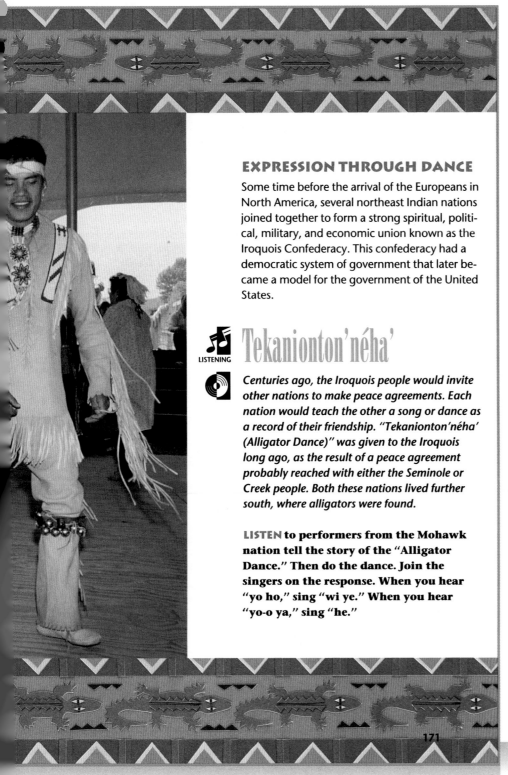

"The music of Native Americans is an important part of our American musical heritage." Have students:

▶ • Tell about performances of Native American music that they have heard or seen.

▶ • Give a final performance of the "Alligator Dance."

LESSON SUMMARY

Informal Assessment In this lesson, students:

OBJECTIVE 1 Performed a traditional Native American dance with "Tekanionton'néha'."

MORE MUSIC: Reinforcement
"Dances of the Summer," page 184 (dances of the world)
"Red River Valley," page 186 (dances of the world)
"Amores hallarás," page 186 (dances of the world)
"Pata Pata," page 187 (dances of the world)
"Grand Entry ," page 331 (Native American)
"Eskimo Ice Cream Dance," page 335 (Native American)
"Garifalia," page 372 (dances of the world)

EXPRESSION THROUGH DANCE

Some time before the arrival of the Europeans in North America, several northeast Indian nations joined together to form a strong spiritual, political, military, and economic union known as the Iroquois Confederacy. This confederacy had a democratic system of government that later became a model for the government of the United States.

Tekanionton'néha'

LISTENING

Centuries ago, the Iroquois people would invite other nations to make peace agreements. Each nation would teach the other a song or dance as a record of their friendship. "Tekanionton'néha' (Alligator Dance)" was given to the Iroquois long ago, as the result of a peace agreement probably reached with either the Seminole or Creek people. Both these nations lived further south, where alligators were found.

LISTEN to performers from the Mohawk nation tell the story of the "Alligator Dance." Then do the dance. Join the singers on the response. When you hear "yo ho," sing "wi ye." When you hear "yo-o ya," sing "he."

171

MOVEMENT: *The"Alligator Dance"*

Formation: double circle—partners standing side-by-side facing counter-clockwise (Girl holds her partner's right elbow with her left hand; boy's right arm is slightly bent.)

Basic Step: When the singing begins, the dancers move forward in a counterclockwise circle using a simple left/right shuffle, like a relaxed jogging step. The feet are lifted slightly, not dragged. Let the drum and rattle set the tempo. Take two steps per beat:

L R L R

Turn: Each time the singers perform the whole note, all of the dancers execute a turn (4 beats). The boy does a basic step in place while turning 360° counterclockwise. At the same time, the girl (still holding partner's elbow) dances a 360° counterclockwise circle around her partner, staying even with him as he turns in place. After finishing one complete 4-beat turn, the dancers resume the basic step.

UNIT FOUR
LESSON 7

RELATED ARTS | MOVEMENT | THEATER | VISUAL ARTS |

LESSON PLANNER

FOCUS Harmony

OBJECTIVE
OBJECTIVE 1 Play I and V chord roots in C major to accompany a song

MATERIALS
Recordings
Listening: Taos Round Dance   CD4:11
Hoe Ana   CD4:8
Yonder Come Day   CD4:4
Movin' On   CD4:16

Instruments
keyboard, recorder, or resonator bells

Resources Resource Master 4 • 5 (practice)

   ▶ = **BASIC PROGRAM**

TOGETHER

People of many different cultures can live together in harmony in the United States. By singing and playing chords, you can create rich musical harmony.

You have sung chords and played chord roots. You can also play complete chords on pitched instruments. The most frequently used chords in a major key are the chords built on the first, fourth, and fifth steps of the major scale. To build each chord, begin with the scale step.

A G major chord is built on the first step of the G major scale. Because this scale step is on a line, the other two notes in the chord will be on the two lines above it.

172

MEETING **INDIVIDUAL** NEEDS

ALTERNATE TEACHING STRATEGIES

OBJECTIVE 1 Have students practice singing the numbers of the chord roots in rhythm as they play. It may also be helpful to assign chords to students in two groups, with one group playing I and the other playing V.

MOVEMENT: *"Yonder Come Day"*

Add a traditional 8-beat gospel-choir step to the song.

Beat 1: Step L with the L foot.

Beat 2: Clap.

Beat 3: Touch R foot next to the L foot.

Beat 4: Clap.

Beat 5: Step R with the R foot.

IN HARMONY

The IV chord will be built on the fourth scale step, which, in G major, is C.

This is a C major chord. Because the scale step is in a space, the other two notes in the IV chord will be in the two spaces above it.

What is the fifth step of the G major scale? What pitches will be in the chord? D; D-F♯-A

PLAY these chords on keyboard or bells.

"Tell if you hear a harmonic accompaniment in these two pieces." Have students:

▶ • Discuss "Taos Round Dance" CD4:11 (page 166), and "Hoe Ana" CD4:8 (page 164). ("Taos Round Dance" uses a monophonic melody line [no harmony]. There is a harmonic accompaniment with "Hoe Ana.")

"Some cultures create harmonic effects like those we're used to hearing; others create music with no harmony at all. Today, you'll continue to explore harmony, learning how to build chords."

2 DEVELOP

1. Review "Yonder Come Day" CD4:4 (pp. 154–155). Play roots of I and V chords in C major as an accompaniment. Have students:

▶ • Sing Part 1 to review the melody.

• Sing these chord roots as you play the entire chords (or with the recording).

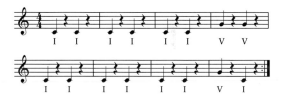

• Play the chord roots on keyboard, recorder, or resonator bells.

OBJECTIVE 1 Informal Assessment
• Play the chord roots as an accompaniment to "Yonder Come Day."

2. Construct I, IV, and V chords in G major. Have students:

▶ • Read about chord construction.

• Play the G (I), C (IV), and D (V) chords on keyboard or resonator bells. (See *Extra Help* below.)

Beat 6: Clap.

Beat 7: Touch L foot next to R foot.

Beat 8: Clap.

Continue this step-clap pattern throughout the song.

EXTRA HELP: *Constructing Triads*

Have students work in pairs to help each other construct each triad on available instruments.

UNIT FOUR
LESSON 7

continued from previous page

3. Add sung and spoken vocal parts to "Yonder Come Day." Have students:

• Learn to sing Parts 2 and 3.

• Read the rhythms of Part 4 by patting the rhythms and then saying the words.

• Speak Part 5 below, clapping and snapping as directed:

perform four times

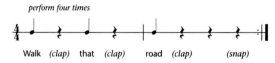

Walk (clap) that (clap) road (clap) (snap)

• Divide into five groups. (Assign each group a part.) Perform the piece seven times through, using parts as outlined:

1. Part 1 only
2. Parts 1 and 2
3. Parts 1, 2, and 3
4. Parts 1 and 4
5. Parts 1, 2, and 3
6. Parts 1, 4, and 5
7. Parts 1, 2, and 3

3 APPLY

Introduce "Movin' On" CD4:16. **Play I, IV, and V harmonic accompaniment as a group project, then sing with harmonic accompaniment.** Have students:

▶ • Listen to "Movin' On." Then sing the song.

Use the I, IV, and V chords to accompany "Movin' On." Play a chord on the first beat of each measure.

Words and Music by
Raymond R. Hannisian

1. There is a voice___ that has no name;___
2. The night has mu-sic that calls to me___
3. Speak to me soft-ly but tell me no lies;___

It comes with eve-ning___ or be-hind the rain:___
A-cross the can-yons___ of an end-less sea.___
I see to-mor-row___ shin-ing in your eyes.___

"I have no time— now to stop and ex-plain;___
I seek the shad-ows of yes-ter-day;___
"I have no time— now to stop and ex-plain;___

I just keep mov-in'___ 'cause it helps to
To-day can't hold me,___ and I must be
I just keep mov-in'___ 'cause it helps to

ease___ the pain."___
on___ my way.___
ease___ the pain."___

174 A HERITAGE OF HARMONY

MEETING **INDIVIDUAL** NEEDS

IMPROVISATION: *Barred Instruments*

Have students create a minor section for "Yonder Come Day" by following these steps.

Step 1 Play the rhythm of Part 4 on the A bar with alternating hands.

Step 2 Starting on A, play the rhythm of Part 4 using any of the following notes: A C D E G A'.

Step 3 Incorporate this section into the piece wherever they think it will sound best. (This will add an eighth section to the performance.)

PLAYING INSTRUMENTS: *Recorder and Handbells*

Recorder and handbell parts to accompany "Movin' On" can be found on **Resource Master 4 • 5**.

GUITAR: *"Movin' On"*

Have students play the I, IV, and V chords on guitar—G, C, and D (or D7) chords—to accompany "Movin' On."

long____ a qui - et road that wan - ders by, and
found____ a si - lent can - yon full of stars and
ev' - ry - where I go a - cross the land, I

I have smiled and won - dered where it goes.
in my heart I heard them tell - ing
stand so proud - ly in the sun and

me I was home.____ The gen - tle winds, The rains that fall,

The tall - est trees, I'm part of it all.____ 3. I've

say, "I am home." 4. I've say, "I am home."____

LESSON SUMMARY

Informal Assessment In this lesson, students:

OBJECTIVE 1 Played a harmonic accompaniment to "Movin' On" using I, IV and V chords in G major.

OBJECTIVE 2 Played the melodic bass line resulting from chord inversions to accompany "An American Hymn."

MORE MUSIC: Reinforcement
"Auld Lang Syne," page 319 (play I, IV, V in F; Scottish immigrants)

"*John B.* Sails," page 347 (play I, IV, V in G; Caribbean immigrants)

Verse 1—Arms reach up, out, then down on the phrase *slowly opens like a rose.*

—Walk slowly to form a road shape (two lines curving from top left of risers to bottom right, the distance apart being greater at the bottom than at the top), creating this shape on *Along a quiet road that wanders by*, and *I have smiled and wondered where it goes.*

Verse 2—Students forming the road sit as a soloist walks "on the road" from the top left to the bottom right.

—Small groups stand on each of the following phrases until the entire group is standing: 1) *the gentle winds;* 2) *the rains that fall;* 3) *the tallest trees;* 4) *I'm part of it all.*

Verse 3—All look up to same corner at the rear of the auditorium on *I've seen the silver mountaintops.*

—Draw a large arc with right arm indicating *and golden prairies on my way.*

—Walk, spreading out to all parts of the risers on *ev'rywhere I go across the land, I stand so proudly in the sun and say, "I am home."*

Verse 4—Remain spread out across risers, returning to first groupings on *I am home.*

UNIT FOUR
LESSON 9

RELATED ARTS | MOVEMENT | THEATER | VISUAL ARTS

LESSON PLANNER

OBJECTIVES
To review songs, skills, and concepts learned in Unit 4 and to test students' ability to:
1. Read and perform rhythms in § meter
2. Recognize the first five steps of a minor scale

MATERIALS
Recordings

Away to America	CD3:24
Hoe Ana	CD4:8
Dance for the Nations	CD3:32
American Dream	CD4:1
Unit 4 Assessment A	CD4:18–21
Unit 4 Assessment B	CD4:22–25

Instruments pitched instruments

Resources
Resource Master 4 • 6 (assessment)
Resource Master TA • 1 (assessment)
Resource Master—staff paper

▶ = **BASIC PROGRAM**

REVIEW

CELEBRATING
AMERICAN MUSIC

We celebrate the music that has come together in the United States to create our heritage in sound. From the music of the Native Americans who have lived here for thousands of years to the music of the many people who have come to this land and made it their home, we have built our great musical heritage. Over the years, people have been drawn "Away to America."

180

MEETING **INDIVIDUAL** NEEDS

PROGRAM IDEA: *Our Musical Heritage* THEATER 🎭

This review can be enjoyed in the classroom or presented as a simple program. Additional materials from Unit 4, *Celebrations*, or the *Music Library* may be added as well as original work from the students.

Have students celebrate America's musical heritage using some of the statements on page 180 as a script. Choose readers for each line of narration. As each line is read, follow it with a performance of the appropriate song. Where applicable, have students add instrumental accompaniments.

For an additional activity, have students or family members with direct ties to the cultures represented give background for some or all of the songs. Students can also supplement the unit songs with songs, stories, dances, and poems from their own heritage, based on their own research and on interviews with family and friends.

For scenery, have students create a mural with large pictures representing various cultures and a large map showing the general locations. Some students might wish to wear clothing from their own or other cultures.

We celebrate with the music that makes our feet dance and our spirits soar. Sing and dance to "Dance for the Nations."

We celebrate the meeting of the music of different cultures in this great land. For example, "El tambor" comes to us from Panama, in Central America. "Hoe Ana" comes to us from Tahiti, an island in the South Pacific Ocean.

When we celebrate the "American Dream," we celebrate with music, our heritage in sound.

Unit 4 Our Musical Heritage **181**

REVIEW

1. Review beats divided into threes and § meter with "Away to America" CD3:24 **(pp. 140–141), and "Hoe Ana"** CD4:8 **(p. 164).** Have students:

▶ • Listen to "Away to America" and tell whether the beats are divided into twos or threes. (threes) Then sing the song.

▶ • Listen to "Hoe Ana." Tell the meter. (§ ; beats divided into threes) Sing the song.

2. Review the first five steps of the major and minor scales with "Dance for the Nations" CD3:32 **(p. 150) and "Hoe Ana."** Have students:

• List the pitches in the first two lines of "Dance for the Nations" from lowest to highest. (C♯ D E F G A B♭)

• Starting from D (tonic or home pitch of the scale), list the first five pitches and play them on a pitched instrument. Then find the location of the half step and tell whether this is a major or minor scale pattern. (D E F G A; between steps 2 and 3; minor)

▶ • Sing and dance "Dance for the Nations." (See Lesson 2, pages 150–151, *Movement*, or *Enrichment* below.)

• Repeat bullets 1 and 2 above for the first line of "Hoe Ana." (C♯ D E F♯ G A B C♯; D E F♯ G A; between steps 3 and 4; major)

3. Identify major and minor in "American Dream" CD4:1 **(pp. 151–153) and reinforce unit theme.** Have students:

• Sing "American Dream" and listen for which section is in major and which is in minor. (A— minor, B—major, form is A B A B)

• Use the song as a starting point to reflect on the unit's theme of musical heritage. (Optional: Celebrate America's musical heritage by performing unit materials with a narration, as in the *Program Idea* at the bottom of page 180.)

ENRICHMENT: *"Dance for the Nations"*

Without the recording, have students add interludes between each repetition of the song during which students take turns improvising melodies on D E F G A. At the same time, have dancers improvise solo movement. The improvisations should be about the length of the song.

UNIT FOUR
LESSON 9

ASSESSMENTS A AND B CD4:18–25

Different recorded examples for Assessments A and B allow for two uses of the same set of questions. When appropriate, recorded examples for Assessment A use familiar musical examples with which students have worked for the given concept. The recorded examples for Assessment B use musical selections the students have not previously worked with for the concept, encouraging the application of knowledge to new material.

The pupil page is intended for those who wish to assess quickly with the whole class or in small groups. Each assessment may be used as a pretest or as a final review before presenting the written test (**Resource Master 4 · 6**).

ANSWERS	
ASSESSMENT A	**ASSESSMENT B**
1. b	a
2. a	b
3. b	d
4. c	d

CHECK IT OUT

1. Do you hear the first five steps of a minor scale?

   a. Yes   b. No

2. Do you hear the first five steps of a minor scale?

   a. Yes   b. No

3. Which rhythm do you hear?

   a.
   b.
   c.
   d.

4. Which rhythm do you hear?

   a.
   b.
   c.
   d.

MEETING **INDIVIDUAL** NEEDS

PORTFOLIO ASSESSMENT

To evaluate students' portfolios, use the Portfolio Assessment form on **Resource Master TA · 1**. See page 136B for a summary of Portfolio Opportunities in this unit.

EXTRA HELP: *Creating a Melody*

Have students look at the last note of each melodic phrase and make sure that the first note of the following phrase is very close to it in pitch. This will result in a more pleasing and smooth melody line.

SOCIAL STUDIES CONNECTION: *Family Tree*

After students have chosen pieces of music to represent their family's musical heritage, have them make a family tree. Each branch should show the name of a song, the name of the person from whom it was collected, and the song's country or place of origin.

You might also have volunteers locate on a large map or globe the countries in which some of the songs originated.

CREATE

A Musical Celebration

CLAP the rhythm shown by the notation below. Read the poem in the rhythm shown.

Words by H. Wilburr

Sing A - mer - i - cans, glad - ly sing

While the bells of free - dom ring!

Hail our flag on land and sea.

Sing that here we all are free!

CREATE your own melody, following these directions.

- Use pitches from the C major scale.

C D E F G A B C' D' E'

- Avoid large leaps. If you do choose a leap, follow it with step-wise motion.
- In measure 4 use pitches D' E' D'. In measure 8 use pitches E D C.

SING the melody you have created. Your composition is now another part of America's sound heritage.

Write

In this unit, we have explored many contributions to the musical heritage of the United States. Choose four or five pieces of music that represent your family's heritage. Name each piece and briefly explain why you chose it.

Unit 4 *Our Musical Heritage* **183**

CREATE AND WRITE

1. Read and compose a melody for a poem in § meter. Have students:

- Apply their knowledge of § meter to clap the rhythm shown, then read the poem as instructed on page 183.

- Working in pairs, follow the directions on page 183 to use the pitches of the C major scale to create a melody for the words of the poem. (Optional: Have students notate the melody on staff paper, available in the Resource Master booklet.

- Practice the melody on a pitched instrument, then sing it for the class.

2. Explore our musical heritage. Have students:

▶ • Discuss how different groups have contributed to this country's musical heritage. (You might have students write a narrative about how people from different cultures feel about their own musical heritage, written from the point of view of a person from each culture.)

▶ • Follow the instructions on page 183 to write about their family's musical heritage.

RELATED ARTS | MOVEMENT | THEATER | VISUAL ARTS

LESSONLINKS

Dances of the Summer *(30 min)*

OBJECTIVE Listen and dance to music for the summer season

Reinforcement (all selections in this Encore) dances of the world, *page 171*

MATERIALS
Recordings
Sumer Is Icumen In (listening)   CD4:26
Yagi Bushi (listening)   CD4:27

Red River Valley *(15 min)*

OBJECTIVE Listen and move to an American folk dance

MATERIALS
Recording Red River Valley (listening)   CD4:28
Resources Resource Master 4 • 7 (practice)

Pata, Pata *(15 min)*

OBJECTIVE Listen and move to a South African song by Miriam Makeba

MATERIALS
Recording Pata, Pata by M. Makeba (listening)   CD4:29

Amores hallarás *(15 min)*

OBJECTIVE Listen and move to an Ecuadorean folk dance

MATERIALS
Recording Amores hallarás (listening)   CD4:30

ENCORE
DANCES OF OUR WORLD

  LISTENING **Sumer Is Icumen In**

Late Medieval (c. 1310)

The farandole *is the oldest European folk dance still in existence today. Popular in France and Italy during medieval times, it was a simple dance that was often accompanied by song. As time went on, the farandole became more and more complicated. Performers had to master a difficult series of steps, turns, and twists. Many Mediterranean and South American dances are similar to the farandole.*

LISTEN to a song which may have accompanied the farandole.

184

MEETING **INDIVIDUAL** NEEDS

MOVEMENT: *Farandole*

Formation: Lines of 6–8 people; the first person leads the rest through the following figures in a free-form dance, doing the farandole step on page 185 above.

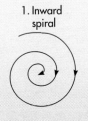   

1. Inward spiral   2. Outward spiral   3. Arches   4. Circle

MOVEMENT: *"Yagi Bushi"*

Preparation: Have students practice walking to the rhythm below, then add the hand rhythm to the walk.

Foot rhythm: $\frac{4}{4}$ ♩   ♩   ♩   𝄽   ‖

Hand rhythm: $\frac{4}{4}$ ♫   𝄽   ♩   𝄽   ‖

Final Form: Repeat movements on the bottom of page 185 throughout song.

Formation: Dancers facing in a clockwise circle, the Bon towel (a patterned cloth) around their necks like a stole. (Use scarfs, towels, or strips from sheets.)

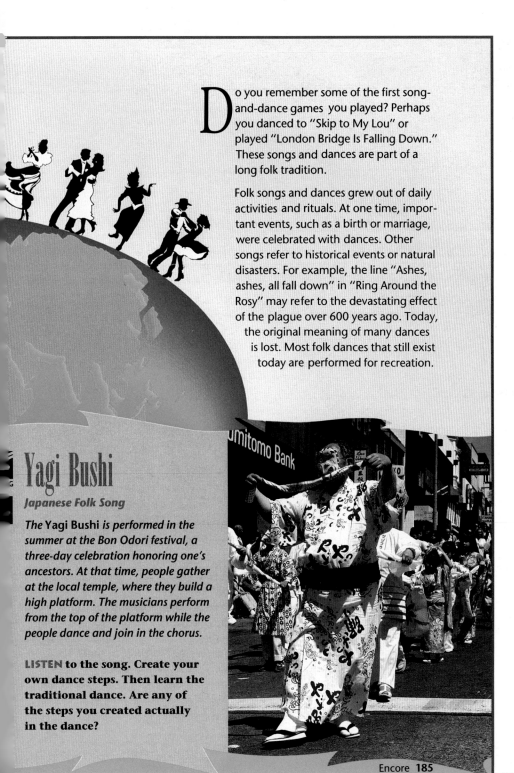

D o you remember some of the first song-and-dance games you played? Perhaps you danced to "Skip to My Lou" or played "London Bridge Is Falling Down." These songs and dances are part of a long folk tradition.

Folk songs and dances grew out of daily activities and rituals. At one time, important events, such as a birth or marriage, were celebrated with dances. Other songs refer to historical events or natural disasters. For example, the line "Ashes, ashes, all fall down" in "Ring Around the Rosy" may refer to the devastating effect of the plague over 600 years ago. Today, the original meaning of many dances is lost. Most folk dances that still exist today are performed for recreation.

Yagi Bushi
Japanese Folk Song

The Yagi Bushi is performed in the summer at the Bon Odori festival, a three-day celebration honoring one's ancestors. At that time, people gather at the local temple, where they build a high platform. The musicians perform from the top of the platform while the people dance and join in the chorus.

LISTEN to the song. Create your own dance steps. Then learn the traditional dance. Are any of the steps you created actually in the dance?

Encore 185

Dances of the Summer

1. Listen to "Sumer Is Icumen In" CD4:26, **music used to accompany a medieval dance.** Have students:

• Read page 184, then tell experiences they have had seeing folk dances.

• Describe the farandole (fɑ ɾɑ̃ dɔl). (a medieval folk dance)

• From the picture, describe how the dance might work. (line dance, forming spirals and circles)

• Listen to "Sumer Is Icumen In" (**su** mər ɪs ɪ **ku** mən ɪn), a medieval English canon with two ostinato bass parts. (The title means "Summer is Coming," and the song describes various summertime activities—plants growing, animals caring for their young, birds singing.)

• Learn this farandole step, then try it with the song:

R   L   RLR   L   R   LRL

2. Listen to "Yagi Bushi" CD4:27, **Japanese dance music. Create dance steps, then learn the traditional dance.** Have students:

• Read about the Yagi Bushi (**ya** gi **bu** shi) and the Bon Odori (**bon** o **do** ɾi) festival.

• Listen to the music, imagining how people might dance to it.

• In pairs, create dance movements that fit the music.

• Perform their dance for the class.

• Learn the traditional dance. (See *Movement* on the bottom of pages 184–185.)

Beat Step	Hands
1. R foot crosses over L.	Clap ♫ over L shoulder.
2. Step L foot in place.	⁂
3–4. Return R foot; ⁂	Clap ♩ in front; ⁂
5. L foot crosses over R.	Clap ♫ over R shoulder.
6. Step R foot in place.	⁂
7-8. Return L foot; ⁂	Clap ♩ in front; ⁂
9. Step R foot forward.	Clap ♫ out in front.
10. Step L foot in place.	⁂
11–12. Return R foot; ⁂	Clap ♩ in front; ⁂
13. Step L foot forward.	R hand swings towel off neck.
14. Step R foot in place.	L hand grabs other end of towel.

Beat Step	Hands
15. Return L foot.	Position towel in front horizontally, chest height, palms facing out.
16. ⁂	⁂
17–19. Step R foot forward, L foot forward, R foot forward.	Rotate towel with both hands, like pedaling a bicycle. (3 times)
20. Step L foot in place.	Freeze hands.
21–23. Step R foot, L foot, R foot backward.	Twirl towel toward body. (3 times)
24. Step L foot in place.	Hook towel over head.

ENCORE
MULTICULTURAL PERSPECTIVES

continued from previous page

Red River Valley CD4:28

Listen to an American folk-dance song and demonstrate basic square-dance movements. Have students:

• Tell what they know about square dancing. (Students may say that it is a type of American folk dancing performed by groups of four couples who follow the directions of a caller.) Then read page 186.

• Listen to "Red River Valley," noting the square-dance directions given by the caller.

• Demonstrate the *do si do* or promenade. (See *Movement* below. Optional: For the complete square dance of "Red River Valley," see **Resource Master 4 • 7**.)

Pata, Pata CD4:29

Listen to an African song and learn a touch-step movement. Have students:

• Listen to "Pata, Pata" (**pa** ta **pa** ta).

• Move to the music using the basic touch-step motion. (Tap the right foot to the right, then return it next to the left foot; repeat with left foot.) (See *Movement* below.)

🎵 Red River Valley *American Folk Dance*

Square dancing *is popular in many parts of the United States. Many of the steps came from European folk dances. Each group of four couples forms a square. The caller, who gives the steps, can use a known version of a dance or combine steps to create a new one.*

You may be familiar with some of the square-dance calls—do si do or promenade. Try some of them with a partner.

LISTEN to "Red River Valley," a popular folk dance.

🎵 Amores hallarás *Ecuadorian Folk Dance*

In Ecuador and throughout the Andes, festivals are a time to visit with friends and neighbors. People come to the festivals to buy and sell products during the day and to sing and dance at night. The amores hallarás describes the courtship, in earlier times, of young people in some parts of the Andean region.

The steps used in this folk dance are very traditional. Listen to the guitar or the drum ostinato at the beginning of the dance. How would you move to the rhythm ♩ ♩ ♩?

186 DANCES OF OUR WORLD

MEETING **INDIVIDUAL** NEEDS

MOVEMENT: *"Red River Valley"*

Have students practice these square-dance steps.

Promenade: Have students walk in pairs, holding hands, in a counterclockwise direction using a smooth, gliding walk.

Swing: 1) Partners stand right sides together, girl's right hand in boy's left hand at shoulder height, boy's right hand on girl's left waist, turning clockwise, or 2) holding hands and circling in a clockwise direction, leaning back slightly, keeping right feet close together and using the left foot to turn in a galloping rhythm.

MOVEMENT: *"Pata, Pata"*

Formation: Standing in place; lines are optional.

Beats 1–4: Touch R foot sideways right and snap fingers to the right side (at the same time). Return R foot and clap hands in front of body. Repeat on L side.

Beats 5–8: Turn toes out and raise arms and pull elbows in; turn heels out and lower arms. Repeat.

Beats 9–12: Raise R knee in front of the body; touch R foot sideways right. Raise R knee; step R foot next to L foot.

Beats 13–16: Kick L foot out, then circle counterclockwise in place (L foot, R foot, L foot), ending in starting position. Repeat the 16-beat pattern until song's end.

Pata Pata *by Miriam Makeba*

When Miriam Makeba, a famous South African singer, wrote "Pata Pata," she was thinking of a dance done in her homeland. The recording of the song was very successful in the United States in the late 1960s. The dance became popular as well.

LISTEN to "Pata Pata." *Pata* means "touch" in Zulu and Zhosa. The basic motion in this dance is touch, step.

Amores hallarás CD4:30

Listen to "Amores hallarás," an Ecuadorean folk dance, and move to the rhythm. Have students:

• Tell where Ecuador is (South America) and locate it on a map. Find the Andes on the map.

• Look at the ♩ ♩ ♩ rhythm as they listen to the ostinato (first 16 beats of the song) and suggest ways to move to this rhythm. Watch as volunteers demonstrate some of the suggestions.

• Listen to "Amores hallarás" (a **mo** ɾes a ya **ɾas**) ("Love Can Be Found"). Listen again, clapping the ♩ ♩ ♩ rhythm.

• Learn the basic eight-beat step for the dance—right, left, right, hop (RLRH); left, right, left, hop (LRLH). Practice the step alone and with a partner. (For the complete folk dance, see *Movement* below.)

MOVEMENT: *"Amores hallarás"*

Formation: Single circle facing inward, alternating boy and girl; boys on the right. Join hands. Boys have scarfs.
A Section: Step in place—RLRH-LRLH-RLRH-LRLH.
B Section: Circle facing counterclockwise, crossing left foot in front of right foot—RLRH-LRLH-RLRH-LRLH-RLRH. (20 beats) **C Section:** Repeat Section B, moving clockwise, crossing right foot in front of left. (Begin with LRLH.) **D and E Sections:** Move toward center of circle—RLRH-LRLH. Back out of circle—RLRH-LRLH. (16 beats) Repeat. **F Section:** Dancers move closer to their partners, stepping in place—RLRH-LRLH. **G Section:** Partners stand with R shoulders together and move clockwise in their

own circle—RLRH-LRLH-RLRH-LRLH-RLRH.
H Section: Repeat G, but with shoulders together and moving counterclockwise. (Begin with LRLH.) **I Section:** Boy kneels on L knee and presents scarf to partner with R hand. Girl takes end of scarf in L hand and dances counterclockwise around boy—RLRH-LRLH-RLRH-LRLH. **J Section:** Boy stands and passes scarf around girl's shoulders. Partners dance side by side, boy's R hand holding girl's R hand on her shoulder, L hands joined in front—RLRH-LRLH-RLRH-LRLH. (Boy is still holding scarf in both hands; the scarf passes around his neck and her shoulders.) **K Section:** Couples dance away from circle until end.

Encore DANCES OF OUR WORLD **187**

ON STAGE

MULTICULTURAL PERSPECTIVES

Through exposure to diverse materials, students develop an awareness of how people from many cultures create and participate in music. This unit includes:

Asian/Asian American

- **Eka Tala (excerpt)**, South Indian theater music, 216
- **Prologue to *Mahabharata* (excerpt)**, traditional Indonesian music, 219

European/European American

- **There's No Business Like Show Business**, by American Irving Berlin, 188
- **Another Op'nin', Another Show**, by American Cole Porter, 191
- **Look Around**, by Americans Cy Coleman, Betty Comden, Adolph Green, 192
- **Summertime**, by George and Ira Gershwin, 195
- **Won't You Charleston with Me?**, by British composer Sandy Wilson, 197
- **Comedy Tonight**, by Stephen Sondheim, 198
- **One**, by Americans M. Hamlisch and E. Kleban, 200
- **Pumping Iron, Starlight Express, I Am the Starlight, The Light at the End of the Tunnel,** by Britons Andrew Lloyd Webber and Richard Stilgoe, 205, 207, 208, 210
- **Opening Scene from *Gianni Schicchi***, by Italian Giacomo Puccini, 213
- **Firenze è come un albero fiorito**, by Giacomo Puccini, 214
- **O mio babbino caro**, by Giacomo Puccini, 215
- **Ladro! Ladro!**, by Giacomo Puccini, 215
- **Our Time**, by American Stephen Sondheim, 222
- **Give My Regards to Broadway**, by American George M. Cohan, 226

Hispanic/Hispanic American

- **De este apacible rincón**, zarzuela aria by Spanish composer Federico Moreno Torroba, 220

For a complete listing of materials by culture throughout the book, see the Classified Index.

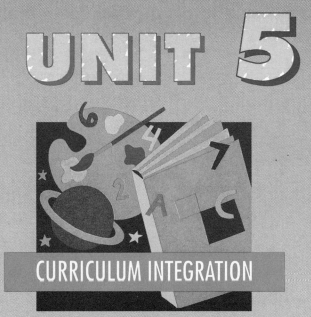

UNIT 5

CURRICULUM INTEGRATION

Activities in this unit that promote the integration of music with other curriculum areas include:

Art

- Design a forum for hometown, 199B

Mathematics

- Determine profit/loss of a theatrical performance, 195A
- Draw and classify plane figures, 195A
- Design a forum for hometown, 199B
- Take measurements and use a formula to find average speeds, 207B
- Play a coordinate game, 211A

Reading/Language Arts

- Write an editorial, 195B
- Write words containing a suffix, 199B
- Write a character sketch, 207B
- Write an autobiographical sketch, 211A
- Write new lyrics, 226
- Write a synopsis of a musical, 231

Science

- Model the first day of summer to compare hours of daylight and darkness, 195B
- Analyze data from a homemade air pollutant collector, 199A
- Explore force using a block and spring scale, 207A
- Explore air resistance, 207A
- Research sources of energy, 211B

Social Studies

- Make a "Time Capsule" bulletin board for hometown, 199A
- Play a map distance game, 211B
- Produce a shadow-puppet musical or opera, 219

PLANNER

ASSESSMENT OPTIONS

Informal Performance Assessments

Informal Assessments correlated to Objectives are provided in every lesson with Alternate Strategies for reteaching. Frequent informal assessment allows for ongoing progress checks throughout the course of the unit.

Formal Assessment

An assessment form is provided on pupil page 230 and Resource Master 5•8. The questions assess student understanding of the following main unit objectives:

- Identify vocal range of soprano, alto, tenor, bass
- Recognize lighter and heavier vocal tone colors
- Identify appropriate interpretive elements by which a singer can project the mood or style of a song (tempo, dynamics, tone color, articulation)

Music Journal

Encourage students to enter thoughts about selections, projects, performances, and personal progress. Some journal opportunities include:

- Critical Thinking, TE 189, TE 210
- Decide on song interpretation, 198
- Describe vocal interpretation, 205, 207, TE 210, 211, 214–215
- Think It Through, 213

Portfolio Opportunities

Update student portfolios with outcome-based materials, including written work, audiotapes, videotapes, and/or photos that represent their best work for each unit. Some portfolio opportunities in this unit include:

- Sing Another Op'nin' *marcato*, with solo singers, TE 191 (audiotape)
- Sing Look Around *legato*, 192 (audiotape)
- Sing Look Around and Comedy Tonight with group interpretation, TE 198, 199 (audiotape)
- Improvisation: Syncopated Interludes, TE 203 (audiotape)
- Play harmonic accompaniment to Pumping Iron, 206 (audiotape)
- Write comparison of musical and opera, TE 215
- Play *Kathakali* rhythm, 217 (audiotape)
- Play in Balinese style, TE 219 (audiotape)
- Write down singer's interpretation choices, 220
- Prepare solo interpretation of Our Time, TE 224 (audiotape)
- Enrichment: The Composer's Workshop, TE 224 (audiotape)
- Check It Out, 230; Resource Master 5•8
- Portfolio Assessment (Resource Masters TA•1–5), 230
- Create, 231
- Write, 231

MY MUSIC NOTEBOOK

UNIT 5 CONCEPT

		LESSON 1 CORE p.188	LESSON 2 CORE p.196	LESSON 3 p.200
FOCUS		Style/Tone	Style, interpretation	Rhythm
SELECTIONS		There's No Business Like Show Business (poem) Another Op'nin', Another Show Look Around Summertime (listening)	Another Op'nin', Another Show Won't You Charleston with Me? Look Around Comedy Tonight	Comedy Tonight One Won't You Charleston with Me?

MUSICAL ELEMENTS	CONCEPTS	UNIT OBJECTIVES Bold = Tested			
EXPRESSIVE QUALITIES	Dynamics	• **Identify appropriate dynamics**	• *Choose dynamics to recite poem (E/D)*	• **Review definition of dynamics (I)** • **Choose dynamics for songs (P/Rf/C)**	• Sing chosen dynamics (Rf)
	Tempo	• **Identify appropriate tempo**		• **Review definition of *tempo* (I)** • **Choose tempo for songs (P/Rf/C)**	• Sing chosen tempo (Rf)
	Articulation	• **Identify appropriate articulation**	• **Hear, discuss, and sing legato and marcato (E/D/I)** • Create "legato" and "marcato" movement (P)	• **Choose articulation for songs (P/Rf/C)**	• Sing chosen articulation (Rf)
TONE COLOR	Vocal/ Instrumental Tone Color	• **Identify soprano, alto, tenor, bass vocal ranges** • **Identify appropriate vocal tone color** • **Identify lighter and heavier vocal tone color**	• *Choose tone color to recite poem (E/D)* • **Hear, describe, identify soprano, alto, tenor, bass, and unchanged voice (E/D/I)** • **Hear and describe lighter and heavier vocal tone color (E/D)** • *Play pitched and unpitched instrument accompaniment*	• **Choose tone color for songs (P/Rf/C)** • **Review lighter/heavier tone color (I)**	• **Recognize unchanged and bass voices (Rf)** • Sing chosen tone color (Rf)
DURATION	Beat/Meter		• *Walk to beat*		• Recognize beats with no new sound • *Move to beat*
	Rhythm	• Recognize syncopation • Play South Indian rhythms			• Pat, clap, and play rhythm patterns with ♫ and syncopation • Recognize syncopation
PITCH	Melody			• Sing pitch letter names in bass clef	
	Harmony	• Perform harmonic accompaniment		• Sing in 2 parts	
	Tonality major/minor		• Hear major and minor	• Hear major	• Hear major
DESIGN	Texture			• Sing in 2 parts	
	Form/ Structure	• Recognize motive	• *Make up repeated movement motive*	• *Make up repeated movement motive*	
CULTURAL CONTEXT	Style/ Background	• Compare opera and musical • Play in Balinese style	• Learn about musicals, lyricists, opera • *Composers: Irving Berlin, Cole Porter, Cy Coleman, George Gershwin* • *Learn about Kiss Me Kate, Porgy and Bess* • *Lyricists: Betty Comden and Adolph Green*	• *Composers: Sandy Wilson, Stephen Sondheim* • *Chareer: Music Journalist*	• Composer: Marvin Hamlisch • *Musical: A Chorus Line* • *Career: Songwriter*

Learning Sequence: E = Explore, D = Describe, I = Identify, P = Practice, Rf = Reinforce, Rd = Read, C = Create   See also *Program Scope and Sequence*, page 432.

OVERVIEW

LESSON 4 CORE p.204	LESSON 5 CORE p.208	LESSON 6 p.212	LESSON 7 p.216	LESSON 8 p.222
Musical drama/tone color/ expressive use of the voice	Musical drama/musical style	Tone color/style	Style	Style
Pumping Iron (listening) Starlight Express (listening)	Starlight Express (listening) I Am the Starlight (listening) The Light at the End of the Tunnel (listening)	Pumping Iron (listening) *Gianni Schicchi* Opening Scene (listening) Firenze è come un albero fiorito (listening) O mio babbino caro (listening) Ladro! Ladro! (listening)	Eka Tala (listening) Prologue to Mahabharata (listening) De este apacible rincón (listening)	Comedy Tonight Our Time One Give My Regards to Broadway
• Review dynamics (Rf)	• Recognize dynamics (Rf)	• Recognize dynamics (Rf)	• Discuss dynamics as element of interpretation (Rf) • Recognize dynamics (Rf)	• Choose and sing dynamics (C) • Recognize dynamics (Rf)
• Review tempo (Rf)	• Recognize tempo (Rf)	• Recognize tempo (Rf)	• Discuss tempo as element of interpretation (Rf) • Recognize tempo (Rf)	• Choose and sing tempo (C) • Recognize tempo (Rf)
• Review legato and marcato (Rf)	• Recognize articulation (Rf)	• Recognize articulation (Rf)	• Discuss articulation as element of interpretation (Rf) • Recognize articulation (Rf)	• Choose and sing articulation (C) • Recognize articulation (Rf)
• Review vocal ranges, categories, tone color (Rf) • Discuss vocal tone color (Rf) • Play chords on pitched instruments	• Compare vocal tone colors (Rf) • Recognize instrumental accompaniment style • *Play melodic motives*	• Recognize vocal categories (Rf) • Recognize vocal tone colors (Rf) • Recognize mood projected by orchestra	• Discuss tone color as element of interpretation (Rf) • Recognize vocal tone color (Rf) • Hear and learn about Indian percussion • Play Indian percussion pattern • Play barred instruments	• Choose and sing with vocal tone color (C) • Recognize vocal tone color (Rf) • *Choose instrumentation for song*
			• Tap 4-beat pattern	
	• Recognize and clap syncopated patterns		• Discuss rhythm as element of music • Recognize changing rhythm patterns	• *Choose and play rhythm patterns for accompaniment*
• Review meaning of sharp	• *Make up short melodies*		• Discuss pitch as element of music	• *Make up melody for poem*
• Play harmonic accompaniment • Review I, IV, V chords in C major • Play chord roots				• Learn harmony part • *Choose chords for song*
• Review C major scale				
• Play harmonic accompaniment			• Discuss texture as element of music • Play 2-part ostinato pattern	• Sing solo and in 2 parts • *Choose texture for accompaniment*
• Play along with verse-refrain song	• Recognize motive in song	• Compare musical and opera	• Discuss form as element of music	
• *Composer: Andrew Lloyd Webber* • *Musical:* Starlight Express	• Recognize gospel call-and-response style	• Learn about opera • *Composer: Giacomo Puccini* • *Learn about* Gianni Schicchi	• Learn about South Indian and Indonesian theater music; shadow puppets; the Mahabharata; Shiva statue; zarzuela • Define *style* • *Composer: Federico Moreno Torroba*	• *Learn about* Merrily We Roll Along

UNIT 5 PLANNER

SKILLS		LESSON 1 CORE p.188	LESSON 2 CORE p.196	LESSON 3 p.200
CREATION AND PERFORMANCE	Singing	• *Recite poem with appropriate tone color and dynamics* • Sing legato and marcato • Sing solos • Sing in 2 parts	• Sing marcato and legato • Sing songs with chosen tempo, dynamics, tone color	• Sing songs with chosen tempo, dynamics, tone color
	Playing	• *Play poem accompaniment*		• Pat and clap syncopated patterns
	Moving	• *Perform "legato" and "marcato" movement*	• *Do Charleston* • *Perform group dance*	• *Do chorus line kicks*
	Improvising/ Creating	• *Improvise poem accompaniment* • *Create poem interpretation with dynamics and tone color* • *Create "legato" and "marcato" movement*	• Create song interpretations • *Create group dance with movement motive*	• *Improvise syncopated patterns*
NOTATION	Reading		• Read pitch letter names in bass clef	• Read syncopated patterns
	Writing			
PERCEPTION AND ANALYSIS	Listening/ Describing/ Analyzing	• *Evaluate poem interpretations* • Explain difference between lyricist and lyrics • Describe vocal articulation • Choose song articulation	• Define vocal tone color • Choose and compare song interpretations (dynamics, tempo, articulation, tone color) • *Identify and show repeated phrases*	• Identify vocal categories • Identify syncopation

  TECHNOLOGY

SHARE THE MUSIC VIDEOS

Use videos to reinforce, extend, and enrich learning.
· **Lesson 1, pp. 189–192:** Musical Expression (creating and interpreting, articulation); Making a Music Video (part songs)
· **Lesson 2, p. 196:** Musical Expression (dynamics, tempo, interpretation)
· **Lesson 3, p. 202:** Making a Music Video (popular music)
· **Lesson 4, p. 207:** Making a Music Video (ideas to videotape)
· **Lesson 7, p. 219:** Sounds of Percussion (gender wayang)
· **Encore, p. 232:** Musical Expression (Georges Bizet, *Carmen*)

MUSIC WITH *MIDI*

MIDI technology allows students to manipulate musical elements and make musical decisions with this song:
· **Lesson 8, p. 226: Give My Regards to Broadway**

MUSICTIME™

This notational software develops students' music reading and writing skills through activities correlated to these lessons:
· **Lesson 3, Project 1 (create syncopated accompaniment)**
· **Lesson 5, Project 2 (practice back-up singing)**
· **Lesson 8, Project 3 (compose a melody for a poem)**

OVERVIEW

LESSON 4 CORE p.204	LESSON 5 CORE p.208	LESSON 6 p.212	LESSON 7 p.216	LESSON 8 p.222
	• *Sing from memory*			• Sing chosen interpretation • Sing solo • Sing in 2 parts
• Play chord roots • Play chord accompaniment	• *Play motives* • Clap syncopated pattern		• Play Indian percussion pattern • Play barred instrument ostinatos	• *Play pitched and unpitched accompaniments*
		• Act out connecting scenes in opera	• *Perform shadow-puppet-like movements*	• *Move to song*
	• *Create 5-note motives*		• *Create shadow-puppet-like movements*	• Create movement to song • *Create poem setting, including melody, harmony, accompaniment*
	• *Read pitch letter names*			• *Read rhythm patterns*
	• *Write pitch letter names*			• *Write song melody and accompaniment*
• Describe attitude and mood of characters in musical • Describe and compare vocal tone colors	• Identify motive in song • Describe and compare vocal tone colors • Describe song mood, compare to other songs, and identify musical elements that project mood • Analyze choice of voice category • Identify musical elements that project contrasting moods	• Identify vocal category, tempo, dynamics, tone color, and articulation, and describe how they fit mood • Identify mood projected by accompaniment • *Write review of opera* • Compare musical and opera	• Identify changing rhythm patterns • Compare two ostinatos • Identify interpretive choices • Compare and contrast 3 musical styles • Describe meaning of style	• Choose and evaluate song interpretations

UNIT 5 PLANNER

MUSIC ACE™

Music Ace reinforces musical concepts and provides ear-training opportunities for students.
· **Lesson 2, p. 196: Lesson 13 (bass clef); Lesson 14 (ledger lines above the bass clef)**

UNIT FIVE
LESSON 1

RELATED ARTS | MOVEMENT | THEATER | VISUAL ARTS |

LESSON PLANNER

FOCUS Style/Tone color

OBJECTIVES
OBJECTIVE 1 Sing a Broadway-show tune with appropriate articulation (tested)
OBJECTIVE 2 Signal to identify the vocal range of a soloist as a soprano (tested)

MATERIALS
Recordings
Another Op'nin', Another Show   CD4:31
Look Around   CD4:33
Look Around (performance mix)   CD4:34
Listening: Summertime from
   Porgy and Bess by G. and
   I. Gershwin   CD4:32

Instruments pitched instruments

Resources
Resource Master 5 • 1 (practice)
Recorder Master R • 19 (pitches D E F F♯
   G A B C' D')

VOCABULARY
musical, lyricist, lyrics, articulation, marcato, legato, changed voice, soprano, alto, tenor, bass, unchanged voice, cambiata, opera

▶ = **BASIC PROGRAM**

U N I T 5

from
There's No Business Like Show Business

There's no bus'ness like show bus'ness
    like no bus'ness I know.
Trav'ling thru the country will be thrilling,
Standing out in front on opening nights,
Smiling as you watch the theatre filling,
And there's your billing out there in lights.
There's no people like show people,
They smile when they are low.
Yesterday they told you you would not go far,
That night you open and there you are,
Next day on your dressing room they've hung a star
Let's go on with the show.

—Irving Berlin

188

MEETING **INDIVIDUAL** NEEDS

SPECIAL LEARNERS: *Attending a Musical Production*

In this unit, teach students functional skills to increase their chances of enjoying theater productions with friends or family. Activities could include using local newspapers or the telephone to find out what will be performed, where it will appear, dates and times, and the price of tickets. Encourage independent activity outside of class to get this information. (For example, some students will be able to make phone calls to check dates and times, others can bring in newspapers.) Friends can work together in gathering information.

IMPROVISATION: *Instrumental Accompaniment*

Divide the class into groups and have each group improvise its own instrumental accompaniment to a reading of "There's No Business Like Show Business" by another group. The words can be read freely, without using the song's original rhythm. Provide each group with one pitched and two unpitched instruments of the students' choice. Remind them of some possibilities for the instruments. For pitched instruments, they might play glissandi, tremolos, or random seconds. For unpitched instruments, they might highlight key words or punctuate the end of the verse.

ON STAGE

189

"For centuries, the musical stage has brought pleasure to people. For the next several lessons, you will have a chance to take part in musical theater as both performer and audience. To begin, try to imagine how it feels to be in a Broadway theater just as the curtain is about to go up." Have students:

▶ • Read "There's No Business Like Show Business."

▶ • Name some ingredients of musical theater productions. (singing, dancing, costumes, scenery, lighting, dialogue, playing instruments)

"One of the most important ingredients of the musical stage is singing. It's important that each song is not only sung with the words, pitches, and rhythms correct, but also with the overall effect that the composer intended. In this lesson, listen for this overall effect."

BIOGRAPHY: *Irving Berlin* THEATER

Irving Berlin (1888–1989), a native of Russia, was the youngest of six children born to a Jewish cantor and his wife. The family later emigrated to New York's Lower East Side. In his childhood, Berlin worked as a street singer and as a singing waiter. In his late teens, he began to write song lyrics. Eventually, he learned to play the piano by ear, acquiring the ability to put music to his lyrics, though he never learned how to read or write notes. In all, Berlin wrote the words and music to over fifteen hundred songs for music hall, stage, and screen. "There's No Business

Like Show Business," written for the 1946 musical *Annie Get Your Gun*, has become the unoffical anthem of show business.

CRITICAL THINKING: *Creating an Interpretation*

Have students discuss various tone colors and dynamics that they think convey the appropriate mood and spirit of the words from "There's No Business Like Show Business." Write their ideas on the board. Then, have them take turns consciously using various tone colors in reading all or part of the lyrics (hushed and breathy, forceful and bright). Evaluate the effectiveness of each interpretation.

UNIT FIVE
LESSON 1

Curtain Up!

Many different combinations of music and drama are found all around the world. These works can include singing, dancing, costumes, scenery, lighting, instruments, and spoken words.

Musicals are plays that contain songs and dances. They developed in the United States around 1900. Many famous musicals were written In the 1940s and 1950s, including *The Sound of Music* by Rodgers and Hammerstein and *My Fair Lady* by Lerner and Loewe.

190

continued from previous page

2 DEVELOP

1. Introduce the topic of the musical theater.
Have students:

▶ • Read pages 190–191 and name some musicals they may have seen.

▶ • In their own words, explain the difference between *lyricist* and *lyrics*.

MEETING **INDIVIDUAL** NEEDS

BIOGRAPHY: *Cole Porter* THEATER

Cole Albert Porter (1892–1964) was an American composer and lyricist. The grandson of a millionaire, he was an only child. His early interest in music was encouraged by his mother. He studied piano and violin and began to compose. By the time he was eleven years old, Porter had composed an operetta and had had a piano piece published. Porter wrote college shows during his student days at Yale and Harvard, then set his sights on Broadway. From the 1930s through the 1950s, Porter was a dominant Broadway and Hollywood composer. His sparkling, sophisticated out-

put was a reflection of his glittering lifestyle. A riding accident in 1937 resulted in continuing pain throughout the rest of his life, yet he went on to produce some of his best work, including *Kiss Me, Kate.*

BACKGROUND: *Kiss Me, Kate* THEATER

Kiss Me, Kate (1948) is in the form of a play-within-a-play. It was inspired by real-life bickering between married actors during a performance of Shakespeare's "The Taming of the Shrew." At the time, Porter had not had a theatrical success for a number of years and was worried about doing the show, but one of the scenarists persuaded him to try. The

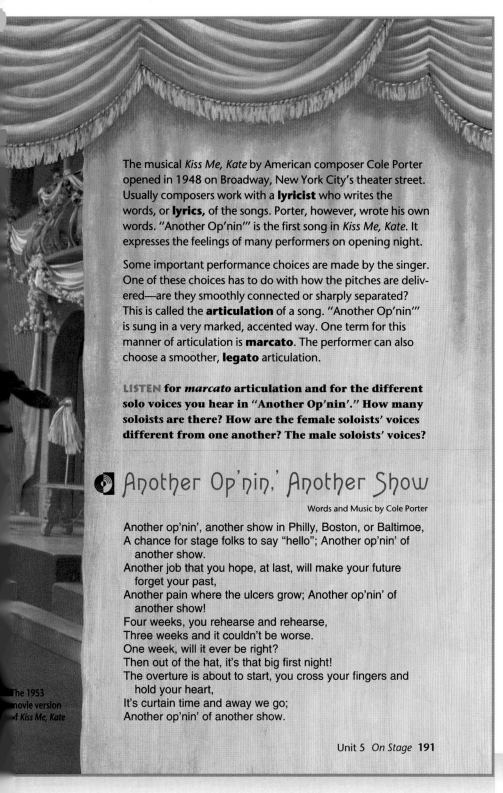

The musical *Kiss Me, Kate* by American composer Cole Porter opened in 1948 on Broadway, New York City's theater street. Usually composers work with a **lyricist** who writes the words, or **lyrics,** of the songs. Porter, however, wrote his own words. "Another Op'nin'" is the first song in *Kiss Me, Kate*. It expresses the feelings of many performers on opening night.

Some important performance choices are made by the singer. One of these choices has to do with how the pitches are delivered—are they smoothly connected or sharply separated? This is called the **articulation** of a song. "Another Op'nin'" is sung in a very marked, accented way. One term for this manner of articulation is **marcato**. The performer can also choose a smoother, **legato** articulation.

LISTEN for *marcato* articulation and for the different solo voices you hear in "Another Op'nin'." How many soloists are there? How are the female soloists' voices different from one another? The male soloists' voices?

Another Op'nin,' Another Show

Words and Music by Cole Porter

Another op'nin', another show in Philly, Boston, or Baltimoe,
A chance for stage folks to say "hello"; Another op'nin' of
   another show.
Another job that you hope, at last, will make your future
   forget your past,
Another pain where the ulcers grow; Another op'nin' of
   another show!
Four weeks, you rehearse and rehearse,
Three weeks and it couldn't be worse.
One week, will it ever be right?
Then out of the hat, it's that big first night!
The overture is about to start, you cross your fingers and
   hold your heart,
It's curtain time and away we go;
Another op'nin' of another show.

The 1953 movie version of *Kiss Me, Kate*

Unit 5 *On Stage* **191**

2. Introduce "Another Op'nin', Another Show" CD4:31**. Listen for articulation.** Have students:

- • Listen to "Another Op'nin', Another Show" and discuss the marcato articulation.

- • Answer the questions about the number and vocal qualities of the solo singers. (4; for both the men and women, one has a higher, lighter quality, the other a lower, heavier quality)

- • Sing the first phrase of the song marcato, then legato, and discuss how the mood changes as the articulation changes.

- • Sing the song marcato as a class, then assign some students to the solo parts and sing the song again.

result was the biggest musical comedy success of Porter's career. His lyrics combined Shakespearean language with his Broadway music, resulting in songs rich with the wit and elegance typical of his best work.

MOVEMENT: *"Another Op'nin', Another Show"*

Preparation: Have students walk with the beat using energetic, abrupt (marcato) movement. They should change direction sharply every four steps, sometimes changing body facing as well, sometimes not. Then have them create ways of "saying" hello with movement—shaking hands, waving, and so on. Next, have partners choreograph the song using "marcato" movement and their ways of gesturing hello. Partners should also create two body designs (poses), one for *Another op'nin'* and one for *another show*. One partner might strike a pose at a higher level, while the other strikes the pose at a lower level. They should strike these same poses each time the words are sung.

Final form: Partners get together in groups of six to teach each other what they have created. Have them look through the words and pick out phrases that suggest pantomime and choreograph gestures—for example, *Another pain where the ulcers grow*. The group then puts all the ideas together to make a dance, filling in the spaces with walking patterns.

UNIT FIVE
LESSON 1

continued from previous page

3. Introduce "Look Around" CD4:33. **Sing with appropriate articulation.** Have students:

▶ • Read about *The Will Rogers Follies*.

▶ • Listen to "Look Around" and discuss its meaning.

▶ • Try singing the first phrase using marcato and legato articulation. Recognize legato as the appropriate articulation for this song.

OBJECTIVE 1 Informal Assessment

▶ • Sing the melody of "Look Around" with legato articulation.

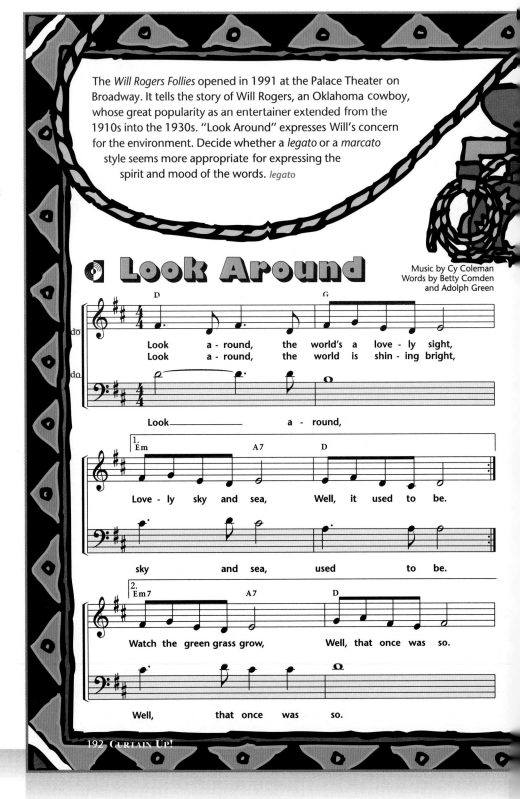

The *Will Rogers Follies* opened in 1991 at the Palace Theater on Broadway. It tells the story of Will Rogers, an Oklahoma cowboy, whose great popularity as an entertainer extended from the 1910s into the 1930s. "Look Around" expresses Will's concern for the environment. Decide whether a *legato* or a *marcato* style seems more appropriate for expressing the spirit and mood of the words. *legato*

Look Around

Music by Cy Coleman
Words by Betty Comden
and Adolph Green

Look a-round, the world's a love-ly sight,
Look a-round, the world is shin-ing bright,
Look a-round,

Love-ly sky and sea, Well, it used to be.
sky and sea, used to be.

Watch the green grass grow, Well, that once was so.
Well, that once was so.

192 CURTAIN UP!

MEETING **INDIVIDUAL** NEEDS

ALTERNATE TEACHING STRATEGY

OBJECTIVE 1 Remind students to sustain all of the vowels as long as possible before singing the consonants following them. Have them sing a few phrases of "Look Around" in a very disconnected, marcato style and discuss how it feels. Then, sing phrases again in legato style and compare the effect of the two articulations.

BIOGRAPHIES: *Three Broadway Giants*

American composer Cy Coleman (b. 1929) began his career as a child giving piano concerts, one of which took

place at Carnegie Hall when he was seven years old. His jazz-influenced scores have been heard in many Broadway shows, including *Sweet Charity*. American lyricists Betty Comden (b. 1915) and Adolph Green (b. 1915) met in college and got their start performing in nightclubs. Their musicals include a version of *Peter Pan*. They have worked on several shows with Coleman, including *The Will Rogers Follies*, a musical biography of the cowboy Will Rogers. Presented like a variety show, complete with a chorus line and a dog act, it won a 1991 Tony Award.

4. Create legato movement for "Look Around." Have students:

▶ • Working alone, develop smooth, sustained (legato) movement for the first two measures, *Look around, the world's a lovely sight*. (Have them use their arms and torso to show "looking around." They should explore:

1. changes of levels—high/low/middle;
2. changes of focus—where they are looking, where the movement is directed;
3. changes of direction;
4. appropriateness of the movement to the spirit of the song.)

▶ • Work with a partner to create a movement motive (a short, descriptive movement) to be done every time the measures beginning with *Look around* are heard. (To choreograph the entire song, see *Movement* below.)

MOVEMENT: *"Look Around"*

Preparation: After partners create the movement motive for "Look Around" in *Develop 4*, have them face each other and take turns mirroring each other using "legato" movements. Have them try this with a walk, still mirroring, creating a symmetrical design with their pathways.

Final form: Have students practice the "Look Around" motive, then create the rest of the movement using phrases at least two measures long. Some of the movement should be in place, mirroring with partners. Some should be walking—in unison or mirroring each other.

VOCAL DEVELOPMENT: *Singing in Legato Style*

Singing songs in a lyrical, legato style requires the breath control and support to move from note to note in a smooth, connected manner. Remind students to maintain correct posture for singing and to breathe deeply for singing. Then have them sustain an *s-s-s-s* for eight beats while you play and sing the melody of each two-bar phrase of "Look Around." Next have them sing each two-bar phrase while keeping the air flow constant as they did to sustain the *s-s-s-s*. They should sustain vowels as long as possible before singing the consonants.

continued from previous page

5. Identify vocal ranges in "Another Op'nin', Another Show" and "Look Around." Have students:

▶ • Read about vocal ranges. (Optional—Use **Resource Master 5 • 1** so students can see and hear the vocal ranges in notation.)

▶ • Listen to "Another Op'nin', Another Show," then tell what voice categories they hear. (in order: mixed voices, soprano, alto, tenor, soprano and alto together, bass, tenor, and alto)

▶ • Tell what type of voice is used for the melody line of "Look Around." (unchanged voices)

3 APPLY

Introduce "Summertime" CD4:32. **Identify vocal range of soloist.** Have students:

▶ • Read about *Porgy and Bess*.

▶ • Listen to "Summertime" and try to identify the vocal range of the soloist.

OBJECTIVE 2 Informal Assessment
• Listen as you name each vocal range (soprano, alto, tenor, and bass), raising a hand to identify the vocal range of the soloist. (soprano)

194 CURTAIN UP!

MEETING **INDIVIDUAL** NEEDS

ALTERNATE TEACHING STRATEGY

OBJECTIVE 2 Have students listen to "Summertime" again, paying attention to the soloist. Then, play "Another Op'nin', Another Show" and have students compare the voice categories they hear to that in "Summertime." If possible, invite guest singers to come sing for the students or take them to see a local production of a musical, discussing the vocal range of each singer afterward.

BACKGROUND: *Porgy and Bess*

The story of the opera is based on a novel by DuBose Heyward. Heyward also co-wrote the lyrics with Ira Gershwin, the composer's brother. The opera takes place in Catfish Row, a waterfront tenement section of Charleston, South Carolina. Porgy (**por** gi), a disabled beggar, finds Bess, falls in love with her, and loses her to another man when she is lured away to New York. As the opera ends, Porgy is heading for New York, determined to find her.

If you were to try out for a singing part in a musical, you would be asked, "What voice are you?" Each of the adult voice categories has a different range. The four major adult, or **changed voice**, categories are **soprano, alto, tenor,** and **bass**.

The range of a young voice is usually in about the same range as the adult soprano. This category is called **unchanged voice**. However, the category of a person's voice may change several times during the pre-teen and teen years. One special stage for boys is when their voices first start to change. This type of voice is called **cambiata**, or changing voice.

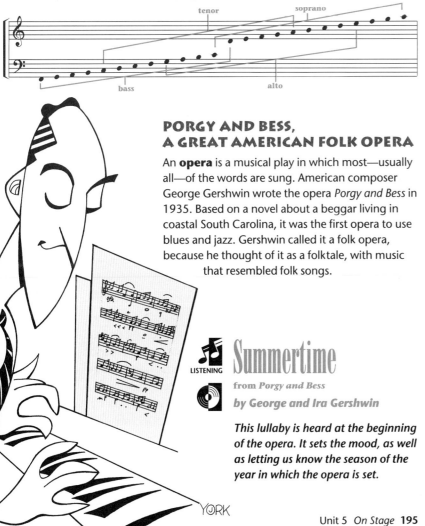

PORGY AND BESS, A GREAT AMERICAN FOLK OPERA

An **opera** is a musical play in which most—usually all—of the words are sung. American composer George Gershwin wrote the opera *Porgy and Bess* in 1935. Based on a novel about a beggar living in coastal South Carolina, it was the first opera to use blues and jazz. Gershwin called it a folk opera, because he thought of it as a folktale, with music that resembled folk songs.

LISTENING

Summertime

from *Porgy and Bess*
by George and Ira Gershwin

This lullaby is heard at the beginning of the opera. It sets the mood, as well as letting us know the season of the year in which the opera is set.

YORK

4 CLOSE
"Pretend you're hearing a singer try out for a part in a musical. What are two of the things you'd have to look for?" (style and range) Have students:

▶ • Name two kinds of articulation. (legato, marcato)

▶ • Name the adult vocal ranges. (soprano, alto, tenor, bass)

"Think about style and range in your own singing as you sing 'Look Around' once again."

LESSON SUMMARY

Informal Assessment In this lesson, students:

OBJECTIVE 1 Sang "Look Around" with appropriate articulation.

OBJECTIVE 2 Signaled to identify the vocal range of the soloist in "Summertime" as a soprano.

MORE MUSIC: Reinforcement
"Haiku Calendar," page 284 (accompany poem)
"America," page 287 (legato; patriotic)
"Música indígena," page 327 (legato/marcato, movement; spring)
"Jarabe tapatío," page 328 (movement)
"Jubilate Deo," page 413A (voice categories)

As a Broadway musical, *Porgy and Bess* met with mixed reviews when it opened, but soon became extremely popular with audiences all over the world. Now generally regarded as a preeminent work of the American musical theater, it is currently performed in the opera houses of the United States and Europe. In the 1950s it was also made into a movie.

BIOGRAPHY: *George Gershwin*

THEATER

Composer George Gershwin (1898–1937) was born in Brooklyn. He showed early evidence of talent at the piano and, by the age of 16, was playing the piano in music stores to demonstrate the sheet music that was for sale. He composed many popular songs himself over the years, both individual songs and songs for a number of Broadway productions and Hollywood movies. His composition *Rhapsody in Blue* used jazz in a concert piece for piano and a jazz orchestra, and was sensationally successful. It still remains one of the standards of the concert repertoire. Tragically, Gershwin died at the age of 38 of an inoperable brain tumor.

ACROSS the

MATHEMATICS

NET PROFIT OR LOSS

"There's No Business Like Show Business"

PAIR   **15–30 MIN**

MATERIALS: number cube, calculator

Each pair of students manage a theater company that has a 600-seat theater. They can sell:

- 300 seats at $40 a seat
- 300 seats at $20 a seat

The expenses for putting on each performance are $12,000.

Have students find whether the theater company makes a profit or loss for one performance. To determine the number of tickets sold, each partner rolls the number cube three times. They arrange the three numbers in any order to get a three-digit number that is not over 300. Before rolling, each partner decides whether his or her three-digit number will be the $40 seats or the $20 seats.

Students can extend this activity for a week of performances.

COMPREHENSION STRATEGY: Compare and contrast

MATHEMATICS

PLANE FIGURES

"Another Op'nin', Another Show"

GROUP   **15 MIN OR LESS**

MATERIALS: maps (North America), plastic wrap or sheet of acetate (transparency), pens, crayons, drawing paper; optional – string

Have students place a flattened sheet of plastic wrap over a map of the continental United States and locate *Philly, Boston*, and *Baltimore*. Have them plot these points on the plastic wrap and draw lines between the points to create a "squashed" triangle. Have them reproduce the triangle on drawing paper, labeling the points and trying to classify the triangle. (scalene, obtuse)

Have them find other groups of cities—groups of four, five, six, and so on—to make other plane figures—quadrilaterals, pentagons, hexagons, and so on. The figures need not be regular (with equivalent sides). Students might also create figures by using string to connect points on a map.

COMPREHENSION STRATEGIES: Visualizing, classifying

CURRICULUM

LANGUAGE ARTS

EDITORIAL

"Look Around"

INDIVIDUAL   **15–30 MIN**

Based on the theme of "Look Around," have students think about how the world—perhaps starting with their community—has changed in their own time. They can focus on issues such as pollution, government, or human rights. For example: Has pollution increased? Is litter more visible today than just a few years ago? Are people doing things to make the world better for all?

Have students write an editorial about how things are changing. The editorial should start with an opinion and include information to support the view. Remind students that the power of persuasive language can convince readers that the writer's opinions are correct.

COMPREHENSION STRATEGY: Expressing point of view

SCIENCE

THE LONGEST DAY

"Summertime"

GROUP   **15–30 MIN**

MATERIALS: globe, clay, flashlight, timer (or watch with second hand)

Have students model the first day of summer (summer solstice) to compare hours of daylight and darkness. They place a dot of clay on a globe at their location. With room lights dimmed, one student aims a flashlight at the Tropic of Cancer (23½°N) on a globe, holding the light about 30 cm from the globe and parallel to the table top. The globe is at a 23½° tilt, with the Tropic of Cancer in direct line with the flashlight beam, the North Pole "leaning" toward the flashlight.

One student rotates the globe counterclockwise at a slow, steady rate. Another student times how long the dot of clay is in the lit portion of the rotation (day) and in the dark portion (night). Students can estimate hours of daylight by using this proportion:

$$\frac{\text{seconds in light}}{\text{total seconds}} \times 24 = \text{hrs of day}$$

COMPREHENSION STRATEGIES: Using a model, compare and contrast

ACROSS THE CURRICULUM

UNIT FIVE
LESSON 2

RELATED ARTS | MOVEMENT | THEATER | VISUAL ARTS |

LESSON PLANNER

FOCUS Style, interpretation

OBJECTIVE
OBJECTIVE 1 Choose appropriate tempo, dynamics, tone color, and articulation for a song (tested)

MATERIALS
Recordings
Another Op'nin', Another Show	CD4:31
Won't You Charleston with Me?	CD4:35
Look Around	CD4:33
Comedy Tonight	CD4:36

Resources
Resource Master 5 • 2 (practice)
Resource Master 5 • 3 (practice)
Resource Master 5 • 4 (practice)
Recorder Master R • 20 (pitches C D E F
  G A B♭ C' D')

VOCABULARY
interpretation, dynamics, tempo

▶ = BASIC PROGRAM

THE CHOICE IS YOURS!

The term **interpretation** refers to the performance choices made by a singer or other performers. The words and music are already given by the composer and lyricist. Sometimes they will also write suggestions in the music for **dynamics** (the degrees of loud and soft) and **tempo** (the speed of the beat). Often, however, these and other decisions are left up to the singer's judgment. You must determine, for example, whether to sing a song with a *legato* or a *marcato* articulation. You must also decide on the vocal tone color that you will use to best express the idea and spirit of a song. Should it be bright or dark, breathy or full-voiced, floating or full, light or heavy?

The Boy Friend, a 1953 musical by Sandy Wilson, makes fun of British manners and musicals of the 1920s. The story takes place at an elegant girls' school. "Won't You Charleston With Me?" is an invitation to do the Charleston, the dance craze of the time.

196

MEETING **INDIVIDUAL** NEEDS

VOCAL DEVELOPMENT: *Singing in Marcato Style*

Performing songs with a marcato quality requires the use of the abdominal muscles to achieve the accented articulation. The following vocalise will develop this vocal skill.

Continue up by half steps to A.

Ha - ha   ha - ha   ha   *(breathe)*   Ha - ha   ha - ha   ha   *(breathe)*

Have students put their hands on their abdominal muscles and experiment with laughing, first like a silly child, then like Santa Claus. They should notice the contraction of the abdominal muscles as they laugh. Then have them put their hands on their abdomens and sing the vocalise, making certain that the abdominal muscles contract. Finish by having them sing "Won't You Charleston with Me?" concentrating on singing the notes of the melody in an accented manner.

BIOGRAPHY: *Sandy Wilson* THEATER

British composer Alexander Galbraith (Sandy) Wilson (b. 1924) began writing songs while still in college. He had his greatest success in 1953 with the London production of his musical *The Boy Friend*, for which he wrote the music,

Julie Andrews on
stage in *The Boy Friend*

What vocal tone colors would you choose for this song?
Compare your ideas with the recording.

Won't You CHARLESTON with Me?

Words and Music by Sandy Wilson

Won't you Charleston with me?
Won't you Charleston with me?
And while the band is playing that
Old vo-de-o-do,
Around we will go,
Together we'll show them
How the Charleston is done.
We'll surprise ev'ryone.
Just think what Heaven it's going to be
If you will Charleston, Charleston with me.

Unit 5 *On Stage* **197**

"In the last lesson, you learned the difference between two musical performance techniques that were important in singing a song as it was intended to be sung." Have students:

▶ • Recall legato (smooth, connected, expressive) and marcato (very marked, accented).

▶ • Remember which seemed to be more appropriate for an energetic performance of "Another Op'nin', Another Show." (marcato)

▶ • Sing "Another Op'nin', Another Show" CD4:31 with marcato articulation.

"In this lesson, you're going to discover other choices that a singer makes in order to best project the meaning of a song."

2 DEVELOP

1. Introduce "Won't You Charleston with Me?" CD4:35. **Predict interpretation decisions.** Have students:

▶ • Read pages 196–197, then talk about what is meant by vocal tone color. (the quality of a singer's sound) (Optional: See **Resource Master 5 • 2** for a fuller explanation of various tone colors and lighter and heavier vocal mechanisms.)

▶ • Predict vocal interpretive decisions for "Won't You Charleston with Me?" as you list them on the board—tempo, dynamics, tone color, articulation. (Optional: Use **Resource Master 5 • 3** for individual predictions.)

▶ • Listen to the song and test their predictions.

▶ • Compare their predictions with the interpretation on the recording.

▶ • Learn the song by listening again and echoing parts of the song, then singing as much as they can of the entire song.

---

the lyrics, and the book, which told a funny story about falling in love. The musical was later produced on Broadway.

MOVEMENT: *"Won't You Charleston with Me?"*

Formation: scattered—partners, facing one another or standing side by side (After learning the steps below, students can put together their own sequence of steps.)

Basic Step: Take step on L foot and swing arms L, then touch R toe in front, and swing arms R. Then take a step on R foot (arms swing L) and touch L toe in back (arms swing R). Lean away from the tapping foot each time.

Step 2: Stand with feet about four inches apart. Shift weight forward to the balls of the feet and turn toes inward and heels outward. Lift R foot slightly. With weight still on balls of feet, put heels inward, turning toes out and return R foot to floor. Repeat, lifting L foot.

Arm movement for Step 2: Cross arms, placing L hand on R knee and R hand on L knee. As heels come together, hands uncross and R hand goes to R knee and L hand goes to L knee. As heels go outward, hands cross, going to opposite knee again. Look at partner, not knees.

UNIT FIVE
LESSON 2

continued from previous page

2. Review "Look Around" CD4:33 **(pp. 192–193). Practice making interpretive decisions.** Have students:

▶ • Recall whether marcato or legato are appropriate articulation for "Look Around." (legato)

▶ • Decide what the tempo, dynamics, and tone color should be. (Accept reasonable answers, but try to come to a group consensus.)

▶ • Sing the melody of "Look Around" using the group interpretation.

3. Read pitch letter names in bass clef and sing "Look Around" in two parts. Have students:

• Note that part of the countermelody is in the bass clef. Read the pitch letter names of the notes in Measures 1–4. (A, B, C#, D)

• Learn the countermelody. (When students are secure singing the melody and countermelody separately, have them sing both parts together.)

3 APPLY

Introduce "Comedy Tonight" CD4:36. **Choose articulation, dynamics, tempo, and tone color.** Have students:

▶ • Read page 198.

OBJECTIVE 1 Informal Assessment

▶ • Decide on appropriate interpretive choices for "Comedy Tonight" and record them—articulation (legato or marcato), dynamics, tempo, and tone color.

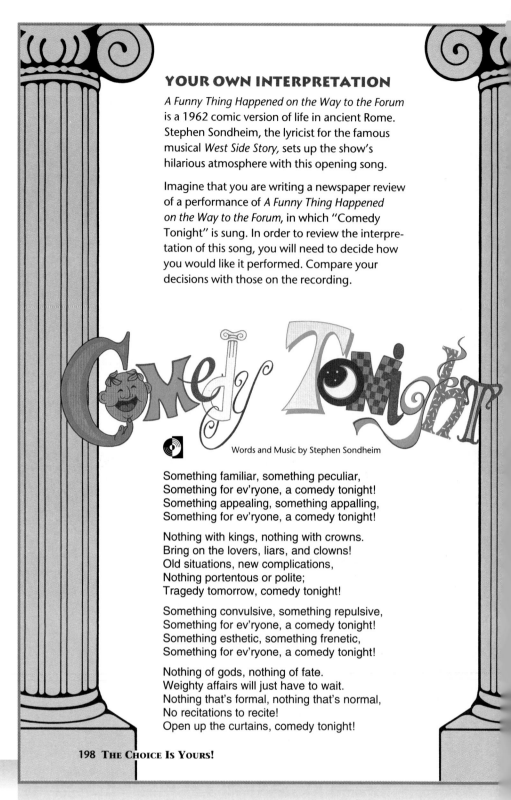

YOUR OWN INTERPRETATION

A Funny Thing Happened on the Way to the Forum is a 1962 comic version of life in ancient Rome. Stephen Sondheim, the lyricist for the famous musical *West Side Story*, sets up the show's hilarious atmosphere with this opening song.

Imagine that you are writing a newspaper review of a performance of *A Funny Thing Happened on the Way to the Forum*, in which "Comedy Tonight" is sung. In order to review the interpretation of this song, you will need to decide how you would like it performed. Compare your decisions with those on the recording.

Comedy Tonight

Words and Music by Stephen Sondheim

Something familiar, something peculiar,
Something for ev'ryone, a comedy tonight!
Something appealing, something appalling,
Something for ev'ryone, a comedy tonight!

Nothing with kings, nothing with crowns.
Bring on the lovers, liars, and clowns!
Old situations, new complications,
Nothing portentous or polite;
Tragedy tomorrow, comedy tonight!

Something convulsive, something repulsive,
Something for ev'ryone, a comedy tonight!
Something esthetic, something frenetic,
Something for ev'ryone, a comedy tonight!

Nothing of gods, nothing of fate.
Weighty affairs will just have to wait.
Nothing that's formal, nothing that's normal,
No recitations to recite!
Open up the curtains, comedy tonight!

198 THE CHOICE IS YOURS!

MEETING **INDIVIDUAL** NEEDS

ALTERNATE TEACHING STRATEGY

OBJECTIVE 1 Help students discover "clues" to appropriate interpretation in "Comedy Tonight." For example, they might read the words to note the rhythm and probable character of the song.

BIOGRAPHY: *Stephen Sondheim*

American composer and lyricist Stephen Sondheim (b. 1930) is considered one of his generation's most innovative creators of musical theater. He became interested in theater as a teenager, when he struck up a friendship with Oscar Hammerstein II. He showed Hammerstein his first musical when he was 15 years old. Hammerstein told him it was the worst thing he had ever read, then proceeded to tell him point-by-point what was wrong. Rather than being discouraged, Sondheim listened and learned. At 27, Sondheim was invited by Leonard Bernstein to write the lyrics to his musical *West Side Story*. It became a hit show, then a movie.

The first Broadway musical for which Sondheim wrote both lyrics and music was *A Funny Thing Happened on the Way to the Forum*, which opened in 1962. The show won a Tony award for best musical, ran for more than two years, and was made into a movie in 1966.

Zero Mostel (top) and Jack Gilford in the 1966 film of *A Funny Thing Happened on the Way to the Forum*

▶ • Listen to the song to check their decisions. (Optional: Use **Resource Master 5 • 4**, on which the student plays the role of a critic writing a review of the performance.)

▶ • Compare their answers and discuss them. (Possible interpretation: marcato articulation, medium-loud dynamic level, medium-fast tempo, bright tone color)

4 CLOSE

"In this lesson, you made some of the same choices a professional singer makes to perform a song as effectively as possible." Have students:

▶ • Review the choices involved in determining interpretation. (dynamics, tempo, tone color, articulation)

"Let's vote on each interpretation choice for 'Comedy Tonight,' then use the top choices to sing the song."

LESSON SUMMARY

Informal Assessment In this lesson, students:

OBJECTIVE 1 Chose appropriate tempo, dynamics, tone color, and articulation for "Comedy Tonight."

MORE MUSIC: Reinforcement

"De colores," page 328 (interpretation; spring)
"Fussreise," page 357 (articulation)
"Lobster Quadrille," page 390 (articulation, dynamics)
"The Gypsy Man," page 394 (dynamics)

MOVEMENT: *"Comedy Tonight"* MOVEMENT

Have students divide into four groups. Each group will take one verse and create a group shape for each idea in the verse (such as *something familiar* or *something peculiar*), as if they were showing still photographs of the idea. Once they have the static images, they should work out transitional movements from one image to another. It is a good idea to have some locomotion (moving through space). When a phrase repeats, the movement should also repeat. After groups show what they have created to the rest of the class, the class should choose a movement motive to represent the phrase *comedy tonight*. (This gives the same cohe-

siveness to the choreography that musical motives can give a score.) Finish with a performance of the entire song, with each group contributing their verse.

CAREERS: *Music Journalist*

As students act as critics, introduce them to the career of music journalist. This kind of writer needs to know about both music and writing. Music journalists review records and concerts and write stories about musicians. Music journalists often get their start writing for a school or local paper. Most have a college degree.

ACROSS the

TIME CAPSULE

"Won't You Charleston With Me?"

GROUP   **30 MIN OR LONGER**

MATERIALS: poster board, markers, tape, glue; optional—student selections to mount on poster

The Charleston was a dance craze of the 1920s. It has become one of the symbols of that time. Have students think about today—this current year in their own hometown. What symbols would they use to represent their town today, as a legacy for people in the future?

Have students work in groups to answer this question by preparing a "Time Capsule" bulletin board display. Each group can think of things to represent their town today. They might include news clippings, maps, photographs, essays, and polls of favorite songs and films. Each group should organize their ideas and collect or write their contributions. Then groups meet together to determine which of the collected items best represent their town. They mount them on a poster display and add written commentary and labels.

COMPREHENSION STRATEGIES: Expressing points of view, organizing and displaying information

EXPLORE POLLUTION

"Look Around"

WHOLE CLASS   **30 MIN OR LONGER**

MATERIALS: cardboard strips (2 cm x 10 cm), tape, string, hand lens

Have students make air pollutant "collectors." To make a collector, they tape or staple together four cardboard strips to make a square frame. Then they stretch clear tape across the frame, three pieces of tape all in the same direction. Then they tie a string around one corner of the cardboard frame and hang frames wherever they wish. The tape collects solid particles from the air.

Have students decide where to hang their collectors—near windows, outside at various points around school, near vents. Any student may make one, two, or more collectors, labeling each one with the student's name and the collector's location.

They hang the collectors for a day and examine the tape with a hand lens. Have students describe what they see, compare each other's results, and determine which test sites had the most pollution and offer possible explanations.

COMPREHENSION STRATEGY: Compare and contrast

CURRICULUM

LANGUAGE ARTS

SUFFIX GAME

"Comedy Tonight"

PAIR   **15–30 MIN**
MATERIALS: slips of paper or index cards, timer (or watch with second hand); optional—dictionary

Sondheim uses suffixes to create fun rhyming pairs in this song: *appealing/appalling*; *situations/complications*; *convulsive/repulsive*.

Have students work in pairs to write each of these suffixes on a separate card: *-able, -age, -al, -ance, -ant, -ent, -eous, -er, -est, -ful, -ible, -ion, -ious, -ish, -ive, -ize, -less, -ly, -or, -ous, -ten, -th, -ty, -ward,* and *-y.*

Partners may use a dictionary to review meanings of the suffixes. Then they play a game. Cards are placed face down in a draw pile. Each player picks a card and has two minutes to write as many words as possible with the selected suffix. Then players exchange lists and tally scores—1 point for each word, 2 extra points for any two words that have an equal number of syllables and one syllable other than the suffix that sounds alike (such as *convulsive* and *repulsive*). They play again with new suffixes.

COMPREHENSION STRATEGY: Building vocabulary

MATHEMATICS/ART

DESIGN

"Comedy Tonight"

INDIVIDUAL   **15–30 MIN**
MATERIALS: graph paper, rulers, protractors, compasses, tape, pencils

The Roman Forum was the section of ancient Rome that was the government center. Among the structures located there were the Senate House, the Hall of Records, many temples, a public speaker's platform, and many arches. They were positioned around a marketplace.

Have students imagine that they could design a forum for their own hometown. Besides government buildings, they could add libraries, museums, theaters, and convention centers. Have them design a forum by drawing plane figures on graph paper. They can choose different figures for the various buildings. The figures should be regular, with sides and angles of equal measures. (Students can tape together two or more sheets of graph paper to increase the forum area—and to have more room for drawing.)

COMPREHENSION STRATEGY: Exploring spatial relationships

UNIT FIVE
LESSON 3

RELATED ARTS | MOVEMENT | THEATER | VISUAL ARTS

LESSON PLANNER

FOCUS Rhythm

OBJECTIVE
OBJECTIVE 1 Clap a syncopated rhythm pattern with a song

MATERIALS
Recordings

Comedy Tonight	CD4:36
One	CD4:37
Won't You Charleston with Me?	CD4:35
Recorded Lesson: Interview with Marvin Hamlisch	CD4:38

▶ = **BASIC PROGRAM**

Marvin Hamlisch wrote the musical *A Chorus Line* in 1975. In the story, a group of dancers are trying out for parts in a Broadway musical. As each performer appears, the audience learns about the sacrifices and frustrations of professional Broadway dancers. At the end of *A Chorus Line*, the dancers who have been chosen for the parts perform in the new musical, which features the song "One."

Music by Marvin Hamlisch
Words by Edward Kleban

One sin-gu-lar sen-sa-tion, ev'-ry lit-tle step she takes,—

One thrill-ing com-bi-na-tion, ev'-ry move that she makes.

One smile and sud-den-ly no-bod-y else will do.

You know you'll nev-er be lone-ly with you know who.

200

MEETING **INDIVIDUAL** NEEDS

BACKGROUND: *A Chorus Line* THEATER

None of its orginators expected to make any money from *A Chorus Line*. It was to be a small Off-Broadway show of innovative musical theater; Hamlisch was originally paid only $900 for the score. The show is set in the backstage of a theater sometime in 1975 where an unseen director is auditioning a group of dancers for a Broadway show. Critics loved the funny and original story, as well as the music, and within a few months *A Chorus Line* had moved to a large theater on Broadway, where it ran for more than 10 years to become one of the longest-running productions in Broad-

way history. It received a Pulitzer Prize in drama and nine Tony awards, and the original cast recording received a gold record.

MOVEMENT: *"One"* MOVEMENT

Basic Step (chorus-line kick): In twos, students stand side by side and hold hands. With the weight on the L foot, they slightly bend their knees (1 beat) and then kick the R foot as high as they can, straightening L knee (1 beat). Then repeat on the other side. When students are comfortable with this and the height of their kicks match, they begin to

One mo-ment in her pres-ence and you can for-get the rest,—

For the girl is sec-ond best—— to none, son,

Ooh! Sigh! Give her your at - ten - tion, Do I

real - ly have to men - tion She's the one?——

RHYTHMS FROM BROADWAY

Here are some dotted rhythm patterns heard in two songs from musicals. This rhythm comes from "One."

This rhythm from "Won't You Charleston with Me?" comes from the dance, the Charleston.

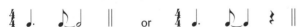

CLAP the melodic rhythm of "Old vo-de-o-do," also from "Won't You Charleston With Me?"

The first three notes shown are a "short-long-short" combination. This is one kind of syncopated rhythm pattern. Syncopation occurs when stressed sounds are heard in unexpected places, such as between beats.

Unit 5 *On Stage* **201**

"Let's begin by singing 'Comedy Tonight.' Keep the beat in your own way as you sing." Have students:

▶ • Sing "Comedy Tonight" CD4:36 (page 198).

• Decide if there are beats in the melody with no new sound on them. (yes)

"In this lesson, you're going to learn more about a rhythm that you just sang in "Comedy Tonight" and review a rhythm you already know."

2 DEVELOP

1. Introduce "One" CD4:37. **Pat dotted rhythm pattern.** Have students:

▶ • Listen to the recording and identify the vocal category. (unchanged)

• Follow you in patting the rhythm of the introduction with alternating hands. (The rhythm is the first dotted rhythm pattern on page 201. A varied version is found in the coda of the recording.)

• Recognize the ♫ pattern. (See Unit 3, Lesson 4, pages 106–109.)

• Find sections in "One" with syncopation. (mm. 2, 3, 6, 10, 14, 18, 19, 20, 25, 27)

▶ • Read page 200, then sing "One."

2. Review "Won't You Charleston with Me?" CD4:35 **(p. 197). Introduce syncopation.** Have students:

▶ • Sing "Won't You Charleston with Me?"

• Look at the two rhythms from "Won't You Charleston with Me?" on page 201.

• Try patting the first rhythm as they sing the song (on *Won't you* and *Charles-ton*).

• Clap the rhythm of *Old vo-de-o-do*.

change their body facing to the left on the R-foot kick and to the right when on the L-foot kick. They can also try this holding each other's waists or with arms over shoulders.

Variation 1: Instead of raising the whole leg as in Step 1, the knee is raised.

Variation 2: Bend both knees, raise R knee, bend knees, kick R leg to left. Repeat with L leg to right.

Variation 3 (jump-hop step): Jump on both feet, hop on left foot and kick right (at same time), jump on both feet, hop right and kick left.

Final Form: Have four pairs work together in a "chorus line" to put the steps together (in groupings of two, four, or eight of the same step). For an ending, they can try the "domino" or "wave effect" by lunging forward and/or pretending to take their hats off one after another.

continued from previous page

3. Meet the composer of "One." Have students:

▶ • Read about Marvin Hamlisch.

Recorded Lesson CD4:38

▶ • Listen to "Interview with Marvin Hamlisch" and hear about his musical training and career as a composer.

▶ • Sing "One" again.

3 APPLY

Review "Comedy Tonight." Identify and clap the syncopated rhythm. Have students:

▶ • Sing "Comedy Tonight," keeping the beat.

• Find places with a "short-long-short" syncopated pattern. (There are 26 in all. Each time the words *Something* or *Nothing* are sung, these two notes and the note following them create the syncopated pattern, quarter note-half note-quarter note in $\frac{2}{2}$ meter. The pattern also appears seven more times with different words: *Bring on the; li-ars, and; Old sit-u-; new com-pli-; Weight-y af-, just have to; No re-ci-.*)

OBJECTIVE 1 Informal Assessment

• Sing the song again, clapping this ostinato:

Meet MARVIN HAMLISCH

When Marvin Hamlisch (b. 1944) was very young, his parents noticed his musical talent. At the age of six, he began taking piano lessons at The Juilliard School of Music in New York City. Hamlisch loved to listen to musicals and rock 'n' roll. At age 7 he began to write his own songs. By the time he reached the sixth grade, Hamlisch could play songs on the piano after hearing them a few times on the radio. Later on, Hamlisch realized how much he loved to write songs and decided to become a composer.

Marvin Hamlisch has written the music for three musicals: A Chorus Line, They're Playing Our Song, *and* The Goodbye Girl. *He has also composed music for more than forty movies. He has won three Academy Awards, or Oscars, for his film music.*

202 INTERMISSION

MEETING **INDIVIDUAL** NEEDS

ALTERNATE TEACHING STRATEGY

OBJECTIVE 1 Notate the syncopated rhythm pattern for "Comedy Tonight" on the board. Have half the class step with the beat as the other half claps the rhythm. Then switch. Play the recording and have them try this twice, first without singing, then while singing along. Finally, have everyone clap the rhythm as they sing.

CAREERS: *Songwriter*

Use the interview with Marvin Hamlisch to introduce students to the career of songwriter. A songwriter may write the lyrics, melody, or both. Songwriters work in different ways. Some write the music first, then try to find appropriate lyrics. Others write the lyrics first, then try to compose the perfect tune. Some compose at the same time every day, while others wait until an idea strikes them. Once the song is finished, the songwriter must market it. She or he looks for a music publisher or recording act. Usually the songwriter makes a demonstration cassette to play for managers, performers, or publishers. The demo should be professional and show off the tune to its best advantage.

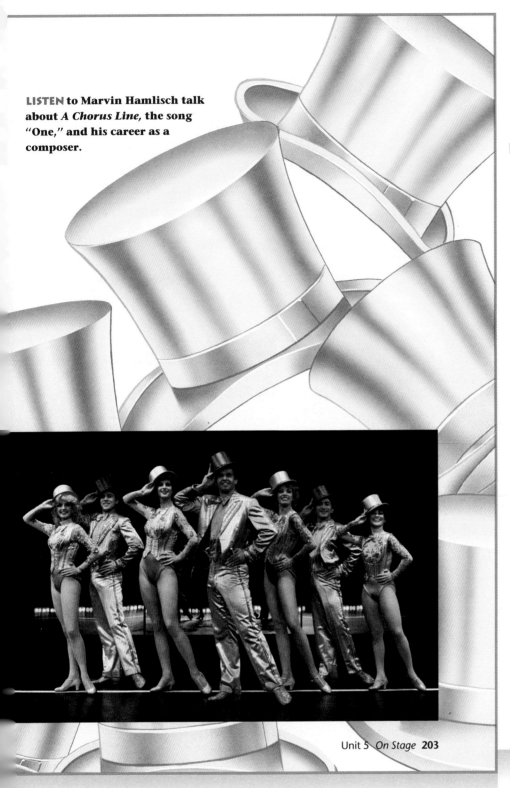

LISTEN to Marvin Hamlisch talk about *A Chorus Line,* the song "One," and his career as a composer.

4 CLOSE

"What kind of rhythm did you learn in this lesson?" (syncopated rhythm)

"Clap some syncopated patterns with me." (Choose two or three rhythm patterns to clap.)

Have students:
▶ • Sing "Comedy Tonight" again.

LESSON SUMMARY

Informal Assessment In this lesson, students:

OBJECTIVE 1 Clapped a syncopated rhythm pattern with "Comedy Tonight."

MORE MUSIC: Reinforcement
"Old Ark's A-Moverin'," page 332 (syncopation)

"Every Morning When I Wake Up," page 334 (syncopation)

"Follow the Drinkin' Gourd," page 370 (syncopation)

IMPROVISATION: *Syncopated Interludes*

Have students review the syncopated rhythm pattern they clapped with "Comedy Tonight" and use it in improvisations, either as an ostinato or as an interlude between repetitions of other songs.

ENRICHMENT: *More Practice with Syncopation*

Have students try walking the beat while clapping the melodic rhythm of "Comedy Tonight." Students might also try making up their own syncopated patterns to clap with the song.

RELATED ARTS [MOVEMENT] [THEATER] [VISUAL ARTS]

LESSON PLANNER

FOCUS Musical drama/Tone color/
Expressive use of the voice

OBJECTIVES
OBJECTIVE 1 Perform a harmonic accompaniment to a song from chordal
notation
OBJECTIVE 2 Describe the vocal tone
color of a singer (tested)

MATERIALS
Recordings
Listening: Pumping Iron from
Starlight Express by R. Stilgoe
and A. Lloyd Webber   CD5:1
Listening: Starlight Express
from *Starlight Express* by
R. Stilgoe and A. Lloyd Webber   CD5:2

Instruments
guitar, keyboard, or resonator bells

Resources Recorder Master R • 21
(pitches C D E F F♯ G A B♭ C' D')

▶ = **BASIC PROGRAM**

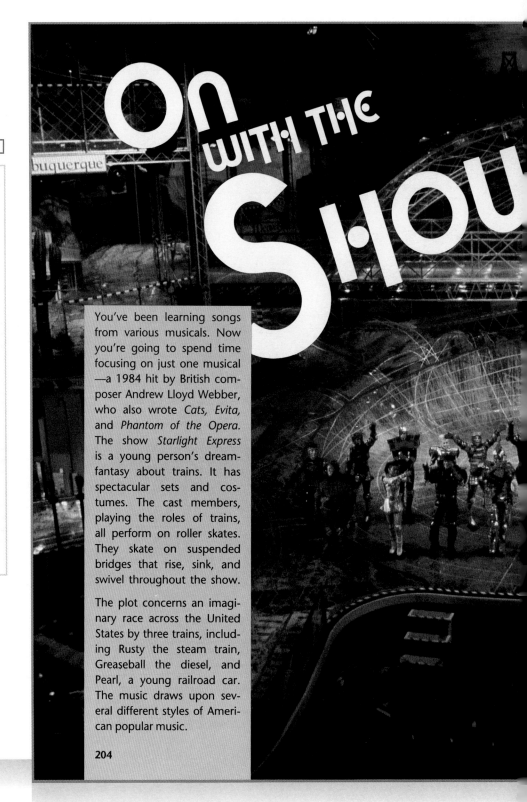

ON WITH THE SHOW

You've been learning songs from various musicals. Now you're going to spend time focusing on just one musical—a 1984 hit by British composer Andrew Lloyd Webber, who also wrote *Cats, Evita,* and *Phantom of the Opera*. The show *Starlight Express* is a young person's dream-fantasy about trains. It has spectacular sets and costumes. The cast members, playing the roles of trains, all perform on roller skates. They skate on suspended bridges that rise, sink, and swivel throughout the show.

The plot concerns an imaginary race across the United States by three trains, including Rusty the steam train, Greaseball the diesel, and Pearl, a young railroad car. The music draws upon several different styles of American popular music.

204

MEETING **INDIVIDUAL** NEEDS

VOCAL DEVELOPMENT: *Caring for the Voice*

Explain to students that no matter which vocal color is used to express a particular song, the sound must be produced correctly and the voice cared for in a sensible way to maintain a healthy singing voice. For example, musical performers such as those in *Starlight Express* would not be able to sing nightly if they did not maintain good vocal health habits. These include getting plenty of rest, drinking a good deal of water to keep the vocal chords hydrated, warming up the voice before each performance, singing without forcing

the voice, and maintaining good breath support throughout the performance.

THEATER
BIOGRAPHY: *Andrew Lloyd Webber*

British composer Andrew Lloyd Webber (b. 1948) was the son of London University's Dean of Music and spent his childhood listening to classical music. His first work on Broadway was the 1971 musical *Jesus Christ Superstar*, which he wrote together with collaborator Tim Rice. They got the show to the stage in an unusual way; they couldn't

🎵 LISTENING 💿 Pumping Iron

by Richard Stilgoe and Andrew Lloyd Webber

In "Pumping Iron," Greaseball, the defending cross-country race champion, describes his great diesel power.

Greaseball

DESCRIBE the attitude that Greaseball portrays in the song. List several words that describe the quality of Greaseball's voice.

1 GET SET

"Think about what affects vocal tone color." Have students:

▶ • Review vocal range—SATB ranges, changed vs. unchanged ranges (page 195); articulation—legato vs. marcato style (page 191); vocal tone color—heavy, light, dark, rough, smooth, and so on (page 196).

"In this lesson, you will focus on how vocal tone color is used as an expressive device to help portray the characters in a famous musical."

2 DEVELOP

1. Introduce "Pumping Iron" CD5:1. Identify the way the composer uses vocal tone color and style to heighten the emotional impact. Have students:

▶ • Read and discuss the information on *Starlight Express*.

▶ • Listen to "Pumping Iron."

▶ • Discuss the attitude that Greaseball portrays in the song. (aggressive, confident, strong-willed, ambitious)

▶ • List several words that describe the tone color of Greaseball's voice. (dark, rough, intense) Decide if Greaseball is using a heavy or light tone color. (heavy)

find anyone to produce the show, so they decided to do it on a record instead. When the record sold in the millions, they found a producer. Both Rice and Lloyd Webber (along with Stephen Sondheim) have dominated musical theater ever since. Lloyd Webber's other hits include *Cats, Evita,* and *Phantom of the Opera.*

BACKGROUND: *Starlight Express* THEATER

In writing a musical, Lloyd Webber has said that he is more interested in creating exciting visual effects than in the plot.

Starlight Express is a good example of his approach. It was first planned as a concert for schools, until director Trevor Nunn had the idea of staging it with roller-skating "trains." The London production opened in 1984 and was an instant hit. In a reconstructed theater, the performers skated around, behind, in front of, and over the audience.

UNIT FIVE
LESSON 4

continued from previous page

2. Play a harmonic accompaniment with "Pumping Iron." Have students:

• Review the C major scale and the I, IV, and V chords. (In C Major, I, IV, and V are C, F, and G. See Unit 2, Lesson 1, pages 51–53 and Unit 4, Lesson 7, pages 172–173.)

• Review the meaning of a sharp (Unit 2, Lesson 1, page 52), then find the chord with the sharp. (F♯ in Lines 2 and 5)

• Say the chord roots in rhythm, then transfer the rhythm pattern to resonator bells or keyboard, playing only the chord roots.

OBJECTIVE 1 Informal Assessment

• Play the roots of the chords each time the refrain occurs on the recording. (Measures 11–22; after D.S. refrain extends through coda) (Repeat, giving all students a turn if possible.)

• Review the strum patterns.
• Take turns playing the chords with the recording on guitar, keyboard, or resonator bells.

3 APPLY

Introduce "Starlight Express" CD5:2. **Describe vocal tone color.** Have students:

▶• Continue to read the story.

▶• Listen to "Starlight Express."

▶• Discuss the mood that Rusty portrays in the song. (fear, uncertainty)

PERFORM this accompaniment to "Pumping Iron."

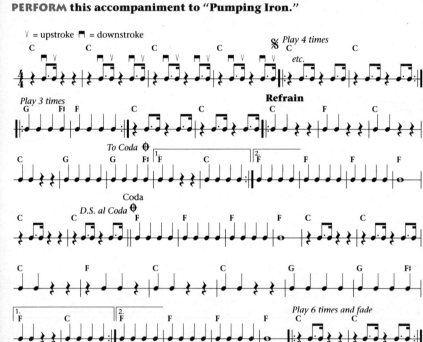

MEETING **INDIVIDUAL** NEEDS

ALTERNATE TEACHING STRATEGIES

OBJECTIVE 1 To help students get ready to play at the refrain, tell them to listen for the words *hear me knock, hear me knock, hear me knock* right before the refrain begins.

OBJECTIVE 2 Comparing Rusty's tone color to Greaseball's may help students to focus on Rusty's special qualities. Place the following analysis on the board, asking for student input:

"Pumping Iron"	"Starlight Express"
General Mood	
Greaseball—confidence	Rusty—fear, uncertainty
Use of Vocal Tone Color	
heavier, dark, rough	lighter, floating, bright
Voice Category	
Bass-Baritone	Tenor

▶ • Write words that describe Rusty's vocal tone color. (floating, bright) Then raise hands to indicate agreement or disagreement with the descriptions given by other class members. (You may wish to collect the papers in order to evaluate the answers of individual class members.)

4 CLOSE

"In this lesson, you heard two songs that were contrasts of mood and vocal tone color." Have students:

▶ • Discuss with a neighbor how each song uses mood and vocal tone color to develop each character.

▶ • Vote on which song they would like to hear again, based on which character they prefer, then listen to the song.

LESSON SUMMARY

Informal Assessment In this lesson, students:

OBJECTIVE 1 Performed a harmonic accompaniment to "Pumping Iron" from chordal notation.

OBJECTIVE 2 Described the vocal tone color of a singer in "Starlight Express."

MORE MUSIC: Reinforcement

"Garden of the Earth," (listening) page 324 (vocal tone color, voice categories; spring)

THE STORY CONTINUES . . .

Starlight Express
by Richard Stilgoe and Andrew Lloyd Webber

The underdog in the cross-country race is Rusty, an old-fashioned steam locomotive. In the first stage of the race, Rusty loses because Greaseball has used dirty tricks. Discouraged, Rusty decides not to enter the next stage. Rusty's love interest, the young railroad car named Pearl, doesn't understand the real reason why he lost and deserts him. Poppa, an old steam engine, tells Rusty about the Starlight Express, a mysterious force that can help him win. Rusty is inspired to reenter the race.

WRITE **down some words that describe Rusty's vocal tone color.**

Rusty

SPECIAL LEARNERS: *Playing Chordal Accompaniments*

Teach students to locate, identify, and play simplified chordal accompaniments from printed music. First, teach functional skills that will enable students to play fewer chords and parts of chords. Instruct students to read and play only the first letter name (the chord root) in each of the chord symbols (for example, play the pitch D when they see the symbol D7) and to play only the chord root that occurs on the first beat if it sounds harmonically correct throughout the measure. For more practice, try this on keyboard with "Look Around" (pp. 192–194) and "One" (pp. 200–201).

GUITAR: *"Pumping Iron" Accompaniment*
Standard Tuning

Easy F

4-string C

Easy G

Easy F#

D Major Tuning This activity is easier in D major tuning. Use F—3rd fret, F#—4th fret, and G—5th fret.

ACROSS the

SCIENCE

FORCE

"Pumping Iron"

PAIR   **15 MIN OR LESS**

MATERIALS: spring scale with a hook, wooden block, clay, string, rubber band

Force is a push or a pull. The amount of force used to move an object can be measured with a spring scale. Have a pair of students wrap a rubber band around a small wooden block. They tie a string to the rubber band and attach the free end of the string to the hook of a spring scale, so that they can pull the block by pulling the scale.

Have them pull the block at a constant rate over several kinds of surfaces (concrete, tiled floor, carpet) for about a meter. How does the amount of force change? Repeat with a mass of clay on the block. How do the results differ? (The rougher the surface, the greater the force used. The greater the mass, the greater the force used.)

COMPREHENSION STRATEGY: Compare and contrast

SCIENCE

AIR RESISTANCE

"Pumping Iron"

INDIVIDUAL   **15 MIN OR LESS**

MATERIALS: cardboard square

The faster the engine in the song (or any object) moves, the greater a force of resistance the engine meets from the air around it.

Have them wave a cardboard square in the air so they can feel the air resistance. (CAUTION: They should be over an arm's length away from anyone.) How can they bend the cardboard to increase the force they feel? How can they decrease the force?

Have them write about the results. In their report, they might include ways in which cars, the space shuttle, buses, and planes are designed to reduce the effects of air resistance.

(Bending the cardboard inward increases air resistance, bending it outward decreases it. Vehicles are designed with smooth, sloping surfaces to reduce air resistance.)

COMPREHENSION STRATEGY: Compare and contrast

CURRICULUM

MATHEMATICS

AVERAGE SPEED

"Pumping Iron"

PAIR   **15 MIN OR LESS**

MATERIALS: two meter sticks, tape, marble or golf ball, timer (or watch with second hand)

Have students work in pairs to find the average speed of a marble. They start by making a marble "path." They tape two meter sticks end to end and lay them along the edge of a room, with enough room for a marble to roll between the sticks and the wall. At one end, one student sets the marble in motion along the path. At the other end, the partner is timing the marble.

The speed changes. As the marble travels in its path, it slows down. The students find the average speed for the course by:

average speed = $\dfrac{2 \text{ meters}}{\text{time (seconds)}}$

They can try this several times, with greater and lesser starting speeds— by using more or less force to get the marble going.

COMPREHENSION STRATEGIES: Using formulas, taking measurements

LANGUAGE ARTS

CHARACTER SKETCH

"Starlight Express"

INDIVIDUAL   **15–30 MIN**

Ask students if they ever had to turn to someone for help with a problem. Perhaps they could not finish an assignment or had a difficult decision to make. Did they turn to someone special whom they knew they could depend on, such as a friend, a relative, or a teacher?

Have them write about that special person. Have them explain in a character sketch:

- Why did they need help?
- Why did they pick that special person to ask for help? What is that person like?
- What did that person do to help?
- What effect did the help have?
- Would they ask that person for help again?

COMPREHENSION STRATEGY: Main ideas

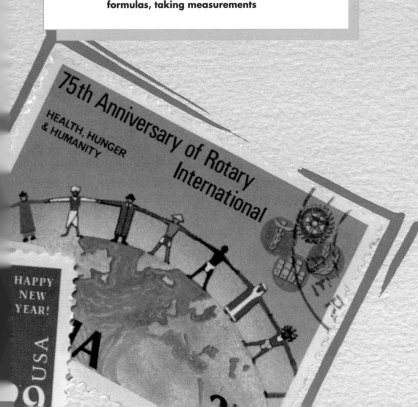

UNIT FIVE
LESSON 5

RELATED ARTS | MOVEMENT | **THEATER** | VISUAL ARTS |

LESSON PLANNER

FOCUS Musical drama/Musical style

OBJECTIVES

OBJECTIVE 1 Count the number of times a two-measure motive is sung in a recording

OBJECTIVE 2 List musical characteristics that project the mood of a song (tested)

MATERIALS
Recordings
Listening: Starlight Express from *Starlight Express* by R. Stilgoe and A. Lloyd Webber **CD5:2**
Listening: I Am the Starlight from *Starlight Express* by R. Stilgoe and A. Lloyd Webber **CD5:3**
Listening: The Light at the End of the Tunnel from *Starlight Express* by R. Stilgoe and A. Lloyd Webber **CD5:4**

Instruments keyboard or resonator bells

Resources Recorder Master R • 22 (pitches C D E F G A B♭ C' D')

▶ = **BASIC PROGRAM**

WHAT'S THE MOTIVE?

In music dramas like musicals and operas, a motive is sometimes used to represent an important character or idea. The musical motive can be sung or played by the orchestra. Each time the motive returns, we are reminded of the other times we heard it. In *Starlight Express*, for example, this motive becomes the musical symbol for the mysterious force, the Starlight Express. Listen for it in the song "Starlight Express."

DETERMINE the pitch letter names of this musical motive.

F F F G   E G E C

I Am the Starlight
LISTENING

by Richard Stilgoe and Andrew Lloyd Webber

In "I Am the Starlight," the voice of the Starlight Express tells Rusty about the true source of its power.

COUNT the repetitions of the Starlight Express motive. How many times is it sung in this song?

THE STORY CONTINUES...
Pearl, now aware that Greaseball used dirty tricks to win the first stage of the race, returns to be Rusty's coach in the final stage.

208

MEETING **INDIVIDUAL** NEEDS

ALTERNATE TEACHING STRATEGY

OBJECTIVE 1 Place the two-measure motive on the board. Each time the motive is heard in the music, point in sequence to the notes that comprise the motive. Listen a second time and repeat the activity, having students raise hands each time the motive is heard.

ENRICHMENT: *Finding the Motive*

Remind students that the motive is often present in instrumental sections such as the introduction and accompaniments. Tell them that the "Starlight Express" motive

changes pitches and there are a few variants in the rhythm. Then have them count the total number of times the motive is heard. (13 times in all: 7 in the introduction, 4 in the song, and 2 in the coda)

BUILDING SELF-ESTEEM: *A "Starlight" Message*

Have students write a short message to themselves, describing what is powerful about them and how they can use that power to attain personal goals. The message can be added to an ongoing Self-Esteem Journal to be read only by the student, unless he or she wishes to share.

1 GET SET

"When words are set to music, the emotion and meaning of the words touch our minds and spirits. Composers often use a motive in more than one song as a subtle reminder of the main features of the story." Have students:

• Say the pitch letter names of the two-measure motive on page 208 as you (or a volunteer) play it for the class.

• Listen to "Starlight Express" CD5:2 (page 207), noting the repetitions of this motive.

"Repeating the motive gives the drama a sense of continuity, even if the composer changes its dynamics or tone color."

2 DEVELOP

Introduce "I Am the Starlight" CD5:3. **Listen for a repeated melodic motive.** Have students:

▶ • Read page 208 and listen to "I Am the Starlight."

▶ • Compare the vocal tone color of the Starlight Express voice to that of Rusty. (Starlight Express—heavier, thicker, darker; Rusty—lighter, thinner, brighter)

▶ • Discuss the message that the voice of the Starlight Express is sending to Rusty. (The power is real and is contained in Rusty's heart and mind.)

• Play the two-measure motive on page 208 on resonator bells or keyboard.

OBJECTIVE 1 Informal Assessment
• Count the number of times they hear the "Starlight Express" motive sung in the song itself. (4)

SPECIAL LEARNERS: *Memorizing Melodies*

Playing the two-measure motive for "Starlight Express" can give students experience in performing short melodies from memory. First, have students practice the motive (preferably on a keyboard) until it is memorized. Then, have each student make up five-note (or shorter) melodies to be used as "motives" in their own future improvised pieces. Have pairs of students play and help each other write down the pitch letter names of the notes in their motives for reference. (Keep the written notation in a folder for students to refer to.)

Students should try playing their motives from memory and practice playing or singing them at home. Have partners practice their motives with each other until they are memorized. Then have each partner learn the other's motive.

UNIT FIVE
LESSON 5

continued from previous page

3 APPLY

Introduce "The Light at the End of the Tunnel" CD5:4. **Identify musical characteristics that reflect the mood of a song.** Have students:

▶ • Continue to read the story.

▶ • Listen to "The Light at the End of the Tunnel" and describe the vocal tone color of Poppa, who leads the singing. (light, bright)

• Listen again, clapping the syncopated pattern each time it is heard.

▶ • Discuss the mood portrayed in the song (celebration), and compare with other celebratory music, such as holiday or patriotic songs.

OBJECTIVE 2 Informal Assessment
• Identify the musical characteristics that project the mood of celebration. (fast tempo, gospel style, emphasis on syncopated rhythms, colorful and bright accompaniment, jubilant call-and-reponse style, generally loud dynamic level)

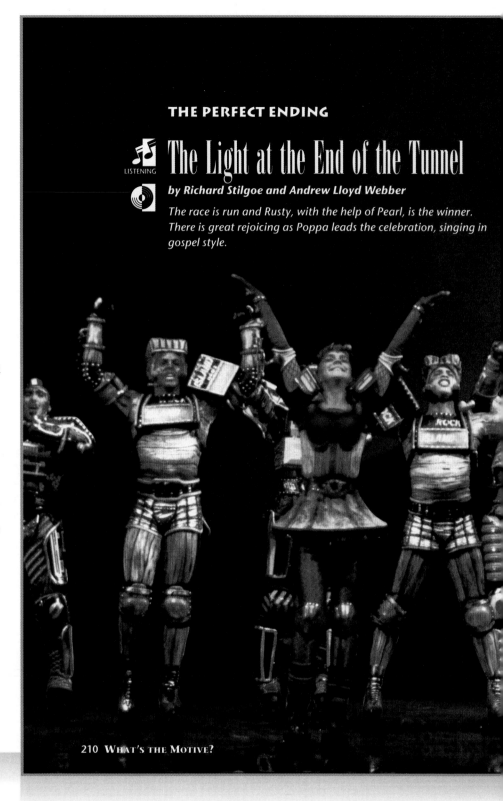

THE PERFECT ENDING

🎵 The Light at the End of the Tunnel
LISTENING

by Richard Stilgoe and Andrew Lloyd Webber

The race is run and Rusty, with the help of Pearl, is the winner. There is great rejoicing as Poppa leads the celebration, singing in gospel style.

210 WHAT'S THE MOTIVE?

MEETING **INDIVIDUAL** NEEDS

ALTERNATE TEACHING STRATEGY

OBJECTIVE 2 Have students brainstorm a list of musical characteristics or elements and write them on the board. (tone color, dynamics, tempo, articulation) Then play a few pieces for them, such as "Starlight Express" and "I Am the Starlight." After each listening, have volunteers place a one- or two-word description on the list next to the appropriate characteristic. Repeat the activity with "The Light at the End of the Tunnel."

CRITICAL THINKING: *Composer's Intent*

Have students discuss why Andrew Lloyd Webber set the voice of The Starlight Express as a bass and Rusty as a tenor. Do they agree or disagree with his choice? Is this a stereotypical use of bass (low, heavy) and tenor (mid-range, light)?

CLAP this syncopated
pattern each time you hear it
in "The Light at the End of the Tunnel."

DESCRIBE the mood expressed in this song. Identify
the musical characteristics that project this mood.

4 CLOSE

"Songs such as the ones you've heard from *Starlight Express* can express many moods or emotions." Have students:

▶ • List on the board three popular songs that have different moods, then list beside each title those musical characteristics that help to identify each of the songs.

LESSON SUMMARY

Informal Assessment In this lesson, students:

OBJECTIVE 1 Counted the number of times they heard a two-measure motive sung in "I Am the Starlight."

OBJECTIVE 2 Listed musical characteristics that projected the mood of "The Light at the End of the Tunnel."

MORE MUSIC: Reinforcement

"Earth Day Every Day," page 322 (syncopation, interpretation; spring)
"Bamboo," page 340 (syncopation)
"Keep Your Lamps!" page 407 (syncopation)

DRAMA CONNECTION: *Style*

Help the class develop a definition for the word "style" using their own ideas and a dictionary. If possible, show sections from video tapes of *Starlight Express, The Boy Friend,* and *A Chorus Line.* If these are unavailable, have students listen to the songs in the unit while looking at the accompanying pictures in the pupil book. Discuss the style of each musical by comparing the music and images. Make a list of descriptive words for each musical (realistic, flashy, exciting, simple, fantasy). Have students discuss what production elements they could change if they were

going to stage *Starlight Express* in a different style (costumes, music, settings). Ask students why they think style is important. (It can influence the choice of production elements; it can determine the type of audience the show will draw.)

ACROSS the

AUTOBIOGRAPHY

"I Am the Starlight"

INDIVIDUAL   **15–30 MIN**

Based on the words of the song, *the power within you*, have students think about:

- something they do better than anything else;
- something they have achieved after working very hard;
- a hobby, sport, or school subject in which they try hard to do their very best.

In an autobiographical sketch, have them describe any of these interests or achievements. They may include how or why they started this special activity, and why they keep working at it. What is their goal when they work at it? What are their future goals?

COMPREHENSION STRATEGY: Expressing point of view

TUNNEL GAME

"The Light at the End of the Tunnel"

PAIR   **15–30 MIN**

MATERIALS: graph paper, number cube, two different colored pencils, rulers

Preparation: Students draw an *x-axis* and a *y-axis*, centered on a sheet of graph paper and label each axis from -6 to +6.

To play: Each player chooses a different colored pencil. One player plots a dot at (-6, +6) and the other at (+6, -6). Each player, in turn, rolls the number cube twice to get an ordered pair of numbers. The player must decide to make one of the two numbers positive and the other negative. They plot a dot at the point located by the ordered pair and draw a "tunnel"—a straight line between the starting point and the new point.

Players alternate to get four turns each, each time using the newly plotted point as the starting point. The player who draws the longer "tunnel" wins.

COMPREHENSION STRATEGY: Making decisions

CURRICULUM

SOURCES OF ENERGY

"The Light at the End of the Tunnel"

GROUP   **30 MIN OR LONGER**

MATERIALS: research materials

Besides being used in engines, steam is used in many power plants to help produce electricity. Water is heated to produce steam, which turns a turbine. The turbine spins a generator, resulting in electricity. The source of the heat that produces the steam can be the burning of fuel (coal) or a nuclear reaction.

Have students work in groups to find out about the benefits and potential hazards of producing electricity by either of these methods. Have other groups research other means of producing electricity—by harnessing solar energy, wind, running water, and geothermal energy. Have them draw diagrams of how each method operates and report their results in a class presentation. Have them compare the methods for safety and usefulness.

COMPREHENSION STRATEGIES: Expressing points of view, compare and contrast

MAP RACE

"The Light at the End of the Tunnel"

PAIR   **15–30 MIN**

MATERIALS: large fold-out map of any continent, string, number cubes, clay, buttons

Preparation: Two players lay a string along a map to plot a zigzag route across a continent. The route must go through five major cities. At each city, they place a dot of clay on the string.

To play: Each player, in turn, rolls the cube three times and uses the numbers to form a three-digit number—the distance (in miles or kilometers) that the player moves a marker (button) along the route. Players use the map scale to determine the distance (rounded to the nearest ten). As they approach a dot on the route, players must land within 50 units (before or after) of the dot in order to pass the dot on that given turn. Thus, players may try to form the greatest three-digit distances, or lesser distances, to help them land near a dot. The first player to reach (or go beyond) the end of the route wins.

COMPREHENSION STRATEGY: Making decisions

LESSON PLANNER

FOCUS Tone color/Style

OBJECTIVES
OBJECTIVE 1 Complete a chart comparing tempo, dynamics, tone color, articulation and voice category in two operatic arias

OBJECTIVE 2 Write a paragraph comparing and contrasting the characteristics of an opera with those of a musical

MATERIALS
Recordings
Listening: Pumping Iron from *Starlight Express* by R. Stilgoe and A. Lloyd Webber   CD5:1
Listening: *Gianni Schicchi* Opening Scene by G. Puccini   CD5:5
Listening: Firenze è come un albero fiorito from *Gianni Schicchi* by G. Puccini   CD5:6
Listening: O mio babbino caro from *Gianni Schicchi* by G. Puccini   CD5:7
Listening: Ladro! Ladro! from *Gianni Schicchi* by G. Puccini   CD5:8

Resources
Resource Master 5 • 5 (background)
Resource Master 5 • 6 (practice)

VOCABULARY
aria

▶ = **BASIC PROGRAM**

OPERA
A Grand Tradition

Giacomo Puccini

Operas were first written around 1600. Many operas heard today were written in the 1700s and 1800s by composers such as Mozart, Wagner, and Verdi. Most operas are plays in which all the words are sung. A few, like *Porgy and Bess*, have spoken text. Operas contain solo songs, called **arias**, vocal groups, sung text, and sections for the orchestra alone. Some include dances. The singers must train for years in order to develop the beautiful, strong sound needed to fill a large opera house, where no electronic equipment is used to make the voices louder.

Many operas end tragically, but some are funny and end quite happily. The short comic opera *Gianni Schicchi* was written by the Italian composer Giacomo Puccini. It had its first performance in New York in 1918. Puccini's operas, such as *La Bohème, Tosca,* and *Madama Butterfly*, are known for their beautiful melodies and dramatic plots.

The Granger Collection

212

MEETING **INDIVIDUAL** NEEDS

BIOGRAPHY: *Giacomo Puccini* THEATER

Italian composer Giacomo Puccini (1858–1924) was born into a family of musicians. His father died when Giacomo was still a child, but his mother was able to obtain a royal grant to pay for his musical education. His teachers encouraged his composing, and he had his first opera performed when he was still in his mid-twenties. He became the most popular opera composer of his time. Several of his operas, including *La Bohème* (la bo **em**), *Tosca* (**tɔs** ka), and *Madama Butterfly*, became classics that are widely performed today.

BACKGROUND: *Gianni Schicchi*

Gianni Schicchi, set in Florence in 1299, is Puccini's only comedy. While working on the opera, Puccini was afraid that "ancient Florence does not suit me, nor is it a subject that would appeal much to the public at large." Happily, he was wrong; both the critics and the public loved the comic opera from its first performance.

Buoso and his family in the opening scene of *Gianni Schicchi*

Gianni Schicchi
Opening Scene
by Giacomo Puccini

The story takes place hundreds of years ago in Florence, Italy. An elderly, wealthy man, Buoso, has just died moments before. Members of his scheming, greedy family are gathered round, pretending to mourn.

THINK IT THROUGH

How does the music played by the orchestra give the impression that the relatives are not sincere?

The family's weeping soon gives way to worrying about Buoso's will. One of them has heard that Buoso left most of his estate to a nearby monastery. They find the will and discover that what they feared is true. They are to receive only small inheritances, rather than larger shares of Buoso's vast wealth !

"What are the four main adult vocal categories?" (soprano, alto, tenor, bass) "Listen for one of these vocal categories in this song." Have students:

▶ • Listen to "Pumping Iron" CD5:1 (page 205).

▶ • Name the vocal category of the soloist in "Pumping Iron." (bass)

"You've been hearing adult voices in Broadway musicals. Today, you're going to hear them in a different kind of musical stage presentation."

2 DEVELOP

1. Introduce "Opening Scene" CD5:5. **Learn basic characteristics of opera.** Have students:

▶ • Read about opera, *Gianni Schicchi* (**jyan** ni **skik** ki), and Giacomo Puccini (**jya** ko mo put **chi** ni).

▶ • Look at the pictures and follow the story in the book as they listen to "Opening Scene." (Optional: Have some students read and act out the connecting sections between the excerpts on **Resource Master 5 • 5**, which contains a plot summary of *Gianni Schicchi*. See *Background* below for a summary of the "Opening Scene" action.)

▶ • Discuss the *Think It Through* question. (Possible answer: The orchestra plays very delicate, short notes; the music does not sound sad or serious.)

BACKGROUND: *Summary of Opening Scene*

This sets the comic tone of the opera. Rinuccio (ri **nut** chi o) and the other relatives are around the body of the wealthy Buoso (**bwɔ** zo), who has just died. The other relatives are weeping, but it soon becomes apparent that they are more concerned for their inheritance than Buoso's death. Each relative tries to outdo the others in their mourning. The first says, "I'll weep for days and days." The next says, "For days? For months!" The next, "Months? For years and years!" Finally, ". . . for all my life!"

As they talk, Gherardo's child is playing in the room and the adults occasionally shoo him away. (Gherardo is Buoso's nephew.) The scene ends as an aunt named Zita (**tsi** ta) says crossly, "Portatecelo voi, Gherardo, via!" (pɔr **ta** te **chɛ** lo voi ge **rar** do via)—"Take the child away, Gherardo!"

continued from previous page

2. Introduce "Firenze è come un albero fiorito" CD5:6 **and "O mio babbino caro"** CD5:7. **Compare stylistic elements of the two arias.** Have students:

▶ • Continue following the story.

▶ • Listen to Rinuccio's aria "Firenze è come un albero fiorito" (fi **ɾɛn** tse ɛ **ko** me un **al** be ɾo fyo **ɾi** to).

▶ • Listen to Lauretta's (lau **ɾet** ta) aria "O mio babbino caro" (o **mi** o ba **bi** no **ka** ɾo).

OBJECTIVE 1 **Informal Assessment**
• On a piece of paper, indicate the tempo, dynamics, tone color, articulation, and voice category of the arias of Rinuccio and Lauretta. (Collect the papers after the conclusion of the opera.) (Optional: Use **Resource Master 5 • 6**, which has a style chart for students to fill in.)

3. Introduce "Ladro! Ladro!" CD5:8. **Discuss interpretation.** Have students:

▶ • Listen to "Ladro! Ladro!" (**la** dɾo).

▶ • Discuss how the singers' interpretations fit the mood of this part of the story. (show anger: heavy, rough tone color, loud dynamics)

The family reads Buoso's will.

LISTENING

Firenze è come un albero fiorito

from *Gianni Schicchi*
by Giacomo Puccini

One of the less greedy relatives, Rinuccio, is in love with Lauretta. His family has forbidden him to marry her because she is too poor to have a dowry—money given by a bride's father to her bridegroom. Rinuccio tells the family that he has sent for the only person who can help them get Buoso's money—Gianni Schicchi, Lauretta's father. The family does not like the idea of asking for help from a lowly peasant, but Rinuccio sings an aria in which he convinces them that Schicchi is quite clever, always playing tricks and practical jokes. Then Lauretta and Schicchi arrive and the family tries to get Schicchi's help.

LISTEN to this aria. What type of voice does Rinuccio have? Describe the tempo, dynamics, tone color, and articulation in Rinuccio's aria.
tenor

Lauretta and Rinuccio

214 OPERA: A GRAND TRADITION

MEETING **INDIVIDUAL** NEEDS

ALTERNATE TEACHING STRATEGIES

OBJECTIVE 1 Briefly review the meaning of each of the terms (tempo, dynamics, tone color, articulation, and voice category) and alert students to what they should listen for. Then let them hear the arias again.

OBJECTIVE 2 Play the ending of *Starlight Express* ("The Light at the End of the Tunnel," page 210) and the ending of *Gianni Schicchi* ("Ladro! Ladro!"). Discuss how the two differ. Note that in the opera the characters are not only singing a song, but also "talking" to each other. By contrast, "The Light" is strictly a song that can be separated from its dramatic setting. Have students work together to correct or complete their comparisons.

CRITICAL THINKING: *Writing a Review*
THEATER

Discuss why newspapers have writers who review musicals, operas, and other art forms. (To help theatergoers decide whether to see the performance, to help the artists improve) Then have students write a review of *Gianni Schicchi*. They should include a plot summary, a critical discussion of the music, and their opinion of each. They should also explain why they would or would not recommend the opera.

O mio babbino caro
from *Gianni Schicchi*
by Giacomo Puccini

Schicchi does not want to help the family because he is disgusted by their greed and their treatment of Lauretta. Lauretta begs him to do so, however, so she can have the money for a dowry and marry Rinuccio.

DESCRIBE **the tempo, dynamics, tone color, and articulation you hear in Lauretta's aria.**

Schicchi finally agrees to help and devises a scheme. Since no one else knows that Buoso has died, he will impersonate him and dictate a new will. When the doctor comes, Schicchi jumps into the bed and pretends to be Buoso. Having fooled the doctor, Schicchi sends for the lawyer and dictates a new will. However, instead of making sure that the relatives get the money, he tells the lawyer that the choicest property is to go to Gianni Schicchi! The family can say nothing lest they get into trouble for assisting in the plot.

Ladro! Ladro!

from *Gianni Schicchi*
by Giacomo Puccini

After the lawyer leaves, the relatives explode in fury, calling Schicchi a thief. Schicchi kicks them out of the house. Now Lauretta and Rinuccio will have the money to get married.

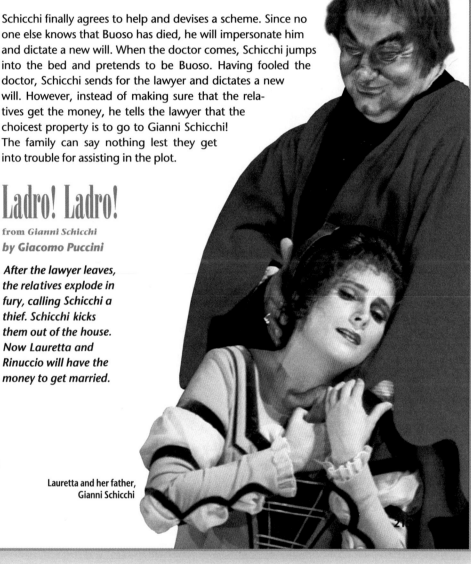

Lauretta and her father, Gianni Schicchi

3 APPLY

Compare a Broadway musical to an opera.
Have students:

OBJECTIVE 2 **Informal Assessment**
▶ • Compare a musical to an opera, writing at least one difference and one similarity. (*Different*—The music in musicals is more like popular songs, music in operas is usually more complicated and serious; Operas are usually all sung, but there is likely to be spoken dialogue in musicals. *Same*—costumes, scenery; tell stories with music; combine dramatic and musical impact; can have dancing)

4 CLOSE

"You've just compared a musical to an opera. Now share your answers." Have students:
▶ • Share some of their answers before turning in their papers.

LESSON SUMMARY

Informal Assessment In this lesson, students:

OBJECTIVE 1 Compared tempo, dynamics, tone color, articulation, and voice category in "Firenze è come un albero fiorito" and "O mio babbino caro."

OBJECTIVE 2 Wrote a paragraph comparing and contrasting the characteristics of an opera and those of a musical.

MORE MUSIC: **Reinforcement**
Excerpts from *Carmen*, page 232 (opera, voice categories, interpretation)
"Garden of the Earth," page 325 (voice categories, interpretation; spring)

BACKGROUND: Gianni Schicchi

Summary of "Firenze è come un albero fiorito" ("Florence is like a blossoming tree"—Rinuccio's aria, as sung by Plácido Domingo): Rinuccio claims that newcomers to Florence, like Gianni Schicchi, will make the city richer and more splendid, just as soil and water nourish a tree.

Summary of "O mio babbino caro" ("Oh, my dear Daddy"—Lauretta's aria, the opera's "hit song," as sung by Ileana Cotrubas): Lauretta begs her father to cooperate with the relatives' plot so that she can have a dowry (money or property given to the husband's family at a wedding). Her last line is "Babbo, pietà, pietà . . ." (pye **ta**). ("Daddy, have pity, have pity!")

Summary of "Ladro! Ladro!" ("Thief! Thief!"): The furious relatives scream "Thief! Thief!" at Gianni Schicchi for tricking them and keeping Buoso's best property for himself. They try to steal things from the house, which now belongs to Schicchi. Schicchi chases them away, yelling, "Get out! Go!" Now that Schicchi is rich, his daughter will have her dowry. Lauretta and Rinuccio are happy that now they can be married. (The End)

RELATED ARTS MOVEMENT THEATER VISUAL ARTS

LESSON PLANNER

FOCUS Style

OBJECTIVES
OBJECTIVE 1 Play a rhythm from South Indian musical theater
OBJECTIVE 2 Play in the style of the Balinese *gender wayang*
OBJECTIVE 3 Identify interpretive choices of an opera singer

MATERIALS
Recordings
Listening: Eka Tala (excerpt) CD5:9
Recorded Lesson: Rhythms of the *Kathakali* Music Drama CD5:10
Listening: Prologue to *Mahabharata* (excerpt) CD5:11
Listening: De este apacible rincón from *Luisa Fernanda* by F. Moreno Torroba CD5:12

Instruments
drums and metallophones or other barred instruments

VOCABULARY
zarzuela

▶ = **BASIC PROGRAM**

Theatrical Traditions

Long before anyone ever thought of Broadway musicals or opera, other kinds of musical theater were enjoyed in different parts of the world.

🎵 **LISTENING**

Eka Tala (Excerpt)
South Indian Theater Music

Kudiyattam *is the oldest kind of musical drama that is still in existence today. It comes from South India and is said to be over 1,000 years old. Kudiyattam is associated with the Hindu religion. The lines are chanted, rather than sung.*

Four instrumentalists accompany the movement in Kudiyattam. Two performers play pot-shaped drums, while one plays an hourglass-shaped drum. The fourth person plays a small pair of cymbals. Listen for the instruments in "Eka Tala." Once you hear a regular rhythm, tap your fingers together on each stressed beat. In Indian music, a rhythm pattern is called a **tala.**

LISTEN for four beats in each group of the "Eka Tala."

216

MEETING **INDIVIDUAL** NEEDS

ALTERNATE TEACHING STRATEGY

OBJECTIVE 1 Have students practice the rhythm on page 217, using such body percussion as patting on knees. Then transfer the rhythms to any sound source. Students may also make up their own speech pattern (either syllables or words) to go with the rhythm.

MULTICULTURAL PERSPECTIVES: *Shiva*

The bronze Shiva (**shi** va) plays an hourglass drum as he dances, thus creating the world. In one left hand he holds the flame of destruction that will end this age. Another

hand is raised in a gesture of protection. The fourth hand points to his uplifted foot, signifying salvation. With his four arms in motion, Shiva demonstrates the continuing cycle of life—creation, preservation, and destruction. The statue was created in the twelfth century A.D.

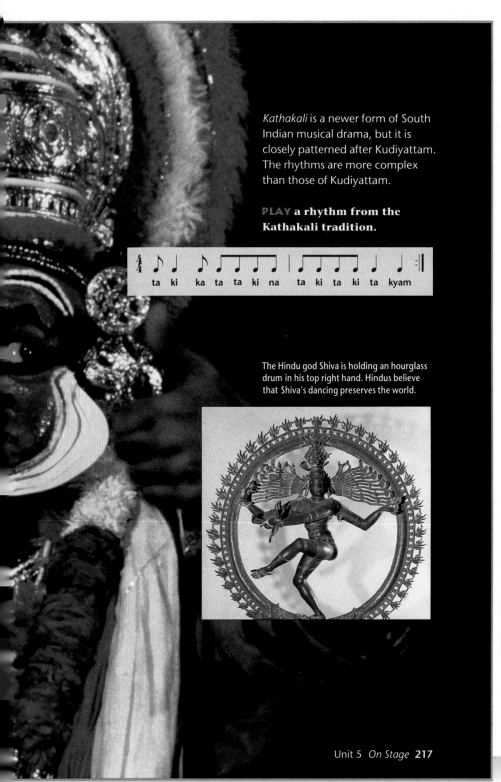

Kathakali is a newer form of South Indian musical drama, but it is closely patterned after Kudiyattam. The rhythms are more complex than those of Kudiyattam.

PLAY a rhythm from the Kathakali tradition.

4/4	♪ ♩	♪	♫♫		♫♫♫ ♩	♩ :‖
	ta ki	ka ta	ta ki na	ta ki ta ki ta	kyam	

The Hindu god Shiva is holding an hourglass drum in his top right hand. Hindus believe that Shiva's dancing preserves the world.

Unit 5 *On Stage* 217

"You have been learning elements of music that will help you sing a song in the style intended by its composer." Have students:

▶ • Name four expressive elements that a performer must consider in determining how to sing a song. (tone color, dynamics, articulation, and tempo)

• Name four other elements of music. (pitch, rhythm, form, and texture)

• Write all eight elements on the board.

"Today, you're going to hear music in which these elements are used in different ways to create three very different kinds of music. Think about how they are different, and also how they are alike, as you listen."

2 DEVELOP

1. Introduce "Eka Tala" (excerpt) CD5:9. **Play a rhythm in the *Kathakali* tradition.** Have students:

▶ • Read about the *Kudiyattam* (ku **di** ya tam) theater and find India on a map.

• Listen to "Eka Tala" (**e** ka **ta** la) and tap fingers together on each stressed beat, listening for the *tala* (rhythm pattern).

• Listen for changing rhythm patterns. (After about 43 seconds they change on almost every first beat.)

▶ • Read about *Kathakali* (ka ta **ka** li) drama.

OBJECTIVE 1 Informal Assessment
Recorded Lesson CD5:10

▶ • Listen to "Rhythms of the *Kathakali* Music Drama" and play the *Kathakali* rhythm on page 217 as directed.

MULTICULTURAL PERSPECTIVES: *The Kudiyattam*

The pot-shaped *mizhavu* (mi **la** vu), heard in the recording, has a body made of copper with a drumhead of cowhide. The drum is placed in a wooden frame and the player sits on the edge of this frame to play the drum, striking it with bare hands. The copper body creates a very resonant sound. The *idakka* (i da ka) has two heads, one on each end. The two heads are laced together across the hourglass-shaped body. The laces are squeezed or relaxed slightly by one arm, to raise or lower the pitch of the drum. The front head is said to represent the sun; the back head, the moon. The *talam* (**ta** lam) are a small pair of cymbals with a very clear tone color. They are used to play the stressed beats of the *tala*.

continued from previous page

**2. Introduce "Prologue to *Mahabharata*"
(excerpt) CD5:11. Learn about the *gender
wayang*.** Have students:

▶ • Read about the *wayang kulit* (wɑ **yang**
ku **lɪt**) theater and the *dalang* (dɑ **lang**).

▶ • Find Indonesia and Bali on a map.

▶ • Listen to a *gender wayang* (gən **der**
wɑ **yang**) as it plays "Prologue to *Mahabharata*" (mɑ **hɑ bɑ** ɾɑ tɑ).

INDONESIAN SHADOW PUPPET THEATER

The *wayang kulit* theater, or shadow puppet theater, is very popular in Indonesia. A storyteller, called the *dalang*, recites ancient Indian and Indonesian stories as he manipulates puppets behind a screen. A light behind the screen causes the puppets to cast shadows. The audience sees only the shadows of the puppets, moving as if by themselves. Some people are allowed to sit in special seats where they can see the puppets and the dalang in action behind the screen. Instrumentalists and a singer accompany the show. The dalang also plays percussion instruments with his foot and conducts the musicians as well. He is highly respected for these abilities. Many different puppets are used. They are made of beautifully decorated, painted, and elaborately cut leather.

218 THEATRICAL TRADITIONS

MEETING **INDIVIDUAL** NEEDS

ALTERNATE TEACHING STRATEGY

OBJECTIVE 2 Have each group clap the rhythm of their pattern separately as they count the eighth notes (1 and 2 and . . .). Then have them play each part separately, still counting. Finally, have them combine the two parts again, counting quietly.

MULTICULTURAL PERSPECTIVES: *Mahabharata*

The *Mahabharata* is an epic poem of India that tells of deeds done by great and strong heroes aided by the gods, just as the Greek epics of Homer do. At least two thousand years old, the story tells of five brothers who marry the same princess, fight a long and bloody war to win a kingdom, then give it all up for a spiritual quest. In the end, they are reunited in heaven. The epic contains the *Bhagavad-gita* (**bɑ** gɑ vɑd **gi** tɑ) ("Song of God"), which presents the core teachings of the Hindu religion. Epics are the oldest form of poetry. The epic is recited orally and is always accompanied by music.

The music for the wayang kulit theater is provided by an instrumental group called *gender wayang*. The gender wayang consists of four metallophones.

🎵 Prologue to *Mahabarata* (Excerpt)
LISTENING

Traditional Indonesian Music

Listen to the gender wayang as it opens a shadow puppet performance in Bali, one of the islands of Indonesia. Listen carefully and you will hear the crickets in the background of this outdoor performance, recorded live.

PLAY patterns on metallophones or other barred instruments to create a sound like that of the gender wayang.

These performers come from Java. Java is a neighbor of Bali and the two islands have related shadow puppet theater traditions.

Unit 5 *On Stage* **219**

3. Play in Balinese style. Have students:
• Divide into two groups, each to learn one of the following patterns on metallophones or other barred instruments.

OBJECTIVE 2 Informal Assessment
• Combine the two patterns and repeat several times to play a short piece in Balinese style.

SOCIAL STUDIES CONNECTION: *Shadow Puppets* 🎭 THEATER

Shadow puppets are flat, jointed figures of cardboard, tin, or leather measuring about 20 inches in height or less. The figures are moved from below the stage by means of rods attached to the puppets. A strong light is projected from the back of the stage onto the puppets, which appear as silhouettes on a taut white cloth at the front of the stage. Have students produce a shadow-screen musical or opera, using an overhead projector or other light source. Students might make shadow puppets of the characters in *Gianni Schicchi* (Lesson 6, pages 212–215) and prepare a shadow-screen version of the opera's story.

MOVEMENT: *"Prologue to Mahabharata"* 🎭 THEATER

Have students look at the shadow puppet on the pupil page, noting where the rods connect to the puppet and make movement possible. (at the wrists, with hinges at the shoulder and elbow joints) Have them practice moving their own elbow and shoulder joints as though they were being operated by a dalang. Then have pairs of students devise puppet-like movements to stage a mock battle (a common puppet-theater subject) to the music. If a sheet and flashlight are available, students can perform the movements on one side of the sheet, while from the other, the rest of the class watches the shadows.

Unit 5 ON STAGE **219**

UNIT FIVE
LESSON 7

continued from previous page

4. Introduce "De este apacible rincón"
CD5:12. Identify probable choices in interpretation by an opera singer. Have students:

▶ • Read about *zarzuela* (saɾ **swe** la).

▶ • Remember what a solo in opera is usually called. (aria) Then read about Javier's (xa **vyeɾ**) aria "De este apacible rincón" (de **es** te a pa **si** ble ɾin **kon**) from *Luisa Fernanda* (**lwi** sa feɾ **nan** da).

▶ • Recall the interpretation choices a singer makes in order to sing a song in the style intended by the composer and watch as a volunteer writes these on the board. (tone color, tempo, dynamics, articulation)

OBJECTIVE 3 Informal Assessment

▶ • Listen to the aria, writing down the choices of interpretation that they think Plácido Domingo might have made. (tone color—bright; tempo—medium fast; dynamics—medium loud to loud; articulation—contrasting between slightly legato and marcato)

▶ • Share their answers for each element.

3 APPLY

Compare styles of music. Have students:

▶ • As a class, or in groups, briefly compare and contrast the three styles of music heard in the lesson. (Only general impressions are needed to help students focus on what they heard. *Alike*—they are all related to musical drama; *Different*—they are different in almost every other way: instruments, rhythms, and so on.)

ZARZUELA: THE OPERA OF SPAIN

Zarzuela is a type of Spanish opera that combines spoken dialogue with music. It takes its name from the Palace of La Zarzuela near Madrid. Lively and exciting festivals that included these musical productions took place at La Zarzuela as early as 1629. Zarzuelas remain popular today.

LISTENING

De este apacible rincón   *from Luisa Fernanda*
by Federico Moreno Torroba

Listen for Spanish rhythms in this brilliant aria, sung by the famous Spanish tenor Placido Domingo. In the aria, a well-to-do man named Javier—now far away from home—remembers the peaceful corner of Madrid where he spent his childhood dreaming of success and wealth.

What choices in interpretation did Placido Domingo make in order to project the feeling of the song effectively?

The variety of musical theater productions around the world is almost endless. Here are some scenes from a few more.

A zarzuela performance in Spain

220 THEATRICAL TRADITIONS

MEETING **INDIVIDUAL** NEEDS

ALTERNATE TEACHING STRATEGY

OBJECTIVE 3 Review the possible interpretive choices. Then play the recording of Javier's aria again and have students write down their choices, working in pairs this time.

BIOGRAPHY: *Federico Moreno Torroba*

Spanish composer Federico Moreno Torroba (fe ðe ɾi ko mo **re** no to **ro** ba), 1891–1982, was also a conductor and music critic. Moreno Torroba's first music lessons were with his father. He studied organ and the art of teaching music. As a young man, he became interested in composing. Spain had never been a country with a strong operatic tradition, and he wanted to write a true Spanish opera. He experimented with serious operas, but was most successful with light operas in the zarzuela style. His many stage works include *Luisa Fernanda* (1932), one of the most popular zarzuelas ever written.

Japanese *Noh* drama

Richard Wagner's opera
Die Walküre

Chinese opera

Gilbert and Sullivan's operetta
H.M.S. Pinafore

Unit 5 *On Stage* **221**

• Decide what is meant by "different styles of music" and what creates these different styles. (Communicate the idea that style is the *combination* of the ways in which all the musical elements are used: dynamics, tone color, tempo, pitch, rhythm, form, articulation, and texture.)

4 CLOSE

"In this lesson, you discovered what creates musical style." Have students:

▶ • Take turns singing phrases from songs in the unit, while volunteers list which elements of musical style are heard.

LESSON SUMMARY

Informal Assessment In this lesson, students:

OBJECTIVE 1 Played a rhythm derived from *Kathakali*, a South Indian musical theater.

OBJECTIVE 2 Played in the style of the Balinese *gender wayang*.

OBJECTIVE 3 Identified interpretive choices that an opera singer made in singing "De este apacible rincón."

MORE MUSIC: Reinforcement
"Diwali Song," page 315 (Indian music)

MULTICULTURAL PERSPECTIVES: *Zarzuela* MOVEMENT

Zarzuela is a special type of Spanish musical stage production, similar to an operetta. Its musical sections alternate singing and dancing, with some spoken dialogue in between. Zarzuela is noted for its beautiful and exuberant melodies, which sound somewhat like Spanish folk songs. The term "zarzuela" comes from the Spanish word *"la zarza"* (lɑ **sɑr** sɑ), a thorny bush. King Philip IV built a palace on a mountain full of zarza bushes during the first half of the seventeenth century; the palace took on the name of the surrounding bushes and came to be known as the Palace of La Zarzuela. Because of the king's love for entertaining, the palace soon became a center for Spanish theater and music, and the operettas written for the king took on the palace's name. Zarzuelas remain very popular in Spain to this day.

LESSON PLANNER

FOCUS Style

OBJECTIVE
OBJECTIVE 1 Evaluate interpretative
choices for a song

MATERIALS
Recordings
Comedy Tonight   CD4:36
Our Time   CD5:13
Our Time (performance mix)   CD5:14
One   CD4:37
Give My Regards to Broadway   CD5:15

Resources
Resource Master 5 • 4 (practice)
Resource Master 5 • 7 (practice)

Technology Music with MIDI: Give My
Regards to Broadway

▶ **= BASIC PROGRAM**

CURTAIN CALLS

"Our Time" is from the 1981 musical *Merrily We Roll Along* by Stephen Sondheim. In the song, a group of recent high school graduates look forward to their lives as adults.

LISTEN for the way tempo, dynamics, articulation, and tone color are used to project the feelings and thoughts of the song.

OUR TIME

Words and Music
by Stephen Sondheim

1. Some-thing is stir - ring, shift-ing ground.— It's just be - gun.—
2. Feel how it qui - vers, on the brink,— ev' - ry - thing!—

Edg - es are blur - ring all a - round, and
Gives you the shiv - ers, makes you think— there's

yes - ter - day— is done.——— Feel the flow,—
so much stuff— to sing.—— And you and me,—

222

MEETING **INDIVIDUAL** NEEDS

BACKGROUND: *Merrily We Roll Along*

The musical *Merrily We Roll Along* is based on a 1930s play of the same name. It tells of two songwriting partners who realize their dream of success, then eventually drift apart. The story is told in a unique way: the action begins in the present and each scene goes a step backwards in time. The audience sees the sad ending of the story—the break-up of the songwriting team—before seeing the happy, hopeful beginning of the characters' careers. The musical ends with the main characters up on a roof in 1957, watching the Soviet *Sputnik* satellite, looking forward to a new

era of space flight and to their future success. Since we already know what will happen to the characters, this happy ending is a bit sad at the same time. When the musical appeared on Broadway in 1981, it was not well received and had only a brief run. Since that time, it has been performed many times in college and community theaters.

hear what's hap-pen-ing. We're what's hap-pen-ing._
we'll be sing-ing it like the birds,____ me with mu-sic and

Don't you know?_ We're the mov-ers and we're the shap-ers,
you the words,_

we're the names_ in to-mor-row's pa-pers, up to us_ now to

show 'em.___ It's

our time,_ breathe it in.__ Worlds to change_ and

Unit 5 *On Stage* **223**

1 GET SET

"You've been hearing musical stage presentations in several styles and thinking about how to interpret a song." Have students:

▶ • Recall the interpretive choices they made for "Comedy Tonight." (See Lesson 2, p. 198, *Apply*.)

▶ • Sing "Comedy Tonight" CD4:36, on page 198.

"Today, you'll learn another song by Stephen Sondheim and select elements of interpretation for it. You'll also choose interpretative elements for a song by one of the most famous American songwriters of all time."

2 DEVELOP

1. Introduce "Our Time" CD5:13. Practice describing interpretation of a song. Have students:

▶ • Read page 222 and listen to "Our Time."

▶ • Discuss the meaning of the song.

• Describe the tempo, dynamics, tone color, and articulation on the recording.

▶ • Sing the melody.

MOVEMENT: *"Our Time"* THEATER

Preparation: Have students work in pairs to find three different ways to express the idea of "me and you," using gesture and movement. Suggestions: Point to one another, pat partner's back as if buddies, give a "high five" or a complicated handshake.

Final Form: Have partners perform their three ideas for the class, then have each half of the class use the ideas to choreograph the end of the song from *It's our time on the block* . . . . They should create variations on *me and you*

each time it is heard. To create variations using the same gestures and movement, they can change group spatial design (how the group is arranged), body facing, and levels (high, low). The movement can be done in one place or with locomotion.

continued from previous page

2. Sing "Our Time" as a solo with expressive choices. Have students:

• Decide on their own interpretation of "Our Time" and prepare a solo version of their interpretation (Verse 1 only).

• Listen as several students are chosen at random to sing their solo for the class. (Ask students to explain their choices after singing the solo.)

3. Sing "Our Time" in two parts. Have students:

• Learn the harmony part to "Our Time" (in the second half of the song). (When students are secure singing the melody and harmony separately, have them sing both parts together.)

224 CURTAIN CALLS

MEETING **INDIVIDUAL** NEEDS

COOPERATIVE LEARNING: *Interpretation of "One"*
Have students work in cooperative groups of three or four on their interpretation of "One," then present the song to the class as a group. Set a time limit of 10 minutes in which to prepare the interpretation. Assign one student in each group to record decisions on tempo, dynamics, tone color, and articulation. You may wish to give each group a copy of "One" so that the recorder may write the group's interpretative decisions directly above the notation.

ENRICHMENT: *The Composer's Workshop*
Have students follow the directions on **Resource Master 5 • 7** to set a poem to music, using the composer's tools—tempo, instrumentation, dynamics, melody, harmony, and rhythm.

Long a-go— all we had— was that fun-ny feel - ing say- ing some - day we'd send 'em reel - ing. Now it looks— like we can.———— Some day just— be-gan.——— It's our time— on the block.— Give us room— and start the clock.— Our time,— com - ing through!— Me and you,— pal, me and you!— Me and you!— Me and you!— Me and you!— Me and you!— Me and you!— Me and you!— Me and you!— Me and you!—

4. Review "One" CD4:37 **(pp. 200–201). Describe their own interpretations of a song.** Have students:

▶ • Sing "One."

▶ • Describe how they would interpret the song (tempo, dynamics, tone color, and articulation) and evaluate their descriptions.

▶ • Decide as a class how to interpret the song.

▶ • Sing the song again, incorporating any changes in interpretation that they have de-cided to make as a class. (You may want them to develop movement for the song, or repeat any movement that they developed in Lesson 3, pages 200–201, *Movement*.)

DRAMA CONNECTION: *Interpretation*

In order for a singer to interpret a song in musical theater, he or she must understand the scene and the circumstance of the character. Ask students to describe the setting and define the circumstance of the characters who sing "Our Time." (high-school graduates dreaming about the future) Have students listen to the recording and decide how the performance reflects the characters' situation. They should notice dynamics, tone color, tempo, and articulation. (Pop tone color, quick tempo, and crisp articulation reflect char-acters' youth and optimistic anticipation of future.)

Have students experiment with interpretation. Pick a song that most students know or can easily learn (such as "Greensleeves"). Have students create several different scenes and characterizations and then interpret the song for each situation.

continued from previous page

3 APPLY

Introduce "Give My Regards to Broadway"
CD5:15. Choose an appropriate interpretation. Have students:

▶ • Read about "Give My Regards to Broadway."

▶ • Decide on appropriate interpretation (legato or marcato articulation, dynamics, tempo, and tone color) for this song.

OBJECTIVE 1 Informal Assessment

▶ • Listen to the recording and evaluate the performers' stylistic choices for the song. (As in Lesson 2, page 198, the student plays the role of a critic writing a review, who must fill in how the performer did with regard to interpretation. Optional: Have students fill in their interpretation on **Resource Master 5 • 4**.)

• Listen to the song to check their decisions, then compare their answers and discuss them. (Possible answers: marcato, medium-loud dynamic level, bright tone color, medium-fast tempo)

• Identify the meter signature and find the syncopated pattern. (²⁄₂; page 227—Measures 25, 27, 33, 41, 49, 57)

▶ • Sing "Give My Regards to Broadway" with an interpretation planned by the class.

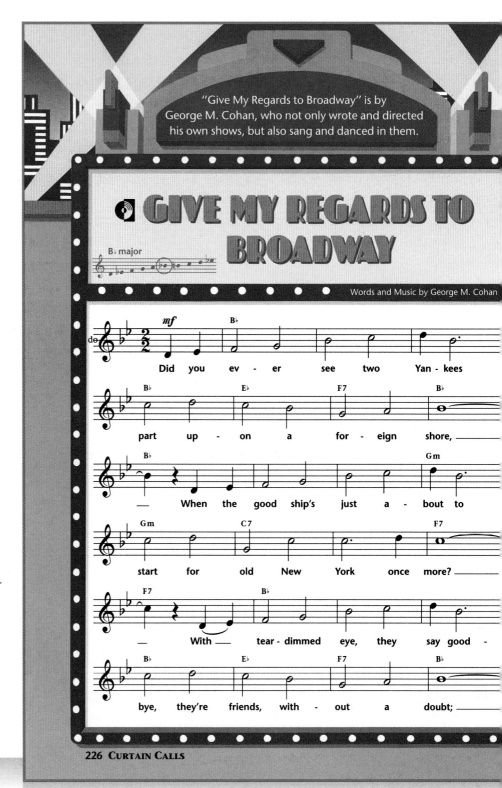

"Give My Regards to Broadway" is by George M. Cohan, who not only wrote and directed his own shows, but also sang and danced in them.

GIVE MY REGARDS TO BROADWAY

B♭ major

Words and Music by George M. Cohan

Did you ev - er see two Yan - kees part up - on a for - eign shore, When the good ship's just a - bout to start for old New York once more? With tear - dimmed eye, they say good - bye, they're friends, with - out a doubt;

226 CURTAIN CALLS

MEETING **INDIVIDUAL** NEEDS

ALTERNATE TEACHING STRATEGY

OBJECTIVE 1 Dynamics, articulation, tempo, and tone color are ways in which performers reflect the meaning of the words. Have students study the words of the song to see whether or not they agree with the performer's choices.

BIOGRAPHY: *George M. Cohan*

American composer George M. Cohan (1878–1942) was also a director, dancer, and singer. His life in the theater began at age nine, when he appeared in vaudeville shows with his family. As an adult, he often starred in his own

musicals, becoming the most famous American theater personality of his generation. Today, he is best remembered as the writer of "Give My Regards to Broadway," "Over There," and "Yankee Doodle Boy" (also known as "Yankee Doodle Dandy"). The syncopated rhythm and the strong feeling of the meter in "Give My Regards to Broadway" are typical of his songs.

LANGUAGE ARTS CONNECTION: *New Words*

Have students write new words for "Give My Regards to Broadway," substituting the name of the school for

When the man on the pier shouts, "Let them

clear," as the ship strikes out.

Refrain
mf

— Give my re-gards to Broad-

way, re-mem-ber me to Her-ald Square; ___

Tell all the gang at For-ty - Sec-ond Street that

I will soon be there. ___ Whis-per of

how I'm yearn - ing to min-gle with the old time

throng; ___ Give my re-gards to old Broad-

way and say that I'll be there 'ere long. ___

"In the future, you should be able to make in-formed choices about how a song should be sung and to perform songs as the composer wants them to be sung." Have students:

▶ • Stand and sing "Give My Regards to Broad-way" as if they were performing it on stage. (You may wish to assign solo parts to add in-terest to the song and to give students practice singing solo.)

LESSON SUMMARY

Informal Assessment In this lesson, students:

OBJECTIVE 1 Evaluated the performers' interpretive choices for "Give My Re-gards to Broadway."

MORE MUSIC: Reinforcement
"Shall I Dream a Dream?," page 380 (interpretation)
"Soft Shoe Song," page 383 (interpretation)

"Broadway" and similarly changing such other terms as "Herald Square" and "Forty-Second Street." This could be a farewell to the school, or the school year itself. For example:

Give my regards to Park School.
Remember me to Nurse Sinclair.
Tell all the gang down in the office that I'll
No longer be there!
Whisper of how I'm yearning
To get outside and play some ball.

Give my regards to old Park School
And say I won't see them till fall!

MOVEMENT: *"Give My Regards to Broadway"*

Have students choreograph this song. They can use steps from "Another Op'nin', Another Show" (p. 191) and "One" (p. 200), arm-movement ideas from "Look Around" (p. 193), the visual image idea from "Comedy Tonight" (p. 199), and the variation idea from "Our Time" (p. 222). After performing, have students share how choreographing and dancing together influences other aspects of their lives.

UNIT FIVE
LESSON 9

RELATED ARTS MOVEMENT THEATER VISUAL ARTS

LESSON PLANNER

OBJECTIVES
To review songs, skills, and concepts learned in Unit 5 and to test students' ability to:
1. Identify vocal range of soprano, alto, tenor, bass
2. Recognize lighter and heavier vocal tone colors
3. Identify appropriate interpretive elements with which a singer can project the mood or style of a song (tempo, dynamics, tone color, articulation)

MATERIALS
Recordings
Another Op'nin', Another Show   CD4:31
Comedy Tonight   CD4:36
Look Around   CD4:33
Listening: I Am the Starlight
   from *Starlight Express* by
   R. Stilgoe and A. Lloyd Webber CD5:3
Give My Regards to Broadway   CD5:15
Unit 5 Assessment A   CD5:16–19
Unit 5 Assessment B   CD5:20–23

Resources
Resource Master 5 • 8 (assessment)
Resource Master TA • 1 (assessment)

▶ = **BASIC PROGRAM**

REVIEW

THE STAGE IS YOURS

Musical theater productions have enchanted audiences for thousands of years in many parts of the world. Musicals have been enjoyed in the United States since the beginning of the 1900s. Sing "Another Op'nin', Another Show" to get the feeling of being on stage on opening night.

Musicals can be funny, or they can send a serious message. Sing "Comedy Tonight" and "Look Around," then compare the moods of these two songs.

"I Am the Starlight" tells us that we have the power to make the things that we wish for come true. Listen for the motive that is a musical symbol for the Starlight Express.

It's time to leave the theater for now. Sing "Give My Regards to Broadway" to salute New York's center of theater magic.

Stephen Sor

Andrew Lloyd Webber

228

MEETING **INDIVIDUAL** NEEDS

PROGRAM IDEA: *A Broadway Revue* 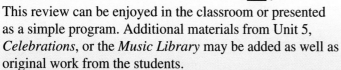 THEATER

This review can be enjoyed in the classroom or presented as a simple program. Additional materials from Unit 5, *Celebrations*, or the *Music Library* may be added as well as original work from the students.

Have students present a revue of the Broadway show tunes in Unit 5 complete with soloists, small groups, and dancers. They can open with "Another Op'nin', Another Show" and close the show with "Give My Regards to Broadway."

If time permits, have students write dialogue connecting the songs. For an added touch, the revue might have a loose plot. For example, it could tell the story of a star looking back on her or his life on the stage.

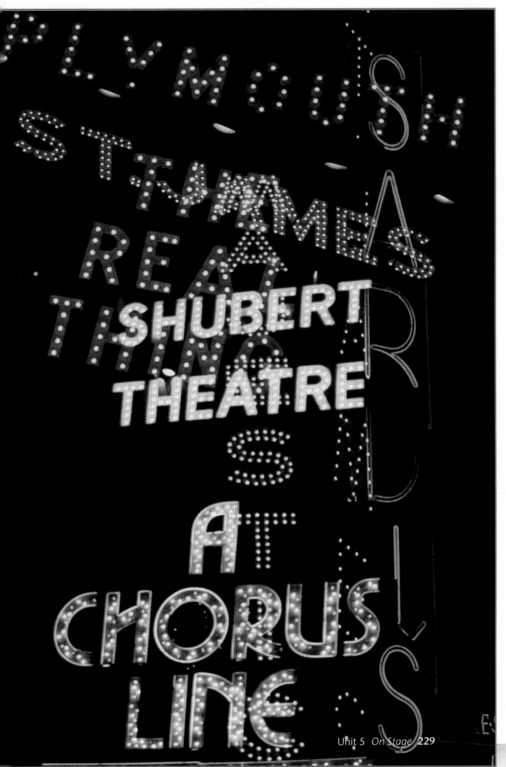

REVIEW

1. Review vocal ranges with "Another Op'nin', Another Show" CD4:31 **(p. 191).** Have students:

▶ • Tell the names of the four adult vocal categories. (soprano, alto, tenor, bass)

▶ • Listen to "Another Op'nin', Another Show" and tell what voice categories they hear. (in order: mixed voices, soprano, alto, tenor, soprano and alto together, bass, tenor, and alto) Sing the song.

2. Review articulation with "Comedy Tonight" CD4:36 **(p. 198) and "Look Around"** CD4:33 **(pp. 192–193).** Have students:

▶ • Sing "Comedy Tonight" and "Look Around" and compare their moods. Tell appropriate choices of articulation, dynamics, tempo, and tone color for each. ("Comedy Tonight"— marcato, medium-loud dynamic level, medium-fast tempo, bright tone color; "Look Around"—legato, medium-slow tempo, medium dynamic level, smooth, light tone color)

3. Review motive with "I Am the Starlight" CD5:3 **(pp. 208–209).** Have students:

• Tell what a motive is. (a brief melody or rhythm that is easily recognized)

• Clap the rhythm of the motive that represents the Starlight Express on page 208.

• Listen for the motive in "I Am the Starlight," then sing the song.

4. Reinforce unit theme with "Give My Regards to Broadway" CD5:15 **(pp. 226–227).** Have students:

▶ • Discuss musical theater around the world, giving examples from the unit. (Optional: Review unit materials by presenting a revue of show songs as in the *Program Idea* on the bottom of page 228.)

▶ • Sing "Give My Regards to Broadway."

UNIT FIVE
LESSON 9

ASSESSMENTS A AND B CD5:16–23

Different recorded examples for Assessments A and B allow for two uses of the same set of questions. When appropriate, recorded examples for Assessment A use familiar musical examples with which students have worked for the given concept. The recorded examples for Assessment B use musical selections the students have not previously worked with for the concept, encouraging the application of knowledge to new material.

The pupil page is intended for those who wish to assess quickly with the whole class or in small groups. Each assessment may be used as a pretest or as a final review before presenting the written test (**Resource Master 5 • 8**).

ANSWERS	
ASSESSMENT A	**ASSESSMENT B**
1. a	c
2. d	c
3. a	a
4. b	a

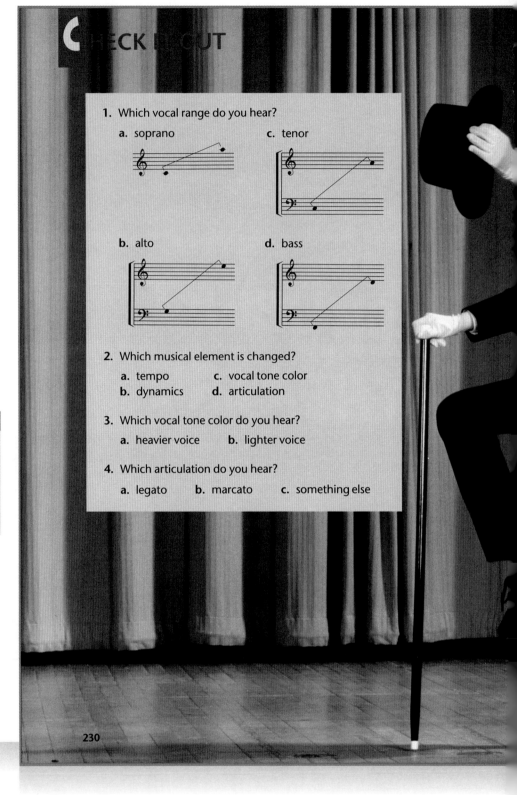

CHECK IT OUT

1. Which vocal range do you hear?
   - **a.** soprano
   - **c.** tenor
   - **b.** alto
   - **d.** bass

2. Which musical element is changed?
   - **a.** tempo
   - **c.** vocal tone color
   - **b.** dynamics
   - **d.** articulation

3. Which vocal tone color do you hear?
   - **a.** heavier voice
   - **b.** lighter voice

4. Which articulation do you hear?
   - **a.** legato
   - **b.** marcato
   - **c.** something else

230

MEETING **INDIVIDUAL** NEEDS

PORTFOLIO ASSESSMENT

To evaluate students' portfolios, use the Portfolio Assessment form on **Resource Master TA • 1**. See page 188B for a summary of Portfolio Opportunities in this unit.

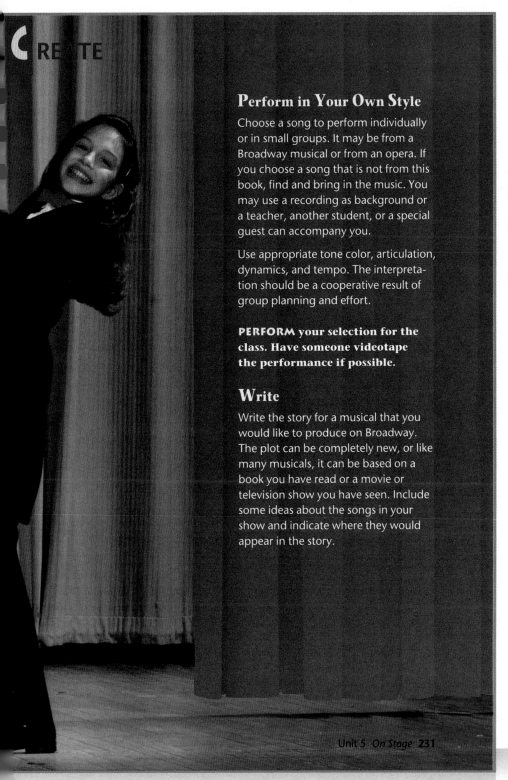

CREATE

Perform in Your Own Style

Choose a song to perform individually or in small groups. It may be from a Broadway musical or from an opera. If you choose a song that is not from this book, find and bring in the music. You may use a recording as background or a teacher, another student, or a special guest can accompany you.

Use appropriate tone color, articulation, dynamics, and tempo. The interpretation should be a cooperative result of group planning and effort.

PERFORM your selection for the class. Have someone videotape the performance if possible.

Write

Write the story for a musical that you would like to produce on Broadway. The plot can be completely new, or like many musicals, it can be based on a book you have read or a movie or television show you have seen. Include some ideas about the songs in your show and indicate where they would appear in the story.

CREATE AND WRITE

1. Perform a song in own style. Have students:

▶ • Review how performers express a composer's intent through stylistic choices.

▶ • Choose a song to perform in their own styles, as directed on page 231. Practice, then perform their selections for the class.

2. Write a story for a Broadway musical. Have students:

▶ • Tell about any musicals they may have seen and briefly describe the plots.

▶ • Discuss the ingredients of a Broadway musical. (story, main characters, songs, dances, costumes, and so on)

▶ • Follow the instructions on page 231 to create musicals they would like to produce on Broadway, including ideas about songs for the show.

LANGUAGE ARTS CONNECTION: *Synopsis*

Tell students that a synopsis, or summary, of a book or play is often used to sell the work to a producer(s). Have them look at their ideas for musicals again, with an eye to making them more interesting and attention-getting. Is the idea dramatic enough? Is the setting interesting? Are there too many main characters for the audience to follow? It might help to exchange synopses with another student and offer rewrite suggestions.

LESSONLINKS

Carmen *(10 min)*

OBJECTIVE Learn about the opera *Carmen*

Prelude *(15 min)*

OBJECTIVE Listen for instruments in excerpt, identify and clap some of the rhythms

Reinforcement opera, *page 215*

MATERIALS
Recording Prelude from *Carmen*
(excerpt) by G. Bizet (listening)   CD5:24

Arias from *Carmen* *(20 min)*

OBJECTIVE Listen to excerpts, noting voice category and expressive qualities

Reinforcement opera, voice categories, interpretation, *page 215*

MATERIALS
Recordings
Seguidilla from *Carmen* (excerpt)
by G. Bizet (listening)   CD5:25
Toreador Song from *Carmen*
(excerpt) by G. Bizet (listening)   CD5:26

ℰNCORE

The Story of Carmen

Georges Bizet

An opera is a play that combines drama with song and dance to tell a story. Set in Spain, the opera *Carmen* by Georges Bizet is the tragic story of a gypsy woman, Carmen. The colorful cast of characters includes Don José, an army corporal whose love for Carmen leads to his destruction. His rival for Carmen's affection is the heroic bullfighter Escamillo. Micaëla, who loves Don José, is as calm and easygoing as Carmen is lively and demanding. Captain Zuniga is the law-abiding superior of Don José.

 LISTENING **Carmen** *(excerpts)* *by Georges Bizet*

 A prelude is an introduction the orchestra plays before the curtain goes up and the opera begins. In the Prelude to Act 1 of **Carmen,** *Bizet uses contrasting rhythm patterns, tempos, and dynamics to create the atmosphere for the story. You will hear one of the musical themes return later in the opera. What instrument families are featured in the prelude?* strings, percussion, brass

CLAP the rhythm patterns on the next page. Which one features the dotted rhythm?

232

MEETING **INDIVIDUAL** NEEDS

BIOGRAPHY: *Georges Bizet*

French composer Georges Bizet (ʒɔrʒ bi ze), 1838–1875, grew up in a family of professional musicians. His father was a singing teacher and a composer, and his mother was an exceptional pianist. His musical talent was discovered at an early age, and by the time he was nine he was enrolled at the Paris Conservatory, the youngest student in the class. As a young man, he won top prizes in competitions on piano and organ. At the age of twenty he won the Prix de Rome, a world-famous composition award. As he grew older, he struggled to make a living as a composer. His first operas were failures, but he was able to sell a few works for orchestra, which gave him the heart to keep composing. *Carmen* was his fifth opera. It was based on an 1845 short story by a French writer.

BACKGROUND: *Carmen*

Carmen tells the story of Don José (dɔn xo se) and the beautiful gypsy Carmen. After falling in love with Carmen, Don José follows her into the mountains, where she has joined a gang of smugglers. When he discovers that she loves the bullfighter Escamillo (es ka mi yo), he is so

LISTEN to the Prelude and identify the order in which the rhythm patterns appear. The dynamic markings will help you. A rhythm pattern may occur more than once. C, A, C, B, C

Carmen - Act I. - Scene V. N°1

Carmen

Learn about the opera *Carmen*. Have students:

• Read page 232 and tell the difference between a play, an opera, and a musical. (Plays don't usually have songs, operas usually have all sung words, musicals usually have songs and spoken words.)

• Tell about any operas they have seen or heard and their stories. (*Porgy and Bess*, page 195; *Gianni Schicchi*, pages 212–215)

Prelude CD5:24

1. Listen for instruments, then perform rhythm patterns from the Prelude. Have students:

• Read about the Prelude on page 232, then listen to it and answer the question about the instruments featured.

• Look at rhythm pattern A and tell which measures contain the same rhythm. (1 and 3) Then clap the pattern.

• Look at rhythm pattern B and tell which measures contain the same rhythm as Measure 1. (5, 7) Then clap the pattern.

• Look at rhythm pattern C and tell which measures contain the same rhythm. (1, 2, 3) Then clap the pattern.

• Tell which pattern contains dotted rhythms. (Pattern B)

2. Listen to the Prelude and identify rhythm patterns. Have students:

• Look at Patterns A, B, and C, noting the dynamic markings and telling what they mean. (*p* —soft; *ff*—very loud)

• Listen to the Prelude and tell in which order they hear the patterns. (Some are repeated.)

jealous he wants to kill Escamillo. Instead, as the last act ends, he stabs Carmen to death as Escamillo is fighting a bull. When *Carmen* was first performed, its intense plot and innovative musical style were criticized. Soon, however, the opera became a success all over the world. Interestingly enough, Bizet wrote the score, full of Spanish flavor, without ever having been to Spain. His knowledge of Spanish music came from books at the Paris Library.

PLAYING INSTRUMENTS: *Ostinato Patterns*

Have students use unpitched rhythm instruments to play the rhythm patterns in their books.

ENCORE

continued from previous page

Arias from *Carmen*

1. Listen and discuss two opera arias. Have students:

• Read page 234, then listen to "Seguidilla" **CD5:25**.

• Tell the name of this kind of solo song in an opera, then discuss the melody of the selection. (Aria; the melody has a wide range and complex contour, including large leaps and vocal ornaments.)

• Read about the "Toreador Song" **CD5:26**, then listen for the rhythm from the Prelude in this aria. (Pattern B)

• Tell the voice category of Escamillo. (bass)

• Discuss the singer's tone color and articulation and why it might be appropriate for the character of a bullfighter.

SEGUIDILLA

Carmen is arrested after attacking another woman. Don José is ordered by Captain Zuniga to take her to prison. Left alone with Don José, Carmen tries to persuade him to set her free. In the aria (an extended solo song) "Seguidilla," Carmen succeeds in coaxing Don José to let her go. As Act I ends, Carmen escapes and Don José is arrested for helping her escape.

234 CARMEN

MEETING **INDIVIDUAL** NEEDS

CRITICAL THINKING: *Opera Plots*

Discuss how operas have many intense, dramatic moments. The plots have many strange turns and may seem melodramatic (like a soap opera) to many listeners. In addition, they are often set in exotic locales. Ask: Why might a composer choose this type of plot? (to place the characters in situations in which they feel intense emotions so that they can sing emotional arias; to provide opportunities for dramatic, exotic scenery and costumes; to provide opportunities for dances, big choruses, and other ensemble singing; to satisfy the audience's taste for spectacle)

DRAMA CONNECTION: *Conflict*
THEATER

Most stories include some form of conflict. Using the *Background* information on pages 232–233, have students determine the central conflict in the opera *Carmen* (Don José's jealousy over Carmen's love for Escamillo). Then discuss how this conflict is set up and how it is resolved. (Don José falls in love with Carmen; Don José stabs Carmen to death.) Have students discuss the use of conflict in other musical theater works represented in this unit. Then invite them to analyze a book or television show for the set up, central conflict, and resolution.

2. Learn about how *Carmen* concludes.
Have students:

- Read about the conclusion of the story.

- Discuss why an opera composer might want to choose a story with a tragic ending. (Tragedy provides powerful emotions to express with music.)

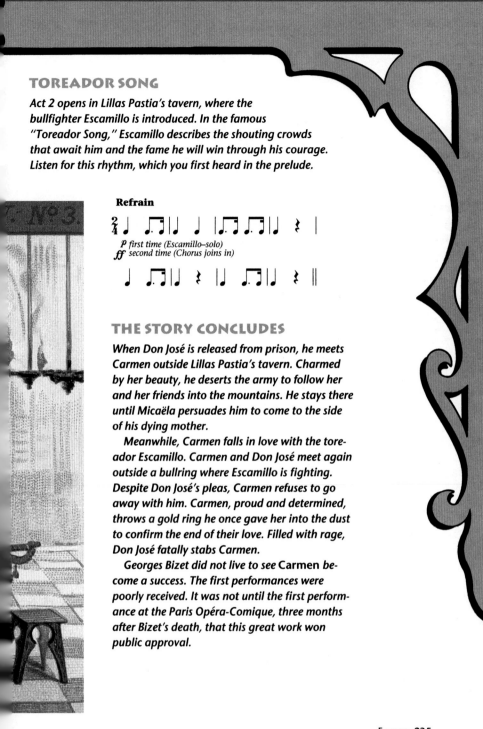

TOREADOR SONG

Act 2 opens in Lillas Pastia's tavern, where the bullfighter Escamillo is introduced. In the famous "Toreador Song," Escamillo describes the shouting crowds that await him and the fame he will win through his courage. Listen for this rhythm, which you first heard in the prelude.

Refrain

$\boldsymbol{p}$ first time (Escamillo–solo)
$\boldsymbol{f\!f}$ second time (Chorus joins in)

THE STORY CONCLUDES

When Don José is released from prison, he meets Carmen outside Lillas Pastia's tavern. Charmed by her beauty, he deserts the army to follow her and her friends into the mountains. He stays there until Micaëla persuades him to come to the side of his dying mother.

Meanwhile, Carmen falls in love with the toreador Escamillo. Carmen and Don José meet again outside a bullring where Escamillo is fighting. Despite Don José's pleas, Carmen refuses to go away with him. Carmen, proud and determined, throws a gold ring he once gave her into the dust to confirm the end of their love. Filled with rage, Don José fatally stabs Carmen.

Georges Bizet did not live to see **Carmen** *become a success. The first performances were poorly received. It was not until the first performance at the Paris Opéra-Comique, three months after Bizet's death, that this great work won public approval.*

Encore **235**

ART CONNECTION: *Pointillism*
VISUAL ARTS

During the late 1800s, artists experimented with new ways of applying color to their canvases. These artists were especially concerned with capturing the ever-changing impressions of light. One painter, Georges Seurat (1859–1891), did a scientific analysis of color and developed a technique known as *pointillism.* In this technique, the artist applies paint in many dots of pure color, relying on the eye and mind of the viewer to mix the color. The illustration above is done in a pointillistic style.

Have students look up a reproduction of Georges Seurat's masterpiece, *Sunday Afternoon on the Island of La Grande Jatte,* in the library. Have them record their observations of the work. Point out that the dimensions of the actual painting are 6' 9" x 10'. Measure an area of a classroom wall to show the grand size of this canvas. Discuss the amount of effort and time Seurat must have spent in creating this work.

FROM RAG TO RAP

UNIT 6

MULTICULTURAL PERSPECTIVES

Through exposure to diverse materials, students develop an awareness of how people from many cultures create and participate in music. This unit includes:

African American

- **It Don't Mean a Thing**, by Duke Ellington and Irving Mills, 247
- **Jump**, by Jermaine Dupri as recorded by Kris Kross, 279
- **Royal Garden Blues,** by Clarence Williams and Spencer Williams, 243

European and European American

- **Alexander's Ragtime Band**, by American Irving Berlin, 239
- **Bandstand Boogie**, by Americans Barry Manilow, Bruce Sussman, and Charles Albertine, 255
- **Birthday,** by Britons John Lennon and Paul McCartney, 262
- **Blowin' in the Wind**, by American Bob Dylan, 259
- **Boogie Woogie Bugle Boy,** by Americans Don Raye and Hughie Prince, 251
- **Fly Like an Eagle**, by American Steve Miller, 265
- **From a Distance**, by American Julie Gold, 275
- **Rocky Top**, by Americans Boudleaux Bryant and Felice Bryant, 268

Hispanic/Native American

- **Uirapurú do Amazonas,** by Brazilian/Maue Indian Gaudencio Thiago de Mello, 276

For a complete listing of songs by culture throughout the book, see the Classified Index.

CURRICULUM INTEGRATION

Activities in this unit that promote the integration of music with other curriculum areas include:

Math
- Graph data based on song survey, 236

Reading/Language Arts
- Create new words for song, 227
- Interpret lyrics and create new words for a song, 255
- Research and write a report on an issue of the 1960s, 262
- Write an essay about a difficult decision, 271
- Write an essay tracing popular music from 1900s to today, 278

Science
- Discuss and come up with possible solutions to save rain forests, 277
- Make a list of technology used in everyday life, 272

Social Studies
- Locate events, music, and people from the 1900s–1990s on a time line, 238, 243, 247, 250, 254, 258, 264, 270, 274
- Research ways to help the homeless, 265

PLANNER

ASSESSMENT OPTIONS

Informal Performance Assessments

Informal Assessments correlated to Objectives are provided in every lesson with Alternate Strategies for reteaching. Frequent informal assessment allows for ongoing progress checks throughout the unit.

Music Journal

Encourage students to enter thoughts about selections, projects, performances, and personal progress. Some journal opportunities include:

- Critical Thinking: Point of View, TE 243
- Critical Thinking: Compare and Contrast, TE 259
- Critical Thinking: Changing Styles, TE 269
- Think It Through, 276

Portfolio Opportunities

Update student portfolios with written work, audiotapes, videotapes and/or photos that represent their best work for each unit. Some portfolio opportunities in this unit include:

- Performance of music from each time period (audiotape), 240–241, 244–245, 248–249, 253, 256–257, 261, 267, 272–273, 277
- Cooperative Learning: Improvising the Blues (audiotape), TE 244
- Playing Instruments: Bass Guitar (Resource Master 6•7, audiotape), TE 259
- Performance of Rocky Top (audiotape), 268–269
- Enrichment: Shooting a Music Video (Resource Masters 6•11, 6•12, 6•13, audio/videotape), TE 276

6

		LESSON 1 p.236	LESSON 2 p.242	LESSON 3 p.246	LESSON 4 p.250
	FOCUS	Style/Rhythm	Style/Harmony	Style/Rhythm	Style/Harmony
	SELECTIONS	Alexander's Ragtime Band 1900s and 1910s Medley (listening)	Royal Garden Blues 1920s Medley (listening)	It Don't Mean a Thing 1930s Medley (listening)	Boogie Woogie Bugle Boy 1940s Medley (listening)

CONCEPTS AND SKILLS

CULTURAL CONTEXT	Style/ Background	• Hear and discuss music and events from the 1900s and 1910s • Hear and learn about ragtime • Hear Dixieland jazz • *Poet: Eloise Greenfield* • *Composer: Irving Berlin*	• Hear and discuss music and events from the 1920s • Hear and learn about blues • *Career: disk jockey*	• Hear and discuss music and events from the 1930s • Hear swing-style jazz • *Composer/performer: Duke Ellington* • *Learn about women in big bands*	• Hear and discuss music and events from the 1940s • *Learn about boogie woogie* • *Career: guitar maker*
CREATION AND PERFORMANCE	Singing		• Sing solo	• *Imitate good vocal models*	• *Sing solo and in small groups*
	Playing	• Perform percussion playalongs	• Perform pitched instrument playalong • *Play blues on pitched instruments*	• Play percussion playalong	• Play D, G, and A chords on guitar • Perform pitched instrument playalong
	Moving	• *Perform ragtime dance*	• Perform pantomime to song • *Dance the Charleston*	• *Perform basic swing steps*	• *Perform movement variations*
	Improvising/ Creating	• *Create ragtime dance*	• Create pantomime to song • *Improvise blues*	• *Create rhythm patterns*	• *Create movement variations*
PERCEPTION AND ANALYSIS	Listening/ Describing/ Analyzing	• Recognize syncopation	• Recognize blues chord changes	• Discuss swing-style music	• Discuss lyrics and feel of song • Compare guitar fingerings

TIMELINE	**1900-1919**	**1920s**	**1930s**	**1940s**

 **TECHNOLOGY**

SHARE THE MUSIC VIDEOS

Use videos to reinforce, extend, and enrich learning.
- **Lesson 1, pp. 236–241:** Blending Musical Styles (American pop); Musical Expression (jazz); Making a Music Video (styles of different eras)
- **Lesson 2, pp. 243–244:** Blending Musical Styles (blues)
- **Lesson 3, p. 246:** Musical Expression (swing)
- **Lesson 4, p. 251:** Blending Musical Styles (bebop); Musical Expression (bebop)
- **Lesson 5, p. 254:** Blending Musical Styles (rock 'n' roll)

- **Lesson 7, pp. 264–368:** Blending Musical Styles (country and western); Making a Music Video (popular music)
- **Lesson 8, pp. 270–271:** Creating Musical Moods (technology and pop music); Signing, Grades 3–6 (The Greatest Love of All)
- **Lesson 9, pp. 275–279:** Making a Music Video (ideas to videotape, performance technology); Signing, Grades 3–6 (From a Distance); Blending Musical Styles (fusion styles); Creating Musical Moods (synthesizers, composing/creating)

SKILLS OVERVIEW

LESSON 5 p.254	LESSON 6 p.258	LESSON 7 p.264	LESSON 8 p.270	LESSON 9 p.274
Style/Harmony	Style/Form	Style/Harmony	Style/Harmony	Style
Bandstand Boogie 1950s Medley (listening)	Blowin' in the Wind 1960s Medley (listening) Birthday (listening)	Fly Like an Eagle 1970s Medley (listening) Rocky Top	The Greatest Love of All 1980s Medley (listening)	From a Distance Uirapurú do Amazonas Two-chord Rock (listening) Jump (listening)
• Hear and discuss music and events from the 1950s • Hear rock 'n' roll • *Learn about American Bandstand* • *Learn about electric guitar technology*	• Hear and discuss music and events from the 1960s • Hear folk-rock, rock songs • *Composer/performer: Bob Dylan*	• Hear and discuss music and events from the 1970s • Hear rock, country and western, disco songs • *Composer/performer: Steve Miller* • *Learn about country and bluegrass music*	• Hear and discuss music and events from the 1980s • Hear pop, rock songs	• Hear and discuss music and events from the 1990s • Hear pop, rap, and Brazilian/Maue Indian songs • *Career: record producer*
	• Sing solo	• Sing in 2 parts	• *Choose and sing song interpretation*	
• Play guitar chords • Perform pitched instrument playalong	• Play guitar chords • Perform pitched instrument playalong • *Play bass guitar*	• Play guitar chords • Perform pitched instrument playalong	• Play guitar chords • Perform pitched instrument playalong	• Perform pitched instrument playalongs • *Clap and pat rhythm patterns with songs* • Perform recorder playalong • *Make and play rain sticks*
• *Perform hand-jive movements with song*	• *Learn sixties-style dances*	• *Perform ten step*		• Perform rap-style dance
• *Create new song lyrics*		• *Arrange and perform in rock style*	• *Create and sing song interpretation*	• *Create and play rain sticks* • *Improvise song accompaniment* • *Create and perform in music video*
• Compare and contrast rock 'n' roll with popular music today • Compare musical elements of two songs • Recognize rondo form	• Decide on song interpretation • Recognize form • *Compare and contrast songs*	• Compare songs	• Compare songs • *Play aural chord identification game*	• Recognize repeated phrases • Recognize synthesizer sound • Compare rap and other types of popular music • Write essay tracing popular music from the 1900s to today
### 1950s	### 1960s	### 1970s	### 1980s	### 1990s

UNIT 6 PLANNER

MUSIC WITH *MIDI*

MIDI technology allows students to manipulate musical elements and make musical decisions.

MUSICTIME™

Use MusicTime to develop students' music reading and writing skills in this unit.

MUSIC ACE™

Music Ace reinforces musical concepts and provides ear-training opportunities for students.
· **Lesson 2, p. 242: Lesson 20 (accidentals)**

LESSON PLANNER

FOCUS Style/Rhythm

OBJECTIVE
OBJECTIVE 1 Read and perform a percussion playalong

MATERIALS
Recordings
Recorded Lesson: A Sound
  Capsule: The 1900s and 1910s   CD5:27
Alexander's Ragtime Band   CD5:28
Listening: 1900s and 1910s
  Medley   CD5:29

Instruments unpitched percussion

Resources Resource Master 6 • 1
  (practice)

VOCABULARY
ragtime, jazz

▶ = **BASIC PROGRAM**

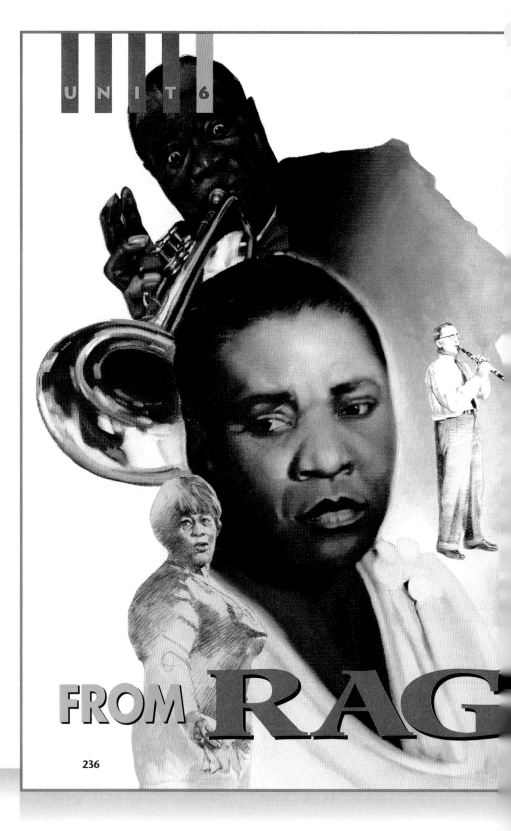

UNIT 6

FROM **RAG**

236

MEETING **INDIVIDUAL** NEEDS

BIOGRAPHY: *Eloise Greenfield*

American poet Eloise Greenfield (b. 1929) loved music, movies, and books as a child. In her early twenties, she decided to become a writer. At the same time she discovered that there were few books about African Americans, and she wanted to change that. Her first try at writing consisted of three short stories that no one wanted to publish. She almost gave up, but told herself that writing takes talent *and* practice. Her first poem was not published until she was in her mid-thirties, and it was 1972 before her first book was published. She has now written more than 15 books for children, including fiction, biographies, and poetry. Several of her books have won awards.

Way Down in the Music

I get way down in the music
Down inside the music
I let it wake me
        take me
Spin me around and make me
Uh-get down

Inside the sound of the Jackson Five
Into the tune of Earth, Wind and Fire
Down in the bass where the beat comes from
Down in the horn and down in the drum
I get down
I get down

I get way down in the music
Down inside the music
I let it wake me
        take me
Spin me around and shake me
I get down, down
I get down

—Eloise Greenfield

TO RAP

237

"Think about how music makes Eloise Greenfield feel as you read her poem." Have students:

▶ • Read and discuss "Way Down in the Music." (The music moves Greenfield and makes her want to dance. If necessary, tell students that the Jackson Five was the band that made Michael Jackson a child pop star and that Earth, Wind and Fire was a popular group in the 1970s.)

▶ • Try to recognize the popular musicians of the 1900s–1990s pictured on pages 236–237. (counterclockwise from upper left: Louis Armstrong—trumpeter and singer, Bessie Smith—singer and composer, Ella Fitzgerald—singer, Benny Goodman—clarinetist and bandleader, Gloria Estefan—singer, Dolly Parton—singer and composer, Elvis Presley—singer)

▶ • Name some of their favorite pop-music groups and try to explain how the music makes them feel.

"Today you're going to hear some popular music from your great-grandparents' day."

MATHEMATICS CONNECTION: *Song Contest*

Have students organize a "favorite song" contest. Each student has a chance to name a favorite song and tell why it is a favorite. Have volunteers tabulate the choices on the board. For example:

Song	No. of Votes
"Jump"	///
"Hoe Ana"	/

Then have students choose a way to graph the data to show the favorites. (A bar graph, pictograph, or circle graph will work best.) If there are too many songs to make a meaningful graph, students should organize the songs by categories such as rap, country and western, rock, and folk, then graph the categories.

continued from previous page

2 DEVELOP

1. Introduce music and events from the 1900s and 1910s. Have students:

Recorded Lesson CD5:27

▶ • Listen to "A Sound Capsule: The 1900s and 1910s" to learn about events and music from that period.

▶ • Name a few events from the 1900s and 1910s. (Optional: Have students complete the word puzzle with names and key events from the Recorded Lesson on **Resource Master 6 · 1**.)

▶ • Discuss each event, including how people communicated before the telephone and how important this invention was.

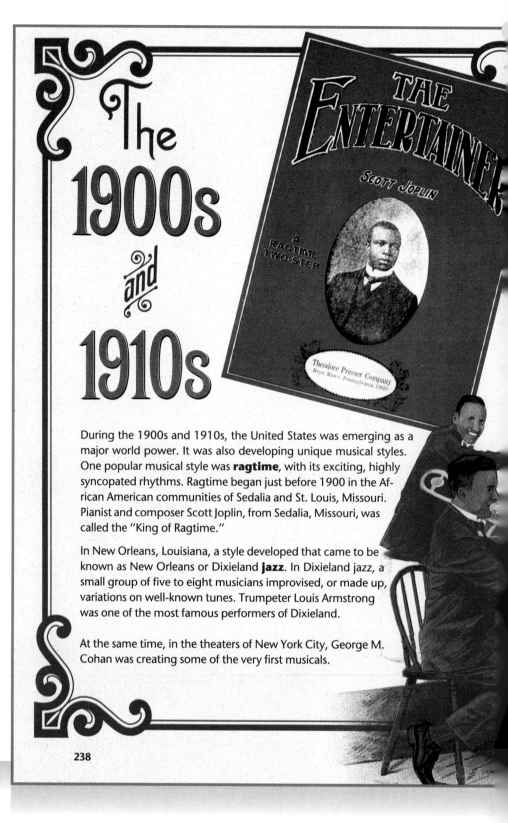

The 1900s and 1910s

During the 1900s and 1910s, the United States was emerging as a major world power. It was also developing unique musical styles. One popular musical style was **ragtime**, with its exciting, highly syncopated rhythms. Ragtime began just before 1900 in the African American communities of Sedalia and St. Louis, Missouri. Pianist and composer Scott Joplin, from Sedalia, Missouri, was called the "King of Ragtime."

In New Orleans, Louisiana, a style developed that came to be known as New Orleans or Dixieland **jazz**. In Dixieland jazz, a small group of five to eight musicians improvised, or made up, variations on well-known tunes. Trumpeter Louis Armstrong was one of the most famous performers of Dixieland.

At the same time, in the theaters of New York City, George M. Cohan was creating some of the very first musicals.

238

MEETING **INDIVIDUAL** NEEDS

SOCIAL STUDIES CONNECTION: *Time Line*

Hang up a large sheet of paper and draw a time line. Mark off the decades of the twentieth century. Ask students to locate events and people in "A Sound Capsule: The 1900s and 1910s" on the time line, as well as other important events from this time period. (1901—President McKinley assassinated; 1914—World War I begins in Europe; 1917—United States enters the war; 1917—first democratic government in Mexico; 1918—World War I ends) As the unit progresses, have students add to the time line as they study the music and culture of each time period

BIOGRAPHY: *Irving Berlin.*

See Unit 5, Lesson 1, page 189, *Biography*.

BACKGROUND: *Ragtime Style*

Classic ragtime originated just before 1900. (See Unit 3, Lesson 5, page 110, *Background*.) By 1910, the music was so popular that many composers started writing a more simplified form of ragtime. Performed by pianists, banjoists, small orchestras, and military bands, a large part of American popular music was made up of this type of ragtime, of which "Alexander's Ragtime Band" is an example.

Alexander's Ragtime Band

Words and Music by Irving Berlin

Oh, ma honey, Oh ma honey, Better hurry and let's meander
Ain't you goin', Ain't you goin', To the leader man, ragged meter man?
Oh, ma honey, Oh ma honey, Let me take you to Alexander's grand stand,
    brass band,
Ain't you comin' along?

Come on and hear, Come on and hear Alexander's Ragtime Band,
Come on and hear, Come on and hear, It's the best band in the land,
They can play a bugle call like you never heard before,
So natural that you want to go to war;
That's just the bestest band what am, honey lamb,
Come on along, Come on along, Let me take you by the hand,
Up to the man, Up to the man, who's the leader of the band,
And if you care to hear the Swanee River played in ragtime,
Come on and hear, Come on and hear Alexander's Ragtime Band.

Unit 6 *From Rag to Rap* 239

2. Introduce "Alexander's Ragtime Band"
CD5:28. **Review syncopation and sing music from the 1900s and 1910s.** Have students:

▶ • Read page 238 about ragtime and jazz.

▶ • Listen to the recording and follow the words to "Alexander's Ragtime Band."

• Review syncopation (see Unit 5, Lesson 3, page 201) and find examples of syncopated rhythms in the music. (*hur-ry and*, *take you to*, *That's just the*)

▶ • Sing "Alexander's Ragtime Band." (Have students start by echo-singing several of the individual vocal lines in "Alexander's Ragtime Band" to reinforce the vocal part. You might also have sections of the class sing designated sections of the song, taking care to have everyone singing at some point.)

MOVEMENT: *"Alexander's Ragtime Band"*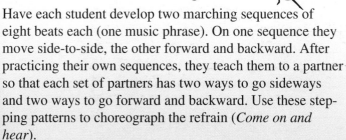

Have each student develop two marching sequences of eight beats each (one music phrase). On one sequence they move side-to-side, the other forward and backward. After practicing their own sequences, they teach them to a partner so that each set of partners has two ways to go sideways and two ways to go forward and backward. Use these stepping patterns to choreograph the refrain (*Come on and hear*).

If time permits, they can add pantomime/gestures suggested by the lyrics, such as the *bugle call* or *come along*. For a final performance, students might wear straw hats and carry canes, broomsticks, or rhythm sticks. One pattern might involve twirling the cane, tossing it from hand to hand, or tapping rhythms on the floor.

PLAYING INSTRUMENTS: *Unpitched*

Have students pat this rhythm with "Alexander's Ragtime Band" and then transfer it to unpitched instruments.

UNIT SIX
LESSON 1

continued from previous page

3. Introduce "1900s and 1910s Medley"
CD5:29. Play rhythm patterns with music from the 1900s and 1910s. Have students:

▶ • Listen to "1900s and 1910s Medley" ("Palm Leaf Rag" by Scott Joplin, "Sugarfoot Stomp" by Joe "King" Oliver, and "Yankee Doodle Boy" by George M. Cohan).

• Read and pat (using alternating hands) the rhythm patterns found in the "1900s and 1910s Medley" playalong.

• Transfer the rhythm patterns to unpitched percussion instruments.

• Perform the rhythm patterns with the recording of "Palm Leaf Rag," the first selection from the "1900s and 1910s Medley."

3 APPLY

Perform a percussion playalong with "1900s and 1910s Medley." Have students:

• In small groups, practice the playalong on various percussion instruments.

OBJECTIVE 1 Informal Assessment
• Perform the rhythm patterns with the entire recording of "1900s and 1910s Medley."

PERFORM a percussion accompaniment to the "1900s–1910s Medley."

LISTENING

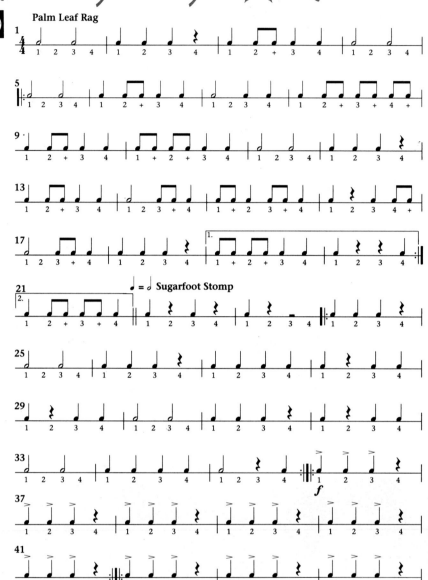

240 THE 1900s AND 1910s

MEETING **INDIVIDUAL** NEEDS

ALTERNATE TEACHING STRATEGY

OBJECTIVE 1 Assign small sections (as small as one or two measures if necessary) in the medley playalong to different students and have them practice each pattern as near to tempo as possible. Encourage them to gradually learn to play connecting sections until they can play a larger section. Then select individual students or groups to perform with various sections of the medley. Some students may find it helpful to create simpler rhythm patterns to play.

SPECIAL LEARNERS: *Rhythm Patterns*

As an alternate to patting the rhythms, have students practice a downward strumming motion (on the quarter and half notes) and a down/up motion (on the eighth-note pairs), then play "air" guitar with "1900s and 1910s Medley." This will help prepare students for the guitar playalongs in Lessons 4–9 of this unit.

Yankee Doodle Boy

4 CLOSE

"In this lesson, you sang a song, performed rhythm patterns, and learned about some of the events which took place during the time period 1900–1919." Have students:

▶ • Discuss some of the musical, historical, and cultural characteristics of this time period.

• Perform the medley again, using unpitched percussion instruments.

LESSON SUMMARY

Informal Assessment In this lesson, students:

OBJECTIVE 1 Read and performed a percussion playalong with "1900s and 1910s Medley."

MORE MUSIC: Reinforcement

"Soft Shoe Song," page 383 (1900s and 1910s popular style)

PLAYING INSTRUMENTS: *Percussion*

After students have mastered the rhythms in the "1900s and 1910s Medley" playalong, ask them to try to play or sing popular songs of today (in ⁴⁄₄ meter with tempos comparable to that of the playalong) using rhythms from the playalong as accompaniment patterns.

LESSON PLANNER

FOCUS Style/Harmony

OBJECTIVES
OBJECTIVE 1 Identify chord changes in a blues I-IV-V accompaniment
OBJECTIVE 2 Read and perform chord roots on pitched instruments

MATERIALS
Recordings
Recorded Lesson: A Sound
  Capsule: The 1920s   CD5:30
Royal Garden Blues   CD5:31
Listening: 1920s Medley   CD5:32

Instruments
guitar, recorder, keyboard, resonator bells, or band instruments in the key of C

Resources
Resource Master 6 • 2 (practice)
Playing the Guitar G • 21 (blues)
Recorder Master R • 23 (pitches G A B♭ B C' D')

VOCABULARY
blues

▶ = **BASIC PROGRAM**

THE 1920s

The 1920s have often been called the Roaring Twenties. World War I, described as "the war to end all wars," was over. People were relieved and lighthearted. The country seemed prosperous, and the world was filled with a sense of optimism: people felt that things would get better and better. Much popular music of the 1920s portrayed this lightheartedness. Dixieland jazz increased in popularity. The Charleston, with its lively music, was the favorite dance of the time.

242

MEETING **INDIVIDUAL** NEEDS

MULTICULTURAL PERSPECTIVES: *The Blues*

The blues is a style of music that began in America in the late 1800s and early 1900s with roots in African American spirituals and work songs. Most blues songs tell of feelings of loneliness and sadness. The singers tell of their struggles with love or against racism. The twelve-bar blues progression is a pattern often heard in the blues. (See Unit 3, Encore, page 132, *Multicultural Perspectives*.) In C major, the chord pattern is: C C C C F F C C G G C C. The blues has influenced many types of modern music—from jazz composers such as Duke Ellington and Quincy Jones to classi-cal composers such as Aaron Copland. Rock 'n' roll artists such as Elvis Presley recorded blues songs in the 1950s. In the 1960s, rock stars such as the Beatles and The Rolling Stones also drew on the blues tradition.

SOCIAL STUDIES CONNECTION: *Time Line*

Continue the time line begun in Lesson 1, page 238, *Social Studies Connection*. Ask students to locate events and people in "A Sound Capsule: The 1920s" on the time line, as well as other events. (1924—Immigration Bill; 1929—stock market crash)

Not all music of the 1920s was lighthearted, however. The **blues**, a style created by African American musicians, usually expressed sorrow but looked with hope to the future.

Royal Garden Blues

Words and Music by
Clarence Williams and Spencer Williams

Hon, don't you hear that trombone moan?
Just listen to that saxophone.
Gee, hear that clarinet and flute,
Cornet a-jazzin' with a mute.
Makes me just throw myself away
When I hear 'em play.

That weepin' melancholy strain,
Say, but it's soothin' to the brain.
Just wanna get right up and dance,
Don't care, I'll take most any chance.
No other blues I'd care to choose
But Royal Garden Blues.

Singer Gertrude "Ma" Rainey, pictured with her band in 1925, has been called "the mother of the blues."

Unit 6 *From Rag to Rap* **243**

"Let's set the scene for some 1920s music." Have students:

▶ • List any events, music, dancing, movies, and so on, that they associate with the 1920s while you write their ideas on the board without comment. (possible answers: President Calvin Coolidge, stock market crash, jazz music, Charleston dance, silent movies, short "bobbed" hair on women) (At the end of the lesson, they can add to and correct the list as necessary.)

"Today you're going to learn more about the 1920s. When the lesson is done, we'll return to the list to add or delete items."

2 DEVELOP

1. Introduce music and events from the 1920s. Have students:

▶ • Read page 242.

Recorded Lesson CD5:30
▶ • Listen to "A Sound Capsule: The 1920s" to learn about events and music from the 1920s.

▶ • Discuss their impressions of the decade. (Optional: Have students circle key events from the Recorded Lesson on **Resource Master 6 • 2**.)

2. Introduce "Royal Garden Blues" CD5:31. **Sing music from the 1920s.** Have students:

▶ • Listen to the recording and follow the words to the song.

▶ • Sing "Royal Garden Blues." (Optional: Provide solo-singing practice by assigning students to take turns singing various lines as solos.)

▶ • In small groups, make up a pantomime suggested by the lyrics of the song, focusing on the instruments mentioned and the feeling of wanting to dance.

CAREERS: *Disc Jockey*

Use the radio theme of "A Sound Capsule: The 1920s" to introduce students to the career of disc jockey. A disc jockey introduces the records, commercials, and news that are aired on a radio station. Sometimes the disc jockey picks out the music for his or her show. They must, however, choose records from a playlist put together by the station's program or music director. To become a disc jockey, you need to develop your own special style of speaking. Most disc jockeys begin on school or college radio stations, then audition for professional work by sending taped shows to commercial radio stations.

CRITICAL THINKING: *Point of View*

The young people of the 1920s often shocked their parents, who thought that all the younger generation was interested in was fun and dancing. But the young people felt that they might as well have fun, since the world had just finished fighting a war. Ask students to write an essay in the form of a debate between an older and younger person from this time, expressing both points of view in a fair manner.

UNIT SIX
LESSON 2

continued from previous page

3. Introduce "1920s Medley" CD5:32. Identify chord changes in the second selection. Have students:

• Listen to "Lost Your Head Blues" (second selection) from "1920s Medley." Count the number of measures out loud for the first verse (after the 4-measure introduction). (1-2-3-4, 2-2-3-4, 3-2-3-4, etc., to 12-2-3-4)

• Tell how many measures are in one verse of the song. (12—Measures 44–55) (Explain that a common blues chord progression is 12 measures long. It is known as the twelve-bar blues: I I I I IV IV I I V V I I.)

• Tell the key (F), pitch letter names of the chord roots (F, B♭, C), and the scale-step number of each chord root (1, 4, 5).

OBJECTIVE 1 Informal Assessment

• Listen and identify chord changes in "Lost Your Head Blues" by holding palms-down when they hear a I chord, thumbs-up on on IV chord, and palms-up on V chord. (Verse 1: I I I I IV IV I I V V I I V; Verse 2: I I I I IV IV I I V V I V—The V chords at the end of each verse lead into the next section.)

3 APPLY

Listen to "1920s Medley" and play music from the 1920s. Have students:

▶ • Listen to "1920s Medley" ("Charleston" by Cecil Mack and Jimmy Johnson, "Lost Your Head Blues" by Bessie Smith, "Travelin' Blues" by Jimmy Rodgers and Shelly Lee Alley).

PERFORM the "1920s Medley" on recorder, keyboard, or bells.

LISTENING

1920s Medley

244 THE 1920s

MEETING INDIVIDUAL NEEDS

ALTERNATE TEACHING STRATEGIES

OBJECTIVE 1 Draw a chart of the twelve-bar blues progression on the board or overhead indicating the chord sequence. Point to each measure and have students follow closely to aid them in hearing the chord changes. Another strategy is to play chords (some repeated, some changing) on a keyboard or guitar without letting students see your fingers. Challenge students to tell when you are playing the same chord and when you are changing chords.

OBJECTIVE 2 Write the pitch letter names of chord roots on the board. Have students play the chord roots as you point to the correct pitch.

MOVEMENT: *Charleston*

Practice the Charleston with the first song of "1920s Medley." (See Unit 5, Lesson 2, page 197, *Movement.*)

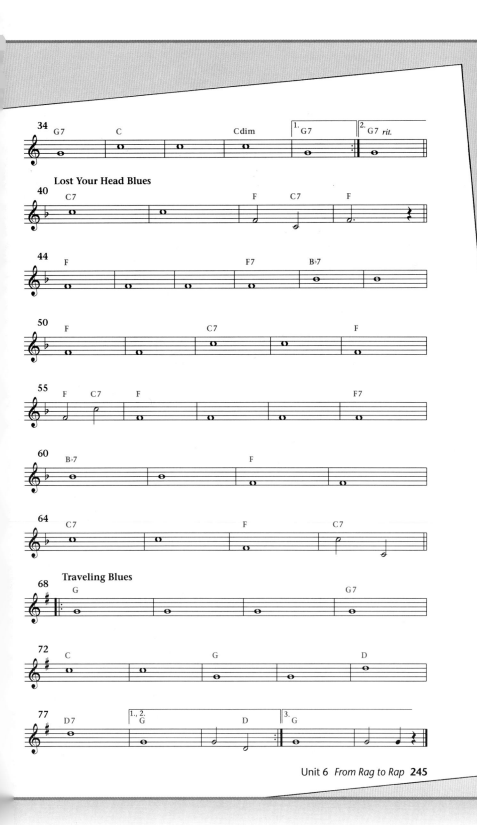

- Read and speak the pitch letter names of the chord roots used in "1920s Medley."
- Transfer the chord roots to pitched instruments by fingering each pitch as they speak it. Perform the pitches with the recording of "Charleston" from the "1920s Medley."

OBJECTIVE 2 Informal Assessment
- Perform the chord root pitches with the recording of "1920s Medley."

4 CLOSE

"Look at the list of 1920s events and music on the board. Do you have anything to add to or remove from the list?"
Have students:

▶ • Add to and correct the list as necessary. (See *Get Set* on page 243.)

"Now play the '1920s Medley' once more for fun."

LESSON SUMMARY

Informal Assessment In this lesson, students:

OBJECTIVE 1 Identified chord changes in an I-IV-V blues accompaniment to "Lost Your Head Blues" from "1920s Medley."

OBJECTIVE 2 Read and performed chord roots on pitched instruments with "1920s Medley."

MORE MUSIC: Reinforcement
"A Blues Montage," page 134 (style—blues)

COOPERATIVE LEARNING: *Improvising the Blues*

Explain to students that the scale used to play the blues is different from our major or minor scales. Place the following pitches from the blues scale on the board.

Have students work in cooperative groups of four to improvise a blues melody on pitched instruments, using the pitches notated on the board. Have each group form two pairs, one to improvise a blues melody and one to play the twelve-bar blues in G major (G, C, and D chords or chord roots) on keyboard or another pitched instrument. The part improvising the blues melody should be the predominant part. Both pairs should listen to each other's work and discuss the results. You may wish to have the groups switch roles and parts.

LESSON PLANNER

FOCUS Style/Rhythm

OBJECTIVE
OBJECTIVE 1 Read and perform a percussion playalong to a 1930s medley

MATERIALS
Recordings
Recorded Lesson: A Sound
   Capsule: The 1930s   CD6:1
It Don't Mean a Thing (If It Ain't
   Got That Swing)   CD6:2
Listening: 1930s Medley   CD6:3

Instruments unpitched percussion
instruments

Resources
Resource Master 6 • 3 (practice)
Recorder Master R • 24 (pitches D E F F♯
   G A B♭)

VOCABULARY
swing

▶ = **BASIC PROGRAM**

Woody Guthrie

The 1930s were a time of economic and social difficulties. Many people experienced the severe hardships of the Great Depression. These hardships were reflected in some of the music. Folksingers like Woody Guthrie and blues musicians like Bessie Smith sang of the tough times. But not all music was sad. A new style of jazz developed, called **swing**. Swing was dance music. It was performed by big bands—bigger than the Dixieland groups of the 1920s. With such large bands, swing music had to be carefully composed and arranged. A band leader coordinated the performance. Duke Ellington was one of the most famous band leaders and composers of the time. Clarinetist and bandleader Benny Goodman also helped mold the sounds of the swing era.

Duke Ellington

246

MEETING **INDIVIDUAL** NEEDS

BIOGRAPHY: *Duke Ellington*

Edward Kennedy Ellington (1899–1974) received his nickname, "Duke," as a teenager because of his elegant dress and manners. He was playing in bands by 1923 and soon became the leader of his own band. Radio broadcasts from New York's Cotton Club from 1927 to 1931 made Ellington and his band famous. The music he wrote for the club's floor shows uncovered his talent for instrumental tone color. Meanwhile, he joined forces with Irving Mills (1894–1985), who managed the band in the twenties and thirties, published its music, and sometimes took

co-composer credits. But it was Ellington and the band who wrote the music—all the players contributed ideas, although Ellington was in charge. As the years went on, Duke wrote longer compositions and music for film.

VOCAL DEVELOPMENT: *"It Don't Mean a Thing"*

Play the recording of "It Don't Mean a Thing" with the balance set to emphasize the vocals, and ask students to listen without singing. Encourage students to imitate the voices in the recording as they sing the song again. It may be helpful for students to count the *doo wahs* (four per line; eight total), until they feel the pattern.

IT DON'T MEAN A THING
(IF IT AIN'T GOT THAT SWING)

Words and Music by Duke Ellington and Irving Mills

What good is melody, what good is music,
If it ain't possessin' something sweet?
It ain't the melody, it ain't the music.
There's something else that makes the
  tune complete.

It don't mean a thing if it ain't got that swing,
doo wah, doo wah, doo wah, doo wah,
doo wah, doo wah, doo wah, doo wah.
It don't mean a thing, all you got to do is sing,
doo wah, doo wah, doo wah, doo wah,
doo wah, doo wah, doo wah, doo wah.
It makes no diff'rence if it's sweet or hot,
Just give that rhythm ev'rything you got.
Oh, It don't mean a thing if it ain't got
  that swing,
doo wah, doo wah, doo wah, doo wah,
doo wah, doo wah, doo wah, doo wah.

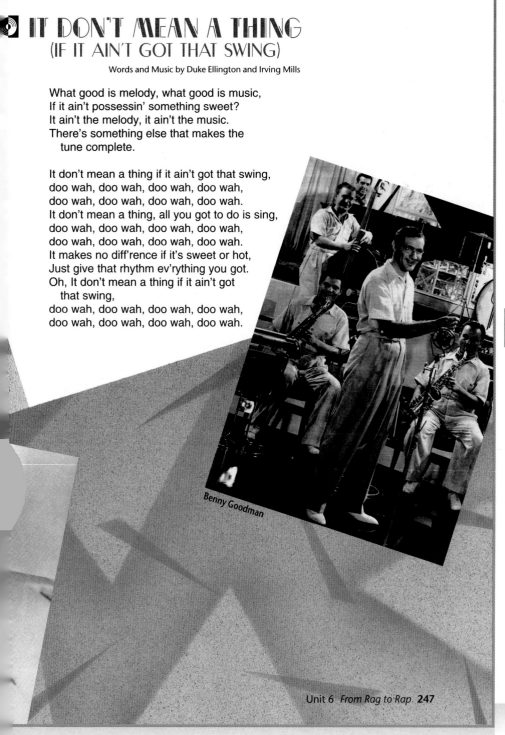

Benny Goodman

1 GET SET

"When was the last time you saw a movie?"
Have students:

▶ • Discuss what people did for entertainment
before video players and television. (possible
answers: went to the movies, listened to radios, danced, sang, and played instruments,
read books, had parties, viewed plays and
other performances, created own games)

"Today we're going to hear music from the
1930s, a time in which the Hollywood film industry became big business. Many Americans
went to the movies at least once a week."

2 DEVELOP

**1. Introduce music and events from the
1930s.** Have students:

Recorded Lesson CD6:1

▶ • Listen to "A Sound Capsule: The 1930s" to
learn about music and events of the 1930s.

▶ • Name and discuss events from the 1930s.
(Optional: Have students unscramble the letters to answer questions about key events from
the Recorded Lesson on **Resource Master
6 • 3**.)

**2. Introduce "It Don't Mean a Thing (If It
Ain't Got That Swing)" CD6:2. Sing music
from the 1930s.** Have students:

▶ • Listen to the recording and follow the words
to "It Don't Mean a Thing."

• Talk about the song's style, including why
swing music is so danceable. (Possible answer:
In swing music, the rhythms are often uneven
or syncopated, and make people feel like
moving.)

▶ • Sing "It Don't Mean a Thing (If It Ain't Got
That Swing)."

MOVEMENT: *"It Don't Mean a Thing"* MOVEMENT

Have students try basic swing dance steps. First have them
practice a toe-heel step on the right foot. Step with the ball
of the foot, then bring the heel down. (2 beats)
Basic Step Toe-heel on R foot, toe-heel on L foot. (4
beats) Step R foot back, then step L foot in place. (2 beats)
Variation Change the toe-heel steps to

Then step R foot back, L foot in place. (2 beats)

Practice ways these steps can be done with a partner. Examples: Facing each other holding both hands or facing
each other with the girl's right hand holding the boy's left.
Students should notice that the dance instructions are given
for the girl; the boy does opposite footwork.

SOCIAL STUDIES CONNECTION: *Time Line*

Continue the time line begun in Lesson 1, page 238, *Social
Studies Connection.* Ask students to locate events and people in "A Sound Capsule: The 1930s" on the time line, as
well as other events. (1933—Hitler becomes Nazi dictator
in Germany; 1939—World War II begins)

UNIT SIX
LESSON 3

continued from previous page

3 APPLY

Introduce "1930s Medley" CD6:3. **Perform rhythm patterns with music from the 1930s.** Have students:

▶ • Listen to "1930s Medley." ("Take the A Train" by Duke Ellington and Billy Strayhorn, "Sing, Sing, Sing" by Louis Prima —made famous by Benny Goodman.)

• Read and pat (using alternating hands) the rhythm patterns found in "1930s Medley."

• Transfer the rhythm patterns to percussion instruments.

• Perform the rhythm patterns with the recording of "Take the A Train" from "1930s Medley."

OBJECTIVE 1 Informal Assessment
• Perform the rhythm patterns with the recording of "1930s Medley."

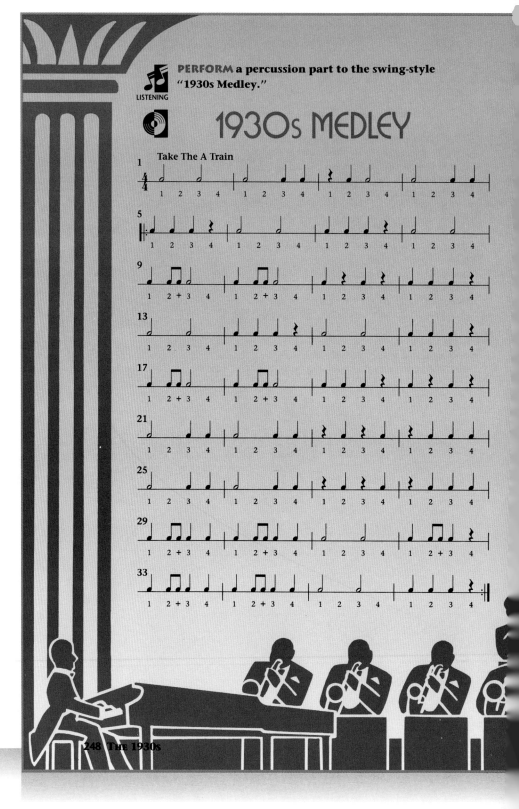

PERFORM a percussion part to the swing-style "1930s Medley."

LISTENING

1930s MEDLEY

248 THE 1930s

MEETING **INDIVIDUAL** NEEDS

ALTERNATIVE TEACHING STRATEGY

OBJECTIVE 1 Have students isolate individual rhythm patterns and practice each pattern up to tempo. When they have mastered the individual patterns, have them put the patterns together. You might also have students create simpler rhythm patterns to use.

BACKGROUND: *Women in Big Bands*

Women played an important role in big-band music. Ina Ray Hutton led her own big band. The Sweethearts of Rhythm were an all-woman big band. (See photo on pages 4–5.) Mary Lou Williams was a famous big-band composer and arranger, who also played the piano. Some of her songs were played by other famous musicians like trumpeter Louis Armstrong and clarinetist Benny Goodman. Many great big-band singers were women, including the Andrews Sisters, Ella Fitzgerald, and Sarah Vaughan. (See also Unit 3, Encore, pages 132–133.)

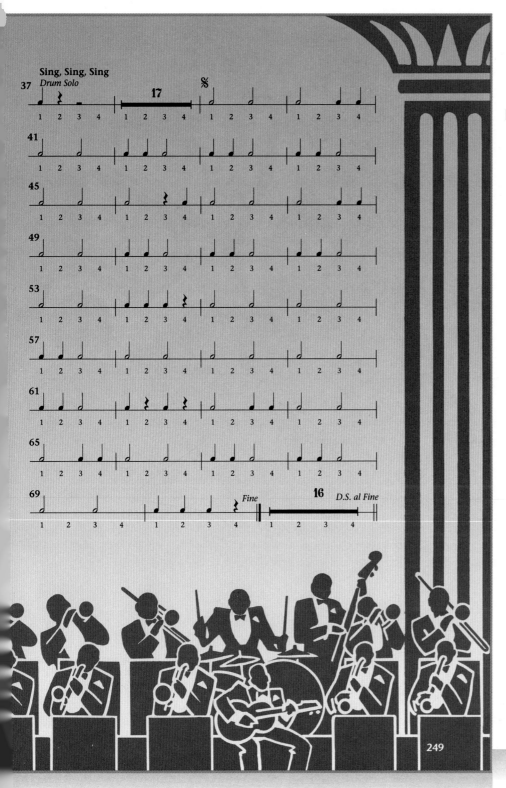

Sing, Sing, Sing

249

"In this lesson, you sang a song from the 1930s and performed rhythm patterns using percussion instruments." Have students:

▶ • Discuss "It Don't Mean a Thing (If It Ain't Got That Swing)" and some of the characteristics of the 1930s. (Encourage students to consider why danceable music was important to a society that liked to socialize.)

• Perform "1930s Medley" again using percussion instruments.

LESSON SUMMARY

Informal Assessment In this lesson, students:

OBJECTIVE 1 Read and performed a percussion playalong with "1930s Medley."

MORE MUSIC: Reinforcement
"The Lion Sleeps Tonight," page 348 (1930s popular style)

LANGUAGE ARTS CONNECTION: *Hard Times*

The Great Depression created many hardships for people, but it also brought them closer together. Ask students to write an essay telling how hard times bring people closer together. Encourage them to use examples from recent times, such as community reactions to widespread unemployment in the early 1990s or the flooding caused by the Mississippi River in 1993.

LESSON PLANNER

FOCUS Style/Harmony

OBJECTIVE
OBJECTIVE 1 Read and perform chords on pitched instruments

MATERIALS
Recordings
Recorded Lesson: A Sound Capsule: The 1940s	CD6:4
Boogie Woogie Bugle Boy	CD6:5
Listening: 1940s Medley	CD6:6

Instruments
guitar, keyboard

Resources Resource Master 6 • 4 (practice)

VOCABULARY
bebop

▶ = **BASIC PROGRAM**

THE 1940s

The Andrews Sisters

250

MEETING **INDIVIDUAL** NEEDS

BACKGROUND: *"Boogie Woogie Bugle Boy"*

"Boogie Woogie Bugle Boy" was written as part of the boogie-woogie craze that swept America in the late thirties and early forties. Boogie woogie is a style of jazz piano playing that is basically a fast blues chord progression with a steady "eight-to-the-bar" bass accompaniment. In slower tempos, a dotted eighth-sixteenth bass pattern is used:

In faster tempos, straight eighths are used:

The song "Boogie Woogie Bugle Boy" has had a life spanning several decades. First it was a hit for the three Andrews sisters, a trio that sang in close harmony and was one of the most popular female groups ever. (They sold 60 million records.) Then in 1972, Bette Midler's enthusiastic version of the song reached No. 8 on the record charts.

Popular music in the 1940s allowed people to escape from some of the grim events of World War II. Big band music continued to be popular, led by such famous musicians as Glenn Miller, Count Basie, Stan Kenton, Benny Goodman, Tommy and Jimmy Dorsey, and Duke Ellington. Famous vocalists included the Andrews Sisters, Ella Fitzgerald, and Frank Sinatra.

In the later 1940s, performers like saxophonist Charlie Parker and trumpeter Dizzy Gillespie created a new kind of jazz called **bebop**. Bebop bands had only a few members, and improvisation was an important part of the band's playing style. Bebop harmonies were more complex than those in most swing music.

BOOGIE WOOGIE BUGLE BOY

Words and Music by Don Raye and Hughie Prince

He was a famous trumpet man from out Chicago way,
He had a "boogie" style that no one else could play.
He was the top man of his craft.
But then his number came up, and he was gone with the draft.
He's in the army now a-blowin' reveille,
He's the BOOGIE WOOGIE BUGLE BOY of Company B.

They made him blow a bugle for his Uncle Sam,
It really brought him down because he couldn't jam.
The captain seemed to understand
Because the next day the "cap" went out and drafted a band,
And now the comp'ny jumps when he plays reveille,
He's the BOOGIE WOOGIE BUGLE BOY of Company B.

A toot! A toot! A toot diddle ah-da toot.
He blows it eight to the bar in "boogie" rhythm.
He can't blow a note unless a bass and guitar are playin' with 'im.
He makes the comp'ny jump when he plays reveille,
He's the BOOGIE WOOGIE BUGLE BOY of Company B.

He puts the boys to sleep with "boogie" ev'ry night,
And wakes them up the same way in the early bright.
They clap their hands and stamp their feet
Because they know how he plays when someone gives him a beat,
He really breaks it up when he plays reveille,
He's the BOOGIE WOOGIE BUGLE BOY of Company B.
A toot! A toot! (etc.)

Unit 6 *From Rag to Rap* **251**

1 GET SET

"Where do you usually hear new songs first?" (radio, TV, and/or from friends)
"If you said radio, you would have fit right into the 1940s!" Have students:

▶ • Discuss why the radio has remained a popular source of news and culture for over 50 years. (Point out that radio was also popular in the 1920s and 1930s. Stress that throughout all these decades, people listened to the radio with as much interest as they watch television today, if not more. Favorite radio shows, such as *The Lone Ranger*, had a large and loyal listening audience.)

2 DEVELOP

1. Introduce music and events from the 1940s. Have students:

Recorded Lesson CD6:4
▶ • Listen to "A Sound Capsule: The 1940s" to learn about events and music from the 1940s.

▶ • Name a few events from the 1940s. (Optional: Have students match key events and people from the Recorded Lesson on **Resource Master 6 • 4.**)

▶ • Briefly discuss each event, including the importance of radio shows in communicating news, sports, and cultural events.

2. Introduce "Boogie Woogie Bugle Boy" CD6:5. **Sing music from the 1940s.** Have students:

▶ • Listen to the recording and follow the words to "Boogie Woogie Bugle Boy."

▶ • Discuss the lyrics and feel of the song. (You might have students contrast this song with one from another lesson such as "Alexander's Ragtime Band," page 239.)

▶ • Sing "Boogie Woogie Bugle Boy." (Optional: See *Enrichment* below.)

SOCIAL STUDIES CONNECTION: *Time Line*

Continue the time line begun in Lesson 1, page 238, *Social Studies Connection*. Ask students to locate events and people in "A Sound Capsule: The 1940s" on the time line, as well as other events. (1941—United States enters World War II; 1945—World War II ends; 1948—Israel is founded; 1949—birth of the People's Republic of China)

MOVEMENT: *"Boogie Woogie Bugle Boy"*

Have partners explore new variations for the swing dance steps from Lesson 3, page 247, *Movement*. For example,

they could slowly rotate as they do the two-handed step, making a complete circle pathway in about eight repetitions. Another possibility is doing the steps side by side, with the same body facing. The girl could "wind in" close to the boy, then "wind out" (turn toward, then away), her right hand in his left hand.

ENRICHMENT: *Solo Singing*

Provide solo-singing practice by assigning different soloists to each *A toot! A toot! A toot diddle ah-da toot*. Have different small groups sing *He's the BOOGIE WOOGIE BUGLE BOY of Company B.*

LESSON 4

continued from previous page

3. Introduce D, easy G, and A chords on guitar. Have students:

• Read page 252.

• Read and finger the D, easy G, and A chords on the guitar. (If possible, restring a guitar in the reverse manner for left-handed students. They can then strum with the left hand and finger the strings with the right hand.)

• Compare the fingerings for the three chords, stating similarities and differences.

3 APPLY

Introduce "1940s Medley" CD6:6. Experience music from 1940s and play chords on a pitched instrument. Have students:

▶ • Listen to "1940s Medley" ("Boogie Woogie Bugle Boy"—see page 251, "String of Pearls" by Jerry Gray, "Chattanooga Choo Choo" by Harry Warren, "In the Mood" by Joe Garland).

• Read and speak the names of the chords used in "1940s Medley."

• Transfer the chord names to pitched instruments, such as guitar or keyboard, by fingering each chord as they speak it.

• Perform the correct chords with the recording of "Boogie Woogie Bugle Boy" from the "1940s Medley."

OBJECTIVE 1 Informal Assessment

• Perform some or all of the correct chords with the recording of "1940s Medley."

PERFORM the "1940s Medley" on guitar.

Hold the guitar as shown. The fingers of your left hand should be above the open strings.

PLAY the D, G, and A chords.

Notice where to place your fingers on the strings. The fingers are numbered from the index finger (1) to the little finger (4).

The X at the top of the chord diagram indicates that the string is not to be played. A string marked with an O should be played open.

252 THE 1940s

MEETING **INDIVIDUAL** NEEDS

ALTERNATE TEACHING STRATEGY

OBJECTIVE 1 Have students perform one chord only, resting as the others are heard on the recording. Gradually add the other chords until all are being performed.

SPECIAL LEARNERS: *Playing the Guitar*

This unit provides many opportunities for students to play guitar accompaniments. Throughout the unit, give students the choice to play chord roots on guitar, keyboard, or classroom instruments. Make the guitar available to all students and encourage them to experiment with the instrument. If

holding an instrument is difficult, have the seated student use a standard neck strap and brace the instrument with pieces of foam. If students are unable to manipulate the left hand to play chords, retune their guitars to an open tuning and have them use bar chords.

For "1940s Medley," change the tuning of a single guitar from E A D G B E to D A D F♯ A D (D major tuning) and have them use bar chords. (See page 427.) The D chord occurs frequently throughout the medley, so students will have many chances to play along, strumming all or a few of the open-tuned strings.

1940s MEDLEY

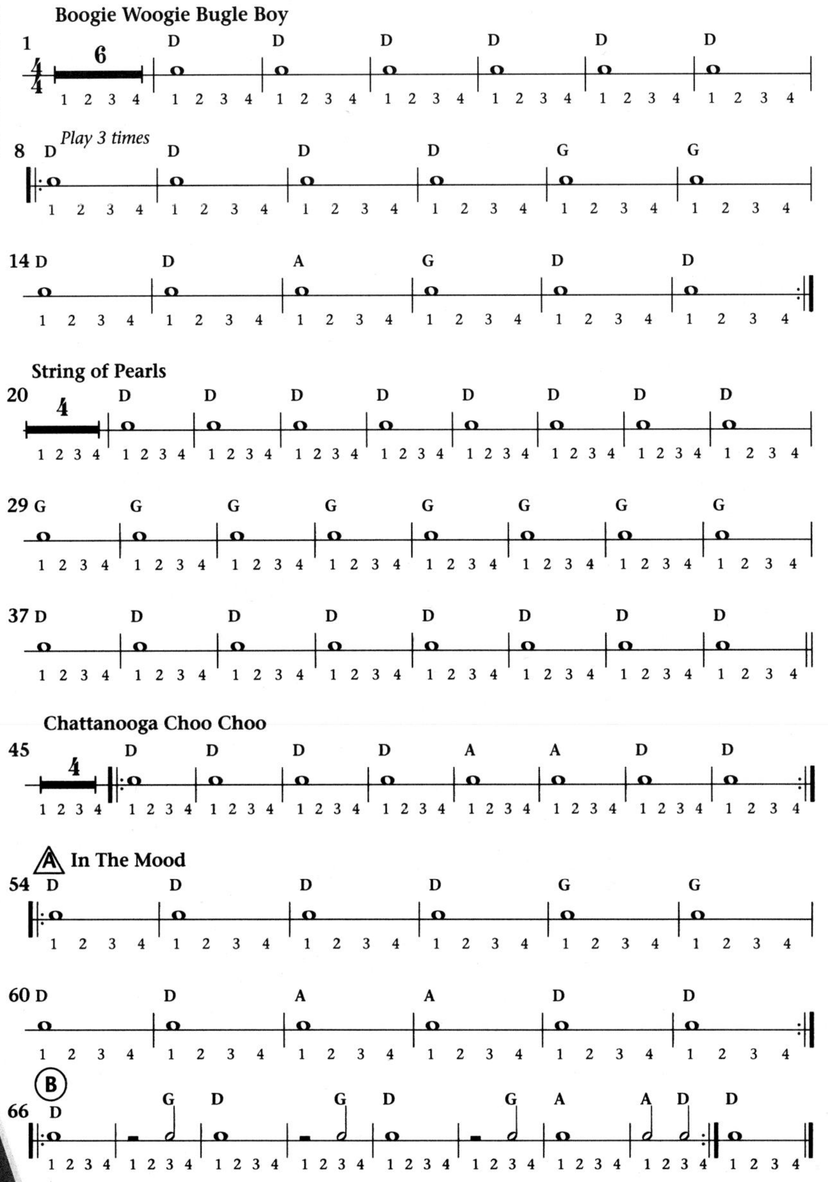

Boogie Woogie Bugle Boy

String of Pearls

Chattanooga Choo Choo

In The Mood

Unit 6 *From Rag to Rap* 253

"Why do you think 'Boogie Woogie Bugle Boy' was written in the 1940s?" (Songs often reflect the culture of their time; the country was at war through half of the decade, so many songs were written about the war.) Have students:

▸ • Discuss some of the characteristics of the 1940s.

• Perform the "1940s Medley" again, using pitched instruments.

LESSON SUMMARY

Informal Assessment In this lesson, students:

OBJECTIVE 1 Read and performed chords on pitched instruments with "1940s Medley."

MORE MUSIC: Reinforcement
"Battle Hymn of the Republic" (listening), page 294 (style—boogie woogie, jazz)

CAREERS: *Guitar Maker*

As students learn guitar chords, introduce them to the career of guitar maker. A guitar maker (or any instrument builder) is usually a craftsperson who loves music. It helps a maker to know how to play the guitar as well as other stringed instruments. To learn how to make a guitar, he or she takes classes, watches other instrument builders, reads books, and examines other instruments. Then she or he makes a practice guitar or two. Some guitar-making jobs are found in musical instrument factories or stores. Other guitar makers have their own workshops, where they take special orders from customers.

BACKGROUND: *"1940s Medley"*

Aside from "Boogie Woogie Bugle Boy" (a hit for the Andrews Sisters), the other songs in this medley were made popular by the Glenn Miller Band. "In the Mood" became the band's biggest hit after a 1939 recording. In live performances of the song, the trumpeters would wave their derbies and the trombonists would whirl their instruments.

RELATED ARTS **MOVEMENT** THEATER VISUAL ARTS

LESSON PLANNER

FOCUS Style/Harmony

OBJECTIVE
OBJECTIVE 1 Read and perform chords on pitched instruments

MATERIALS
Recordings
Recorded Lesson: A Sound Capsule: The 1950s	CD6:7
Bandstand Boogie	CD6:8
Boogie Woogie Bugle Boy	CD6:5
Listening: 1950s Medley	CD6:9

Instruments
guitar, keyboard

Resources
Resource Master 6 • 5 (practice)
Playing the Guitar G • 24 (G C D7 chords)
Playing the Guitar G • 26 (G C D7 chords)

VOCABULARY
rock 'n' roll

▶ = **BASIC PROGRAM**

The 1950s saw the birth of a new, distinctly American musical style called **rock 'n' roll**. Rock 'n' roll had its roots in earlier American music, including blues, gospel, and country styles. Rock 'n' roll really took off when Bill Haley and the Comets recorded "Rock Around the Clock" for the 1955 movie *Blackboard Jungle.* Chuck Berry changed rock 'n' roll by using the guitar as a main, or lead, instrument. Elvis Presley, known as the "King of rock 'n' roll," became a huge star in the 1950s, and his music has remained extremely popular ever since.

Dick Clark, host of the popular 1950s television show American Bandstand

254

MEETING **INDIVIDUAL** NEEDS

SOCIAL STUDIES CONNECTION: *Time Line*

Continue the time line begun in Lesson 1, page 238, *Social Studies Connection.* Ask students to locate events and people in "A Sound Capsule: The 1950s" on the time line, as well as other key events. (1950–1953—Korean War; 1955—Rosa Parks arrested in Alabama for refusing to give her bus seat to a white man; 1956—revolts against Communism in Eastern Europe; 1957—Vietnam War begins with North Vietnam invading South Vietnam; 1957—Ghana is first black African nation to achieve independence from colonial rule)

BACKGROUND: *American Bandstand*

To millions of teenagers in the fifties and early sixties, *American Bandstand* was the television show to watch in the late afternoon. Broadcast from Philadelphia, *American Bandstand* showcased the hottest rock 'n' roll stars as well as giving many musicians their first important break. As the records played, a group of teenagers danced, introducing the latest fashions and the newest dance crazes to the rest of the country. Host Dick Clark became a media star at age 25, with his picture everywhere, even on lunch boxes. In 1963, he moved to Los Angeles, where he now produces television shows.

♪ Bandstand Boogie

Words by Barry Manilow and Bruce Sussman
Music by Charles Albertine

Refrain

*We're goin' hoppin', we're goin' hoppin' today,
where things are poppin', the Philadelphia way;
we're gonna drop in on all the music they play on
the Bandstand. (Bandstand.)*

*And I'll jump and, hey, I may even show 'em my handstand,
because I'm on, because I'm on the American Bandstand.
When we dance real slow I'll show all the guys in the grandstand
what a swinger I am; I am on American Bandstand.*

Refrain

*Whatdaya know, here on the show ready to go, what a pro!
Hey! I'm makin' my mark; Gee, this joint is jumpin'.
They made such a fuss just to see us arrive.
Hey! It's Mister Dick Clark; what a place you've got here,
swell spot, the music's hot here.
Best in the East, give it at least a seventy-five!*

*And now we're hoppin', and we'll be hoppin' all day
where things are poppin' the Philadelphia way,
And you can drop in on all the music they play on the Bandstand.
And we'll rock and roll and
Stroll on American, Lindy Hop and Slop, it's American.
Tune in , I'm on, turn on, I'm in, I'm on! Today, Bandstand.*

255

"What do you know about the 1950s?" (Possible answers: sock hops, Cold War between the United States and U.S.S.R., Elvis Presley, rock 'n' roll) Have students:

▶ • Examine the art on pages 254–255, and briefly discuss the events and people pictured.

"Today you're going to learn the theme song from one of the hit television shows of the fifties—*American Bandstand.*

2 DEVELOP

1. Introduce music and events from the 1950s. Have students:

▶ • Read page 254.

Recorded Lesson CD6:7
▶ • Listen to "A Sound Capsule: The 1950s" to learn about events and music from the 1950s.

▶ • Compare and contrast 1950s rock 'n' roll music to popular music today. (Optional: Have students complete the word puzzle with key names and events from the Recorded Lesson on **Resource Master 6 • 5.**)

2. Introduce "Bandstand Boogie" CD6:8. **Sing music from the 1950s.** Have students:

▶ • Listen to the recording and follow the words to "Bandstand Boogie."

• Compare "Bandstand Boogie" to "Boogie Woogie Bugle Boy" CD6:5 (page 251), comparing rhythm patterns, tempos, and other stylistic elements that make each song representative of its decade.

▶ • Sing "Bandstand Boogie."

▶ • Notice the form of the song (A B A C A coda) and compare this to rondo form.

MOVEMENT: *"Bandstand Boogie"* Hand Jive

Formation: sitting circle

A section: (*We're goin' hoppin'* . . .) Starting on *hoppin'*, pat own legs twice. Pat own L leg with R hand and R leg of neighbor on left with L hand, twice. Pat own legs twice. Pat own R leg with L hand and L leg of neighbor on right with R hand, twice.

B section: (*And I'll jump* . . .) Starting on *jump*, pat own legs twice. Cross arms and pat legs twice. Uncross arms and pat legs twice. Snap fingers twice.

C section: (*Bandstand, Bandstand, Bandstand, Whatdaya know* . . .) Make up own hand-jive movements.

LANGUAGE ARTS CONNECTION: *New Lyrics*

Help students to interpret the lyrics of "Bandstand Boogie." (*Best in the East, give it at least a seventy-five*—the show had a song-rating segment; *Lindy Hop; Slop*—types of dances) Then have them substitute more current slang for some of the words—for example, *swinger* (fresh, cool) or *Lindy Hop* (hip-hop)—to create an updated version of the song.

UNIT SIX LESSON 5

continued from previous page

3. Introduce easy C chord on guitar and review D, easy G, and A chords. Have students:

• Read and describe the fingering for the easy C chord, then finger the easy C chord on the guitar.

• Review the D, easy G, and A chords on the guitar. (See page 252.)

• Practice changing from the C chord to easy G and D, noting how the finger positions change.

3 APPLY

Introduce "1950s Medley" CD6:9. **Experience music from the 1950s and play chords on a pitched instrument.** Have students:

▶ • Listen to "1950s Medley" and discuss the music. ("Rock Around the Clock" by Bill Haley, "Rock and Roll Music" by Chuck Berry, "Hound Dog" by Jerry Lieber and Mike Stoller)

• Read and speak the names of the chords used in the "1950s Medley."

• Transfer the chords to guitar or keyboard by fingering each chord as they speak it.

• Perform the chords with the recording of "Rock Around the Clock" from "1950s Medley."

OBJECTIVE 1 Informal Assessment
• Perform some or all of the chords with the recording of "1950s Medley."

PERFORM a harmonic accompaniment to the "1950s Medley" on guitar.

Play the C chord so that you can use it with the G and D chords. Remember that your fingers are numbered from the index finger (1) to the little finger (4).

Easy C

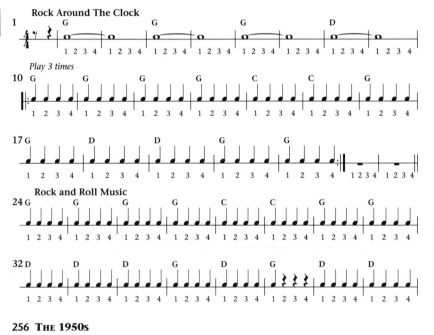

1950s MEDLEY

256 THE 1950s

MEETING **INDIVIDUAL** NEEDS

ALTERNATE TEACHING STRATEGY

OBJECTIVE 1 Assign individual chords to various groups in the class. Write the chord names on the board or overhead. As you point to the chord, each group performs their chord at the correct time. You might also teach this alternate strum pattern with the medley:

BACKGROUND: *The Electric Guitar*

The electric guitar is the newest member of the guitar family. The first known use of pick-ups to amplify sound electrically occurred in the 1920s, but the guitars did not catch on. The first successful electric guitars appeared in the early 1930s, with an electric Hawaiian guitar nicknamed the "Frying Pan" because of the shape of its aluminum body. After World War II, the solid-body guitar began to catch on, as men such as Les Paul and Leo Fender worked on its design. Fender formed the Fender Electrical Instrument Company and in 1948 started to market the "Broadcaster," changing its name to the "Telecaster" in 1950. By the end

4 CLOSE

"In this lesson, you sang a song from the 1950s and added the C chord to the list of chords you can play." Have students:

- Show the fingering for the C chord on guitar.
▶ • Sing "Bandstand Boogie" once more.

LESSON SUMMARY

Informal Assessment In this lesson, students:

OBJECTIVE 1 Read and performed chords on pitched instruments with "1950s Medley"

MORE MUSIC: Reinforcement
Playing the Guitar, page 426

---

40 G   G   C   C   D   D   G   G
1 2 3 4   1 2 3 4   1 2 3 4   1 2 3 4   1 2 3 4   1 2 3 4   1 2 3 4   1 2 3 4

48 G   G   C   C   G   G
1 2 3 4   1 2 3 4   1 2 3 4   1 2 3 4   1 2 3 4   1 2 3 4

54 D   D   D   G   D   G
1 2 3 4   1 2 3 4   1 2 3 4   1 2 3 4   1 2 3 4   1 2 3 4

Hound Dog
Play 4 times

60 G   G   G   G   C   C
1 2 3 4   1 2 3 4   1 2 3 4   1 2 3 4   1 2 3 4   1 2 3 4   1 2 3 4   1 2 3 4

67 G   G   D   C   G   G
1 2 3 4   1 2 3 4   1 2 3 4   1 2 3 4   1 2 3 4   1 2 3 4

Rock Around The Clock
Play 2 times

73 G   G   G   G   C   C   G
1 2 3 4   1 2 3 4   1 2 3 4   1 2 3 4   1 2 3 4   1 2 3 4   1 2 3 4

80 G   D   D   G   G   G   G
1 2 3 4   1 2 3 4   1 2 3 4   1 2 3 4   1 2 3 4   1 2 3 4   1 2 3 4

Unit 6 *From Rag to Rap* **257**

---

of the 1950s, the electric guitar was on its way to becoming one of the world's most popular instruments, thanks to Chuck Berry, B.B. King, Les Paul, Buddy Holly, and others.

TECHNOLOGY IN MUSIC: *Electric Guitar*

Although developed from the acoustic guitar, the sound of the modern electric guitar is produced quite differently. On an acoustic guitar, the plucked strings cause the soundboard to vibrate, which in turn amplifies the sound. When a pick-up is attached to make an electric-acoustic guitar, the pick-up moves up and down with the soundboard vibrations, and the amplified sound is a combination of string and body tones.

On a solid-body electric guitar, the body does not respond to the vibrations of the strings. Instead the vibrations are converted by the pick-ups into electrical impulses. These pass through an amplifier before being emitted as sound through the speakers. Electronic "effects" devices can alter the sound. For example, chorus, delay, and reverberation devices make the sound fuller. Because the electric-guitar body serves only to hold the strings and not to amplify the sound, in theory, electric guitars can be any shape the maker wants.

LESSON PLANNER

FOCUS Style/Form

OBJECTIVES
OBJECTIVE 1 Read and perform chords on guitar
OBJECTIVE 2 Identify form in a popular composition from the 1960s

MATERIALS
Recordings
Recorded Lesson: A Sound
Capsule: The 1960s   CD6:10
Blowin' in the Wind   CD6:11
Listening: 1960s Medley   CD6:12
Listening: Birthday by
J. Lennon and P. McCartney   CD6:13

Instruments guitar

Resources
Resource Master 6 • 6 (practice)
Resource Master 6 • 7 (practice)
Recorder Master R • 25 (pitches D E F♯ G A B)
Signing Master S • 6 • 4 (Blowin' in the Wind)

▶ = **BASIC PROGRAM**

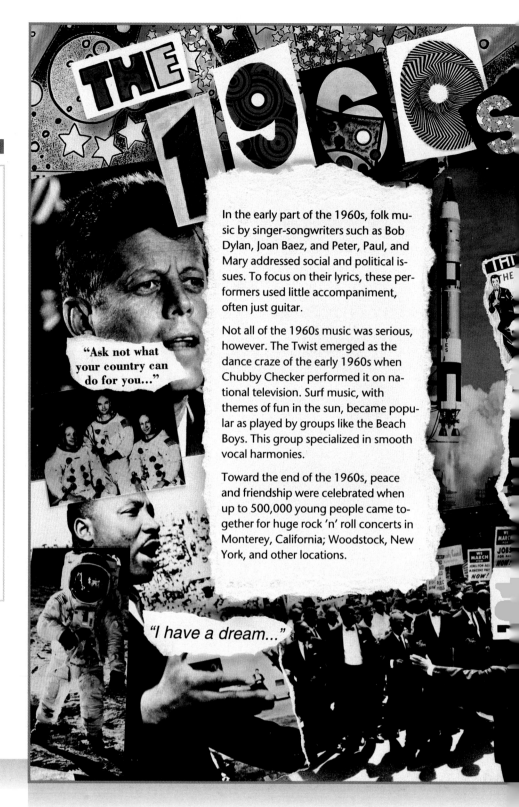

In the early part of the 1960s, folk music by singer-songwriters such as Bob Dylan, Joan Baez, and Peter, Paul, and Mary addressed social and political issues. To focus on their lyrics, these performers used little accompaniment, often just guitar.

Not all of the 1960s music was serious, however. The Twist emerged as the dance craze of the early 1960s when Chubby Checker performed it on national television. Surf music, with themes of fun in the sun, became popular as played by groups like the Beach Boys. This group specialized in smooth vocal harmonies.

Toward the end of the 1960s, peace and friendship were celebrated when up to 500,000 young people came together for huge rock 'n' roll concerts in Monterey, California; Woodstock, New York, and other locations.

"Ask not what your country can do for you..."

"I have a dream..."

MEETING **INDIVIDUAL** NEEDS

SOCIAL STUDIES CONNECTION: *Time Line*

Continue the time line begun in Lesson 1, page 238, *Social Studies Connection.* Ask students to locate events and people in "A Sound Capsule: The 1960s" on the time line, and other events from this time period. (1961—Berlin Wall is built in Germany; 1961—U.S. supports invasion of Cuba at the Bay of Pigs; 1963—President John F. Kennedy assassinated in Dallas; 1964—Civil Rights Act outlaws segregation in public places; 1965—Voting Rights Act protects the right of all Americans to vote; 1965—Malcolm X assassinated; 1968—Martin Luther King, Jr., assassinated)

CRITICAL THINKING: *Compare and Contrast*

Have students compare and contrast "Blowin' in the Wind" and "Boogie Woogie Bugle Boy." Encourage them to compare such elements as lyrics, mood, tempo, and instrumentation. Discuss whether or not each song represents the era in which it was written. (Bring out that each song is related to the way people dealt with the issue of war.)

SIGNING: *"Blowin' in the Wind"*
Signing Master S • 6 • 4 has sign language for this song.

Blowin' in the Wind

Words and Music by Bob Dylan

How many roads must a man walk down
Before you call him a man?
Yes, 'n' how many seas must a white dove sail
Before she sleeps in the sand?
Yes, 'n' how many times must the cannonballs fly
Before they're forever banned?
The answer, my friend, is blowin' in the wind,
The answer is blowin' in the wind.

How many times must a man look up
Before he can see the sky?
Yes, 'n' how many ears must one man have
Before he can hear people cry?
Yes, 'n' how many deaths will it take 'till he knows
That too many people have died?
The answer, my friend, is blowin' in the wind,
The answer is blowin' in the wind.

How many years can a mountain exist
Before it's washed to the sea?
Yes, 'n' how many years can some people exist
Before they're allowed to be free?
Yes, 'n' how many times can a man turn his head
Pretending he just doesn't see?
The answer, my friend, is blowin' in the wind,
The answer is blowin' in the wind.

"The answer is blowin' in the wind."

Unit 6 *From Rag to Rap* 259

BIOGRAPHY: *Bob Dylan*

Singer-songwriter Bob Dylan (b. 1941) has had many hit records, although his first album only sold 5,000 copies its first year. Born in Minnesota, Dylan has gone through many musical phases. He started as a folk singer in the coffee houses of the late fifties and early sixties, writing civil rights and anti-war songs. "Blowin' in the Wind" was a Top 10 hit for Peter, Paul, and Mary in 1963, selling 320,000 copies in the first eight days of its release. As he achieved success as a folk singer, Dylan changed his sound, adding an electric guitar to accompany his folk lyrics. This move shocked many folk-song fans, but earned Dylan his first

gold record, in 1965. In the next ten years, Dylan released at least one or two records a year. His albums at the end of the seventies showed a gospel influence, as Dylan became a born-again Christian. In recent years, he has toured frequently, playing songs from every phase of his musical development for the large audiences he continues to attract.

PLAYING INSTRUMENTS: *Bass Guitar*

Use **Resource Master 6 • 7** to teach students a bass accompaniment to "Blowin' in the Wind." Then have them play the accompaniment along with the song.

Unit 6 FROM RAG TO RAP **259**

continued from previous page

3. Introduce A7 chord on guitar and review easy C, D, easy G, and A chords. Have students:

• Read and describe the fingering for the A7 chord, then finger the A7 chord on the guitar.

• Review the easy C, D, easy G, and A chords on the guitar using the correct fingering. (See pages 252 and 256.)

• Try playing A7, D, easy G, and easy C in different combinations to see which chord progressions sound pleasing to them.

PERFORM the contrasting styles of the "1960s Medley" on guitar.

Learn the A7 chord so that you can use it with the G, C, and D chords. Remember that your fingers are numbered from the index finger (1) to the little finger (4).

260 THE 1960s

MEETING **INDIVIDUAL** NEEDS

ALTERNATE TEACHING STRATEGY

OBJECTIVE 1 To build ear-training skills while allowing more time to change fingerings, have students play every other measure. They should listen to and identify chord sounds in the in-between measures.

MOVEMENT: *"1960s Medley"*

Have students learn Sixties-style dances to do with the medley. Explain that the dances are done freely, with any variations the dancer cares to work in.

Monkey: Hips move from side to side (feet remaining in place) while arms alternate up and down straight out in front of chest.

Twist: Twist hips from side to side. Arms are bent at elbows and twisting in opposition to the hips. Feet remain in contact with the floor but weight shifts from one foot to the other.

Watusi: Variation on the twist, but body bends at waist going forward and backward, diagonally, or side to side.

1960s Medley

Satisfaction

Musical notation with chord names D, C, D, C across measures, with counting 1 2 3 4 below each measure.

Roll Over Beethoven
Play 3 times

The Twist
Play 3 times

---

1. Introduce "1960s Medley" CD6:12. **Experience music from 1960s and play chords on guitar.** Have students:

▶ • Listen to "1960s Medley" ("Satisfaction" by the Rolling Stones, "Roll Over Beethoven" by Chuck Berry, "The Twist" by Hank Ballard—made famous by Chubby Checker).

• Read and speak the names of the chords used in the "1960s Medley" playalong.

• Divide into two groups, with one group fingering only the easy C and A7 chords and the other group fingering the D and easy G chords.

• Perform their group's chords with the recording of "Satisfaction" from the "1960s Medley."

OBJECTIVE 1 Informal Assessment

• Perform some or all of the chords with the recording of "1960s Medley."

ART CONNECTION: *Album Covers* 🎨 VISUAL ARTS

Have students study the illustration on page 260. "How would you know that this picture represents the 1960s?" (The bell-bottom trousers; some students might recognize the art style as one popularized by Peter Max on album covers of the 1960s.) Ask students to compare this picture with the general style of popular album covers on CDs and tapes today. Invite students to bring in CDs, records, and tapes with covers they like. Select those suitable for class discussion and ask students to evaluate the various design approaches used.

continued from previous page

2. Introduce "Birthday" CD6:13 **Review rondo form.** Have students:

▶ • Read about and discuss the Beatles and their impact on popular music and musicians in Britain and the United States.

▶ • Review the text and the three sections of "Birthday," then listen to the song.

OBJECTIVE 2 Informal Assessment

• Identify the order of the three sections of "Birthday." (A B C A C A)

• Describe the musical form. (It is similar to rondo form, but has an extra C section after the B section. Review *rondo,* Unit 2, Lesson 3, page 60.)

THE BEATLES: THE BRITISH INVASION

In the 1960s, British rock groups such as the Rolling Stones, the Animals, and the Who began to give concerts in the United States. These groups became extremely popular. The most influential and famous of these groups, however, was the Beatles.

The Beatles changed rock 'n' roll in the 1960s by accompanying their songs with orchestral instruments, instruments from India, and unusual electronic sounds. Their initial American tour in 1964 was a phenomenal success. In less than a decade, the Beatles sold 125 million single records and 85 million albums.

The Beatles

262 THE 1960s

MEETING **INDIVIDUAL** NEEDS

ALTERNATE TEACHING STRATEGY

OBJECTIVE 2 Organize the class into cooperative-learning groups of four students. Within each group each student is given a card A, B, or C. Play "Birthday," having students in each group stand as their individual section is heard. The fourth person in the group is the recorder, who keeps track of the order in which the various sections stand.

LANGUAGE ARTS CONNECTION: *Research Report*

Have students write a report on one of the issues of the 1960s, such as the Vietnam War or the civil rights movement. Encourage students to interview their parents and other adults in addition to conducting library research. If appropriate, their research should include songs that played a large part in the movements, such as "Blowin' in the Wind" or "We Shall Overcome."

FOLLOW the text and figure out the musical form of "Birthday." The song contains three musical sections, which have different words, shown below. A B C A C A

Birthday

LISTENING

Words and Music by John Lennon and Paul McCartney

You say it's your birthday, it's my birthday too, yeah.
You say it's your birthday, we're gonna have a good time.
I'm glad it's your birthday, Happy Birthday to you!

Yes, we're goin' to a party, party.
Yes, we're goin' to a party, party.
Yes, we're goin' to a party, party.

I would like you to dance (Birthday)
Take a cha-cha-cha-chance (Birthday)
I would like you to dance (Birthday)
Dance.

"Birthday" has a form in which the refrain, or A section, returns. This repetition of a musical section serves as a familiar landmark for the listener.

Unit 6 *From Rag to Rap* **263**

---

4 CLOSE

"What's your favorite part of the 1960s?" Have students:

▶ • Discuss the 1960s, including why many songs, shows, and styles from that era are popular today.

▶ • Sing "Blowin' in the Wind."

LESSON SUMMARY

Informal Assessment In this lesson, students:

OBJECTIVE 1 Read and performed chords on guitar with "1960s Medley."

OBJECTIVE 2 Identified form in "Birthday."

MORE MUSIC: Reinforcement
Playing the Guitar, page 426

RELATED ARTS **MOVEMENT** THEATER VISUAL ARTS

LESSON PLANNER

FOCUS Style/Harmony

OBJECTIVE
OBJECTIVE 1 Read and perform chords on pitched instruments

MATERIALS
Recordings
Recorded Lesson: A Sound
   Capsule: The 1970s   CD6:14
Fly Like an Eagle   CD6:15
Listening: 1970s Medley   CD6:16
Rocky Top   CD6:17
Rocky Top (performance mix)   CD6:18

Instruments
guitar, keyboard

Resources
Resource Master 6 • 8 (practice)
Recorder Master R • 26 (pitches
  D E F♯ G A B)

VOCABULARY
heavy metal, disco, country and western

▶ = **BASIC PROGRAM**

The 1970s saw advances in music technology. Amplifiers made music louder and electronic devices changed guitar and keyboard tone colors. This enabled rock bands like Led Zeppelin to create new sounds. They helped start a new style called **heavy metal.** Later in the 1970s, a style called **disco** emerged with performers such as Donna Summer. Disco's strong, steady beat made it easy to dance to. Another style popular in the 1970s was **country and western**. This music, which grew out of earlier country music styles, features the banjo, fiddle, and pedal-steel guitar. The harmonies stay simple so that listeners can focus on the expressive vocal styles of the singers. Singers such as Dolly Parton, Randy Travis, and Garth Brooks have kept country music popular into the 1990s.

264

MEETING **INDIVIDUAL** NEEDS

SOCIAL STUDIES CONNECTION: *Time Line*

Continue the time line begun in Lesson 1, page 238, *Social Studies Connection.* Ask students to locate events and people in "A Sound Capsule: The 1970s" on the time line, as well as other events from this time period. (1970—1st Earth Day celebrated; 1973—U.S. troops leave Vietnam; 1974—President Richard Nixon resigns because of Watergate scandal; 1975—North Vietnam defeats South Vietnam to end Vietnam War; 1979—Soviet Union and U.S. sign a major nuclear weapons control agreement)

SOCIAL STUDIES CONNECTION: *Local Services*

Have students work in groups to find out what services their community provides to the homeless. (soup kitchens, food banks, housing, medical care, and so on) They might wish to contribute in some way, perhaps by organizing a food drive at school to collect canned-food donations for distribution to a local food bank.

SING **this popular song from the mid-1970s.**

Fly Like an Eagle
Words and Music
by Steve Miller

(*Tip top tip.* Doot doot doo doo.)
Time keeps on slippin', slippin', slippin', into the future.
Time keeps on slippin', slippin', slippin', into the future.
I wanna fly like an eagle to the sea:
fly like an eagle, let my spirit carry me.
I want to fly like an eagle till I'm free, right through the
  revolution.

Feed the babies who don't have enough to eat.
Shoe the children with no shoes on their feet.
House the people livin' in the street.
Oh, there's a solution.
Doo doot-n doo doot. Doo doot-n doo doot.

Unit 6 From Rag to Rap **265**

1 GET SET

"What kind of music did people listen to in the 1970s? What kinds of clothes did they wear?" Have students:

▶ • Describe American life in the 1970s. (Possible answers: Presidents Nixon, Ford, and Carter, women's liberation movement, platform shoes, crocheted vests, *The Brady Bunch*, rock music, disco music, heavy metal music)

▶ • Discuss why so much of the 1970s is familiar. (Possible answers: television reruns, "oldies" radio stations, revival of 1970s fashions in the early 1990s)

"Today you're going to sing two different songs that represent music from the Seventies."

2 DEVELOP

1. Introduce music and events from the 1970s. Have students:

Recorded Lesson CD6:14
▶ • Listen to "A Sound Capsule: The 1970s" to learn about events and music from the 1970s.

▶ • Read pages 264–265, then discuss the 1970s, revising or adding to their ideas from the *Get Set*. (Optional: Have students circle famous names from the 1970s on **Resource Master 6 • 8.**)

2. Introduce "Fly Like an Eagle" CD6:15. **Sing music from the 1970s.** Have students:

▶ • Listen to the recording and follow the words to the song.

▶ • Discuss the words to the song, telling what Steve Miller wishes could be done for the poor and homeless.

▶ • Sing "Fly Like an Eagle."

BIOGRAPHY: *Steve Miller*

American guitarist and songwriter Steve Miller (b. 1943) started playing guitar at the age of five, and before he was a teenager was leading a band made up of his brother Jimmy and William 'Boz' Scaggs. After high school graduation, he left Dallas to go to the University of Wisconsin, where he formed another band. During 1965 he began to play Chicago-style blues. He recorded a single, but then retired because of management problems to become a janitor at a record company.

In 1966, Miller went to the West Coast to join the San Francisco music scene, cutting his first rock record within two years. In 1973, his eighth album, *The Joker*, became the No. 2 LP. He retired again to become a farmer, then came back to music in 1976 with *Fly Like an Eagle*. Several songs from the record, including the title track, made the Top 10. He has continued recording mainstream rock songs, but still can be heard playing the blues in his live performances.

UNIT SIX
LESSON 7

continued from previous page

3. Introduce E minor chord on guitar and review C, D, G, A, and A7 chords. Have students:

• Read and describe the fingering for the E minor chord, then finger the E minor chord on the guitar.

• Review the C, D, G, A, and A7 chords on the guitar. (See pages 252, 256, and 260.)

• Practice changing from the E minor chord to one of the other chords on page 267 (G, D, C, and A), noting how the finger positions change.

PERFORM the "1970s Medley" on guitar.

Learn to play the the E minor chord so that you can use it with the G, C, A, and D chords. Remember that your fingers are numbered from the index finger (1) to the little finger (4).

Em

266 THE 1970s

MEETING **INDIVIDUAL** NEEDS

ALTERNATE TEACHING STRATEGY

OBJECTIVE 1 Have students work in pairs or small groups to practice the new chord, Em, as well as to review the chords learned in previous lessons. Then have them say the names of the chords aloud as they play "Already Gone," the first part of "1970s Medley." After they are comfortable with the fingerings, have them try to play "Already Gone" with the recording again.

1970s MEDLEY

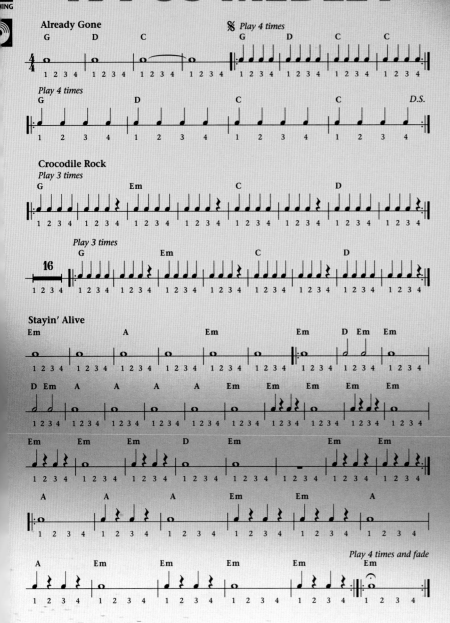

1. Introduce "1970s Medley" CD6:16. **Experience music from the 1970s and play chords on a pitched instrument.** Have students:

▶ • Listen to "1970s Medley" ("Already Gone" by J. Tempchin and R. Strandlund—originally sung by the Eagles, "Crocodile Rock" by Elton John, "Stayin' Alive" by the Gibb Brothers—known as the BeeGees).

• Read and speak the names of the chords used in the "1970s Medley" playalong.

• Transfer the chords to guitar or keyboard by fingering each chord as they speak it.

• Perform the chords with the recording of "Already Gone" from the "1970s Medley."

OBJECTIVE 1 Informal Assessment

• Perform the chords with the recording of "1970s Medley."

continued from previous page

2. Introduce "Rocky Top" CD6:17. **Sing a country-and-western song.** Have students:

▶ • Listen to the recording and follow the words to the song.

▶ • Sing the melody to "Rocky Top."

• Learn the countermelody. (When students are secure singing the melody and countermelody separately, have them put both parts together.)

3. Play chords on a pitched instrument to accompany "Rocky Top." Have students:

• Read and speak the names of the chords used in "Rocky Top."

• Transfer the chords to guitar or keyboard by fingering each chord as they speak it.

• Perform the chords with the recording of "Rocky Top." (These chords may be more challenging than those in the medleys. Students can substitute easy forms of some of the chords for the regular chords. See pages 426–427.)

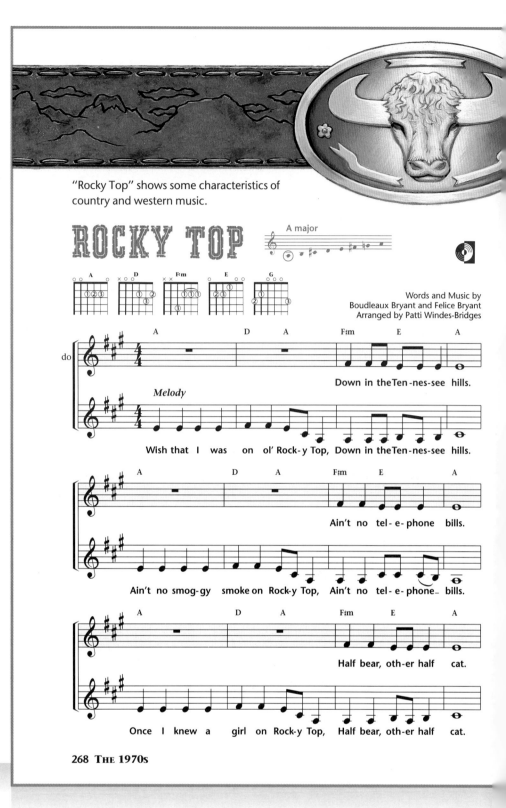

"Rocky Top" shows some characteristics of country and western music.

ROCKY TOP

A major

Words and Music by
Boudleaux Bryant and Felice Bryant
Arranged by Patti Windes-Bridges

Down in the Ten-nes-see hills.

Melody

Wish that I was on ol' Rock-y Top, Down in the Ten-nes-see hills.

Ain't no tel-e-phone bills.

Ain't no smog-gy smoke on Rock-y Top, Ain't no tel-e-phone bills.

Half bear, oth-er half cat.

Once I knew a girl on Rock-y Top, Half bear, oth-er half cat.

268 THE 1970s

MEETING **INDIVIDUAL** NEEDS

MULTICULTURAL PERSPECTIVES: *Country Music*

Country music evolved from the folk music brought to the United States by early settlers from the British Isles. The pioneers put new words to the old melodies to fit their new experiences, singing about lumberjacks, buffalo hunters, outlaws, and cowboys. They also wrote new songs. The songs were passed on orally, often accompanied by the fiddle. Banjos were introduced to the European settlers by enslaved Africans, and became popular by the late 1800s. The guitar joined the fiddle and banjo as the third instrument of the standard country string band after Sears began

selling it through its catalogue in 1894. In the 1920s, the country-music recording industry was born.

MULTICULTURAL PERSPECTIVES: *Bluegrass*

"Rocky Top" was recorded by the Osborne Brothers in 1971 as part of the bluegrass revival at that time. Bluegrass is a type of country music with a down-home, acoustic sound played on stringed instruments such as mandolin, banjo, fiddle, and Dobro (an acoustic slide guitar). It began in the 1940s with Bill Monroe and his Blue Grass Boys. In the 1970s, it was rediscovered by people who disliked the "commercialized" Nashville sound. Many bluegrass

"In this lesson, you heard several songs from the 1970s." Have students:

▶ • Discuss "Fly Like an Eagle," "1970s Medley," and "Rocky Top," looking for similarities and differences.

▶ • Give suggestions as to why one decade produced so many types of music. (different influences, musicians, and cultural exchanges due to more available, cheaper means of transportation as well as media contact)

• Split into three groups to perform "Rocky Top," one group singing the melody, one group singing the countermelody, and one group playing the accompaniment.

LESSON SUMMARY

Informal Assessment In this lesson, students:

OBJECTIVE 1 Read and performed chords on pitched instruments.

MORE MUSIC: Reinforcement
Playing the Guitar, page 426

performers only work at music part-time, often playing at one of the many bluegrass festivals held each year.

CRITICAL THINKING: *Changing Styles*

Have students discuss the musical style of "Rocky Top," including instrumentation, tempo, and other elements that contribute to its country-and-western feel. Then have them work in small groups to consider how they could change it to make it sound more like a rock song from the 1970s. Have them write down their style choices. If possible, have them perform the song in the new style. Which version do they prefer?

MOVEMENT: *The Ten Step*

Formation: double circle—couples side by side, holding hands

Part 1: (Part 1 is a ten-beat step.) **1.** Touch L heel out in front; **2.** Step L foot next to R foot; **3.** Touch R toe back; **4.** Stomp R foot; **5.** Touch R heel out in front; **6.** Bend R knee, crossing R foot over L foot; **7.** Touch R heel out in front; **8.** Step R foot next to L foot; **9.** Touch L heel out in front; **10.** Bend L knee, crossing L foot over R foot.

Part 2: Shuffle forward: L R L; R L R. (Counts are 1 & 2.) Repeat sequence once for a total of four shuffles.

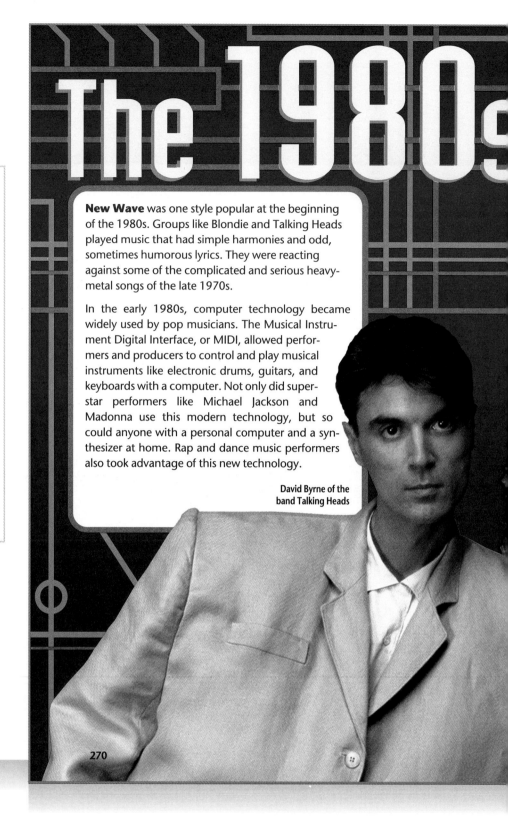

The 1980s

New Wave was one style popular at the beginning of the 1980s. Groups like Blondie and Talking Heads played music that had simple harmonies and odd, sometimes humorous lyrics. They were reacting against some of the complicated and serious heavy-metal songs of the late 1970s.

In the early 1980s, computer technology became widely used by pop musicians. The Musical Instrument Digital Interface, or MIDI, allowed performers and producers to control and play musical instruments like electronic drums, guitars, and keyboards with a computer. Not only did superstar performers like Michael Jackson and Madonna use this modern technology, but so could anyone with a personal computer and a synthesizer at home. Rap and dance music performers also took advantage of this new technology.

David Byrne of the band Talking Heads

270

LESSON PLANNER

FOCUS Style/Harmony

OBJECTIVE
OBJECTIVE 1 Read and perform chords on a pitched instrument

MATERIALS
Recordings
Recorded Lesson: A Sound
  Capsule: The 1980s   CD6:19
The Greatest Love of All   CD7:1
The Greatest Love of All
  (performance mix)   CD7:2
Listening: 1980s Medley   CD7:3

Instruments
guitar, keyboard

Resources
Resource Master 6 • 9 (practice)
Signing Master S • 6 • 5: "The Greatest
  Love of All"

▶ = **BASIC PROGRAM**

MEETING **INDIVIDUAL** NEEDS

SOCIAL STUDIES CONNECTION: *Time Line*

Continue the time line begun in Lesson 1, page 238, *Social Studies Connection.* Ask students to locate events and people in "A Sound Capsule: The 1980s" on the time line, as well as other events from this time period. (1980—birth of Solidarity Union in Poland; 1980—civil war begins in Nicaragua; 1981—Sandra Day O'Connor becomes 1st woman on the Supreme Court; 1989—Berlin Wall is knocked down; 1989–1991—Communist governments collapse in the Soviet Union and Eastern Europe)

BUILDING SELF-ESTEEM: *"The Greatest Love of All"*

Have students discuss how the lyricist of "The Greatest Love of All" feels about herself. Who is her hero/heroine? Where did she find the greatest love of all? Ask them to write an essay entitled "Why I'm a Hero/Heroine" or "Why I Like Myself."

The Greatest Love of All

Words by Linda Creed
Music by Michael Masser

I believe that children are our future;
teach them well and let them lead the way.
Show them all the beauty they possess inside.
Give them a sense of pride, to make it easier;
let the children's laughter remind us how we used
    to be.

Ev'rybody's searching for a hero;
people need someone to look up to.
Never found anyone who fulfilled my need.
A lonely place to be, and so I learned to depend
    on me.

I decided long ago never to walk in anyone's
    shadow.
If I fail, if I succeed, at least I lived as I believe.
No matter what they take from me, they can't take
    away my dignity.

Because the greatest love of all is happening
    to me.
I found the greatest love of all inside of me.
The greatest love of all is easy to achieve.
Learning to love yourself is the greatest love of all.
And if by chance that special place that you've
    been dreaming of
leads you to a lonely place, find your strength
    in love.

Unit 6 *From Rag to Rap* **271**

1 GET SET

"Name a major event that happened to you in the 1980s." Have students:

▶ • Fill in a time line on the board with major events from the 1980s, including events of personal importance such as birth dates.

"Today you're going to learn more about music and events from the 1980s." (Keep the time line on the board for students to add to at the end of class.)

2 DEVELOP

1. Introduce music and events from the 1980s. Have students:

Recorded Lesson CD6:19

▶ • Listen to "A Sound Capsule: The 1980s" to learn about events and music from the 1980s.

▶ • Read page 270, then discuss the music of the 1980s, including how computer technology is being used by musicians. (Musicians use computer software such as sequencers to record or create music, edit it, and control synthesizers in playing it back through MIDI. Computers with MIDI can also synchronize lights and other performance elements with the music. Optional: Have students fill in the time line on **Resource Master 6 • 9** with key events from the 1980s.)

2. Introduce "The Greatest Love of All" CD7:1. **Sing music from the 1980s.** Have students:

▶ • Listen to the recording and follow the words to the song.

▶ • Discuss what the song means.

▶ • Sing "The Greatest Love of All."

LANGUAGE ARTS CONNECTION: *Writing an Essay*

Discuss how "The Greatest Love of All" stresses personal responsibility for success or failure, in living in accordance to one's beliefs. Then have students write essays about a difficult decision they made or a time they stood up for something in which they believed.

SIGNING: *"The Greatest Love of All"*

Signing Master S • 6 • 5 has sign language for this song.

ENRICHMENT: *Interpretation*

Have groups of students decide on their own interpretations for "The Greatest Love of All," then practice and sing them for the rest of the class.

UNIT SIX
LESSON 8

continued from previous page

3. Introduce the A minor chord on guitar and review easy C, D, easy G, A, A7, and Em chords. Have students:

• Look at the fingering for the A minor chord, then finger the chord on the guitar.

• Review the easy C, D, easy G, A, A7, and Em chords on the guitar. (See pages 252, 256, 260, and 266.)

• Practice changing from the A minor chord to the easy G chord, noting how the finger positions change.

3 APPLY

Introduce "1980s Medley" CD7:3. Experience music from the 1980s and play chords on a pitched instrument. Have students:

▶ • Listen to "1980s Medley" and discuss the three songs. ("Born in the U.S.A." by Bruce Springsteen, "Running with the Night" by Lionel Ritchie, "Head Over Heels" by Curt Smith and Roland Orzabal of the group Tears for Fears, "Shake It Up" by Ric Ocasek of The Cars)

• Read and speak the names of the chords used in the "1980s Medley" playalong.

• Transfer the chords to guitar or keyboard by fingering each chord as they speak it.

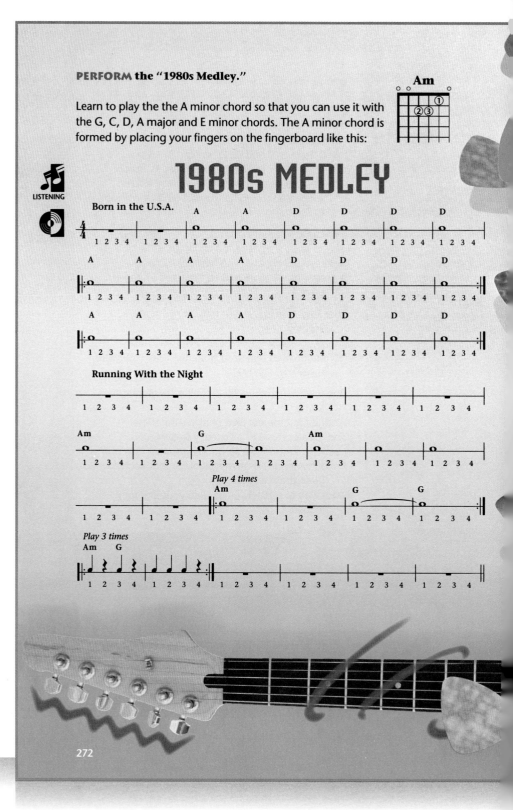

PERFORM the "1980s Medley."

Learn to play the the A minor chord so that you can use it with the G, C, D, A major and E minor chords. The A minor chord is formed by placing your fingers on the fingerboard like this:

272

MEETING **INDIVIDUAL** NEEDS

ALTERNATE TEACHING STRATEGY

OBJECTIVE 1 Play a "Chord Quiz" game. Select a group of five students to be the contestants. Then secretly assign the six chords to six different groups of players. As you point to each group in turn, they play their assigned chord four times. (Start and end the chord progression with a specific chord known to the contestants.) The contestants decide, as a group, what chords they heard and write them down in order. After they share their answers with the class, choose another contestant group and replay.

SCIENCE CONNECTION: *Advances in Technology*

Increase awareness of the wide reach of technology by having students make a list of every machine they have used since the day began. The list may include a clock, furnace, air conditioner, faucet, microwave, toaster, refrigerator, car, bicycle, bus, radio, computer, telephone, television, VCR, and so on. Discuss how we often take for granted innovations that were greeted with amazement just a generation or two ago. Ask students to speculate what inventions will be taken for granted by their children.

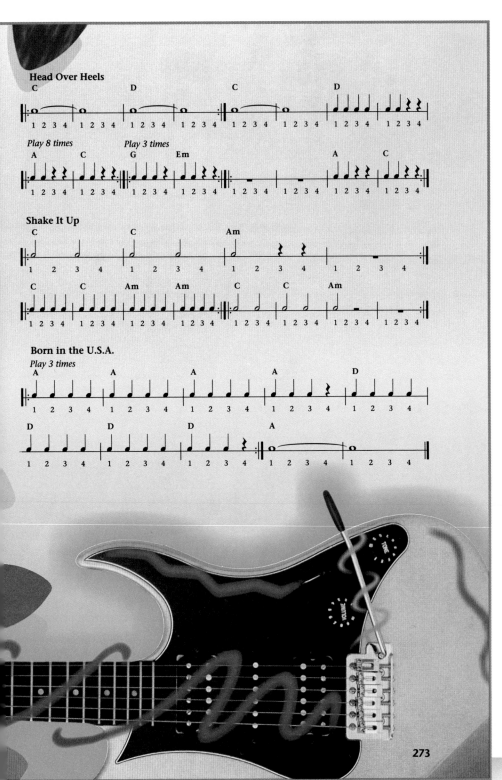

Head Over Heels

Shake It Up

Born in the U.S.A.

273

- Perform the chords with the recording of "Born in the U.S.A" from the "1980s Medley."

OBJECTIVE 1 Informal Assessment
- Perform some or all of the chords with the recording of "1980s Medley."

4 CLOSE

"What would you like to add to the 1980s time line?" Have students:

▶ • Discuss events, inventions, music, and so on as they add them to the time line begun in the *Get Set*.

- Take turns demonstrating the chords they have studied in this unit so far—Am, Em, C, D, G, A, and A7. (See pages 252, 256, 260, and 266.)

LESSON SUMMARY

Informal Assessment In this lesson, students:

OBJECTIVE 1 Read and performed chords on a pitched instrument.

MORE MUSIC: Reinforcement
"Brilliant Corners," page 134 (1980s jazz style)
"The Wind Beneath My Wings," page 385 (1980s popular style)

RELATED ARTS | MOVEMENT | THEATER | VISUAL ARTS |

LESSON PLANNER

FOCUS Style

OBJECTIVE
OBJECTIVE 1 Read and perform chords on guitar

MATERIALS
Recordings
Recorded Lesson: A Sound
 Capsule: The 1990s   CD7:4
From a Distance   CD7:5
Listening: Uirapurú do
 Amazonas by G. Thiago de Mello CD7:6
Listening: Two-Chord Rock by
 J. Roberts   CD7:7
Recorded Lesson: Interview
 with Malcolm-Jamal Warner   CD7:8
Listening: Jump by J. Dupri as
 performed by Kris Kross   CD7:9
Instruments
recorder, guitar, and other pitched instruments

Resources
Resource Master 6 • 10 (practice)
Resource Master 6 • 11 (practice)
Resource Master 6 • 12 (practice)
Resource Master 6 • 13 (practice)
Playing the Guitar G • 11 (G and D
 chords)
Signing Master S • 6 • 6 (From a
 Distance)

VOCABULARY
rap

▶ = BASIC PROGRAM

THE 1990s

•Satellites and other new devices help the people of the 1990s to communicate faster than ever before. In the 1990s, music reflects this ability to be in touch with people everywhere. Many opportunities exist to learn musical styles from all over the world. The next time you go to your local music store, look over the variety of music from other countries.

Rap music, sometimes called *hip-hop,* gained in popularity in the 1990s. It began in the 1970s with young African Americans who would improvise spoken rhymes to the beat of their favorite records. Rap concerts usually involve rappers performing live to a pre-recorded musical background. The music ranges from a simple drum pattern to an entire rock band.

Rap artist Salt (Cheryl James) of the group Salt-n-Pepa

274

MEETING **INDIVIDUAL** NEEDS

SOCIAL STUDIES CONNECTION: *Time Line*

Continue the time line begun in Lesson 1, page 238, *Social Studies Connection.* Ask students to locate events and people in "A Sound Capsule: The 1990s" on the time line, as well as other events. (1990—Iraq invades Kuwait; 1991—United States and other nations invade Iraq, Iraqi army leaves Kuwait; 1993—Clinton becomes president)

SIGNING: *"From a Distance"*

Signing Master S • 6 • 6 has sign language for this song.

SPECIAL LEARNERS: *Advances in the 1990s*

This is an important decade for those people with disabilities; the Americans with Disabilities Act (ADA) was signed into law in 1990. ADA gives civil-rights protection to individuals with disabilities in private-sector employment, public services, public accommodations, transportation, and telecommunications. Individuals with disabilities will be able to get jobs for which they are qualified and will have access to public transportation, hotels, restaurants, schools, and parks. Telecommunication devices for the deaf (TDD) will allow those people to use telephones from their own homes.

At the beginning of the 1990s many people felt a renewed commitment to world peace and understanding. This song expresses that view.

From a Distance

Words and Music by Julie Gold

From a distance, the world looks blue and green,
and the snow-capped mountains white.
From a distance, the ocean meets the stream,
and the eagle takes to flight.
From a distance there is harmony, and it echoes through the land.
It's the voice of hope, it's the voice of peace. It's the voice of everyone.

From a distance, we all have enough,
And no one is in need.
There are no guns, no bombs, and no disease,
No hungry mouths to feed.
From a distance, we are instruments
Marching in a common band;
Playing songs of hope, playing songs of peace,
They're the songs of everyone.
God is watching us, God is watching us,
God is watching us, from a distance.

From a distance, you look like my friend
Even though we are at war.
From a distance I just cannot comprehend
What all this fighting is for.
From a distance there is harmony and it echoes through the land.
It's the hope of hopes, it's the love of loves. It's the heart of everyone.
God is watching us...

Unit 6 *From Rag to Rap*

1 GET SET

"How many types of music can you name?" Have students:

▶ • List types of music for you to write at the top of columns on the board. (classical, rap, blues, country, rock, world beat, folk)

▶ • Write the name of their favorite song in the appropriate column.

"Music today is as diverse as the people in this class. In this lesson, you're going to hear music from the Nineties and learn some of the reasons why Americans listen to so many different kinds of music."

2 DEVELOP

1. Introduce music and events from the 1990s. Have students:

Recorded Lesson CD7:4

▶ • Listen to "A Sound Capsule: The 1990s" to learn about events and music from the 1990s.

▶ • Read page 274, then discuss major events in the 1990s, including those pictured. (Optional: Have students locate countries from the Recorded Lesson on the world map found on **Resource Master 6 • 10.**)

▶ • Try to explain why some of the changes have occurred in popular music and why the music is so diverse. (the interaction that takes place among musicians from around the world via the media and concerts)

2. Introduce "From a Distance" CD7:5. **Sing music from the 1990s.** Have students:

▶ • Listen to the recording and follow the words, listening for repetition of any phrases and statements. (*from a distance, God is watching us*)

• Discuss the repetitions and how they give unity to the song, and how the different verses and contrasting melodies give variety to it.

▶ • Sing "From a Distance."

After discussing ADA, ask students to give examples of the law's effect. (Possible answers: lowered curbs, braille elevator buttons, spaces for wheelchairs in all sections of theaters, baseball parks, and other public facilities, TDD access of television programs)

ENRICHMENT: *Rhythm Pattern*

Have students practice clapping on Beats 2 and 4 of a four-beat measure. Then sing "From a Distance," clapping this pattern each time the section beginning *God is watching us* occurs.

CRITICAL THINKING: *Lyricist's Intent*

Discuss possible interpretations of the words of "From a Distance." One possibility is that from an airplane or spacecraft, the troubles of the world can seem to take on a different perspective. It seems to be the belief of the lyricist that God is watching over us from a similar far-off perspective. The inference might be that having a comprehensive view of the world will promote harmony among people.

UNIT SIX
LESSON 9

continued from previous page

3. Introduce "Uirapurú do Amazonas"
CD7:6. Play along on a pitched instrument.
Have students:

▶ • Read about "Uirapurú do Amazonas"
(i **ɾɑ** pu **ɾu** du ɑ mɑ **zo** nɑs) by Gaudencio Thiago de Mello (gau **den** si o ti **ɑ** go
də **mɛl** lo).

• Listen to the recording, patting the rhythm of
the ostinato accompaniment (quarter/quarter/
half) on page 276 as they try to identify the
instruments.

• Practice the ostinato accompaniment on page
276, then play it with the recording.

▶ • Discuss the *Think It Through* question. (Students might debate the question, with one side
trying to convince the other that the rain forest
must be saved.)

4. Introduce "Two-Chord Rock" CD7:7. **Play**
the recorder. Have students:

▶ • Listen for the synthesizers in "Two-Chord
Rock." (All the instruments, except two electric guitars, are synthesizers—including the
drums, which are sampled.)

• Clap Measures 2 and 19 (third measure of
Line 3) of the recorder part to become familiar
with the syncopated patterns.

• Perform the recorder playalong with "Two-
Chord Rock."

LISTENING Uirapurú Do Amazonas *(excerpt)*
by Gaudencio Thiago de Mello

*In the 1990s many composers and performers combine musical
elements of different world cultures. In this recording you will
hear musical styles from Brazil and the United States. The Brazilian composer Gaudencio Thiago de Mello, who has roots in the
Maue Indian nation of the Amazon, worked together with American saxophonist and composer Paul Winter to create this composition. Thiago de Mello sings in Portuguese, in his native Indian
dialect, and imitates sounds heard in nature.*

*The recording begins with the intricate song of the uirapurú
bird, which is native to the Amazon rain forest of Brazil. Then
Thiago de Mello is heard, singing a song he composed. Paul Winter plays a solo between two of the verses. See if you can name
the instruments you hear in this recording.* guitar, rainstick shaker,
drum, whistles, soprano saxophone

PERFORM this repeated pattern with the song on a
pitched instrument.

THINK IT THROUGH
How can this recording help you convince
someone that the Amazon rain forest must
be saved?

276 THE 1990s

MEETING **INDIVIDUAL** NEEDS

ALTERNATE TEACHING STRATEGY

OBJECTIVE 1 Have the students clap the rhythm of the two
strum patterns until they feel secure with them. Then have
them practice playing the chord pattern by strumming once
per measure. Finally, have them put the strum patterns together with the chords to perform "Two-Chord Rock." Another strategy is to use D major tuning to simplify the
fingering.

PLAYING INSTRUMENTS: *Rain Sticks*

Have students make their own rain sticks. Thoroughly seal
one end of a long cardboard tube (such as that for gift
wrap). Push dowel rods, pencils, or tongue-depressors
through the sides of the tube at about two-inch intervals.
Put tape around each stick to seal each of the openings
completely. Pour about one cup of corn, rice, sand, pebbles,
or other filler into the tube and seal the open end. Cover the
tube with decorated paper. Create the rain sound by slowly
tilting the rain stick, causing the filler material inside to
gently tap against the rods as it falls to the lower end.

Two-Chord Rock by *James Roberts*

Listen for the sound of the latest synthesizers in "Two-Chord Rock."

PERFORM this on recorder with "Two-Chord Rock."

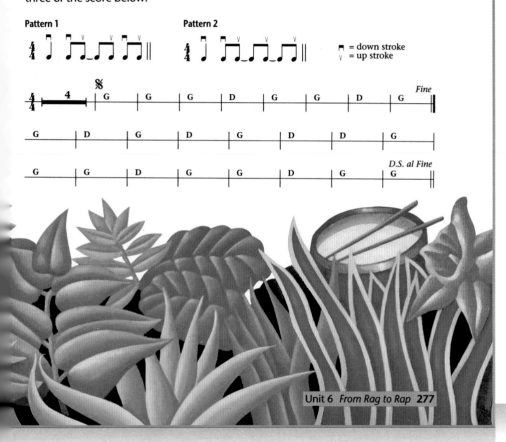

ADD this guitar part.

Strum Pattern 1 for line one and Pattern 2 for lines two and three of the score below.

Pattern 1   Pattern 2

■ = down stroke
V = up stroke

3 APPLY

1. Play guitar chords to accompany "Two-Chord Rock." Have students:

• Review fingerings for the C, D, G, A, Am, A7, and the Em chords on guitar. (See pages 252, 256, 260, 266, and 272.)

• Practice each chord, using the two strum patterns on page 277.

• Read and speak the names of the chords used in the "Two-Chord Rock" playalong, fingering each chord on guitar as they speak it.

OBJECTIVE 1 Informal Assessment
• Perform the chords with "Two-Chord Rock." (Strum Pattern 1 for Line 1 and Pattern 2 for Lines 2–3 of the playalong.)

Continue by tilting the higher end downward. The effect simulates the sound of restful, falling rain. For a performance, students can play their own taped or improvised bird-sounds with an improvised instrumental accompaniment, including the handmade rain sticks.

SCIENCE CONNECTION: *Saving the Rain Forest*
Discuss why the South American rain forests are important. (They are home to millions of kinds of plants and animals. Rain-forest plants give us medicines, pineapples, rubber, chocolate, cinnamon, and nuts. The forests act as "lungs" for the world, cleaning pollutants from the air and giving off tons of oxygen.) They are disappearing, as they are cut down to make lumber and to clear land for ranches.

Challenge students to come up with both local and global solutions. For instance, they can plant seedlings on school property (if allowed). They may be interested in joining the thousands of young people who have raised money to buy acres of rain forest through the Adopt-an-Acre program of The Earth's Birthday Project. Each acre costs about $35. For a teacher's guide write: The Nature Conservancy International Program/1815 North Lynn Street/Arlington, VA 22209–9713.

continued from previous page

2. Introduce "Jump" CD7:9. **Listen to rap music.** Have students:

▶ • Read page 278.

Recorded Lesson CD7:8
▶ • Listen to "Interview with Malcolm-Jamal Warner" as he describes his involvement with rap music.

▶ • Read page 279 and listen to "Jump."

▶ • Discuss rap music, describing how it is different from most other types of popular music in the 1990s. (Rap emphasizes words and rhythm over melody.)

RAP MUSIC IN THE 1990S

MEET
MALCOLM-JAMAL WARNER

Many people know Malcolm-Jamal Warner (b. 1967) as the actor who played Theo in television's "The Cosby Show." In addition to acting, Warner now directs and produces films and videos. He first heard rap music as a child, and it still plays an important role in his musical life. Warner even produces rap albums.

LISTEN as Malcolm-Jamal Warner describes his musical experiences and his involvement with rap music.

278 THE 1990s

MEETING **INDIVIDUAL** NEEDS

CAREERS: *Record Producer*

The interview with Malcolm-Jamal Warner introduces students to the career of record producer. A record producer helps an artist select the songs to be recorded. The producer often chooses the recording engineer and arranger, and hires background musicians. At the recording session, the producer supervises the music's sound, adding personal touches such as a special blend of instruments or vocal harmony. The producer supervises how the recording is "mixed," and then helps choose the singles from the album.

MOVEMENT: *"Jump"*

Have students discuss any rap dancing they may have seen, then work in pairs to create their own dance steps to "Jump." They should work in an energetic, hip-hop style. Movements should be *marcato*—sharp and well-defined, with quick head-and-arm movements. A common step is to slide feet out, slide feet in with right foot in front, then slide feet out, slide feet in with left foot in front. Another step is to slide feet out, slide feet in and bring right knee up, then slide feet out, slide feet in and bring left knee up.

🎵 **LISTENING** **Jump** *(excerpt) by Jermaine Dupri*
💿 *Performed by Kris Kross*

The rap group Kris Kross gets its name from members Chris Smith and Chris Kelly. They are known for wearing their clothes backwards and baggy as well as for their music. Their manager Jermaine Dupri writes the songs for Kris Kross to perform. When their hugely successful 1992 album **Totally Krossed Out** *appeared, Smith and Kelly were 13 years old. Listen for their rap nicknames, "Daddy Mack" and "Mack Daddy," in "Jump," a No. 1 hit.*

Kris Kross

4 CLOSE

"In this lesson, you sang a song about peace and hope, played a pattern with a Brazilian song, played the recorder and guitar with a rock song, and heard a rap song. How would you describe the music of the 1990s?" (Possible answers: varied, eclectic, many cultures influencing each other) Have students:

• Perform the recorder and/or guitar playalong with "Two-Chord Rock."

LESSON SUMMARY

Informal Assessment In this lesson, students:

OBJECTIVE 1 Read and performed chords on guitar with "Two-Chord Rock."

MORE MUSIC: Reinforcement

Performance Technology, page 280 (1990s technology)
"Grand Entry," page 331 (summer)
"Amoeba," pages 413K-L (technology, music of the 1990s)

After each pair has created several steps, encourage two pairs to create a routine together. They should aim for precise movement in unison.

ENRICHMENT: *Music Video*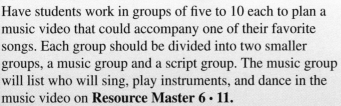

Have students work in groups of five to 10 each to plan a music video that could accompany one of their favorite songs. Each group should be divided into two smaller groups, a music group and a script group. The music group will list who will sing, play instruments, and dance in the music video on **Resource Master 6 • 11.**

The script group will write the sequence of scenes that go along with the music. Pass out **Resource Masters 6 • 12** and **6 • 13** to assist the script group in its planning. If a video camera is available, students can use their plans to shoot the video. Have a representative of the script group act as a director to give cues (using **Resource Master 6 • 13,** "Music Video Shooting Sheet") to the camera operator.

LANGUAGE ARTS CONNECTION: *From Rag to Rap*

Have students write an essay using the information and songs in this unit to trace popular music from the 1900s to today.

Performance

LESSONLINKS

Performers at a Rock Concert *(10 min)*

OBJECTIVE Learn about performers at a rock concert

Reinforcement 1990s technology, *page 279*

Amplified Sound *(10 min)*

OBJECTIVE Learn how sound can be electronically amplified

Reinforcement 1990s technology, *page 279*

Special Effects *(10 min)*

OBJECTIVE Learn how special effects can change the atmosphere of the stage

MATERIALS
Other flashlights, cellophane, and/or other materials to create visual special effects

Reinforcement 1990s technology, *page 279*

The Rolling Stones

280

MEETING **INDIVIDUAL** NEEDS

BACKGROUND: *The History of Rock Music*

Rock has origins in African American rhythm and blues. One of the first international rock hits was "Rock Around the Clock," performed by Bill Haley and the Comets (see page 15). By the mid-1960s, folk rock became popular with singers such as Bob Dylan. His lyrics were inspired by folk songs, but the accompaniment was often electric guitar. Around the same time, the Beatles began experimenting with rock music, adding more complex chord progressions, non-Western musical sounds, and imaginative, socially aware lyrics. The 1970s and 1980s were eclectic, combining rock, blues, and classical music with increased use of technology. (See also Lessons 5–9, pages 254–279.)

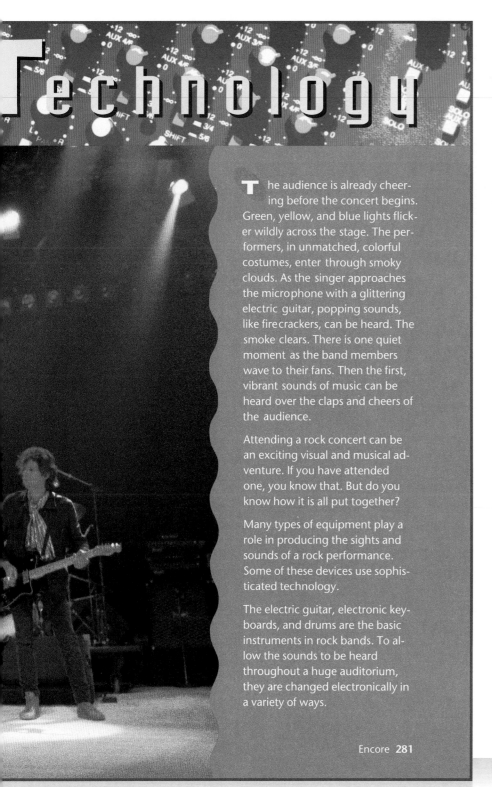

Technology

T he audience is already cheering before the concert begins. Green, yellow, and blue lights flicker wildly across the stage. The performers, in unmatched, colorful costumes, enter through smoky clouds. As the singer approaches the microphone with a glittering electric guitar, popping sounds, like firecrackers, can be heard. The smoke clears. There is one quiet moment as the band members wave to their fans. Then the first, vibrant sounds of music can be heard over the claps and cheers of the audience.

Attending a rock concert can be an exciting visual and musical adventure. If you have attended one, you know that. But do you know how it is all put together?

Many types of equipment play a role in producing the sights and sounds of a rock performance. Some of these devices use sophisticated technology.

The electric guitar, electronic keyboards, and drums are the basic instruments in rock bands. To allow the sounds to be heard throughout a huge auditorium, they are changed electronically in a variety of ways.

Encore **281**

Performers at a Rock Concert

Learn about the performers at a rock concert. Have students:

• Read pages 280–281 and name different kinds of musicians in the photograph. (singer, keyboard player, guitarist, drummer)

• Tell about their experiences attending a rock concert or watching one on television.

• Tell how sounds are heard at large concerts. (sounds are changed electronically)

SCIENCE CONNECTION: *How Ears Hear*

Have students research the path of sound in the human ear. Students might make a diagram showing how sound waves enter the ear and are then conducted by the small bones (hammer, anvil, stirrup) to the cochlea, or inner ear, then to the brain via auditory nerve signals.

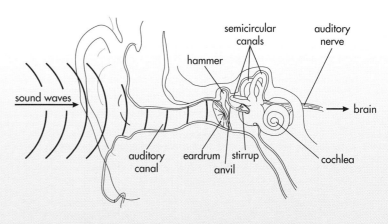

ENCORE

continued from previous page

Amplified Sound

Learn how sound can be electronically amplified. Have students:

• Read pages 282–283 and tell about times they have used a microphone.

• Briefly discuss amplification. (Ask if anyone knows the name for the measure of a sound level—decibel.)

• Guess the decibel level for watching television (55 decibels), cars on a busy street (85 decibels), and a rock concert (100–110 decibels).

• Understand that the sounds in concerts are amplified, using special equipment. (See *Technology in Music* on the bottom of page 283.)

The band U2 in concert

MEETING **INDIVIDUAL** NEEDS

SCIENCE CONNECTION: *Hearing Damage*

Discuss with students that hearing can be damaged by many things, including exposure to loud noises over a long period. People who work in noisy places or who often listen to loud music may suffer a gradual hearing loss. Ask for ideas to avoid this sort of hearing damage. (Avoid loud noises as much as possible, wear ear protectors in noisy places, do not turn the volume on headsets up too high.) Point out that musicans in rock groups sometimes wear earplugs to avoid damaging their hearing.

CAREER: *Sound Engineer*

Sound engineers usually work in recording studios. For concerts, however, a sound engineer arrives ahead of the musicians—to unload, set up, and test the equipment. He or she takes care of the soundboard (mixer) and also works the board for a musical group on tour. During the show, the engineer controls the volume of the entire group and may also highlight different instruments or vocalists by adjusting the tone color or volume output. Engineers usually have training in electronics from a recording or broadcast school.

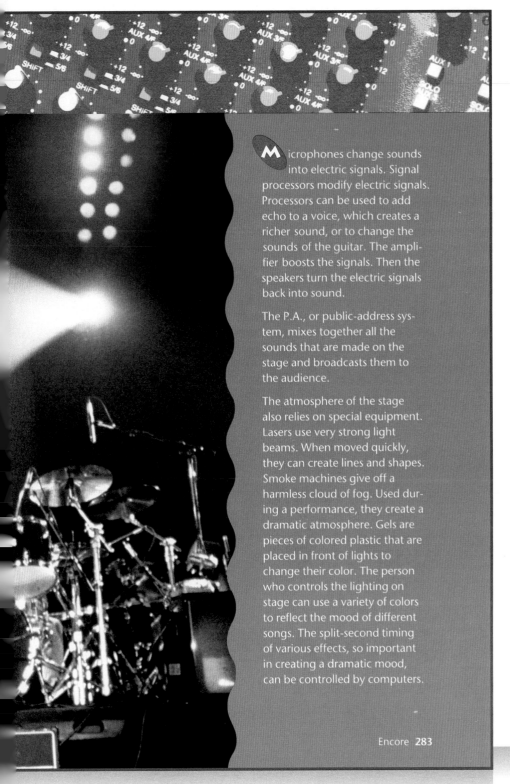

Microphones change sounds into electric signals. Signal processors modify electric signals. Processors can be used to add echo to a voice, which creates a richer sound, or to change the sounds of the guitar. The amplifier boosts the signals. Then the speakers turn the electric signals back into sound.

The P.A., or public-address system, mixes together all the sounds that are made on the stage and broadcasts them to the audience.

The atmosphere of the stage also relies on special equipment. Lasers use very strong light beams. When moved quickly, they can create lines and shapes. Smoke machines give off a harmless cloud of fog. Used during a performance, they create a dramatic atmosphere. Gels are pieces of colored plastic that are placed in front of lights to change their color. The person who controls the lighting on stage can use a variety of colors to reflect the mood of different songs. The split-second timing of various effects, so important in creating a dramatic mood, can be controlled by computers.

Encore 283

Special Effects

Learn how technology can be used to change the atmosphere on the stage and create a special effect. Have students:

• Name different effects a rock band might use. (light shows using lasers, smoke machines, colored gels on lights)

• Tell about different effects they have seen at a concert or on television.

• Discuss briefly how computers might control the effects. (They can be programmed to time the effects to match the music.)

• In small groups, create a visual effect that might be used in a rock concert. (Students can use flashlights, colored cellophane, and so on.)

TECHNOLOGY IN MUSIC: *Sound System*

A complex system of electronic devices is used so that the audience can hear the music at a rock concert. The sounds of the instruments and vocalists are converted to electrical signals by microphones. The signals are carried through cables to amplifiers, which boost the signals. The signals pass through a mixer, which adjusts the sound and balances it for stereo between the public address system (PA) speakers. The mixer insures that no performer is too loud or too soft, and that the sound hits the listeners' ears from many directions. A crossover unit divides the signals, feeding them to speakers specially designed for low, middle, and high sounds. A second mixer feeds a private mix from backstage to monitors (speakers) at the musicians' feet, so they can hear their own performance.

CELEBRATIONS

CELEBRATIONS!

The *Celebrations* section provides music and lessons for patriotic, seasonal, and holiday celebrations from a wide variety of cultures. These materials are collected in a separate section for integration at the appropriate time, providing flexibility, depending on:
- calendar schedules, standard or year-round
- school guidelines about holiday observance
- special interests of students

INTEGRATED LESSONS FOR CONCEPT AND SKILL REINFORCEMENT

Reinforcement references in *Celebrations* lesson suggestions point out key concepts, skills, and themes for the selections, and provide page references to unit lessons that cover the same ideas.

FLEXIBLE LESSON PLANS

Celebrations lessons include separate activity suggestions for each selection, allowing you to use parts or all of a lesson as time permits. A *Putting It All Together* section at the end of many lessons provides a unifying and creative program idea.

CONTENTS

PLANNER

MULTICULTURAL PERSPECTIVES

Through exposure to diverse materials, students develop an awareness of how people from many cultures create and participate in music. This unit includes:

For a complete listing of songs by culture in this section and throughout the book, see the Classified Index.

		INTRODUCTION p. 284	PATRIOTIC DAYS p. 286	HALLOWEEN p. 296
	SELECTIONS	Haiku Calendar	America • Que bonita bandera • O Canada • The Star-Spangled Banner • Battle Hymn of the Republic (listening) • Battle Hymn of the Republic	The Ghost Ship • Old Abram Brown
CONCEPTS	**Expressive Qualities**		**Dynamics:** Sing *mp, mf, f, ff,* cresc. **Articulation:** Sing melody legato	**Dynamics:** Plan, then sing dynamics for song
	Tone Color	**Instrumental:** Play pitched and unpitched classroom instruments	**Instrumental:** • Play unpitched percussion • Recognize piano, band families • *Play chordal accompaniment on keyboard or autoharp* • *Play snare drum*	**Vocal:** Change tone color in song **Instrumental:** • Perform body percussion • *Play percussion*
	Duration		**Beat/Meter:** • Clap with beat • *Play ⅜ accompaniment* **Rhythm:** • Recognize syncopation • Clap rhythmic patterns • Find ♫ and ♩. ♪	**Meter:** Perform patterns in ⁴ **Rhythm:** • Clap rhythm patterns • Echo body percussion • Sing melody in augmentation
	Pitch	**Melody:** *Play pitches from low to high*	**Melody:** • Trace melodic contour • Recognize steps, skips, and leaps **Harmony:** • Sing melody with descant and countermelody **Tonality:** Recognize F major	**Melody:** • Sing with pitch letter names • Show melodic direction • List pitches in melody **Harmony:** Sing in 3 parts **Tonality:** • Find key change • Recognize tonal center, minor
	Design	**Form/Structure:** *Change Instruments to show form*	**Texture:** • Sing in two parts • Play song accompaniment **Form/Structure:** • Recognize similar phrases • Sing verse-refrain	**Texture:** • Recognize textures • Sing in 2- and 4-part canon • Sing melody in 2 parts **Form/Structure:** Change tone color to show sections
	Cultural Context	List songs of celebration	• Hear jazz style • *Learn about "America," "O Canada"* • *Learn about Puerto Rico* • *Lyricists: Francis Scott Key, Julia Ward Howe*	• *Learn about Halloween* • *Composers: Don Besig, Nancy Price, Benjamin Britten* • *Lyricist: Walter de la Mare*
SKILLS	**Creation and Performance**	**Playing:** Play pitched and unpitched classroom instruments **Creating:** • Create poem accompaniment • Create movement for poem	**Singing:** • Sing legato • Sing in 2 parts • Sing *mp, mf, f, ff,* cresc. **Playing:** • Play percussion • *Play chords* **Moving/Creating:** Create jazz-style movement	**Singing:** • Sing at different dynamic levels • Sing in 3 parts • Sing in 2- and 4-part canon **Playing:** *Play percussion accompaniment* **Creating:** • Create movement to show melody • Create mood for song
	Notation		**Reading:** • *Read pitch syllables from notation* • Read key signature • Find ♫ and ♩ ♪ in song **Writing:** Trace melodic contour	**Reading:** • Read rhythms from notation • Sing using pitch letter names **Writing:** Create movement to show melodic contour
	Perception and Analysis	**Analyzing:** Musically depict expression, repetition, and form of poem	**Listening:** • Identify piano and band • Analyze form and melody • Listen for jazz-style improvisation **Describing:** Describe phrases **Analyzing:** Compare verse and refrain	**Listening:** Recognize different textures **Analyzing:** • Analyze song and decide on appropriate mood • Compare choices with recording

SKILLS OVERVIEW

Italic = Meeting Individual Needs

WINTER p. 300	HANUKKAH p. 303	CHRISTMAS p. 304
Holiday Sing-Along (listening) • Winter Poem (poem)	Ocho Kandelikas	Si me dan pasteles • Silent Night • Carol from an Irish Cabin
	Tempo: Experience accelerando	
Instrumental: Accompany poem	**Instrumental:** • Recognize guitar	**Instrumental:** • Play percussion and melodic ostinatos • Recognize harp as stringed instrument • Perform instrumental sections for song
Meter: Recognize ¾ **Rhythm:** Use ♪ to accompany poem	**Rhythm:** Experience fermata and ties	**Meter:** Recognize ⁶⁄₈ **Rhythm:** • Recognize repeated rhythm pattern • Recognize syncopation • Play rhythmic ostinato • Find ♫♫ in song
Tonality: Recognize songs in minor	**Tonality:** Experience minor	**Melody:** Recognize repeated melodic pattern **Harmony:** Sing 3-part harmony **Tonality:** Recognize major
Form/Structure: Sing song medley	**Texture:** Recognize monophony and homophony **Form/Structure:** *Move to show verse-refrain*	**Texture:** • Sing and compare unison and 3-part textures • Add percussion ostinatos to song **Form/Structure:** Create introduction and coda
• *Learn about winter holidays* • *Poet: Nikki Giovanni*	• Hear guitar played in Spanish style • *Learn about Hanukkah* • *Composer: Flory Jagoda*	• *Learn about a Puerto Rican Christmas* • *Learn about Christmas* • *Composer: Dale Wood*
Playing: Play instruments to accompany poem	**Moving:** *Move to show verse-refrain*	**Singing:** Sing in 3 parts **Playing:** • Play percussion and melodic ostinatos • Play instrumental sections of song **Creating:** Create song sections
		Reading: • Find ♫♫ in song • Find repeated rhythm patterns in notation • *Play notated melodic ostinatos*
Describing: • Describe special winter customs • Discuss use of metaphors in poem	**Listening:** • Identify guitar • Identify monophony and homophony	**Listening:** • Identify homophony • Identify major and minor • Identify harp **Describing:** • Describe texture • Describe ♫♫ and ♫♫ **Analyzing:** Find repeated rhythms

CELEBRATIONS PLANNER

		KWANZAA p. 308	NEW YEAR p. 312	MARTIN LUTHER KING, JR., DAY p. 320
	SELECTIONS	Siyahamba	Bo Hai Huan Ten (listening) • Diwali Song • Haji Firuz • Bashana Haba'ah (listening) • Auld Lang Syne	I Have a Dream
CONCEPTS	**Expressive Qualities**	**Tempo:** Hear moderato		**Dynamics:** Hear and sing *mp*, *f*, *cresc.* **Tempo:** Hear and sing *ritardando* and *a tempo*
	Tone Color	**Instrumental:** Perform percussion accompaniments	**Instrumental:** • Recognize instrument families in Chinese orchestra • Play hand drum and cymbals • Recognize organ • Play pitched instruments	
	Duration	**Beat/Meter:** • Learn patterns in $\frac{4}{4}$ • *Move to beat* **Rhythm:** Learn rhythm patterns	**Beat/Meter:** • Change from $\frac{4}{4}$ to $\frac{6}{8}$ • Recognize and perform $\frac{6}{8}$ • Move to beat **Rhythm:** • Clap and tap rhythm patterns • *Create dance using ♩ and ♩ steps*	**Rhythm:** Clap ♩. ♪ patterns
	Pitch	**Harmony:** Sing 3-part harmony **Tonality:** Recognize major	**Melody:** Find melodic sequences **Harmony:** • Recognize vocal harmony part • Perform I, IV, V chord roots **Tonality:** Recognize F major	
	Design	**Texture:** • Discuss song textures • Add percussion accompaniment	**Form/Structure:** • Analyze phrase structure • Recognize and move to show form	
	Cultural Context	*Learn about Kwanzaa*	Learn about Chinese New Year, Chinese orchestra, Indian drumming, tabla, Diwali, Rosh Hashanah, Hogmanay • *Singer: Hooshang Bagheri* • *Poet: Robert Burns*	*Learn about Dr. Martin Luther King, Jr., and other civil rights leaders* • *Create program with civil rights songs*
SKILLS	**Creation and Performance**	**Playing:** Play percussion accompaniment **Moving:** Move in choir formation	**Playing:** • Play percussion • Play chord roots **Moving:** Perform dances **Creating:** • *Create Chinese instrument* • *Create melodic sequences* • *Create dance*	**Singing:** • Sing *mp*, *f*, *cresc.* • Sing *ritardando* and a tempo • Choose singing style to express lyrics **Playing:** Clap song rhythm patterns **Creating:** *Create program with civil rights songs*
	Notation		**Reading:** • Read notated rhythm pattern • Perform notated chord roots	**Reading:** Find rhythm patterns in notation
	Perception and Analysis	**Describing:** Describe texture changes **Analyzing:** Discuss textural effect of adding voice parts	**Listening:** • Identify Chinese instruments • Listen for recurring rhythm • Identify A B form • Identify vocal harmony part **Describing:** *Describe difference between $\frac{4}{4}$ and $\frac{6}{8}$* **Analyzing:** • Compare $\frac{6}{8}$ meter and Indian dadra • Analyze phrase structure	**Describing:** Identify information in song lyrics

SKILLS OVERVIEW

Italic = Meeting Individual Needs

SPRING p. 322	SPRING p. 326	SUMMER p. 330
Earth Day Every Day (Celebrate) Garden of the Earth (listening) Garden of the Earth	Música indígena (listening) • Jarabe tapatío (listening) • De colores	Grand Entry (listening)
Tempo/Dynamics/Articulation: Choose tempo, dynamics, articulation for song **Articulation:** Show phrases through breathing	**Tempo/Dynamics/Articulation:** Choose tempo, dynamics, articulation of song **Dynamics:** Hear dynamic change **Articulation:** Decide on legato or marcato movement	**Dynamics:** Recognize dynamics **Tempo:** Recognize tempo
Vocal: • Choose tone color for song • Recall adult voice categories • Hear tone color of Russian singers • Recognize unchanged voices and cambiata **Instrumental:** Describe tone color of soprano saxophone	**Instrumental:** *Play percussion accompaniment*	**Instrumental:** Hear Native American drumming **Vocal:** *Distinguish solo singer from unison chorus*
Meter: • Find meter signature changes • Recognize ¾ **Rhythm:** • Recognize syncopation • Recognize repeated rhythm pattern	**Meter:** • Recognize ²/₄ with change to ³/₄ • Recognize ⁶/₈	**Beat:** Hear accents
Melody: Recognize similar phrases		
Form/Structure: • Recognize and show phrases • Show song sections	**Form/Structure:** • Recognize A B form • Show A B A form with movement	**Form/Structure:** *Recognize form*
• *Learn about Earth Day* • *Composer/Performers: John Denver, Paul Winter*	• *Learn about Cinco de Mayo* • *Composer: Manuel María Ponce* • *Learn about "Jarabe tapatío" and "De colores"*	*Learn about Native American powow*
Singing: • Show phrases by breathing at ends • Sing chosen song interpretation **Creating:** Create song interpretation	**Singing:** Sing chosen song interpretation **Moving:** • Move in A B A form • Learn Mexican dance step **Creating:** • Create dance in A B A form • Create song interpretation • *Create words to fit song rhythm*	
Reading: Recognize repeated rhythm pattern in notation	**Reading:** Tell meter from signature	
Listening: Find syncopation • Discuss vocal tone color • Identify ¾ meter **Describing:** Describe tone color of soprano saxophone **Analyzing:** • Decide on song interpretation • Compare interpretations • Discuss reasons for meter changes in song • Analyze phrase structure	**Listening:** • Identify meter • Identify change in dynamics • Identify A B form **Analyzing:** • Decide on marcato or legato movement • Decide on interpretation choices for song • Compare interpretations	**Listening:** • Listen for accents • Recognize dymanic changes • Recognize tempo changes **Analyzing:** • Compare processionals • *Analyze form*

CELEBRATIONS
INTRODUCTION

LESSONLINKS

Haiku Calendar *(20 min)*

OBJECTIVE Discuss seasonal celebrations and add instrumental and/or "found" sounds to enhance the expressive qualities of a poem

Reinforcement accompanying a poem, *pages 145, 195*

Haiku Calendar

Leaf, brown in the wind
Taps like a bird on the pane
Presaging Autumn.

Leaf, sunk in the soil,
Spends winter dying; new life
Mounts from its leaching.

Leaf, loosing its sheath
Into the warm air unfurls
Green in Spring's morning.

Leaf drinks air and light,
Channels rain, feeds its parent
Great tree of Summer.

Leaf, brown in the wind
Taps like a bird on the pane
Presaging Autumn.

—*Pamela Gillilan*

284

MEETING **INDIVIDUAL** NEEDS

IMPROVISATION: *"Haiku Calendar"*

First have students decide on an instrument to be played each time the word *leaf* occurs in any verse. (for example, finger cymbals) Then form four groups of students and have each decide on sounds for their assigned verse. Perform the poem with all the groups accompanying. (The first and last verses would be identical, since the verses are exactly the same.) Following are some possibilities.

Verses 1 and 5: light taps on a wood block

Verse 2: low drum sounds

Verse 3: sounds from lowest to highest pitches on the piano (or, with three players—lowest to highest pitches on metallophones; first on the bass, then on the alto, and finally on the soprano)

Verse 4: freely improvised sounds on glockenspiel suggesting air, light, rain, and the *Great tree of summer*

Haiku Calendar

1. Read the poem and discuss seasonal celebrations. Have students:

• Take turns reading each verse of "Haiku Calendar."

• Discuss each verse. (Bring out that the cyclical nature of the poem is in keeping with that of the seasons and that each verse relates to a particular season by describing what happens to a leaf during that season.)

• Talk about the seasons of the year and list celebrations of various cultures that fall within each. Share their favorite celebration and give reasons why it is their favorite.

• Work in groups to make a list of songs that they enjoy singing for different celebrations.

2. Add instrumental and/or "found" sounds to enhance the expressive qualities of the poem. Have students:

• Plan instrument and/or "found" sounds to be played on or after important words and phrases in the poem to enhance its expressive quality. (See *Improvisation* on the bottom of page 284.)

• Perform the poem with their accompaniment. (Some classes may be interested in developing group choreography for the poem, each individual representing a leaf.)

LANGUAGE ARTS CONNECTION: *Haiku*

Haiku is an unrhymed verse-form from Japan that is often about nature. A haiku usually contains seventeen syllables in three lines: Line 1 has five syllables, Line 2 seven, and Line 3 five. In "Haiku Calendar," Gillilan has linked four haikus (one repeated) into a poem describing the seasons. Have students analyze the poem by counting the number of syllables in each line of one verse, by noting that each verse is a complete thought/poem, and so on. Then have them write their own haiku.

SCIENCE CONNECTION: *Leaves*

Talk about the life cycle of a leaf as described in "Haiku Calendar." In the fall, the leaf dies and the plant becomes dormant to survive the winter. The dead leaf nourishes other life as its nutrients are leached out into the soil. In the spring, a new leaf grows. The green chlorophyll in the leaf captures energy from the sun. Through photosynthesis, the plant uses sunlight to produce sugar, providing it with the food it needs to grow. Students might enjoy drawing the life cycle of a leaf to illustrate the poem. They might also research and diagram the process of photosynthesis.

CELEBRATIONS
PATRIOTIC DAYS

RELATED ARTS | MOVEMENT | THEATER | VISUAL ARTS

SELECTIONS

LESSONLINKS

America *(15 min)*

OBJECTIVE Sing a patriotic song in F major with legato articulation in two parts

Reinforcement
flat key signatures, *page 101*
legato articulation, *page 195*

MATERIALS
Recordings
America   CD7:10
America (performance mix)   CD7:11

Resources
Playing the Guitar G • 22 (patriotic)
Recorder Master R • 27 (pitches E F G A
   B♭ C' D')

Every nation has songs to express patriotism. Besides celebrating our country and its achievements, we sing and listen to music that honors other countries as well.

286

MEETING **INDIVIDUAL** NEEDS

BACKGROUND: *"America"*

The words for "America" were written in 1831 by Samuel Francis Smith for a church school in Boston as part of an Independence Day celebration. Smith used the melody to Britain's "God Save the Queen." The song continues to be popular because it evokes feelings of patriotism.

PLAYING INSTRUMENTS: *Keyboard*

Have students use a keyboard or an autoharp to play the chords written above the descant. Point out the ¾ meter, having students play chords on either the down beat or the quarter-note beat for each measure.

PITCH SYLLABLES: *"America"*

Have students sing the last four phrases of the melody (from *Land where my . . .*) using pitch syllables (*do re mi fa so la*) and hand signs.

The words to "America" were first used at a Fourth of July picnic in Boston. The music is the same as the British national anthem "God Save the Queen."

America

Music by Henry Carey
Words by Samuel F. Smith

My coun - try, land of

My coun - try 'tis of thee, Sweet land of

lib - er - ty, Of thee I sing. Land

lib - er - ty, Of thee I sing. Land where my

of the pil - grim's pride,

fa - thers died, Land of the Pil - grim's pride,

From ev' - ry moun - tain - side, let free - dom ring.

From ev' - ry____ moun - tain - side Let____ free - dom ring.

Celebrations *Patriotic Days* **287**

America CD7:10

Sing a patriotic song in F major with legato articulation in two parts. Have students:

• Read pages 286–287 and give their own definitions of patriotism. (a love for one's country)

• Read the words to "America" aloud and discuss their meaning. (The words tell of the many generations of Americans who have felt pride in their country.)

• Look at the key signature, tell how to find *do*, and tell what the key is. (one flat; count down from the last flat, which is *fa*; F major)

• Listen to the recording, following the melody in their books and tell whether the articulation is legato or marcato. (legato) Then sing the melody using legato articulation.

• Sing the descant. (When students are secure singing both parts separately, have them try singing them together.)

LANGUAGE ARTS CONNECTION: *Paraphrasing*

Discuss what it means to paraphrase, then have students paraphrase "America," rewriting the words in language commonly used today. The paraphrasing need not fit the melody.

PATRIOTIC DAYS

continued from previous page

LESSON**LINKS**

Qué bonita bandera (*30 min*)

OBJECTIVE Analyze and sing a patriotic Puerto Rican song with syncopation and play rhythmic accompaniment

Reinforcement syncopation, *page 157*

MATERIALS
Recordings
Qué bonita bandera (What a
  Beautiful Flag)   **CD7:12**
Recorded Lesson: Pronunciation
  for "Qué bonita bandera"   **CD7:13**

Instruments
claves, congas, güiros

Qué bonita bandera   CD7:12

1. Analyze the song. Have students:

• Listen to "Qué bonita bandera."

• Tell how many times the phrase *qué bonita bandera* is repeated. (three; six with the repeat)

• Describe what is musically the same and what is different about the phrase. (First and third phrases are the same; the second has the same melodic shape, but is higher.)

• Clap the rhythm of the phrase, *es la bandera Puertoriqueña*, then sing the melody of this phrase in the verse and refrain.

Puerto Rico is a special political unit. It is not officially a state, yet its people are citizens of the United States. This song about Puerto Rico shows the pride that Puerto Ricans feel for the flag of their land. Unlike many patriotic songs that sound like marches or hymns, this music reflects the syncopated rhythms of Puerto Rican music.

The flag of Puerto Rico was designed about 100 years ago.

Flaming red flowers adorn the tropical trees of Puerto Rico.

288 HANDS ACROSS THE WATER

MEETING **INDIVIDUAL** NEEDS

BACKGROUND: *Puerto Rico*

Puerto Rico is an island just east of Haiti and the Dominician Republic that helps form the boundary between the Atlantic Ocean and the Caribbean Sea. The name *Puerto Rico* means "rich port" in Spanish. After nearly 450 years under Spanish control, Puerto Rico became a commonwealth of the United States on July 25, 1952. As a commonwealth, its citizens are United States citizens and may freely enter and leave the United States. However, they may not vote in presidential elections while they are living in Puerto Rico.

At home, Puerto Ricans govern themselves; they have their own constitution, governor, and legislation.

EXTRA HELP: *Substitute Instruments*

The following items may be used as substitute percussion instruments. Claves—two dowels, or the edge of a wooden desk played with a pencil; güiro—edge of a spiral notebook played with pencil, or cheese grater played with butter knife; conga—upside-down trash can.

QUÉ BONITA BANDERA
What a Beautiful Flag

Puerto Rican Folk Song
English Version by MMH

C minor

Spanish: A-zul, blan-ca y co-lo-ra-da, y'en el
Pronunciation: α sul βlan ka i ko lo ɾa ða yen el
English: See our flag of blue, white and red. In the

me-dio tie-ne u-na es-tre-lla. Bo-ni-ta, se-
me ðio tye neu naes tre ya bo ni ta se
mid-dle, there is a star. A beau-ti-ful

ñor-es, es la ban-de-ra Puer-to-ri-que-ña.
nyor es es la βan de ɾa pwer to ɾi ke nya
ban-ner, my friend, the flag of Puer-to Ri-co.

Refrain
que-ña. Qué bo-ni-ta ban-de-ra,
ke nya ke βo ni ta βan de ɾa
Ri-co. *Qué bo-ni-ta ban-de-ra,*

Qué bo-ni-ta ban-de-ra, Qué bo-ni-ta ban-
ke βo ni ta βan de ɾa ke βo ni ta βan
Qué bo-ni-ta ban-de-ra, Qué bo-ni-ta ban-

de-ra es la ban-de-ra Puer-to-ri-que-ña.
de ɾa es la βan de ɾa pwer to ɾi ke nya
de-ra, the beau-ti-ful flag of Puer-to Ri-co.

Celebrations *Patriotic Days* **289**

---

2. Sing the song. Have students:

Recorded Lesson CD7:13

• Listen to "Pronunciation for 'Qué bonita bandera.'"

• Sing "Qué bonita bandera."

3. Identify syncopation. Have students:

• Recall the definition of syncopation. (See page 154.)

• Clap the beat as they listen to the song, noting where sounds are stressed between beats. (Measures 1, 3, 5, 7, 9, 11, 13, 15)

4. Play rhythmic accompaniments to the song. Have students:

• Clap the claves rhythm, using the words if needed.

ban - de - ra muy lin - da

• Pat the conga rhythm on their knees, alternating hands and patting the last beat on their thighs.

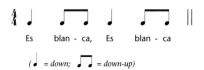

qué bo - ni - ta

(♩ = rim)

• Practice the güiro part with the right hand scraping up and down the left arm in this pattern—*down-down-up, down-down-up*.

Es blan - ca, Es blan - ca

(♩ = down; ♫ = down-up)

• Divide into four groups and try all three rhythms together, with one group singing.

• Transfer to claves, congas, and güiros. (See *Extra Help* on the bottom of page 288 for substitute instruments.)

• Select singers and percussionists and give a performance of the complete piece. (See *Playing Instruments* below.)

PLAYING INSTRUMENTS: *"Qué bonita bandera"*

Perform the song, using the following form:
—Instruments begin, entering every four measures in this order: claves, conga, güiro
—Sing song (instruments play throughout)
—Interlude: four measures of instruments alone
—Repeat song (instruments play throughout)

PRONUNCIATION: *"Qué bonita bandera"*

α f**a**ther	e ch**a**otic	i b**ee** o **o**bey
u m**oo**n	β b without lips touching	ð **th**e
ɾ flipped r	ī rolled r	

CELEBRATIONS

PATRIOTIC DAYS

continued from previous page

LESSON LINKS

O Canada *(15 min)*

OBJECTIVE Sing a two-part song accompanied by band, including piano

Reinforcement
instrument families in a band, *page 7*
recognize the sound of the piano,
page 97

MATERIALS
Recordings
O Canada   CD7:14
O Canada (performance mix)   CD7:15
Recorded Lesson: Pronunciation
for "O Canada"   CD7:16

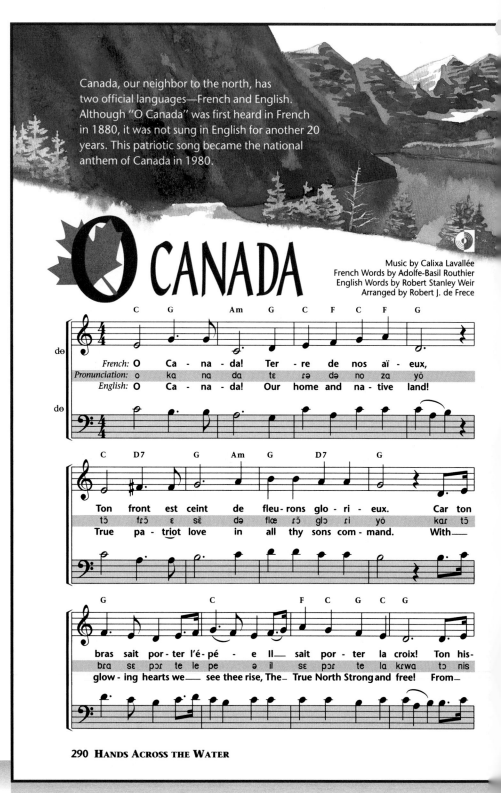

Canada, our neighbor to the north, has two official languages—French and English. Although "O Canada" was first heard in French in 1880, it was not sung in English for another 20 years. This patriotic song became the national anthem of Canada in 1980.

O CANADA

Music by Calixa Lavallée
French Words by Adolfe-Basil Routhier
English Words by Robert Stanley Weir
Arranged by Robert J. de Frece

290 HANDS ACROSS THE WATER

MEETING **INDIVIDUAL** NEEDS

BACKGROUND: *"O Canada"*

The song "O Canada" was adopted as the national anthem in 1980. The song itself was composed by Canadian musician Calixa Lavallée (kɑ lɪks ə lɑ va le) in 1880. A judge, Sir Adolphe Basile Routhier (ɑ **dɔlf** bɑ **zil** ɾu thi **e**), wrote the French lyrics the same year. It was first sung at a skating rink in Québec City and was very popular in French-speaking Canada before another judge, Robert Stanley Weir, composed the English lyrics in 1908. Outside Canada, the anthem is often heard at North American hockey games (when a Canadian team is playing).

PRONUNCIATION: *"O Canada"*

ɑ f<u>a</u>ther	e ch<u>a</u>otic	ɛ p<u>e</u>t	i b<u>ee</u>	o <u>o</u>bey
ɔ p<u>aw</u>	ə <u>a</u>go	ö lips form [o] and say [ɛ]
œ lips form [ɔ] and say [ɛ]		ɾ flipped r
ü lips form [u] and say [i]		ʒ plea<u>s</u>ure
~ nasalized vowel

O Canada CD7:14

1. Learn the song in unison. Have students:

- Listen to "O Canada."
- Discuss the prominent theme in the words of the anthem. (*We stand on guard for thee.*)
- Sing the melody on the syllable *lo.*

Recorded Lesson CD7:16
- Listen to "Pronunciation for 'O Canada.'"
- Sing the melody.

2. Listen for instruments accompanying the song. Have students:

- Tell which keyboard instrument is accompanying the recording. (piano)
- Tell what kind of group is heard in the recording and what instrument families are included. (band; brass—trumpets, trombone, tuba; percussion—piano, drums; string—electric bass) Tell which instrument family usually found in a band is missing. (woodwind)

3. Practice and sing in two parts. Have students:

- Practice the countermelody (for cambiatas).
- Sing the song. (When students are secure singing the melody and countermelody separately, have them sing both parts together.)

SOCIAL STUDIES CONNECTION: *Draw a Map*

Have students draw a map of Canada, labeling the different provinces and their capitals. You might want to divide the class into small teams, with each team researching one of the provinces. Then have each team summarize their findings.

CELEBRATIONS

PATRIOTIC DAYS

continued from previous page

LESSONLINKS

The Star Spangled Banner *(30 min)*

OBJECTIVE Identify similar phrases and show melodic contour

Reinforcement melodic contour, *page 21*

MATERIALS
Recording The Star-Spangled Banner   **CD7:17**

During the War of 1812, Francis Scott Key observed a British attack in Baltimore Harbor. When he saw that the Americans had successfully defended Fort McHenry, he was moved to write a poem. He later set the poem to music, using a popular British tune. The United States Congress adopted the song as the National Anthem in 1931.

THE STAR-SPANGLED BANNER

Words by Francis Scott Key
Music attributed to J. S. Smith

1. Oh! — say, can you see, by the dawn's ear - ly light, What so proud - ly we hailed at the twi - light's last
2. On the shore, dim - ly seen through the mists of the deep, Where the foe's haugh - ty host in dread si - lence re -
3. Oh, — thus be it ev - er when — free men shall stand Be - tween their loved homes and the war's des - o -

292 HANDS ACROSS THE WATER

MEETING **INDIVIDUAL** NEEDS

BIOGRAPHY: *Francis Scott Key*

Francis Scott Key (1779–1843), a lawyer by profession, wrote the words to the "Star-Spangled Banner." Its original title was "The Defense of Fort McHenry." The song was written on the back of an envelope while Key was on an American ship during the War of 1812. Key was on board the ship to plead for a friend's release from the English. When he saw the American flag still flying over Fort McHenry in the morning, he was moved to write the lyrics. The music is an English tune.

LANGUAGE ARTS CONNECTION: *Write an Essay*

Have students write about a meaningful memory of "The Star-Spangled Banner." This could be an event when they were moved by the national anthem or when a particular singer's interpretation of the song had an effect on them. If students have no such memories, have them write about a time they heard the song played (where they were, what they were doing, why the song was played).

The Star-Spangled Banner
CD7:17

1. Identify similar phrases. Have students:

• Tell the meaning of the song. (The fact that the flag was still flying meant that the Americans were still in control of Fort McHenry.)

• Listen to the song, identifying phrases with the same melody. (*Oh! say . . . gleaming* and *Whose broad stripes . . . streaming*)

• Echo-sing some of the more difficult phrases in the song in two-measure units. (for example, Lines 1 and 2; the transition from *gallantly streaming* to *And the rockets' red glare*; and so on)

• Sing the song. (Remind them to open their mouths in a round shape, as if singing "aw," on the high notes.)

2. Show melodic contour. Have students:

• Review melodic contour, steps, skips, and leaps. (See Unit 1, Lesson 4, page 18.)

• Sing the first two lines (*Oh! say . . . gleaming*), tracing the melodic contour in the air with their hand.

• Identify steps, skips, and leaps in the same lines. (skips at the beginning and end, with a few steps and leaps in the middle)

• Sing the whole song, noticing steps, skips, and leaps. (Challenge them to find the widest leap—between *streaming* and *And*.)

Celebrations *Patriotic Days* 293

ART CONNECTION: *Symbols of America* VISUAL ARTS

Have students brainstorm symbols that represent the United States. (the flag "Old Glory," the bald eagle, Uncle Sam, the Statue of Liberty, the rattlesnake flag "Don't Tread on Me," the Great Seal of the United States) Discuss how the symbols also stand for principles we care about, such as freedom for all, courage, and national pride. Then have students use some of the symbols or new ones of their own choosing to make flags or banners for the classroom or their

rooms at home. They can pencil a design on a yard of muslin, then color it in with felt-tip markers. (To hold the muslin still for drawing, tape the corners to a table or other rigid surface.)

CELEBRATIONS

PATRIOTIC DAYS

continued from previous page

LISTENING Battle Hymn of the Republic

played by the Monty Alexander Trio

Monty Alexander is a jazz pianist who was born in Jamaica. His trio first performed this jazz version of "Battle Hymn of the Republic" at the Montreux Jazz Festival in Switzerland. Alexander says that he had very little idea of what he was going to play when he first sat down at the piano. He knew he wanted to feature the "Battle Hymn" in some way. Listen to his improvisation on this well-known patriotic tune.

Julia Ward Howe wrote the poem "Battle Hymn of the Republic" in 1862, during the Civil War. The tune was based on the song "John Brown's Body," also from the Civil War period.

294

LESSONLINKS

Battle Hymn of the Republic (listening) *(15 min)*

OBJECTIVE Listen to and analyze a jazz version of "Battle Hymn of the Republic" featuring the piano

Reinforcement
keyboard instruments—piano, and jazz style, *page 119*
boogie woogie style, *page 253*

MATERIALS
Recording Battle Hymn of the
Republic (listening)   CD7:18

Resources
Resource Master C • 1 (listening map)
Listening Map Transparency T • 10
Recorder Master R • 28 (pitches G C' D')

Battle Hymn of the Republic *(15 min)*

OBJECTIVE Sing and analyze a patriotic song in verse-refrain form with dotted rhythms, then sing it in two parts

Reinforcement
verse-refrain form, countermelody, *page 25*
dotted rhythms, *page 113*

MATERIALS
Recordings
Battle Hymn of the Republic   CD7:19
Battle Hymn of the Republic
  (performance mix)   CD7:20

MEETING **INDIVIDUAL** NEEDS

EXTRA HELP: *"Battle Hymn," Jazz Version*

The following is a guide to the style and sections:

Style: The piano plays in boogie-woogie style, the bass plays walking bass (steady notes). Each statement of the theme is 16 measures. The accents are on Beats 2 and 4.

Form: Introduction, theme, six variations

Introduction: Free tempo and meter presenting the verse of the song

Sections 1–2: The refrain melody is heard clearly, played by the piano. The pianist fills in the space between phrases of the melody (in Measures 4, 8, 12, and 15–16 of each statement) with single notes and chords.

Sections 3–5: The melody is no longer heard clearly. The pianist improvises new melodies for the chord pattern of the refrain. The piano accompaniment changes to chords from walking bass. Gradually Alexander plays more elaborately, ending section 5 with call-and-response between hands.

Section 6: Melody is played dramatically with piano tremolos, a half-step higher than before.

Section 7: More improvisation over the refrain chords

Battle Hymn of the Republic

Music by William Steffe
Words by Julia Ward Howe

B♭ major

m f s l t d r m

BATTLE HYMN
of the Republic

mp B♭

Mine eyes have seen the glo-ry of the com-ing of the Lord;

E♭ B♭

He is tram-pling out the vin-tage where the grapes of wrath are stored;

B♭ *cresc.*

He has loosed the fate-ful light-ning of his ter-ri-ble swift sword;

mf cresc. E♭ F B♭

His truth is march-ing on.

Refrain *f* B♭ E♭ B♭

Glo-ry, Glo-ry, Hal-le-lu-jah! Glo-ry, Glo-ry, Hal-le-lu-jah!

f

Glo-ry, Glo-ry! Glo-ry, Hal-le-lu-jah.

B♭ *ff* E♭ F B♭

Glo-ry, Glo-ry, Hal-le-lu-jah! His truth is march-ing on!

ff

Glo-ry, Glo-ry! His truth is march-ing on.

Celebrations *Patriotic Days* **295**

Battle Hymn of the Republic (listening) CD7:18

Analyze a jazz version of "Battle Hymn of the Republic" featuring piano. Have students:

• Listen to the introduction, guessing the song. Name the keyboard instrument. (piano)

• Listen to the music, noting the number of times the melody (refrain only) is stated or improvised. (seven times, excluding the introduction) (Optional: Use **Listening Map Transparency T • 10** or **Resource Master C • 1**, which is a listening map of the song.)

• Listen again for the jazz-style improvisation by the piano and bass. (See *Extra Help* on the bottom of page 294.)

Battle Hymn of the Republic CD7:19

1. Sing and analyze a song in verse-refrain form with dotted rhythms. Have students:

• Find measures in the notation of the verse that are exactly the same as measures in Part 1 of the refrain. (last $2\frac{1}{4}$ measures)

• Clap the rhythm of the verse, then count how many times the dotted eighth-sixteenth rhythm pattern occurs. (20) Find the dotted quarter-eighth rhythm pattern in the song. (refrain)

• Listen to the song, singing along with the melody as able.

• Divide into two groups and sing different sections to hear the verse-refrain relationship. (One group sings the verse at the same time that the other sings the refrain.)

2. Sing the song in two parts. Have students:

• Find dynamic markings in the song. Then sing the melody, focusing on dynamics.

• Learn Part 2 of the refrain. (When students are secure singing the melody and counter-melody separately, have them sing both parts together.)

BIOGRAPHY: *Julia Ward Howe*

Julia Ward Howe (1819–1910) was a social reformer who wrote the words to the "Battle Hymn of the Republic" after visiting Civil War camps outside of Washington, D.C. *The Atlantic Monthly* published the song the following spring, and it soon became a major war song for the Union army. Howe also worked for world peace and women's right to vote.

PLAYING INSTRUMENTS: *Snare Drum*

Introduce students to the snare drum, teaching them a simple roll pattern to accompany "Battle Hymn of the Republic."

MOVEMENT: *Create a Jazz Version*

MOVEMENT

Monty Alexander's version of "Battle Hymn" invites a different kind of movement based on jazz and African rhythms. Have students work in pairs. One student is the leader and moves freely to the music in place while the other imitates the movement. When one 16-measure section is completed, the other student becomes the leader and the first follows his or her motions. Continue to switch leaders for the first six statements of the theme and then allow both to do their own best motions simultaneously for the last variation.

CELEBRATIONS

HALLOWEEN

RELATED ARTS MOVEMENT | THEATER | VISUAL ARTS

SELECTIONS
THE GHOST SHIP, *page 296*
OLD ABRAM BROWN, *page 299*

HAUNTED NIGHT

Most people have at least one scary story to tell on the right occasion. This song is the ghostly tale of a haunted ship.

E minor (modulates)

m, s, l, t, d r m

The Ghost Ship

Words and Music by Don Besig and Nancy Price

mf B   Em   D   C

1. Now lis - ten well as a tale I tell of a night I
(2.)   then I spied off the star-board side a— strange, mys-

C   B   Em   D

shook with fear.___ We were sail - ing west on the o - pen sea,
ter - ious sight.___ I___ froze with fear as it drift - ed near

C   Bm   Em

head - in' home from a long,— long year.___ I was stand - ing
like a ghost in the dark— of night.___ I could see a

296

MEETING **INDIVIDUAL** NEEDS

BACKGROUND: *Halloween*

Halloween began in ancient Britain and western Europe as a Celtic festival that observed the beginning of winter and the Celtic New Year, November 1. The Celts believed that the souls of the dead returned to earth for this evening. The people lit bonfires and wore costumes made from animal skins. Later, in the A.D. 800s, the Catholic Church established All Saints' Day on November 1. The evening before All Saints' Day became known as "All Hallows' Eve" or "All Hallow e'en." The festival came to colonial America with the early British settlers who brought their customs with them—among them the wearing of costumes and bobbing for apples on Halloween.

BIOGRAPHIES: *Don Besig and Nancy Price*

American composer Don Besig (b. 1936) taught vocal music in public schools for 25 years before leaving to compose full-time. Most of his works are for chorus. He often collaborates with Nancy Price (b. 1958), a high school choral director in upstate New York. Besig also loves musical theater, a field in which he has worked as a director, choreographer, and designer.

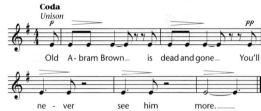

• Create movement in the spirit of the song to show melodic direction and perform it while singing. (For example, they can begin at a low level and slowly get higher. On the coda, all can sink lower until they are on the floor.)

2. Sing in canon and in augmentation and perform body percussion patterns. Have students:

• Listen again to identify how the composer arranged the song, using different textures for each repetition of the melody (unison two times; two-part canon two times; four-part canon two times; one group in unison two times as the other sings twice as slow once; coda)

• Form four groups. Sing the song in two-part canon (two groups on each part) and four-part canon (one group on each part).

• Echo you in performing a body percussion pattern for whole note, half note, quarter note, and eighth note. Then form four groups. Each group performs one of the note values with a different body percussion sound. (See *Playing Instruments* below.)

• Learn what augmentation means. (rhythms performed twice [or more] as slowly as the original version)

• Divide into two groups, with one group singing in unison two times as the other sings twice as slow (in augmentation) once. Notice that in the augmented version most beats of the song have one sound rather than two. (The vocal coda is notated here for your convenience.)

PLAYING INSTRUMENTS: *Reinforce ⁴⁄₄ Meter*

Have students practice the following patterns, echoing you.

Stamp:

Pat:

Clap:

Snap:

(alternating hands—left/right)

Have students do the entire pattern four times, echoing you. Then have students form four groups. Each group performs one of the note values with a different body percussion sound. Finally, have them transfer their pattern to a percussion instrument of their choice. For example:

○—gong, triangle, or suspended cymbal;
♩—rattle/shaker (cabasa, tambourine, or güiro); ♩—drum;
♫—wood sound (temple block, log drum, or woodblock)

Use these instruments as an accompaniment for "Old Abram Brown." Add one sound for each section of the song: unison—gong; 2-part canon—add drum; 4-part canon—add rattle/shaker; augmentation—add wood sound.

CELEBRATIONS
WINTER

LESSON LINKS

Holiday Sing-Along *(15 min)*

OBJECTIVE Sing a medley of holiday favorites, listening for minor keys and $\frac{3}{4}$ meter

Reinforcement
minor, *page 81*
$\frac{3}{4}$ meter, *page 81*

MATERIALS
Recordings Holiday Sing-Along (listening)   CD7:24

Resources Resource Master C • 2 (text)

Happy Holidays

Some winter holiday customs are quite old, having passed from one generation to the next. Both Christmas and Hanukkah have been celebrated for many hundreds of years. The customs of Kwanzaa, a newer holiday, are becoming more widely observed each year.

Although the celebrations of winter vary, one thing is the same. The joyful spirit of family, friendship, hope, and peace is an important part of each celebration.

DESCRIBE special customs that you or someone you know observe for the winter holidays.

300

MEETING **INDIVIDUAL** NEEDS

BACKGROUND: *Winter Holidays*

Winter is a season of great festivity. Many current celebrations had their roots in ceremonies honoring the return of light, when the year turns toward spring. In the Northern Hemisphere, this happens around December 21 or 22 on the shortest day of the year—the one with the fewest hours of sunshine. People prayed for warmth and light; the Feast of Lights was celebrated by people in many different regions around the world. A typical celebration saw lighted candles carried in a procession; they represented the life-giving power of the sun. Afterwards, people would gather to feast and socialize. Singing and dancing were often a part of these celebrations.

Holiday Sing-Along CD7:24

Sing a medley of holiday favorites, listening for minor keys and ⅜ meter. Have students:

• Read pages 300–301 and describe special winter customs.

• Listen to "Holiday Sing-Along" and name the songs contained in the medley. ("Deck the Hall," "The Holly and the Ivy," "We Three Kings," "Angels We Have Heard on High," "God Rest Ye Merry Gentlemen," "Joy to the World," "Silent Night," "Wasn't That a Mighty Day?", "We Wish You a Merry Christmas")

• Review verses to the songs that may be unfamiliar, then sing along with the recording. (Optional: The song lyrics are found on **Resource Master C • 2**.)

• Tell which songs are in ⅜ meter. ("The Holly and the Ivy," "We Three Kings," "We Wish You a Merry Christmas"; "Silent Night" is in ⁶⁄₈ meter, which may sound like ⅜)

• Tell which songs are in minor. ("We Three Kings" and "God Rest Ye Merry Gentlemen")

Holiday Sing-Along
Traditional Holiday Songs

Singing songs, or caroling, has been part of winter celebrations for centuries. Carols are generally simple yet festive tunes. Many carols, such as "Joy to the World" and "Angels We Have Heard on High," tell of the Christmas story. Others, such as "Deck the Hall," describe holiday customs.

SING along with these holiday favorites.

Celebrations *Winter Holidays* **301**

MATHEMATICS CONNECTION: *Holiday Cookies*

Have students bring in favorite holiday cookie recipes. Have them imagine they are making cookies for a school assembly. They can work in groups to solve the problem of how they would make enough cookies. (First they need to determine how many cookies they need in all. Then the problem can be solved in a number of ways—either making one batch of enough recipes to reach the desired total of cookies, or doubling some recipes, and so on.) For an added challenge, provide them with the prices of ingredients and have them figure how much the cookies would cost.

CELEBRATIONS

WINTER

continued from previous page

LESSON**LINKS**

Winter Poem *(poem) (20 min)*

OBJECTIVE Accompany a poem about winter, using sixteenth notes

Reinforcement sixteenth-note rhythms, *page 81*

Ocho Kandelikas *(20 min)*

OBJECTIVE Sing and experience accelerando, and identify monophonic and homophonic textures

Reinforcement monophony and homophony, *page 77*

MATERIALS
Recordings Ocho Kandelikas
(Eight Candles)   CD7:25
Recorded Lesson: Pronunciation
for "Ocho Kandelikas"   CD7:26

Resources Recorder Master R • 29
(pitches D E G A D')

Winter Poem

Accompany a poem about winter, using sixteenth notes. Have students:

• Write key words from the poem on the board, such as *snowflake fall*, *i kissed it*, *web of snow*, and *spring rain*.

• Choose instrument sounds to represent each set of words, making sure to include sixteenth-note rhythms. (See page 67.)

Holidays are not the only reason to celebrate in winter. The beauty of snow and other seasonal elements often inspire poetry and music.

WINTER POEM

once a snowflake fell
on my brow and i loved
it so much and i kissed
it and it was happy and called its cousins
and brothers and a web
of snow engulfed me then
i reached to love them all
and i squeezed them and they became
a spring rain and i stood perfectly
still and was a flower

—Nikki Giovanni

302

MEETING **INDIVIDUAL** NEEDS

BACKGROUND: *Nikki Giovanni*

American poet Nikki Giovanni (b. 1943) became active in the civil rights movement in college. Her poems and essays often touch on African American issues. An energetic, down-to-earth person, she reads her poetry around the country, as well as teaching creative writing. An album of her poetry read over gospel music sold more than 100,000 copies. Giovanni's first book of children's poetry was written for her son. She has since published several books of poems for children as well as books of essays and poems for adults.

MULTICULTURAL PERSPECTIVES: *Hanukkah*

Hanukkah, the "festival of lights," celebrates a Jewish victory over the Syrians in A.D. 165. It is said that, after the victory, as they cleaned the Temple of Jerusalem, the Jews found a small amount of oil to light their holy lamps. This oil miraculously lasted for eight days. Hanukkah commemorates that event by the lighting of a special eight-branched candelabrum each night of the eight-day event. A helper candle is used to light one candle the first night, two the second, and so on. During the holiday, people sing, dance and often exchange gifts. They also make donations to the poor.

The words of this Hanukkah song are in Ladino. This is a language that blends ancient Hebrew, medieval Spanish, and Arabic with Slavic, Greek, French, and Turkish words.

OCHO KANDELIKAS
EIGHT CANDLES

Words and Music by Flory Jagoda
English Version by MMH

Ladino: Ha - nu - kah lin - da 'sta a - ki
Pronunciation: xɑ nu kɑ lin dɑ stɑ ɑ ki
English:
1. Han - uk - kah time be - gins to - night.
2. So man - y par - ties we can share,
3. De - li - cious pies for us to eat.

— o - cho kan - del - as par - a mi. mi. Ah.
o cho kan del as pɑ ɾɑ mi mi ɑ
— Eight can - dles here for me to light. light.
— With joy and glad - ness in the air. air. } Ah.
— Al - monds and hon - ey for a treat. treat.

U - na kan - del - li - ka, dos kan - del - i - kas, tres kan - del - i - kas,
u na kan de li ka dos kan de li kas tres kan de li kas
One— kan - de - li - ka, Two kan - de - li - kas, Three kan - de - li - kas,

kua - tro kan - del - i - kas, sin - ko kan - del - i - kas, seysh kan - del - i - kas,
kwa tro kan de li kas sing ko kan de li kas sesh kan de li kas
Four— kan - de - li - kas, Five— kan - de - li - kas, Six kan - de - li - kas,

sie - te kan - dle - i - kas, o - cho kan - del - as par - a mi.
sie te kan de li kas o cho kan de las pɑ ɾɑ mi
Sev - en kan - de - li - kas, Eight can - dles here for me to light.

Celebrations *Winter Holidays* **303**

• Play the sounds they chose as a volunteer reads the poem.

• Discuss the poem, noting how Giovanni uses metaphors. (*a web of snow; i was a flower*)

Ocho Kandelikas CD7:25

1. Sing and experience accelerando. Have students:

• Read about Ladino.

• Tap with the beat as they listen to recognize accelerando (a gradual speeding-up of the beat). (On the second ending, Measure 5 begins slower. An accelerando reaches the original tempo by Measure 12. Last two measures of the refrain are back in original tempo.)

Recorded Lesson CD7:26
• Listen to "Pronunciation for 'Ocho Kandelikas.'"

• Say the numbers 1–8 in Ladino as you point to each number written on the board. (*una, dos, tres, kuatro, sinko, seysh, siete, ocho*)

• Learn to sing the song.

2. Identify monophonic and homophonic textures. Have students:

• Listen to the recording and identify the instrument accompanying the song. (guitar—played in Spanish style)

• Recall the meaning of the texture terms monophony, homophony, and polyphony. (See pages 74–75.)

• Listen again and tell the texture of the first measure of each verse and then the texture of the rest of each verse and the refrain (single melody—monophony; melody with accompaniment—homophony)

BIOGRAPHY: *Flory Jagoda*

Flory Jagoda was born in the former country of Yugoslavia to a Sephardic Jewish family. (Sephardic Jews, or Sephardim, are descendants of a group of European Jews who originally settled in Spain and Portugal.) She learned many Sephardic songs from her grandmother, who in turn passed down songs she had learned from her ancestors. Jagoda now lives in Virginia. She often performs alone or with her son and two daughters, giving concerts of Ladino songs. She has also recorded two albums.

MOVEMENT: *"Ocho Kandelikas"*

Have students walk or dance in a circle, counterclockwise for four measures, then clockwise for four measures. During the refrain, have eight students go to the center and improvise their own candle-like movements using colored scarves.

PRONUNCIATION: *"Ocho Kandelikas"*

ɑ f**a**ther   e ch**a**otic   i b**ee**   o **o**bey   u m**oo**n
ɾ flipped r   x slightly guttural h, *Spanish* ba**j**o

CELEBRATIONS

WINTER

continued from previous page

LESSONLINKS

Si me dan pasteles *(20 min)*

OBJECTIVE Discuss a song's cultural context, sing the song in parts, discuss its texture, and play a percussion accompaniment

Reinforcement texture, *page 77*

MATERIALS
Recordings
Si me dan pasteles (When You Bring Pasteles)   **CD8:1**
Si me dan pasteles (performance mix)   **CD8:2**
Recorded Lesson: Pronunciation for "Si me dan pasteles"   **CD8:3**

Si me dan pasteles CD8:1

1. Discuss the song's cultural context.
Have students:

• Discuss foods mentioned in the song as part of Puerto Rican culture. (The meat and vegetable patties sometimes have a wrapping made from plantain leaves; rice is also a part of many Puerto Rican meals.)

• Name foods from their cultural heritage that are eaten on holidays.

Pasteles are meat-and-vegetable patties that are eaten at holiday time. When carolers go from house to house in Puerto Rico, they often receive pasteles as gifts. Children hurry home with these special treats so they can be enjoyed while they're still hot!

SI ME DAN PASTELES
WHEN YOU BRING PASTELES

Puerto Rican Folk Song
Arranged by
Alejandro Jiménez

304 HAPPY HOLIDAYS

MEETING **INDIVIDUAL** NEEDS

BACKGROUND: *"Si me dan pasteles"*

"Si me dan pasteles" is traditionally sung during the Christmas season, especially around the time of January 6, Three Kings Day (the celebration of the Epiphany). The song is often sung by strolling carolers. The house owner will offer the carolers a gift of holiday delicacies such as pasteles. Pasteles are a combination of cooked plantain and meat made into a pattie and wrapped in plantain leaves. Those who cannot afford meat fill them with rice or other fillers. (The *cuchara* mentioned in the song means spoon.) The Christmas dinner often begins with pasteles as well. The

dinner is eaten after Midnight Mass, in the early hours of Christmas morning.

EXTRA HELP: *Vocal Ostinatos*

Play the vocal ostinato parts on resonator bells or keyboard to help students learn to sing them.

PRONUNCIATION: *"Si me dan pasteles"*

a f<u>a</u>ther	e ch<u>a</u>otic	i b<u>ee</u>	o <u>o</u>bey
ß b without lips touching		ð <u>the</u>	ɾ flipped r
ɾ̄ rolled r	x slightly guttural h, *Spanish* ba<u>j</u>o		

Si me dan a - rroz— no me den cu - cha - ra,
si me ðan a ros no me ðeng ku cha ra
If you give me rice ones,— don't give me cu - cha - ra,

Le lo lai, le lo lai,
le lo lai le lo lai

que ma - má me di - jo— que se lo lle - va - ra.
ke ma ma me ði xo ke se lo ye βa ra
My ma - má has told me— "Bring them straight home to me!"—

le lo lai, le lo lai.
le lo lai le lo lai

Interlude

Le lo lai, le lo lai. Le lo lai, le lo lai.
le lo lai le lo lai le lo lai le lo lai

Le lo lai, le lo lai. Le lo lai, le lo lai.
le lo lai le lo lai le lo lai le lo lai

2. Sing a song in parts and discuss its texture. Have students:

• Listen to the song and identify where the melody and rhythm of Measure 1 returns. (Measures 3, 5, 7) Listen for repeated parts of the interlude. (Measures 11–12 are the same as Measures 9–10.)

• Listen again, for syncopation (defined on page 154). (between Beats 3–4 of Measures 1–8)

Recorded Lesson CD8:3

• Listen to "Pronunciation for 'Si me dan pasteles.'"

• Sing the melody of the song.

• Learn Parts 2 and 3. (When students are secure singing the parts separately, have them sing all parts together.) Then tell the difference in texture between singing the melody alone and with all the parts. (The texture gets thicker.)

3. Add percussion ostinatos. Have students:

• Divide into groups and learn the following ostinatos.

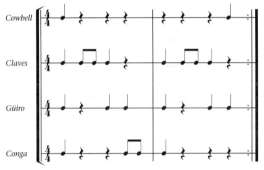

• Divide into two groups. One group plays the percussion accompaniment as the other sings Part 1 of the song.

• Add Parts 2 and 3 of the song for a final performance. Then discuss the effect that adding percussion parts has on the texture. (The texture gets even thicker.)

PLAYING INSTRUMENTS: *Pitched*

Add one or both of the following ostinatos to "Si me dan pasteles," using any pitched instruments:

CELEBRATIONS

WINTER

continued from previous page

LESSON LINKS

Silent Night *(30 min)*

OBJECTIVE Sing the song, identify homophonic texture, and explore § rhythm patterns

Reinforcement
homophony, *page 77*
§ meter, *page 161*

MATERIALS
Recordings
Silent Night (Stille Nacht)   CD8:4
Recorded Lesson: Pronunciation
   for "Silent Night (Stille Nacht)"   CD8:5

Resources Playing the Guitar G • 15
   (Silent Night); G • 16 (Holiday)
Recorder Master R • 30 (pitches G A
   C' D')

Carol from an Irish Cabin *(30 min)*

OBJECTIVE Sing a song in minor and §
meter; create an introduction and coda

Reinforcement
minor, *page 73*
§ meter, ♪♪♪ *page 161*

MATERIALS
Recordings Carol from an Irish
   Cabin   CD8:6

Instruments pitched instruments

Resources
Orff Orchestration O • 8
Recorder Master R • 31 (pitches D F G A
   B♭ C' D')

On Christmas Eve of 1818, Joseph Mohr wrote the words to "Silent Night" and asked his friend to write the music. The church organ wasn't working, so Franz Gruber wrote a simple setting and used a guitar to accompany the voices. From its modest beginnings, "Silent Night" spread throughout the world.

MEETING **INDIVIDUAL** NEEDS

BACKGROUND: *Christmas*

Christmas is a Christian holiday celebrating the birth of Jesus Christ. The date of December 25 was probably influenced by existing Roman holidays, which celebrated the end of the harvest season. On these holidays, people decorated their homes with greens and exchanged gifts. The person who gave children gifts was first known as St. Nicholas, a tall, thin gentleman. American poet Clement Clarke Moore first portrayed the present-day Santa—a jolly, stout person—in a poem, "An Account of a Visit from St. Nicholas" (" 'Twas the Night Before Christmas"), which appeared in the *Troy Sentinel* in 1823.

PRONUNCIATION: *"Silent Night"*

ɑ f<u>a</u>ther	e ch<u>a</u>otic	i b<u>ee</u>	ɪ <u>i</u>t
o <u>o</u>bey	ɔ p<u>aw</u>	u m<u>oo</u>n	ʊ p<u>u</u>t
ə <u>a</u>go	ɾ flipped r	x guttural h, *German* Ba<u>ch</u>	

Carol from an Irish Cabin

Music by Dale Wood
Words Anonymous

G minor

m, s, l, t, d r m

Gm ... Dm

1. The cold wind blows o - ver the heath- er,_____
2. The clean snow falls soft - ly, falls soft - ly,_____
3. So let there be no fear of dark-ness,_____

Gm ... Dm

The salt wind blows o - ver the sea,_____ The—
The snow crys - tals cov - er the moor._____ Let
And let there be no fear of sea;_____ Let the

B♭ ... F

harsh wind blows down from the moun- tains,_____ And
wan - der - ers lost and grown wea - ry,_____ Find
star guide the lost and for - sak - en,_____ Safe

Gm ... Dm ... Gm

blows a white Christ - mas to me._____
wel - come at my cab - in door._____
o - ver the moor - lands to me._____

The lilting quality of Irish folk music is heard in "Carol from an Irish Cabin" with its dotted rhythms and ⅜ meter. The spirit of the Christmas season expressed in the song offers a warm welcome to the weary traveler.

Celebrations *Winter Holidays* **307**

Silent Night CD8:4

1. Sing the song. Have students:

• Read and discuss page 306.

Recorded Lesson CD8:5

• Listen to "Pronunciation for 'Silent Night.'" Sing the song.

2. Identify homophonic texture and explore ⅜ rhythm patterns. Have students:

• Listen to the recording and tell the texture. (melody with accompaniment—homophony)

• Determine that the song is in major.

• Notice the time signature and tell its meaning. (⅜; see page 141)

• Notice the frequency of the rhythm: ♪♪ (If possible, play it for students with straight eighths, then, as written. Have them describe the difference in effect.)

• Find the repetition of rhythm patterns. (Measures 1 and 2; 3 and 4; 5–6 and 7–8)

Carol from an Irish Cabin
CD8:6

1. Sing the song in minor and ⅜ meter. Have students:

• With books closed, listen to "Carol from an Irish Cabin" and determine that it is minor.

• Listen to the recording and identify the accompanying instrument. (harp) Tell the instrument family to which it belongs. (string)

• Read page 307 about the rhythm and meter. Find the dotted rhythms in the song, then echo you as you clap the rhythm of the song.

• Sing the song.

2. Create an introduction and coda. Have students:

• Work in cooperative groups to create an instrumental introduction and coda to set the mood for the song. (for example, tremolos on G and D and shakers or vocal wind-sounds to give the feeling of a chilly wind) Perform their introduction and coda with the song.

BIOGRAPHY: *Dale Wood*

Dale Wood (b. 1934) was born in Glendale, California. His musical career began when, at the age of 13, he won a national hymn-writing competition. Wood is currently editor of *The Sacred Music Press* and lives in Northern California. He specializes in choral music and especially likes writing for children's voices. In his free time, he enjoys gourmet cooking and camping.

ORFF: *"Carol from an Irish Cabin"*

See **O • 8** in *Orchestrations for Orff Instruments*.

LANGUAGE ARTS CONNECTION: *Song Book*

Have students collect stories and songs when they see family members during holiday get-togethers. With songs from this lesson, they can put these into books to share as gifts. Have them complete the books by writing a paragraph introducing each song. The paragraph might share a personal memory of the song and/or tell its history.

# CELEBRATIONS

WINTER

continued from previous page

LESSONLINKS

Siyahamba *(30 min)*

OBJECTIVE Discuss the texture of a song, sing it in three parts, and perform a percussion accompaniment

Reinforcement texture, *page 77*

MATERIALS
Recordings
Siyahamba	**CD8:7**
Siyahamba (performance mix)	**CD8:8**
Recorded Lesson: Pronunciation for "Siyahamba"	**CD8:9**

Instruments
percussion instruments (conga drums, cabasa or shaker, güiro, agogo bells, cowbell, and log drum)

Kwanzaa is a seven-day holiday, between December 26 and January 1, which celebrates the values of African American families, communities, and culture. Candles are lit each day of Kwanzaa to symbolize the seven basic principles of the holiday. The song "Siyahamba" celebrates the first two principles—Unity and Self-Determination. It is a traditional Zulu song that has been used as a South African freedom song.

ADD this solo part.

308 HAPPY HOLIDAYS

MEETING **INDIVIDUAL** NEEDS

MULTICULTURAL PERSPECTIVES: *Kwanzaa*

Kwanzaa (**kwan** zɑ) is a Swahili word that means "first." Kwanzaa is a cultural holiday created by Maulana Karenga in 1966 to celebrate the universal values of African Americans. The holiday is based on African harvest festivals. During the seven days of Kwanzaa, from December 26 to January 1, the seven principles of Kwanzaa are observed. Among these are Umoja (u **mo** jɑ)—unity; Kujichagulia (**ku** ji **cha** gu **li** ɑ)—self-determination; and Ujima (u **ʒi** mɑ)—collective work and responsibility. On each of the seven days a candle is lit and people discuss the idea for that day and give each other homemade or homegrown gifts.

MOVEMENT: *"Siyahamba"*

Have students sing the song in a choir formation using an easy swaying body movement. The body movement should remain subtle, leaning gently to the left, then to the right, in a rocking motion or with small steps from side to side.

SIYAHAMBA
We Are Marching

African Folk Song
Arranged by
Robert J. de Frece

Zulu: Si - ya - hamb' e - ku - kha -nye - ni kwen-khos' si - ya-
Pronunciation: si ya ham bɛ ku ka nye ni kwɛn kos si ya
English: We are march - ing in the light of God. We are

Si - ya - hamb' e - ku - kha -nye - ni kwen-khos' si - ya-
si ya ham bɛ ku ka nye ni kwɛn kos si ya
We are march - ing in the light of God. We are

Si - ya - hamb' e - ku - kha -nye - ni kwen-khos' si - ya-
si ya ham bɛ ku ka nye ni kwɛn kos si ya
We are march - ing in the light of God. We are

hamb' e - ku - kha- nye - ni kwen- khos'. Si - ya - Si - ya-
ham bə ku ka nye ni kwɛn kos si ya si ya
march -ing in the light of God. We are We are

hamb' e - ku - kha- nye - ni kwen- khos'. Si - ya - nye - ni kwen- khos', si - ya-
ham bə ku ka nye ni kwɛn kos si ya nye ni kwɛn kos si ya
march -ing in the light of God. We are the light of God, We are

hamb' e - ku - kha- nye - ni kwen- khos'. Si - ya - nye - ni kwen- khos', si - ya-
ham bə ku ka nye ni kwɛn kos si ya nye ni kwɛn kos si ya
march -ing in the light of God. We are the light of God, We are

G major
s₁ l₁ d r m f s

Celebrations *Winter Holidays* **309**

Siyahamba CD8:7

1. Discuss the texture of the song and sing it in three parts. Have students:

• Listen to the song and discuss the textural effect of adding additional voice parts. (texture goes from thin to thick)

• Decide if it is in major or minor. (major)

Recorded Lesson CD8:9

• Listen to "Pronunciation for 'Siyahamba.'"

• Try singing each of the voice parts, then divide into three groups and practice one part per group. (When students are comfortable singing each part separately, have them try putting the three parts together.)

PRONUNCIATION: *"Siyahamba"*

ɑ f<u>a</u>ther   ɛ p<u>e</u>t   i b<u>ee</u>   o <u>o</u>bey
u m<u>oo</u>n   ə <u>a</u>go

CELEBRATIONS
WINTER

continued from previous page

2. Perform a percussion accompaniment.

● Learn the percussion parts below.

Conga drums

low   high   low

Cabasa or shaker (can play sixteenths.)

Güiro

Scrape   Tap

Agogo bells

Cowbell

The sheet music lyrics:

ham - ba___ Oh___ si - ya -
ham ba si ya
march - ing.___ Oh___ We are

ham - ba, hamb' - e - ku - kha - nye - ni, ham - ba si - ya -
ham ba ham bɛ ku ka nyɛ ni ham ba si ya
march - ing, march - ing, we are march - ing, march - ing we are

ham - ba, hamb' - e - ku - kha - nye - ni, ham - ba si - ya -
ham ba ham bɛ ku ka nyɛ ni ham ba si ya
march - ing, march - ing, we are march - ing, march - ing we are

Last time to Coda

hamb' e - ku - kha - nye - ni kwen - khos',___ Si - ya -
ham bɛ ku ka nyɛ ni kwɛn kos si ya
march - ing in the light___ of God,___ We are

hamb' - e - ku - kha - nye - ni kwen - khos', nye - ni kwen - khos', si - ya -
ham bɛ ku ka nyɛ ni kwɛn kos nyɛ ni kwɛn kos si ya
march - ing in the light___ of God,___ the light of God, We are

hamb' - e - ku - kha - nye - ni kwen - khos', nye - ni kwen - khos', si - ya -
ham bɛ ku ka nyɛ ni kwɛn kos nyɛ ni kwɛn kos si ya
march - ing in the light___ of God,___ the light of God, We are

310 HAPPY HOLIDAYS

MEETING **INDIVIDUAL** NEEDS

PRONUNCIATION: *"Siyahamba"*

a f<u>a</u>ther	ε p<u>e</u>t	i b<u>ee</u>	o <u>o</u>bey
u m<u>oo</u>n	ə <u>a</u>go		

ART CONNECTION: *Interpretation*
VISUAL ARTS

Have students discuss the Alston painting. What is depicted? (a family) What might the family represent? (strong African American culture) Bring out that Alston probably had several levels of interpretation in mind and that these levels are what make a work of art interesting.

ENRICHMENT: *Program Idea*
THEATER

The songs in this lesson are ideal for a program entitled "Winter Holidays Around the World." Have students sing the songs as strolling carolers, moving around the auditorium or from classroom to classroom. If possible, have them create costumes appropriate to the various cultures represented.

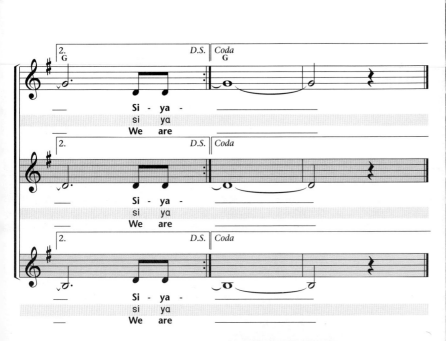

FAMILY

Charles Alston worked in many different styles. His painting *Family* is an abstract representation of mother, father, and children. As an adult, Alston returned to the South, where he grew up, to photograph African Americans at work and at home. These pictures of southern life in the 1930s became the basis of his "family" paintings. Alston felt closest to his works that protested the discrimination against African Americans, yet celebrated their culture.

Family by Charles H. Alston, 1955. Collection of WHITNEY MUSEUM OF AMERICAN ART, NEW YORK, Purchase, with funds from the Artists and Students Assistance Fund, photography by Bill Jacobson, NY

• Divide into two groups. One group plays the percussion accompaniment as the rest sings the song. (One person sings a soprano solo.) Discuss the texture of the performance. (solo—thin; gets thicker and thicker with voices and instruments)

Form:

Soprano solo sings A section 2 times alone.

Choir: A section (4 times)

1st time—conga drums

2nd time—add cabasa or shaker, and güiro

3rd time—add agogo bells and cowbell

4th time—add log drum (improvising)

B Section (Measure 5): Choir with solo descant on repeat. Instruments continue.

At the *D.S.* the choir performs sections A and B, as written, with repeats (including solo descant on repeat of B section). At the end of the song, all percussion stops on Beat 3 of the second measure. (The cowbell will play on the third beat for that time only.)

ART CONNECTION: *Family Portraits* VISUAL ARTS

Throughout history artists have created family portraits. Have students bring in examples of family portraits from home, from art books, or from magazines. Discuss the different media used to create the portraits (most common are paintings and photographs). Have students identify portraits that contrast in style (formal vs. informal, realistic vs. abstract). Have students write paragraphs comparing the purpose and style of one portrait with Charles Alston's painting. (Alston's work celebrates family life of southern African Americans; style is abstract, with obscured or distorted facial features and flattened space.)

CELEBRATIONS

NEW YEAR

LESSONLINKS

Bo Hai Huan Ten *(15 min)*

OBJECTIVE Identify instrument families in a Chinese orchestra and rhythmically accompany and move to music played by the orchestra

Reinforcement
Chinese New Year, *page 97*
Chinese orchestral instruments, *page 29*
Chinese Music, Chinese immigrants, *page 157*

MATERIALS
Recording Bo Hai Huan Ten
   (listening)   CD8:10

Instruments
medium hand drums, medium cymbals

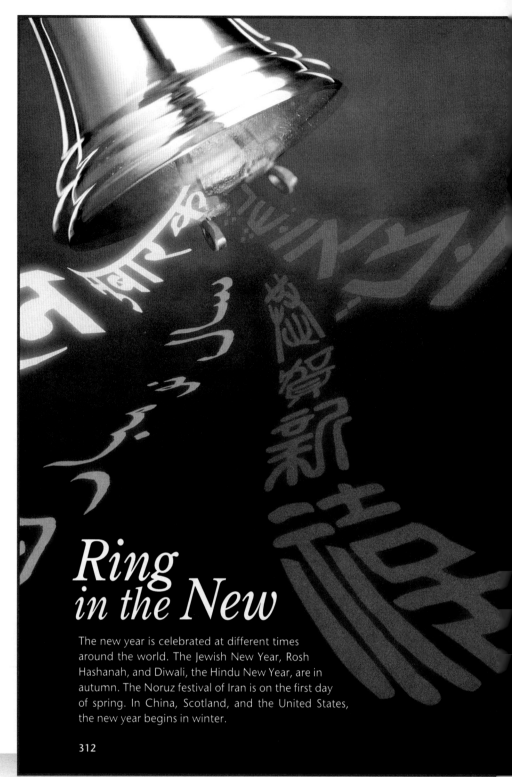

Ring in the New

The new year is celebrated at different times around the world. The Jewish New Year, Rosh Hashanah, and Diwali, the Hindu New Year, are in autumn. The Noruz festival of Iran is on the first day of spring. In China, Scotland, and the United States, the new year begins in winter.

312

MEETING **INDIVIDUAL** NEEDS

SOCIAL STUDIES CONNECTION: *New Year*

Ask students to guess what these dates have in common: January 1, March 21, April 14, September 10. (They are all dates for New Year's Day in various cultures [U.S.A., Iran, India, Ethiopia], along with other variable dates based on lunar calendars.) Have students create a list of traditions associated with New Year celebrations. You might have them research various New Year traditions as well as researching other calendars (such as the Chinese lunar calendar) and calendar systems. Have them share findings.

MULTICULTURAL PERSPECTIVES: *Chinese New Year*

The new year for the Chinese begins with the second new moon after the beginning of winter. The date may fall any time between mid-January and mid-February. Each new Chinese year is named after one of the 12 animal symbols on the Chinese zodiac, such as the monkey, ox, rabbit, and rooster. The personality of the animal for which the year is named is thought to affect what happens during that year. The Chinese New Year is a time for family reunions and for honoring ancestors. It is also a giant birthday celebration; the Chinese traditionally add a year to their age on New Year's Day, no matter when they were born.

A Chinese orchestra such as the one which plays "Bo Hai Huan Ten" includes woodwinds similar to flute and oboe; plucked, bowed, and hammered strings; and a variety of unpitched percussion instruments.

The Chinese Music Society of North America

LISTENING

Bo Hai Huan Ten

Traditional Chinese New Year Music

You will hear the instruments of the Chinese orchestra played with energy and a sense of festivity in this piece that celebrates the new year. The title means "Jubilation All Around" in English.

PLAY this rhythm along with the recording.

Cymbals and
medium
hand drums

gong
hə
shing
shi

Bo Hai Huan Ten CD8:10

1. Discuss New Year's celebrations. Have students:

• Look at the characters/words for "Happy New Year" on page 312. (From left to right: Hindi, Farsi, Chinese, and Hebrew; for pronunciation key, see *Pronunciation* below. The characters and/or words are also printed on pages 313, 314, 316, and 318.)

• Read about New Year's celebrations, then tell about their own family traditions.

2. Identify instrument families in a Chinese orchestra. Have students:

• Listen for the instruments in the Chinese orchestra and tell what families they hear. (Strings, woodwinds, percussion; see *Multicultural Perspectives* below for a list of instruments in the recording.)

• Tell which instrument family found in western orchestras was not heard. (brass)

3. Rhythmically accompany a Chinese New Year song. Have students:

• Read about the Chinese orchestra and "Bo Hai Huan Ten" (bo haɪ huɑn tɛn).

• Read and clap the rhythm pattern at the bottom of page 313.

• Listen for the rhythm pattern on page 313 in "Bo Hai Huan Ten," noting where it occurs. (It occurs 5 times altogether.)

• Listen again, walking to the beat around the room and clapping the pattern when it occurs.

• Transfer the rhythm pattern to hand drums and cymbals (some students on each) and play with the recording. In between patterns, move expressively to the music. (See *Extra Help* below for instrument ideas.)

MULTICULTURAL PERSPECTIVES: *Chinese Instruments*

The instruments pictured on page 313 include erhu, gaohu, zhonghu, and gehu (stringed instruments in the range of western violin, viola, and cello), yangqin (hammered dulcimer), sheng (a reed instrument with anywhere from 17 to 36 pipes), pipa (lute), suona (a reed instrument similiar to the oboe), and percussion (gongs, cymbals, drum). In the background to the far left is the zheng, a Chinese zither. Not pictured here, but heard on the recording of "Bo Hai Huan Ten," are the di (flute) and qinqin (a plucked string instrument).

PRONUNCIATION: *Happy New Year*

See the Chinese pronunciation of "Happy New Year" on page 313.

   i b<u>ee</u>   o <u>o</u>bey   ə <u>a</u>go

EXTRA HELP: *Make a Chinese Instrument*

Have students try to make a Chinese instrument such as a gong or hand drum. They can experiment with different sounds made by hitting wood, metal plates, or cans with pieces of wood or metal, then play rhythms with "Bo Hai Huan Ten."

continued from previous page

साल मुबारक

sal mu ba rak

LESSON LINKS

Diwali Song *(30 min)*

OBJECTIVE Sing an Indian song, hear a keyboard instrument, and play a six-beat Indian rhythm pattern

Reinforcement
keyboard instruments, *page 97*
⁶⁄₈ rhythm patterns, *page 165*
Music from India, *page 221*

MATERIALS
Recordings
Diwali Song   CD8:11
Recorded Lesson: Pronunciation
  for "Diwali Song"   CD8:12
Recorded Lesson: Playing Indian
  Music on the Tabla   CD8:13

Diwali Song CD8:11

1. Sing an Indian song and hear a keyboard instrument. Have students:

• Read about the New Year in India, then compare it to other New Year celebrations.

• Listen for the keyboard instrument in the recording and tell whether it sounds like a piano, organ, or harpsichord. (organ—it is a harmonium, a portable organ)

Recorded Lesson CD8:12
• Listen to "Pronunciation for 'Diwali Song.'"

• Sing the song.

Diwali is the first day of the new year in India. Also called the Festival of Lights, it is an autumn festival that many people of the Hindu religion celebrate. Families fill clay saucers with oil, light them, and place them in windows and along roads and streams. The lights guide Lakshmi, the Hindu goddess of prosperity, to each home.

Batik print of Lakshmi.

314 RING IN THE NEW

MEETING **INDIVIDUAL** NEEDS

MULTICULTURAL PERSPECTIVES: *The Tabla*

The tabla is a two-piece drum set with a bass and a treble drum that is one of India's most important instruments. Both drumheads are made of goat skin with a small patch of metal powder pasted in the middle to alter the sound of the drum and reduce vibrations. The body of the treble drum is made from wood; the body of the bass drum is made from metal. The treble drum is tuned to the tonal center of the song and played with the fingers of the right hand. The bass drum is played with the fingers of the left hand. The sounds are combined into rhythm patterns or *talas* (see

page 216). The six-beat *dadra tala* is heard on the recording of "Diwali Song."

ENRICHMENT: *New Year Ceremony*

Have the students list the reasons for celebrating the new year (starting anew, reflecting on goals and intentions) and create their own New Year ceremony. For example, they might write about a personal quality they would like to change and then throw the paper away, or think about something they would like to accomplish and seal it in an envelope to open a year later.

Diwali Song

Collected by
Kathy B. Sorensen
As sung by Chhanda Chakroborti

Hindi: दी प ज ला ओ दी प ज ला ओ आ ज दी वा ली
Pronunciation: di pə ja la o di pə ja la o a jə di wa li
English: **Light up your lamps, come light them to-day, the day of Di-wa-li**

दी प ज ला ओ दी प ज ला ओ
re di pə ja la o di pə ja la o
Re.——— **Light up your lamps, come light them to-day. The**

Fine

आ ज दी वा ली रे खु शी खु शी स ब हें स ते आ ओ
a jə di wa li re ku shi ku shi sa va hã sə te ao
day of Di-wa-li Re. Ev'-ry-one smil-ing and hap-py, Ah-oh

आ ज दी वा ली रे आ ज दी वा ली
a jə di wa li re a jə di wa li
To-day, Di-wa-li—— Re, to-day, Di-wa-li,

D.C. al Fine

आ ज दी वा ली आ ज दी वा ली रे
a jə di wa li a jə di wa li re
to-day, Di-wa-li, To-day, Di-wa-li Re.———

Celebrations *New Year* **315**

---

2. Play a six-beat Indian rhythm pattern.
Have students:

Recorded Lesson CD8:13

• Listen to "Playing Indian Music on the Tabla," in which Dhananjay (Jay) Patankar describes the tabla and demonstrates Indian rhythmic patterns.

• Try playing the six-beat dadra pattern notated below. (Have students tap on their desk, using the right hand for the treble drum and the left hand for the bass drum, as described in the recorded lesson.)

L R R R L L L

• Tell which western European meter is most like the six-beat dadra pattern. (§ meter has six pulses, so it is the closest western European equivalent to dadra. However, dadra is not based on western rhythms such as eighth notes, and it does not have two dotted quarter beats divided into threes like § meter.)

• Divide into two groups for a performance of "Diwali Song." One group sings the song and one group plays the dadra pattern on their desks.

PRONUNCIATION: *Happy New Year*

See the Hindi pronunciation of "Happy New Year" on page 314.

a f<u>a</u>ther   u m<u>oo</u>n   ɾ flipped r

PRONUNCIATION: *"Diwali Song"*

a f<u>a</u>ther   e ch<u>a</u>otic   i b<u>ee</u>   o <u>o</u>bey   u m<u>oo</u>n
ə <u>a</u>go   ɾ flipped r   ~ nasalized vowel

MULTICULTURAL PERSPECTIVES: *Diwali*

Diwali is the name of a group of five Hindu holidays that come all together at the end of October or the beginning of November, usually at the end of the Indian rainy season. This is one of the many festivals of lights found throughout the world. Lights are kept lit throughout Diwali, so that Lakshmi, the Hindu goddess of prosperity, can find her way to every home. Hundreds of clay saucers are filled with oil and a cotton cord is placed in each for a wick. These lamps are then placed everywhere. Indian villages glow with flickering lights throughout the five days of Diwali.

CELEBRATIONS

NEW YEAR

continued from previous page

LESSON**LINKS**

Haji Firuz *(30 min)* 4Div

OBJECTIVE Identify meter and key signature, explore the melodic structure of, and sing a song from Iran

Reinforcement
melodic contour, *page 21*
flat key signatures, *page 101*
§ meter, *page 165*

MATERIALS
Recordings
Haji Firuz   CD8:14
Recorded Lesson: Pronunciation
   for "Haji Firuz"   CD8:15

Haji Firuz CD8:14

1. Identify meter and key signature in a song from Iran. Have students:

• Look at the notation and tell the closest western European meter and key to those of "Haji Firuz." (§ ; one flat—F major; Note that these are only approximate. Iranian music does not use the western concepts of meter or key.)

sɔ le no mo bɑ ræk

In Iran, the first day of spring begins the new year. It is called Noruz, which means "new day." Preparations for Noruz begin about two weeks earlier, when everyone plants a *sabzeh.* Seeds of wheat, barley, or lentils are sprouted in a small container.

The 13 days of Noruz are a time of great celebration—songs, dances, games, gifts, and visiting. Families and friends gather for picnics, where they are entertained by clowns, folk singers, dancers, comic actors, and acrobats. The final day of Noruz is time to throw the sabzeh into the water to send bad luck away.

An Iranian American family celebrates Noruz in Verona Park, New Jersey.

316 RING IN THE NEW

MEETING **INDIVIDUAL** NEEDS

ENRICHMENT: *Rhythm Patterns for "Haji Firuz"*

Play a pattern on their knees with their hands, patting both, right, left, right, while saying text below:

Ring   tam - bou - rine.   Ring   tam - bou - rine.

Then play the same pattern while reciting different text:

Pass   the   al - monds.   Pass   the   al - monds.

Discuss the difference in feeling between the two texts. (The first brings out the feeling of three beats to a measure in the right hand—the syllables *ring, tam-, -ine;* the second brings out the feeling of two beats to a measure in the left hand—the syllables *pass, al-.*) Have students play the pattern along with "Haji Firuz" and think one of the texts while playing the pattern. In their opinion, which seemed to fit the song better?

PRONUNCIATION: *Happy New Year*

See the Farsi pronunciation of "Happy New Year" on page 316.
   ɑ f<u>a</u>ther   æ c<u>a</u>t   e ch<u>a</u>otic   o <u>o</u>bey   ɔ p<u>a</u>w

Haji Firuz is one of the entertainers of Noruz. He wears a baggy red shirt and pants with a cone-shaped hat, and, he usually plays a tambourine.

Haji Firuz

As Collected and Sung by Hooshang Bagheri
English Version by MMH

F major
t, d r m f s

Pronunciation: ha ji fi ɾuz æm mæn   sɔ li yɛ ɾuz æm   mæn
English: Ha - ji Fi - ruz I am!   Ev' - ry year I come 'round.

ha ji fi ɾuz æm mæn   sɔ li yɛ ɾuz æm   mæn
Ha - ji Fi - ruz I am!   Ev' - ry year I come 'round.

Instrumental

sɔɛ e no vi ni ɔ mæd e di ke xɔɛ ti ɔ mæd
Cel - e - brate a fine new year, Cel - e - brate, the time is here.

sha di ko nid pa be ku bid dæst bə zæ nid ke ɔ mæd
Stamp your feet, and clap your hands and Cel - e - brate the fine new year.

Persian:
حاجی فیروزم من   سالی یه روزم من
حاجی فیروزم من   سالی یه روزم من
سال نو و عید آمده   عیدی که خواستی آمده
شادی کنید   پا بکوبید   دست بزنید که عید آمده

Celebrations *New Year* **317**

2. **Explore the melodic structure of an Iranian song.** Have students:

• Look at the notation and tell how "Haji Firuz" is performed. (an instrumental section between two sung sections)

• Listen to "Haji Firuz," following the notation and sharing their thoughts about how the melody is constructed. (Students might see that many phrases are followed by another phrase with the same rhythms and with the same melodic contour a step lower.)

• Tell what a *sequence* is. (a connected series; one element coming right after another element) (Tell them that in music, a melodic sequence is a phrase with the same rhythm and melodic contour as the previous phrase, but different pitches.)

• Compare the first four measures with the second four. (The second four measures are a sequence of the first, beginning a step lower.)

• Find sequences in the instrumental section. (Measures 10 and 11 are sequences of Measure 9; Measures 13–16 form a sequence of Measures 9–12.)

• Tell how many measures long the sequence is in Line 6 (1 measure).

3. Sing the song. Have students:

• Read about the Noruz (no **ɾuz**) celebration, and discuss how the new year is celebrated in Iran. (The family in the picture on page 316 is at an outdoor picnic, traditional for the last day of the celebration. They are eating Iranian desserts and drinking hot tea from glasses.)

• Sing "Haji Firuz" on the vocable *la*.

Recorded Lesson CD8:15
• Listen to "Pronunciation for 'Haji Firuz.'"
• Sing the song.

SCIENCE CONNECTION: *Plant a Sabzeh*

Part of the Noruz celebration is planting a *sabzeh* (**sab** se). Bring in some wheat or barley berries and/or lentils. (These can be found at health food stores.) Have students spread a thick layer of seeds on top of a can filled with dirt. Water and place in a sunny location. The seeds will sprout and look like green grass.

ENRICHMENT: *Melodic Sequences*

Have students create melodies to play or sing based on sequences in the key of F.

BIOGRAPHY: *Hooshang Bagheri*

Dr. Hooshang Bagheri (hu **shæng** gɛ ba gɛ **ri**) teaches at the California State University in Northridge, California, where he is on the faculty of the School of Education.

PRONUNCIATION: *Haji Firuz*

ɑ f_ather	æ c_at	e ch_aotic	ɛ p_et	i b_ee
ɪ i_t	o _obey	ɔ p_aw	u m_oon	ə _ago
ɾ flipped r	x guttural h, *German* Ba_ch			

CELEBRATIONS

NEW YEAR

continued from previous page

LESSON LINKS

Bashana Haba'ah *(20 min)*

OBJECTIVE Perform a circle dance to a song in A B form with harmony part

Reinforcement harmony, *page 97*
A B form, *page 13*

MATERIALS
Recording Bashana Haba'ah by
N. Hirsch (listening)   CD8:16

Auld Lang Syne *(15 min)*

OBJECTIVE Accompany a song in F major with I, IV, and V chord roots

Reinforcement flat key signatures, *page 101*
I-IV-V chords, *page 179*

MATERIALS
Recording Auld Lang Syne   CD8:17

Instruments drum; Optional—bass/tenor pitched instruments (hand bells, resonator bells, guitar, Autoharp, tenor recorder)

Resources Signing Master S • 6 • 7

Bashana Haba'ah CD8:16

1. Prepare for a dance. Have students:

• Walk freely around the room to a steady quarter-note drumbeat provided by a student.

• Walk to a half-note beat.

שָׁנָה טוֹבָה וּמְאוּשֶׁרֶת
shana tova uməushɛrɛt

Rosh Hashanah, the Jewish New Year, is celebrated throughout the world. It comes in September or October. The holiday begins at sundown and lasts for ten days. A prayer called the *kiddush* is recited before the evening meal. The meal includes foods with special meanings. For instance, honey symbolizes a sweet year ahead.

Yom Kippur is the last day of the Jewish New Year season. It is a time to ask forgiveness and remember to live better lives in the new year.

LISTENING

Bashana Haba'ah

by Nurit Hirsh

Listen to a Hebrew song of hope that tells about the good things to come. The English translation of "Bashana Haba'ah" is "In the Year to Come."

Sounding the shofar, or ram's horn, is an impressive moment during Rosh Hashanah.

318 RING IN THE NEW

MEETING **INDIVIDUAL** NEEDS

BACKGROUND: *Rosh Hashanah*

Rosh Hashanah (**rosh** hɑ **shɑ** nɑ) or "Head of the Year" is the Jewish New Year, which is celebrated in either September or October. It falls on the first two days of the lunar month of Tishrei. The days of Rosh Hashanah are considered holy days. They are a time to pray and reflect on the past year and make plans for the new one to come. Families go to the synagogue for special services, which begin with the blowing of the *shofar* (**sho** fɑr) or trumpet made from a ram's horn. Then families gather at home for a special meal, which features fish dishes to symbolize "plenty."

MOVEMENT: *Choreograph a Dance*

MOVEMENT

Have students make up their own dance for "Bashana Haba'ah." They should use four half-note steps and eight quarter-note steps as the basis for their movement.

PRONUNCIATION: *Happy New Year*

See the Hebrew pronunciation of "Happy New Year" on page 318.

ɑ f<u>a</u>ther	ɛ p<u>e</u>t	o <u>o</u>bey	u m<u>oo</u>n
ə <u>a</u>go	ɾ f<u>li</u>pped ɾ		

Happy New Year

New Year's Eve in Scotland is known as Hogmanay. At midnight, the front door is opened to send out the old year and bring in the new year. Friends and family join in good wishes, sing "Auld Lang Syne," and hang up the new calendar.

F major

s, l, d r m s l d'

Auld Lang Syne

Scotch Air
Words by Robert Burns

Verse

1. Should auld ac - quain - tance be for - got, And
2. And here's a hand, my trust - y frien', And

nev - er brought to mind? Should auld ac - quain - tance
gie's a hand o' thine; We'll tak' a cup o'

be for - got, And days of auld lang syne?
kind - ness yet, For auld lang syne.

Refrain

For auld lang syne, my dear, For auld lang syne;

We'll tak' a cup o' kind - ness yet For auld lang syne.

Celebrations *New Year* 319

---

2. Perform a circle dance to a song in A B form with a harmony part. Have students:

- To the half-note beat, step R foot to right and touch L foot, then step L foot to left and touch R foot. Then try it to the quarter-note beat.

- Practice a drum pattern of four half-note beats followed by eight quarter-note beats.

- Listen to "Bashana Haba'ah" (ba **sha** na ha ba 'a), tell the form and which section has a vocal harmony part. (A B; B)

- Learn movements using circle formation, hands joined, then perform with the music:

   A section: Move counterclockwise four slow steps (8 beats), seven quick steps (7 beats). Turn to face clockwise on the eighth beat. (16 beats altogether)

   Repeat in the opposite direction. Face center. (16 beats)

   B section: Walk four quick steps to center and four quick steps back to place (8 beats). Then step R, touch L, step L, touch R (4 beats). Beginning with R foot, turn clockwise in place (4 beats). Repeat all B section movements.

Auld Lang Syne CD8:17

Accompany a song in F major. Have students:

- Read page 319, then listen to "Auld Lang Syne," singing along as able.

- Tell the key. (F major) Hum the roots of the I, IV, and V chords with the verse or play them on bass/tenor pitched instruments:

Beats: 4 4 4 4 4 4 2 2 4

Chords: I - V - I - IV - I - V - IV - V - I

Roots: F - C - F - B♭ - F - C - B♭ - C - F

- Form two groups, one singing the melody and the other singing or playing the chord root accompaniment on the verse. Read the chords for the refrain, playing the roots while others sing the song.

BACKGROUND: *Hogmanay*

Hogmanay (hag mə ne) is the traditional New Year's Eve celebration in Scotland. Some think the word comes from an Old French term, meaning "new year with mistletoe." The first person or "first foot" to enter the house in the new year is the "first footer" and he or she can bring good luck to the family. Tradition calls for the person to come empty-handed—except for a lump of coal to add to the fire.

SIGNING: *"Auld Lang Syne"*

Signing Master S • 6 • 7 has sign language for this song.

BIOGRAPHY: *Robert Burns*

Poet Robert Burns (1759–1796) is considered the national poet of Scotland. His poems often deal with love and friendship. He wrote the words to "Auld Lang Syne" (Old Long Since) after hearing an old man singing them.

CRITICAL THINKING: *Compare and Contrast*

Have students summarize the common motifs in the various new year celebrations in this lesson (cleaning house, eating special food, asking forgiveness, making resolutions) and reflect on the diverse expression of universal themes.

CELEBRATIONS

MARTIN LUTHER KING, JR., DAY

RELATED ARTS [MOVEMENT] [THEATER] [VISUAL ARTS]

SELECTION
I HAVE A DREAM, *page 320*

LESSON LINKS

I Have a Dream (20 min)

OBJECTIVE Sing a song with dotted rhythms and discuss and relate the lyrics to Dr. Martin Luther King, Jr.

Reinforcement dotted rhythm patterns, *page 109*

MATERIALS
Recording I Have a Dream   CD8:18

Resources Signing Master S • 6 • 8

A Dream o

In the summer of 1963, Dr. Martin Luther King, Jr., delivered his "I Have a Dream" speech to over 200,000 Americans in Washington, D.C. The speech defined the basis of the civil rights movement. Dr. King's words still carry deep meaning for all people.

I Have a Dream

Words and Music by Teresa Jennings

Majestically

1. There was a man in A-mer-i-ca who had a dream, they say, that all the peo-ples of the earth could live in peace some-day. 2. And King. "I have a dream," this great man used to say. "I have a dream." His words would light the way.

when he spoke to the gath-ered crowds, his heart and soul would sing. This gra-cious man, this gen-tle man. This Mar-tin Luth-er King.

1. The

320

MEETING **INDIVIDUAL** NEEDS

BIOGRAPHY: *Dr. Martin Luther King, Jr.*

Dr. Martin Luther King, Jr. (1929–1968) was the foremost leader of the civil rights movement in the United States during the 1950s and 1960s. Dr. King's early involvement with civil rights for African Americans came in 1955 when he helped organize a boycott aimed at ending segregated seating on Montgomery (Alabama) city buses. (The boycott began when Rosa Parks was arrested for refusing to move to the back of a public bus.) In 1956 the U.S. Supreme Court ruled in a related case that segregation in public transportation was illegal.

After moving to Atlanta in 1960, King continued to speak out and use nonviolent means to protest against racial discrimination. His most famous speech, "I Have a Dream," was given in Washington, D.C., in 1963. From 1964 to 1968, Dr. King continued to expose and challenge policies and practices that limited the freedom of African Americans as well as others. In 1968 while organizing a march in Memphis, Dr. King was assassinated.

SIGNING: *"I Have a Dream"*

Signing Master S • 6 • 8 has sign language for this song.

reedom

with growing intensity

time he lived— was a trou-bled time— when peo-ple could not
so he tried— to tell us all;— his words with peace would

see in spite of all— our diff-'ren-ces,— we have the right to
ring. This hon-est man,— this no-ble man.— This Mar-tin Luth-er

be. 2. And King. "I have a dream," this great man used to say.
dream," to live in har-mon-y.

"I have a dream." His words would light the way. "I have a
"I have a dream" that

molto rit.   *a tempo*

all of us are free! Are free!

C major (modulates)

Celebrations *Martin Luther King, Jr., Day* **321**

I Have a Dream CD8:18

Sing a song with dotted rhythms and discuss Dr. Martin Luther King, Jr. Have students:

• Tell what they already know about Dr. Martin Luther King, Jr.

• Listen to "I Have a Dream," following along in their books.

• Find dotted quarter-eighth rhythm patterns in the song and clap the rhythm of the measures in which they are found. (Measures 4, 8, 23, 27)

• Identify something new they learned about Dr. King from the lyrics of the song. Discuss the contributions of Dr. King to all people. (See *Biography* on the bottom of page 320.)

• Relate the meaning of the text to the style of singing the song. Sing along as they are able, trying to communicate the meaning of the lyrics in an expressive manner.

LANGUAGE ARTS CONNECTION: *Writing an Essay*

Have students write an essay explaining what M.L. King, Jr., meant by these words: "The ultimate measure of a man is not where he stands in moments of comfort and convenience, but where he stands at times of challenge and controversy."

ENRICHMENT: *Program Idea*

Have students research and dramatize some of the important events from King's life to present as a program. Have them add songs such as "I Have a Dream" at appropriate places. They might also include some songs of the civil rights movement such as "We Shall Overcome."

SOCIAL STUDIES CONNECTION: *Leading Citizens*

Write these names on the board: Abraham Lincoln (president of the United States, author of the Emancipation Proclamation), Geronimo (Native American leader), Cesar Chavez (migrant farm workers' leader), Susan B. Anthony (women's voting rights' leader). Have students identify and describe each person, or choose one person to research in depth, focusing on how each worked to make life better for others. This project can also be a term report.

CELEBRATIONS

SPRING

RELATED ARTS `MOVEMENT` `THEATER` `VISUAL ARTS`

SELECTIONS
EARTH DAY EVERY DAY (CELEBRATE), *page 322*
GARDEN OF THE EARTH *(listening), page 324*
GARDEN OF THE EARTH, *page 325*

LESSONLINKS

Earth Day Every Day (Celebrate)
(20 min)

OBJECTIVE Discuss interpretation and changing meter in a song, find syncopation, and sing the song

Reinforcement
syncopation, *page 211*
interpretation of a song, *page 211*

MATERIALS
Recording Earth Day Every Day
(Celebrate)   CD8:19

Resources Recorder Master R • 32
(pitches D E G A)

C major

r, m, f, s, l, t, d r m

John Denver is one of many musicians bringing attention to the environment through their songs. What is the primary message of Denver's song?

Earth Day Every Day
(CELEBRATE)

Words and Music
by John Denver

Slowly, freely

Cel- e- brate morn- ing,   the   cry of a loon on a lake in the night,

dreams that are born in the dawn's ear- ly   light,—   cel- e- brate morn- ing.

Cel- e- brate   liv- ing,   the   laugh- ter that sings in the heart of a child,

free- dom that flies to the call of the   wild,—   cel- e- brate liv- ing.

322

MEETING **INDIVIDUAL** NEEDS

BACKGROUND: *Earth Day*

The first Earth Day was celebrated on April 22, 1970, as an expression of concern about the environment. All over the United States, people paused to enjoy the outdoors and to come up with solutions for its problems. They planted trees and picked up trash. They learned about recycling paper, bottles, and cans. They thought of ways to conserve resources such as electricity, oil, and water. The celebration proved a popular one, and today it is still celebrated in the United States and other countries.

BIOGRAPHY: *John Denver*

John Denver (b. 1943) was born Henry John Deutchendorf, Jr., in New Mexico. While studying architecture at Texas Tech, he became involved with folk music. Hoping to break into the music business, Denver moved to Los Angeles where he played in numerous clubs. His first album *Rhymes and Reasons* included the hit song "Leaving on a Jet Plane." His first hit single was "Take Me Home, Country Roads." An ardent environmentalist, Denver makes his home in Colorado.

Earth Day Every Day CD8:19

1. Discuss interpretation and changing meter in a song. Have students:

• Name things that are being celebrated in the lyrics of "Earth Day Every Day." (morning, living, evening, Earth Day) Then find a reference to "The Star Spangled Banner" in the lyrics. (*the dawn's early light*)

• Give their favorite image from the song, and suggest ways to interpret the song to match the mood of the lyrics, choosing tempo, articulation, dynamics, and tone color. (They may choose different interpretations for the two sections of the song.)

• Listen to the song and compare their choices with those on the recording.

• Form groups of four to find changes of meter signature in the song. (Measures 2, 3, 4, 6, 7, 8, 9, 11, 15, 16)

• Tell what the meter signatures are and in which part of the song they occur. ($\frac{4}{4}$, $\frac{5}{4}$, $\frac{3}{4}$, $\frac{2}{4}$; the first part) Then tell why John Denver might have used meter changes in the song. (Possible answer: to give the first section a free feeling, as if in a pleasant dream)

2. Find syncopation and sing the song. Have students:

• Listen to the music again and tell where they hear syncopation (placing stresses on weak beats or parts of beats that are normally unstressed) in the second part of the song, starting at *Celebrate Earth Day*. (each time the words *Earth Day* are sung, and in the phrases *land and sea* and *you and me*)

• Sing the song.

Celebrations *Spring* **323**

SCIENCE CONNECTION: *Recycling*

Have students find out how your community practices recycling. They can work in pairs to write ten questions related to recycling and the environment, then use these questions to interview a person involved with the local recycling program. Have students report their findings to the rest of the class. Suggest they use charts and/or demonstrations as appropriate. To learn more about recycling in general, students can send a postcard requesting information to the Environmental Defense Fund—Recycling/257 Park Ave. South/New York, NY 10010.

CELEBRATIONS

SPRING

continued from previous page

LESSONLINKS

Garden of the Earth (listening)
(15 min)

OBJECTIVE Listen for tone color (vocal and instrumental)

Reinforcement
vocal tone color, *page 207*
vocal categories, *page 207*

MATERIALS
Recording Garden of the Earth by
P. Winter (listening)   CD8:20

Garden of the Earth *(15 min)*

OBJECTIVE Identify phrases and vocal category, and sing a song

Reinforcement
vocal categories, *page 215*

MATERIALS
Recordings
Garden of the Earth   CD8:21
Recorded Lesson: Pronunciation
for "Garden of the Earth"   CD8:22

Resources Signing Master S • 6 • 9

SPRING GARDENING Natalia Goncharova painted *Spring Gardening* around 1908. It combines an abstract approach to painting with influences from Russian folk art. Later, her paintings became even more abstract. Goncharova also designed sets and costumes for Russian ballets.

LISTENING

Garden of the Earth

Paul Winter Consort and the Pokrovsky Singers

Paul Winter took his group on tour to Russia in 1986. There he met a popular group dedicated to singing ancient Russian village music. The two groups of musicians from different nations worked together to create a new style. They developed a unique sound, combining Western harmonies with ancient Russian songs. Making music together was a way of expressing friendship and getting to know each other.

324 OUR PLANET, OUR HOME

MEETING **INDIVIDUAL** NEEDS

BIOGRAPHY: *Paul Winter*

Paul Winter's (b. 1939) music combines many different musical styles, such as jazz and folk, with sounds of nature and animals. Winter began playing the drums when he was five. By the time he was 12, he had tried many different instruments and decided the saxophone was his favorite. He attended Northwestern University, where he formed a sextet.

In 1986, Winter and his group, the Paul Winter Consort, went on a tour of the Soviet Union. There he met the Dmitri Pokrovsky Singers when they performed with the

Consort at Moscow University. The two groups decided to make a record together, and in 1987 they began recording. As they recorded, Winter's group improvised new melodies and added percussion instruments to the Pokrovsky Singers ancient songs and chants. Together they created new and unusual music, including "Garden of the Earth."

ART CONNECTION: *A World Garden* VISUAL ARTS

Have students use the title of the song "Garden of the Earth" as a starting point for creating a "world garden." First have students draw an outline map, showing Earth's

E♭ major

s, l, d r m f s l

Garden of the Earth

Traditional
Russian Folk Song
Words by Paul Winter
and Paul Halley

Russian: Ой ты сад, ты мой сад, Сад зе-
Pronunciation: uɪ tɪ sat tɪ mɔɪ sat sat zi

English: 1. There's a gar - den 'round the Earth, There's a
(2.) voi - ces, ma - ny tongues, from the
(3.) glo - ry of the Earth, for the

лё - нень - кий, Ты за - чем ра - но цве-
lyɔn nyɛn ki tɪ za chɛm ɪɑ nə tsvi

home be - neath the sun; In the beau - ty of this
moun - tains to the sea; Sing of beau - ty all a-
glo - ry of the sun; We will sing of life to-

тёшь, О - сы - па - ешь - ся.
tyɔsh ɑ sɪ pɑ yɛsh syɑ

gar - den, We will hear_____ a thou- sand songs. 2.Ma - ny one.
round_ us, in this an - cient har - mo - ny. 3.For the
ge - ther, and for - ev - er live as

Celebrations Spring **325**

Garden of the Earth (listening) CD8:20

Listen for tone color. Have students:

• Read about how "Garden of the Earth" was created, then listen to the recording.

• Discuss the tone color of the Russian singers. (The tone color, typical in southern Russia and parts of Eastern Europe, is a heavier, brighter, more "forward" sound than that to which students may be accustomed.)

• Recall the adult voice categories, which also classify saxophones. (soprano, alto, tenor, bass) Listen again and describe the tone color of the soprano saxophone. (light, smooth, floating)

• Listen again and tell the meter. ($\frac{3}{4}$)

Garden of the Earth CD8:21

Identify phrases and vocal category, and sing a song. Have students:

• Listen to "Garden of the Earth," singing along as able.

Recorded Lesson CD8:22
• Listen to "Pronunciation for 'Garden of the Earth.'"

• Sing the song.

• Decide on the number and length of the phrases. (3, short-short-long: Phrase 1—*There's a garden . . .*; Phrase 2—*There's a home . . .*; Phrase 3—*In the beauty . . .*)

• Notice what is alike about Phrases 1 and 2. (almost the same melody and rhythm.) Notice what is alike about all three phrases. (Each starts with the following rhythm.

)

• Recall how to show phrases in singing. (take a breath only at the end of each phrase)

• Sing the song again, showing the phrases by breathing at the correct places. Tell the category to which their voices belong. (unchanged voices, perhaps cambiatas)

---

continents. Then have them draw images mentioned or suggested by the song on their map.

ENRICHMENT: *Phrase Length*

The point of observing phrase lengths is to help students become aware that the greater length of the last phrase adds to the rhythmic interest of the song in a way that having all phrases the same length would not. To illustrate this, have students read the words of the first English verse, changing *of this garden* to *of this earth* so that there are four phrases of the same length and rhythm. The effect of the song, if the rhythm were like this, would probably be considered quite monotonous, especially when repeated for three verses. Then have the students say the words as written, noting and discussing the difference in the effect.

SIGNING: *"Garden of the Earth"*

Signing Master S • 6 • 9 has sign language for this song.

PRONUNCIATION: *"Garden of the Earth"*

ɑ f**a**ther	ɛ p**e**t	i b**ee**	ɪ **i**t
ɔ p**aw**	u m**oo**n	ə **a**go	ɪ̄ rolled r

CELEBRATIONS

SPRING

RELATED ARTS [MOVEMENT] [THEATER] [VISUAL ARTS]

SELECTIONS
MÚSICA INDÍGENA *(listening), page 327*
JARABE TAPATÍO *(listening), page 328*
DE COLORES, *page 328*

LESSONLINKS

Música indígena *(15 min)*

OBJECTIVE Create legato or marcato movement for a dance in A B A form

Reinforcement
legato/marcato movement, *page 195*
A B A form, *page 161*

MATERIALS
Recording Música indígena by
M. M. Ponce (listening)   CD8:23

Resources Resource Master C • 3
(practice)

THE FIFTH OF MAY

Cinco de Mayo means "fifth of May." This national holiday of Mexico honors the day, more than 100 years ago, when the Mexicans won a major battle against the French.

Celebrations of Cinco de Mayo take place in the United States as well as in Mexico. The holiday is a festive springtime event in New York, Los Angeles, El Paso, and anywhere there are communities of Mexican-Americans.

MEETING **INDIVIDUAL** NEEDS

MULTICULTURAL PERSPECTIVES: *Cinco de Mayo*

On May 5, 1862, in the town of Puebla, Mexico, a small group of Mexicans won a decisive battle against the invading French army. In Mexico and Mexican American communities in the United States, Cinco de Mayo (**sing** ko ð e **ma** yo) is celebrated with a fiesta. People wear their best clothes or traditional costumes. There are dances, mariachi music, food, decorations of green, white, and red (the colors of the Mexican flag), contests, performances, and the breaking of the piñata (a crepe-paper figure built around a clay

pot). In some Mexican towns, a mock battle is staged between soldiers dressed as French and Mexican soldiers.

BIOGRAPHY: *Manuel María Ponce*

Mexican composer Manuel María Ponce (man **wel** ma ɾia **pon** se), 1882–1948, was a pianist and composer of symphonies, chamber music, and songs. As a child he studied piano in Mexico City and in Europe. He gave his first concert of his own compositions the year he turned 30. His compositions remain popular, especially in Mexico. One of his songs, "Estrellita," has such a catchy melody that it is often mistaken for a folk song.

♪ LISTENING

Música indígena *by Manuel Maria Ponce*

Manuel Maria Ponce, who is often called the "father of modern Mexican music," drew on the folk music of his native country for his compositions. The title of this piece means "indigenous music." You will hear the sound of music that originates or occurs naturally in Mexico—music that is indigenous to Mexico.

—Celebrations Spring **327**

Música indígena CD8:23

Create legato or marcato movement for a dance in A B A form. Have students:

• Listen to "Música indígena" (**mu** si kʌ ɪn **di** he nʌ) while quietly tapping with the beat on their legs. Try to tell the meter. (²₄, with a ³₈ measure at the end of the A section and in the middle of the B section)

• Raise their right hands when the music becomes soft.

• Raise their left hands when the opening music returns.

• Tell the form of the music. (A B A)

• Decide whether this music should have legato or marcato movement for each section to fit its mood. (See Unit 5, Lesson 1.) Learn the A section for the following dance and create the B section movement, using the style of movement they chose. (Optional: Use the rhythm accompaniment on **Resource Master C • 3** as a guide.)

Form concentric circles with partners standing side by side, moving solemnly to the music as follows:

A section—Walk 7 beats clockwise. Turn to face the opposite direction on Beat 8.

Walk 7 beats counterclockwise and face partner on Beat 8.

Raise and lower hands. (4 beats)

Rest 2 beats (second time—1 beat).

B section—Partners use mirroring to create a B section for the dance. The partner on the inside of the circle begins to move arms to reflect the music while the outside partner mirrors the movement.

A section—Repeat original movement, only this time raise and lower hands three times. (11 beats)

SOCIAL STUDIES CONNECTION: *Geography*

Have students locate Mexico on a map and find the town of Puebla where the battle of Cinco de Mayo was fought. "Jarabe tapatío" (page 328) was originally from the people called Los Tapatíos who live on the outskirts of Guadalajara (gwa da la **xa** ɾa), the capital of Jalisco (xa **lis** ko). Have students locate Jalisco and Guadalajara.

ENRICHMENT: *"Música indígena"*

Have students create words to the music celebrating Cinco de Mayo. Use **Resource Master C • 3**.

LANGUAGE ARTS CONNECTION: *Spanish Words*

Discuss Spanish words such as fiesta (**fyɛ** sta), mariachi (ma ɾi **a** chi), tortilla (toɾ **ti** ya), piñata (pi **nya** ta), sombrero (som **bɾe** ɾo), and amigo (a **mi** go). Have students use a dictionary to find their original meaning or origin. Discuss how non-English words become a common part of the English vocabulary through usage. Create a bulletin board with an illustrated list of Spanish words that have become a part of our everyday vocabulary.

Celebrations SPRING: The Fifth of May **327**

continued from previous page

LESSON LINKS

Jarabe tapatío *(listening) (30 min)*

OBJECTIVE Learn a traditional Mexican dance-step

Reinforcement
movement, *page 195*
§ meter, *page 145*

MATERIALS
Recording Jarabe tapatío
(listening)   CD8:24

De colores *(15 min)*

OBJECTIVE Decide on interpretation and then sing a traditional Mexican song

Reinforcement
interpretation, *page 199*
§ meter, *page 145*

MATERIALS
Recordings
De colores (Many Colors)   CD8:25
Recorded Lesson: Pronunciation
for "De colores"   CD8:26

Technology Music with MIDI

Jarabe tapatío CD8:24

1. Learn the Jarabe step. Have students:

• Read about "Jarabe tapatío" (χɑ ɾɑ βe tɑ pɑ **ti** o) and the Jarabe dance.

LISTENING Jarabe tapatío

Mexican Folk Melody

The jarabe is the national dance of Mexico. Jarabe means "mixture." The dance features several melodies and tells the story of a courtship. Toward the end of the dance, the man throws down his sombrero and the woman dances on it. Then she picks up the sombrero and puts it on to symbolize her acceptance of the man's proposal.

In the 1970s "De colores" became a theme song for Mexican Americans who were striving for fair treatment in this country. Why would a song about the beauty of different colors be used in a struggle for equal rights?

DE COLORES
MANY COLORS

Spanish Folk Song
English Version
by MMH

Spanish: 1. De co-lo-res, de co-lo-res se vis-ten los
Pronunciation: de ko lo ɾes ðe ko lo ɾe se βis ten los
English: 1. Oh, the col-ors! Oh, the col-ors we see in the
2. Hear the roost-er, hear the roost-er who sings, "qui-ri,

cam-pos en la pri-ma-ve-ra. De co-
kam pos en la pri ma βe ɾa de ko
blos-som-ing fields in the spring-time. All the
qui-ri, qui-ri, qui-ri, qui-ri." Now the

328 THE FIFTH OF MAY

MEETING **INDIVIDUAL** NEEDS

BACKGROUND: *"Jarabe tapatío"* MOVEMENT

Jarabe tapatío is the national dance of Mexico. Originally it was a lengthy dance done by the Independence fighters, but it was shortened so that more people would be able to learn it. However, it still contains a great variety of difficult steps. Jarabe tapatío is remembered for its specific symbol of the sombrero and the distinct relationship between partners. The dance tells the story of courtship with the final acceptance of the proposal.

BACKGROUND: *"De colores"*

"De colores" is a popular children's song in Mexico that took on a new meaning in the early 1970s. Because "De colores" was a symbol of their Mexican heritage, it became a theme song for the civil rights movement by Mexican Americans who were striving for fair treatment in the United States. There is also significance in the words about a world of many colors, which came to represent a world where all races and creeds would be treated equally.

- Learn a simplified version of the basic Jarabe step (Verbal Cue—*heel, toe, toe*):

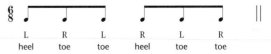

2. Practice the Jarabe step with the music.
Have students:

- Listen to the recording and tell the meter. (§)
Then try the Jarabe step again, stepping on the balls of the feet rather than the toes.

- Practice the Jarabe step with the music, both in place and traveling forward.

- Form couples, facing each other, with the boy clasping hands behind his back, the girl holding skirt in both hands to the side and slightly forward.

- Beginning with the left heel, do Jarabe steps in place (Measures 1–7). On Measure 8, stamp left foot beside right without shifting weight.

- Repeat the same step for the repeat of Measures 1–8, only move in a circular pathway, traveling clockwise to exchange places with partner. Right shoulders pass. (The repeat is done with a different step in the original.)

De colores CD8:25

Decide on interpretation and then sing a traditional Mexican song. Have students:

- Discuss images in the song and why the song was used by Mexican Americans in the struggle for equal rights.

- Decide on intepretation choices to fit the mood of the song (tempo, dynamics, articulation, tone color). Then listen to "De colores," following the notation. Compare their interpretation with that on the recording.

- Tell the meter. (§)

Recorded Lesson CD8:26
- Listen to "Pronunciation for 'De colores.'"

- Sing the song.

PLAYING INSTRUMENTS: *Percussion*

To add authentic Latin American percussion sounds, have students play maracas, claves, güiro, or cabasa to the beat of the music while they sing "De colores."

PRONUNCIATION: *"De colores"*

ɑ f<u>a</u>ther	e ch<u>a</u>otic	i b<u>ee</u>	o <u>o</u>bey
u m<u>oo</u>n	β b without lips touching		ð <u>the</u>
ɾ flipped r	x slightly guttural	h, *Spanish* b<u>aj</u>o	

LANGUAGE ARTS CONNECTION: *Color Poems*

"De colores" tells about the colors of the rainbow that light up the sky. Have students write a poem about the colors of the rainbow or a poem that includes descriptions of the many colors of nature.

ENRICHMENT: *Program Idea*

Have your own Cinco de Mayo celebration with a performance of "Música indígena," "Jarabe tapatío," and "De colores." Decorate the stage in green, red, and white. Break a piñata and pass out candy or party favors to the guests.

ᴄELEBRATIONS

SUMMER

RELATED ARTS `MOVEMENT` `THEATER` `VISUAL ARTS`

SELECTION
GRAND ENTRY *(listening), page 331*

LESSONLINKS

Grand Entry *(15 min)*

OBJECTIVE Hear a Native American song and learn about Native American drumming style

Reinforcement
summer, *page 279*
Native American music, *page 171*

MATERIALS
Recording Grand Entry (Powwow)
(listening)   CD8:27

Summertime

Long ago, many Plains Indians lived in small villages during the winter. When warm weather arrived, several villages gathered together to celebrate. These gatherings were the ancestors of the modern-day event known as the powwow.

Today, people from many different Native American nations participate in powwows. The largest ones take place during the summer months. The powwow is a time to reunite with friends and family and enjoy events such as rodeos, sports, feasts, and dancing contests.

Powwows usually have several categories of dance competition. Two of the most common are the Traditional and Fancy Dance. Traditional dances are based on steps that have been danced for hundreds of years. Fancy Dances feature newer Native American dance styles.

Men's Fancy Dancers competing at a powwow in Wyoming.

330

MEETING **INDIVIDUAL** NEEDS

MULTICULTURAL PERSPECTIVES: *Powwows*

Contemporary powwows are usually intertribal. They provide a way for Native Americans to maintain their heritage. During a powwow, people dance, sing, eat, make and sell crafts, and visit with friends. Powwows also offer non-Indian people a chance to learn about Native American traditions.

ENRICHMENT: *Form of "Grand Entry"*

Have students analyze the form of "Grand Entry," telling how many times the song is repeated and what distinguishes the beginning of the repetitions. (4; each repetition begins with a solo by Gary Fields) Then ask students how many distinct sections they can identify in the song. (4; the form is A A B C D B C, repeated four times. Students might note that the A section is sung first by the solo singer, then repeated in unison.)

Grand Entry CD8:27

Listen to a Native American song and learn about Native American drumming style.
Have students:

• Read about powwows and "Grand Entry."

• Listen to "Grand Entry" and talk about the meaning of the drum to Native Americans, according to Gary Fields. (It is similar to the heartbeat.)

• Tell whether they hear any accents at the beginning when the drum plays. (Very slight accents on every other beat may give a feeling of $\frac{2}{4}$.)

• Tell if the dynamics of the drum vary. (yes)

• Listen again, noting how the tempo varies toward the end of the song and what is different about the drum playing when the tempo changes. (As the tempo gets faster, the drum is played louder and faster. The tempo change is cued by the strong drum accents.)

• Compare the selection to other processionals they have heard, such as "The Wedding March" or "Pomp and Circumstance." (All have a strong, steady beat.)

Energetic movements are characteristic of both Men's and Women's Fancy Dance.

LISTENING

Grand Entry

Traditional Native American Music

Each powwow begins with the Grand Entry. As special music plays, the dancers enter the arena. The order of their entry depends on the category of dance in which they are participating.

Gary Fields's heritage is Native American. His knowledge of Native American music comes from living on reservations in America and Western Canada. He has learned many Native American songs. Listen as he describes the music and events of the Grand Entry.

Celebrations *Summer* **331**

SOCIAL STUDIES CONNECTION: *Native Americans*

Have students research some of the contributions of Native Americans to the world. Among these are the domestication of a large number of wild plants, including maize (corn), beans, and squash, that today feed many people around the world. The Iroquois Confederacy was one of the first democratic governments in the world. Certain groups are well-known for crafts such as carving, rug- or basket-weaving, pottery, and jewelry making. Encourage students to report on their research creatively. They might speak from the point of view of a Native American, cook a Native American meal, or demonstrate a craft.

Music LIBRARY

MORE MUSIC!

The *Music Library* is a collection of anthologies for use throughout the year. It includes more songs and listening selections for:
- reinforcement of specific concepts and skills
- extra practice
- alternate materials

INTEGRATED LESSONS FOR CONCEPT AND SKILL REINFORCEMENT

Reinforcement references in *Music Library* lesson suggestions point out key concepts, skills, and themes for the selections, and provide page references to unit lessons that cover the same ideas.

CONTENTS

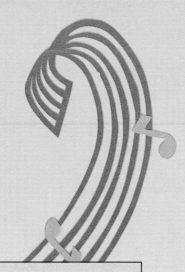

PLANNER

MULTICULTURAL PERSPECTIVES

Through exposure to diverse materials, students develop an awareness of how people from many cultures create and participate in music. This unit includes:

For a complete listing of songs by culture, see the Classified Index.

The Boatman

Sing the song CD8:28. Have students:

• Perform this pattern to the quarter-note beat: pat, clap; pat, clap; pat, clap; pat, snap. Then perform the pattern with the song.

• Tell the pitch that is *do* and the pitch letter names of the notes. (G; G A B)

• Sing the melody with the pitch syllables *do re mi*, then with the words.

• Find the chord labels above the notation and tell their Roman numeral names. (G—I; D—V; see page 31.) Listen as you play the chords with the song, signaling chord changes.

Reinforcement
dotted rhythms, *page 113*
I and V chords, *page 33*

Old Ark's A-Moverin'

1. Introduce the song CD8:29. Have students:

• Listen to the song, patting with the beat. Then clap the rhythm of the song.

• Divide into two groups, one to clap the rhythm, the other to pat with the beat. Switch and repeat activity.

• Review the definition of syncopation. (See page 154.) Tell which measures contain syncopation and clap the syncopated pattern. (Measures 1, 5 of the sung part; Measures 1, 3, 5 of the spoken part)

• Tell what *D.C. al Fine* means. (Go back to the beginning and stop at *Fine*—end.)

• Tell the form. (A B A)

• Optional—Use **Playing the Guitar G • 23.**

MEETING **INDIVIDUAL** NEEDS

BACKGROUND: *"Old Ark's A-Moverin'"*

Many spirituals are based on stories from the Bible. (See Unit 1, Lesson 7, page 30, *Multicultural Perspectives*.) In "Old Ark's A-Moverin'," the Old Ark represents the ship that Noah built to save his family and two of each of the world's animals from a great flood. In the Biblical account, the flood was caused by rain that lasted forty days and forty nights.

ENRICHMENT: *"Hotaru Koi"*

Using Dynamics: This song is a good one to sing with a crescendo/decrescendo effect, as if the fireflies were appearing one by one, then disappearing into the night.

Singing in Canon: Have students sing "Hotaru Koi" as a two-part canon. At first, have the second group enter when the first group begins singing Measure 3. Then, have students sing the song with the second group entering just one beat later than the first group.

Hotaru Koi
Come, Firefly

Four-tone

Japanese Folk Song
English Version by MMH

Japanese: ほ ほ ほ た る こい
Pronunciation: ho ho ho ta ɾu koi
English: Ho! Ho! Fire - fly, please come!

あっ ち の み ず は に が い ー ぞ
at chi no mi zu wa ni ga i zo
You will find the wa - ter bad o - ver there.

こっ ち の み ず は あ ま い
kot chi no mi zu wa a ma i
All of the wa - ter's good here, near to

ぞ ほ ほ ほ た る
zo ho ho ho ta ɾu
me! Ho! Ho! Fire - fly, please

こい や ま み ち こい あん ど の
koi ya ma mi chi koi an do no
come! On the moun - tain road, Come once a -

ひ か り で ま た こ い こい
hi ka ɾi de ma ta ko i koi
gain and bring your ti - ny lan - tern light!

Music Library *Reading Anthology* **333**

---

2. Sing the song. Have students:
- Tell the pitch that is *do*. (G)
- Tell how many pitches are in the song, then name the pitches using pitch letter names and pitch syllables. (3; G A B; *do re mi*)
- Sing the song, first with pitch syllables, then with the words.

Reinforcement
syncopation, *page 203*
A B A form, *page 69*

Hotaru Koi

1. Introduce the song CD8:30. Have students:
- Read the words, then describe what the singer is trying to do. (Talk the firefly into coming closer.) Decide what *Ho* might represent in the song (the blinking of the fireflies) and how that might help determine how *Ho* should sound (light and delicate).
- Note the meter signature and the rhythms used. ($\frac{2}{4}$; quarter notes and rests, pairs of eighth notes, dotted eighth-sixteenth)
- Clap the rhythm of the song.

2. Sing the song. Have students:
- Note the key signature (no sharps or flats) and decide on the probable tonal center (A— *la*, since it begins and ends on this pitch.)
- Scan the song to see what pitches are used and tell their pitch letter names (*mi so la ti*; E G A B), then echo you on various combinations of *mi so la* and *ti*.
- Sing the song with pitch syllables.

Recorded Lesson CD8:31
- Listen to "Pronunciation for 'Hotaru Koi.'"
- Sing the song.

Reinforcement
dotted rhythms, *page 113*
la tonal center, *page 73*

PRONUNCIATION: *"Hotaru Koi"*

a f<u>a</u>ther e ch<u>a</u>otic i b<u>ee</u> o <u>o</u>bey
ɔ p<u>a</u>w u m<u>oo</u>n ɾ flipped r

PLAYING INSTRUMENTS: *Recorder*

See **R • 1**, **R • 3**, and **R • 15** in *Playing the Recorder* for "The Boatman." See **R • 4**, **R • 11**, and **R • 16** for "Old Ark's A-Moverin'." See **R • 5** for "Hotaru Koi."

ENRICHMENT: *Rhythm Syllables*

Have students read the rhythm of "Hotaru Koi" using rhythm syllables, saying *ta* for ♩, *ti ti* for ♫ , and *tim ka* or *tim ri* for ♪♫ Students can also sing the song in canon, as marked.

ORFF: *"Boatman," "Old Ark's A-Moverin'," and "Hotaru Koi"*

See **O • 9**, **O • 10**, and **O • 11** in *Orchestrations for Orff Instruments*.

RELATED ARTS **MOVEMENT** THEATER VISUAL ARTS

Every Mornin' When I Wake Up

Sing in canon CD8:32. Have students:

• Identify the type of song. (a canon)

• Note the meter and the rhythms used. (⁴₄; quarter and eighth notes, tied notes, syncopation— ♪ ♩ ♪)

• Echo you, saying the words in rhythm.

• Note the key signature (no sharps or flats) and decide on the tonal center. (C *do*)

• Echo you on each phrase with pitch syllables.

• Sing the song with pitch syllables, then with the words in unison, then canon. (Optional: Add an introduction using the vocal ostinatos on **Resource Master RA • 1**.)

Reinforcement syncopation, *page 203*

Nobody Knows the Trouble I've Seen

Practice a syncopated pattern, then sing the song. Have students:

• Look at the ♪ ♩ ♪ syncopated pattern, then listen to the song CD8:33 (unison) and tell how many times it occurs. (three)

• Listen once more, following the notation and clapping the rhythm pattern when it occurs. Identify the word or words that are associated with this pattern. (*No-bod-y*)

• Sing the word *nobody* when it occurs as they listen to the song, then sing the whole song.

Reinforcement syncopation, *page 157*

MEETING **INDIVIDUAL** NEEDS

BIOGRAPHY: *Avon Gillespie*

"Every Mornin' When I Wake Up" was written by one of the best-known teachers of Orff Schulwerk in the United States, Avon Gillespie, who died in 1989. A dancer and choral conductor, as well as a teacher, he traveled throughout the country doing workshops and courses for teachers, sharing his techniques for joyful music learning.

ORFF: *Every Mornin' When I Wake Up*

See **O • 12** in *Orchestrations for Orff Instruments.*

PLAYING INSTRUMENTS: *Recorder*

See **R • 5** and **R • 18** in *Playing the Recorder* for "Every Mornin' When I Wake Up." See **R • 6**, **R • 9**, and **R • 11** for "Nobody Knows the Trouble I've Seen."

ENRICHMENT: *Partner Song*

Sing "Nobody Knows the Trouble I've Seen" as a partner song with "This Train" and "Swing Low, Sweet Chariot" (*Share the Music*, Grade 5, pages 58 and 162). (Use "Nobody Knows" Version 2 CD8:34.)

ESKIMO
Ice Cream Dance

Yupik Song
Collected and Transcribed by Ben Snowball

Yupik: Yu a - e kum kun a a - e kum kun Yu
Pronunciation: yu ɑ e kʌm kʌn ɑ ɑ e kʌm kʌn yu

wal__ e kum kun__ a o e kum kun A__ yo ko e ya ha
wal e kʌm kʌn ɑ o e kʌm kʌn ɑ yo ko e ya hɑ

A yo ko e ya ha Ya a ha a ya. Yu ya.
ɑ yo ko e ya hɑ ya a hɑ ɑ ya yu ya

Pentatonic

m, s, l, d r m

Drum Accompaniment

Music Library *Reading Anthology* **335**

Eskimo Ice Cream Dance

1. Sing the song CD8:35. Have students:

• Listen to the song.

Recorded Lesson CD8:36
• Listen to "Pronunciation for 'Eskimo Ice Cream Dance.'"

• Listen to the song again, following along.

• Sing along with the recording.

2. Learn the movement. Have students:

• Learn the movements for the A section. (The dance is done in a straight line. Dancers should bounce lightly throughout. They are accompanied by drummers playing hand drums with the beat behind the dancers. The drum head faces downward, then both sides of the rim are tapped with a long dowel rod to simulate the technique used with Eskimo drums.)

Measure 1: Wave hands forward (R-L-R-hold). (The waving motion represents the women waving good-bye to the men as they go whaling.)
Measure 2: Keep L hand on waist. Wave with R hand twice to left, then twice to right at shoulder height.
Measure 3: Wave hands forward (L-R-L-hold).
Measure 4: Repeat Measure 2.
Measure 5: With both hands, do a motion as if washing clothes—twice down left, twice up left.
Measure 6: Washing clothes motion twice down right, twice up right.
Measure 7: Wave R-L-R-L.
Measure 8: One washing motion down left, then hold.

• Learn the movements for the B section. (See *Movement* below.)

• Sing the song with the dance. (The A section, which is heard three times, gets a little faster each time.)

Reinforcement Native American music, *page 171*

MOVEMENT

MOVEMENT: *"Eskimo Ice Cream Dance"*

B section: Movements are done in pantomime, one per beat. *Measure 9*—stir counterclockwise twice. *Measure 10*—stir, rest, lick R palm, hold. *Measure 11*—lick back of R hand, hold, put "bowl" down, hold. *Measure 12*—pick up "parka" on R side, hold, put "parka" over head, hold. *Measure 13*—pick up "bowl" on L side, hold, put "bowl" in L arm, hold. *Measure 14*—walking motion with R hand out, in, out, in. *Measure 15*—dip R hand into "bowl," serve to guest, dip, serve. *Measure 16*—dip, serve, dip, eat (lick palm). *Measure 17*—dip, eat, dip, eat. *Measures 18–19*—with hands on hips, swallow, rest, swallow, rest, swallow, rest three beats.

BACKGROUND: *"Eskimo Ice Cream Dance"*

"Eskimo Ice Cream Dance" was collected by the Native Alaskan singer Ben Snowball. The words mention dancing, drumming, and ice-cream making. In the native language, the ice cream is known as *akutaq* (ɑ ku tɔk). The recipe is: "Whip caribou fat or moose fat . . . until fluffy. Stir in seal oil, sugar, fresh berries, shredded fish, and snow. Share with friends."

PRONUNCIATION: *"Eskimo Ice Cream Dance"*

ɑ f<u>a</u>ther   e ch<u>ao</u>tic   o <u>o</u>bey   u m<u>oo</u>n
ʌ <u>u</u>p

Music Library READING ANTHOLOGY **335**

MUSIC LIBRARY
READING ANTHOLOGY

Oh, How Lovely Is the Evening

Sing the song as a round and with a melodic ostinato CD8:37. Have students:

• Listen to the song and tell the meter. (¾) Tell how many beats a dotted half note gets in ¾. (3)

• Listen again, singing along as able.

• Tell the instrument family they hear in the recording. (string)

• Sing the song as a three-part canon.

• Play Line 3 on resonator bells or other pitched instruments to accompany the song.

Reinforcement canon, *page 73*
string family, *page 29*

Jubilate Deo

1. Introduce the song CD8:38. Have students:

• Name the meter signature and explain its meaning.(¢ or cut time—Note values are cut in half, the half note gets one beat.)

• Tap the rhythm.

• Name the key and tell where the half steps occur. (C; *mi-fa* and *ti-do*; E-F and B-C)

• Sing the following with pitch letter names, then pitch syllables (hold each for two beats): C' D' E' D' C' B A G F E D C; *do' re' mi' re' do' ti la so fa mi re do*

• Sing the song with pitch letter names and pitch syllables.

• Practice singing the melody through with vowel sounds only. (*oo, ee, ah, eh,* and *oh*)

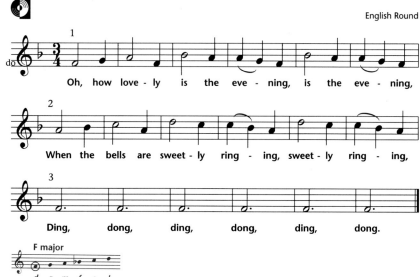

Oh, How Lovely Is the Evening

English Round

Oh, how love-ly is the eve-ning, is the eve-ning,

When the bells are sweet-ly ring-ing, sweet-ly ring-ing,

Ding, dong, ding, dong, ding, dong.

F major
d r m f s l

Jubilate Deo

Music by Michael Praetorius
Text from Psalm 65

Latin: Ju - bi - la-te De-o. Ju-bi-la-te De - o. Al - le-lu - ia!
Pronunciation: yu bi la tɛ dɛ ɔ yu bi la tɛ dɛ ɔ al lɛ lu ya

C major
d r m f s l t d' r' m'

336

MEETING **INDIVIDUAL** NEEDS

ENRICHMENT: *"Oh, How Lovely Is the Evening"*

This song, brought from England by colonists, has been a part of American song literature for many years. Have students sing it in trios, with each member representing a different generation—parents, grandparents, and great-grandparents.

PLAYING INSTRUMENTS: *Recorder*

See **R · 21** in *Playing the Recorder* for "Oh, How Lovely Is the Evening."

ENRICHMENT: *"Jubilate Deo"*

Have students sing in canon. On a signal, have them stop and sustain the pitch they are singing, listening carefully to tune up the harmony. Use this ostinato for cambiata voices:

do so, so, do
Al - le - lu - ia

PRONUNCIATION: *"Jubilate Deo"*

ɑ f<u>a</u>ther ɛ p<u>e</u>t i b<u>ee</u> ɔ p<u>aw</u> u m<u>oo</u>n

COME, FOLLOW ME!

Words and Music by John Hilton

2. Sing the song. Have students:

• Listen to "Jubilate Deo," paying attention to the Latin pronunciation. (The text means "Rejoice in the Lord, Alleluia!")

• Practice pronunciation of the text.

• Sing the song with text in unison. (When students are comfortable singing in unison, have them try singing the song as a canon.)

Reinforcement C major scale, *page 65*

Come, Follow Me!

1. Introduce the song CD8:39. Have students:

• Tell what type of song it is. (canon)

• Tell the key from the signature. (two flats—B♭ major)

• Look at the song to see which pitches in the scale are used. (all of them—including high *re* and *mi*)

• Find the dotted quarter-eighth combinations and review how to perform them.

• Sing the song with pitch syllables, then with words.

2. Sing the song in canon. Have students:

• Listen to the recording with attention to how it sounds in canon. (Note that all voices should end at the same time and that only on the ending is the fermata to be used.)

• Listen again, singing along with Group 1.

• Listen again, singing along with Group 3.

• Form three groups and sing the song in canon as written.

• Recognize how the texture changes as more voice parts are added. (It becomes thicker.)

Reinforcement
flat key signatures, *page 101*
dotted rhythms, *page 113*

MOVEMENT: *"Come, Follow Me!"* Canon

Have students create a dance that can be done in canon. The movements should be simple in order to provide a clear visual picture of the canon. For example:

Formation: three groups in three lines, facing one another, the lines forming three sides of a rectangle, but far enough apart so that none of the lines will intrude on another line's floor space

Lines 1–2: Eight steps forward (ending with a step-close).

Lines 3–4: Two side-close steps to the right, followed by two side-close steps to the left.

Lines 5–6: Eight steps backward to starting place.

BACKGROUND: *"Come, Follow Me!"*

The English produced many canons and rounds, especially during the Renaissance period. Canons were the "pop songs" of the day, and contests were held regularly to see who could write the best and most interesting canon. Many of the canons have survived to the present day. "Come, Follow Me!" was written during this period and communicates some of the excitement and fun that these early part songs created.

MUSIC LIBRARY
READING ANTHOLOGY

Dona nobis pacem

1. Introduce the song CD8:40. Have students:

• Identify the meter as ¾ and identify the various rhythm patterns.

• Tap the rhythm.

• Identify the key signature as F major and sing the melody with numbers or pitch syllables.

2. Analyze the melody. Have students:

• Find the lines that have the same rhythm. (Lines 4 and 6)

• Find the lines that have repeated notes. (Lines 1, 2, 3, 4, and 6)

• Find the lines that are entirely stepwise. (Lines 3 and 4)

• Find the lines that are stepwise except for one skip. (Lines 2 and 5)

3. Sing the song. Have students:

• Listen to the recording and identify the singing as a cappella (not accompanied).

• Practice the Latin pronunciation and sing with words. (Remind students to sing the phrases with one breath.)

• Sing the long notes (dotted half notes) with a sense of forward direction and sustained intensity. (When students are comfortable singing in unison, have them try singing the song in canon.)

Reinforcement

¾ , *page 81*
reading rhythms, *page 17*

Dona Nobis Pacem — Latin Hymn

338

MEETING **INDIVIDUAL** NEEDS

BACKGROUND: *"Dona nobis pacem"*

This Latin hymn, which dates to the sixteenth century, is one of the most well known of all canons. Its text means "Give us peace." The slurred notes in the melody help to give it a smooth and flowing character.

PRONUNCIATION: *"Dona nobis pacem"*

ɑ f*a*ther   ɛ p*e*t   i b*ee*   ɔ p*aw*

MOVEMENT: *"Dona nobis pacem"* Canon

Formation: three concentric circles, facing counterclockwise, clockwise, and counterclockwise. The innermost circle is Group 1, the middle circle is Group 2, the outermost circle is Group 3.

Dance: Each group moves forward in its circle with a step, touch, touch with the beat when it begins singing. Each circle stops moving when the group finishes singing the song.

Oh, Sinner Man

African American Spiritual

1.,6. Oh, sin-ner man, where you gon-na run to?
2. Oh, sin-ner man, rock's a - gon-na hide you.
3. Run to the sea, sea will be a - boil-ing.
4. Run to the Lord, Lord, won't you hide me?
5. Oh, sin-ner man, you ought to be a - pray-ing.

Oh, sin-ner man, where you gon-na run to?
Oh, sin-ner man, rock's a - gon-na hide you.
Run to the sea, sea will be a - boil-ing.
Run to the Lord, Lord, won't you hide me?
Oh, sin-ner man, you ought to be a - pray-ing.

Oh, sin-ner man, where you gon-na run to?
Oh, sin-ner man, rock's a - gon-na hide you.
Run to the sea, sea will be a - boil-ing.
Run to the Lord, Lord, won't you hide me?
Oh, sin-ner man, you ought to be a - pray-ing.

All on that day.

Ostinato

Oh, sin-ner man! Oh, sin-ner man!

Oh, sin-ner man! On that day.

Oh, Sinner Man

1. Introduce the song and its rhythms CD9:1.
Have students:

• Clap the rhythm of the song, noticing which measures contain sixteenth notes. (Measures 1–6 of the melody; 1, 3, 5 of the ostinato)

• Divide into two groups. Group 1 claps the first measure of each line of the song. Group 2 claps the second measure of each line. Clap together on Line 4, then switch parts.

• Sing the melody with the recording, listening for the featured instrument family. (string—guitar, banjo, fiddle, string bass)

2. Learn a rhythmic accompaniment. Have students:

• Practice these parts in three groups.

Group 1—Sing the song.

Group 2—Pat the pattern below.

Group 3—Clap the pattern below.

• Sing the song as volunteers play the Group 2 rhythm on drum, the Group 3 rhythm on claves or other appropriate instruments. (Optional: Use "Oh, Sinner Man" Performance Mix CD9:2.)

• Learn the vocal ostinato. (When students are secure singing the ostinato and melody separately, have them sing both parts together.)

Reinforcement
reading sixteenth notes, *page 57*
country stringed instruments, *page 29*

ORFF: *"Dona nobis pacem"*

See **O · 13** in *Orchestrations for Orff Instruments.*

PLAYING INSTRUMENTS: *Recorder*

See **R · 21** in *Playing the Recorder* for "Dona nobis pacem." See **R · 17** and **R · 22** for "Oh, Sinner Man."

CRITICAL THINKING: *"Oh, Sinner Man"*

Have students discuss the imagery used in the text of the song. What is the special day? (Judgment Day) Who could be the *sinner man* be? Ask students why they think enslaved African Americans used this imagery in the song.

ENRICHMENT: *"Oh, Sinner Man"*

Have students create words and rhythm for a spoken B section. For example:

I ran in the morning, I ran at night.

I kept running faster 'til I saw the light.

I ran for my children. I ran for me.

I ran and I ran 'cause I had to be free.

RELATED ARTS MOVEMENT THEATER VISUAL ARTS

Bamboo

1. Introduce the song and its rhythms CD9:3.
Have students:

• Tell the form. (verse-refrain)

• Working with a partner, study the notation in order to identify measures in the verse that have the same rhythms as other measures. (Measures 1–3, 9–11, and 25–27 are the same; Measures 5, 6, 13, and 14 are the same; Measure 7 is the same as Measure 15.)

• Identify measures with syncopation. (1–3, 9–11, 25–27)

• Listen to the song, lightly clapping the rhythms in Measures 1 and 5.

• Listen again, then sing the song.

2. Create ostinatos to accompany the song.
Have students:

• Create ostinatos using parts of the repeated rhythm patterns that they identified.

• Play the ostinatos on unpitched percussion instruments—including clicking and shaking instruments—to accompany the song. (Suggestions: Use an ostinato with a rhythm different from the one being sung; use ostinatos that contrast with that part of the song; for example: quarter and half notes for the verse, eighth and quarter notes for the refrain.)

• Use ostinatos to create dance steps for the verse and refrain. (See *Movement* below.)

Reinforcement
verse-refrain form, *page 61*
syncopation, *page 211*

Bamboo

G mixolydian

Words and Music by Dave Van Ronk

1. You take a stick of bam-boo, You take a stick of bam-boo, You
(2.) trav - el on the riv - er, You trav - el on the riv - er, You
(3.) home's a - cross the riv - er, My home's a - cross the riv - er, My

take a stick of bam-boo, You throw it in the wa-ter,
trav - el on the riv - er, You trav - el on the wa-ter, } Oh——
home's a - cross the riv - er, My home's a - cross the wa-ter,

Oh—— Han –nah—— { You take a stick of bam-boo, You
You trav - el on the riv - er, You
My home's a - cross the riv - er, My

take a stick of bam-boo, You take a stick of bam-boo, You
trav - el on the riv - er, You trav - el on the riv - er, You
home's a - cross the riv - er, My home's a - cross the riv - er, My

throw it in the wa-ter,
trav - el on the wa-ter, } Oh—— Oh—— Han - nah!——
home's a - cross the wa-ter,

Refrain

Riv - er,———— She come down.————

340

MEETING **INDIVIDUAL** NEEDS

MOVEMENT: *"Bamboo"*

Have partners or small groups use at least two ostinatos to create their dance steps. Provide these guidelines:

—Keep the movement simple with very few steps that use eighth-note rhythms.

—For the most part, move "in place" to facilitate the singing.

—Use walking steps part of the time.

ORFF: *"Bamboo"*

See **O • 14** in *Orchestrations for Orff Instruments.*

PLAYING INSTRUMENTS: *Recorder*

See **R • 15** and **R • 19** in *Playing the Recorder* for "Bamboo." See **R • 5**, **R • 12**, and **R • 17** for "I Got a Letter."

Riv- er,_____ She come down._____ { 2. You
3. My

down._____ You take a stick of bam-boo, You take a stick of bam-boo, You

take a stick of bam-boo, You throw it in the wa-ter._____

I Got a Letter

South Carolina Singing Game

1. I got a let-ter this morn - ing,
2. I wrote a let-ter this morn - ing, } Oh, yes;
3. I mailed a let-ter this morn - ing,

I got a let-ter this morn - ing,
I wrote a let-ter this morn - ing, } Oh, yes.
I mailed a let-ter this morn - ing,

Four-tone

l, d r m

I Got a Letter

Introduce the song CD9:4. Have students:

• Practice clapping on Beats 2 and 4.

• Clap the pattern as they listen to the song.

• Listen to the recording as they follow the written notation.

• Sing the song with the recording.

• Identify the pitches used in the melody (E G A B), focusing on the final pitch of the song (E—*la*—6). (If students are having difficulty understanding the concept of *la* as the tonal center, explain that a melody that centers on *la* is said to be in a minor key. Play other melodies that are minor and have them sing the final pitch.)

Reinforcement minor keys, *page 73*

PLAYING INSTRUMENTS: *Pitched*

Have students play the pitched instrument parts on **Resource Master RA • 2** with "I Got a Letter." The notes in the chords in the handbell/xylophone/keyboard parts can be divided among two or three students. You may wish to have students play the recorder descant on **R • 5** with these parts.

ORFF: *"I Got a Letter"*

See **O • 15** in *Orchestrations for Orff Instruments*.

MUSIC LIBRARY
READING ANTHOLOGY

De allacito carnavalito

Sing the song CD9:5. Have students:

• Clap the rhythm of the song.

• List the pitches from low to high, then tell the key from the signature and first and last pitches. (A C D E G A C; A minor)

• Sing the song with pitch syllables and then with pitch letter names.

Recorded Lesson CD9:6

• Listen to "Pronunciation for 'De allacito carnavalito.'"

• Sing the song.

Reinforcement
A minor, *page 105*
reading rhythms, *page 17*

Fortune

Sing the song CD9:7. Have students:

• Read the words of the song in rhythm.

• Tell the tonal center. (F) Then find pitches below *do*. (*ti,* in Measure 2; *so,* in Measure 4)

• Sing the song with pitch syllables.

• Listen to the recording, singing along with Group 1. (When students are secure in unison, have them form groups and sing in two-part, then four-part canon.)

• Tell the texture of the song sung in unison and in canon. (monophony; polyphony—see pages 74–75)

Reinforcement texture, *page 77*

MEETING **INDIVIDUAL** NEEDS

BACKGROUND: *"Fortune"*

Composers often wrote short canons as gifts to dinner hosts. This song by German composer Ludwig van Beethoven (1770–1827) was probably composed for such an occasion. Whatever the reason for their composition, Beethoven's works remain among the most performed music ever written.

PRONUNCIATION: *"De allacito carnavalito"*

ɑ f**a**ther	e ch**a**otic	i b**ee** o **o**bey
ß b without lips touching	ð <u>the</u>	ɾ flipped r
x slightly guttural	h, *Spanish* b**a**jo	

ENRICHMENT: *Augmentation and Diminution*

Have students sing "O musique" with the note values doubled. Explain that this is called "augmentation." (See page 299.) Then have one group sing in augmentation as the other sings with the regular values, both groups stepping to the same beat in place or moving around the room. Switch roles and repeat. Next, have students sing with the note values cut in half, or in "diminution." Have one group sing in diminution as the other sings with the regular values, again stepping to the beat. Finally, form three groups and, still stepping to the beat, have one group sing with regular note values, one in augmentation, and one in diminution.

O musique

French Folk Song
English Version by MMH

French: O mu-si-que no-tre a-mie, Sour-ce pure et frai - che.

Pronunciation: o mü zi kə nɔ trɑ mi sur sə pü ɾe frɛ shə

E minor

m, s, l, t, d r m s

Autumn Canon

Words and Music by Lajos Bárdos
Translated by Sean Deibler

1. Fly, fly, fly, the leaf takes leave of the branch, breez - es are strong, win - ter is com - ing.

2. Cry, cry, cry, the tears come soft - ly be - hind, turn - ing to frost, touch - ing my heart.

D minor

l, t, d r m f s l

Music Library *Reading Anthology* **343**

O musique

Sing in canon CD9:8. Have students:

• Listen to "O musique." (The words mean, "Music, our friend, pure and fresh spring.")

• Decide on the tonal center. (E minor—the song ends on *mi* instead of *la*.)

Recorded Lesson CD9:9

• Listen to "Pronunciation for 'O musique.'"

• Sing the song with the recording, singing with Group 1 during the canon. (When students are ready, have them form four groups and sing in four-part canon as indicated.)

Reinforcement minor, *page 153*

Autumn Canon

Sing the song CD9:10. Have students:

• Name the scale (D minor) and sing a de-scending minor scale with numbers or pitch syllables. (8 7 6 5 4 3 2 1; *la so fa mi re do ti, la,*)

• Name the meter signature (2/2 or cut time) and discuss its meaning. (See page 336.)

• Tap the rhythm of the song, then sing with numbers or pitch syllables.

• Sing the song with the text.

Reinforcement minor scale, *page 165*

ENRICHMENT: *"Autumn Canon"*

Have students discuss the text and "tone painting" (the use of musical elements to describe the text). Play the recording, having them pay attention to the "tone painting." (slow, sustained notes and dissonance [harsh sounds] to describe autumn and the coming of the harsh winter) Then form two groups. Group 1 sings or plays a B♭. Group 2 sings or plays an A to illustrate dissonance. Finally, have them sing the song in canon, stopping when this half-step interval occurs between the two groups (Group 1: *leave* in Measure 6; Group 2: *fly* in Measure 3). Sing the entire song in three-part canon.

BIOGRAPHY: *Lajos Bárdos*

Hungarian composer and conductor Lajos Bárdos (b. 1899) studied with Kodály at the Budapest Academy, where he later taught for many years. His work consists mostly of choral music. As a choral conductor, he toured widely with his choruses, which became internationally known.

PRONUNCIATION: *"O musique"*

α f<u>a</u>ther	e ch<u>a</u>otic	ɛ p<u>e</u>t	i b<u>ee</u>
o <u>o</u>bey	ɔ p<u>a</u>w	u m<u>oo</u>n	ə <u>a</u>go
ɾ flipped r	ü lips form [u] and say [i]		

MUSIC LIBRARY
READING ANTHOLOGY

De Lanterna na Mão

1. Introduce the song CD9:11, **and create a rhythmic accompaniment.** Have students:

• Listen to the recording and identify the instruments. (guitar, Brazilian-style percussion)

• Describe the mood of the accompaniment.

• Choose unpitched instruments for ostinatos that can help sustain the mood.

• Develop two simple two-measure ostinatos to accompany the song, one for the A section and another for the B section. (Students can use rhythms found in the melody as below.)

• Practice the patterns on the chosen instruments, then play them with the song.

2. Sing the song. Have students:

• List the pitches of the B section from low to high and tell the key. (A B C D E F G A; A minor)

Recorded Lesson CD9:12
• Listen to "Pronunciation for 'De Lanterna na Mão.'"

• Sing the song, then add the ostinatos.

Reinforcement
Brazilian percussion, *page 13*
minor scale, *page 105*

344

MEETING **INDIVIDUAL** NEEDS

PLAYING INSTRUMENTS: *Pitched*

An instrumental part for "De Lanterna na Mão" can be found on **Resource Master RA • 3**. It may be played on alto recorder, bass xylophone, keyboard, piano, cello, or another low-pitched instrument.

PRONUNCIATION: *"De Lanterna na Mão"*

ɑ f<u>a</u>ther	e ch<u>a</u>otic	ɛ p<u>e</u>t	i b<u>ee</u>
ɪ <u>i</u>t	o <u>o</u>bey	ɔ p<u>a</u>w	u m<u>oo</u>n
ɾ flipped r	ʒ plea<u>s</u>ure	~ nasalized vowel	

PLAYING INSTRUMENTS: *Recorder*

See **R • 19** and **R • 22** in *Playing the Recorder* for "De Lanterna na Mão."

ENRICHMENT: *Conducting*

Show students the pattern for conducting in duple meter and have them conduct "De Lanterna na Mão."

Spring Rain

Sung as a round. End when first part has sung lines 1-3 twice.

Words and Music by Laura MacGregor
Arranged by Robert J. de Frece

1. Lis - ten now; hear the rain, soft - ly on the hill - side.

2. Slow - ly the fog comes rol - ling, cov' - ring the fields.

3. By the trees I sit, list' - ning to the rain, wait - ing for the sun.

Optional ostinato for cambiatas.
Enter as Voice 4.

Rain fal - ling soft - ly down, gen - tle rain.

A minor

Spring Rain

1. Introduce the song CD9:13**.** Have students:

• Listen to the song.

• Tell the meter signature. (¾)

• Decide on the tonal center and mode (A minor—note that the song begins and ends on *mi*, rather than *la*.)

2. Sing the song. Have students:

• Listen again to the song, singing along as they are able.

• Practice each line by echoing you.

• Sing the song with the recording.

3. Introduce the cambiata ostinato. Have students:

• Listen to the recording, with attention to the cambiata part.

• Sing the melody as those with lower or changing voices sing the cambiata part.

4. Sing the song in canon with the cambiata part. Have students:

• Form four groups to sing the song in canon. One group, which should be made up of those with lower or changing voices, is to sing the ostinato. The other three groups sing the song in canon. All groups are to end at the same time when the first group has sung the song through twice. (Optional: Use "Spring Rain" Performance Mix CD9:14.)

Reinforcement ¾ meter, minor, *page 81*

BIOGRAPHY: *Laura MacGregor*

Laura MacGregor, the composer of "Spring Rain," is a general music teacher in northern British Columbia. She graduated from, and took her Orff Schulwerk training at, the University of Alberta in Canada. The canon was composed when she was an undergraduate student at the university.

RELATED ARTS | MOVEMENT | THEATER | VISUAL ARTS

The Gypsy Rover

Sing the song and learn the movement

CD9:15. Have students:

• Listen to the song, singing along with the refrain. Retell the story in their own words.

• Sing the song.

• Learn the dance. (See *Movement* below for the verse movements.)

Formation: Gypsy   Father
(square)   **1**   **3**
             4   **2**
    Suitor   Lady

Form: four verses, each followed by a refrain (as in the song)

Refrain:

1. Take four steps forward and back, toward and away from partner. (2 measures)

2. Take four steps forward and back, toward and away from corner. (2 measures)

3. Join hands and circle clockwise, returning home. (5 measures)

Reinforcement verse-refrain form, ledger lines, pitch letter names, *page 25*

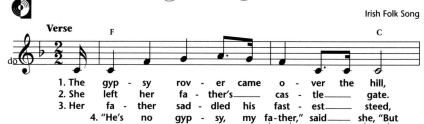

The Gypsy Rover

Irish Folk Song

Verse

1. The gyp - sy rov - er came o - ver the hill,
2. She left her fa - ther's cas - tle gate.
3. Her fa - ther sad - dled his fast - est steed,
4. "He's no gyp - sy, my fa - ther," said she, "But

Bound through the val - ley so shad - y. He whis - tled and he sang till the
Left her own true lov - er. She left her ser - vants and
Rode by the riv - er Clyde. Drew near to a man - sion
lord of the free - lands all o - ver, And I will stay till my

green woods rang, And he won the heart of a la - dy.
her es - tate. To fol - low the gyp - sy rov - er.
with great speed, Found the gyp - sy and his la - dy.
dy - ing day with my whist - ling gyp - sy rov - er."

Refrain

Ly - de - o, ly - de - o, da - day, Ly - de - o, Ly - de - ay - de; He

whis - tled and he sang till the green woods rang, And

he won the heart of a la - dy.

346

MEETING **INDIVIDUAL** NEEDS

MOVEMENT: *"The Gypsy Rover"*
The folk-style dance tells the story in movement.

Verse 1	**Verse 2**	**Verse 3**	**Verse 4**
Gypsy (1) circles clockwise, passes Father (3), does two-hand swing with Lady (2), and goes home.	Lady (2) circles clockwise, passes the Suitor (4), does two-hand swing with Gypsy (1), and goes home.	Father (3) circles clockwise, passes Lady (2), does two-hand swing with Suitor (4), and goes home.	Both (3) and (4) circle clockwise while (1) and (2) do a two-hand swing. All go home.

John B. Sails

G major

G   C   D7

Folk Song from the Bahama Islands

1. Oh, we come on— the sloop *John B.* My grand-fa-ther and
2. The— first mate, — he got sad, Feel-in' aw-f'ly
3. The— poor cook, — he got fits, And throw 'way — all the

me. A-round Nas-sau Town we— did roam.
bad, Cap-tain come a-board took him a-way.
grits, Then he took and — eat up all of the corn.

Walk-in' all night, Just see-in' the sights,
Please let me a-lone, And let— me go home,
Please let me go home, I want— to go home.

Well, I feel so break-up, — I want— to go home.
Well, I feel so break-up, — I want— to go home.
Well, this is the worst — trip Since I — was born.

Refrain

So hoist up — the *John B.* sails, See how — the main-s'l

set. Send for — the Cap-t'n a-shore, Let — me go

Music Library Song Anthology **347**

John B. Sails

1. Introduce the song CD9:16. Have students:

• Look at the song and notice that it is in verse-refrain form. Then look at and listen to the song to discover if the verse and refrain have the same or different melodies. (same)

• Listen again, singing along as able.

2. Add a chordal accompaniment. Have students:

• Notice what the chord letters above the staff in the song are. (G, C, D7)

• Write the spelling of each chord on the board: G chord: G B D

    C chord: C E G

    D7 chord: D F♯ A C

• Practice playing the chords on guitar, auto-harp, or with a soft tremolo on resonator bells or barred instruments. (Each student plays one pitch as you or a student points to the chord names as they occur in the song. They are to play whenever the leader points to the chord name in which their assigned pitch is found.)

(Optional: Use **Playing the Guitar G • 27**. Optional: **Technology**—Use Music with MIDI.)

3. Sing in two parts. Have students:

• Echo you on each phrase of the harmony part for "*John B.* Sails."

• Sing the entire harmony part with the recording. (When students are comfortable singing each part separately, have them form two groups and sing the parts together.) (Optional: Use "*John B.* Sails" Performance Mix CD9:17.)

Reinforcement
verse-refrain form, *page 13*
I, IV, V chords in G, *page 179*

PLAYING INSTRUMENTS: *Recorder*

See **R • 20** in *Playing the Recorder* for "Gypsy Rover."

BACKGROUND: *"John B. Sails"*

The story told in "*John B.* Sails," of a trip at sea and of wishes to return home, is typical of calypso songs. Most calypso songs were improvised for amusement and self-expression, then passed on orally. (For more information about calypso music, see the bottom of page 365, *Multicultural Perspectives*.)

PLAYING INSTRUMENTS: *Unpitched*

Add Latin American percussion to "*John B.* Sails."

D7		G	C

home.　　Please let— me go home,　　I want — to go home.

| C | G | D7 | G |

Well, — I feel so break—up, — I want— to go home.

The Lion Sleeps Tonight

1. Introduce the song CD9:18. Have students:

• Listen to the song, which was first recorded in 1939.

• Sing the chord roots below, singing scale numbers (I, IV, or V) on Beats 1 and 3 only. (Each chord is heard for one measure. This 4-measure pattern repeats many times:

　　Measure 1—I; Measure 2—IV;
　　Measure 3—I; Measure 4—V)

• Sing the 4-measure chord-root pattern using the words and rhythm of the song. (Cambiatas can sing the G an octave lower.)

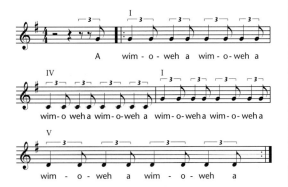

A　wim - o - weh a　wim - o - weh a

wim - o weh a wim - o - weh a　wim - o - weh a wim - o - weh a

wim - o - weh　a　wim - o - weh　a

• Learn the other three accompaniment parts on page 348. (Have students notice that each part moves only a step up or a step down.)

• Optional—Use **Playing the Guitar G • 18.**

The Lion Sleeps Tonight

Accompaniment

Words and Music by Solomon Linda
Arranged by Robert J. de Frece

G major

s, l, t, d r m f s

| G | C | D |

G

A　wim - o - weh a　wim - o - weh a　wim - o - weh a　wim - o - weh a

C

A　wim - o - weh a　wim - o - weh a　wim - o - weh a　wim - o - weh a

A　wim - o - weh a　wim - o - weh a

348

MEETING **INDIVIDUAL** NEEDS

LANGUAGE ARTS CONNECTION: *"John B. Sails"*

Have students create words from their own experience for the first eleven measures of the verse. For example:

Oh, we came to the school today

And thought we would see a play.

But when we arrived we heard that it wouldn't go on.

It would have been fun

For every one.

Now our chance to see it is over and gone.

EXTRA HELP: *Part Singing*

To help students sing the parts in "The Lion Sleeps Tonight," have an alto xylophone or keyboard play along with each part. Have each group of students stand in a circle around the pitched instrument, played by a student who can successfully play the part. This reinforcement should help students to perform their parts successfully.

ENRICHMENT: *Descant*

Have students learn the descant for the refrain and sing it with "The Lion Sleeps Tonight."

Begin w/
Boys & Girls Sep
(   )
The Lion Sleeps Tonight
    (listen — What Movie?)
Books out — Solo Sing w/
        Recording
have fun!
Music Symbols — Bingo /
        Worksheet HW

2. Sing in five parts. Have students:

• Divide into five groups. (Group 1 sings the melody. Groups 2, 3, and 4 sing the three-part accompaniment. Group 5—including cambiatas—sings the chord root part and may be doubled on a bass instrument an octave lower.)

• Sing "The Lion Sleeps Tonight" according to the following form:

  1. Introduction (solo or group)—Verse 1 and Refrain, unaccompanied.

  2. Chord roots plus Parts 2, 3, and 4: two times through.

  3. Chord roots and Parts 2, 3, and 4 continue. Melody enters. Sing the accompaniment *piano* during the A section (verse) and *forte* during the B section (refrain).

  4. After Verse 3, repeat the refrain four times, getting softer and softer. Finish by having everyone stop on the first beat of the first measure, humming the I chord.

Reinforcement
I, IV, V chords, *page 175*
1930s popular music styles, *page 249*

In the jun-gle, the might-y jun-gle,
Near the vil-lage, the peace-ful vil-lage, } the li-on sleeps to-night.
Hush, my dar-ling, don't fear, my dar-ling, }

Refrain

Ee_____ um_ mum_ a-way_____

Descant (optional)

Ee_____ um_ mum_ a-way_____

Music Library *Song Anthology* **349**

BACKGROUND: *"The Lion Sleeps Tonight"*

This popular song had its origins as a Zulu song by Solomon Linda of Johannnesburg, South Africa. His group The Evening Birds made a recording of the song, then known as "Mbube," in 1939. The song had such an impact in South Africa that a cappella singing was identified by the name "mbube" for many years. The American folk singer Pete Seeger heard the song and changed the word "Mbube" to "Wimoweh." The song was recorded by Seeger's group The Weavers in 1950 and became a big hit on American radio. More recent recordings have been made by African groups such as Ladysmith Black Mambazo, the most popular men's a cappella group in South Africa.

PLAYING INSTRUMENTS: *Recorder*

See **R • 13** in *Playing the Recorder* for "The Lion Sleeps Tonight."

Orion

1. Introduce the song and practice identifying change of meter CD9:19**.** Have students:

• Listen to and discuss the song. (You may wish to explain that the composer wrote "Orion" to make people aware of the dangers of air pollution.)

• Tell the meter signature. ($\frac{4}{4}$)

• Look at the notation, observing the change of meter to $\frac{3}{4}$ in the second section.

• Listen to the song and signal when they hear a change of meter.

2. Follow a score that includes first and second endings. Have students:

• Find the first and second endings.

• Listen to the song, following the notation.

Pentatonic

l, d r m s l d'

Words and Music by James Zimmermann

1. O - ri - on is a - ris - ing, You can see his stars a - blaz-
(2.) day is get - ting cold - er, And I real - ly start to won-

ing in the mid - dle of a clear - eyed coun - try
der why they're cloud - ing all the coun - try skies to

sky. And it's nev - er too sur - pris - ing that the
gray. The— world is get - ting old - er, You can

sky is still a - maz - ing way out here where noth - ing
hear it in the thun - der and the rain might come and

hides it from my eyes. }
chase it all a - way. }
And sleep - ing out -

side in a bag as a kid, it seems like the

350

MEETING **INDIVIDUAL** NEEDS

LANGUAGE ARTS CONNECTION: *Definitions*

Work as a class to define unfamiliar words and phrases in "Orion." Have a few students working with dictionaries to verify each definition. For example, define who or what *Orion* is (a constellation), tell what is meant by *clear-eyed country sky*, and explain what *wane* means (a period in which the moon seems to be disappearing—from full moon to new moon).

SCIENCE CONNECTION: *Constellations*

Orion is a constellation, that is, a group of stars named for an object, person, or animal. The Orion constellation is visible in the northern hemisphere during the winter months of January and February. The ancient Greeks and Romans saw Orion as a hunter. The three bright stars in a row in the middle were Orion's belt and another group of stars to the right formed his hunter's bow. Early people told stories about Orion and about the other constellations that they named. Today astronomers, sailors, and others still use many of the ancient constellations to indicate locations in the night sky.

best thing that I ev - er did; And chas - ing the

sha - dows and the tracks in the snow, don't you

1.
know?

2. The know?

Coda
The moon is on the wane, And it

looks like it might rain, or may - be snow.

And how are we to stay here if there's

no room left to play here or to

grow. Don't you know? Don't you know?

3. Identify the key the song is in and sing the song. Have students:

• Look at the first section of the song. Tell what key the song is in and why. (C major; there are no sharps or flats and the tonal center is C.)

• Sing the song.

• Note the scale pitches used (*la₁ do re mi so la do₁*) and recognize that the melody is pentatonic.

• Have some students accompany "Orion" by playing a descending C major scale twice in whole notes (eight measures each time, 16 measures total) on pitched instruments during the first 4/4 section while the rest of the class sings.

Reinforcement
C major, *page 53*
4/4 and 3/4, *page 81*

Have students find out more about the Orion constellation. As part of their report, they might make a model of Orion by punching holes in black construction paper to show the position of the stars.

ENRICHMENT: *Constellation Compositions*

Have students find and draw constellation of their choice, then use the configuration to devise a melodic motive. They can use the motive as the opening pitches of a complete melody they compose. Students born under the same sign could work together on this.

MUSIC LIBRARY
SONG ANTHOLOGY

RELATED ARTS | MOVEMENT | THEATER | VISUAL ARTS |

Shenando'

1. Introduce the song CD9:20. Have students:

• Read the text, learn about chanteys (see *Movement* below), and tell what they think the tempo is and why. (Answers will vary. Tempo is slow due to the slow, steady pushing needed to turn the capstan. Also the text tells of the sailor's love for Shenandoah's daughter.)

• Find the ♩.♪, ♪♩., ties, and upbeats. (Each phrase begins with an upbeat.)

• Tap the rhythm. (Lines 1 and 3 have the same rhythm.)

• Name the key (E♭ Major) and sing the melody with numbers or pitch syllables.

• Sing the melody.

2. Sing the song in two parts. Have students:

• Sing the melody with individual students singing lines 1 and 3 of each verse.

• Practice the countermelody. (When students are secure singing the melody and countermelody separately, have them sing both parts together.) (Optional: Use "Shenando'" Performance Mix CD9:21.)

• Optional—Use **Playing the Guitar G • 19**.

Reinforcement flat key signatures, *page 101*

American Sea Chantey

1. Oh, Shen-an-do', I long to hear you.
2. Oh, Shen-an-do', I love your daugh-ter.
3. Oh, Shen-an-do', I'm bound to leave you.

A - way, a - way you roll-ing riv-er.

Oh, Shen-an-do', I long to hear you.
Oh, Shen-an-do', I love your daugh-ter.
Oh, Shen-an-do', I'll not de-ceive you.

A - way, we're bound a - way. 'Cross the

A - way, a - way,

wide Mis - sou - ri.

'Cross the wide Mis - sou - ri.

E♭ major

s, d r m f s l t d'

352

MEETING **INDIVIDUAL** NEEDS

BACKGROUND: *"Shenando'"*

Tradition has it that "Shenando'" is about a trader who fell in love with the daughter of the Native American Chief Shenandoah. The trader then took her "'Cross the wide Missouri." The haunting melody made the song popular among riverboat workers, who regularly traveled American rivers such as the Missouri and the Mississippi.

SOCIAL STUDIES CONNECTION: *Maps*

Have students find the Missouri River on a map and list cities that developed along its banks.

MOVEMENT: *"Shenando'"*

Have students do research on the different types of chanteys and the type of work the seamen were performing when they sang the songs. For example, "Shenando'" is a capstan chantey. A *capstan*, shaped like a vertical cylinder, is a device for lowering or hoisting the anchor. The cable to which the anchor is attached is wound around the capstan. This was then rotated manually by the seamen pushing spokes attached to the cylinder as they sang a capstan chantey.

Then have students sing "Shenando'," imitating the work motions the seamen might be doing while singing.

Las mañanitas
The Morning Song

F major

s, t, d r m f s

Mexican Folk Song
English Version by MMH

F

C7

Spanish: És - tas son las ma - ña - ni - tas que can -
Pronunciation: es ta son las ma nya ni tas ke kan
English: Now we sing las ma - ña - nl - tas, as King

F   B♭   F

ta - ba el Rey Da - vid, a las mu - cha - chas bo -
ta βael rei ða βið a las mu cha chaz βo
Da - vid long a - go sang a song to greet the

Dm   F   Gm   C7   F

ni - tas se las can - ta - mos a - sí: Des -
ni tas se las kan ta mos a si des
morn - ing, to greet the sun - light's first glow. A -

C7   F

pier - ta, mi bien, des - pier - ta, mi -
pyer ta mi βyen des pyer ta mi
wak - en, dear one, a - wak - en and

C7   F   B♭

ra que ya a - ma - ne - ció, Ya los pa - ja - ri - tos
ra ke ya a ma ne syo ya los pa xa ri tos
wel - come the ros - y dawn. Now the birds are sweet - ly

F   Gm   C7   F

can - tan, la lu - na ya se me - tió.
kan tan la lu na ya se me tyo
sing - ing, the sil - ver moon - light has gone.

Music Library *Song Anthology* **353**

Las mañanitas

1. Introduce the song CD9:22. Have students:

• Listen to the song and tell the language of the text. (Spanish)

Recorded Lesson CD9:24

• Listen to "Pronunciation for 'Las mañanitas.'"

• Memorize the words, filling in phrases as you speak the words, leaving out words at the end of each phrase.

• Sing the song. (Optional: Use "Las mañanitas" Performance Mix CD9:23.)

2. Move in ⅜ meter. Have students:

• Using colorful scarves, practice conducting in triple meter. (See *Enrichment* below.)

• Create a movement pattern in triple meter as individuals or in small groups while listening to the song.

• Perform their movements with the song, singing along as able.

Reinforcement ⅜ meter, *page 81*

MULTICULTURAL PERSPECTIVES: *Mexican Parties*

"Las mañanitas" is sung in Mexico to celebrate a birthday. Mexican children often celebrate birthdays or name days (the day of the Catholic saint for whom the child is named) with piñata parties. The piñata, a decorated clay jar, is hung from a tree or ceiling. Each child is blindfolded in turn and given a stick to swing at the piñata. When it breaks, everyone gathers up the sweets and toys that fall out.

PLAYING INSTRUMENTS: *Recorder*

See **R · 22** in *Playing the Recorder* for "Las mañanitas."

ENRICHMENT: *Conducting*

Have students conduct in triple meter with "Las mañanitas":

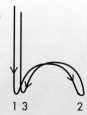

1 3   2

PRONUNCIATION: *"Las mañanitas"*

ɑ f<u>a</u>ther	e ch<u>a</u>otic	i b<u>ee</u> o <u>o</u>bey
u m<u>oo</u>n	β b without lips touching	ð <u>the</u>
ɾ flipped r	x slightly guttural h, *Spanish* b<u>a</u>jo	

MUSIC LIBRARY
SONG ANTHOLOGY

Soon Ah Will Be Done

1. Introduce the song and practice identifying the dotted eighth-sixteenth rhythm CD9:25. Have students:

• Focus on the difference between ♫ and ♫ by thinking of the first two notes of the first three phrases of "The Star Spangled Banner" (pages 292–293). (♫ —*Oh* and *By the;* ♫— *What so*)

• Listen to "Soon Ah Will Be Done" while patting with the beat.

• Decide which of the rhythms above is found in the refrain of the song. (♫)

• Listen again, then describe the hopes and feelings portrayed in the music and the text, including the difference in mood between the verse and refrain. (The music of the refrain is softer and reflects a sense of calm, while the verses are louder and reflect greater passion.)

Soon Ah Will Be Done

African American Spiritual
Arranged by Robert J. de Frece

Refrain

Soon ah will be done-a with the trou-bles of the world,
Soon ah will be done-a with the trou-bles of the world,

Trou-bles of the world,——— the trou-bles of the world,
Trou-bles of the world,——— the trou-bles of the world,

Soon ah will be done-a with the trou-bles of the world,
Soon ah will be done-a with the trou-bles of the world,

B minor

354

MEETING **INDIVIDUAL** NEEDS

MULTICULTURAL PERSPECTIVES: *Dialects*

English was not the native language of enslaved Africans who were brought to the United States. African Americans developed their own dialects, or regional ways of speaking English, influenced by the sound of their native languages. For example, the word *ah* in the title of "Soon Ah Will Be Done" represents an African American dialect pronunciation of *I*. A complete version of the refrain words in this dialect might be written: *Soon ah will be done-a wid de troubles ob de worl'*. Students may wish to try singing the refrain with this pronunciation.

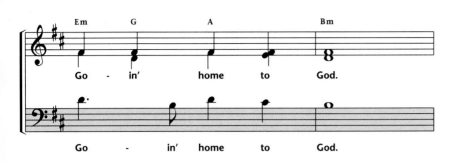

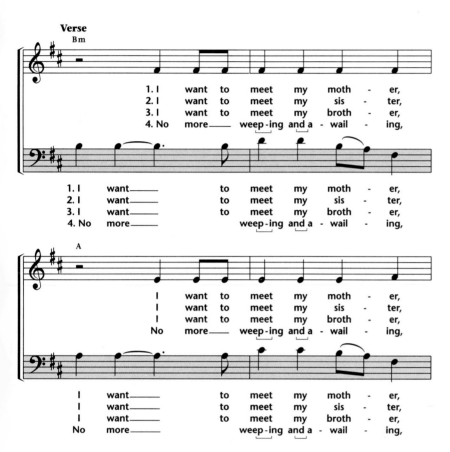

2. Sing the melody and differentiate between ♪♪ and ♪♪ Have students:

• Sing the melody of the refrain, concentrating on the dotted eighth-sixteenth rhythm.

• Say the words of the text in even eighth notes.

• Describe how the two rhythms are different. (In ♪♪ the notes are held for an equal amount of time; in ♪♪ the first note is held longer.)

• Sing the melody of the verses.

3. Sing the song in two parts. Have students:

• Note that the second part (for cambiatas) is in the bass clef, then follow on the notation as you or a volunteer plays the part.

• Sing the cambiata part as able. (When students are secure singing the melody and cambiata part separately, have them sing the two parts together.) (Optional: Use "Soon Ah Will Be Done" Performance Mix CD9:26.)

MUSIC LIBRARY
SONG ANTHOLOGY

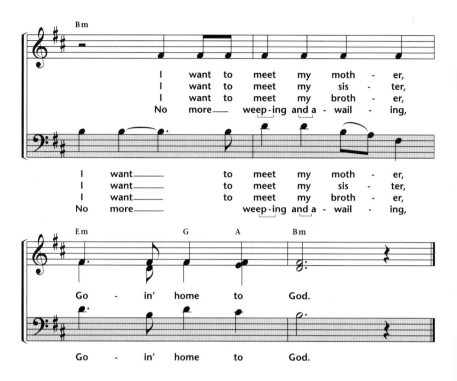

continued from previous page

4. Sing the song with attention to mood and style. Have students:

• Volunteer to sing solos in the verses.

• Sing the song, emphasizing the contrasts of mood and style between the verses and refrain by having different singers perform the verses solo, but having the entire class sing the refrain.

Reinforcement
verse-refrain form, *page 61*
dotted rhythms, *page 127*

356

MEETING **INDIVIDUAL** NEEDS

MULTICULTURAL PERSPECTIVES: *Spirituals*
See Unit 1, Lesson 7, page 30, *Multicultural Perspectives*.

Fussreise

1. Introduce the song CD9:27 (German) CD9:28 (English). Have students:

• Look at the words and discuss their meaning. (They are an expression of happiness and joy by a hiker wandering on a beautiful morning through the countryside. You may wish to go over some of the poetic language in the English translation: *thro'*—through; *o'er*—over; *Adam*—biblical figure, the first human; *thou*—you; *oft*—often; *dost*—do; *thy*—your; *naught*—nothing; *boon*—gift.)

• Listen to the song to decide whether it should be sung in a legato or marcato style. (The accompaniment suggests a light marcato style.)

BACKGROUND: *"Fussreise"*

"Fussreise" is an example of an art song, or *Lied*. Famous composers of this genre include Franz Schubert, Robert Schumann, and Hugo Wolf. These songs had a strong literary basis, with most of the lyrics coming from poets of the time. Because of this, the texts were very important. The best of the songs blend the poet, character, scene, and singer into a dramatic whole that enhances the poem's meaning. This song, composed in the 1880s, is an expression of the joy of being outside and taking a walk in the beautiful German countryside. The actual poem was written by Eduard Mörike (1804–1875) in the mid-1800s.

PRONUNCIATION GUIDE: *"Fussreise"*

ɑ f<u>a</u>ther	e ch<u>a</u>otic	ɛ p<u>e</u>t	i b<u>ee</u>
ɪ <u>i</u>t	o <u>o</u>bey	ɔ p<u>aw</u>	u m<u>oo</u>n
ʊ p<u>u</u>t	ə <u>a</u>go	ç <u>h</u>ue	

ö lips form [o] and say [e]   œ lips form [ɔ] and say [ɛ]

ɾ flipped r   ü lips form [u] and say [i]

x guttural h, *German* Ba<u>ch</u>

MUSIC LIBRARY
SONG ANTHOLOGY

continued from previous page

2. Sing the song. Have students:

Recorded Lesson CD9:29

• Listen to "Pronunciation for 'Fussreise.'"

• Echo-sing the phrases in German or English.

• Find the dotted note rhythms (Measures 5, 14, 21, 35, 40, 48, 50, 52, 55, 56, 58, 73, and 74) and the triplet (Measure 7) and practice saying the words so that these rhythms are performed correctly.

• Sing the song with the appropriate articulation.

Reinforcement articulation, *page 199*

358

MEETING **INDIVIDUAL** NEEDS

PRONUNCIATION GUIDE: *"Fussreise"*

ɑ f<u>a</u>ther	e ch<u>ao</u>tic	ɛ p<u>e</u>t	i b<u>ee</u>
ɪ <u>i</u>t	o <u>o</u>bey	ɔ p<u>aw</u>	u m<u>oo</u>n
ʊ p<u>u</u>t	ə <u>a</u>go	ç h<u>ue</u>	

ö lips form [o] and say [e]   œ lips form [ɔ] and say [ɛ]

ɾ flipped r   ü lips form [u] and say [i]

x guttural h, *German* Ba<u>ch</u>

BIOGRAPHY: *Hugo Wolf*

Austrian composer Hugo Wolf (1860–1903) was one of the outstanding composers of the art song. Although he began composing while still a teenager, it was not until he was in his late twenties that he turned to literature as inspiration for his songs. Several poets, especially German poet Eduard Mörike, inspired him to write a great variety of music, and within three years he had published more than 200 songs. The songs were received well, so he tried his hand at opera, completing his first opera in 1895. The opera was not successful, and in 1897 he composed his last songs and had a mental breakdown that led to his death.

ART CONNECTION: *"Fussreise"*

VISUAL ARTS

Have students draw or cut out magazine pictures of sights the wanderer in the song might observe on a country hike today. Assemble them on a bulletin board to give students the sense of the beauty of nature as an inspiration to poets and composers.

Chíu, chíu, chíu

Sing the song CD9:30. Have students:

• Perform a body percussion pattern with the beat as they listen to the song: pat, clap, snap L, snap R. (Accent Beat 1.)

• Listen again, following the words of the verse on the notation. (*Canta* means "sing"; *pajarito* means "little bird.")

• Sing the melody of the refrain on a neutral syllable such as *loo* or *vee* in order to become familiar with the pitches of the melody.

Recorded Lesson CD9:31
Listen to "Pronunciation for 'Chíu, chíu, chíu.'"

• Sing the song.

Reinforcement dotted rhythms, *page 123*

Uruguayan Folk Song
English Version by MMH

360

MEETING **INDIVIDUAL** NEEDS

PRONUNCIATION: *"Chíu, chíu, chíu"*

ɑ f<u>a</u>ther	e ch<u>a</u>otic	i b<u>ee</u>	o <u>o</u>bey
u m<u>oo</u>n	β b without lips touching		ð <u>the</u>
ɾ flipped r	x slightly guttural h, *Spanish* ba<u>j</u>o		

BACKGROUND: *"Chíu, chíu, chíu"*

Uruguayan folk music often shows the influences of the Spanish, Italian, and German people who colonized Uruguay and intermingled with the few surviving Native American people. "Chíu, chíu, chíu" shares several characteristics with Spanish and Italian folk music. Among these are the short, repeated rhythm patterns and subtle syncopation.

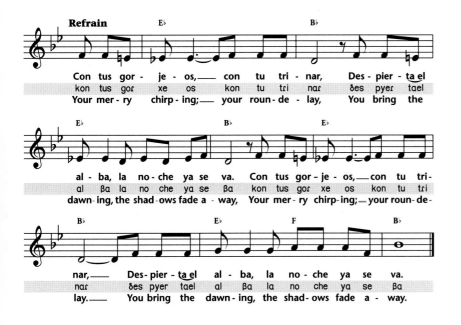

Refrain

Con tus gor - je - os,— con tu tri - nar, Des - pier - ta el
kon tus goɾ xe os kon tu tri naɾ ðes pyeɾ tael
Your mer - ry chirp - ing;— your roun - de - lay, You bring the

al - ba, la no - che ya se va. Con tus gor - je - os,— con tu tri -
al βa la no che ya se βa kon tus goɾ xe os kon tu tri
dawn - ing, the shad - ows fade a - way, Your mer - ry chirp - ing;— your roun - de -

nar,— Des - pier - ta el al - ba, la no - che ya se va.
naɾ ðes pyeɾ tael al βa la no che ya se βa
lay.— You bring the dawn - ing, the shad - ows fade a - way.

MUSIC LIBRARY
SONG ANTHOLOGY

Where'er You Walk

1. Introduce the song CD9:32. Have students:

• Listen to the song.

• Discuss its meaning. (The narrator believes that wherever a friend goes, good things will happen in nature; breezes will blow, trees will form shade, and flowers will grow.)

• Decide on the form. (A B A)

2. Sing along with the song. Have students:

• Listen to the song again, with particular attention to the style and to the multiple notes on the word *shade* in Line 4, and on *crowd* in Line 5. Then echo you in singing these two words.

• Listen again, singing along as able.

3. Practice rhythm patterns in the song. Have students:

• Notice the 32nd notes in the first measure of the A section and in the first measure of the B section. Echo you in singing these rhythms.

• Practice the large leaps in the melody, at first isolated, then as part of the entire phrase in which they appear (for example: *into* toward the end of Line 2, *shall fan* in Line 3, *sit* to *shall* in Lines 4–5, *crowd into* in Line 5, *shall rise* in Line 6, *you turn* in the last line.)

• Sing the song.

Reinforcement
A B A form, *page 69*
melodic contour, *page 21*

MEETING **INDIVIDUAL** NEEDS

BACKGROUND: *"Where'er You Walk"*

This is a solo aria from the opera *Semele* (1744). Handel based the opera on the story of Semele, a figure from classical mythology. Her son Bacchus supposedly discovered how to make wine from grapes.

Virtuoso singing in the baroque period was quite elaborate. The musical content was often felt to be more important than the text. The form of "Where'er You Walk," A B A, was very popular and was known as *aria da capo*. It was usual for the soloist to improvise variations on the repeat of the A section.

BIOGRAPHY: *George Frideric Handel*

German composer George Frideric Handel (1685–1759) wrote some of Europe's best-loved music, including *Messiah* and *Water Music*. He was also one of the great organists of his time. Handel's musical talent was evident from an early age. At the age of 7 he played the organ so well that a duke persuaded his father to let him study music. By the time he was 11, Handel was composing his own sonatas and music for church services. As an adult he took a job as a music master at a German court, while frequently traveling to England. He soon decided to settle permanently in that country, becoming England's most popular composer.

Drill, Ye Tarriers

Words and Music by
Thomas Casey and Charles Connolly

Verse

Cm
1. Oh, ev'-ry morn-in' at sev-en o' clock,— There's a
2. Now, our new fore-man was Jer-ry Mc-Cann,— You can
3. Now, next time pay-day come— a-round,— Jim

Gm
hun-dred tar-ri-ers a- work-in' at the rock, And the
bet that he was sure a blame— mean— man, Last—
Goff a dol-lar— short— was— found, When—

Cm
boss comes a- long and he says, "Keep still! And
week a pre-ma-ture blast went off, And a
asked what— for, came— this re- ply, "You were

Gm
come down heav-y on the cast-iron drill," and
mile in the air— went— big Jim Goff, and
docked for the time— you were up in the sky!" So

Refrain

Cm   Gm   Cm   Gm   Cm
Drill, ye tar-ri- ers, drill, Drill, ye tar-ri- ers, drill.

Eb   Cm
Oh, it's work all day for sug-ar in your tay,

Gm   Cm   Gm   Cm
Down be-hind the rail-way, Oh, drill, ye tar-ri- ers, drill!

C minor
l₁ t₁ d r m s l t d'

Music Library *Song Anthology* **363**

Drill, Ye Tarriers

1. Introduce the song CD9:33. Have students:

• Listen to the song while tapping with the beat, paying attention to the rhythm. (Strong rhythms make the song very robust and lively, like the tarriers.)

• Tell the form and how the number of singers helps them distinguish the sections. (A B or verse-refrain form; verse—solo singer, refrain—group.)

• Tell the story of the song.

• Sing the refrain, then the entire song.

2. Practice identifying minor scale. Have students:

• Play a minor scale on resonator bells (C D Eb F G Ab Bb C') and sing with numbers or pitch syllables. (1 2 3 4 5 6 7 8 or *la, ti, do re mi fa so la*)

• Play a major scale on resonator bells and sing with numbers or pitch syllables to contrast the sound with minor. (C D E F G A B C', 1 2 3 4 5 6 7 8 or *do re mi fa so la ti do'*)

• Listen as you sing the song in C major to compare the sound of major and minor.

3. Add a melodic ostinato. Have students:

• Sing the song, adding the following melodic ostinato to the verses.

Drill, ye tar-ri-ers, drill
la₁ la₁ mi mi mi la₁

• Have the students make up an accompaniment using metallic found-sounds to imitate the drill. Stress the strong beats.

• (Optional: **Technology**—Use Music with MIDI.)

Reinforcement minor and major, *page 165*

PLAYING INSTRUMENTS: *Pitched and Unpitched*

Add these ostinatos to "Drill, Ye Tarriers."

Bass xylophone:

Finger cymbals: (Refrain)

Triangle: (Refrain)

Body percussion:
pat   pat   pat   clap clap
Drill, drill, drill that rock!

BACKGROUND: *"Drill, Ye Tarriers"*

With river traffic being replaced by railroads, paths had to be made through mountains to lay railroad tracks. Many of the men who worked to build the railroads were Chinese and Irish. They drove drills into the rock, making holes for blasting charges. They were given the name "tarriers," possibly because they dug like terriers. By 1890, passenger and freight trains, including the first transcontinental railroad, linked all the major centers of the nation. This song by two Irish Americans tells about their life on the job.

Island in the Sun

1. Play a body-percussion pattern with the song CD10:1. Have students:

• Pat this body-percussion pattern during the verse while listening to "Island in the Sun."

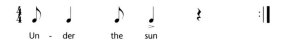

Un - der   the   sun

• Whisper this pattern while listening to the refrain.

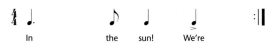

In   the   sun!   We're

• Whisper the pattern again with the tie (leaving out *sun*), creating syncopation (see page 154). Then clap the pattern with the tie and perform with the refrain.

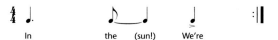

In   the   (sun!)   We're

ISLAND IN THE SUN

Music by Harry Belafonte
Words by Lord Burgess

D major

1. This is my is - land in the sun where my peo - ple have toiled since time be - gun.— Though I may sail on man - y a sea— Her shores will al - ways be home to me.—

Refrain

Oh, is - land in the sun.— Willed to me— by my

Optional Cambiata

fa - ther's hand.— All my days— I will sing in praise— of your

364

MEETING **INDIVIDUAL** NEEDS

PLAYING INSTRUMENTS: *"Island in the Sun"*

Have students learn to play the accompaniment parts to "Island in the Sun" on **Resource Master SA • 1**.

1. Clap the rhythm and speak the words for each instrument.

2. Play the instruments, speaking the words.

3. Use the instrument parts to accompany the song, playing only in the sections indicated.

CRITICAL THINKING: *Performance Decisions*

Have students decide how they might add pitched instruments to the accompaniment for "Island in the Sun" on **Resource Master SA • 1** to help differentiate the verse from the refrain. (Suggestion: Have guitars, resonator bells, etc., play the I, IV, and V7 chords [D, G, A7] in the refrain from the notation.)

ORFF: *"Island in the Sun"*

See **O • 16** in *Orchestrations for Orff Instruments*.

for - ests, wat - ers, your shin - ing sand.

2. I hope the day will nev - er come that I

can't a - wake to the sound of drum.

Nev - er let me miss car - ni - val With ca -

lyp - so songs phil - o - soph - i - cal.

2. Sing the song. Have students:
- Sing the melody.
- Learn the harmony part in the refrain and the optional cambiata, if desired. (After students are comfortable singing each part separately, have them form groups and sing the parts together.) (Optional: Use "Island in the Sun" Performance Mix CD10:2.)

Reinforcement syncopation, *page 157*

MULTICULTURAL PERSPECTIVES: *Calypso Music*

"Island in the Sun" was written by Harry Belafonte in calypso style. Calypso is a lively rhythmic music with African roots. It originated in Trinidad, part of the West Indies, near the end of the nineteenth century. Like spirituals, calypso songs began as a protest against the harsh life of those who worked on the sugar plantations. Enslaved Africans used the music to communicate, to make fun of the slave owners, and to pass on news.

Today, lyrics remain the primary focus of calypso songs. Singers, who often bear colorful names, comment on social and political issues such as elections in Trinidad or racial tensions in New York City (where almost two million West Indians live). Many calypso singers pride themselves on their ability to think up new rhymes off the top of their heads. Each spring a major calypso competition is held in Trinidad, and calypso fever sweeps the country.

PLAYING INSTRUMENTS: *Recorder*

See **R · 18** in *Playing the Recorder* for "Island in the Sun."

MUSIC LIBRARY
SONG ANTHOLOGY

RELATED ARTS **MOVEMENT** ☐ THEATER ☐ VISUAL ARTS

Scarborough Fair

1. Introduce the song CD10:3. Have students:

• Listen to the song, following the notation, to discover the different meters. (²⁄₄ and ⁶⁄₄)

• Tell how many times the meter changed. (4 times)

• Sing the song. (Optional: Technology— Use Music with MIDI.)

2. Explore the Dorian scale and compare it to the minor scale. Have students:

• Play a Dorian scale on resonator bells and sing it with pitch letter names or pitch syllables ascending and descending. (ascending: D E F G A B C D'; *re mi fa so la ti do re'*)

• Discover that "Scarborough Fair" is in the Dorian mode, which can be played on the piano using only white keys from D to D' and sung from *re* to *re'*.

• Take the rhythm from "Scarborough Fair" and improvise a melody using the notes in the Dorian scale, D E F G A B C D', and ending on D. (You may simplify this by having them use only the rhythms of the first phrase.)

• Play and sing the D minor scale (D E F G A B♭ C D') with pitch syllables, then letter names (beginning on *la₁*—D), ascending and descending. (For comparison with minor, the Dorian scale can be sung from *la₁* to *la*, with *fa* raised a half step to *fi*.)

• Sing the Dorian scale once again with letter names.

Reinforcement minor scale, *page 165*

English Folk Song

1. Are you go-ing to Scar-borough Fair?_____
2. Tell her to make me a cam-bric shirt,_____
3. Tell her to wash it in yon-der dry well,_____
4. Tell her to dry it on yon-der thorn,_____
5. Tell him to find me an a-cre of land,_____

Pars-ley,

sage, rose-mar-y and thyme;_____

Re-
With
Where
Which
Be-

mem-ber me to one that lives there,_____ For
out a seam or fine nee-dle-work,_____ And
wa-ter ne'er sprung, not drop of rain fell,_____ And
nev-er bore blos-som since A-dam was born,_____ And
tween the sea foam and the sea sand,_____ Or

she was once a true love of mine._____
then she'll be a true love of mine._____
then she'll be a true love of mine._____
then she'll be a true love of mine._____
nev-er be a true love of mine._____

6. Tell him to plough it with a lam'd horn
Parsley, sage, rosemary and thyme;
And sow it all over with one peppercorn,
Or never be a true love of mine.

D Dorian

366

MEETING **INDIVIDUAL** NEEDS

PLAYING INSTRUMENTS: *"Scarborough Fair"*

Unpitched: Have the students play the following accompaniment with the song.

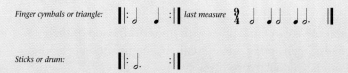

Finger cymbals or triangle: *last measure*

Sticks or drum:

Pitched: Have students sing the following descant with the song, or play it on resonator bells or recorder.

Pars-ley, sage, rose-mar-y and thyme, rose-mar-y and thyme. Re-

mem-ber me to her. She was once a true love of mine, of mine.

ORFF: *"Scarborough Fair"*
See **O • 17** in *Orchestrations for Orff Instruments.*

Shady Grove

Southern Appalachian Folk Song

Refrain

Shad - y Grove, my lit - tle love, Shad - y Grove, I know,

Shad - y Grove, my lit - tle love, Bound for Shad - y Grove.

Verse

1. Cheeks as red as the bloom - ing rose, Eyes of the deep - est brown;
2. Went to see my Shad - y Grove, She was stand - ing in the door,
3. Wish I had a big fine horse, Corn to feed him on,
4. Shad - y Grove, my lit - tle love, Shad - y Grove, I say,

You are the dar - ling of my heart, Stay till the sun goes down.
Shoes and stock - ings in her hand, Lit - tle bare feet on the floor.
Pret - ty lit - tle girl, stay at home, Feed him when I'm gone.
Shad - y Grove, my lit - tle love, Don't wait till the Judg - ment Day!

Shady Grove

1. Introduce the song and its rhythms

CD10:4. Have students:

• Find measures with the ♩♪ and ♪♪♪ patterns in the song and clap them. (♩♪—Measures 1, 3, 5, 9; ♪♪♪—Measures 2, 6, 9, 11, 13, 15)

• Clap the entire song, saying the words in rhythm.

• Name the notes in the song and the tonal center with pitch letter names or pitch syllables. (C D E G A C'; *do re mi so la do'*; the tonal center is D—*re*)

• Sing the song with pitch letter names or pitch syllables, then with the words.

2. Analyze the song. Have students:

• Listen to the song, following the notation. Compare the melodies of the refrain and the verse. (The melodies are the same. The rhythm is different to accommodate the words.)

• Discuss the tempo and mood of the song. (fast tempo; happy, dance-like mood)

3. Explore the *re* pentatonic scale. Have students:

• Play a *re* pentatonic scale ascending and descending on resonator bells. (D E G A C D' C A G E D)

• Notice the arrangement of steps and skips in the scale. (step, skip, step, skip, step)

• Sing the scale with pitch letter names or pitch syllables (D E G A C D'; *re mi so la do re'*)

• Improvise on the *re* pentatonic scale on resonator bells. (Begin and end on *re*.)

Reinforcement dotted rhythms, *page 113*

MOVEMENT: *"Shady Grove"*

Formation: Double circle with couples joining hands in the promenade or skating position and facing counterclockwise.

Refrain: *Measures 1–8*—Couples promenade counterclockwise. (16 steps)

Verse: *Measures 9–12*—Couples swing with right elbows using an easy walking step (8 steps, 2 full circles); *Measures 13–16*—Couples swing with left elbows (2 full circles).

ORFF: *"Shady Grove"*

See **O • 18** in *Orchestrations for Orff Instruments.*

PLAYING INSTRUMENTS: *Recorder*

See **R • 17** in *Playing the Recorder* for both "Scarborough Fair" and "Shady Grove."

ENRICHMENT: *"Shady Grove"*

Have students read and perform the following rhythmic ostinato. Then form two groups; one group to sing "Shady Grove," the other to perform the ostinato on the refrain.

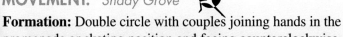

pat   clap   clap

MUSIC LIBRARY
SONG ANTHOLOGY

4Ai, iv; 4Bi, iii; 4Cv

The Kettle Valley Line

Introduce the song and sing in two parts
CD10:5. Have students:

• Listen to the song and decide whether the tonality is major (*do*-centered) or minor (*la*-centered) and what the tonal center is. (minor; *la*-centered; D)

• List the pitches of the melody in the first line from low to high and find the half step. (D E F G A—the first five steps in the D minor scale; E–F—2–3)

• Discuss the story the song tells. (See also *Background* below.)

• Sing Part 1 with the recording.

• Sing Part 2 with the recording. (When students are secure singing each part separately, have them sing both parts together.) (Optional: Use "The Kettle Valley Line" Performance Mix **CD10:6.**)

Reinforcement first five steps of the minor scale, *page 153*

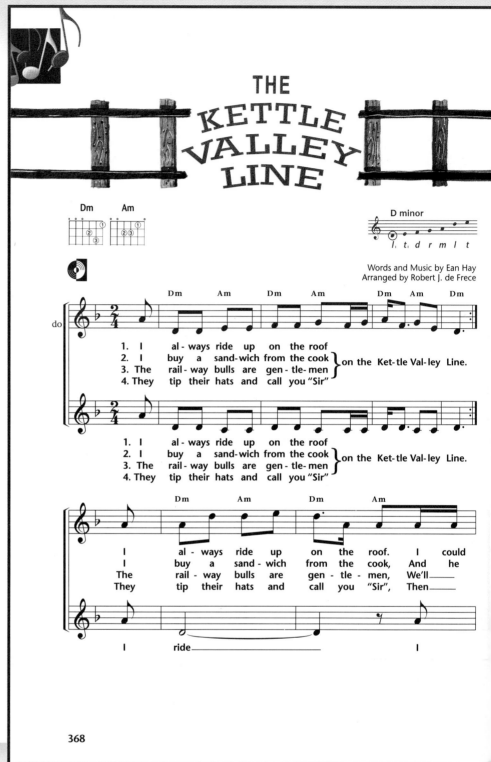

MEETING **INDIVIDUAL** NEEDS

BACKGROUND: *"The Kettle Valley Line"*

The Kettle Valley Line is a railroad route that runs between Lethbridge, Alberta and Hope, British Columbia in Western Canada. From the 1880s to the 1930s, laborers looking for work traveled throughout North America in or on the roofs of empty boxcars to avoid paying the fare. One such worker was composer Ean Hay's father. Ean Hay wrote the words of "The Kettle Valley Line" based on stories his father had told him about his experiences at the end of World War I. The "railway bulls" were police officers who would put the workers in "stir" (jail) if they caught them riding for free.

LANGUAGE ARTS CONNECTION: *Folk Songs*

Long before they were written down in books, folk songs were orally transmitted from one person and place to another. Often notes and words were changed in the process. Sometimes old verses were omitted and new ones made up. Have the students carry on this tradition by making up new verses about traveling on "The Kettle Valley Line." They can change a few words in an existing verse or make up an entirely new verse.

PITCH SYLLABLES: *"The Kettle Valley Line"*

Have students figure out the pitch syllable names of the pitches used in both Parts 1 and 2. Then have them sing the song with pitch syllables, adding hand signs as able.

ORFF: *"The Kettle Valley Line"*

See **O • 19** in *Orchestrations for Orff Instruments*.

MUSIC LIBRARY
SONG ANTHOLOGY

Follow the Drinkin' Gourd

1. Introduce the song CD10:7. Have students:

• Read the song's text and discuss how its words contain encoded directions for enslaved African Americans who planned to escape North to freedom. (See *Background* below.)

• Find eighth-quarter-eighth, eighth-dotted quarter, dotted quarter-eighth, and triplet patterns. Tell how many beats each pattern gets in cut time, or $\frac{2}{2}$. (1 beat)

• Clap the triplet pattern in Measure 7 (at *Follow the*) and the ♪ ♩ ♪ pattern to the same words in Measure 15. (Bring out that the triplet contains equal sounds, while the syncopated pattern in Measure 15 contains unequal sounds—short-long-short.)

• Find ties and tap the rhythm of measures that use them.

• Name the scale. (E minor)

2. Sing the song. Have students:

• Listen to the song, then tell its form. (verse-refrain)

• Sing the song.

FOLLOW THE DRINKIN' GOURD. Words and Music by Paul Campbell. TRO-© Copyright 1951 (renewed) Folkways Music Publishers, Inc., New York, NY. Used by Permission.

370

MEETING **INDIVIDUAL** NEEDS

BACKGROUND: *"Follow the Drinkin' Gourd"*

This is one of the songs associated with the Underground Railroad, the system that helped enslaved African Americans escape to the northern United States or Canada. The "gourd" in the song is the Big Dipper constellation, which is made up of seven bright stars that look like a long-handled drinking cup. The two end-stars in the bowl of the Big Dipper point to the North Star, Polaris, which is at the end of the handle of the Little Dipper. By traveling toward the North Star, the escaping person would eventually reach freedom. When an escape was to take place, additional verses were added that would tell such things as where to meet and at what time.

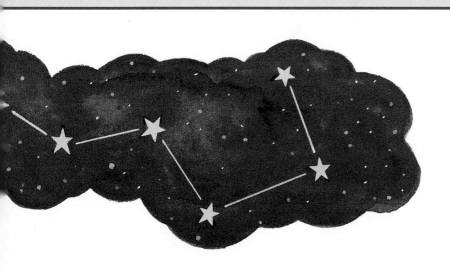

3. Add a melodic ostinato to the song. Have students:

• Sing the syncopated phrase *Drink-in' Gourd* (Measure 12—resting on the last quarter) as a melodic ostinato with the song. Then play the ostinato from the notation on resonator bells or other pitched instruments.

• When ready, divide into three groups for a final performance of the song—Group 1 to sing the melody, Group 2 to sing the ostinato, and Group 3 to play the ostinato on resonator bells or other pitched instruments.

Reinforcement
reading rhythms, *page 17*
call-response/spiritual, *page 119*
syncopation, *page 203*

Refrain

Fol - low_____ the Drink - in' Gourd,_____

Fol - low_____ the Drink - in' Gourd,_____

For the Old Man is a - wait - in' for to

car - ry you to free - dom, Fol - low the Drink - in' Gourd.

SCIENCE CONNECTION: *Steering by the Stars*

Have students do research on the Big Dipper, the Little Dipper, and other constellations to determine how stars were used for direction by African Americans escaping slavery and are still used by others, such as sailors and astronomers. (The North Star, Polaris, is always in the same small area in the sky because it is located above the North Pole. For thousands of years, people have used the Dippers to find the North Star, which they then used to find their way at night.)

LANGUAGE ARTS CONNECTION: *Directions*

Have the students make up a verse to the song that gives encoded directions in the style of "Follow the Drinkin' Gourd." It could name a time and place for a meeting or describe a person who will be "waiting" there.

MUSIC LIBRARY
SONG ANTHOLOGY

RELATED ARTS **MOVEMENT** THEATER VISUAL ARTS

Garifalia

1. Introduce the song CD10:8 **and ʒ meter.**
Have students:

• Perform by rote this rhythm pattern, which is a combination of duple and triple meter:

• Perform the same pattern from notation in ʒ that you have written on the board:

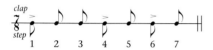

• Perform the pattern as they listen to "Garifalia."

• Perform the pattern again, taking the steps, but thinking the claps. (This will help prepare students to dance to "Garifalia.")

• Say the words in rhythm while performing the pattern.

Greek Folk Song
English Version by MMH

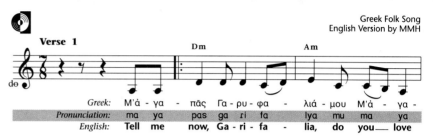

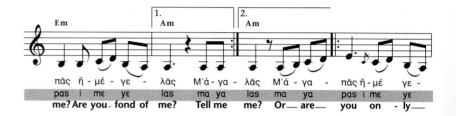

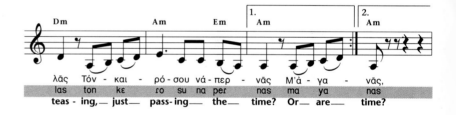

372

MEETING **INDIVIDUAL** NEEDS

BACKGROUND: *"Garifalia"*

"Garifalia" is a playful Greek folk song that has fun with words. Garifalia, a female proper name, also means carnation. The name Basil means the herb as well as being a male proper name.

PRONUNCIATION: *"Garifalia"*

ɑ f**a**ther	ɛ p**e**t	i b**ee**	o **o**bey
u m**oo**n	ð **the**	ɾ flipped r	

πῶ, δέν-σέ-γε - λῶ. Σ'ά-γα - λῶ. Σ'ά - γα - πῶ, δέν-σέ-γε -
po ðen se ye lo sa ga lo sa ga po ðen se ye
nev-er, nev-er— tease! Yes, I tease! You-should— know I love—

λῶ, Σάν-τά - μά-τι-α-μου τά-δυό Σ'ά - γα - δυό.
lo san ta ma ti a mu ta ðyo sa ga ðyo
you, I love— you as my own two eyes! You— should— eyes.

A minor

l, t, d r m l t d' r' m'

---

2. Sing the song and learn a Greek dance.
Have students:

Recorded Lesson CD10:9

• Listen to "Pronunciation for 'Garifalia.'"

• Sing the song.

• Learn a "grapevine" step, common to many Greek dances: (Verbal Cue—*side, back, side, cross, side, back, side, cross*) Step to the side with the right foot, cross behind with the left, step again with the right, then cross in front with the left. Repeat.

• Perform the grapevine step to a ⅞ rhythm pattern. (Step on Beat 1 each time—1 2 3, 1 2, 1 2—as they did before.)

• Dance to "Garifalia." (See *Movement* below.)

Reinforcement
meter, *page 157*
dances of the world, *page 171*

MOVEMENT: *"Garifalia"*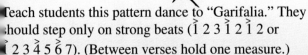

Teach students this pattern dance to "Garifalia." They should step only on strong beats (1̇ 2 3 1̇ 2 1̇ 2 or 1̇ 2 3 4̇ 5 6̇ 7). (Between verses hold one measure.)

Formation: In line or a circle with hands joined at shoulder height, elbows bent, arms in "W" position

Measure 2: Begin the grapevine step moving to the right (Verbal Cue—*side, back, side*).

Measure 3: Continue grapevine step moving right (Verbal Cue—*cross, side, back*).

Measure 4: Take a step to the side with the right foot, point left foot in front of right on Beat 4 and hold (Verbal Cue—*side right, point, hold*).

Measure 5: Step to left on left foot, point right foot in front of left on Beat 4 and hold (Verbal Cue—*side left, point, hold*).

Repeat the four-measure pattern throughout the song, always moving to the right. (If in a line, the farthest person to the right leads the rest in a curving line across the floor and around the room. If in a circle, move counterclockwise.)

MUSIC LIBRARY
SONG ANTHOLOGY

El robalo

1. Introduce the song CD10:10. Have students:

• Pat with the beat on their legs as they listen to the recording.

• Tell the meter and what the meter signature means. (²/₄; two beats to a measure, the quarter note equals one beat)

• Listen again, following the words in the book.

• Sing the melody on a neutral syllable such as *loo* or *vee* in order to become familiar with the pitches of the melody. (For more practice performing the rhythm of the song, see *Extra Help* below.)

2. Sing the song. Have students:

Recorded Lesson CD10:11
• Listen to "Pronunciation for 'El robalo.'"

• Sing the song.

Reinforcement ²/₄ meter, *page 157*

The Haddock

Venezuelan Folk Song
Collected by Francisco Carrero

Spanish: Ya te co-noz-co, Ro-ba-lo por el ca-mi-no que vas, con tus za-pa-ti-cos blan-cos y tus me-dias co-lo-rás. Con tus za-pa-ti-cos blan-cos y tus me-dias co-lo-rás.

Pronunciation: ya te ko nos ko ɾo βa lo poɾ el ka mi no ke βas, kon tus sa pa ti kos βlang kos i tus me ðyas ko lo ɾas. kon tus sa pa ti kos βlang kos i tus me ðyas ko lo ɾas.

English: I rec-og-nize you, Ro-bo-lo, on the high-way where you go. I see your lit-tle white san-dals and your lit-tle socks of red. I see your lit-tle white san-dals and your lit-tle socks of red.

D major

374

MEETING **INDIVIDUAL** NEEDS

PRONUNCIATION: *"El robalo"*

ɑ f<u>a</u>ther   e ch<u>a</u>otic   i b<u>ee</u>   o <u>o</u>bey
u m<u>oo</u>n   β b without lips touching   ð <u>th</u>e
ɾ flipped r

EXTRA HELP: *"El robalo"*

To help students correctly perform the straight eighth notes and the triplet eighth notes in the song, have them:

1. Pat-clap eighth notes in the tempo of the song.

2. Pat-clap-clap triplet eighth notes in the same tempo.

3. Clap the beat, whispering first *1, 2, 1, 2* then *1, 2, 3, 1, 2, 3.*

4. Divide into two groups. Group 1 pats with the beat, Group 2 alternates clapping triplet eighths and straight eighths for one beat each. Then switch roles.

5. Group 1 pats with the beat while Group 2 claps the rhythm of Measures 2–3 a few times, thinking *1, 2, 3, 1, 2* in each measure. Have the students patting with the beat listen for two unequal, then two equal sounds within each measure. Then switch roles.

Words and Music by Joyce Elaine Eilers
Adapted by MMH

When it seems your skies are all gray, ___ and the

When your skies are

trou-bles of the world are here to stay; ___

gray, And trou-ble's here to stay, Just

C minor/C major

A Voice from a Dream

1. Introduce the song CD10:12. Have students:

● Listen to the opening section of the song and decide if it is in major or minor. (minor).

● Listen to the entire song and raise their hands when they hear the change in style and tempo. (Measure 21) Then tell if the new section is in major or minor. (major)

● Sing the *mi fa so la so* pattern that first appears in Measures 25–26 with *Come a-long with me*. Then tell how many times that pattern occurs in the melody with the same or different words. (6; there are slight variants in the rhythms.)

● Sing this pattern with the appropriate words as they listen to the song.

2. Sing the melody. Have students:

● Follow the song in the book as the recording is played, singing the melody as able.

● Tell the form. (A B) Then describe the features that help differentiate the character of the A and B sections. (the change from minor to major, and changes in style and tempo)

● Sing the melody.

SOCIAL STUDIES CONNECTION: *Eastern Venezuela*

"El robalo" comes from the eastern region of Venezuela. Have students find Venezuela on a map and note some of the geographical features of the eastern region. (Part of this region borders the Atlantic Ocean to the east and the Caribbean Sea to the north.) Tell them that the coastal lowland, the region within a few miles of the beaches, is mostly hot and dry. A wall of mountains rises just a few miles inland from the beaches. It was on these beaches that Columbus first stepped foot in South America, on one of his trips to the Americas. The mountains discouraged European exploration of the inland areas for many years.

MUSIC LIBRARY
SONG ANTHOLOGY

continued from previous page

3. Learn the second part. Have students:

• Sing the second part (for cambiatas).

• Divide into two groups, one to practice the melody and one to practice the second part. (When students are secure singing each part separately, have them sing the two parts together.) (Optional: Use "A Voice from a Dream" Performance Mix **CD10:13**.)

Reinforcement major and minor, *page 153*

376

MEETING **INDIVIDUAL** NEEDS

ENRICHMENT: *Bass Clef Notation*

Have students look at the second part for "A Voice from a Dream," noting that it is written in the bass clef. Then listen as you or a volunteer plays the second part on a keyboard instrument, singing along as able. What vocal range does Part 2 work best for? (cambiata, or changing voice) As a

class, have students explore writing the second line of Part 2 in the treble clef. Why is Part 2 written in the bass rather than the treble clef? (Since the part is written for a lower voice, it is easier to read in bass clef. To notate the part in treble clef would require several ledger lines below the lowest line of the staff.)

Come a-long with me,_____ where the sky is blu - er

Come_____ with me,_____

than the deep -est sea,_____ Come with me,_____ Come with

with me, Come with me.

Come with me.

me._____ Come with me._____

Come with me, Come with me.

(Optional)

Music Library *Song Anthology* **379**

RELATED ARTS | MOVEMENT | THEATER | VISUAL ARTS

Shall I Dream a Dream?

1. Introduce the tempo and rhythm of the song CD10:14. Have students:

• Look at the words and decide whether legato or marcato articulation would be appropriate. (See page 191.) Then select tempo, dynamics, and tone color that would be appropriate to the words. (See page 196.)

• Perform a clap-snap-snap-snap pattern with the beat as they listen to the recording, comparing the choices of articulation, tempo, dynamics, and tone color to their own.

• Clap the following rhythm pattern:

• Listen again to the song and clap the rhythm pattern each time it appears in the song. (The pattern appears eight times.)

MEETING **INDIVIDUAL** NEEDS

ENRICHMENT: *Solo Singing and Texture*

Provide students with practice as soloists. Assign each phrase of the first four lines of "Shall I Dream a Dream?" to a different solo singer. Then have all students continue singing the two parts with their assigned groups.

As an additional activity, discuss whether this change in tone color and texture is an effective way to interpret the song and allow students to suggest and try other tone color or textural changes.

Reach-ing for a star drift-ing slow-ly by.

We will find our hap-pi-ness nev-er won-d'ring why.

If you walk be-side me in the days a-head,

If you walk be-side me in the days a-head,

We can climb the high-est hill, we can dream a dream.

We can climb the high-est hill, we can dream a dream.

Now the time has come, time to think it through,

Now the time has come, time to think it through,

Music Library *Song Anthology* **381**

2. Learn the parts to the song. Have students:

• Sing the melody of the song, making sure to use the articulation and other interpretation choices they made earlier. (Optional: Try singing the first four lines in the opposite artic-ulation to test their choice of articulation.)

• Learn the parts of the song. (Assign mem-bers of the class to the high part and low [cam-biata] part and have them practice singing the parts. Emphasize the difference between the $\frac{4}{4}$ ♩ ♩♩ ♩. ♪ ‖ and the $\frac{4}{4}$ ♩ ♩♩ ♩ ♩ ‖ rhythm patterns. When students are secure singing both parts separately, have them sing the parts together.) (Optional: Use "Shall I Dream a Dream?" Performance Mix **CD10:15**.)

Reinforcement
dotted quarter-eighth pattern, *page 113*
interpretation, *page 227*

MUSIC LIBRARY
SONG ANTHOLOGY

MEETING **INDIVIDUAL** NEEDS

LANGUAGE ARTS CONNECTION: *Biographies*

Have students think of someone in their lives who they consider a best friend. Have students read the words of the song, "Shall I Dream a Dream?" Discuss in groups that the song could be describing the encouragement and support given by a friend. Then have them discuss what a best friend means to them and write a biography of a close friend. Students should include some achievement for which that friend has given them support and encouragement.

Words and Music by
Roy Jordan and Sid Bass

Soft Shoe Song

1. Introduce the song CD10:16. Have students:

- Read the words, then recall, or listen as you tell them, what vaudeville and a soft-shoe dance are. (See *Background* below.)

- Look at the song and find the "sand-block" part, which is intended to simulate the sound of a dancer's feet. (The part is located just above the vocal line on page 383, preceded by the syllable *ch*.)

- Note the dotted eighth-sixteenth and triplet rhythms and practice them separately. (Point out that these occur frequently in both the sand-block part and in the melody. Explain that the usually strict three-to-one relationship of the dotted eighth-sixteenth rhythm is more relaxed in this style of music.)

Music Library *Song Anthology* **383**

BACKGROUND: *"Soft Shoe Song"*

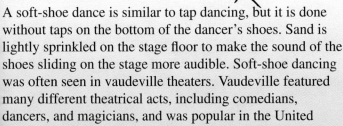

A soft-shoe dance is similar to tap dancing, but it is done without taps on the bottom of the dancer's shoes. Sand is lightly sprinkled on the stage floor to make the sound of the shoes sliding on the stage more audible. Soft-shoe dancing was often seen in vaudeville theaters. Vaudeville featured many different theatrical acts, including comedians, dancers, and magicians, and was popular in the United

States from the 1880s to the early 1930s. In its heyday from the 1900s to the 1920s, vaudeville was the major form of family entertainment. Its popularity declined only with the introduction of talking motion pictures (movies) in the late 1920s.

continued from previous page

2. Listen to the song with attention to style. Have students:

• Listen to the song, noting the relaxed soft-shoe style, the sand-block part (imitating the sound of soft-shoe dancing), and the form of the song.

• Decide on the form. (A B A)

• Sing the melody.

3. Practice the rhythm of the sand-block part. Have students:

• Read the rhythm of the sand-block part, softly saying *ch* for every note and lightly rubbing palms together to simulate the soft-shoe sound. (You might have them first read the rhythm to these words:

> *Let's all do the old soft shoe.*
>
> *Just doo-dle-dee doo-dle the old soft shoe.*
>
> *Doo-dle-dee-doo! Doo-dle-dee-doo!*
>
> *Doo-dle-dee! Doo-dle-dee-doo!)*

• Sing the melody as some students do the sand-block part. (Rub hands together or use sand blocks or a piece of sandpaper in each hand. See *Extra Help* on the bottom of page 385.)

• Take turns performing the sand-block part as others sing the song. (Optional: Use "Soft Shoe Song" Performance Mix **CD10:17**.)

Reinforcement

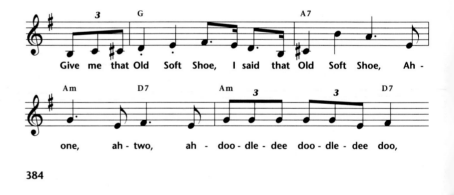

384

MEETING **INDIVIDUAL** NEEDS

MOVEMENT: *"Soft Shoe Song"*

Have students work in small groups to create soft-shoe choreography. This can be done easily by almost anyone while seated. The easy, gentle—almost delicate—style of this dance should always be maintained. All steps are small, especially the hop, and are done with only the ball of the foot, not the heel. Because this dance is done on the ball of the foot, have students warm up their feet and legs (knee bends, ankle extensions, calf stretches, walking) before dancing to avoid tired muscles.

A section: (One hand is on each knee; steps follow the rhythm of the sand-block part.)

Measure 1—Step L, cross R, step L, hop on L (to the rhythm of Measure 1 sand-block part). Repeat in opposite direction.

Measure 2—Beginning with left foot, step the rhythm with alternating feet while moving feet left.

Measure 3—Pat the rhythm with alternating hands.

Measure 4—Beginning with the right foot, step the rhythm with alternating feet, moving feet right to finish in original position.

Measures 5–8—Repeat Measures 1–4, but move feet to the right on Measure 6 and to the left on Measure 8.

Play me that Old Soft Shoe and noth-in' else will do, That's the

ch ch ch

dance my dar-lin' used to do. **do.**

The Wind Beneath My Wings

Words and Music by
Larry Henley and Jeff Silbar

Freely

It must have been cold there in my shad-ow,

to ne-ver have sun-light— on— your face.

You were con-tent to let— me— shine, that's your way,—

you al-ways walked a step— be-hind.

Music Library *Song Anthology* **385**

The Wind Beneath My Wings

1. Introduce the song CD10:18. Have students:

• Read the text of the song, which was written and became popular during the 1980s, and discuss its meaning. (thanking a friend for staying around even though the narrator got all the attention)

• Listen to the song, noticing the repetition of melodies and the rests at the beginnings of most phrases.

• Listen again, singing along as able.

B section:

With palms facing forward at shoulder height, move hands and arms together from side to side in this rhythm (3 times):

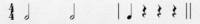

On last two measures of B section, gradually, to the beat, move hands from a head-high position back to hands on knees, as at the beginning of the A section.

Last A section: Same as Measures 1–8. On Beats 2–3 of last measure, clap "out" (one hand extending forward at a time).

EXTRA HELP: *Soft-Shoe Effect*

The soft-shoe sound effect can be simulated by rubbing sand blocks together. Another way to create the effect is rubbing together pieces of fine sandpaper fastened securely to a flat surface. A third way is to brush the head of a textured hand drum with the hand.

continued from previous page

2. Create movement for the song. Have students:

• Suggest ways that they can express the meaning of this song through movement.

• Work in pairs to choreograph parts of the song. (Suggest they create similar movements for similar phrases and contrasting movements for contrasting phrases.)

• Show one other pair their choreography, then work with that pair to complete a dance.

• Divide into two groups, one to sing while the other performs its movement in the smaller groups of four. Repeat, switching roles.

Reinforcement 1980s popular music style, *page 273*

1. So, I was the one with all the glo - ry,
2. It might have ap - peared to go un - no - ticed,

while you were the one with all the strength.
but I've got it all here in my heart.

A beau - ti - ful face with - out a name for so long,
I want you to know I know the truth, of course I know it,

a beau - ti - ful smile to hide the pain.
I would be noth - ing with - out you.

Did you ev - er know that you're my he - ro,

and ev' - ry - thing I would like to be?

I can fly high - er than an ea - gle,

386

MEETING **INDIVIDUAL** NEEDS

BACKGROUND: *"The Wind Beneath My Wings"*

This song was introduced by Bette Midler in the 1989 movie *Beaches*. Midler plays a famous rock singer who sings the song in remembrance of a lifelong friend who dies in her early thirties. The friend leaves behind a young daughter. The rock singer played by Midler becomes the daughter's guardian.

ENRICHMENT: *Conducting*

Have students conduct in quadruple meter with "The Wind Beneath My Wings":

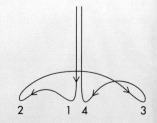

2   1 4   3

'cause you are the wind be-neath my—— wings.

wings.   wind———— be - neath— my— wings.

Fly,——— fly,——— fly a-way,— you let— me fly— so—

high.— Oh,— fly,——— fly——— so

high a-gainst— the sky,— so high— I al - most touch—

— the sky.— Thank— you,— thank— you,— thank

God for you,— the wind be-neath— my— wings.

D major

s, l, t, d r m f s l t d' r'

RELATED ARTS MOVEMENT THEATER VISUAL ARTS

Hashivenu

1. Introduce the song and warm up the voice CD10:19. Have students:

• Read the words and decide what they mean. (a wish to return to God, to be renewed)

• Discover that there are three phrases, each of four measures duration. (Since each phrase begins in a slightly higher vocal register than the previous one, a natural crescendo can occur, peaking at Measure 11 with the word *Chadesh*, which means "renew.")

• Listen to the song, noting the rise and fall of the melody and the meter. (6/8)

• Practice a vocalise that will help them sing the high E♭ without straining. (See *Vocal Development* below.)

2. Sing the song. Have students:

• Sing the pure vowels—*ah, eh, oo*—using the echo patterns on page 388. (Demonstrate both the shape of the mouth and the exact sound of each vowel as in Unit 3, Lesson 2, page 98, *Vocal Development*.)

• Sing the C minor scale, which you print either on a chart or the board, to establish the tonality of the song and discover where the half steps are located.

Recorded Lesson CD10:20
• Listen to "Pronunciation for 'Hashivenu.'"

• Sing the song. (When students are ready, have them try singing in three-part canon.)

Reinforcement
6/8 rhythm patterns, *page 161*
Israeli immigrants, *page 161*

PREPARING TO SING "HASHIVENU"

"Hashivenu" is a traditional Israeli round. The text is chanted on the Jewish Sabbath, during festivals, and at weekday services when the Torah, a set of scrolls containing the first five books of the Old Testament, is returned to its resting place.

The Hebrew text of "Hashivenu" contains several pure vowels. Can you locate them in the song? Sing the following patterns, focusing on the pure vowels in the word "alleluia" (*ah, eh,* and *oo*). Be sure your jaw is open and relaxed.

Israeli Folk Song
Edited by Doreen Rao
English Version by MMH

© Copyright 1987 by Boosey and Hawkes, Inc. Reprinted by permission.

388

MEETING **INDIVIDUAL** NEEDS

VOCAL DEVELOPMENT: *Developing Vocal Range*

Have students practice this vocalise to widen their vocal ranges. Have them breathe deeply, then blow out the "old" air, inhale "new" air, raise their arms above their heads, and make a siren-like sound on *oo* as they lower their arms. (This relaxes the back of the throat, opening up the vocal mechanism.) Now have them sing the vocalise.

Continue up by half steps to F♯

Ah - Oh - Ah - Oh - Ah *(breathe)*   Ah - Oh - Ah - Oh - Ah *(breathe)*

Keep a relaxed jaw on the *ah* vowel. Round the lips only on the *oh* vowel.

Have students bend their knees and "touch" the pitch above their heads when they sing high D and above. Use this same process to sing the high E♭ in "Hashivenu" without straining.

PRONUNCIATION: *"Hashivenu"*

ɑ f<u>a</u>ther	e ch<u>a</u>otic	ɛ p<u>e</u>t	i b<u>ee</u>
ɪ <u>i</u>t	o <u>o</u>bey	u m<u>oo</u>n	ə <u>a</u>go
x guttural h, *Hebrew* <u>H</u>anukkah			

PREPARING TO SING "THE LOBSTER QUADRILLE"

This song is based on a poem by Lewis Carroll, the well-known author of *Alice in Wonderland.* The text describes an invitation for creatures who live on the seashore to join a *quadrille,* a dance for four pairs of partners.

The melody contains several large upward and downward leaps. As you sing the downward leaps, stand on the tips of your toes to help prevent the bottom pitch from sinking into your chest voice. As you sing the upward leaps, bend your knees and pretend to touch the high pitch above your head. This helps prevent straining for the pitch from below.

ea - ger-ly the   you can real - ly have no would not join the

What   mat - ters it how   The   fur - ther off from

Lobster Quadrille

1. Introduce the song CD10:21. Have students:

• Look at the notation beginning on page 390 and identify the expression marks in the song, including articulation markings (the dot under the note stands for staccato, or short; the dot with a line stands for stressed staccato; the line alone stands for a stress; the wedge-shaped mark stands for accent) and dynamic markings (*mp* , *mf* , and crescendo).

• Read the words to the song with expression. (Note: the word *shingle* in line 4 means "beach.")

• Look at the notation and tell where the song changes from one part alone to two parts together.

• Look at the five examples of wide leaps on page 389 and locate them in the song.

• Listen to the song, following along on the notation, then discuss how the expressive markings help to convey the meaning of the text.

MULTICULTURAL PERSPECTIVES: *"Hashivenu"*

The text of "Hashivenu" is from the book of Lamentations, 5:21. This musical setting of the text is associated with the fast day, Tisha B'av, the ninth day of the month of Av in the Hebrew calendar. On that day, which occurs in summer, the entire book of Lamentations is read in remembrance of the destruction of the first and second temples in Jerusalem, as well as the Spanish expulsion of Jews in 1492 and the Holocaust of World War II.

BIOGRAPHY: *Carolyn Jennings*

Composer Carolyn Jennings (b. 1936) teaches piano at St. Olaf College in Minnesota, and is director of a choir there. For many years, she was more interested in playing the piano than composing, although she did compose one piano piece when she was nine. It was when she began directing a children's choir that she began writing and arranging music for choirs. She has since published more than 75 compositions and arrangements for school, church, and community choruses, including "Lobster Quadrille." She has also written music for orchestra, instrumental ensembles, and piano.

MUSIC LIBRARY
CHORAL ANTHOLOGY

continued from previous page

2. Chant the text. Have students:

• Echo as you chant the phrase of the text with the indicated dynamics and articulation and using the following gestures:

Stressed staccato—touch the back of one hand with the fingertips of the other hand with a quick motion, pressing with slight weight to feel the effect of separate, yet slightly stressed, sounds;

Stress—rub one hand over the back of the other hand;

Accent—hit one fist on top of the other.

The Lobster Quadrille

Music by Carolyn Jennings
Words by Lewis Carroll

As though it all made perfectly good sense

"Will you walk a lit-tle fast-er?" said a whit-ing to a snail. "There's a por-poise close be-hind us, and he's tread-ing on my tail. See how ea-ger-ly the lob-sters and the tur-tles all ad-vance! They are wait-ing on the shin-gle, Will you come and join the dance? Will you, won't you, will you, won't you, will you join the dance? Will you, won't you, will you, won't you, won't you join the dance?

C major

390

MEETING **INDIVIDUAL** NEEDS

VOCAL DEVELOPMENT: *Vocalises for Wide Leaps*

Have students practice this vocalise for upward leaps.

Continue up by half steps to F

Ah   Ah   (breathe)   Ah   Ah   (breathe)   Ah   Ah   (breathe)

Sing the *ah* vowel sound with an open, relaxed jaw and with the tongue forward.

Have students bend their knees as they "touch" the high pitch over their heads. (This promotes "going into the body" for the top pitch rather than straining for it from below.)

Practice this vocalise for downward leaps.

Continue up by half steps to E

Oh   Oh   (breathe)   Oh   Oh   (breathe)   Oh   Oh   (breathe)

Sing the *oh* vowel sound with an open relaxed throat and with the tongue forward.

Have students go up on their toes as they sing the low pitch. (This avoids their "sinking into" pitches in the lower, or speaking, range and promotes good breath support.)

You can real-ly have no no-tion how de-light-ful it will be, When they

take us up and throw us, with the lob-sters, out to sea!" ___

Part 2

But the snail re-plied,"Too far, too far," and gave a look a-skance, Said he

thanked the whit-ing kind-ly, but he would not join the dance.

Unison

Would not dance, ___ would not dance. ___ Would ___ not, could not,

would not, could not, would not join the dance, Would ___ not, could not,

would not, could not, could not join the dance. ___

3. Practice the melodic leaps in the song.
Have students:

• Look again at the five examples of wide leaps printed on page 389.

• Sing the first example, *ea-ger-ly the*, making certain to stand on tiptoe when they sing the downward leap from E to G and bending their knees and touching high E when they sing the upward leap from G to E. (See *Vocal Development* on the bottom of page 390.)

• Sing the first six lines of the song, concentrating on singing the wide leaps correctly.

• Practice the leaps in Example 2, then tell how many times they will need to sing the C to E♭ interval in lines 7–8. (three) Sing lines 7–8.

• Practice singing the octave leap in Example 3, maintaining strong breath support to sing the low G.

• Practice the leaps in Examples 4–5. Sing lines 14–17 (pages 391–392), paying special attention to singing the leaps correctly.

• Practice separately the two parts starting at the bottom of page 392. Then sing them together.

BACKGROUND: *"Lobster Quadrille"*

Jennings composed "Lobster Quadrille" with a dance rhythm, since the quadrille itself is a dance. The rhythm she chose, two weak beats followed by a strong beat, seemed to fit the word accents. She chose C major as the key because it is straightforward. But when the whiting talks about being thrown out to sea, the music also moves "out to sea" from C major to A♭ major. And when the whiting asks, *What matters it how far we go?* the melody takes a gleefully large leap. Jennings enjoys "text-painting" in her music, as in "Lobster Quadrille," but indicates that it often happens spontaneously and is not calculated.

BIOGRAPHY: *Lewis Carroll*

"Lewis Carroll" was the pseudonym used by British author Charles Lutwidge Dodgson (1832–1898), the author of *Alice's Adventures in Wonderland* and *Through the Looking Glass*. Both books were written for Alice Liddell, a young friend of his. Dodgson was also a mathematics professor who wrote books on mathematics and logic, and *Alice* contains many mathematical puzzles. He also loved inventing ridiculous words, some of which have become part of the English language.

MUSIC LIBRARY
CHORAL ANTHOLOGY

continued from previous page

4. Warm up the voice and sing the song.
Have students:

• Warm up their bodies and voices through this exercise:

  1. Imagine that they are shooting a basketball through an imaginary hoop.

  2. Bounce an imaginary ball for four beats, saying *bounce* with each beat.

  3. Aim the ball for two beats, shoot for one beat, and stand up on the fourth beat. (Repeat Steps 2–3 three times. The third time, leave hands up after shooting, bring arms down slowly, and sing on *ah*. As arms come down, students should be in a singing posture, with shoulders relaxed and down and feet slightly apart.)

• Sing the song, maintaining the spirit of a dance by singing it lightly and with all the correct rhythms. (Optional: Use "Lobster Quadrille" Performance Mix **CD10:22**.)

Reinforcement
dotted rhythms, *page 123*
articulation, dynamics, *page 199*

392

MEETING **INDIVIDUAL** NEEDS

LANGUAGE ARTS CONNECTION: *Word Play*

Lewis Carroll loved to play with words, as this excerpt from *Alice's Adventures in Wonderland* shows.

> "Take some more tea," the March Hare said to Alice, very earnestly.

> "I've had nothing yet," Alice replied in an offended tone: "so I ca'n't take *more*."

> "You mean you ca'n't take *less*," said the Hatter: "it's very easy to take *more* than nothing."

> "Nobody asked *your* opinion," said Alice.

Read the excerpt to the class (or write it on the board) and have them discuss its meaning. You might ask: How does what Alice means by *more* differ from what the March Hare and the Mad Hatter mean? Challenge interested students to think of another play on words or a pun. (The spelling of *can't* is how Carroll spelled it in the original.)

MOVEMENT: *"Lobster Quadrille"*

In *Alice's Adventures in Wonderland*, the "Lobster Quadrille" is a silly dance that pairs creatures such as a whiting fish and a lobster. The lobster gets thrown out to sea, then brought back to land. The actual quadrille, a kind of square dance, was one of the most difficult of the ballroom dances popular at the time Carroll wrote *Alice*. Carroll was probably poking fun at the difficulty of the dance.

Have students read Chapter 10 of *Alice's Adventures in Wonderland* and then use the description of the Lobster Quadrille in the chapter to create their own pantomime version of the quadrille. The description of the dance is paraphrased below.

Form two lines along the seashore, then clear all the jellyfish out of the way. Each animal has a lobster as a partner. Advance twice, change lobsters, and return to places. Then throw the lobsters as far out to sea as you can, swim after them, turn a somersault in the sea, change lobsters again, and return to land.

The Gypsy Man

1. Introduce the texture and dynamics of the song **CD10:23**. Have students:

• Read the words to the song and discover how the composer varied the music while repeating the text three times. (Part 1 remains the same through all three repetitions; Part 2 changes each time; and in the third repetition a *divisi* [divided] part is added for two measures to produce a thicker texture.)

• Notice that the dynamics change from forte to mezzo forte to piano, which has the effect of following Janisek's trip down the street with a "terraced" or decrescendo effect as he goes further away.

• Listen to the recording, paying special attention to the dynamic markings and to the change in texture.

2. Practice rhythms. Have students:

• Listen as you clap the rhythm pattern in Measure 1.

• Watch as a volunteer writes the pattern on the board, then count the number of times the pattern appears in Part 1 of the song either in clapping notation or in the melody. (13)

• Watch as a volunteer puts a rhythm pattern on the board from Part 1 that is different from the first pattern.

• Clap the melodic rhythm of Part 2.

• Form three groups and clap the melodic rhythm of all three parts.

PREPARING TO SING "THE GYPSY MAN"

The melody of "The Gypsy Man," a Slovakian folk song, contains several repeated melodic patterns. Sing the following melodic patterns and then locate them in the song.

394

MEETING **INDIVIDUAL** NEEDS

VOCAL DEVELOPMENT: *Dynamic Levels*

To begin singing "The Gypsy Man" at a loud dynamic level requires good breath support. The following exercise strengthens the abdominal muscles needed to support the breath.

Have students assume the correct posture for singing, then put one hand on the chest and the other on the abdominal muscles below the waist. Tell them to blow out the "old" air and inhale the "new" air, making certain the inhalation is felt with the bottom hand and not with the top hand (which indicates shallow breathing). Then have them echo as you say *ts* to this rhythm pattern from the song:

Teacher:

Students:

Next, draw on the board this diagram showing the shape of the dynamics in "The Gypsy Man." Blow out the "old" air, inhale the "new," and exhale on *s-s-s* for eight beats following the dynamics of the diagram. (It takes more breath support to sing piano.)

- Follow you through the *Vocal Development* on the bottom of page 394 to warm up their voices.

- Establish tonality by singing the pitch syllables for the F major scale printed on the board or a chart.

do   re   mi   fa   so   la   ti   do¹   do   ti,   la,   so,

- Sing the melodic patterns on page 394 with pitch syllables and locate them in the song.

- Sing through Part 1, applying their understanding of the rhythm, dynamics, and melodic patterns.

4. Discover the shape and phrase structure of the melody. Have students:

- Look at the pitches in Measures 2–3 of Part 1 and tell whether they move in a stepwise pattern or in leaps. (The pitches move primarily by step.)

- Look at the text and melody of Part 1 and decide how long the phrases should be. (The song is arranged in two-measure melodic phrases.)

- Sing Part 1 again, making certain to breathe deeply enough to have breath support for the phrases.

- Divide into two groups to practice the two parts. (Have some students practice the divisi part also.)

- Try singing all three parts together. (Optional: Use "The Gypsy Man" Performance Mix **CD10:24**.)

Reinforcement dynamics, *page 199*

Finally, have students hum a B above middle C, sustaining it for eight beats going from forte to piano, while consciously conserving the breath to have enough support to sustain the piano.

BACKGROUND: *"The Gypsy Man"*

"The Gypsy Man" has the rhythmic interest and vitality typical of Eastern European music. The clapping of measures with the accent on Beats 1 and 4 (rather than Beats 1 and 3) is characteristic of Eastern European folk songs. When singing the song, students should use very crisp and clear articulation.

BIOGRAPHY: *Béla Bartók*

Béla Bartók (**be** la **bar** tɔk), 1881–1945, showed musical talent at a young age. At age four, he could play over forty tunes by ear on the piano. As a young man, he became fascinated by the folk melodies of his native Hungary and traveled throughout his homeland and neighboring countries collecting and recording thousands of tunes on an Edison phonograph. His interest in folk music influenced his own compositions. One of his great achievements was the way that he integrated rhythms and scale structures of Eastern European folk music with Western musical forms.

MUSIC LIBRARY
CHORAL ANTHOLOGY

Old Joe Clark

1. Introduce the song CD10:25. Have students:

• Look at the notation and discover the form of the song. (verse-refrain)

• Listen to the song and discover that the music to the refrain is the same every time it returns; by contrast, the verses are musically similar but not exactly the same.

2. Practice rhythm patterns. Have students:

• Practice the following rhythm, then find it in Parts 1 and 2 of the first refrain. (Write all of the rhythm patterns on the board.)

• Practice this rhythm pattern, locating it in Part 1 of the second refrain.

• Practice this pattern, locating it in Part 2 of Verse 1.

• Practice this pattern, locating it in Part 2 of Verse 3.

PREPARING TO SING "OLD JOE CLARK"

"Old Joe Clark" is a familiar American fiddle tune. It was well known in the midwestern and southern parts of the United States in the late 1890s and early 1900s and is still sung today. In this arrangement, Parts 2 and 3 in Verse 3 make sounds that imitate instruments. The "pling pling-a pling" imitates a banjo, and the "pom pom" imitates the plucked strings of a string bass.

This song is in the Mixolydian mode. This means that it has the sound of a major scale, except that the seventh note of the scale is flatted.

Practice the following melodic patterns. They will help you sing "Old Joe Clark" in tune. Can you locate the patterns in the score?

396

MEETING **INDIVIDUAL** NEEDS

BACKGROUND: *"Old Joe Clark"*

"Old Joe Clark" is a fiddle dance tune. Although folk songs do not require a highly trained voice and should be sung with the emphasis on singing just for enjoyment, the spirit of this dance tune can be enhanced by crisp articulation of the consonants.

VOCAL DEVELOPMENT: *Articulation*

The following vocalise gives students practice in using the articulators, i.e., lips, teeth, and tongue. Have students maintain correct posture for singing. Tell them to breathe "down" as though they were filling up a balloon inside their stomachs and sing the vocalise on one breath.

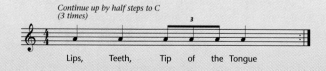

3. Warm up the voice, then practice singing melodic patterns. Have students:

• Warm up their voices. (The performance of this song is enhanced by crisp articulation of the consonants. See *Vocal Development* on the bottom of page 396 for a vocalise to develop articulation.)

• Sing through the Mixolydian mode on *loo* or using pitch syllables to establish tonality. (The Mixolydian mode sounds like a major scale, except that the seventh pitch of the scale is flatted. Alternate methods of singing the Mixolydian mode with pitch syllables are given below.)

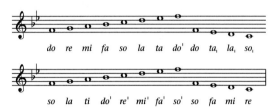

• Practice the melodic patterns on page 396 using a neutral syllable like *loo* for each note. Locate the patterns in the song. (Make certain students correctly sing the E♭ in these patterns, since it occurs throughout the song and the tendency will be to sing E♮.)

4. Prepare to sing the song. Have students:

• Sing through Measures 1–9 of Part 3 as a group, paying special attention to E♭.

• Sing Measures 1–9 of Parts 1–2 as a group, making certain to sing the interval between F and C correctly.

• Divide into two groups and sing the first nine measures of the song.

MUSIC LIBRARY
CHORAL ANTHOLOGY

continued from previous page

5. Identify dynamic markings. Have students:

- Look at the notation and identify the dynamic markings.

- Tell which part is marked the loudest and explain why. (When the melody appears in one of the three parts, that part becomes the loudest; because the melody should be the most prominent.)

Old Joe— Clark, Ain't got long to stay.

'Round and 'round Old Joe Clark, Ain't got long to stay.

'Round and 'round, I ain't got long to stay.

Part 3 Joe Clark's bed meas- ured eight by four. He took his

feath - er bed and— me, I got the floor.

Part 2 Old Joe Clark had a feath - er bed.

Part 3 Joe Clark's bed meas- ured eight by four. He got the

He got the bed and— I got the floor.

feath - er bed and— me, I got the floor.

398

MEETING **INDIVIDUAL** NEEDS

VOCAL DEVELOPMENT: *Expanding Vocal Range*

The following vocalise will help students sing the pitches in "Old Joe Clark" that are higher in their vocal range. It will help them work on open vowels as well. Remind students to shape the vowels correctly as they sing the vocalise. (See Unit 3, Lesson 2, page 98, *Vocal Development.*)

Have students listen as you demonstrate the vocalise:

Continue up by half steps to F

Ah___ Oh Ee Oh Eh *(breathe)*

Have students sing the vocalise, keeping the same vertical shape of the mouth for the *ee* vowel as they did for the *ah*

Part 1 Verse 2
I went down to Joe Clark's house, Nev-er been be-fore.

Part 2
Old Joe Clark had a feath-er bed.

Part 3
Joe Clark's bed meas-ured eight by four. He got the

He slept on the feath-er bed and I slept on the floor.

He got the bed and— I got the floor.

feath - er bed and— me, I got the floor.

Refrain
Old Joe— Clark,——— I say now

'Round and 'round Old Joe Clark, 'Round and 'round.

'Round and 'round it's 'round and 'round I say.

Music Library *Choral Anthology* **399**

6. Practice singing in three parts. Have students:

• Sing through Part 1 of the first verse as a group. Then sing through Parts 2 and 3. (It is helpful for the whole group to sing through each part to find out where the melody appears.)

• Divide into three parts to sing the first verse, making certain that the melody in Part 1, marked *mf*, can be heard.

• (Optional: **Technology**—Use Music with MIDI.)

vowel. (The tendency is to close the mouth to a horizontal position when singing the *ee* vowel.) As they get higher in their range, have them bend their knees and "touch" the high pitch above their heads. (This promotes "going into the body" for the pitch rather than straining for it from below.)

Remind students to keep the same open feeling in the throat as in the vocalise when they sing Part 1 of the refrain and verses.

continued from previous page

7. Practice "word painting." Have students:

• Speak the word *pling*, making certain to speak the *p* and *ng* correctly.

• Clap and speak each *pling* in Part 2 on page 400.

• Sing the *pling*'s, making certain to let each *ng* ring like the strings of a banjo. (See *Vocal Development* below.)

• Repeat the above three bullets for each *pom* in Part 3 on page 400. (The *m* in each *pom* should hum as the strings would on a string bass.)

• Divide into two groups and sing the "instrumental" parts together. (This is similar to *scat* singing. Scat is heard mostly in jazz singing, when the vocalist makes the voice suggest the sound of an instrument.)

MEETING **INDIVIDUAL** NEEDS

VOCAL DEVELOPMENT: *Singing* pling *and* pom

Explain to students that sometimes composers and arrangers write words and music to imitate sounds we hear around us, such as instruments, animals, and noises. In this case, *pling* should sound like a banjo, *pom* like a string bass.

Practice for singing *pling:* Have students sing the following vocalise with the lips protruding in the form of a pout as they sing the *p* and the back of the tongue touching the roof of the mouth lightly as they sing the *ng*. This allows the *ng* to continue singing as the strings of a banjo would.

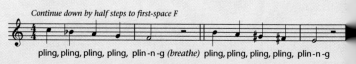

- Look at the last four measures of the song and locate the fermata for each part.

- Divide into three parts and practice the measures with the fermatas.

Practice for singing *pom:* Have students sing the following vocalise with the lips in the same position as it was for the *p* in *pling*, then closed and barely touching for the *m*. This allows the *m* to continue humming or sounding as the strings of a string bass would.

Continue up by half steps to first-space F

pom - pom pom-pom pom_m *(breathe)* pom-pom pom-pom pom_m *(breathe)*

continued from previous page

9. Put it all together to sing the song. Have students:

- Sing the whole song, with particular attention to the rhythmic vitality of this dance tune and to maintaining the dynamic balance between the parts so that the melody is always heard.

Reinforcement verse-refrain form, *page 61*

El zapatero

1. Introduce the song CD10:26 **(English)** CD10:27 **(Spanish).** Have students:

• Read the words and discover that there are three verses and that the words are the same for all three verses.

• Find which musical element changes. (The rhythm is in diminution the second time—the notes are twice as fast.)

• Clap the rhythms on page 404 and locate them in the song. (Pattern 1 is the first two measures of the first refrain; Pattern 2 is the first two measures of the second refrain.)

• Note that the eighth notes become six-teenth notes in Verse 2.

• Look at the notation and discuss the meaning of coda and *D.C. al coda, accel. poco a poco, cresc.,* and *molto accel.* (ending section; go back to the beginning, then skip to the coda when signaled; gradually get faster; get louder; get a lot faster)

• Listen to the song while quietly tapping with the beat and notice that the beat remains the same when the rhythm changes.

2. Warm up the voice and establish the tonality of the song. Have students:

• Warm up the voice. (See *Vocal Development* below.)

• Use pitch syllables to sing the G major scale. (Write the scale on the board.)

G Major Scale

do re mi fa so la ti do' do ti, la, so,

PREPARING TO SING "EL ZAPATERO"

This song was sung in Southern California. How many times are the verse and refrain sung? The words remain the same, but what musical element changes? 3; the rhythm is diminished the second time

Clap the following rhythmic patterns and discover them in the song.

G major

s, t, d r m f s l

EL ZAPATERO
The Shoemaker

Baja Californian Folk Song
Arranged by Carl S. Miller

Verse

mp   G   D7   3

Spanish: Yo le di-je a un za-pa-te-ro que me hi-
Pronunciation: yo le ði xeaun sa pa te ro ke mi
English: I went down to ask the cob-bler if he'd

D   G

cie-ra u-nos za-pa-tos, Con el pi-qui-to re-
sye rau no sa pa tos kon el pi ki to re
make me leath-er san-dals, With the toes as smooth-ly

C   Cm   D7   G   mf

don-do co-mo lo tie-nen los pa-tos. Mal-
ðon do ko mo lo tye nen los pa tos mal
round-ed as a duck bill or a can-dle. A

404

MEETING **INDIVIDUAL** NEEDS

PRONUNCIATION: *"El zapatero"*

a f<u>a</u>ther   e ch<u>a</u>otic   i b<u>ee</u>   o <u>o</u>bey
u m<u>oo</u>n   ð <u>the</u>   ɾ flipped r
x slightly guttural h; *Spanish* ba<u>j</u>o

BACKGROUND: *"El zapatero"*

"El zapatero" (The Shoemaker) can be traced back to southern California, during a time when people still bought shoes and sandals from cobblers, rather than buying factory-made products. The song is about one such shoemaker. The sedate verse is followed by a rapid, tongue-twisting re-frain. The shorter notes in the refrain serve to illustrate the fury vented upon the shoemaker by the customer.

PLAYING INSTRUMENTS: *Percussion*

Have students add a percussion accompaniment to "El zapatero." See **Resource Master CA • 1**.

VOCAL DEVELOPMENT: *Vocal Flexibility*

The following warm-ups will help students sing lightly and with the vocal flexibility needed to maintain the dance-like quality of the music.

Refrain *2nd time accel. poco a poco*

ha - ya el za - pa - te - ro | Co - mo me en - ga - ñó! | Me
a   yael   sa   pa te ro | ko mo meng ga nyo | me
curse up - on the cob - bler | Who will trick and cheat! | The

To Coda

hi - zo los za - pa - tos | Y el pi - qui - to no! | Mal -
i so los sa pa tos | yel pi ki to no | mal
san - dals that he made fit | Some - one el - se's feet! | A

ha - ya el za - pa - te - ro | Co - mo me en - ga - ñó! | Me
a yael sa pa te ro | ko mo meng ga nyo | me
curse up - on the cob - bler | Who will trick and cheat! | The

Verse *mp*

hi - zo los za - pa - tos | Y el pi - qui - to no! | Yo le
i so los sa pa tos | yel pi ki to no | yo le
san - dals that he made fit | Some - one el - se's feet! | I went

di - je a un za - pa - te - ro | Que me hi - cie - ra u - nos za - pa - tos, Con el
ði xeaun sa pa te ro | ke mei sye rau no sa pa tos kon el
down to ask the cob - bler | If he'd make me leath - er san - dals With the

pi - qui - to re - don - do | Co - mo lo tie - nen los pa - tos. | Mal -
pi ki to re ðon do | ko mo lo tye nen los pa tos | mal
toes as smooth - ly round - ed | As a duck bill or a cand - le. | A

3. Sing and identify melodic patterns. Have students:

• Sing these patterns (written on the board), then find them in the melody of the song. (the beginning measures of the verse and the refrain)

so mi do do mi mi mi fa mi re

so, do re mi fa so so la so fa mi re

4. Analyze musical elements. Have students:

• Look at the two-measure phrases of the melody in Verse 1, finding similarities and differences. (The phrase structure is A B A B; the second A has no triplet.)

• Look at the phrase structure of the melody in the first refrain, telling how it compares to the phrase structure of the verse. (It has the same A B A B structure.)

• Tell whether pitches in the refrain move primarily by step or by leap. (step)

5. Sing the melody. Have students:

Recorded Lesson CD10:28

• Listen to "Pronunciation for 'El zapatero.'"

• Practice the refrain, then sing the melody of both the verse and refrain. Tell what musical elements in the refrain are different from the verse, making it sound as if the shoemaker were being scolded. (The dynamic marking changes from *mp* to *mf* and the rhythm consists of shorter notes.)

• Sing the melody of the second verse and refrain, making certain to sing the correct rhythm and dynamics.

Breathing exercise: Have students, using the correct posture for singing, put one hand on their stomachs and laugh so that they feel the stomach muscles moving. Laugh first like Santa Claus (*ho, ho, ho*) and then like a silly person (*hee, hee*). Then have them blow out the "old" air and inhale the "new" so that they feel the expansion at the waist where they felt the laughs. (Have them inhale to the count of three and exhale to the count of five on *s-s-s-s*. Repeat, inhaling to the count of four and exhaling to the count of six.)

Developing crisp articulation: Have students, starting on the pitch A above middle C in unison, sing the following tongue-twister: *She makes a proper cup of coffee in a copper coffee pot.* (Move upward by half steps. Students should keep an open throat as they sing.)

ENRICHMENT: *Performance Suggestion*

You may have students perform the three verses of "El zapatero" in this form: Spanish, English, Spanish; or: English, Spanish, English; or perform all three verses in English.

MUSIC LIBRARY
CHORAL ANTHOLOGY

continued from previous page

6. Add the harmony part to the song.
Have students:

• Look at the harmony part in the first verse and refrain and determine if the phrase structure is the same as for the melody. (no) Offer reasons as to why the arranger might have changed it. (harmonic variety and interest)

• Sing the harmony part as a group, noticing how its melodic content differs from that of the melody. (Harmony part has more leaps and more sharps and flats.)

• When comfortable singing each part separately, divide into two groups and sing both parts of the first verse and refrain, using all the musical skills just practiced—singing correct rhythms, pitches, and dynamics, and shaping the two-measure phrases.

• Sing both parts of Verses 2–3, making certain to keep a steady beat even when the rhythm becomes faster in the second verse.

7. Sing the song. Have students:

• Practice the *la* sounds, keeping the jaw relaxed as described in the *Vocal Development* below.

• Sing the song.

Reinforcement sixteenth notes, *page 81*

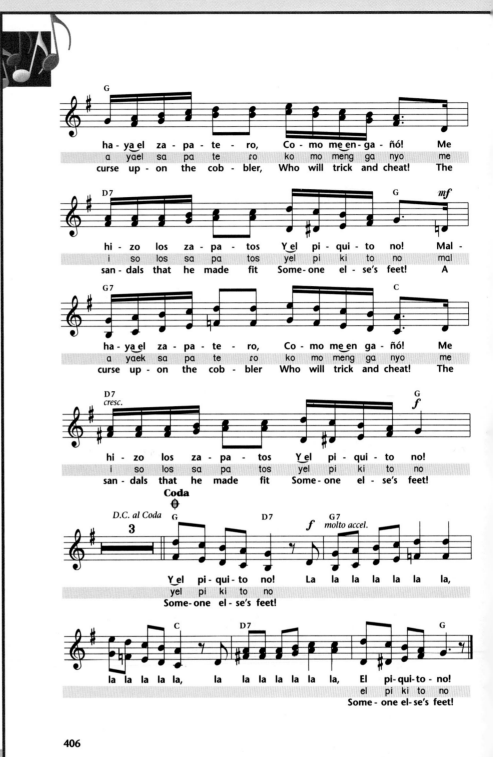

ha - ya el za - pa - te - ro, Co - mo me en - ga - ñó! Me
a yael sa pa te ɾo ko mo meng ga nyo me
curse up - on the cob - bler, Who will trick and cheat! The

hi - zo los za - pa - tos Y el pi - qui - to no! Mal -
i so los sa pa tos yel pi ki to no mal
san - dals that he made fit Some - one el - se's feet! A

ha - ya el za - pa - te - ro, Co - mo me en - ga - ñó! Me
a yaek sa pa te ɾo ko mo meng ga nyo me
curse up - on the cob - bler Who will trick and cheat! The

hi - zo los za - pa - tos Y el pi - qui - to no!
i so los sa pa tos yel pi ki to no
san - dals that he made fit Some - one el - se's feet!

D.C. al Coda **Coda**

Y el pi - qui - to no! La la la la la la la,
yel pi ki to no
Some - one el - se's feet!

la la la la la, la la la la la la la, El pi - qui-to - no!
el pi ki to no
Some - one el- se's feet!

406

MEETING **INDIVIDUAL** NEEDS

VOCAL DEVELOPMENT: *Relaxed Jaw*

A relaxed jaw is necessary for the crisp articulation of this song, especially the *la-la* section. Have students put a hand on their faces just in front of the ear, drop the jaw, and feel the open space of the hinge. Keeping the hand there, have them sing the following vocalise.

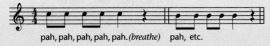

Continue down by half steps to first-space F

pah, pah, pah, pah, pah. *(breathe)* pah, etc.

Sing the vocalise again, concentrating on the open feeling in the back of the throat. Then sing the *la-la* section with the same openness, remembering to flip the *l* sounds. Only the tongue moves as each *la* is sung, not the jaw.

PRONUNCIATION: *"El zapatero"*

ɑ f<u>a</u>ther e ch<u>a</u>otic i b<u>ee</u> o <u>o</u>bey
u m<u>oo</u>n ð <u>the</u> ɾ flipped r
x slightly guttural h; *Spanish* bajo

PREPARING TO SING "KEEP YOUR LAMPS!"

"Keep Your Lamps!" is a traditional African American spiritual. The text reflects the hope for freedom. The syncopated rhythm patterns are typical of this musical style.

Practice the following rhythm patterns and locate them in the song.

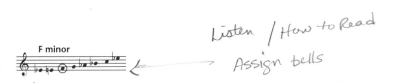

F minor

Listen / How to Read
Assign bells

Keep Your Lamps!

African American Spiritual
Arranged by Andre Thomas

Fm   mf

Keep your— lamps trimmed and burn - ing, keep your

C   Fm   D♭

lamps trimmed and burn - ing, keep your— lamps trimmed and burn-

D♭   Fm   Cm Fm 1.   2.

- ing,——— the time is draw-ing nigh.— Keep your— — Child-ren

Keep Your Lamps!

1. Introduce the song CD10:29 **and review syncopation.** Have students:

• Read the words to the song and discuss what they mean.

• Tell the form of the song. (A A B B C C A A; B—*Children don't get weary*, C—*Long, long journey*)

• Review the meaning of the word *syncopation*. (See Unit 4, Lesson 3, page 154.)

• Practice a syncopated pattern. (While you tap with the beat, have students clap this syncopated pattern written on the board.)

• Clap the syncopated rhythm patterns on page 407 and locate them in the notation.

• Listen to the song while quietly tapping with the beat and notice that many of the words are sung between, rather than on, the beat because of the syncopated rhythm.

2. Warm up the voice and establish the tonality of the song. Have students:

• Warm up their bodies and voices. (See *Vocal Development* below and on the bottom of pages 408–409.)

• Sing the F harmonic minor scale, echoing you. (F G A♭ B♭ C D♭ E♮ F'; *la₁ ti₁ do re mi fa si la*)

• Look at the song and notice how often the E♭ is changed to E♮. Practice the following phrases to prepare for the change in the song. Also, note the change in rhythm between the two phrases.

Keep your— lamps   Keep your lamps

VOCAL DEVELOPMENT: *Relaxation and Posture*

The following exercise promotes relaxation of the body and results in good singing posture. Have students imagine they are toy marionettes with all parts of their bodies attached to strings. Tell them to collapse as you push an imaginary button, and then come up slowly, one vertebrae at a time, to a standing position. Then have them raise their hands above their heads and bring their arms down slowly while sighing on *ah*. Finish the exercise by rolling their shoulders up, back, and down. (The chest should be slightly lifted and the weight evenly distributed between both feet.)

MUSIC LIBRARY
CHORAL ANTHOLOGY

continued from previous page

3. Practice the A section. Have students:

• Look at the notation and tell the texture of the A section. (unison)

• Clap the rhythm of the first eight measures of Part 1 as they sing them.

4. Practice the B section. Have students:

• Look at the text of the B section and decide what the most important word is in the re-peated phrase. (*weary*)

• Sing the first phrase with the intention of moving toward the word *weary*. (When the word *don't* is sung, there needs to be move-ment through the dotted half note. A technique to help students sustain long notes is to have them imagine they are pulling a string from a ball of yarn throughout the duration of the note.)

• Practice Parts 2 and 3 of the B section. (Point out the crescendo/decrescendo dynamic markings above the word *weary*. This con-tributes to the expression of complete weariness.)

• When comfortable singing each part sepa-rately, divide into three groups and sing the B section in three parts.

408

MEETING **INDIVIDUAL** NEEDS

VOCAL DEVELOPMENT: *Breathing Exercise*

Step 1: Have students bend over at the waist, put their hands around their waists, stick their tongues out, and pant like a dog. (Explain that they will feel the diaphragm muscle expanding and contracting. It is this muscle which controls the inhalation and exhalation of breath.)

Step 2: Still bent over, have them blow out the "old" air to the count of five and inhale the "new" air to the count of three. They should feel the waist expanding all around as they inhale.

Step 3: Have them stand up, keeping the hands around the waist. Repeat Step 2, inhaling to the count of four and ex-haling to the count of six. (Breathing in this manner assures that the breath is deep enough to support the singing tone.)

5. Practice the C section. Have students:

• Compare the C section and the A section. (The melody is the same; the words are different and the texture changes when Parts 2 and 3 are added in the last few measures.)

• Practice Parts 2 and 3 of the C section separately.

• Sing all three parts of the C section together.

6. Sing the song in three parts. Have students:

• Look at the notation at the return of the A section and discover the change from the opening A section. (The second ending changes texture with the addition of Parts 2 and 3. There is also a dramatic tempo change with the use of the ritardandos and fermatas before returning to the original tempo at the very end of the song.)

• Practice the three parts in the second ending separately. (When they are comfortable with each part, have them sing all three parts together.)

• Sing the entire song in three parts. (Optional: Use "Keep Your Lamps!" Performance Mix **CD10:30**.)

Reinforcement syncopation, *page 211*

VOCAL DEVELOPMENT: *Vocal Range*

Have students sing the following vocalise. Remind them to keep an openness at the back of the throat as they sing the *oh* and *ah* vowels.

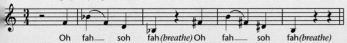

MULTICULTURAL PERSPECTIVES: *Spirituals*

See Unit 1, Lesson 7, page 30, *Multicultural Perspectives*.

PLAYING INSTRUMENTS: *Bongos*

Have students add an accompaniment to "Keep Your Lamps." See **Resource Master CA • 2**.

MUSIC LIBRARY
LISTENING ANTHOLOGY

YOU'RE INVITED

LESSONLINKS

OBJECTIVE Prepare for, attend, and discuss a mock concert, using appropriate audience behavior

Reinforcement instrument families in the orchestra, *page 29*

MATERIALS
Recordings
Recorded Lesson: Interview
  with Ellen Taaffe Zwilich   CD10:31
Celebration for Orchestra (excerpt)
  by E. Zwilich (listening)   CD10:32
Recorded Lesson: Interview
  with Nadja Salerno-
  Sonnenberg   CD10:33
Violin Concerto in E Minor
  Op. 64, Third Movement by
  F. Mendelssohn (listening)   CD11:1
American Salute by M. Gould
  (listening)   CD11:2

Other
Optional—chairs arranged as for an audience at a concert; table with lemonade or fruit juice to serve at intermission

You're Invited:

SYMPHONY ORCHESTRA CONCERT

You enter the concert hall. An usher takes your ticket and shows you to your seat. The program tells you about the compositions you're about to hear and the artists who will perform. You read about the composer of the first piece, *Celebration for Orchestra.*

Meet Ellen Taaffe Zwilich

Ellen Zwilich began composing when she was ten years old. She also played the piano, violin, and trumpet. Zwilich became a professional violinist. Later she won prizes for several of her compositions, including the first Pulitzer Prize ever awarded to a woman composer.

The audience applauds and the orchestra stands in a gesture of respect as the conductor enters. The conductor steps onto the podium, raises the baton, and the concert begins.

At the end of the composition, Ellen Zwilich is called out to share the applause.

410

MEETING **INDIVIDUAL** NEEDS

ENRICHMENT: *Preparing for a Concert*

The preparation given for an actual concert can make a great difference in how meaningful and enjoyable the students' experience is. Before the concert, besides discussing expected behavior, review the instruments of the orchestra with the students, play recordings of the compositions they are to hear, and provide background about the selections, the composers, and the performers. After a concert, have the students discuss the music and how they felt about it, then evaluate the appropriateness of their behavior. Guide them to find out about other concerts in their area. (newspaper, radio stations that specialize in concert music, posters on community bulletin boards) You might have them write a review of the concert, then read a review in the local papers and compare their reactions to those of the professional critic.

BACKGROUND: *About the Program*

Celebration for Orchestra was written by Ellen Taaffe Zwilich for the Indianapolis Symphony on the occasion of the opening of their new performing home, the beautifully renovated Circle Theater, in the center of the city. It was Zwilich's wish to show off the capabilities of both the hall and the orchestra with this composition.

Next is a movement from the Mendelssohn Violin Concerto. The soloist is Nadja Salerno-Sonnenberg.

Meet Nadja Salerno-Sonnenberg

Nadja Salerno-Sonnenberg was born in Rome, Italy. When she was eight, she moved to the United States to study music. She has been a concert violinist for many years and has won awards for her playing.

At the end of the piece, everyone applauds loudly and calls out "Brava" to Nadja Salerno-Sonnenberg in admiration of her playing. Then the conductor waits until the audience is quiet again to begin the next composition. The last piece on the program is a set of variations on "When Johnny Comes Marching Home." When the music ends, the conductor and orchestra take their final bows. You leave the hall, remembering the sounds of the music you heard.

LISTENING

Celebration for Orchestra
Ellen Taaffe Zwilich
(1984)

Violin Concerto in E Minor, Op. 64, Third Movement
Felix Mendelssohn
(1844)

American Salute
Morton Gould
(1944)

Music Library *You're Invited* **411**

TEACHING SUGGESTIONS

1. Prepare for a mock concert by a symphony orchestra. Have students:

• Listen as you explain that they will be attending a mock concert by a symphony orchestra.

• Discuss procedure and behavior at a concert. (For example: give tickets to usher and receive a program, find seats, read the program, listen to the music, applaud at the end of each piece, discuss the music as they sip refreshments at intermission.)

• Make a program and tickets for the concert. (Students can use the information in *Background* on the bottom of pages 410–411, to prepare the program. Some students can act as ushers, identified by arm bands. You might have the room slightly darkened with seat numbers on the chairs corresponding to those on the tickets. Distribute tickets just prior to the "concert." A picture of an orchestra on a stage can be placed in front to represent the performing group.)

2. Attend a mock concert by symphony orchestra. Have students:

Recorded Lesson CD10:31

• Listen to "Interview with Ellen Taaffe Zwilich" to hear Zwilich talk about her career as a composer and introduce *Celebration for Orchestra*.

• Listen to *Celebration for Orchestra* CD10:32.

Recorded Lesson CD10:33

• Listen to "Interview with Nadja Salerno-Sonnenberg" to hear her talk about being a violinist and introduce the violin concerto.

• Listen to Salerno-Sonnenberg play "Violin Concerto in E Minor, Op. 64, Third Movement" CD11:1.

• Finish the "concert" by listening to *American Salute* CD11:2.

• Share their reactions to the concert experience and to the music.

Violin Concerto in E Minor, Op. 64, Third Movement
A concerto is a composition for solo instrumentalist and orchestra. Felix Mendelssohn began this concerto when he was about 29 and completed it when he was 35. It was written for violinist Ferdinand David, who gave the composer much helpful advice. The final movement, heard here, is very spirited and shows off the skill of the solo violinist to great advantage. The work was an instantaneous hit when it premiered on March 13, 1845, in Leipzig, Germany, and is still one of the most popular violin concertos.

American Salute is a set of variations on the nineteenth-century song "When Johnny Comes Marching Home." The four different orchestral families (strings, brass, woodwinds, percussion), are each featured in the work. The tune is first heard three times in its original form, each time louder than the time before; then, in three variants. *Variant 1* is light and soft, at a higher pitch level, with some melodic "embroidery"; *Variant 2* is fast, loud, march-like, yet almost "jazzy"; *Variant 3* uses longer note-values (augmentation)—first very loud, then very soft. The Coda repeats the familiar tune in its original form, but with the tempo increasing to the exciting ending.

MUSIC LIBRARY
LISTENING ANTHOLOGY

SELECTIONS

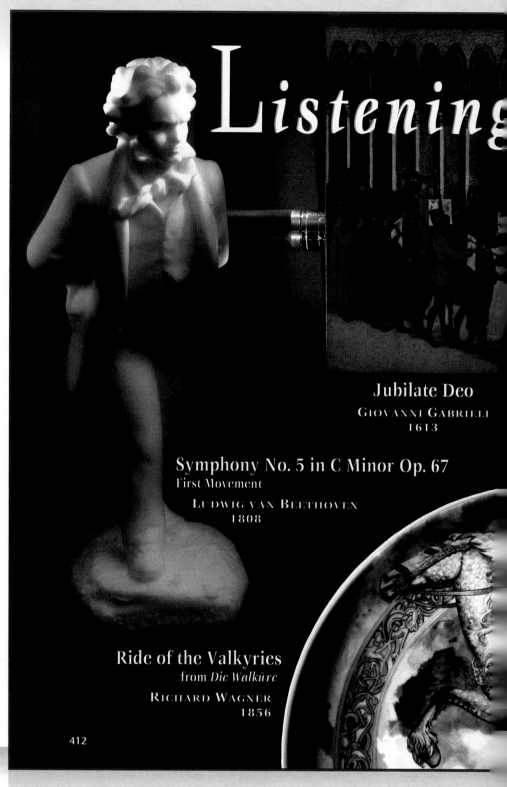

Listening

Jubilate Deo
GIOVANNI GABRIELI
1613

Symphony No. 5 in C Minor Op. 67
First Movement
LUDWIG VAN BEETHOVEN
1808

Ride of the Valkyries
from *Die Walküre*
RICHARD WAGNER
1856

412

MEETING **INDIVIDUAL** NEEDS

LISTENING ANTHOLOGY

Pages 412 and 413 are followed in this Teacher's Edition by six *Listening Anthology* lessons on pages 413A through 413L. Each lesson is based on one of the listening selections shown on these two pages of the Pupil's Edition.

For each listening selection, a Listening Map Transparency and Listening Map Resource Master are available. Students can watch as you point to the symbols on the transparency while the selection is played the first time. On a subsequent listening, students may follow their copies of the maps.

This *Listening Anthology* offers a sample of music performed at concerts and provides strategies that help students become actively involved listeners—and thus, develop appropriate concert etiquette.

You are encouraged to use these listening selections and listening maps often during the school year. One goal might be to choose a number of favorite selections and challenge students to recognize the melody, the title, and the name of the composer by the end of the school year.

All maps are available as Listening Map Transparencies. Listening selections in this program are listed in the Classified Index.

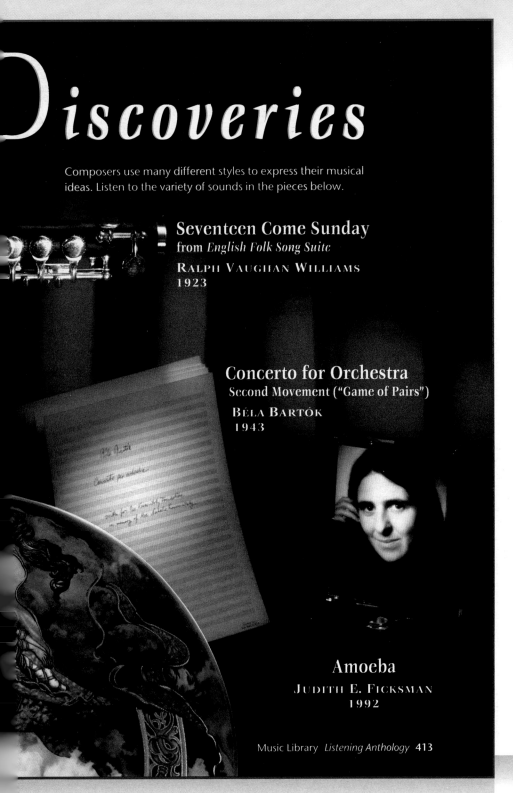

iscoveries

Composers use many different styles to express their musical ideas. Listen to the variety of sounds in the pieces below.

Seventeen Come Sunday
from *English Folk Song Suite*
RALPH VAUGHAN WILLIAMS
1923

Concerto for Orchestra
Second Movement ("Game of Pairs")
BÉLA BARTÓK
1943

Amoeba
JUDITH E. FICKSMAN
1992

Music Library *Listening Anthology* **413**

ABOUT THE PUPIL PAGES
Each listening selection is represented by a picture on the pupil page.

JUBILATE DEO
detail from Renaissance painting, *Procession of the Cross in the Piazza San Marco* by Gentile Bellini (jen **ti** le   bel **li** ni)

SYMPHONY NO. 5
statue of Beethoven

RIDE OF THE VALKYRIES
designer plate (Metropolitan Opera, New York), showing characters from *Die Walküre*—Brünnhilde carrying Sieglinde

SEVENTEEN COME SUNDAY
piccolo

CONCERTO FOR ORCHESTRA
reproduction of a page from composer's autograph (handwritten) score

AMOEBA
digital audiotape and package showing a photograph of the composer

OTHER LISTENING MAPS AVAILABLE
Pupil Edition:
- **Muss i denn,** German March, page 9
- **Ecce gratum** (excerpt) from *Carmina Burana* by *C. Orff,* page 45
- **Alla turca** from **Piano Sonata in A Major, K. 331** *by W. A. Mozart,* page 61
- **Anitra's Dance** from **Peer Gynt Suite** No. 1 *by E. Grieg,* page 79
- **Sonata in G Minor ("The Cat's Fugue")** *by D. Scarlatti,* page 119

- **Fantasia on Greensleeves** *by R. Vaughan Williams,* pages 160–161

Resource Masters:
- **Capriccio espagnol (excerpt)** *by N. Rimsky-Korsakov,* RM 1 • 9
- **Sonata in G Minor ("The Cat's Fugue")** (detailed) by *D. Scarlatti* RM 3 • 4
- **Battle Hymn of the Republic** played by the Monty Alexander Trio RM C • 1

MUSIC LIBRARY
LISTENING ANTHOLOGY

JUBILATE DEO
by Giovanni Gabrieli

LESSONLINKS

OBJECTIVE Recognize the quality of the countertenor (male alto) voice

Reinforcement voice categories, *page 195*

MATERIALS
Recording Jubilate Deo by
G. Gabrieli (listening)   CD11:3

Resources
Listening Map Transparency T • 11
Resource Master LA • 1 (listening map)

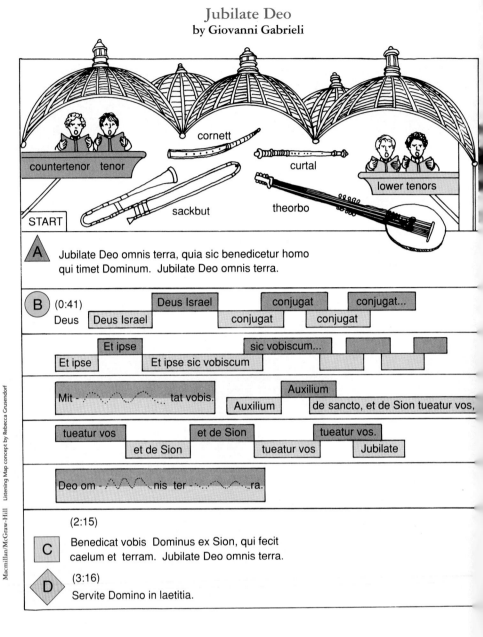

Jubilate Deo
by Giovanni Gabrieli

countertenor   tenor

cornett

curtal

lower tenors

sackbut

theorbo

START

A Jubilate Deo omnis terra, quia sic benedicetur homo qui timet Dominum. Jubilate Deo omnis terra.

B (0:41)
Deus | Deus Israel | Deus Israel | conjugat | conjugat...
conjugat | conjugat

Et ipse | Et ipse | Et ipse sic vobiscum | sic vobiscum...

Mit - .... tat vobis. | Auxilium | Auxilium | de sancto, et de Sion tueatur vos,

tueatur vos | et de Sion | et de Sion | tueatur vos | tueatur vos. | Jubilate

Deo om - .... nis ter - .... ra.

(2:15)
C Benedicat vobis Dominus ex Sion, qui fecit caelum et terram. Jubilate Deo omnis terra.

D (3:16)
Servite Domino in laetitia.

Macmillan/McGraw-Hill   Listening Map concept by Rebecca Grusendorf

MEETING **INDIVIDUAL** NEEDS

EXTRA HELP: *Following the Listening Map*

Have students look at the building design, which is an outline of the roof of the Venetian Cathedral of San Marco (san mar ko), where the selection was performed in the early 1600s. Then point to the singers and instruments heard in the selection. Also point out the A, B, C, and D, which indicate the four parts of the piece.

TRANSLATION: *Latin Text into English*

A section: Let the whole earth rejoice in God, for thus is blessed the man who fears the Lord. Let the whole earth rejoice in God.
B section: May the God of Israel unite you and may he himself be with you. May he send you help from his holiness, and may he protect you (who are) from Zion. Let the whole earth rejoice in God.
C section: May the Lord bless you from Zion, he who made heaven and earth. Let the whole earth rejoice in God.
D section: Serve the Lord with gladness.

TEACHING SUGGESTIONS

Introduce "Jubilate Deo" CD11:3. **Recognize the quality of the countertenor voice.** Have students:

• Name places where they have heard choirs. (concerts, churches, special features on television)

• Learn about the composition. (Explain that "Jubilate Deo" is a *motet*, or sacred piece not designed for a specific service. Its words are drawn from various psalms.)

• Preview the map, locating the three types of male singers' voices (countertenor, tenor, and lower tenors), the pictures of the instruments (cornett, theorbo, curtal, sackbut), and the words to the song (in Latin). (Use **Listening Map Transparency T • 11** and **Resource Master LA • 1**.)

• Listen as you explain that a countertenor is a male singer who can sing the range of a female alto using a controlled *falsetto*, or a "false voice."

• Listen to "Jubilate Deo" (yu bi **la** tɛ **dɛɔ**), watching you follow the map on the transparency. (Note that the antiphonal, or echo, effect in the B section is shown graphically with higher and lower boxes containing Latin text. Optional: Have students point to the singers' voices they hear on **Resource Master LA • 1**.)

OBJECTIVE 1 Informal Assessment
• Have students raise their hands when they hear the countertenor voice.

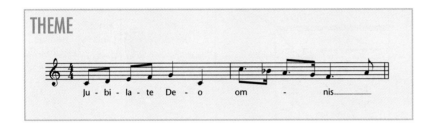

THEME

Ju - bi - la - te De - o om - nis_____

BIOGRAPHY: *Giovanni Gabrieli*

Giovanni Gabrieli (jo **van** ni ga **brysl** i), c. 1556–1612, grew up in the exciting musical climate of Venice, Italy. In 1585 Gabrieli became organist of the famous Cathedral of San Marco. Because there are two choir areas on opposite sides of the cathedral, each with an organ, Gabrieli was able to experiment with compositions for *cori spezzati*, (**kɔ** ɾi spet **tsa** ti) or "separated choirs." These could consist of voices only, instruments only, or a combination of both. Music for *cori spezzati* often sounds as if the separated choirs are echoing each other across a wide space.

BACKGROUND: *Renaissance Instruments*

The instruments used in "Jubilate Deo" were popular during the Renaissance, the musical period lasting from about 1450 to 1600. The cornett (kɔr **nɛt**) is a wooden or ivory horn with six holes and a cup-shaped mouthpiece. The theorbo (thi **ɔr** bo) is a large lute, a guitar-like instrument. The sackbut (**sæk** bʌt) is a brass instrument that developed into the modern trombone. The curtal (**kɜr** tǝl) is an early ancestor of the modern bassoon.

MUSIC LIBRARY
LISTENING ANTHOLOGY

SYMPHONY NO. 5 IN C MINOR OP. 67, FIRST MOVEMENT
by Ludwig van Beethoven

LESSONLINKS

OBJECTIVE Recognize the main motive from Beethoven's Symphony No. 5 in C Minor Op. 67, First Movement

Reinforcement
motive, *page 153*
orchestral instruments, *page 7*

MATERIALS
Recording Symphony No. 5 in C Minor Op. 67, First Movement, by L. van Beethoven (listening) CD11:4

Resources
Listening Map Transparency T • 12
Resource Master LA • 2 (listening map)
Playing the Guitar G • 17 (Beethoven)

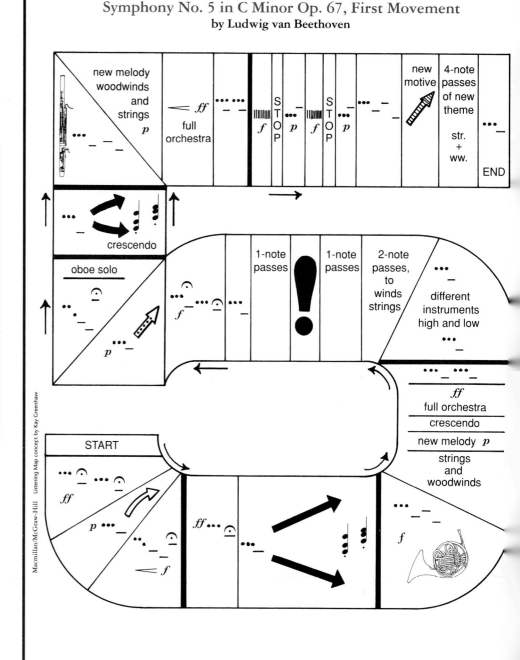

Symphony No. 5 in C Minor Op. 67, First Movement
by Ludwig van Beethoven

Macmillan/McGraw-Hill   Listening Map concept by Kay Greenhaw

MEETING **INDIVIDUAL** NEEDS

EXTRA HELP: *Following the Listening Map*

Point out the START label at the lower left part of the page and have students trace around the numeral 5, following the arrows. As each section is traced, mention main musical events such as the main motive, or the motivic passes from one instrument family to another. Have students identify each instrument pictured. (French horn, bassoon)

BIOGRAPHY: *Ludwig van Beethoven*

Ludwig van Beethoven (**lud** viç ฀an **be** to vən), 1770–1827, was born in Bonn, Germany, where both his

grandfather and father were musicians. In hopes of making him another prodigy like Mozart, Beethoven's father forced him into long hours of keyboard practice.

Beethoven's early years were spent in various court positions. In 1792 he went to Vienna to study, and he remained there the rest of his life. His first major public appearance was in 1795 in Vienna as a composer and pianist. When he began to lose his hearing, he realized that he could no longer be a public performer, so he devoted himself largely to composition. By 1819 he was completely deaf; it was during this last period of his life that he produced some of his greatest compositions.

TEACHING SUGGESTIONS

1. Introduce Symphony No. 5 CD11:4**. Describe what a motive is.** Have students:

• Listen as you sing or play the main motive, labeled "theme," below. Tell whether they have heard the music before and, if possible, identify the composer or title.

• Give their explanations of what the main motive of a music piece is. (It is the most prominent and recognizable short melodic or rhythmic fragment, usually repeated through the piece.)

2. Recognize the motive. Have students:

• Preview the map, looking at the numbering on the listening map, looking at all the different sections and following the arrows from the bottom left of the numeral 5 to the top right. (Use **Listening Map Transparency T • 12** or **Resource Master LA • 2**.)

• Find examples of the three short dots and line, which represent the main motive.

• Look at the map and name different instruments they will hear in the piece. (French horns, strings, woodwinds, full orchestra, oboe, bassoon)

• Listen to the music, watching you follow the map on the transparency.

OBJECTIVE 1 Informal Assessment
• Raise their fingers or give a "V" for victory signal with two fingers each time they hear the main motive.

THEME

BACKGROUND: *Symphony No. 5, First Movement*

The first movement of the fifth symphony was sometimes used as a victory song by Americans and their allies during both world wars. The main motive (• • • ——) translates in Morse Code to a "V" for victory. The work has become one of the most widely performed orchestral works in the world.

PLAYING INSTRUMENTS: *Keyboard*

Using the piano or electronic keyboards, teach students to play the main motive of the first movement of the symphony. You may want to place colored press-on dots on the keys to help students locate the right keys. For example, place red dots on G and E♭, and green dots on F and D. Tell the students to use the red dots for the first group of notes and the green dots for the second group.

MUSIC LIBRARY

LISTENING ANTHOLOGY

RIDE OF THE VALKYRIES
from *DIE WALKÜRE*
by Richard Wagner

LESSON LINKS

OBJECTIVE Identify repeating and contrasting sections in music

Reinforcement
repeating/contrasting sections, brass family, *page 7*

MATERIALS
Recording Ride of the Valkyries from *Die Walküre* by R. Wagner (listening) CD11:5

Resources
Listening Map Transparency T • 13
Resource Master LA • 3 (listening map)

Ride of the Valkyries from *Die Walküre*
by Richard Wagner

① Introduction:

fluttering
woodwinds
and strings

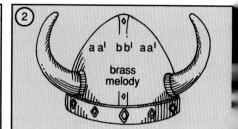

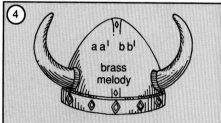

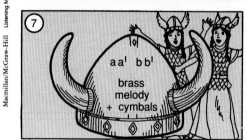

Macmillan/McGraw-Hill   Listening Map concept by Debbie Tannert

---

MEETING **INDIVIDUAL** NEEDS

EXTRA HELP: *Following the Listening Map*

Point out the numbers to help students follow the map. Have them listen for the woodwinds and strings in the introduction. Help students identify the family of instruments that plays the repeated theme shown by the helmets. (brass family) Have students listen carefully to hear the brass instruments. Also point out the women who are singing (and sometimes riding flying horses), explaining that their lyrics are telling part of the story of the opera. Note that Section 7 is drawn with bolder lines to show that the music is in a major key and includes loud, low brass.

BACKGROUND: *Die Walküre* THEATER

Die Walküre is the second of Wagner's cycle of four operas which was meant to be performed on four successive evenings. This saga, *The Ring of the Nibelungs* (**ni** bə **lungz**), is based on Germanic folklore. It was composed over a period of almost thirty years from 1848 to 1874. The god Wotan (**vo** tɑn) has ordered his daughters, known as the Valkyries (**val** kü riz), to bring dead heroes to him. Act III of the opera begins with "Ride of the Valkyries," with the maidens riding through the air, carrying the heroes to their mountaintop castle, Valhalla (val **hɑ** lɑ).

TEACHING SUGGESTIONS

1. Preview the opera. Have students:

• Tell what they know about operas. (They are sung plays.)

• Listen as you tell them that the opera *Die Walküre* (di͞ vɑl **kū** ɾə) is the story of a god who orders his nine daughters to bring heroes who died in battle to him so he can transform them into immortals.

• List words to predict how such a story might sound in music, writing the words on the board. (Answers will vary, but may include powerful, scary, bigger than life, bizarre)

2. Introduce "Ride of the Valkyries" **CD11:5.** Identify repeating/contrasting sections of the music. Have students:

• Preview the map, identifying sections that will be similar, naming the visual clue. (sections 2, 4, 6, and 7—helmet; sections 3, 5, and 8—storm clouds; sections 3, 5, 6, 7, and 8—women in armor singing) (Use **Listening Map Transparency T • 13** or **Resource Master LA • 3**.)

• Point to the letters on the helmets, naming parts that will be similar. (a and a'; b and b')

• Listen as you read the following summary of the German text:

Section 3: "Hey! Over here!" "Heiaha!"
Section 5: "Let the horses graze!" "Who's that with you?" "A dead warrior." "There's another." "The horses are anxious!" "The warriors' fighting has rubbed off on them." (*Laughter.*) "Quiet!" "Hey! What took you so long to get here?" **Section 6:** "Work." "Hoyotoho!" "Heiaha!" (*More Valkyries arrive with dead warriors across their saddles, in a flash of lightning.*) **Section 7:** "Greetings, riders!" "Hoyotoho!" "Heiaha!" **Section 8:** "Hoyotoho!" "Heiaha!"

• Listen to the music, watching as you follow the map.

• Review the descriptive word list on the board, revising it to reflect the music heard. (loud, powerful, galloping rhythms)

OBJECTIVE 1 Informal Assessment
• Signal as they listen again to the music, raising their right hand when they hear a or a' and their left hand when they hear b or b' and patting the beat on their knees during contrasting sections 3, 5, and 8.

THEME

BIOGRAPHY: *Richard Wagner*

Richard Wagner (ɾɪç ɑɾt **vɑg** nəɾ), 1813–1883, was a German operatic composer. He was largely a self-taught musician who sought to create a new form of opera. Until his time, European opera was generally a stop-and-go style of musical theater. A play was told either in sung or spoken words with interspersed musical numbers for solo singers or chorus. Wagner sought a continuous, symphonic sound, with singers weaving into the orchestral fabric. He made extensive use of the *leitmotif* (**lɑɪt** mo͞ tif), in which a musical motive or theme portrays people, objects, or an abstract idea such as love, sorrow, or strength.

ENRICHMENT: *Creating Sound Effects for a Myth*

Wagner's *Die Walküre* is based on a German myth. Have students read myths from another culture and create sound effects or improvise music to accompany the story of the myth as it is read.

SEVENTEEN COME SUNDAY from *ENGLISH FOLK SONG SUITE*
by Ralph Vaughan Williams

LESSONLINKS

OBJECTIVES
OBJECTIVE 1 Recognize repetition and contrast of larger musical sections (A B C B A)
OBJECTIVE 2 Demonstrate knowledge of repeat signs, *D.S.* and *Da Capo* indications, use of first and second endings, and coda
OBJECTIVE 3 Read rhythmic notation to perform an accompaniment on classroom instruments

Reinforcement
repetition/contrast, *page 7*
concert band instruments, *page 7*
D.S., coda, *page 7*

MATERIALS
Recording Seventeen Come Sunday from *English Folk Song Suite* by R. Vaughan Williams (listening)   **CD11:6**

Instruments
rhythm sticks, triangles, finger cymbals, hand drums, crash cymbals

Resources
Listening Map Transparency T • 14
Resource Master LA • 4 (listening map)

Listening Map Transparency T•14 Grade
Use with pages 413G–H.

Seventeen Come Sunday from *English Folk Song Suite*
by Ralph Vaughan Williams

Macmillan/McGraw-Hill   Listening Map concept by Debbie Tannert

Introduction   Play

last time to coda

A $\frac{2}{4}$

B   Bridge   legato

last time Da Capo   tr

1.   2.

Countermelody   **C**

D.S. after repeat

Coda   tr   all

MEETING **INDIVIDUAL** NEEDS

EXTRA HELP: *Following the Listening Map*

Point out the $\frac{2}{4}$ meter signature, reminding students that each measure has two beats. Have students find the repeat signs, the first and second endings, and tell what *Dal Segno* means (go back to the sign 𝄋) and what *Da Capo* means (go back to the start). Point out that no classroom instruments are to be played during the four-measure introduction in the A section nor during the two-measure introduction to the B section. Tell students that the A section rhythm on the map is a simplified version of the melody; the B section rhythm is that of the actual triangle part; the C section rhythm is that of the actual drum part. (Note: A trill is played on the triangle by rolling the beater inside the triangle.)

BIOGRAPHY: *Ralph Vaughan Williams*

English composer Ralph Vaughan Williams (1872–1958) began to write music when he was six, but he did not begin to study it seriously until he had completed his general education and attended the Royal College of Music. In 1903 he began collecting and studying English folk songs. Gradually he incorporated English folk songs into his own music.

TEACHING SUGGESTIONS

1. Introduce "Seventeen Come Sunday" **CD11:6. Recognize repetition and contrast of larger musical sections. Recognize repeat signs, first and second endings, and *Da Capo* and *D.S.* indications.** Have students:

• Recall some of their favorite folk tunes, explaining that the English composer Ralph Vaughan Williams used English folk tunes in this piece.

• Preview the map, having students find the order of sections (A B C B A), repeat signs, first and second endings (in B section), and *Da Capo* and *D.S.* indications. (Use **Listening Map Transparency T • 14** or **Resource Master LA • 4**.)

• Review the meaning of legato. (smooth, connected)

• Find where the countermelody will be heard (in C section), understanding that a countermelody is a contrasting melody heard at the same time as the main melody.

• Listen to the music, watching you follow the map on the transparency.

OBJECTIVE 1 Informal Assessment

• Pantomime playing a flute during the A sections, a clarinet during the B sections, and a tuba during the C section as they listen to the music.

OBJECTIVE 2 Informal Assessment

• Raise one finger on first endings and two fingers on second endings, and say "B" when they reach the *D.S.* indication, "A" when they reach the *Da Capo* indication, and "Coda" when they reach that indication.

2. Perform rhythmic patterns to accompany the music. Have students:

• Echo-clap these rhythm patterns: ♩ 𝄾, and ♫ ♩, explaining they will hear them in the selection.

• Understand that this listening map is a play-along map.

• Preview the map for the symbols for rhythm sticks, triangles, finger cymbals, crash cymbals, and hand drums. (Distribute these instruments to the class.)

• Play along with the piece using the notation on **Transparency T • 14** or **Resource Master LA • 4**.

OBJECTIVE 3 Informal Assessment

• Trade instruments and perform the accompaniment, listening and reading the map.

THEME

Many of his works are concerned with the idea of people as "pilgrims" enduring difficulties through the journey of life.

ENRICHMENT: *⅔ Rhythm Patterns*

Clap different ⅔ rhythm patterns such as the following:

Seventeen Come Sunday

Have students write the rhythm patterns on a piece of paper or on the board.

ENRICHMENT: *A Rhythm Routine*

Have students form pairs and do a ball routine to demonstrate form, beat, and legato in this piece:

A section: Bounce-catch a ball with a partner.

B section: Roll the ball back and forth between the two partners every four beats.

C section: Do chest passes on the strong beats.

MUSIC LIBRARY
LISTENING ANTHOLOGY

CONCERTO FOR ORCHESTRA, SECOND MOVEMENT ("GAME OF PAIRS")
by Béla Bartók

LESSONLINKS

OBJECTIVE Aurally identify pairs of instruments

Reinforcement
orchestral instrument families, *page 29*
texture, *page 29*

MATERIALS
Recording Concerto for Orchestra, Second Movement ("Game of Pairs") by B. Bartók (listening)　　　CD11:7

Resources
Listening Map Transparency T • 15
Resource Master LA • 5 (listening Map)
Musical Instruments Masters—string family, percussion family, woodwind family, brass family

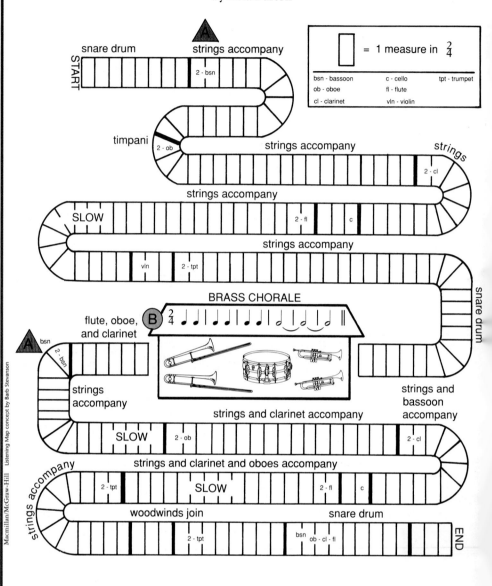

Concerto for Orchestra, Second Movement ("Game of Pairs")
by Béla Bartók

Macmillan/McGraw-Hill　Listening Map concept by Barb Stevanson

MEETING **INDIVIDUAL** NEEDS

EXTRA HELP: *Following the Listening Map*

Follow the path. Have students notice that each space on the path represents one measure in ²⁄₄ meter (each measure gets two beats). Have students point to the A and A'. As you hear the accompanying instrument parts, point to the appropriate names of instruments alongside the path. During the B section, point to the words "brass chorale" and point to the rhythm of the chorale theme each time it is heard.

BIOGRAPHY: *Béla Bartók*

Béla Bartók (**be** la **bar** tɔk), 1881–1945, showed musical talent at a very young age. When he was just four years old he could play over forty tunes by ear on the piano. As a young man, he traveled throughout his native Hungary and neighboring countries collecting and recording thousands of folk songs on an Edison phonograph. In 1940, Bartók moved to the U.S. He lived in New York, spending his time composing, as well as notating the folk music he had recorded. The Concerto for Orchestra was written for and first performed by the Boston Symphony Orchestra in 1944.

TEACHING SUGGESTIONS

1. Introduce Concerto for Orchestra CD11:7. Aurally identify pairs of instruments. Have students:

• Name the four families in the orchestra, then list them on the board. (string, woodwind, percussion, brass)

• Preview the map, noting the A B A form, and have individual students name the instruments from their abbreviations, writing them under the correct family name on the board. (in order of first appearance on the listening map: snare drum, percussion; bassoons, oboes, clarinets, woodwinds; cello, strings; flutes, woodwinds; violin, strings; trumpets, brass) (Use **Listening Map Transparency T • 15** or **Resource Master LA • 5**.)

• Point to the section on the map where they will hear brass instruments in the brass chorale.

• Listen to the music, watching as you follow the map on the transparency.

• Make instrument cards, index cards with names or pictures of the instruments used in the selection. (Optional: Use **Musical Instruments Masters**.)

OBJECTIVE 1 Informal Assessment
• Signal by holding up their card when they hear their instrument.

THEME

ENRICHMENT: *Instrument Matching Game*

Turn the instrument cards used for the Informal Assessment face down and have the students play a matching game in which they must find pairs of instruments by turning over two cards at a time.

MUSIC LIBRARY
LISTENING ANTHOLOGY

AMOEBA
by Judith E. Ficksman

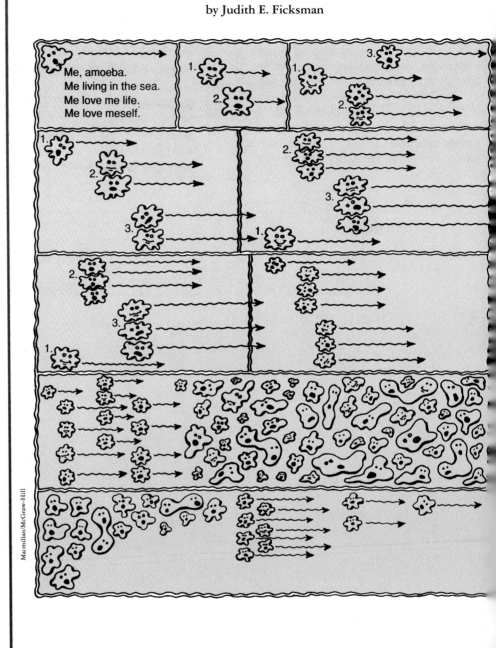

Amoeba
by Judith E. Ficksman

Me, amoeba.
Me living in the sea.
Me love me life.
Me love meself.

Macmillan/McGraw-Hill

LESSONLINKS

OBJECTIVES
OBJECTIVE 1 Show awareness of texture changes from thin to thick as vocal sounds are added and subtracted by the computer

OBJECTIVE 2 Move to show how music can express an idea

Reinforcement music technology in the 1990s, *page 279*

MATERIALS
Recording Amoeba by J. E. Ficksman (listening)　　CD11:8

Resources
Listening Map Transparency T • 16
Resource Master LA • 6 (listening map)

MEETING **INDIVIDUAL** NEEDS

EXTRA HELP: *Following the Listening Map*

Have students notice that each shape represents an amoeba, showing about how many are singing and their relative pitch (high, medium, and low). Point out the last line where amoebas along the top represent a decrease in low and middle voices. The piece ends with one high-pitched amoeba singing.

BACKGROUND: *"Amoeba"*

To compose "Amoeba," Ficksman asked herself: "What would a one-celled organism think if it could? What would it tell us?" She started with the idea that a computer might

be able to model an amoeba's reproductive cycle. To accomplish this, Ficksman chose pitches from the overtone series and used a computer program called "Gravy" to reproduce the melody at different pitch levels. She kept the sounds close together in an octave spread. The piece begins and ends with one amoeba. In its seventh generation, the piece has 64 amoebas—"their voices pulsing like a great wave."

BIOGRAPHY: *Judith E. Ficksman*

Judith E. Ficksman (b. 1958) dreamt as a child of being a writer. In third grade, she began to study the guitar and

TEACHING SUGGESTIONS

1. Learn how human voices and computers can be used to make music. Have students:

• Tell what an amoeba is. (a protist—a one-celled organism)

• Tell what they know about computers.

• Listen as you explain that this piece of music was created by taking one voice singing a short melody and "multiplying" it into many voices using a computer.

2. Introduce "Amoeba" CD11:8. **Move to show how music can express an idea.** Have students:

• Preview the map, having students read the words aloud and pointing out the varying numbers of amoebas on the map.

(Use **Listening Map Transparency T · 16** or **Resource Master LA · 6**.)

• Listen to the music, watching you follow the map on the transparency.

• Tell what idea the composer may have had in mind when she wrote this piece. (to show how amoebas grow and possibly to imagine how they might think)

OBJECTIVE 1 Informal Assessment

• Use finger and hand movements to show increasing and decreasing numbers of amoebas added or taken away by the computer.

OBJECTIVE 2 Informal Assessment

• Use movement to show the story told by the music. (Have students form small groups and use freestyle, creative movement to fit the music. Have groups perform their movements in class to the music.)

THEME

Me, a-moe-ba, me liv-ing in the sea. Me love me life. Me love me-self.

found she loved music. "Amoeba" was composed at Columbia University's computer music studio.

TECHNOLOGY IN MUSIC: *Computers*

The first special-purpose electronic computer was made in 1939 by John V. Atanasoff, an American mathematician and physicist. Early computers were used mainly for mathematical calculations. Modern computers can be programmed to generate graphics and musical sounds. A computer works by taking data and encoding it in the 0's and 1's of the binary numeration system. When the data is translated or decoded, it can become words, numbers, pictures, or music.

SCIENCE CONNECTION: *Life Cycle of an Amoeba*

Have students research amoebas, including how they divide (fission), how they eat (use pseudopods—or "false feet"—to surround and trap food and water), what they eat (mostly other protists), and so on. Students can draw pictures of the division process, labeling the parts of an amoeba.

MATH CONNECTION: *Geometric Progression*

Have students plot the number of amoebas in seven generations (1, 2, 4, 8, 16, 32, 64—not shown on the listening map), then calculate several more generations.

MUSIC LIBRARY

MUSICAL

RELATED ARTS MOVEMENT | THEATER | VISUAL ARTS

LESSONLINKS

OBJECTIVE To produce and perform a musical play that increases awareness of ecological problems and some possible solutions

MATERIALS
Recordings

Where Does It Come From?	CD11:9
There's Just So Much to Go Around	CD11:10
Please, Don't Cut Down the Trees	CD11:11
Keep the Circle Going 'Round	CD11:12
I Can See a Rainbow	CD11:13
Here Come the Earth Kids	CD11:14
Performance Mixes for each selection	CD11:15–20

Resources Resource Master S • 1 (script)

Instruments
chime tree, glockenspiels, metallophones, maracas, cabasa, ocean drum, hand drums, or found objects to simulate these instruments

A group of kids hiking through the woods is dismayed to find a terrible change in the forest they love. The Natural Resources look dirty and full of junk.

Among the kids are the Practical Kid, the Idealistic Kid, the Skeptical Kid, the Apathetic Kid, and the Apathetic Kid's Little Sister. The Apathetic Kid says, "We didn't make this mess. There's nothing we can do." The Forest explains how their actions affect everything around them.

Music by Neil Fishman • Book and lyrics by Harvey Edelman • Story conceived by Harvey and Julie Edelman

WHERE DOES IT COME FROM

Music by Neil Fishman
Words by Harvey Edelman

1.-3. Where does it come from?____ Where does it go? { 1. It's
2. It's

some-thing to con-sid-er,____ some-thing you should know. The
real-ly quite im-por-tant.____ Learn it as you grow. The
3. We should be a-ware that____ we reap____ what we sow. The

414

PRODUCTION SUGGESTIONS

AUDITIONS: "Trying out" for a play is a chance for students to become familiar with the characters, plot, music and dances and to try out their performing skills. Read an audition script for students just before the audition so they can hear pronunciations and the flow of dialogue. (For auditions, use pages in **Resource Master S • 1** on which several characters speak, for example, pages 2 and 8.) Allow students to try out for more than one part and to indicate afterward which part or parts they most want.

In addition to auditioning actor-singers, you will need to audition for the two vocal soloists, the dancers (probably half the cast), and the instrumentalists who will provide sound effects for the Natural Resources. Teach dance and vocal audition-numbers to the entire class before the auditions begin. Encourage students to listen to relevant recordings to prepare themselves. Instrumental auditions should include producing tone-color improvisations for at least two of the Natural Resources.

CREW: Students can volunteer as stagehands or as technicians in charge of special effects, lighting, sets, costumes, and props.

bag that held your lunch, the food you did‑n't munch, the
gas in the fa‑mi‑ly car, the strings on your gui‑tar, your
for‑ests full of trees, wa‑ter in the seas,

plates and cups you left on your tray. A piece of o‑range
bi‑cy‑cle and your fav'‑rite games. The cloth that makes your
an‑i‑mals in ev'ry shape and size. The air that's fresh and

rind, an ap‑ple left be‑hind, the milk you drink,— the
clothes, C‑Ds and vi‑de‑os. Your dad's snow‑plow,— your
clean, ev'‑ry‑thing that's green. Read a book— or

kit‑chen— sink,— things you use each day.
pup‑py's— chow,— more than we could
take a— look,— right be‑fore your

name. Things don't just ap‑pear— then va‑nish in the air.—

Ev'‑ry‑thing comes from some‑thing and al‑ways goes some‑where.—

eyes. Where does it come from?— Where does it go?

TEACHING SUGGESTIONS

1. Introduce the play "Earth Kids." Have students:

• Discuss what they know about Earth's eco‑logical problems. List some of those problems on the board.

• Read page 414 and say what each character might think about ecological problems.

2. Introduce "Where Does It Come From?" CD11:9. Have students:

• Listen to "Where Does It Come From?", fol‑lowing the notation. Discuss how the song's ideas relate to the ecological problems listed.

• Notice differences in the endings of each of the three verses. (different lengths and melodies) Then sing the song.

3. Plan to produce "Earth Kids" as a stage play. Have students:

• Discuss the elements of producing a play. (See the bottom of pages 414–423 and **Resource Master S • 1**.)

• Read the synopsis of the play in their books on pages 414–422, then receive copies of the script (**Resource Master S • 1**).

• Sign up for auditions and crew assignments.

4. Practice Scene I. Have students:

• Prepare to practice their parts in this scene, while the others act as the audience.

• Listen to the overture. (Use "Here Come the Earth Kids," performance mix CD11:20 or your own instrumental version.) As the overture concludes, the five Kids at the back of the au‑ditorium come forward down the center aisle, laughing and improvising dialogue. Some show fatigue through dialogue and gestures, but are revived by stopping in the clearing; their energy levels pick up.

• Speak their assigned parts. (The River Voices can be miked from backstage so that they sound differently from the Kids.)

CASTING: In assigning parts after the auditions, consider acting, dancing and musical skills, physical attributes, and the wishes of each student. Help students feel good about the parts they get by consistently speaking of each role in the play as essential. Avoid using terms such as *leading role* or *small part*. All characters should be cast with proper names, even ones who have only a few lines. The gender of any role can be changed depending on who gets the part; for example, Phyllis could be Phil, or Al could be Alice.

The roles of Jamie and Ian call for expressive acting and solo singing. If the best actor for either role does not have an adequate singing voice, change a few lyrics so the singing can be done by another student or by the full cast. Jamie probably should be smaller than Al since she is his younger sister. Movement quality is crucial in casting the Natural Resources. A Forest character moves differently than a River or Animal character. After part assignments, Natural Resources can make their characters more specific. For example, a Fossil Fuel might be oil. An Animal might be an endangered species such as the spotted owl. New Kids or Natural Resources may be added, or their lines combined, as needed. Nonspeaking roles could include New Kids, additional Natural Resources, dancers for the round, and Kids from the audience for the final song.

continued from previous page

5. Introduce "There's Just So Much to Go Around" CD11:10. Have students:

• Listen to the song, following the notation.

• Discuss the meaning of the lyrics.

• Find the song in the script and which character disagrees with the message. (Scene II; Al)

• Notice which lines of lyrics begin with an eighth rest and which with a quarter rest. (varies from verse to verse)

• Practice speaking the rhythm of Phrase 1, which begins with an eighth rest, and Phrase 2, which begins with a quarter rest.

• Sing the song from the notation.

6. Stage two songs. Have students:

• Learn stage directions: *downstage*—part of the stage nearest the audience; *upstage*—part of the stage farthest from the audience; *stage right*—right part of stage from view of one facing the audience; *stage left*—left part of stage from view of one facing the audience; *stage center*—anywhere on a line between left and right. (These can be combined to indicate a more specific area—for example, *downstage center*.)

• Discuss blocking and staging a song. (See *Blocking* and *Staging a Song* below.)

• Write suggestions for staging "Where Does It Come From?" and "There's Just So Much to Go Around" on the board.

• Sing the songs, trying out some of their ideas.

• Learn the movement for "Where Does It Come From?" (See *Movement* on the bottom of page 417.)

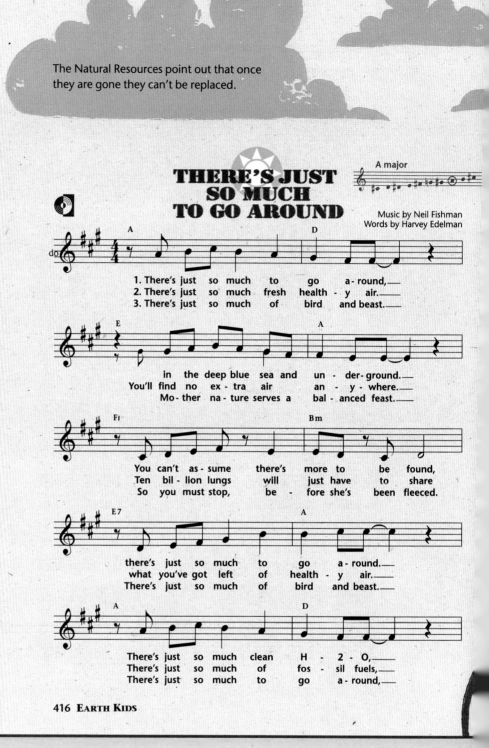

The Natural Resources point out that once they are gone they can't be replaced.

THERE'S JUST SO MUCH TO GO AROUND

A major

Music by Neil Fishman
Words by Harvey Edelman

1. There's just so much to go a-round,___
2. There's just so much fresh health-y air.___
3. There's just so much of bird and beast.___

in the deep blue sea and un-der-ground.
You'll find no ex-tra air an-y-where.___
Mo-ther na-ture serves a bal-anced feast.___

You can't as-sume there's more to be found,
Ten bil-lion lungs will just have to share
So you must stop, be-fore she's been fleeced.

there's just so much to go a-round.___
what you've got left of health-y air.___
There's just so much of bird and beast.___

There's just so much clean H-2-O,___
There's just so much of fos-sil fuels,___
There's just so much to go a-round,___

416 EARTH KIDS

PRODUCTION SUGGESTIONS
THEATER

BLOCKING: To *block* means to establish or chart the stage movement of actors. Where actors stand, where they face, the pathways they take from place to place all affect the audience's perception. (Examples: When Al is expressing a viewpoint different from all the others, he can stand apart from them, emphasizing their differences. When the New Kids arrive, they stay apart from the other group at first because they are strangers.) To keep the audience's attention, actors can cross to another section of the stage just before or as they speak an important line, or they can speak the line downstage (close to the audience).

STAGING A SONG: In a musical, songs are both visual and aural. Staging a song—blocking of singers and dancers, use of props, interpretation—needs to be planned. Staging can emphasize a song's message or the relationship between characters. For example, Ian and Jamie agree about saving the trees, so they can stand close together when they sing "Please, Don't Cut Down The Trees." When the Forests join in, they might also step towards the two singers. In "Where Does It Come From?" the singers can be spaced informally about the stage as they pick up the trash left by the Kids, emphasizing that trash is all over the forest.

that's health-y wat-er if you did not know.___
you de-pend up-on their mol-e-cules.___
in the deep blue sea and un-der-ground.___

Mixed with pol-lu-tants it will not flow.
When they are gone, it's back to the mules,
You can't as-sume, there's more to be found,

There's just so much clean H-2-O.___
so don't you waste our fos-sil fuels.___
there's just so much to go a-round.___

Once there was a ti-ny vil-lage___ with
Once there was a blue-green plan-et,___ a

wa-ter, food, and fuel ga-lore.___ But
won-drous place to work and play.___ Be-

af-ter years of waste and pil-lage___ it's
fore there was a way to ban it,___ pol-

D.C., third time to Fine

gone like the din-o-saur.
lu-tion turned that plan-et grey.

The kids begin to notice that some of the Natural Resources are indeed missing. Little Sister seems tired. The Air wonders if pollution is affecting her. The kids ask how the disappearance of resources will affect life.

Music Library *Musicals* **417**

7. Practice Scene II. Have students:

• Prepare to practice their parts in this scene, while others act as the audience.

• Begin the scene separated from each other and spread out over the entire stage (to help create a restful mood just before the Kids doze off).

• Watch as the Natural Resources, speaking their lines louder and louder, enter from all over the stage and auditorium in groups of similar resources. They move in slow motion to create a dreamlike quality. (See below for movement and sound suggestions.)

• Listen as the Natural Resources sing and dance to "Where Does It Come From?" with Jamie and Ian joining in on Verses 2 and 3.

• Practice the speaking parts as assigned. (The new hikers' entrances should not come close to the path of any of the Natural Resources. The discussion about the canary in a coal mine should be held stage right, away from Jamie.)

• Listen as the Natural Resources, Ian, Jamie, Phyllis, and Skip sing "There's Just So Much to Go Around," using the class's staging ideas as well as those in the script. (During this song, have several of the Natural Resources exit with the same dreamlike movements they used for their entrance. Each should exit at a different point, with at least one of them going into the audience.)

MEETING **INDIVIDUAL** NEEDS

ENRICHMENT: *Entrance of Natural Resources*

Air: *Sound*—chime tree or soft blowing into a mike. *Movement*—The characters do not appear on stage; they are only heard. **Forest:** *Sound*—intermittent shaking of cabasa or maracas (like leaves rustling). *Movement*—stiff, lumbering walk by tall trees; relaxed, swaying walk by underbrush. **River:** *Sound*—slow, quiet glissandos on a glockenspiel or metallophone. *Movement*—flowing. **Animal:** *Sound*—Bear might have a drum, eagle a soft cymbal, small birds a bird whistle. *Movement*—Circulate among the trees at different levels. **Fossil Fuel:** similar to Air and River to represent natural gas and petroleum.

MOVEMENT: *"Where Does It Come From?"*

MOVEMENT

Line 1: (*Where does it come from?*) Right hand sweeps forward and out to right side. (*Where does it go?*) Left hand sweeps forward and out to left side. Repeat gestures each time this is sung.

Verse 1: A few individual Natural Resources hold up items mentioned in the song (bag, food, orange peel) that have been left or thrown by Al.

Verse 2: Jamie and Ian pantomime the lyrics.

Verse 3: Natural Resources make gestures, movements, and perhaps sounds mentioned in the lyrics.

continued from previous page

8. Introduce "Please, Don't Cut Down the Trees" CD11:11, and prepare for solo singing auditions. Have students:

• Look at the notation, noticing the key changes (G major for the A section, E♭ major for the B section and A♭ major for the coda) and the accidentals in the last line of the B section.

• Listen to the recording, following in their books and hearing the key changes.

• Practice the last eight measures of the B section to become comfortable singing the intervals required by the accidentals.

• Sing the song, first as a class and then with varied groupings; for example: girls—A section, boys—B section, all—coda or duets for students interested in auditioning for the solo parts.

The Forest tells the kids why we need to replace the billions of trees that are cut down each year. While we need trees for building houses and making paper and other materials, the trees keep soil from washing away. They keep the atmosphere supplied with oxygen. In tropical areas, rain forests are home to thousands of species of animals and plants.

G major/Modulates

PLEASE DON'T CUT DOWN THE TREES

Music by Neil Fishman
Words by Harvey Edelman

Please, please don't cut down the trees. They look so pret-ty— sway-ing in the breeze. To save the earth they hold the keys, so please don't cut down the trees.

418 EARTH KIDS

PRODUCTION SUGGESTIONS

STUDENT STAGING: Students might need some help to stimulate their staging ideas. If discussion is slow, ask them which words or ideas in the song would be easily pantomimed, how such a pantomime could be done and which characters would do it. Ask them how the Forests' actions would differ from those of Jamie and Ian. Suggest that they find a movement or group spatial arrangement that can be used each time the words *Please don't cut down the trees* are sung.

ACCOMPANIMENTS: Song accompaniments can help set the style of the musical. The performance mixes,

CD11:15–20, give a contemporary sound. You may also use the piano accompaniments or create your own accompaniment by adding guitar, bass, and percussion players from a local high school.

SOUND EFFECTS: There will be two kinds of sound effects—taped river and forest sounds, which are heard in the opening and closing scenes, and the instrumental patterns played for each group of Natural Resources.

1. The strength of their roots keeps the earth in place. The
2. A world with-out trees, I - mag - ine the view. If

breadth of their leaves keeps the sun from my face.
we don't take care, well, it just might come true. So

Stand - ing so tall, limbs o - pen wide,
do what you may, do what you must,

D.C. last time to Coda

they seem to call: There's shel - ter in - side.
day af - ter day we hold na - ture's trust.

Coda

Please, please don't cut down the trees.

They look so pret - ty— sway - ing in the breeze. To

save the earth they hold the keys, so please,—

— oh please, don't cut down the trees.

9. Practice Scene III. Have students:

• Discuss how to stage "Please, Don't Cut Down the Trees," writing their ideas on the board. (See *Student Staging* at the bottom of page 418.) Watch as Jamie, Ian, and the Forests try out some of the ideas.

• Prepare to practice their parts in Scene III, while others act as the audience.

• Begin the scene with Jamie sitting alone on the tree stump, downstage left, with the Natural Resources somewhat distant. Animal 5 approaches tentatively, followed by the others who have speaking lines. As the Forest begins to disappear and as others tell her more about forest problems, Jamie's movements and voice become increasingly agitated. By the time Ian enters, she is very upset.

• Listen as Jamie and Ian sing "Please, Don't Cut Down the Trees." (They could both sing as if pleading with the audience. When Al enters and begins to make "overworked brother"-type remarks, Ian might pull Al to stage right, away from Jamie, showing anger and impatience in his voice and movements.)

SET DESIGN: The contribution of sets (backdrops, flats, large scenery pieces) is as important in creating illusion as that of costumes and props. Since this is a play with more dialogue than action, the set not only needs to "set the scene" visually, but also encourage movement. A tree platform upstage right, like an open tree house, allows actors to change their level and add tension to their movements as they get too near the edge or almost fall while climbing. This platform can be as simple as a sturdy table with cardboard-cutout bushes and a single maple tree cutout in front to disguise it. Another possibility is a plank placed across the upper rungs of two well-braced stepladders, which are concealed by the cardboard cutouts of trees and bushes. Of course, safety must be the most important feature of any platform.

The tree stump downstage left, at a contrasting low level, can be an actual stump or an upside-down trash can that has been padded on the rim for quiet, covered with papier-mâché, and painted to look like the real thing. The rest of the forest atmosphere can be provided by a backdrop painted on cloth or paper and by other trees cut out of large cardboard appliance cartons.

MUSIC LIBRARY
MUSICAL

continued from previous page

10. Introduce "Keep the Circle Going 'Round" CD11:12. Have students:

• Compare definitions of the words *circle, cycle, recycle,* and *round.*

• Read the lyrics of the song and discuss its meaning in light of their definitions. (Nothing in the world ever completely disappears—it only changes form.)

• Listen to the song, following the notation, and notice where the round occurs. (in the refrains after the verses)

• Memorize the refrain.

• Practice it as both a two-part and three-part round. (Parts 2 and 3 enter on the word *circle* of the previous part.)

• Sing the entire song, using this form:
Refrain (repeated)
Verse 1
Refrain as two-part round (repeated)
Verse 2
Refrain as two-part round (repeated as three-part round)
Refrain as two-part round (repeated)

• Learn the dance. (See *Movement* below.)

When the Skeptical Kid wonders what they can do to help, Little Sister suggests that they become Earth Kids and protect their environment. The Idealistic Kid agrees. The Practical Kid hopes it's not too late, then suggests that they begin by cleaning up the area. The Natural Resources teach the kids about recycling—how to reuse certain products instead of throwing them away.

420 EARTH KIDS

MEETING **INDIVIDUAL** NEEDS

MOVEMENT: *"Keep the Circle Going 'Round"*

Refrain: One large circle holding hands, walking one step per beat—first four measures clockwise, next four counterclockwise. On the repeat, break the circle on the last 2 measures and form two informal groups of singers, one upstage right and the other downstage left.

Verse 1: Face the audience to sing, forming two circles by the time the refrain begins again.

Refrain: As above, except each circle starts walking with the singing entrances of the round, resulting in the circles

beginning, changing direction, and ending at different times.

Verse 2: Repeat movement from Verse 1.

Refrain: First time as in the two-part round refrain. On the repeat, break into three circles for the three-part round with students closest to center stage in each of the two circles forming a third circle in the middle of the stage.

Refrain: Return to two circles for first time. On repeat, drop hands, face the audience and finish the song in small groupings all over the stage.

The Resources continue to dwindle. Little Sister dreams of a better future.

I CAN SEE A RAINBOW

A major (modulates)

r, m, f, s, l, t, d

Music by
Neil Fishman
Words by
Harvey Edelman

1. I can see the wilt-ed flow-er bloom and grow in
2. I can see the dense rain for-ests— free from threat of

fresh clean air.— In a land— that's parched and dy-ing—
man's ma-chines.— To an end— where all are hap-py—

I can see— life ev'-ry-where.— I can see— a
I can see— we'll find the means.— I can see— the

world for-got-ten— grow-ing health-y day by day.—
dis-tant chim-neys— not a puff of smoke in sight.—

Through the val-ley, 'cross the moun-tains,— I can see there is a way.—
On the fa-ces of the hun-gry— I can see hope tak-ing flight. —

— I can see— a rain-bow light-ing up— the skies.

Music Library *Musicals* **421**

11. Introduce "I Can See a Rainbow" CD11:13, **and prepare for solo auditions.** Have students:

• Listen to the song, following the notation.

• Notice that the melody in the second eight measures is almost identical to the first eight measures, except that it starts a whole step higher, requiring a key signature change.

• Notice similarities and differences between the first and second endings.

• Sing the song, first as a class and then in several small groups. (All students interested in auditioning for this solo can sing as a small group in preparation for their audition.)

12. Practice Scene IV. Have students:

• Prepare to practice their parts in this scene, while others act as the audience.

• Begin the scene with Jamie talking to the group. She is seated on the tree stump with the others seated on the ground facing her. They are stage center, somewhat downstage of her with their backs to the audience. As each Natural Resource talks to the Kids, it steps closer until the Kids are almost surrounded. The entire group starts to spread apart when Fossil Fuel 4 says, "Actually, it's already started." By the time the introduction to "Keep the Circle Going 'Round" begins, they have formed a large circle to sing the song and do the dance.

• Listen as Jamie sings her solo, "I Can See a Rainbow."

• Watch as all the Natural Resources begin to exit slowly and everyone except Al assumes a trance-like state. Al struggles with Jamie to prevent her from "disappearing" with the Natural Resources while the other Kids slowly sink into their original sleeping positions. The scene ends with all the Kids asleep.

EXTRA HELP: *Projection of Lines*

Projecting lines is essential to the success of a play. Actors should talk to the audience when speaking, even when their lines are directed to an actor at their side. (This is especially important for young actors who are just learning to project their voices.) Speaking lines too quickly is another reason actors are often not understood. Have students imagine that they are speaking their lines to a person in the back of the auditorium.

ENRICHMENT: *Building Recycled Instruments*

The ecological message of this play could be motivation for building instruments out of previously used materials. Ask students to bring items from home that they feel have the potential for making good sounds when struck, plucked, blown, or shook. Provide wire, glue, nails, screws, small pieces of wood, and simple tools for them to work with. Some of these student-made instruments might have sounds appropriate for use in the play.

MUSIC LIBRARY

MUSICAL

continued from previous page

13. Introduce "Here Come the Earth Kids"
CD11:14, clarifying the rhythm and learning the harmony for the refrain. Have students:

• Look at the notation and notice phrases beginning with a rest.

• Listen as you clap half notes and speak the words, demonstrating first the four divisions, then the three divisions per half note, as in every other measure of the verse.

• Clap half notes while you say the words, then clap and say the words.

• Listen to the song while following the notation, then sing the melody.

• Learn and practice the harmony in Measures 3–4 and 7–9 of the refrain.

• Sing the refrain in two parts with the recording.

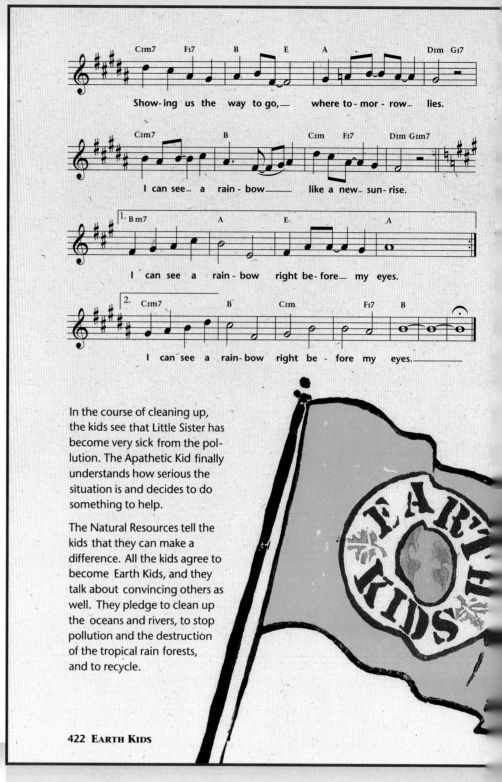

In the course of cleaning up, the kids see that Little Sister has become very sick from the pollution. The Apathetic Kid finally understands how serious the situation is and decides to do something to help.

The Natural Resources tell the kids that they can make a difference. All the kids agree to become Earth Kids, and they talk about convincing others as well. They pledge to clean up the oceans and rivers, to stop pollution and the destruction of the tropical rain forests, and to recycle.

422 EARTH KIDS

PRODUCTION SUGGESTIONS

STAGING THE SONG: The final song "Here Come the Earth Kids" is a message of determination and solidarity. Have the singers mass together in a strong front.

PROPS: Each prop has the potential to give more reality and life to the performance. Props can help an actor create a character or further the plot. For instance, we know something about Al from the number of food items he carries in his backpack. The plot depends on his throwing an apple, lunchbag, and other trash into the forest, since those items will be sung about and used in a later scene.

Each student will have a backpack with a lunch in it. They can put other items in it as well. In fact, students have a chance to develop their characters more fully by creating "stage business" that makes use of props not mentioned in the script. Skip or Phyllis might wear a radio headset that the character adjusts occasionally. (Of course, the director must determine whether or not this detracts from or adds to the scene.) Students can determine from the script what props their characters need and bring them to each rehearsal. Rehearsing with props should begin early because it influences the stage movement.

HERE COME THE EARTH KIDS

Music by Neil Fishman
Words by Harvey Edelman

Verse

1. From our homes and our schools there's a war to be waged.
2. How we live, work, and play will de-ter-mine our fate.

Moth-er na-ture has rules and we've got-ta be-have.
There are dues we must pay be - fore it's too late.

There's no time to take sides, we must work as a team
Ev'-ry-one must take part so we're sure to suc-ceed.

so the earth will a - bide and be home to our dream.
Search your mind and your heart and then fol - low our lead.

Refrain

Make way, here— come— the Earth Kids! We've got the pow-er to

save the world.— To - day here— come— the Earth Kids.

1. Our shin-ing ho-ur, one flag un - furled.— [Fine]
2. furled. Make way, here— [D.S. al Fine]

14. Practice Scene V. Have students:

• Prepare to practice their parts in this scene, while others act as the audience.

• Begin the scene with taped natural sounds of the forest (*not* the ones used for the Natural Resources). Each of the Kids wakes up sleepily but soon "comes to life." As the scene progresses, voices and movement become more energetic and animated. The Kids get excited about being Earth Kids and pick up a lot of trash and stuff it in paper bags left over from their lunches.

• Sing "Here Come the Earth Kids," during which the New Kids re-enter. (Suggestion—repeat the refrain many times while bringing as many students from the audience as possible up onto the stage to join in the singing. They can easily learn the refrain from the repetitions.)

• Conclude the play with the cast singing as they exit down the center aisle. Al, still on stage, stops everyone to hear the Natural Resources call out, "Way to go, Earth Kids." The Kids reply, then cheer and resume singing as they exit.

COSTUMES: For the audience, costumes help make a character and a scene believable. For actors, especially students, costumes can provide "permission" to create their character.

In this play there are two kinds of costumes. The Kids dress like ordinary sixth-grade hikers: sneakers, boots, shorts, jeans, T-shirts, baseball caps. Students will decide individually how their characters would dress and bring that kind of clothing.

Suggestions for the Natural Resources: All of the characters can have a basic costume of sweat suits, or leotard and tights, with a hood of an appropriate color.

Air—No costume is needed since this part consists of a voice from a backstage mike. *River*—The basic costume is blue with matching socks on hands and feet. Each character holds a long piece of fabric that he or she moves so that it ripples like flowing water. *Forest*—Trees and bushes wear the basic costume in appropriate shades of green, with cardboard or fabric leaves, vines, or lichens attached. *Fossil Fuel*—Billows of light fabric surround the Natural Gas character and silky, flowing fabric is worn by Liquid Petroleum. *Animal*—Ears, tails, paws, and wings can be attached as necessary.

RECORDER

PLAYING THE RECORDER CORRELATION

A summary of lessons in the *Playing the Recorder* booklet referenced throughout this Teacher's Edition follows.

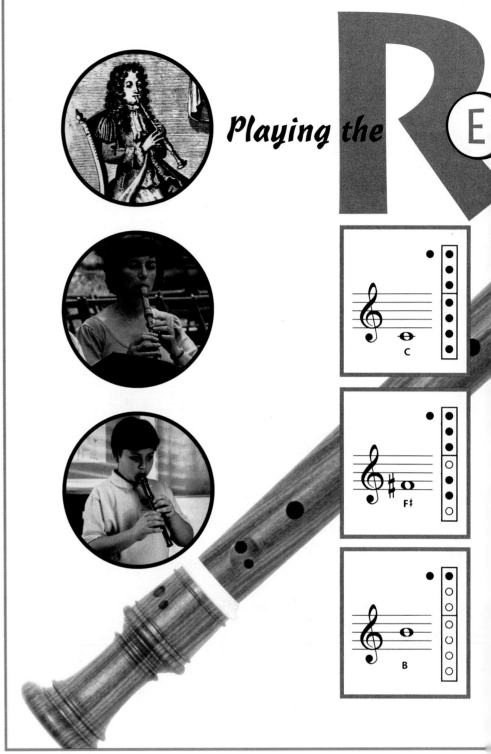

GUITAR

GUITAR CHORDS

Guitar chords are presented in the pupil book with the following songs:

Unit 1

Unit 2

Unit 6

Music Library

See the Classified Index, Instruments, for other Guitar activities in this book.

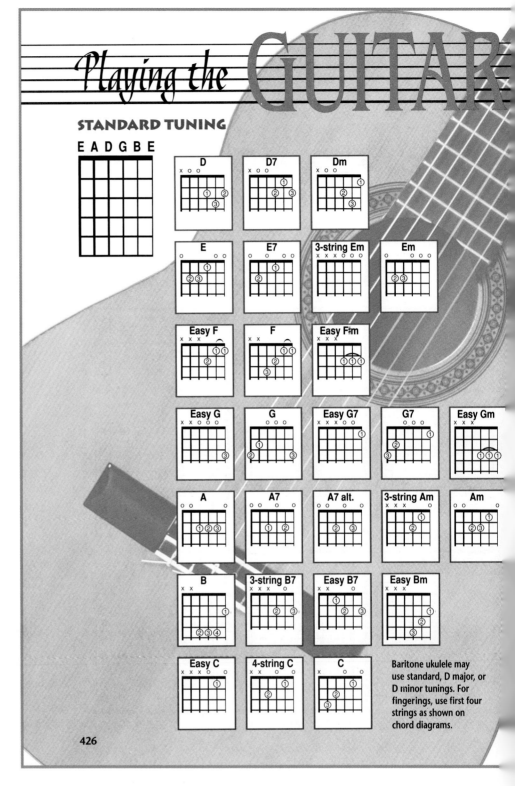

STANDARD TUNING

E A D G B E

Baritone ukulele may use standard, D major, or D minor tunings. For fingerings, use first four strings as shown on chord diagrams.

426

ALTERNATE TUNING IN MAJOR AND MINOR

Frets are indicated by the letter *f* and a number (f7 = 7th fret).

D MAJOR TUNING

D A D F♯ A D

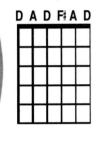
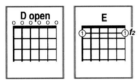
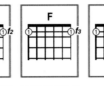

D MINOR TUNING

D A D F A D

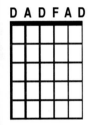
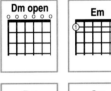
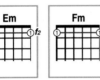

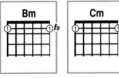

427

PLAYING THE GUITAR CORRELATION

A summary of Guitar lessons referenced throughout this Teacher's Edition follows.

Unit 1	Playing the Guitar	Guitar Objective
Lesson 3, 14	G•8	Down and up strums; eighth-note rhythm
Lesson 6, 26	G•1	Introduction; Easy C, Easy G7 (Standard)
Lesson 6, 26	G•2	"Old Blue" (key of C)
Lesson 6, 26	G•3	D Major tuning; D A/A7; "Old Blue" (key of D)
Lesson 7, 30	G•4	Chord roots; "A Ram Sam Sam"
Unit 2		
Lesson 3, 58	G•6	Easy Em/Em,Easy B7/B; "Wade in the Water"
Lesson 5, 66	G•12	Am, Em, B (D Minor tuning); "Tumbai"
Lesson 6, 70	G•7	D Minor tuning; 6/8; major and minor
Lesson 6, 70	G•14	Review; "Hava Nagila"
Lesson 8, 78	G•5	Easy G/G chord; 2/4; "Mama Don't 'Low"
Unit 4		
Lesson 1, 136	G•13	Fast 6/8; "Pat Works on the Railway"
Lesson 3, 154	G•20	Syncopation, E, full B7/B, "This Train"
Lesson 4, 158	G•7	D Minor tuning; 6/8; major and minor
Lesson 5, 162	G•10	D7; 3/4; "Sandy McNab"
Lesson 8, 176	G•25	Bass accompaniment, second position, "Deep Blue Sea"
Lesson 8, 176	G•9	Full G; Thumb/Brush strum; "Cripple Creek"
Lesson 8, 176	G•28	Bass with 2 strings plucked; "Wadaleeacha"
Unit 6		
Lesson 2, 242	G•21	Blues Shuffle Strum, "Joe Turner Blues"
Lesson 5, 254	G•24	Review; "Amazing Grace"
Lesson 5, 254	G•26	Bass runs; "The Wabash Cannonball"
Lesson 9, 274	G•11	Tie; accent; "Old Blue" (key of G)
Celebrations		
Patriotic, 286	G•22	Chord roots (Standard and D Major tuning),Thumb/Brush strum, "America the Beautiful"
Christmas, 306	G•15	A (Standard); E7; "Silent Night"
Christmas, 306	G•16	Common time, "What Child is This?," "Pat-a-Pan"
Music Library		
332	G•23	Tablature review; hammer-on and pull-off; "Old Ark's A-Moverin'"
347	G•27	Calypso strum; "*John B.* Sails"
348	G•18	4-string C/C chord; "The Lion Sleeps Tonight"
352	G•19	Cut time; full C (Standard); "Deep Blue Sea"
413C	G•17	Tablature and melody playing (Standard and D Major tuning); "Ode to Joy"

GLOSSARY

GLOSSARY

A

accent a stress on a given pitch or chord, **108**

accordion a kind of portable organ held by straps over the shoulders, **108**

aria a solo song in an opera, **212**

arranger a person who makes decisions about how style, instrumentation, tempo, harmony, and dynamics can be changed in a piece of music, **36**

articulation the manner in which sounds are performed, for example, smoothly connected or sharply separated, **191**

B

band an instrumental ensemble that usually consists of brass, woodwind, and percussion instruments, **5**

bass clef (𝄢) a clef used to show low pitches, **124**

bebop a style of jazz that developed in the mid-1940s. It is performed by small groups and focuses on improvisation, **251**

big band the ensemble used for swing jazz, usually consisting of woodwinds, brass, and percussion instruments, as well as string bass, **5**

blues a style of music that began in America in the early twentieth century, with roots in African American spirituals and work songs, **243**

C

cambiata the stage when boys' voices first begin to change and they can sing some slightly lower pitches than before, **195**

canon a musical form in which a melody is imitated exactly in one or more parts, similar to a round, **52**

chamber music music played by a small ensemble, **112**

D

changed voice an adult singing voice, usually categorized as soprano, alto, tenor, or bass, **195**

chord three or more pitches sounded together, **30**

coda an ending section to a piece of music, **5**

countermelody a contrasting melody that goes with a melody, **24**

countersubject a melody that is heard with the subject in a fugue, **118**

country and western a style of American music, **264**

D

disco a style of popular dance music that developed in the 1970s, with a strong, steady beat for dancing, **264**

duo-pianists two performers who play music for two pianos, **125**

dynamics the degree of intensity and loudness of sound, **196**

E

envelope the shape of a sound from its beginning to its end, **115**

episode the section of a fugue in which the main melody is not heard, **118**

F

flat (♭) a symbol meaning to lower a tone a half step, **52**

fortepiano an early kind of piano that was smaller and quieter than those used in concerts today, **113**

fugue a composition in which three or more voices enter one after the other and imitate the main melody in various ways according to a set pattern, **118**

G

grand staff the set of two staffs used for piano music that includes very low as well as very high notes, **124**

H

half step the smallest distance between pitches in most western music; the distance between a pitch and the next closest pitch on a keyboard, **51**

harpsichord an early keyboard instrument with strings that are plucked when the keys are pressed, **96**

heavy metal a style of rock 'n' roll music that developed in the 1970s, using loud and distorted electrically produced sounds, **264**

I

instrumentation the choice of instruments in a piece of music, **36**

interpretation choices made by the performer that help make a musical performance more effective, **196**

interval the distance between two pitches, **51**

introduction a section of a piece, **8**

inverted chord a chord played with a note other than the root in the bass, **176**

J

jazz a type of popular American music with roots in African American spirituals, blues, and ragtime, borrowing rhythms from Africa and Latin America and melodies from Europe, **238**

K

key signature sharps or flats placed at the beginning of each staff, **70**

L

ledger lines lines drawn above and/or below a staff to show pitches that are higher and/or lower than those on the staff, **25**

legato a kind of articulation in which pitches are smoothly connected, **191**

lyricist a person who writes the words to songs, **191**

lyrics the words of a song, **191**

M

major scale a scale with *do* as the tonal center, with half steps between steps three and four, and seven and eight, **51**

marcato a kind of articulation in which pitches are sharply separated, **191**

march form a form that usually has sections AABB Trio Trio, **8**

mazurka a Polish dance, always in ¾ meter, **108**

melodic contour the upward or downward movement, or shape, of a melody, **18**

minor scale a scale with *la* as its tonal center, with half steps between steps two and three, and five and six, **70**

motive a small building-block of melody or rhythm, **150**

musical a musical theater production featuring a story told with singing and dancing, **190**

N

new wave a style of music popular in the early 1980s, featuring simple harmonies and often humorous lyrics, **270**

O

opera a drama with costumes and scenery, in which all or most of the text is sung, **195**

orchestra a large instrumental ensemble that usually includes members of the string, woodwind, brass, and percussion families, **5**

organ a keyboard instrument whose sound is produced by air forced through pipes, **95**

P

pedal point a single pitch held for a long time under changing chords or scales, **102**

Glossary **429**

piano a keyboard instrument whose sound is produced by hammers hitting stretched strings, **97**

pitch the highness or lowness of a tone, **18**

player piano a kind of mechanical piano that plays by itself, **110**

prepared piano a way of changing the sound of the piano by placing items such as pieces of paper, coins, spoons, or erasers on or between the strings, **122**

R

ragtime a style of music in which the melody is strongly syncopated while the accompaniment keeps a steady beat, **238**

rap a style of music that developed in the 1970s, involving spoken rhymes usually heard with a background of recorded music, **274**

relative minor a minor key having the same key signature as the major key three half steps higher; for example, A minor is the relative minor of C major, **103**

rock 'n' roll a style of music that developed in the 1950s, based on blues, gospel, and country music styles, **254**

root the pitch on which a chord is built, **31**

S

scale an ordered series of pitches, **51**

sharp (♯) a symbol meaning to raise a pitch a half step, **52**

stretto a technique used in a fugue in which the subject enters quickly in several voices, overlapping with itself, **118**

subject the main melody in a fugue, **118**

swing a kind of jazz that developed in the 1930s, played by big bands, **246**

syncopation a type of rhythm in which stressed sounds occur on weak beats or between beats, **154**

synthesizer an electronic keyboard instrument that can produce new sounds or imitate the sound of any other instrument, **104**

T

tala a rhythm grouping used in music from India, **217**

tempo the speed of the beat, **196**

texture the way melody and harmony combine to create layers of sound, **28**

tie (⌣) a musical sign that joins two notes of the same pitch into a single sound equal to their total duration, **28**

tonal center the pitch around which the melody of a piece seems to center; often the last pitch in a melody, **52**

tone color the special sound of each instrument or voice, **5**

treble clef (𝄞) a clef used to show high pitches, **124**

triad a chord with three pitches, each one of which is two steps away from the other, **31**

trio a part of march form and some dance forms that contrasts with earlier sections, **8**

U

unchanged voice the voice of a young person that has not changed to an adult voice, **195**

unison all perform the same part, **66**

V

verse-refrain form a song form in which the words of the verse change following each repetition of the refrain; the verse and refrain usually have different melodies, **12**

W

whole step a distance equal to two half steps, **51**

Z

zarzuela a kind of Spanish opera, **220**

SHARE THE *Music* SEQUENCING:

T hroughout *Share the Music* careful sequencing promotes successful music learning. Lesson-to-lesson and unit-to-unit, students enjoy enriching musical experiences that lead them through carefully planned sequence stages. The *Program Scope and Sequence* shows these stages for tested objectives and outlines presentation of other selected concepts. Specific activities are presented in the Unit Planners.

PREPARE

Experience the concept in all perceptual modalities (visual, aural, kinesthetic) without labeling it and without conscious attention being drawn to it.

Imitate and explore the concept, without labeling, gradually leading toward and ultimately reaching an understanding of it.

Describe the concept, characterizing it in students' own words, gestures, and/or pictures.

PROGRAM SCOPE AND SEQUENCE

MUSICAL ELEMENTS	CONCEPTS	UNIT 1 *MUSIC MAKERS*	UNIT 2 *MUSICAL ADVENTURES*	UNIT 3 *THE KEYBOARD CONNECTION*	UNIT 4 *OUR MUSICAL HERITAGE*
EXPRESSIVE QUALITIES	Dynamics	• Experience a variety of dynamics levels *(throughout)*			
	Tempo	• Experience a variety of tempos *(throughout)*			
	Articulation	• Experience a variety of articulations *(throughout)*			
TONE COLOR	Vocal/ Instrumental Tone Color	• Experience, explore, describe, label, practice identifying (L1), reinforce (L2–3, 6–9), create with (L8–9) band instruments and families* • Experience, explore describe, label, practice identifying (L1), reinforce (L8–9) orchestral instrument families* • Experience piano (L1, 8), organ (L7)	• Maintain orchestral instruments (L1, 4, 8) • Experience piano (L3, 7) • Body percussion (L2–3, 5–7) • Pitched (L1–6, 8–9) and unpitched (L2–3, 6–9) classroom instruments • Small instrumental (L1, 5, 7–9) and vocal (L6) ensembles	• Explore, describe, identify (L1), practice (L2), reinforce (L2–9) sounds of keyboard instruments (pipe and electric organs, harpsichord, piano, synthesizer, thumb piano, player piano, accordion), and how sounds are produced* • Body percussion (L4–5) • Pitched (L2, 4, 6–9) and unpitched (L4–5, 7) classroom instruments • Small instrumental (L7–8) and vocal ensembles (L6)	• Maintain band (L1) • Native American vocal tone color and drumming (L6) • Ukulele (L5) • Body percussion (L1–7, 9) • Pitched (L2, 4–5, 7–9) and unpitched (L1, 3–4) classroom instruments • Small instrumental (L1–2, 4–5, 8–9) and vocal ensembles (L5–6)

AN OVERVIEW

LABEL

Identify and label the concept by name. Introduce hand sign, gesture, or symbol as appropriate.

APPLY

Practice the concept, using known material, now with the label or name used.

Reinforce the concept with new material, with label used.

Read or interpret visual representation, consciously using the concept.

Create, consciously applying understanding of the concept.

Maintain the understanding with more new material.

Bold = Tested Strand   ★ = Assessment of Tested Objective

UNIT 5 *ON STAGE*	UNIT 6 *FROM RAG TO RAP*	CELEBRATIONS	ENCORE/MUSIC LIBRARY
• **Explore, describe (L1), label, practice (L2), reinforce (L2–8), create (L2, 8–9) appropriate dynamics***	• Maintain appropriate dynamics (L1–9)	• **Reinforce appropriate dynamics (287, 298, 323, 329)**	• **Reinforce appropriate dynamics (380, 389, 394)**
• **Explore, describe (L1), label, practice (L2), reinforce, create (L2, 8–9) appropriate tempo***	• Maintain appropriate tempo (L1–9)	• **Reinforce appropriate tempo (323, 329)**	• **Reinforce appropriate tempo (380)**
• Explore, describe, label, practice (L1), reinforce (L2–8), create (L2, 8–9) appropriate articulation*	• Maintain appropriate articulation (L1–9)	• **Reinforce appropriate articulation (323, 327, 329)**	• **Reinforce appropriate articulation (357, 380, 389)**
• **Maintain orchestra (L6)** • **Explore, describe, label, practice identifying (L1), reinforce (L3) adult, cambiata, and unchanged voice ranges*** Explore, describe (L1), label, practice (L2), reinforce (L2, 4–5, 7–9), create (L2, 8–9) lighter/heavier tone color* Explore (L1), describe, label, practice (L2), reinforce (L2–8), create (L2, 8–9) appropriate vocal tone color* Indian percussion, Indonesian metallophones (L7)	• **Maintain band (L1–9)** • **Maintain keyboard (L2, 4–9), synthesizer (L9)** • Maintain appropriate vocal tone color (L1–9) • Guitar (L4–9), recorder, bells (L2) • Percussion (L1, 3) • Electric guitar (L5–8) • Electric bass (L6) • Body percussion (L1, 3, 9) • Pitched (L2, 4–9) and unpitched (L1, 3, 9) classroom instruments • Small instrumental (L2, 5, 7) and vocal ensembles (L2, 6–7)	• **Reinforce keyboard instruments (291, 294–295, 314)** • **Reinforce families of band (291)** • **Reinforce appropriate vocal tone color (323, 329)** • **Reinforce voice ranges (325)** • Russian vocal tone color (325) • Soprano saxophone (325)	• **Reinforce percussion (86)** • **Reinforce keyboard instruments (132)** • Rock music technology (280) • **Reinforce strings (336, 339), percussion (344), brass (413E)** • **Reinforce orchestra (410, 413C, 413I), band (413G)** • **Reinforce voice ranges (413A)** • **Reinforce appropriate vocal tone color (380)** • Electronic music (413K)

(continued on next page)

MUSICAL ELEMENTS	CONCEPTS	UNIT 1 MUSIC MAKERS	UNIT 2 MUSICAL ADVENTURES	UNIT 3 THE KEYBOARD CONNECTION	UNIT 4 OUR MUSICAL HERITAGE
DURATION	Beat/Meter	• Experience ⁶⁄₈	• ³⁄₄ and ⁴⁄₄ (L1–8), ²⁄₄ (L1, 8) • Beats with ♪ (L2)	• ³⁄₄ (L4)	• Explore, describe, identify, practice (L1), reinforce, read (L1, 4, 5, 9), create (L1, 4, 9) patterns in ⁶⁄₈ * • Patterns in ³⁄₄ (L1, 3, 5)
	Rhythm	• Experience, imitate (L1–2), describe, label, practice, reinforce (L3, 8), read (L4–5, 8), create (L7, 9) patterns with ♪ ♪ ♩ ♩ 𝅝 and rests* • Experience ♬♬ (L2) ♫ (L6); ♫ (L1, 2, 5–7) and ♩. ♪ (L7)	• Explore, identify (L2–3), practice, reinforce, read, create patterns with ♬♬ ♫ ♫ (L2–3, 5–9)* • Experience ♫ (L2, 6) and ♩. ♪ (L2–3)	• Explore, describe, label, identify, practice (L4), reinforce, read, create (L4–5, 7–9) rhythm patterns with ♫ and ♩. ♪*	• Maintain patterns with ♬♬ ♫ ♫ (L1, 3); ♫ and ♩. ♪ (L3–4) • Syncopation with ties (L3, 5, 7)
PITCH	Melody	• Experience (L1–3), explore, describe, label, practice (L4), reinforce (L4, 7), read (L5, 8), notate (L5), create with (L5, 9) treble staff pitches*	• Half and whole steps (L1) • Flat and sharp (L1) • Melodic contour (L1)	• Maintain treble staff pitches (L1, 4, 8) and create melodies (L4, 7, 9) • Half and whole steps • Pitches in bass clef (L8)	• Pitches in bass cleff (L2) • Melodic motive (L2) • Half and whole steps
	Harmony	• Harmony part (L2) • I and V chords in C major (L7)	• I, IV, V chord roots (L7) • 3-part canon (L6)	• Presence or absence of harmony (L1)	• I and V chords (L5) • I, IV, and V chords (L7–8) • Chord inversion (L8)
	Tonality major/minor	• Experience major and minor (L1–8) • Explore major scale (L7) • Experience whole and half steps in major (L1–3, 5–9) and minor (L1) scales	• Imitate, describe, identify (L1), practice (L2), reinforce (L4, 6, 8), read (L4), create with major (L9) scale* • Imitate, describe, identify, practice (L6), reinforce (L8) minor scale • Imitate, describe, identify whole and half steps in major (L1, 6, 8) and minor scales (L6, 8) • Tonal center (L1)	• Reinforce and read major (L2–3, 8) and minor (L3) scales • Practice half steps in major and minor scales (L3) • Tonal center from key signature (L2–3, 8)	• Maintain major and minor scales (L2, 5–8) • Reinforce understanding of half steps in major and minor scales (L2, 5)* • Create in minor (L7)
DESIGN	Texture	• Melody and countermelody (L5) • Thick and thin texture (L6), textural change (L8) • 2-part songs (L4–7)	• Textural change, monophony, homophony, polyphony (L7) • 2- (L4) and 3-part songs (L6–7)	• Polyphony (L6) • 2-part songs (L1, 6)	• Solo vs. group texture (L6), unaccompanied vs. accompanied texture (L6–7) • 2- (L2) and 3-part songs (L5, 7)
	Form/ Structure	• Experience, explore, describe, label, practice, reinforce (L1), read (L2) contrasting and repeating sections • Introduction and coda (L1, 2) • March form (L2) • A B or verse-refrain form (L2–3, 5–6, 8)	• Identify, practice (L5), reinforce, read (L8), create (L8–9) A B A form* • Canon (L1, 6, 7) • Verse-refrain form (2–3, 8) • A A B A form (L4, 5) • Rondo form (L3, 8)	• Rondo form (L5) • Fugue (L6)	• Maintain A B A form (L4) • Maintain repeating and contrasting sections (L6, 8) • Melodic motive (L2)
CULTURAL CONTEXT	Style/ Background	• Bands and orchestras from a variety of cultures (L1–9)	• Baroque (L1), Classical (L3), Romantic (L2, 4, 8) styles • Folk songs from Liberia (L2), Israel (L5–7), Turkey (L6–7) • Pop singer Whitney Houston (L1)	• Baroque (L1–2, 6), Classical (L2, 5), Romantic (L4), 20th-century experimental (L7) styles • Jazz (L6, 8), gospel (L6) • Uganda (L7) • Jazz pianist Ellis Marsalis (L6)	• Native American songs, poetry, dance (L6) • Folk songs from Panama (L1), Georgia Sea Islands (L3), Taiwan (L3), Renaissance England (L4), Tahiti (L5)

Bold = Tested Strand   * = Assessment of Tested Objective

UNIT 5 ***ON STAGE***	UNIT 6 ***FROM RAG TO RAP***	CELEBRATIONS	ENCORE/MUSIC LIBRARY
(L1, 3–5, 7–8)	• $\frac{4}{4}$ (L1–9)	• **Reinforce $\frac{6}{8}$ (305, 306, 315, 316, 329)** • Patterns in $\frac{4}{4}$ (299) • $\frac{3}{4}$ (301)	• **Reinforce $\frac{6}{8}$ (388)** • $\frac{3}{4}$ (338, 345, 353, 374), $\frac{9}{4}$ (366), $\frac{7}{8}$ (372), $\frac{4}{4}$ to $\frac{3}{4}$ (351), $\frac{9}{4}$ to $\frac{6}{4}$ (366)
laintain ♩. ♪ and ♫ Syncopation with ties and ♪♩♪ (L3, 5)	• **Maintain ♪ ♪ ♩ 𝅗𝅥 𝅝 and rests (L1, 3)**	• **Reinforce ♩. ♪ (295, 321) and ♫ (295)** • **Reinforce ♪ ♩ ♩. 𝅗𝅥 𝄾 (297)** • **Reinforce rhythms with ♪ (302)** • Syncopation with ties (288, 323) • Augmentation (298)	• **Reinforce ♩. ♪ and ♫ (332, 333, 337, 354, 360, 367–368, 380, 383, 389)** • **Reinforce ♪ ♪ ♩ 𝅗𝅥 𝅝 and rests (332–345, 371, 404)** • Syncopation with ♪ ♩ ♪ (332, 334, 340, 371, 407) and with ties (364, 371, 407)
Pitches in bass clef (L2) Melodic motive (L5)	• Blues melodic improvisation (L2)	• **Reinforce pitches in treble clef (297, 298)** • Melodic contour (293, 317)	• **Reinforce pitches in treble clef (332–345)** • Melodic contour (362)
, IV, V chords (L4)	• Chordal accompaniments	• I, IV, ˙ :hords (319) • Melody and countermelody (295)	• I and V chords (332) • I, IV, V chords (347–348)
laintain major scale (L4)	• Blues scale (L2)	• **Reinforce minor (298, 301, 306)** • Tonal center from key signature (287, 316, 319)	• **Reinforce major (337, 363, 375), and minor (333, 341–344, 363, 366, 375)** • Tonal center from key signature (337, 352)
Planning texture (L8) 2-part songs (L1, 8)	• Melody and accompaniment (L1–9) • 2-part songs (L7)	• Thinner/thicker texture (305, 309), monophony (303), homophony (303, 306)	• Monophony, polyphony (342)
Movement motives (L1, 2) Verse-refrain form (L4) Motive (L5)	• 12-bar blues (L2)	• **Reinforce A B A form (327)** • Verse-refrain form (295) • A B form (319)	• Movement motive (43) • Listening map (43) • **Reinforce A B A form (332, 362, 384)** • Canon (336) • Verse-refrain form (340, 347, 354, 396) • Theme and variations (411) • Motive (413C)
American (L1–3, 7–8) and British (L2, 4–5) musicals; opera (L6); Indian, Indonesian, Spanish musical theater (L7) Composer Marvin Hamlisch (L3)	• Popular music styles from the 1900s through 1990s (L1–9), including ragtime, jazz, blues, swing, bebop, rock 'n' roll, country and western, disco, heavy metal, new wave, rap	• Jazz (294) • Native American music (330) • Seasonal and patriotic music from a wide variety of cultures (American, Puerto Rican, Canadian, Latino, German, Irish, South African, Chinese, Indian, Iranian, Israeli, Scottish, Russian, Mexican, Native American) (284–331)	• Medieval music (42) • Drumming in various cultures (86–89) • Blues and jazz (132) • Folk dances of the world (184) • Opera (232) • Technology of rock concert (280–283) • Concert etiquette (410) • Composer Ellen Taaffe Zwilich (410) • Violinist Nadja Salerno-Sonnenberg (411) • Renaissance, Classical, Romantic, and 20th-century styles (410, 412)

PROGRAM SCOPE AND SEQUENCE

OVEMENT SCOPE AND SEQUENCE

A SEQUENCED APPROACH TO MOVEMENT

Share the Music presents movement in a systematic way, to encourage students to develop movement skills as they learn music concepts and skills. This **Movement Scope and Sequence**, a first for any music series, shows how movement skills are sequenced throughout the lessons.

MOVING: A PRIMARY MODE OF LEARNING

All children are born tactile and kinesthetic learners, discovering their world through touch and movement. Visual and auditory learning become important, but some children remain primarily "movement" or kinesthetic learners. On the playground, hand jive, jump rope, hopscotch, ball tossing, and other movement games are the activities of choice. This energy, interest, and enthusiasm is available to us in the classroom: to present musical concepts in a fresh way, to get students physically involved in skill development, to motivate, illustrate, and educate.

PARALLELS BETWEEN MUSIC AND MOVEMENT

Movement can provide clarity and reinforce understanding in music. Experiencing beat in movement can help a student learn to play an ostinato. Drawing the melodic contour in the air can help a child sing a melody. Creating a dance in A B A C A form can prepare students to hear rondo form.

ELEMENTS OF MOVEMENT		UNIT 1 FOCUS: SPACE	UNIT 2 FOCUS: TIME
SPACE	**Level**	• Do a low turn (L1) • Perform high and low level movement (L2) • Contrast levels (L4)	
	Direction	• Change direction (L1, 2, 4, 6) • Move towards/away; move clockwise (L6)	• Move in opposite directions (L5, 7)
	Pathway	• Trace air pathways with arm, explore air pathways with ribbon wand (L4)	• Trace air pathways with arm (L1) • Make a circle pathway on floor (L7)
	Range	• Change range to show dynamic changes (L1)	
	Body Design	• Learn correct posture for singing (L1)	• Freeze (L2)
	Body Facing	• Face forward, backward, and sideways (L1, 2) • Turn at different levels (L4, 8) • Move side by side; face partner (L6)	• Move front to front and back to back (L3) • Choose partner facing (L3, 5, 7) • Change facing to show phrases (L7)
GROUP FORMATIONS		• Group spatial variations (L1, 8) • Circle (L2, 6) • Square (L6)	• Circle (L5, 6, 7)
LOCOMOTOR		• Walk (L1, 4, 6, 8) • Jump and hop (L2) • Leap (L2, 4) • Stamp and perform footwork, run (L8)	• Walk (L3, 5) • Jump (L4)
NONLOCOMOTOR		• Bounce knees; mime instrument playing (L1) • Perform body percussion (L1, 7) • Stretch (L2) • Learn hand signs (L5) • Twist (L8)	• Use sign language (L1) • Do a "hand-feet" dance (L2, 4) • Perform body percussion (L3, 7) • Use hand signs (L4)
TIME		• Step-snap, touch-step, move body to the beat (L1) • Walk, snap, or clap to a rhythm (L3, 6, 8) • Pat ♩♩♩♩ (L3) • Contrast tempo (L4)	• Pat with alternating hands (L2), tap (L5), pat to the beat (L8) • Clap, tap, or pat to a rhythm (L1, 2, 5, 6) • Pat ♩♩♩♩ (L2, 3) • Move in slow motion (L4)
FORCE/QUALITY		• Use contrasting force (L1)	• Use sustained and percussive movements (L3)
RELATIONSHIPS		• Follow the leader (L1, 2, 4) • Create group choreography (L1, 3, 8) • Mirror, move in unison (L4) • Head and side couple (L6) • Move with a partner (L8)	• Create group choreography (L3, 5) • Move with a partner (L5, 7) • Move in unison (L7)
DANCE SKILLS		• Perform a modified grapevine step (L1) • Jazz walk (L2) • Samba (L2) • Exchange places, promenade, and practice an elbow swing (L6)	• Learn a hand-feet kick step (L2) • Do the cancan (L4)

UNIT 3 FOCUS: **PARTNER/ GROUP RELATIONSHIPS**	UNIT 4 FOCUS: **BODY FACING**	UNIT 5 FOCUS: **CHOREOGRAPHY**	UNIT 6 FOCUS: **POPULAR DANCE STYLES**
• Raise/lower arms (L2)	• Raise/lower arms (L2, 3)	• Do high and low level poses (L1) • Change levels (L1, 8)	
• Move away/towards (L1) • Move clockwise (L2) • Move counterclockwise (L2, 6)	• Change directions (L1, 8)	• Change directions (L1, 8)	
• Dance circle, snake-like, and zigzag floor pathways (L7)			• Dance in a circular floor pathway (L4)
• Take large steps (L1)			
• Practice correct posture (L1)		• Create poses for lyrics (L1) • Practice correct posture (L1) • Create a group shape (L2)	
• Vary body facing (L1) • Move forward and backward (L2); front to front (L5); side by side (L5, 7); and front to back (L7)	• Explore facing variations (L1) • Turn (L1, 2) • Face forward and backward (L1, 3) • Move side by side (L1, 6) • Face center of circle; reverse body facing (L2) • Do a 4-beat turn (L6)	• Change body facing (L1) • Move side by side (L3)	• Move forward and backward (L1); side to side (L1, 4, 7) • Do a spin-turn (L4)
• Three straight lines; three concentric circles (L2, 3) • Line, circle, snake-like, zigzag (L7)	• Scattered (L2) • Group shape (L2) • Kick-line (L3) • Spatial variations (L8)	• Scattered (L2) • Group shape (L2) • Kick-line (L3) • Spatial variations (L8)	• Scattered (L4, 7) • Circle (L5)
• Walk (L1, 2, 4) • Do a side-crossing walk variation (L5)	• Walk (L1, 2, 3)	• Walk (L1, 6, 8) • Create locomotion (L2) • Jump, hop (L3)	• March (L1) • Walk (L4)
• Use sign language (L1)	• Perform body percussion (L1, 3) • Use sign language (L2) • Move head/arm (L3) • Make a paddling-arm movement; perform gestures (L5)	• Mime lyrics; change focus (L1) • Choreograph gestures (L1, 8) • Cross arms (L2) • Do a knee kick (L3) • Lunge (L3) • Perform body percussion (L7)	• Twirl/toss cane (L1) • Mime lyrics, perform gestures (L1); mime instrument playing (L2) • Learn hand jive (L5) • Sign (L6) • Twist hips, move arms, bend and straighten at waist (L6) • Perform foot/leg gestures (L7)
• Perform a gospel-choir step to the beat (L3) • Walk, learn a mazurka step to the beat (L4) • Pat alternating hands to show a rhythm (L4); clap to a rhythm (L4, 5)	• Clap first beat of measure (L1) • Tap, clap, or pat alternating hands to a rhythm (L1, 3) • Pat, clap, clap-snap, or pat-clap to the beat (L1, 2, 3) • Do a gospel-choir step to the beat, clap-snap to a rhythm (L7)	• Walk to the beat (L1, 3) • Pat or clap to a rhythm (L3, 5, 7) • Tap stressed beat; perform body percussion (L7)	• Tap or pat to a rhythm (L1) • Pat to the beat (L4)
		• Use abrupt, energetic, or sustained movements (L1) • Swing arms (L2)	
Cross foot over foot, open foot out to the side (L1) Create group choreography (L1, 7) Move in unison; move in canon (L2, 3) Move with a partner (L5)	• Create movement variations with a partner (L1) • Move in unison; move in canon (L2)	• Walk in unison, mirror (L1) • Choreograph with a partner (L1, 2) • Create group choreography (L1, 8) • Move with a partner (L2, 3, 7)	• Move with a partner (L3, 6, 7)
Learn a gospel-choir step (L3) Do the mazurka (L4)	• Learn the two step (L1) • Pivot (L2) • Shuffle (L6) • Do a gospel-choir step (L7)	• Learn the Charleston (L2) • Create a movement motive (L2) • Dance in a kick-line (L3) • Act out a scene (L6) • Create puppet-like movement (L7)	• Learn a swing-dance step (L3) • Do the monkey, twist, and watusi (L6) • Shuffle (L7)

MOVEMENT GLOSSARY

alignment   The position of body parts in relation to each other. Of special importance to good singing is the position of the vertebrae, head, shoulders, and feet in relation to each other.

ballroom dance   Any among a group of dance styles in which couples move while holding each other. These dances vary widely in their tempos, steps, body facings, and holds. Examples: waltz, fox trot, tango, rumba, samba.

body facing   The spatial orientation of body surfaces, most often the front.

> Whether or not one is moving, **body facing** exists at all times. The term refers to where various body surfaces are in relation to an outside reference.
>
> 1   partner or opposing line
>   · *front to front*
>   · *front to back*
>   · *back to back*
>   · *side by side*—with same or opposite outside reference
>   · *same*—both facing the same outside reference
>   · *opposite*—each facing opposite outside references
> 2   direction or line of motion
>   · *forward*—front facing the line of motion
>   · *backward*—back facing the line of motion
>   · *sideways*—side facing the line of motion
> 3   the area in which the person is located
>   · *front*—where the leader stands
>   · *back*—opposite to front
> 4   the group formation
>   · *inward*—toward the center of a circle or square
>   · *outward*—away from the center of a circle or square
>   · *clockwise*—to the left in a circle
>   · *counterclockwise*—to the right in a circle

body percussion   The sounds created by using body parts as percussion instruments. Examples: pat, clap, snap, rub, stamp.

body shape   The design created by placement of body parts.
   curved rounded lines predominant
   angular straight and bent lines predominant

broken circle   A line of dancers with a leader who leads the group in curved pathways (often circular). The curved pathway remains unclosed.

Charleston   An up-tempo popular dance style that originated in the 1920s. Characterized by fast, bouncy footwork (knees twist in and out, heels swing outward) and a variety of arm movements.

circle dance   A dance done in circle formation without partners.

circle formation   A number of individuals standing or sitting equidistant from a center point.

close   Bring one foot next to the other. Can be done with or without transferring weight (either a step or a touch).

concentric circle formation   Circles inside other circles, without partners.

dance   A series of body movements usually performed to music. A dance can be structured or improvisatory, and may include visually perceptible themes (steps, gestures, or spatial designs) that are repeated and developed throughout its duration.

dancing   Doing a dance or moving with control over the form and visual design of body movements.

direction   The spatial orientation of the line of motion.

> When there is a line of motion, **direction** occurs. If an individual is still, there is no direction, only body facing. A direction is always in relation to a point of reference. The most common directions are:
>
> 1   in relation to a partner or facing line
>   · *toward*—approaching a partner or line
>   · *away from*—separating from a partner or line
> 2   in relation to a circle formation
>   · *clockwise*—following the hands of a clock
>   · *counterclockwise*—reverse of clockwise
>   · *in*—toward the center of the circle
>   · *out*—away from the center of the circle
> 3   in relation to an imaginary vertical line
>   · *up*—higher
>   · *down*—lower
>
> *Forward, backward,* and *sideways* are body facings in relation to the line of motion and are not directions.

do-si-do   Partners begin by facing each other, then move toward each other, pass right shoulders, step to the right, walk backward, pass each other again by the left shoulders, and return to facing position. Often done with arms folded across chest.

double circle   A partner formation of concentric circles. Partners stand side by side or front to front. Dancers in the inside circle are connected to partners in the outside circle by holding a hand or both hands and/or moving together.

echo   Copy a movement after the leader completes it.

elbow swing   Link elbows (right or left) with partner and turn.

facing partner   Front-to-front body relationship.

floor pattern or pathway   An imaginary line resulting from locomotion across the floor.

formation   A group spatial arrangement or design.

Every dance or singing game has a traditional spatial arrangement called a **formation** that determines how the participants will stand or sit at the beginning of the dance or game. Some of these include:

- *broken circle*
- *circle*
- *double circle*
- *concentric circles*
- *line*
- *longways set* or *contradance lines*
- *scattered*
- *square*
- *square of four*

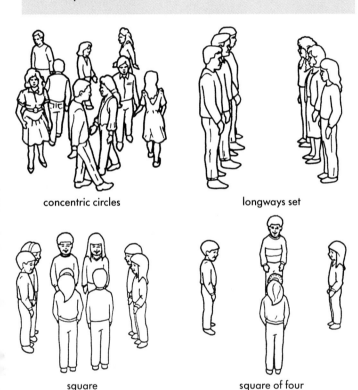

concentric circles

longways set

square

square of four

four-beat turn   Complete turn in place taking four beats and four steps.

gallop   A $\frac{6}{8}$ locomotor combination of a step and a leap. The step gets a quarter-note value; the leap gets an eighth-note value ($\quarternote$ $\eighthnote$). The same foot always leads in a gallop.

gospel choir step   A particular series of movements done by a gospel choir during singing.

beat 1	beat 2	beat 3	beat 4
step	clap	touch	clap

grapevine step   A series of weaving foot movements (cross/side/back/side): 1) Left foot crosses right; 2) right foot steps open to right; 3) left foot steps in back of right; 4) right foot steps open to right. Step can be done to the left by crossing the right foot in front of the left to begin. A *modified grapevine step* begins with an open step to the side followed by a cross step either in front or in back.

group shape or group design   The spatial outline created by a gathering of people. Related to formation but not all group shapes are traditional formations.

hand feet   Using the hands to replicate the movement of the feet.

hand jive   Rhythmic clapping, slapping, and patting hand movements performed with chants and songs.

hand signs   Specific hand gestures used to communicate. Both Native American sign language and sign language for the deaf provide an extensive lexicon of specific hand signs. Hand signs are also used to signal pitch syllables.

head couple   The partners at the head of the set or the end nearest the source of music.

high five   Gesture used as a greeting or a congratulation in which two people clap their right hands, maintaining contact as they raise their hands upward.

improvise   Create (movement) spontaneously, without prior planning.

in place   In self space; without leaving home base.

in step   Moving in unison with other movers.

jazz step or walk   A series of foot movements: 1) Step with the right foot; 2) touch the left foot to the floor; 3) step with the left foot; 4) touch the right foot to the floor. Finger snaps are often done with the touches.

jog   A slow-run variation where the knees come up a bit and the movement has a bouncy quality.

keep the beat   Move with each underlying pulse.

leader   The person who chooses or creates the movement for others to copy or follow.

leap   A basic locomotor movement in which weight is transferred from one foot to the other, with a moment in which neither foot is on the floor. A leap differs from a run because it is done for either height or distance, not speed.

line dance   Dance in which participants move next to one another, either side by side or front to back, forming a straight line. There are no partners.

locomotion   Going from one place to another, or traveling.

Movement that allows us to get somewhere is called **locomotion.** Most locomotion involves the feet. Basic locomotor movements that use alternate feet include:

- *walk*
- *run*
- *leap*

Basic locomotor movements that do not alternate feet include:

- *hop*
- *jump*

Other common forms of locomotion combine two of the basic forms and are distinguished by their rhythm.

- *gallop* step/leap, uneven rhythm (♩ ♪)
- *slide* sideways gallop
- *skip* step/hop, uneven rhythm (♩ ♪)
- *step-hop* similar to skip, even rhythm (♫ or ♩ ♩)

Forms of locomotion that do not involve the feet include *crawl, scoot,* and *roll.* These are not considered basic forms.

longways or contradance set   Parallel lines of dancers usually facing each other.

lunge   A large steplike movement forward or to the side that feels like a fall. The back foot does not leave the ground and weight is divided between the two feet.

march   A walk variation in ⅜ or ⅘ that uses quick military-style steps. Alternate knees are raised and lowered with each step. One step for each underlying beat.

mirror   Strive to move in perfect unison. Can be done by facing partners or by a group, usually with a designated leader. Mirroring without a leader is possible with practice.

movement exploration   Improvised motion to discover movement possibilities, usually relating to a concept. Example: Explore different partner facings and holds.

movement motive   A short movement phrase with distinctive time, space, and force characteristics that can be repeated and varied in the development of a dance composition.

movement ostinato   A repeating movement pattern.

movement quality   The characteristic of movement that results from the interplay of time and force. Examples: strong, light, sudden, percussive, sustained, shaky, swinging, vibratory.

movement variation   A movement that has been changed but still maintains its original character. Example: an arm gesture done with the opposite arm, or at a different level or tempo.

nonlocomotor   Movement that does not involve traveling from one place to another. Sometimes called *axial movement* because it occurs around an axis at a joint in the body. Examples: bend, twist, stretch, sway, swing, reach.

pantomime   Movement, especially gestures, used to simulate an activity without the objects that would usually be present. Example: playing a trumpet without the trumpet.

pat   Tap thighs with both hands.

pathway   An imaginary line created by movement.

percussive   A quality of movement created by a quick, short, explosive movement that stops instantly.

pivot   A change of body facing in which the ball of one foot remains fixed to a spot on the floor while the other foot changes location.

posture   Body alignment.

processional   A group of people moving together in formation, often in step with each other and with music of some kind, as in a parade. Usually ceremonial in nature, with spectators.

promenade   To perform this movement, a couple walks side by side, usually with skaters' hold.

range of movement   The size of a movement, or how much area is required to execute a movement. Examples: large, small.

samba   A Latin ballroom dance style popular in the 1930s and 1940s in which partners tilt forward on the backward steps and backward on the forward steps.

scattered formation   A group of individuals or couples spaced randomly around the movement area.

self space   The area that an individual occupies. Used by that person only.

set   A formation for dancing. Examples: longways or contradance set, square set.

shared space   The total area through which more than one person is moving.

shuffle   Walk variation in which the feet maintain constant contact with the floor, making a soft, scuffy sound. Used in Native American and country-dance styles.

side couples   The couples to the side of the head and foot couples in a square set.

side-touch   A movement sequence: 1) step out to the side with one foot; 2) tap the other foot next to the first but without a weight transfer.

sign language   Communication involving movement, most often of the hands, and no spoken words.

signing   Most commonly refers to use of American Sign Language for the Deaf. Signing has become a feature of many concerts that include songs.

Skaters' hold

skaters' hold   A traditional position for dance in which partners stand side by side with same body facing, holding right hand with right hand and left hand with left hand to the front. This can be achieved easily by partners facing one another, shaking right hands and holding, doing the same with the left hands, and then facing the same way without dropping hands.

skip   A $\frac{6}{8}$ locomotor combination of a step and a hop. The step has the value of a quarter note and the hop has the value of an eighth note ($\quarternote$ $\eighthnote$). The leading foot alternates.

square of four   Four dancers, each forming one side of a square.

square set   Four dancers or four couples, each forming one side of a square and facing a partner or another couple.

stand   An upright position with one foot or both feet as base of support.

step   A basic form of locomotion in which weight is transferred completely from one foot to the other. A series of steps is *walking*.

step-close-step   A movement sequence: 1) step in any direction with one foot; 2) the other foot steps next to the first foot; 3) step out with the first foot.

step-hop   A $\frac{6}{8}$ dance step similar to a skip, except that each movement gets a full beat (even rhythm $\quarternote\quarternote$).

step in place   Walk without going anywhere.

steps   Locomotor combinations and/or sequences making up a dance.

step-touch   A dance step in which weight is transferred to one foot on one beat and the other foot taps the floor on the next beat without transferring weight. Variations of this include step-lift and step-kick.

stretch   Reach away from the center of the body with one or more body parts. This movement puts joints into extension.

style   A quality of movement or a particular way movement elements are combined that make a dance (or other creative form) recognizable as unique. Styles can be influenced by the origin of the dance (example: Appalachian clogging), by the kind of music (example: jazz dance), or by the dancer (example: the style of Kris Kross).

supporting foot   The foot that bears weight or supports the body.

sustained   A continuous quality of movement with no sudden changes. Usually occurs with a slow to moderately slow tempo.

sway   Shift weight from one foot to the other without taking feet from the ground. Typically used with a slow to moderate tempo.

swing   A dance step in which partners join hands or link elbows and turn around each other.

swing (dance)   A dance style introduced in the 1930s and popular for several decades. Typified by jazz dancing with vigorous movement. The jitterbug and lindy hop are two dances in this style.

ten step   Country-style partner dance performed to music in $\frac{2}{4}$ or $\frac{4}{4}$, characterized by a sequence of ten single-beat foot movements.

through space   Moving out of self space into shared space.

touch   Tap the floor with a foot without transferring weight to that foot.

trace   Go over a preexisting line. Example: Using a finger, trace the melodic contour of a phrase of music shown in a book.

traditional dance   A dance performed by a particular ethnic group that has been handed down as a custom from generation to generation. Examples: the Iroquois Alligator Dance, the Polish mazurka.

travel   Locomote or go from one place to another. Examples: walk, run.

twist   Turn a body part against a fixed point or point of resistance.

twist (dance)   A dance popular in the 1960s in which the hips twist from side to side as the arms move in opposition to the hip movement. The feet remain in contact with the floor but the weight shifts from one foot to the other.

two-step   A popular dance which actually uses three steps (step/close/step) in a duple rhythm ($\eighthnote\eighthnote$ $\quarternote$).

unison movement   At least two people moving identically.

walk   A series of steps or alternating transferences of weight from one foot to the other. There is never a moment when both feet are off the ground.

walk variations   The ways in which the basic walking step can be altered.

> Basic locomotor forms can be executed in countless ways. Some **walk variations** have well-known names: march, jog, shuffle, strut, stroll. Regardless of the variation, the basic locomotor form is still a walk.

weight transference   A change in the body part that supports the weight of the body. Examples: A step changes the supporting surface from one foot to the other foot; sitting down changes the supporting surface from the feet to the buttocks.

MULTICULTURAL PERSPECTIVES

Share the Music is committed to teaching and spreading the joy of music through the expressions of many cultures. The musical selections in the series and the approaches to teaching music reflect our pluralistic society and the diversity of cultures.

As a multiculturally infused music series, *Share the Music* celebrates diverse modes of cultural expression. Varied vocal styles, for example, are used as appropriate. Students learn about both lighter and heavier vocal registers and determine which is most culturally appropriate for selected materials.

Students experience many facets of culture, including dance, fine arts, holidays, instruments, and aspects of daily life.

Making Multicultural Music Accessible in the Classroom

Share the Music includes authentic materials along with support tools to make them easy to use.

- **Context Information** leads students to respect, appreciate, and understand diverse peoples and cultures. This background is presented throughout the pupil books and in *Meeting Individual Needs.*

- **Recorded Interviews** bring musicians from diverse backgrounds into the classroom to introduce new material in a familiar, friendly way.

Easing the Use of Non-English Languages

In keeping with our commitment to presenting authentic music, *Share the Music* incorporates songs in over 60 languages. Songs in their original languages encourage positive self-esteem by honoring the languages of many cultures. With these songs, teachers receive important tools for using various languages with ease.

- **Recorded Pronunciation lessons** accompany every non-English song. In these lessons, a native speaker teaches students how to pronounce song words.

- **Singable English translations,** where appropriate, provide an alternative to using the original language.

- **The International Phonetic Alphabet** provides pronunciation at the point of use, underlaid beneath song notation. For each song, a customized key on the teacher's page provides a quick reference for pronunciation. In Grades 1–2, the pronunciation is printed on the reduced pupil page in the Teacher's Edition only.

Using the International Phonetic Alphabet (IPA)

The International Phonetic Alphabet (IPA) was developed in 1888 to facilitate the accurate pronunciation of all languages. It is commonly used by linguists, singers, and speech pathologists. IPA provides one consistent set of symbols for sounds from diverse languages, including non-English sounds that other phonetic systems fail to take into account. Thus, it helps provide greater multicultural authenticity. In IPA, each symbol represents one sound, and diacritic marks are minimized.

The IPA used in *Share the Music* was simplified by a linguist, working with over 100 multicultural experts, to retain English consonants wherever possible and to incorporate 12 main vowel symbols used in IPA. Special sounds that have no English equivalent are represented with special symbols. The use of simplified IPA limits the number of symbols students encounter, encouraging ease of use and success.

As the first major textbook series to use IPA, *Share the Music* helps students easily attain a greater degree of multicultural authenticity in their pronunciation of diverse languages.

PRONUNCIATION KEY

Simplified International Phonetic Alphabet

VOWELS

ɑ	f**a**ther	o	**o**bey	æ	c**a**t	ɔ	p**a**w
e	ch**a**otic	u	m**oo**n	ɛ	p**e**t	ʊ	p**u**t
i	b**ee**	ʌ	**u**p	ɪ	**i**t	ə	**a**go

SPECIAL SOUNDS

β	say *b* without touching lips together; *Spanish* nue**v**e, ha**b**a
ç	**h**ue; *German* i**ch**
ð	**th**e; *Spanish* to**d**o
ņ	sound **n** as individual syllable
ö	form [o] with lips and say [e]; *French* adi**eu**, *German* sch**ö**n
œ	form [ɔ] with lips and say [ɛ]; *French* c**oeu**r, *German* pl**ö**tzlich
ɾ	flipped r; bu**tt**er
ī	rolled r; *Spanish* pe**rr**o
ɭ	click tongue on the ridge behind teeth; *Zulu* ŋ**c**wele
ü	form [u] with lips and say [i]; *French* t**u**, *German* gr**ü**n
ɵ	form [ʊ] with lips and say [ɪ]
x	blow strong current of air with back of tongue up; *German* Ba**ch**, *Hebrew* **H**anukkah, *Spanish* ba**j**o
ʒ	plea**s**ure
'	glottal stop, as in the exclamation "uh oh!" ['ʌ 'o]
~	nasalized vowel, such as French b**on** [bõ]
˥	end consonants *k*, *p*, and *t* without puff of air, such as s**k**y (no puff of air after *k*), as opposed to **k**ite (puff of air after *k*)

OTHER CONSONANTS PRONOUNCED SIMILAR TO ENGLISH

ch	**ch**eese	ny	o**ni**on; *Spanish* ni**ñ**o
g	**g**o	sh	**sh**ine
ng	si**ng**	ts	boa**ts**

BIBLIOGRAPHY

African American Music (See also Multicultural Music)

Bebey, Francis. *African Music: A People's Art.* Chicago: Chicago Review Press, 1975.

Edet, Edna S. *The Griot Sings: Songs from the Black World.* Collected and adapted. New York: Medgar Evers College Press, 1978.

Glass, Paul. *Songs and Stories of Afro-Americans.* New York: Grosset & Dunlap, 1971.

Johnson, James Weldon, and J.R. Johnson, eds. *The Books of American Negro Spirituals.* 2 vols. in 1. Jersey City, N.J.: Da Capo Press, 1977.

Jones, Bessie, and Bess L. Hawes. *Step It Down: Games, Plays, Songs, and Stories from the Afro-American Heritage.* Athens, Ga.: Univ. of Georgia Press, 1987.

Nketia, Joseph H. *The Music of Africa.* New York: W.W. Norton & Co., 1974.

Southern, Eileen. *The Music of Black Americans.* 2d ed. New York: W.W. Norton & Co., 1983.

Cooperative Learning

Gibbs, Jeanne. *Tribes: A Process for Social Development and Cooperative Learning.* Santa Rosa, Calif.: Center Source Publications, 1987.

Johnson, David W., Robert T. Johnson, and Edythe Johnson Holubec. *Circles of Learning: Cooperation in the Classroom.* Alexandria, Va.: Association for Supervision and Curriculum Development, 1984.

Slavin, Robert E. *Cooperative Learning: Student Teams.* 2d ed. Washington, D.C.: National Education Association, 1987.

Dalcroze (See also Movement)

Abramson, Robert M. *Rhythm Games.* New York: Music & Movement Press, 1973.

Aronoff, Frances W. *Move with the Music: Songs and Activities for Young Children, A Teacher-Parent Preparation Workbook Including Keyboard.* New York: Turning Wheel Press, 1982.

Bachmann, Marie-Laure. *Dalcroze Today: An Education Through and into Music.* Oxford: Clarenon Press, Oxford University Press, 1991.

Jaques-Dalcroze, Émile. *Rhythm, Music, and Education.* rev. ed. Translated by Harold F. Rubenstein. London: The Dalcroze Society, 1980.

Early Childhood Music

Andress, Barbara. *Music Experiences in Early Childhood.* New York: Holt, Rinehart & Winston, 1980.

Aronoff, Frances W. *Music and Young Children: Expanded Edition.* New York: Turning Wheel Press, 1979.

Bayless, Kathleen M., and Marjorie E. Ramsey. *Music: A Way of Life for the Young Child.* 3d ed. Columbus, Ohio: Merrill Publishing Co., 1987.

Birkenshaw, Lois. *Music for Fun, Music for Learning: For Regular and Special Classrooms.* 3d ed. Toronto: Holt, Rinehart & Winston of Canada, 1982.

McDonald, Dorothy C., and Gene M. Simons. *Musical Growth and Development: Birth Through Six.* New York: Schirmer Books, 1989.

Nye, Vernice T. *Music for Young Children.* 3d ed. Dubuque, Iowa: William C. Brown Publisher, 1983.

Kodály

Choksy, Lois. *The Kodály Context.* Englewood Cliffs, N.J.: Prentice-Hall, 1981.

———. *The Kodály Method: Comprehensive Music Education from Infant to Adult.* 2d ed. Englewood Cliffs, N.J.: Prentice-Hall, 1988.

Daniel, Katina S. *Kodály Approach, Method Book One.* 2d ed. Champaign, Ill.: Mark Foster Music Co., 1979.

———. *Kodály Approach, Method Book Two.* Champaign, Ill.: Mark Foster Music Co., 1986

———. *Kodály Approach, Method Book Three.* Champaign, Ill.: Mark Foster Music Co., 1987.

———. *Kodály Approach, Method Book Two—Song Collection.* Champaign, Ill.: Mark Foster Music Co., 1982.

Szonyi, Erzsébet. *Musical Reading and Writing.* Translated by Lili Halápy. Revised translation by Geoffrey Russell-Smith. 8 vols. London and New York: Boosey & Hawkes Music Publishers, 1973–1979.

Listening

Copland, Aaron. *What to Listen for in Music.* New York:
McGraw-Hill Book Co., 1988.

Hoffer, Charles R. *The Understanding of Music.* 5th ed. Belmont, Calif.: Wadsworth Publishing Co., 1985.

Miller, Samuel D. "Listening Maps for Musical Tours." *Music Educators Journal 73* (October 1986): 28–31.

Movement (See also Dalcroze)

Boorman, Joyce L. *Creative Dance in the First Three Grades.* Toronto: Harcourt Brace Jovanovich, Canada, 1969.

———. *Creative Dance in Grades Four to Six.* Toronto: Harcourt Brace Jovanovich, Canada, 1971.

———. *Dance and Language Experiences with Children.* Toronto: Harcourt Brace Jovanovich, Canada, 1973.

Joyce, Mary. *First Steps in Teaching Creative Dance to Children.* 2d ed. Mountain View, Calif.: Mayfield Publishing Co., 1980.

Weikart, Phyllis. *Teaching Movement and Dance: Intermediate Folk Dance.* Ypsilanti, Mich.: High/Scope Press, 1984.

Multicultural Music (See also African American Music)

Anderson, William M. *Teaching Asian Musics in Elementary and Secondary Schools.* rev. ed. Danbury, Conn.: World Music Press, 1986.

Anderson, William M., and Patricia Shehan Campbell. *Multicultural Perspectives in Music Education.* Reston, Va.: Music Educators National Conference, 1989.

Fulton Fowke, Edith, and Richard Johnston. *Folk Songs of Canada.* Waterloo, Ontario, Canada: Waterloo Music Company, 1954.

George, Luvenia A. *Teaching the Music of Six Different Cultures.* rev. ed. Danbury, Conn.: World Music Press, 1988.

Heth, Charlotte, ed. *Native American Dance: Ceremonies and Social Traditions.* Washington, D.C.: National Museum of the American Indian, Smithsonian Institution with Starwood Publishing, Inc., 1992.

Horse Capture, George P. *Powwow.* Cody, Wyo.: Buffalo Bill Historical Center, 1989.

Rhodes, Robert. *Hopi Music and Dance.* Tsaile, Ariz.: Navajo Community College Press, 1977.

Speck, Frank G., Leonard Broom, and Will West Long. *Cherokee Dance and Drama.* Norman, Okla.: University of Oklahoma Press, 1983.

Titon, Jeff Todd, ed. *Worlds of Music: An Introduction to the Music of the World's Peoples.* 2nd ed. New York: Schirmer Books, 1992.

Orff

Frazee, Jane, and Kent Kreuter. *Discovering ORFF: A Curriculum for Music Teachers.* Valley Forge, Pa.: European American Music Distributors Corp., 1987.

Keetman, Gunild. *Elementaria, First Acquaintance with Orff-Schulwerk.* Valley Forge, Pa.: European American Music Distributors Corp., 1974.

Keller, Wilhelm. *Introduction to Music for Children.* Translated by Susan Kennedy. Valley Forge, Pa.: European American Music Distributors Corp., 1974.

Nash, Grace C., Geraldine W. Jones, Barbara A. Potter, and Patsy S. Smith. *Do It My Way: The Child's Way of Learning.* Sherman Oaks, Calif.: Alfred Publishing Co., 1977.

Orff, Carl, and Gunild Keetman. *Music for Children.* English version adapted from Orff-Schulwerk by Margaret Murray. 5 vols. London: Schott & Co., 1958–1966.

———. *Music for Children.* Canadian (North American) version adapted from Orff-Schulwerk by Doreen Hall and Arnold Walter. 5 vols. London: Schott & Co., 1956.

Regner, Hermann, ed. *Music for Children.* Vol. 2, *Orff-Schulwerk.* Valley Forge, Pa.: European American Music Distributors Corp., 1977.

Shamrock, Mary. "Orff Schulwerk: An Integrated Foundation." *Music Educators Journal 72* (February 1986): 51–55.

Recorder

King, Carol. *Recorder Roots* (Books I–II). Memphis, Tenn.: Memphis Musicraft Publications, 1978 and 1984.

Signing

Gadling, Donna C., Pastor Daniel H. Pokorny, and Dr. Lottie L. Riekehof. *Lift Up Your Hands: Inspirational and Patriotic Songs in the Language of Signs.* Washington, D.C.: National Grange, 1975.

Kannapell, Barbara M., and Lillian B. Hamilton. *Songs in
Signed English.* Washington, D.C.: Gallaudet College Press, 1973.

Riekehof, Lottie L. *The Joy of Signing.* 2d ed. Springfield, Mo.: Gospel Publishing House, 1987.

Sternberg, Martin. *American Sign Language.* New York: Harper & Row Publishers, 1987.

Weaks, Donna Gadling. *Lift Up Your Hands.* Vol. 2, *Favorite Songs with Sign Language Interpretation.* Washington, D.C.: National Grange, 1980.

Special Learners

Atterbury, Betty W. *Mainstreaming Exceptional Learners in Music.* Englewood Cliffs, N.J.: Prentice-Hall, 1990.

Cassidy, J.W., and W.L. Sims. "What's In a Name?" *General Music Today* 3 (3–1990). 23–24, 32.

Darrow, Alice-Ann. "Music for the Deaf." *Music Educators Journal* 71 (February 1985): 33–35.

Graham, Richard M., and Alice S. Beer. *Teaching Music to the Exceptional Child: A Handbook for Mainstreaming.* Englewood Cliffs, N.J.: Prentice-Hall, 1980.

Hughes, J.E. "Sing everyone." *General Music Today,* 4 (2–1991), 8–9.

Jellison, J.A. "A Content Analysis of Music Research with Handicapped Children and Youth (1975–1986): Applications in Special Education." In C.K. Furman (ed.), *Effectiveness of Music Therapy Procedures: Documentation in Research and Clinical Practice* (pp. 223–279). Washington, D.C.: National Association for Music Therapy, 1988.

———. "Functional Value as Criterion for Selection and Prioritization of Nonmusic and Music Educational Objectives in Music Therapy." *Music Therapy Perspectives,* 1 (2–1983), 17–22.

———, B.H. Brooks, and A.M. Huck. Structure Small Groups and Music Reinforcement to Facilitate Positive Interactions and Acceptance of Severely Handicapped Students in Regular Music Classrooms." *Journal of Research in Music Education* 39 (1984), 322–333.

———. "Talking About Music: Interviews with Disabled and Nondisabled Children." *Journal of Research in Music Education,* 39 (1991), 322–333.

———. "Writing and Talking About Children with Disabilities. *General Music Today,* 4 (1–1990), 25–26.

Lam, Rita C., and Cecilia Wang. "Integrating Blind and Sighted Through Music." *Music Educators Journal* 68 (April 1982): 44-45.

Pennington, H.D. "Acceptance and Expectations of Disabled Students in Music Classes" *General Music Today* 5 (1–1991), 31.

Technology

JVC Video Anthology of World Music and Dance. Victor Company of Japan and Smithsonian/Folkways Recordings, 1991. Distributed by New England Networks, 61 Prospect Street, Montpelier, Vt. 05602

MetroGnomes' Music (MS-DOS, 640K, CGA, or better display, 3.5" or 5.25" drive, hard drive and sound card recommended). Fremont, Calif.: The Learning Co.

Note Play (MS-DOS/Windows, MIDI keyboard optional). Available through Educational Resource, Elgin, Ill.

Piano Works (MS-DOS, 640K, CGA, or better display, 3.5" or 5.25" floppy drive and hard drive, MIDI interface and keyboard). Bellevue, Wash.: Temporal Acuity Products.

Soloist (MS-DOS, 286K, Sound Blaster sound card, microphone). Ibis Software, available through Educational Resource, Elgin, Ill.

Vocal Development/Choral Music

Bartle, Jean Ashworth. *Lifeline for Children's Choir Directors.* Toronto: Gordon V. Thompson Music, 1988.

Cooksey, John M. *Working with the Adolescent Voice.* St. Louis: Concordia Publishing House, 1992.

Heffernan, Charles W. *Choral Music: Technique and Artistry.* Englewood Cliffs, N.J.: Prentice-Hall, 1982.

May, William V., and Craig Tolin. *Pronunciation Guide for Choral Literature.* Reston, Va.: Music Educators National Conference, 1987.

Rao, Doreen. *Choral Music Experience Education Through Artistry.* Vol. 1, *Artistry in Music Education;* Vol. 2, *The Artist in Every Child;* Vol. 5, *The Young Singing Voice.* New York: Boosey & Hawkes, 1987.

Swears, Linda. *Teaching the Elementary School Chorus.* Englewood Cliffs, N.J.: Prentice-Hall, 1984.

OPTIONS FOR SCHEDULING Grades K–5 (See p. 446 for Grade 6.)

FOR MUSIC SPECIALISTS Music Once a Week

9- or 12-month schools

UNIT 1	UNIT 2	UNIT 3	UNIT 4	UNIT 5	UNIT 6
CORE Lessons 1, 2, 4, 5	CORE Lessons 1, 2, 4, 5	CORE Lessons 1, 2, 4, 5	CORE Lessons 1, 2, 4, 5	CORE Lessons 1, 2, 4, 5	CORE Lessons 1, 2, 4, 5
Lesson 9 Review and Assessment (optional)	Lesson 9 Review and Assessment (optional)	Lesson 9 Review and Assessment (optional)	Lesson 9 Review and Assessment (optional)	Lesson 9 Review and Assessment (optional)	Lesson 9 Review and Assessment (optional)

IN ADDITION TO CORE LESSONS, CHOOSE FROM	
ACROSS THE CURRICULUM	Curriculum integration activities after CORE Lessons 1, 2, 4, 5
ENCORE	After each unit
CELEBRATIONS	Seasonal, holiday, patriotic songs to integrate into the units
MUSIC LIBRARY	Reading Anthology Song Anthology Choral Anthology (Grades 5 and 6) Listening Anthology Musicals

OUR AUTHORS RECOMMEND:

SEQUENCED INSTRUCTION for ONCE-A-WEEK LESSONS

TIME FRAME (36 weeks / 36 lessons)

- CORE Lessons 1, 2, 4, 5 in all six units in consecutive teaching order
- Review and Assessment—Lesson 9 in each unit (optional)
- Selections from ACROSS THE CURRICULUM, ENCORE, CELEBRATIONS, and MUSIC LIBRARY

FOR MUSIC SPECIALISTS Music Twice a Week

9- or 12-month schools

UNIT 1	UNIT 2	UNIT 3	UNIT 4	UNIT 5	UNIT 6
CORE Lessons 1, 2, 4, 5	CORE Lessons 1, 2, 4, 5	CORE Lessons 1, 2, 4, 5	CORE Lessons 1, 2, 4, 5	CORE Lessons 1, 2, 4, 5	CORE Lessons 1, 2, 4, 5
Non-CORE Lessons 3, 6, 7, 8	Non-CORE Lessons 3, 6, 7, 8	Non-CORE Lessons 3, 6, 7, 8	Non-CORE Lessons 3, 6, 7, 8	Non-CORE Lessons 3, 6, 7, 8	Non-CORE Lessons 3, 6, 7, 8
Lesson 9 Review and Assessment	Lesson 9 Review and Assessment	Lesson 9 Review and Assessment	Lesson 9 Review and Assessment	Lesson 9 Review and Assessment	Lesson 9 Review and Assessment

IN ADDITION, CHOOSE FROM	
ACROSS THE CURRICULUM	Curriculum integration activities after CORE Lessons 1, 2, 4, 5
ENCORE	After each unit
CELEBRATIONS	Seasonal, holiday, patriotic songs to integrate into the units
MUSIC LIBRARY	Reading Anthology Song Anthology Choral Anthology (Grades 5 and 6) Listening Anthology Musicals

OUR AUTHORS RECOMMEND:

SEQUENCED INSTRUCTION for TWICE-A-WEEK LESSONS

TIME FRAME (36 weeks / 72 lessons)

- CORE and Non-CORE lessons in all six units in consecutive teaching order
- Selected activities from *Meeting Individual Needs* sections of lesson
- Review and Assessment—Lesson 9 in each unit
- Selections from ACROSS THE CURRICULUM, ENCORE, CELEBRATIONS, and MUSIC LIBRARY

TO ORGANIZE TEACHING BY SPECIFIC THEMES, SEE THE *THEMATIC* INDEX AT THE BACK OF THIS BOOK.

OPTIONS FOR SCHEDULING

FOR CLASSROOM TEACHERS Grades K–5
9- or 12-month schools

UNIT 1	UNIT 2	UNIT 3	UNIT 4	UNIT 5	UNIT 6
CORE Lessons 1, 2, 4, 5 ▶ Basic Program activities	CORE Lessons 1, 2, 4, 5 ▶ Basic Program activities	CORE Lessons 1, 2, 4, 5 ▶ Basic Program activities	CORE Lessons 1, 2, 4, 5 ▶ Basic Program activities	CORE Lessons 1, 2, 4, 5 ▶ Basic Program activities	CORE Lessons 1, 2, 4, 5 ▶ Basic Program activities

IN ADDITION TO CORE LESSONS, CHOOSE FROM

ACROSS THE CURRICULUM	Curriculum integration activities after CORE Lessons 1, 2, 4, 5
ENCORE	After each unit
CELEBRATIONS	Seasonal, holiday, patriotic songs to integrate into the units
MUSIC LIBRARY	Reading Anthology Song Anthology Choral Anthology (Grades 5 and 6) Listening Anthology Musicals

OUR AUTHORS RECOMMEND:
SEQUENCED INSTRUCTION for ONCE-A-WEEK LESSONS

TIME FRAME (36 weeks / 36 lessons)

- Basic Program activities shown with ▶ symbol from CORE Lessons 1, 2, 4, 5 in all six units in consecutive teaching order
- Selections from Non-CORE lessons, ACROSS THE CURRICULUM, ENCORE, CELEBRATIONS, and MUSIC LIBRARY

FOR CLASSROOM TEACHERS Grade 6
9- or 12-month schools

CORE UNIT 1 Music Makers	UNIT 2 Musical Adventures	UNIT 3 The Keyboard Connection	UNIT 4 Our Musical Heritage	UNIT 5 On Stage
CORE Lessons 1–8 ▶ Basic Program activities	CORE Lessons 1, 2, 4, 5 ▶ Basic Program activities	CORE Lessons 1, 2, 4, 5 ▶ Basic Program activities	CORE Lessons 1, 2, 4, 5 ▶ Basic Program activities	CORE Lessons 1, 2, 4, 5 ▶ Basic Program activities

IN ADDITION TO CORE LESSONS, CHOOSE FROM

UNIT 6 FROM RAG TO RAP	Eras of American music history
ACROSS THE CURRICULUM	Curriculum integration activities after CORE lessons
ENCORE	After each unit
CELEBRATIONS	Seasonal, holiday, patriotic songs to integrate into the units
MUSIC LIBRARY	Reading Anthology Song Anthology Choral Anthology (Grades 5 and 6) Listening Anthology Musicals

OUR AUTHORS RECOMMEND:
SEQUENCED INSTRUCTION for ONCE-A-WEEK LESSONS

TIME FRAME (36 weeks / 36 lessons)

- Basic Program activities shown with ▶ symbol from CORE lessons in Units 1–5 in consecutive teaching order
- Selections from Unit 6, Non-CORE lessons, ACROSS THE CURRICULUM, ENCORE, CELEBRATIONS, and MUSIC LIBRARY

Basic Program activities for classroom teachers can be taught with a minimum background in music.

TO ORGANIZE TEACHING BY SPECIFIC THEMES, SEE THE *THEMATIC INDEX* AT THE BACK OF THIS BOOK.

OPTIONS FOR SCHEDULING Grade 6 (See p. 444 for Grades K–5.)

FOR ELEMENTARY OR MIDDLE SCHOOL MUSIC SPECIALISTS
9- or 12-month schools

CORE UNIT 1 Music Makers	UNIT 2 Musical Adventures	UNIT 3 The Keyboard Connection	UNIT 4 Our Musical Heritage	UNIT 5 On Stage
CORE Lessons 1–8	CORE Lessons 1, 2, 4, 5	CORE Lessons 1, 2, 4, 5	CORE Lessons 1, 2, 4, 5	CORE Lessons 1, 2, 4, 5
ALSO INCLUDE FOR TWICE A WEEK OR DAILY				
	Non-CORE Lessons 3, 6, 7, 8	Non-CORE Lessons 3, 6, 7, 8	Non-CORE Lessons 3, 6, 7, 8	Non-CORE Lessons 3, 6, 7, 8
Lesson 9 Review and Assessment	Lesson 9 Review and Assessment	Lesson 9 Review and Assessment	Lesson 9 Review and Assessment	Lesson 9 Review and Assessment

IN ADDITION, CHOOSE FROM	
UNIT 6 FROM RAG TO RAP	Eras of American music history
ACROSS THE CURRICULUM	Curriculum integration activities after CORE lessons
ENCORE	After each unit
CELEBRATIONS	Seasonal, holiday, patriotic songs to integrate into the units
MUSIC LIBRARY	Reading Anthology Song Anthology Choral Anthology Listening Anthology Musicals

FOR SEQUENCED INSTRUCTION, OUR AUTHORS RECOMMEND:

FOR ELEMENTARY MUSIC SPECIALISTS

TIME FRAME (twice a week, 36 lessons per semester)

- Unit 1 lessons in consecutive teaching order
- CORE lessons in Units 2–5 in consecutive teaching order
- Review and Assessment, Lesson 9, in Units 1–5
- Selections from Unit 6, ACROSS THE CURRICULUM, ENCORE, CELEBRATIONS, and MUSIC LIBRARY
- Selected activities from *Meeting Individual Needs* sections of lessons

FOR MIDDLE SCHOOL MUSIC SPECIALISTS

TIME FRAME (daily, 45 lessons per 9-week course)

- Unit 1 lessons in consecutive teaching order
- CORE lessons in Units 2–5 in consecutive teaching order
- Selected Non-CORE lessons in Units 2–5
- Review and Assessment, Lesson 9, in Units 1–5
- Selections from Unit 6, ACROSS THE CURRICULUM, ENCORE, CELEBRATIONS, and MUSIC LIBRARY
- Selected activities from *Meeting Individual Needs* sections of lessons

FOR MIDDLE SCHOOL MUSIC SPECIALISTS

TIME FRAME (daily, 90 lessons per semester)

- Unit 1 lessons in consecutive teaching order
- CORE and Non-CORE lessons in Units 2–5 in consecutive teaching order
- Review and Assessment, Lesson 9, in Units 1–5
- Selections from Unit 6, ACROSS THE CURRICULUM, ENCORE, CELEBRATIONS, and MUSIC LIBRARY
- Selected activities from *Meeting Individual Needs* sections of lessons

For Grades 7 and 8: The Grade 6 book can be used flexibly in Grades 7 and 8.

TO ORGANIZE TEACHING BY SPECIFIC THEMES, SEE THE *T*HEMATIC INDEX AT THE BACK OF THIS BOOK.

THEMATIC INDEX

CLASSIFIED INDEX

Velez, Glen, 89
Warner, Malcolm-Jamal, 278
Williams, Mary Lou, 133

poets
Burns, Robert, 319
Carroll, Lewis, 391
de la Mare, Walter, 298
George, Phil, 168
Giovanni, Nikki, 302
Greenfield, Eloise, 236
Horne, Frank, 90
Johnson, Georgia Douglas, 46
Millay, Edna St. Vincent, 146
O'Shaughnessy, Arthur, 1
Updike, John, 110

Body Percussion. *See* Creative
Activities; Duration/Rhythm; Ostinatos;
Playalong Accompaniments

Canons. *See* Rounds/Canons

Careers

arranger
Jones, Quincy, 36
Williams, Mary Lou, 133

composer
Bach, Johann Sebastian, 103
Bagley, E. E., 13
Bárdos, Lajos, 343
Bartók, Béla, 395, 413I
Beethoven, Ludwig van, 413C
Berlin, Irving, 189, 238
Besig, Don, 65, 296
Bizet, Georges, 232
Britten, Benjamin, 298
Cage, John, 123
Carmichael, Hoagy, 95
Chopin, Frédéric, 109
Cohan, George M., 226
Coleman, Cy, 192
Davis, Mac, 55
Denver, John, 322
Dylan, Bob, 259
Ellington, Duke, 246
Ficksman, Judith E., 413K
Gabrieli, Giovanni, 413B
Gershwin, George, 195
Gillespie, Avon, 334
Grieg, Edvard, 78
Hamlisch, Marvin, 202
Handel, George Frideric, 362
Haydn, Franz Joseph, 112, 113
Jacquet de la Guerre, Elisabeth-Claude, 97
Jagoda, Flory, 303
Jennings, Carolyn, 389
Jennings, Teresa, 2
Kaplan, Artie, 92
Lloyd Webber, Andrew, 204–205
MacGregor, Laura, 345
Miller, Steve, 265
Monk, Thelonious, 124
Morrison, Van, 24
Mozart, Wolfgang Amadeus, 60, 99
Offenbach, Jacques, 56
Orff, Carl, 42
Peterson, Oscar, 105
Ponce, Manuel María, 326
Porter, Cole, 190
Puccini, Giacomo, 212
Rimsky-Korsakov, Nicolai, 28–29
Rodgers, Richard, 115

Saint-Saëns, Camille, 62
Scarlatti, Domenico, 119
Sondheim, Stephen, 198
Sousa, John Philip, 144
Torroba, Federico Moreno, 220
Vaughan Williams, Ralph, 160, 413G
Velez, Glen, 89
Wagner, Richard, 413F
Williams, John, 138
Williams, Linda, 141
Williams, Mary Lou, 133
Wilson, Mark, 147
Wilson, Sandy, 196–197
Winter, Paul, 324
Wolf, Hugo, 358
Wood, Dale, 307
Zwilich, Ellen Taaffe, 410

concert violinist
Salerno-Sonnenberg, Nadja, 411

drummer
Roach, Max, 134
Velez, Glen, 89

folk musician
Bagheri, Hooshang, 317

guitarist
Memphis Minnie, 132

lyricist, 191
Comden, Betty, 192
Green, Adolph, 192
Hart, Lorenz, 115
Key, Francis Scott, 292
Knox, Jane Foster, 147
Price, Nancy, 296
Sondheim, Stephen, 198

other
disc jockey, 243
guitar maker, 253
music journalist, 199
piano tuner-technician, 93
sound engineer, 282

pianist
Donegan, Dorothy, 133
Jarrett, Keith, 135
Labèque, Katia and Marielle, 125
Marsalis, Ellis, 114
Williams, Mary Lou, 133

pop singer
Houston, Whitney, 50

record producer
Warner, Malcolm-Jamal, 278

songwriter
Davis, Mac, 55

Choral Music. *See* Part Songs

Chords
building, 172–173
changes
identifying, 244
listening for, 32, 332
chord roots, 31, 162–163, 164–165,
172–173, 176–177, 206, 319, 348
definition, 30
guitar
A minor, 272
A7, 260–261
C G D, 256
D G A, 252, 253
E minor, 266–267
review, 256, 260, 266, 272, 277
inverted, 176–177
I–V, 31, 162–163, 164–165

I–IV–V, 177, 178, 206
playing, 126, 174, 319
reading, 277

Classroom Instruments. *See*
Instruments, Playing

Classroom Management
"Battle Hymn," jazz version, 295
concert behavior, 410
creating a melody, 182
following the listening map, 413A, 413C,
413E, 413G, 413I, 413K
form identification problems, 64
musicals, staging, 414–423
part singing, 348
performing in fugal style, 119
projection of lines, 421
soft-shoe sound effect, 385
substitute instruments, 288
triplet eighth notes, 374
vocal ostinatos, 304
writing dialogue, 84

Clefs
bass, 124–125, 148, 165, 198, 355, 376
treble, 19, 124

Composers. *See* Biographies; Listening
Selections

Conducting
$\frac{2}{4}$, 344
$\frac{3}{4}$, 353
$\frac{4}{4}$, 386

Cooperative Learning
accompaniment patterns, 74
arranging songs, 36
composing a melody, 126
creating movement, 45, 68, 137
designing a production, 83
El Capitán, 145
form, listening for, 262
improvising accompaniments, 41
improvising the blues, 245
interpretation of One, 224
melodic bass line, 178
minimalist music, 123
special learners, 6, 58
writing rondeau poem, 61

Creative Activities. *See also*
Dramatizations/Pantomimes; Instruments,
Making; Performance, For
arranging a song, 36
art or construction, 43, 76–77, 81, 131, 133,
175, 219, 285, 293, 324, 359
body percussion, 16–17, 141
choreography, 4–5, 41, 45, 69, 185, 199, 223,
227, 278–279, 318, 386
composing, 122, 224
A B A form, 85
melodies, 126, 136, 183, 209, 351
creating song interpretations, 225
melodies, improvising, 317
moving to show concept or element
augmentation and diminution, 342
bass line, 95
beat, 3, 313
chord changes, 32
contrast and repetition, 2
contrasting sections, 413F
descending scale, 56
form, 6, 68–69, 262

snare drum, 8–9, 39
steel drums, 32
string bass, 5
synthesizer, 104
tambourine, 88
trombone, 5, 8–9, 38–39
trumpet, 5
tuba, 8–9
ukulele, 165

Instruments, Making,
86–87, 122, 276–277, 313, 421

Instruments, Playing. *See also*
Playalong Accompaniments; the booklets
Orchestrations for Orff Instruments, Playing the Guitar, Playing the Recorder, under separate cover
bass guitar, 259
bells, 25, 31, 62, 100, 136–137, 148, 173, 206, 209, 336, 363
body percussion, 299, 360, 364
classroom, 22, 31, 34, 36, 41, 52, 56, 81, 109, 162–163, 177, 178, 181, 188–189, 284–285, 297, 363, 366
drums, 57, 335
guitar, 32, 54, 75, 81, 154, 158, 162, 174, 176, 206, 207, 252, 260–261, 266–267, 272, 277, 347, 352, 413C
handbells, 174
keyboard, 80, 94, 100, 103, 126–127, 128–129, 173, 206, 209, 252, 286, 413D
Orff, 24, 31, 57, 59, 67, 142, 298, 307, 333, 334, 339, 340, 341, 364, 366, 369
percussion, 404
percussion, barred, 25, 174
percussion, unpitched, 11, 13, 15, 33, 75, 88, 107, 144, 157, 160, 162–163, 203, 233, 239, 241, 248, 289, 299, 310, 329, 347
pitched, 305, 341, 344, 351, 371
prepared piano, 122
rain sticks, 276
recorder, 14, 18, 22, 26, 30, 34, 46, 50, 52, 54, 62, 66, 69, 73, 90, 98, 106, 107, 110, 136, 146, 158, 162, 174, 188, 196, 204, 208, 242, 246, 258, 264, 277, 286, 294, 302, 306, 322, 333, 334, 336, 339, 340, 344, 347, 349, 365, 367
ukulele, 165

Keyboard. *See* Instruments, Playing

Limited English-Proficient Students. *See* Non-English Language Selections

Limited Tone Songs
four-tone
Hotaru Koi (*mi so la ti*), 333
I Got a Letter (*la, do re mi*), 341
pentatonic
De allacito carnavalito (The Carnival Is Coming), 342
Eskimo Ice Cream Dance, 335
Fung Yang Song, 20
Keep the Circle Going 'Round, 420
Orion, 350
Shady Grove, 367
three-tone
Old Ark's A-Moverin' (*do re mi*), 332
Tee galop pour Mamou (Gallop On to Mamou) (*do re mi*), 107

Listening Maps. *See also* Listening Map Transparencies, under separate cover

in pupil book
Alla turca from Piano Sonata in A Major, K. 331 by W. A. Mozart, 61
Anitra's Dance from *Peer Gynt Suite No. 1* by E. Grieg, 79
Ecce gratum (excerpt) from *Carmina Burana* by C. Orff, 45
Fantasia on Greensleeves by R. Vaughan Williams, 160–161
Muss i denn, (German March), 9
Sonata in G Minor ("The Cat's Fugue") by D. Scarlatti (general), 119

in Resource Masters
Battle Hymn of the Republic, The, played by the Monty Alexander Trio, C•1
Capriccio espagnol (excerpt) by N. Rimsky-Korsakov, 1•9
Sonata in G Minor ("The Cat's Fugue") by D. Scarlatti (detailed), 3•4

in Teacher's Edition and Resource Masters
Amoeba by J. E. Ficksman (LA•6), 413K–413L
Concerto for Orchestra, Second Movement ("Game of Pairs"), by B. Bartók (LA•5), 413I–413J
Jubilate Deo by G. Gabrieli (LA•1), 413A–413B
Ride of the Valkyries from *Die Walküre* by R. Wagner (LA•3), 413E–413F
Seventeen Come Sunday from *English Folk Song* Suite by R. Vaughan Williams (LA•4), 413G–413H
Symphony No. 5 in C Minor Op. 67, First Movement, by L. van Beethoven (LA•2), 413C–413D

Listening Selections
by composer
Bach: Prelude in A Minor, 102
Bagley: National Emblem, 13
Bartók: Concerto for Orchestra, Second Movement, 413I
Beethoven: Symphony No. 5 in C Minor, Op. 67, First Movement, 413C
Bizet: *Carmen* (excerpts), 232
Cage: Three Dances for Two Amplified Prepared Pianos (excerpt), 123
Carmichael: Heart and Soul, 94
Chopin: Mazurka, Op. 68, No. 3, 109
Dupri: Jump, 279
Ficksman: Amoeba, 413K
Gabrieli: Jubilate Deo, 413A
Gershwin: Summertime from *Porgy and Bess,* 195
Gould: American Salute, 411
Grieg: Anitra's Dance from *Peer Gynt Suite No. 1,* 79
Haydn: Trio No. 39 Finale ("Gypsy Rondo"), 113
Hirsh: Bashana Haba'ah, 318
Jacquet de la Guerre: Rondeau, 96
Jarrett: Montage of Performance Styles, 135
Lennon and McCartney: Birthday, 263
Makeba: Pata Pata, 187
Mendelssohn: Violin Concerto in E Minor Op. 64, Third Movement, 411
Monk: Brilliant Corners, 134
Monk: Rhythm-a-ning, 125
Mozart: Alla turca from Sonata in A major, 60
Offenbach: Cancan from *Gaité parisienne,* 56

Orff: Ecce gratum (excerpt) from *Carmina Burana,* 44
Ponce: Música Indígena, 327
Puccini: Firenze è come un albero fiorito from *Gianni Schicchi,* 214
Puccini: *Gianni Schicchi* (opening scene), 213
Puccini: Ladro! Ladro! from *Gianni Schicchi,* 215
Puccini: O mio babbino caro from *Gianni Schicchi,* 215
Purcell: Canon, 52
Rimsky-Korsakov: Capriccio espagnol (excerpt), 29
Roberts: Two-Chord Rock, 277
Rodgers and Hart: This Can't Be Love, 115
Saint-Saëns: Tortoises from *The Carnival of the Animals,* 63
Samite: Kakokolo, 120
Sands: Tune in a CAGe, 53
Scarlatti: Sonata in G Minor ("The Cat's Fugue"), 119
Sousa: El Capitán, 145
Stilgoe and Lloyd Webber: I Am the Starlight, 208
Stilgoe and Lloyd Webber: The Light at the End of the Tunnel, 210
Stilgoe and Lloyd Webber: Pumping Iron, 205
Stilgoe and Lloyd Webber: Starlight Express, 207
Thiago de Mello: Uirapurú Do Amazonas, 276
Torroba: De este apacible rincón from *Luisa Fernanda,* 220
Vaughan Williams: Fantasia on Greensleeves, 160
Vaughan Williams: Seventeen Come Sunday from *English Folk Song Suite,* 413G
Wagner: Ride of the Valkyries from *Die Walküre,* 413E
Williams: Liberty Fanfare (excerpt), 139
Zwilich: Celebration for Orchestra, 411
by title
Alla turca from Sonata in A major by W. A. Mozart, 60
American Salute by M. Gould, 411
Amoeba by J. Ficksman, 413K
Amores hallarás, 186
Anitra's Dance from *Peer Gynt Suite No. 1* by E. Grieg, 79
Bashana Haba'ah by N. Hirsh, 318
Battle Hymn of the Republic, The, played by the Monty Alexander Trio, 294
Birthday by J. Lennon and P. McCartney, 263
Blues Montage, A, 134
Bo Hai Huan Ten, 313
Brilliant Corners by T. Monk, 134
Cancan from *Gaité parisienne* by J. Offenbach, 56
Canon by H. Purcell, 52
Capriccio espagnol (excerpt) by N. Rimsky-Korsakov, 29
Carmen (excerpts) by G. Bizet, 232
Celebration for Orchestra by E. Zwilich, 411
Concerto for Orchestra, Second Movement ("Game of Pairs"), by B. Bartók, 413I
De este apacible rincón from *Luisa Fernanda* by F. Torroba, 220

Literature. *See* Alphabetical Index of Literature

Mainstreaming. *See* Special Learners

Meet (interviews with musicians). *See* Biographies; Recorded Interviews

Melody. *See* Pitch

Meter. *See* Duration/Rhythm; Pitch and Rhythm Index

MIDI. *See* Technology

Minor/Modal Songs

Motive
definition, 150, 208, 229, 413D
listening for, 209, 229
melodic, 43, 150, 208–209, 413D

Movement. *See also* Creative Activities; Dramatizations/Pantomimes

Style

Baroque
  English, 52, 362
  French, 96
  German, 102
  Italian, 119
bebop, 251
blues, 134, 243, 244
boogie woogie, 250
Broadway musical, 190–191, 229
calypso, 347, 365
carols, 301
Classical
  Austrian, 60, 113
  German, 413C–413D
chanteys, 352
comparing, 220–221
country and western, 264, 268
disco, 264
electronic, 413K–413L
folk. See Folk Music; Multicultural Materials
gospel, 116
heavy metal, 264
jazz, 114, 115, 125, 134, 238, 247, 294
kathakali, 216
kudiyattam, 216
Lied, 357
listening for, 134, 375
march, 9, 13, 145
Medieval, English, 184
musical theater, 211, 233
  American, 195
  Balinese, 219
  English, 205, 207, 208, 210
  South Indian, 216
  Spanish, 220
Native American music, 166, 171, 330, 335
new age, 324
new wave, 270
opera, 195, 212–213, 214, 233, 413F
orchestral. See Instrumental/Vocal Ensembles
popular music, 275
popular. See also Pop Music, Past/Present
  American, 53, 94, 244, 248, 252, 256, 260, 267, 272
  English, 262
  ragtime, 110–111, 238
rap, 274, 278
Renaissance
  English, 158, 337
  German, 336
  Italian, 413A
rock 'n' roll, 14, 254–255, 258, 277, 280
Romantic
  French, 56, 63, 232
  German, 411, 413E–413F
  Italian, 213
  Norwegian, 79
  Polish, 109
  Russian, 29
samba, 10
spiritual, African American, 30, 58, 76, 117, 154, 332, 334, 339, 354, 370, 407
survey, 246–247
twentieth century
  American, 123, 139, 411, 413K–413L

English, 160, 205, 207, 208, 210, 413G–413H
German, 44
Hungarian, 413I–413J
Italian, 213–215
Mexican, 327
wayang kulit, 218
world music, 276
zarzuela, 220

Technology. See also Music Ace, MusicTime; and Share the Music videos, referenced in the Unit openers

Music with MIDI
Alleluia, 98
De colores, 328
Drill, Ye Tarriers, 363
Give My Regards to Broadway, 226
Greensleeves, 158
John B. Sails, 347
Joshua Fit the Battle of Jericho, 58
Old Joe Clark, 396
Scarborough Fair, 366
Walk Together, Children, 30

other
computers, 271, 413L
discussing, 48
electric guitar, 257
MIDI, 270
performance, 280–283
sound system, 283
synthesizer, 105, 277

Tempo
accelerando, 303
choosing, 196–197, 198–199, 224–225, 226, 231, 329, 352, 380
listening for, 44, 210, 214–215, 222–223, 230, 259, 331, 367, 375
rubato, 108

Texture
added parts, 309
arrangements, 36
body percussion, 75, 299
changing, 75
choosing, 297, 380
countermelody, 27
definition, 28, 74
fugue, 118
harmonic accompaniments, 174, 177
identifying, 76, 342
instrumental accompaniment, 31, 93
listening for, 28–29, 34, 76–77, 97, 125, 167, 173, 303, 305, 307, 311, 337, 394
stringed instruments, 28
vocal, 71

Theater. See Curriculum Integration, drama

Theme
orchestral, 413D
rondo, 60–61, 112

Tone Color. See also Instruments, Identifying; Instruments, Playing; Recorded Lessons
choosing, 220, 380

definition, 5
drums, 89
electric organ, 116
identifying, 116
instrumental, 4, 6
keyboard, 96, 112, 115, 129, 130
listening for, 44, 115, 259
piano, 116
prepared piano, 122
sand block, 383
soprano saxophone, 325
stringed instruments, 27
vocal, 167
  choosing, 196–197, 198–199, 220, 224–225, 226, 231, 297, 329
  countertenor, 413B
  describing, 206–207
  identifying, 205
  listening for, 197, 209, 213, 214–215, 222–223, 229, 230
  Russian singers, 325
  speaking voice, 189
  voice types, 214

Visual Arts. See Fine Art Reproductions and Architecture

Vocal Development
articulation, 191, 192–193, 195, 198, 396
  legato, 193, 287
breathing, 66
  for chest voice, 154
  exercise, 408
caring for the voice, 204
countermelody, 20
dynamics, 298, 394–395
enunciation, 70, 298, 400
intonation, 298
matching pitch, 102
posture and breathing, 1G
pronunciation
  Latin, 337, 338
ranges, 7
  identifying, 194–195, 229, 230
  listening for, 234
ranges, developing, 388
ranges, expanding, 158–159, 398
relaxation and posture, 407
relaxed jaw, 406
shaping vowel sounds, 98
singing in marcato style, 196
singing in tune, 140
style, 246
upward leaps, 48
vocal flexibility, 404–405
vocal models, 116
vocal range, 409
vocalises for wide leaps, 390

Whole Language. See Curriculum Integration

Writing Notation
chords, 30, 224
melodic notation, 24, 123, 126, 131, 183, 224
notating compositions, 85, 224
notating Native American music, 167
pitch letter names, 24, 123, 209
rhythm patterns, 16, 33, 41, 141, 143, 155

PITCH AND RHYTHM INDEX

The Pitch and Rhythm Index provides a listing of songs for teaching specific rhythms or pitches. Songs that use only the rhythms or pitches under the heading are labeled *entire*. Specific measure numbers are indicated in parentheses when the rhythms or pitches apply to part of a song. The letter *a* indicates that the anacrusis to the measure is included.

Pitch Index: The pitch index is organized by teaching sequence. Within each category, the pitch sets are arranged alphabetically.

Rhythm Index: The headings in the rhythm index are listed by duration, from shortest to longest. Rhythms in § meter are grouped together at the end of the index. Other known rhythms used in the specified measures are listed after the meter signature of each entry.

Pitch

RE

do re mi

Boatman, The (entire), 332
Haji Firuz (1–4, 17–20), 317
Harmony (descant) (1–6, 9–14), 92
Old Ark's A-Moverin' (entire), 332
Tee galop pour Mamou (entire), 107

do re mi so

Kakokolo (1–8), 121
Trav'ler (a17–20), 147

do re mi so la

A Zing-a Za (a9–16), 11
Walk Together Children (1–8), 30

SO₁

so₁ do

Hoe Ana (cambiata) (entire), 164

so₁ do re mi

Gypsy Rover, The (a1–2, 10–11), 346

so₁ do re mi so

Please, Don't Cut Down the Trees (a42–50), 418

LA₁

la₁ do re mi

I Got a Letter (entire), 341

la₁ do re mi so

Fung Yang Song (9–15), 21

so₁ la₁ do

Lean on Me (a25–26, a29–30), 126
Yonder Come Day (Part 3) (entire), 154

so₁ la₁ do re mi

Accentuate the Positive (a1–2, 5–10, 13–16, 25–26, 29–32), 6
I Believe in Music (a6–9), 54
Yonder Come Day (Part 1) (1–3, 5–8), 154

so₁ la₁ do re mi so

You Sing for Me (a17–28), 27

so₁ la₁ do re mi so la

Auld Lang Syne (entire), 319

DO'

do re mi so la do'

Shady Grove (entire), 367
A Zing-a Za (a9–17), 11

la₁ do mi so la do'

Every Mornin' When I Wake Up (entire), 334

la₁ do re mi so la do'

De allacito carnavalito (The Carnival Is Coming) (entire), 342
Orion (entire), 350

so₁ do re mi so do'

Day-O (3–4, 9–18, 21–31), 32

so₁ la₁ do re mi so la do'

Fung Yang Song (entire), 20

MI₁

mi₁ so₁ la₁ do re mi

Eskimo Ice Cream Dance (entire), 335

mi₁ so₁ la₁ do re mi so la

Keep the Circle Going 'Round, (entire) 420

FA

do re mi fa so

El tambor (The Drum) (a5–9, a14–17), 142
Harmony (1–6, 9–14), 92
Lion Sleeps Tonight, The (melody) (entire), 348
O Canada (Part 1) (1–4, a9–12), 290
Hoe Ana (descant) (entire), 164
Old Joe Clark (Part 1) (1–8), 396
Old Joe Clark (Part 2) (1–25, 34–97), 396
Siyahamba (We Are Marching) (a6–10), 310

do re mi fa so la

Alleluia (1–8), 98
America (7–14), 287
Dona Nobis Pacem (9–16), 338
I Believe in Music (17–32) (entire), 54
Island in the Sun (melody) (5–12, 17–24), 364
Lobster Quadrille, The (1–5, 21–25, 103–105, a118–123), 390
Look Around (melody) (1–3, 5–8, 11–14, 19–22, a25–28), 192
Music for the World (1–4, 9–12), 34
O Canada (1–4, a9–14, 17–20), 290
Oh, How Lovely Is the Evening (entire), 336

do re mi fa so la do'

Lobster Quadrille, The (1–5, 21–32, 57–71, 97–105, a116–129), 390

la₁ do mi fa so la

Said I Wasn't Gonna Tell Nobody (entire), 117

mi fa so

Yonder Come Day (Part 2) (entire), 154

mi fa so la ti do'

America (descant) (entire), 287

so₁ do re mi fa so

Gypsy Man, The (Part 1) (entire), 394
I Shall Sing (refrain) (entire), 24
John B. Sails (melody) (a1–7, 9–10, 16–22, 25–26), 347
Lion Sleeps Tonight, The (a5–16), 348
Star-Spangled Banner, The (a29–32), 292
Where Does It Come From? (1–7, a13–15, a21–31), 414

so₁ do re mi fa so la

El zapatero (The Shoemaker) (melody) (a9–33), 404

so₁ la₁ do re mi fa so

Garden of the Earth (entire), 325
Gypsy Rover, The (entire), 346
Movin' On (entire), 174
Nobody Knows the Trouble I've Seen (entire), 334
Siyahamba (We Are Marching) (entire), 309
You Sing for Me (Part 1) (a17–32), 26
Wind Beneath My Wings, The (1–11, 13–27, 29–31, 45–55), 385

TI

do re mi fa so la ti do'

A Zing-a Za (entire), 11
Come, Follow Me! (1–8), 337
Here Come the Earth Kids (1–16), 423
Music for the World (1–16), 34
Shall I Dream a Dream? (Part 1) (1–8, 17–20, 25–28, 33–36, 41–52), 380
Trav'ler (a11–24), 147

do re mi fa so la ti do' re'

Flying Free (entire), 64

do re mi fa so la ti do' re' mi'

Here Come the Earth Kids (entire), 423
Hymn to Freedom (entire), 104
Jubilate Deo (entire), 336

do re mi fa so la ti do' re' mi' fa'

Come, Follow Me! (entire), 337
Silent Night (Stille Nacht) (entire), 306

la₁ ti₁ do re mi fa

Si me dan pasteles (When You Bring Pasteles) (entire), 304

la₁ ti₁ do re mi fa so la

Autumn Canon (entire), 343

PROGRAM CONSULTANTS

Contributing Writer
Janet McMillion
St. Louis, MO

Consultant Writers
Teri Burdette, Signing
Gaithersburg, MD

Brian Burnett, Movement
Toledo, OH

Robert Duke, Assessment
Austin, TX

Joan Gregoryk,
Vocal Development/Choral
Washington, D.C.

Judith Jellison,
Special Learners/Assessment
Austin, TX

Jacque Schrader, Movement
Annapolis, MD

Kathy B. Sorensen,
International Phonetic Alphabet
Salt Lake City, UT

Mollie Tower, Listening
Austin, TX

Consultants
Lisa DeLorenzo, Critical Thinking
Upper Montclair, NJ

Nancy Ferguson, Jazz/Improvisation
Somerville, TN

Judith Nayer, Poetry
New York, NY

Marta Sanchez, Dalcroze
Pittsburgh, PA

Mollie Tower, Reviewer
Austin, TX

Robyn Turner, Fine Arts
Austin, TX

Multicultural Consultants
Judith Cook Tucker
Danbury, CT

JaFran Jones
Bowling Green, OH

Oscar Muñoz
Olympia, WA

Marta Sanchez
Pittsburgh, PA

Edwin J. Schupman, Jr.,
of ORBIS Associates
Spokane, WA

Mary Shamrock
Northridge, CA

Kathy B. Sorensen
Salt Lake City, UT

Visual and Performing Arts Contributors
Barbara Becker, Visual Arts
Los Angeles, CA

Karen Goodkin, Visual Arts
San Francisco, CA

David Robinson, Theater
Stockton, CA

Arlene Shmaeff, Visual Arts
Oakland, CA

Sue Walton, Theater
San Francisco, CA

Ancillary Contributors
Angela Broeker, Resource Masters
New Wilmington, PA

Teri Burdette, Signing
Gaithersburg, MD

Cindy Hall, Recorder
Whitefish Bay, WI

Jo Ella Hug, Recorder
Missoula, MT

Eleanor T. Locke, Songs to Sing and Read
Oakland, CA

Jerry Snyder, Playing the Guitar
Monte Sereno, CA

Patti Windes-Bridges, Playing the Guitar
Cave Creek, AZ

Lesson Contributors
Our thanks to these music educators for their contributions of classroom-tested lessons, materials, and strategies.

Sylvia Arieta (El Paso, TX), Margie King Barab (New York, NY), Patti Beckham (Lake Oswego, OR), Nancy Boone (Murfreesboro, TN), Ruth Boshkoff (Bloomington, IN), Madeline S. Bridges (Nashville, TN), Jay Broeker (New Wilmington, PA), Susanne Burgess (Memphis, TN), Randy DeLelles (Las Vegas, NV), Virginia Ebinger (Los Alamos, NM), Carol Erion (Alexandria, VA), Rhona Ewbank (Pasadena, TX), Cindy Hall

(Whitefish Bay, WI), Ruth Pollock Hamm (Mayfield, OH), Carol Huffman (North Olmsted, OH), Sarah Kastendieck (Fort Collins, CO), Susan Kennedy (San Francisco, CA), Robert Kikuchi-Yngojo (San Francisco, CA), Laura Koulish (New York, NY), Jeff Kriske (Las Vegas, NV), Judy Mahoney-Green (Albuquerque, NM), David Means (Northfield, MN), Karen Medley (Memphis, TN), Ellen Mendelsohn (New Milford, NJ), Isabel Miranda (Oxnard, CA), Janet L. S. Moore (Tampa, FL), Grace Nash (Tallahassee, FL), Konnie Saliba (Cordova, TN), Vicky Salmon (Pasadena, CA), Marcelyn Smale (St. Cloud, MN), Anna Marie Spallina (New York, NY), Todd Thompson (Northfield, MN), Wendy Ulmer (Woolrich, ME), Joy Yelin (Yonkers, NY), Alexis A. Zolczer (Orchard Park, NY)

Across the Curriculum Contributors
Our thanks to these teachers for their classroom-tested Across the Curriculum activities.

Patti Beckham (Lake Oswego, OR), Brenda Cook (Bakersfield, CA), Mary Jo Gardere (Dallas, TX), Elaine Hewes (Blue Hill, ME), Carol Huffman (North Olmsted, OH), Jane Livingston (Veazie, ME), Alice Bremer Moersch (Northfield, MN), Marilyn Moore (Normal, IL), Diane De Nicola Orlofsky (Troy, AL), Mary Sturbaum (Bloomington, IN)

Listening Map Contributors
Our thanks to these Texas educators for contributing listening maps to *Share the Music*.

Marilyn Buckner, Debra Erck, Kay Greenhaw, Rebecca Grusendorff, Melody A. Long, Sally K. Robberson, Diane Bethea Steele, Barb Stevanson, Debbie Tannert

National Music Advisory Committee
Our thanks to these music specialists, classroom teachers, and administrators for their valuable contributions in the development of *Share the Music*.

Betty Adkins (Shreveport, LA), Susan Ahmad (Alpharetta, GA), Carol Albright (Holidaysburg, PA), Earl Alexander (Lake Charles, LA), George Alter (Kansas City, MO), Claude Anderson (East Chicago, IN), Kathy Anderson (Mt. View, CA), Thom Antang (Campbell, CA), Christine Aparicio-Chaulsett (Los Angeles, CA), Sylvia Arieta (El Paso, TX), Saundra Ashworth (San Antonio, TX), Missy Atterbury (Edmond, OK), Eleanor Avant (Columbia, SC), Patti Beckham (Lake Oswego, OR), Sue Bertsche (Chicago, IL), Maureen Best (Chatham, IL), Patsy Biendenfield (Houston, TX), Ron Blackgrave (Indianapolis, IN), Victor Bobetsky (Hartford, CT), Judy Boelts (Fairbanks, AK), Earlene Brasher (Decatur, GA), Pat Brown (Knoxville, TN), Teddye Brown (Arlington, TX), Bruce Brumley (Mt. Sterling, KY), Bryan Burton (West Chester, PA), Doris Butler (Florence,

KY), Bettie Carroll (Dayton, OH), Jo Ellen Clow (Broken Arrow, OK), Deborah Cook (Roselle, NJ), Nancy Cox (Altus, OK), Robert Crisp (Detroit, MI), Don Davis (Jacksonville, AR), William Downes (Louisville, KY), Neiltje Dunham (Nashua, NH), Mary Frances Early (Atlanta, GA), Donya Easterly (Clear Creek, TX), Marie Esquibel (Albuquerque, NM), Laura Floyd-Cole (Carson, CA), Renée Forrest (Madison, WI), Enrique Franco (Los Angeles, CA), Sister Pat Gilgum (St. Louis, MO), Michelle Goady (Dallas, TX), Cathy Graham (Antioch, TN), Brian Halverson (San Antonio, TX), Katherine Heide (Kenosha, WI), Debbie Hess (Bloomington, IN), Peggy Horner (Altoona, PA), Anne-Marie Hudley (Bronx, NY), Karen Huff (Granville, OH), Jo Ella Hug (Missoula, MT), Janice Hupp (Wichita, KS), Joan Jemison (Minneapolis, MN), Steven Johns (Nokomis, FL), Sandy Jude (Winchester, KY), Nancy Kielian-Boyd (East Grand Rapids, MI), Dorothy Kittaka (Ft. Wayne, IN), Tom Kosmala (Pittsburgh, PA), Margaret B. LaFleur (Minneapolis, MN), Guido Lavorata (Chandler, AZ), Joanne Lawrence (Ellicott City, MD), Brenda Lucas (Lexington, KY), Lana Manson (Chicago Heights, IL), Doug Martin (Atlanta, GA), Sheridan Matheison (Lexington, MA), Cindy McCaskill (Boulder, CO), Sherry McKelfresh (Ft. Collins, CO), Dorothy Millard (Skokie, IL), Clayton Miller (New Rochelle, NY), Ruth Millner (Dallas, TX), Violeta Morejon (Miami, FL), Jim Morris (Athens, GA), Denise Moulton (Richardson, TX), Sharon Munson (Delavan, WI), Kathleen Myers (Altoona, PA), Darolyne Nelson (Tempe, AZ), Hal Nelson (Tampa, FL), Larita Owens (Topeka, KS), Mary Ozanne (Plano, TX), Paula Pheasant (Tyrone, PA), Josephine Poelinitz (Chicago, IL), Pam Price (Grapevine, TX), Yolanda Rippetoe (San Antonio, TX), Marcia Rober (Arlington, TX), Joe Royster (Lake City, FL), Juyne Sauer (Houston, TX), Ruth Sauls (Austin, TX), Kathleen Shepler (Louisville, KY), Linda Singleton (Nashville, TN), Gloria Sousa (Monterey, CA), Gwen Spells (Marietta, GA), Sue Stanger (Los Angeles, CA), Gwendolyn Staten (Indianapolis, IN), Doris Stewart (Muncie, IN), Judy Svengalis (Des Moines, IA), Rose Marie Terada (Boulder, CO), Doris Terry (Macon, GA), Jean Thomas (Chattanooga, TN), Bonnie Thurston (Santa Cruz, CA), Doug Turpin (St. Louis, MO), Robert Ullom (Columbus, OH), Dianne Vernon (Dallas, TX), Barbara Waite (Evansville, IN), Mamie Watson (San Antonio, TX), Timothy Waugh (Bluefield, WV), Craig Welle (Houston, TX), Jo Welty (Amarillo, TX), Joann Whorwell (Kokomo, IN), Euranie Williams (Dallas, TX), Tobizena Williams (Dallas, TX), Charles W. Winslow, Jr. (Richardson, TX), Melinda Winther (Spokane, WA), Mary Wright (Omaha, NE), Pam Ziegler (Austin, TX)

Multicultural Advisors

Dennis Waring, Ethnomusicologist, Wesleyan University, Middletown, CT

Shailaja Akkapeddi (Hindi), Edna Alba (Ladino), Gregory Amobi (Ibu), Thomas Appiah (Ga, Twi, Fanti), Deven Asay (Russian), Vera Auman (Russian, Ukrainian), David Azman (Hebrew), Lissa Bangeter (Portuguese), Britt Marie Barnes (Swedish), Dr. Mark Bell (French), Brad Ahawanrathe Bonaparte (Mohawk), Chhanda Chakroborti (Hindi), Ninthalangsonk Chanthasen (Laotian), Julius Chavez (Navajo), Lin-Rong Chen (Mandarin), Anna Cheng (Mandarin), Rushen Chi (Mandarin), T. L. Chi (Mandarin), Michelle Chingwa (Ottowa), Hoon Choi (Korean), James Comarell (Greek), Lynn DePaula (Portuguese), Ketan Dholakia (Gujarati), Richard O. Effiong (Nigerian), Nayereh Fallahi (Persian), Angela Fields (Hopi, Chemehuevi), Gary Fields (Lakota, Cree), Siri Veslemoy Fluge (Norwegian), Katalin Forrai (Hungarian), Renee Galagos (Swedish), Linda Goodman, Judith A. Gray, Savyasachi Gupta (Marati), Elizabeth Haile (Shinnecock), Mary Harouny (Persian), Charlotte Heth (Cherokee), Tim Hunt (Vietnamese), Marcela Janko (Czech), Raili Jeffrey (Finnish), Rita Jensen (Danish), Teddy Kaiahura (Swahili), Gueen Kalaw (Tagalog), Merehau Kamai (Tahitian), Richard Keeling, Masanori Kimura (Japanese), Chikahide Komura (Japanese), Saul Korewa (Hebrew), Jagadishwar Kota (Tamil), Sokun Koy (Cambodian), Craig Kurumada (Balkan), Cindy Trong Le (Vietnamese), Dongchoon Lee (Korean), Young-Jing Lee (Korean), Nomi Lob (Hebrew), Sam Loeng (Mandarin, Malay), Georgia Magpie (Comanche), Mladen Marič (Croatian), Kuinise Matagi (Samoan), Hiromi Matsushita (Japanese), Jackie Maynard (Hawaiian), David McAllester, Ellen McCullough-Brabson, Mike Kanathohare McDonald (Mohawk), Khumbulani Mdlefshe (Zulu), Martin Mkize (Xhosa), David Montgomery (Turkish), Kazadi Big Musungayi (Swahili), Professor Akiya Nakamara (Japanese), Edwin Napia (Maori), Hang Nguyen (Vietnamese), Richard Nielsen (Danish), Wil Numkena (Hopi), Eva Ochoa (Spanish), Drora Oren (Hebrew), Jackie Osherow (Yiddish), Mavis Oswald (Russian), Dr. Dil Parkinson (Arabic), Kenny Tahawisoren Perkins (Mohawk), Alvin Petersen (Sotho), Phay Phan (Cambodian), Charlie Phim (Cambodian), Aroha Price (Maori), Marg Puiri (Samoan), John Rainer (Taos Pueblo, Creek), Lillian Rainer (Taos Pueblo, Creek, Apache), Winton Ria (Maori), Arnold Richardson (Haliwa-Saponi), Thea Roscher (German), Dr. Wayne Sabey (Japanese), Regine Saintil (Bamboula Creole), Luci Scherzer (German), Ken Sekaquaptewa (Hopi), Samouen Seng (Cambodian), Pei Shin (Mandarin), Dr. Larry Shumway (Japanese), Gwen Shunatona (Pawnee, Otoe, Potawatomi), Ernest Siva (Cahuilla, Serrano [Maringa']), Ben Snowball (Inuit), Dr. Michelle Stott (German), Keiko Tanefuji (Japanese), James Taylor (Portuguese), Shiu-wai Tong (Mandarin), Tom Toronto (Lao, Thai), Lynn Tran (Vietnamese), Gulavadee Vaz (Thai), Chen Ying Wang (Taiwanese), Masakazu Watabe (Japanese), Freddy Wheeler (Navajo), Keith Yackeyonny (Comanche), Liming Yang (Mandarin), Edgar Zurita (Andean)

ACKNOWLEDGMENTS

Grateful acknowledgment is given to the following authors, composers, and publishers. Every effort has been made to trace the ownership of all copyrighted material and to secure the necessary permissions to reprint these selections. In the case of some selections for which acknowledgment is not given, extensive research has failed to locate the copyright holders.

Hooshang Bagheri for *Haji Firuz.* Copyright © Hooshang Bagheri.

Elizabeth Barnett for *Travel* by Edna St. Vincent Millay. From COLLECTED POEMS, HarperCollins. Copyright 1921, 1948 by Edna St. Vincent Millay. Reprinted by permission of Elizabeth Barnett, literary executor.

Irving Berlin Music Company for *Alexander's Ragtime Band* by Irving Berlin, page 239. Copyright © 1911 by Irving Berlin. Copyright Renewed. International Copyright Secured. Used by Permission. All Rights Reserved. For *There's No Business Like Show Business* by Irving Berlin, page 188. Copyright © 1946 by Irving Berlin. Copyright renewed. International Copyright Secured. Used by Permission. All Rights Reserved.

Boosey & Hawkes, Inc. for *Autumn Canon* by L. Bardos. © Copyright 1933 by Magyar Korus, Budapest; Copyright Renewed. Copyright & Renewal assigned 1950 to Editio Musica Budapest. Reprinted by permission of Boosey & Hawkes, Inc. English translation © Sean Deibler. For *Concerto for Orchestra* by Béla Bartók. Copyright © 1946 by Hawkes & Son (London) Ltd. Copyright Renewed. Reprinted by permission of Boosey & Hawkes, Inc. For *The Lobster Quadrille* by Carolyn Jenkins. © 1990 by Boosey & Hawkes, Inc. Reprinted by permission. For *Old Abram Brown.* Text by Walter de la Mare from TOM TIDDLER'S GROUND. Music by Benjamin Britten. © Copyright 1936 by Boosey & Co., Ltd.; Copyright Renewed. Reprinted by permission of Boosey & Hawkes, Inc. For *Old Joe Clark,* arr. by Mary Goetze. © 1984 by Boosey & Hawkes, Inc. Reprinted by permission. For *Seventeen Come Sunday* from ENGLISH FOLK SONG SUITE by Ralph Vaughan Williams. Copyright © 1924 by Boosey & Co. Ltd. Copyright renewed. Reprinted by permission of Boosey & Hawkes, Inc.

Cherio Corp. for *Bandstand Boogie,* Words by Barry Manilow and Bruce Sussman, Music by Charles Albertine. © 1954 (Renewed), 1975 CHERIO CORP. All Rights Reserved. Used by Permission.

Cherry Lane Music Publishing Company, Inc. for *Day-O* by Irving Burgie and William Attaway. ©1955, Renewed 1983 Cherry Lane Music Publishing Company, Inc./Lord Burgess Music Publishing Co. This Arrangement © 1994 Cherry Lane Music Publishing Company, Inc./Lord Burgess Music Publishing Co. For *Earth Day Every Day (Celebrate)* by John Denver. Copyright © 1990 Cherry Mountain Music (ASCAP). International Copyright Secured. All Rights Reserved.

CPP/Belwin, Inc. for *Carol from an Irish Cabin* by Dale Wood. Copyright © 1970 by BELWIN-MILLS PUB. CORP., c/o CPP/BELWIN, INC., Miami, FL 33014. International Copyright Secured. Made in U.S.A. All Rights Reserved. For *Every Morning When I Wake Up* by Avon Gillespie. Copyright © 1976 BELWIN MILLS PUBLISHING CORPORATION. All Rights Assigned to and Controlled by BEAM ME UP MUSIC. International Copyright Secured. Made in USA. All Rights Reserved. Used by Permission of CPP/BELWIN, INC., P.O. Box 4340, Miami, FL 33014. For *From a Distance* by J. Gold. © 1987 WING AND WHEEL MUSIC & JULIE GOLD MUSIC (BMI). All Rights Administered by IRVING MUSIC, INC. (BMI). International Copyright Secured. Made in USA. All Rights Reserved. For *The Greatest Love of All* by Michael Masser and Linda Creed. Copyright © 1977 by GOLD HORIZON MUSIC CORP., A Division of Filmtrax Copyright Holdings Inc. and GOLDEN TORCH MUSIC CORP., A Division of Filmtrax Copyright Holdings Inc. International Copyright Secured. Made in USA. All Rights Reserved. For *It Don't Mean a Thing (If It Ain't Got That Swing),* D. Ellington & I. Mills. © 1932 (Renewed 1960) Mills Music, Inc., c/o EMI MUSIC PUBLISHING, worldwide print rights controlled by CPP/BELWIN, INC., Miami, FL 33014. Used by Permission. All Rights Reserved. For *Trav'ler* by Mark Foster and Jane Foster Knox. Copyright © 1988 Studio 224, Inc., c/o CPP/BELWIN, INC., Miami, FL 33014. International Copyright Secured. Made in USA. All Rights Reserved. For *A Voice from a Dream* by Joyce Elaine Eilers. Copyright © 1976 Schmitt Music Center, Inc., c/o CPP/BELWIN, INC., Miami, FL 33014. International Copyright Secured. Made in USA. All Rights Reserved.

Sean Deibler for *Autumn Canon* by L. Bardos. © Copyright 1933 by Magyar Korus, Budapest; Copyright Renewed. Copyright & Renewal assigned 1950 to Editio Musica Budapest. Reprinted by permission of Boosey & Hawkes, Inc. English translation © Sean Deibler.

Judith E. Ficksman for *Amoeba,* Copyright © 1992 by Judith E. Ficksman, New York. All Rights Reserved.

Flat Town Music Co. for *Tee galop pour Mamou.* © 1990 Flat Town Music Co.

Geordie Music Publishing Co. for *Shady Grove.* © 1952 Jean Ritchie, Geordie Music Publishing Co.

Pamela Gillilan for *Haiku Calendar* by Pamela Gillilan. Copyright © Pamela Gillilan.

HarperCollins Publishers for *Way Down in the Music,* text only, from HONEY, I LOVE by Eloise Greenfield. Text Copyright © 1978 by Eloise Greenfield.

Harwin Music Co. for *Ac-cent-tchu-ate the Positive.* Lyric by Johnny Mercer. Music by Harold Arlen. © 1944 (Renewed) HARWIN MUSIC CO. All Rights Reserved. Used By Permission.

Mary E. Hay for *Kettle Valley Line* by Ean Hay. Used by permission.

Hinshaw Music, Inc. for *American Dream* by Ed Harris. Copyright © 1988 by Hinshaw Music, Inc. Reprinted by permission. For *Keep Your Lamps!* Copyright © 1982 by Hinshaw Music, Inc. For *Shall I Dream a Dream?* by Julie Knowles. Copyright © 1990 by Hinshaw Music, Inc. Reprinted by permission.

House of Bryant Publications for *Rocky Top* by Boudleaux Bryant and Felice Bryant. © 1967 HOUSE OF BRYANT Publications, P.O. Box 570, Gatlinburg, TN 37738. International Copyright Secured. Made in U.S.A. All Rights Reserved.

Flory Jagoda for *Ocho Kandelikas* by Flory Jagoda. © 1981 Flory Jagoda.

Mattie Catherine Johnson for *Love Letter to America* by Mattie Catherine Johnson. © 1992 Mattie Catherine Johnson.

Alfred A. Knopf, Inc. for *Player Piano* from THE CARPENTERED HEN AND OTHER TAME CREATURES by John Updike. Copyright 195. by John Updike. Reprinted by permission of Alfred A. Knopf, Inc.

Jeff Kriske for *The Old Ark's A-Moverin'* (Orff arrangement of spiritual). Copyright © Jeff Kriske.

Little, Brown and Company for *The Tortoise* from VERSES FROM 1929 ON by Ogden Nash. Copyright 1950 by Ogden Nash. Copyright © renewed 1977 by Frances Nash, Isabel Nash Everstadt, and Linell Nash Smith. First appeared in The New Yorker. By permission of Little, Brown and Company.

Living Earth Music for *Garden of the Earth.* Words by Paul Winter and Paul Halley, arr. by Dimitri Pokrovsky. © 1987 Living Earth Music (BMI).

Laura MacGregor for *Spring Rain* by Laura MacGregor. © 1987 Laura MacGregor.

McLain Family Music for *You Sing for Me* by Raymond McLain, McLain Family Music, BMI.

MCA Music Publishing for *Boogie Woogie Bugle Boy.* Words and Music by DON RAYE AND HUGHIE PRINCE. © Copyright 1940, 1941 by MCA MUSIC PUBLISHING, A Division of MCA, INC., 1755 Broadway, New York, NY 10019. Copyright renewed. Rights administered by MCA MUSIC PUBLISHING, A Division of MCA, INC. USED BY PERMISSION. ALL RIGHTS RESERVED. For *The Old Piano Roll Blues* by Cy Coben. © Copyright 1949 by Leeds Music. All rights administered by MCA MUSIC PUBLISHING, A Division of MCA, INC. New York, NY 10019.

William Morrow & Co., Inc. for *Winter Poem* from MY HOUSE by Nikki Giovanni. Text copyright © 1972 by Nikki Giovanni. By permission of William Morrow & Co., Inc.

Music Sales Corporation for *Blowin' in the Wind*, Music & Lyrics by Bob Dylan. Copyright © 1962 Warner Bros. Copyright renewed 1990 Special Rider Music. International Copyright Secured. All Rights Reserved. Used by Permission. For *El Zapatero* from CANCIONES DE LOS NIÑOS compiled by Carl S. Miller. Copyright © 1978 by Shawnee Press, Inc. (ASCAP). International Copyright Secured. All Rights Reserved. Used by permission. For *Flying Free* by Don Besig. Copyright © 1979 Shawnee Press, Inc. (ASCAP). International Copyright Secured. All Rights Reserved. For *Carifalia*, compiled by Susan and Ted Alevizos. Used by Permission of Oak Publications, a division of Music Sales Corporation (ASCAP). International Copyright Secured. All Rights Reserved. For *The Ghost Ship* from REFLECTIONS OF A LAD AT SEA. Music by Don Besig, Lyrics by Don Besig & Nancy Price. Copyright © 1982 Shawnee Press, Inc. International Copyright Secured. All Rights Reserved. Used by Permission. For *Movin' On* by Raymond R. Hannisian. Copyright © 1969 Malcolm Music (BMI). International Copyright Secured. All Rights Reserved.

Myers Music Corp. and Golden Rule Music Admin. Ltd. for *Rock Around the Clock* by Max Freedman and Jimmy DeKnight. Copyright © 1952 (Renewed) 1980 Myers Music Corp. & Capano Music Company. All Rights Reserved. Used by Permission.

Plank Road Publishing, Inc. for *Dancin' on the Rooftop* by Teresa Jennings. © 1992 Plank Road Publishing, Inc. All Rights Reserved. For *I Have a Dream* by Teresa Jennings. © 1990 Plank Road Publishing, Inc. All Rights Reserved. For *Tune in a CAGe* by Norm Sands. © 1991 Plank Road Publishing. All Rights Reserved.

Plymouth Music Co., Inc. for *The Gypsy Man* (aka *The Highwayman*) by Béla Bartók, arr. Benjamin Suchoff. Copyright © 1969, 1980 Plymouth Music Co., Inc., 170 N.E. 33rd Str., Ft. Lauderdale, FL 33334.

Revelation Music Publishing Corp. & Rilting Music, Inc. for *Our Time* by Stephen Sondheim from MERRILY WE ROLL ALONG. Copyright 1981, 1983 and 1984 by Revelation Music Publishing Corp. & Rilting Music, Inc. A Tommy Valando Publication. International Copyright Secured. Made in U.S.A. All Rights Reserved.

Samite Music Company for *Kakokolo* by Samite. Copyright © 1988 Samite Music Company.

Shapiro, Bernstein & Co., Inc. for *Royal Garden Blues* by Clarence Williams and Spencer Williams. Copyright MCMXIX Shapiro, Bernstein & Co., Inc., New York. Copyright renewed. Used by Permission. For *Soft Shoe Song* by Roy Jordan and Sid Bass. © 1951 Shapiro, Bernstein & Co., Inc., New York. Renewed. Used By Permission.

Norman Simon Music for *Harmony* by Artie Kaplan and Norman J. Simon © 1972. Reprinted courtesy of Thrice Music, Inc., and Norman Simon Music, a division of Ennanden Prod. Inc.

Kathy B. Sorensen for *Diwali Song*, *Hoe Ana*, and *Tsing Chun U Chü*, collected and transcribed by Kathy B. Sorensen. © 1991 Kathy B. Sorensen.

Sundance Music for *Away to America* by Linda Worsley. Copyright © 1983 Sundance Music.

Thrice Music, Inc. for *Harmony* by Artie Kaplan and Norman J. Simon © 1972. Reprinted courtesy of Thrice Music, Inc., and Norman Simon Music, a division of Ennanden Prod. Inc.

Tomi Music Co., Inc. for *Hymn to Freedom* by Oscar Peterson and Harriette Hamilton. Copyright © 1963, 1989 by Oscar Peterson, Harriette Hamilton.

Warner Bros. Publications Inc. for *Another Op'nin', Another Show* by Cole Porter. © 1949 (Renewed) Chappell & Co. (ASCAP). All Rights Reserved. Used by Permission. For *Bamboo* by Dave Van Ronk. © 1962 (Renewed) PEPAMAR MUSIC CORP. All Rights Reserved. Used by Permission. For *Comedy Tonight* by Stephen Sondheim. © 1962 (Renewed) Stephen Sondheim (ASCAP) Burthen Music Co., Inc. (ASCAP) Owner of Publication and Allied Rights Throughout the World, Chappell & Co. (ASCAP) Sole Selling Agent. All Rights Reserved. Used by Permission. For *Fly Like an Eagle*. Words and Music by Steve Miller. © 1976 SAILOR MUSIC. All Rights Reserved. Used by Permission. For *I Believe in Music* by Mac Davis. © 1970, 1972 SCREEN GEMS-EMI MUSIC INC. & SONGPAINTER MUSIC. All Rights Reserved. Used by Permission. For *I Shall Sing* by Van Morrison. © 1970 WB Music Corp. & Caledonia Soul Music. All Rights Reserved. Used by Permission. For *Lean on Me* by Bill Withers. © 1972 INTERIOR MUSIC (BMI). All Rights Reserved. International Copyright Secured. Used by Permission. For *Look Around*. Music by Cy Coleman. Lyrics by Betty Comden and Adolph Green. Copyright © 1991 NOTABLE MUSIC CO., INC. and BETDOLPH MUSIC COMPANY. All Rights administered by WB MUSIC CORP. From the Musical Production THE WILL ROGERS FOLLIES. All Rights Reserved. Used by Permission. For *One Moment in Time* (words only) by Albert Hammond and John Bettis. Copyright © 1987 ALBERT HAMMOND MUSIC & JOHN BETTIS MUSIC (ASCAP). All Rights on behalf of ALBERT HAMMOND MUSIC for the World excluding U.K./Eire, PRS territories & Japan Administered by WB MUSIC CORP. All Rights on behalf of JOHN BETTIS MUSIC for the World excluding Japan Administered by WB MUSIC CORP. All Rights Reserved. Used by Permission. For *The Wind Beneath My Wings* by Larry Henley and Jeff Silbar. Copyright ©

1982 WARNER HOUSE OF MUSIC & WB GOLD MUSIC CORP. All Rights Reserved. Used by permission. For *Won't You Charleston with Me* (words only) by Nancy Wilson. Copyright by Chappell & Co. All Rights Reserved. Used by permission.

World Music Press for *Amores Hallarás*, traditional choreography by Elizabeth Villareal, from a SINGING WIND: FIVE MELODIES FROM ECUADOR. Copyright © 1988 World Music Press. Used by permission. For *Si Me Dan Pasteles*. © 1986 Alejandro Jimenez/World Music Press, P.O. Box 2565, Danbury, CT 06813. Used by permission. For *Yonder Come Day*, lyrics by Judith Cook Tucker. ©1985 World Music Press/Judith Cook Tucker.

Wren Music Co. and American Compass Music Corp. for *One* from A CHORUS LINE, Music by Marvin Hamlisch, Lyric by Edward Kleban. © 1975 MARVIN HAMLISCH and EDWARD KLEBAN. All Rights Controlled by WREN MUSIC CO. and AMERICAN COMPASS MUSIC CORP. All Rights Reserved. Used by Permission.

James Zimmerman for *Orion* by James Zimmerman. © 1972 James Zimmerman. All Rights Reserved.

COVER DESIGN: Designframe Inc., NYC

COVER PHOTOGRAPHY: Jade Albert for MMSD

Cover Set Design by Mark Gagnon Synthesizer courtesy of Kurzweil Music System/Young Chang America, Inc. Stand courtesy of Ultimate Support System, Inc.

ILLUSTRATION
Unit Planner Logo Art: Zita Asbaghi
Celebrations and Music Library Planner Art: Jenny Vainisi
Technology Logo: Menny Borovski
Movement Glossary Illustrations: Network Graphics

PHOTOGRAPHY
All photographs are by the Macmillan/McGraw-Hill School Division (MMSD) except as noted below.

Across the Curriculum Backgrounds: Scott Harvey for MMSD

Titus Kana for MMSD: 7A, 21A, 37A, 69B, 97A, 101B, 109A, 109B, 113A, 145B, 153A, 153B, 161B, 165B, 195A, 207A. Anne Nielsen for MMSD: xv (b.l. inset), 13A, 17A, 17B, 21B, 25B, 29B, 33B, 53A, 57B, 65A, 145A, 195B, 199B, 211A. Mark A. Philbrick for MMSD: xiv (b.). Robert Matheu/Retna Ltd.: xv (t.r.). Jim Stratford for MMSD: xiv (t.,m.).

ART **&** **P**HOTO **C**REDITS

COVER DESIGN: Designframe Inc., NYC

COVER PHOTOGRAPHY: Jade Albert for MMSD

Cover Set Design by Mark Gagnon
Synthesizer courtesy of Kurzweil Music System/Young Chang America, Inc. Stand courtesy of Ultimate Support System, Inc.

ILLUSTRATION
Steven Adler, 158-159, 190-191; Victoria Allen, 32-33; Don Baker, 180-181; Johanna Bandle, 284-285; George Baquero, 272-275; Andrea Baruffi, 78-79; Karen Bell, 200; Doron Ben-Ami, 84-85, 94-95; Steven Bennett, 64, 90, 176, 313-314, 316, 318-319; Robert Bergin, 212-213; Robert Burger, 226-227, 252-253; Dave Calver, 222-225; Ben Carter, 168-169; Harvey Chan, 140-141; Bradley Clarke, 66-67; Adam Cohen, 34-35; Sally Comport, 188-189; Margaret Cusack, 288-289; Jerry Dadds, 142-143; Tom Daly, 248-249; Jeanne de la Houssay, 86-89, 162-163; Brian Dugan, 172-173, 202-203; Andrea Eberbach, 24-25; Jon Ellis, 268-269; Kerna Erickson, 116-117; Cynthia Fitting, 302-303; Nancy Freeman, 82-83; Barbara Friedman, 36-37; Brad Gaber, 76-77; Chris Gall, 296-297; Linda Gist, 136-137; Joan Greenfield, 304-305; Ken Hamilton, 146-149; Janet Hamlin, 14-15; John Hart, 414-423; Ed Heins, 42-45; Eileen Hine, 164-165; Bill Hobbs, 150-153; Catherine Huerta, 166-167; Neal Hughes, 160-161; Susan Huls, 26-27, 198; Bruce Hutchinson, 206-207; Paul Jermann, 10-13; W.B. Johnston, 298-299; Mark Kaplan, 110-115, 210-211, 228; Greg King, 108-109; Mike Kowalski, 290-291; Elliot Kreloff, 126-127; Lingta Kung, 156-157; Roger Leyonmark, 242-243; Keith Lo Bue, 48-49, 100-101; Roberta Ludlow, 278-279; Fred Lynch, 276-277; Rob MacDougall, 254, 256-257; Scott MacNeill, 250-251; Vickie Maloney, 124-125; Barbara Maslen, 328-329; John Mattos, 132-135; Julia McLain, 244-245; Dave Miller, 326-327; Kristen Miller, 170-171; Jonathan Milne, 178-179; J.T. Morrow, 62-63, 260-265; Christy Mull, 8-9; Alan J. Nahigian, 6-7, 38-39, 238-239; Susan Nees, 128-131; Tom Nikosey, 232-235; Stephen Osborn, 18-19; Julie Pace, 286; Nan Parsons, 60-61; Rodica Prato, 324-325; Mike Radencich, 292-293; Melaine Reim, 30-31; Anna Rich, 0-1; Ronald Ridgeway, 258-259; Ray Roberts, 46-47; Christian Rodin, 16-17, 196-197; Barbara Roman, 52-53; Marlene Ruthen, 313, 315, 316, 317, 318, 319; Lissi Sigillo, 68-69; Peter Spacek, 118-119; Richard Sparks, 154-155; Sandra Speidel, 72-73; Victor Stabin, 208-209; Tom Starace, 112-113; Jim Starr, 322-323, 410-411; Gary Symington, 40-41; David Taylor, 144-145; Joseph Taylor, 184-187, 306-307; Juan Tenorio, 246-247; Leyla Torres, 174-175; Jenny Vainisi, 56-57; Mei Wang, 20-21; Elsa Warnick, 64-65; Vicki Wehrman, 58-59, 70-71; Peter Wells, 22-23; Dean Williams, 236-237; David Wisniewski, 218-219; Ted Wright, 192-194; Deborah Yellen, 74-75; Jeff York, 194-195.

Tech Art by TCA Graphics, Inc.

PHOTOGRAPHY
All photographs are by the Macmillan/McGraw-Hill School Division (MMSD) except as noted below.

i: instruments, Jim Powell Studio for MMSD. iv-v: instruments, Jim Powell Studio for MMSD. vi: t.l. instruments, Jim Powell Studio for MMSD. **Unit 1** 2: t. Bill Waltzer for MMSD. 4-5; Institute of Jazz Studies/Rutgers University. 8: Tony Stone Images. 10: Luis Villota/Stock Market. 13: Doug Bryant. 16-17: Morton Tadder/Archive Photos. 28-29: William Waterfall/Stock Market. 32-33: Dave Bartruff. 37: Edie Baskin/Onyx. 42: British Library, ADD Ms 18851. folio 184V. 43: The Bettmann Archive. **Unit 2** 50-51: Edie Baskin/Onyx. 51: b.r. Chuck Jackson Photo; t.r. Nick Elgar/London Features International. 54: t.r. Chris Michaels/FPG; t.l. Superstock. 56: Philadelphia Museum of Art: The Henry P. McIlhenny Collection in memory of Frances P. McIlhenny. 60: Scala/Art Resource. 76-77: t. Richard Kelly for MMSD. 77: b. © 1993 Craig Molenhouse. 80-81: b. Karen Meyers for MMSD; t. Jim Powell Studio for MMSD. 87, 88: Bill Waltzer for MMSD. 89: Glenn Velez. **Unit 3** 90-91: Scala/Art Resource. 92-93: Karen Meyers for MMSD. 95: Church Organ: Metropolitan Museum of Art, Purchase, Margaret M. Wess Gift, in memory of her father, John B. McCarty, 1982 (1982.54). 96: Metropolitan Museum of Art, The Crosby Brown Collection of Musical Instruments 1884 (1982.54). 96-97: l. Steinway & Sons. 97: r. Courtesy Yamaha International, Keyboards Division. 99: Giraudon/Art Resource; b. FPG. 102-103: Bridgeman/Art Resource. 104: t. Yamaha Corporation of America. 104-105: b. The Bettmann Archive. 107: Sydney Byrd. 109: Scala/Art Resource. 110-111: QRS Music Rolls Inc., Buffalo, NY. 112: Art

Resource. 113: Metropolitan Museum of Art, Gift of Geraldine C. Herzfeld, in memory of her late husband, Monroe Eliot Hemerdinger, 1984. 114: Steve Pumphrey/Onyx. 116: Lisa Seifert. 120: Gerald Bourin/Explorer. 120-121: British Museum. 122, 123: John Cage/Artservices/Lovely Music. 125: M. Rosenstiehl/Sygma. 128: b. Ken Karp for MMSD; t. QRS Music Rolls Inc., Buffalo, NY. 129: b. Karen Meyers for MMSD; t. Giraudon/Art Resource. 130: l. Tony Freeman/PhotoEdit; r. Steinway & Sons. 132: Hooks Bros. © Michael Ochs Archives/Memphis Music & Blues Museum. 133: t. Michael Ochs Archives; b. American Stock/Archive Photos. 134, 135: Gene Martin. **Unit 4** 143: Tom & Michele Grimm/International Stock. 162-163: Jim Powell Studio for MMSD. 165: Ken Karp for MMSD. 167: Mark A. Philbrick for MMSD. 168-169: Mark Lagerstrom. 170-171: Kevin King. 172, 173: Karen Meyers for MMSD. 175: David Muench. 177: Karen Meyers for MMSD. 181: r. Tom Owen Edmunds/The Image Bank; m. Jack Vartoogian; l. Bob Daemmrich/Stock Boston. 182: Phyllis Picardi/International Stock Photography, Ltd. 184: Musée National des Arts et Traditions Populaire © R.M.N. 185: Carol Simowitz. 186: M.L./Retna Ltd. 187: t. Blair Seitz/Photo Researchers, Inc.; b. Douglas Mason/Woodfin Camp & Associates, Inc. **Unit 5** 190-191: The Kobal Collection/Superstock. 196-197: Springer/The Bettmann Archive. 199: The Kobal Collection/Superstock. 203: Ron Scherl © 1982. 204-205, 207, 210-211: Martha Swope. 212: The Granger Collection. 213: The Bettmann Archive. 214, 215: Ron Scherl. 216-217: Ian Berry/Magnum. 217: inset Art Resource. 220: Jack Vartoogian. 221: t.l. Jack Vartoogian; t.r. Ron Scherl/The Bettmann Archive; m.r. Wu Gang/Gamma Liaison; b.l. Lee Snider/Photo Images. 228: l. E.J. Camp/Outline; r. Steve Granitz/Retna Ltd. 229: Obremski/The Image Bank. 230-231: Karen Meyers for MMSD. 232: Culver Pictures. 233, 234-235: The Bettmann Archive. **Unit 6** 238: The Granger Collection. 241: Bill Waltzer for MMSD. 243: Michael Ochs Archives. 246: t.l. Woody Guthrie Publications; b.r. Michael Ochs Archives. 247: Frank Driggs Collection. 252: Bill Waltzer for MMSD. 254: Culver Pictures. 255: Michael Ochs Archives. 258: t.l., b.l. Photofest; m.l. Brown Brothers; b.l. inset, m.r. NASA; t.r. Star File Photos; b.r. Photoworld/FPG International. 259: t.l., m.l., b.l., b.r., b.m. Photofest; t.r. The King Collection/Retna Ltd.; m.b. Star File Photos; t.m. James Pickerell/Black Star. 262: Zimmerman/FPG. 266: Bill Waltzer for MMSD. 270: Deborah Feingold/Outline Press. 271: F. Reglain/Gamma Liaison. 272-273: Jim Powell Studio for MMSD. 278: Bill Bernstein/Outline. 279: Kriss Kross/Outline. 280-281: Michael Putland/Retna Ltd.; t. DOD Electronics. 282-283: Stills/Retna Ltd.; t. DOD Electronics. **Celebrations** 286: Bill Hickey/The Image Bank. 288: l. A. Perez Bourse; r. Walter H. Hodge/Peter Arnold. 300-301, 304, 305: Nancy Palubniak for MMSD. 308: Chester Higgins, Jr./New York Times. 308-309 bkgnd., 310-311 bkgnd.: David Young-Wolff/PhotoEdit. 311: r. *Family* by Charles Alston, Collection of Whitney Museum of American Art, New York/Photography by Bill Jacobson, N.Y. 313: By permission of the Chinese Music Society of North America, Chicago, U.S.A. 314: l. Air India Library; r. Ken Karp for MMSD. 316: Bob Krist for MMSD. 318: Richard T. Nowitz. 320: The Bettmann Archive. 321: Flip Schulke/Black Star. 324: t. Tate Gallery/Art Resource; b. Ben Simmons/Paul Winter Consort/Living Music. 326: Black Star. 328: Bob Daemmrich Photos. 330: The Image Bank. 331: Tony Freeman/PhotoEdit. **Music Library** 410: Britain Hill Photography. 411: Christian Steiner. 412: r. Art Resource. 412-413: t. Courtesy The Selmer Company; b. Hutschenreuther U.S.A. 413: l. © 1946 by Hawkes & Son (London) Ltd. Copyright renewed. Reprinted by permission of Peter Bartok and Bela Bartok, Jr. and Boosey & Hawkes, Inc.; r. MMSD. 424: t. The Bettmann Archive; m. Herb Snitzer Photography; b.l. Ken Karp for MMSD.

Macmillan/McGraw-Hill School Division thanks The Selmer Company, Inc., and its Ludwig/Musser Industries and Glaesel String Instrument Company subsidiaries for providing all instruments used in MMSD photographs in this music textbook series, with exceptions as follows. MMSD thanks Yamaha Corporation of America for French horn, euphonium, acoustic and electric guitars, soprano, alto, and bass recorders, piano, and vibraphone; MMB Music Inc., St. Louis, MO, for Studio 49 instruments; Rhythm Band Instruments, Fort Worth, TX, for resonator bells; Courtly Instruments, NY, for soprano and tenor recorder; Elderly Instruments, Lansing, MI, for autoharp, dulcimer, hammered dulcimer, mandolin, Celtic harp, whistles, and Andean flute.

438

THEMATIC CORRELATIONS TO READING SERIES

Macmillan/McGraw-Hill: *Spotlight on Literacy* © 1997

The following materials from Share the Music may be used with each unit in Macmillan/McGraw-Hill's Spotlight on Literacy.

THEMATIC CORRELATIONS TO READING SERIES

Macmillan/McGraw-Hill: *Spotlight on Literature* © 1997

The following materials from Share the Music may be used with each unit in Macmillan/McGraw-Hill's Spotlight on Literature.

UNIT 1 • Living and Learning. *Learning experiences can lead to new understanding and insights. In school, students study math and social studies. But they also learn about who they are and how they fit in.*

Accentuate the Positive, 6
Family (painting), 311
Flying Free, 64
Greatest Love of All, The, 271
I Believe in Music, 54
I Shall Sing, 24
Lean on Me, 126
Navajo Courtship Song (listening), 167
One Moment in Time, 49
Our Time, 222
We Are the Music Makers (excerpt) (poem), 1
Wind Beneath My Wings, The, 385
You Sing For Me, 26

UNIT 2 • Quests. *Finders and seekers experience a sense of awe at the wonders of our world. Any valuable discovery is worth the effort to find it.*

American Dream, 151
Fly Like an Eagle, 265
Garifalia, 372
I Have a Dream, 320
John B. Sails, 347
Light at the End of the Tunnel, The, from *Starlight Express* by R. Stilgoe and A. Lloyd Webber (listening), 210
One Moment in Time, 49
Orion, 350
Our Time, 22
Shall I Dream a Dream?, 380
Trav'ler, 147
Travel (poem), 146
Voice from a Dream, A, 375

UNIT 3 • Determination. *Self-assurance and determination will help you achieve the seemingly impossible. An unflagging belief in yourself and your own abilities can make even the most difficult goal achievable.*

Comedy Tonight, 198
Follow the Drinkin' Gourd, 370
I Have a Dream, 320
I Shall Sing, 24
Keep Your Lamps!, 407
Our Time, 222

Ride of the Valkyries from *Die Walküre* by R. Wagner (listening), 413E
Siyahamba (We Are Marching), 309

UNIT 4 • Time. *Time is both the outline that frames our lives and the yardstick with which we measure them. Time is something that we can neither see nor feel, but it has a profound effect on our lives.*

1900s–1910s Medley (listening/playalong), 240
1920s Medley (listening/playalong), 244
1930s Medley (listening/playalong), 248
1940s Medley (listening/playalong), 253
1950s Medley (listening/playalong), 256
1960s Medley (listening/playalong), 162
1970s Medley (listening/playalong), 267
1980s Medley (listening/playalong), 272
Auld Lang Syne (American New Year song), 319
Away to America, 140
Bashana Haba'ah by N. Hirsh (Jewish New Year music) (listening), 318
Birthday by J. Lennon and P. McCartney (listening), 263
Bo Hai Huan Ten (Traditional Chinese New Year music) (listening), 313
Diwali Song (Indian New Year song), 315
Fly Like an Eagle, 265
Haiku Calendar (poem), 284
Haji Firuz (Iranian New Year song), 317
Keep the Circle Going 'Round, 420
Movin' On, 174
One Moment in Time, 49
Our Time, 222
Rock Around the Clock, 15
Sound Capsule: The 1900s and 1910s, A (recorded lesson), 238
Sound Capsule: The 1920s, A (recorded lesson), 243
Sound Capsule: The 1930s, A (recorded lesson), 247
Sound Capsule: The 1940s, A (recorded lesson), 251
Sound Capsule: The 1950s, A (recorded lesson), 255
Sound Capsule: The 1960s, A (recorded lesson), 259

Sound Capsule: The 1970s, A (recorded lesson), 265
Sound Capsule: The 1980s, A (recorded lesson), 271
Sound Capsule: The 1990s, A (recorded lesson), 275
There's Just So Much to Go Around, 416
Winter Poem (poem), 302

See also Unit 6: From Rag to Rap, 236–283

UNIT 5 • Belonging. *To be part of a community is one of the most basic human needs. Even if it's not a conventional family unit, everyone needs a place to fit in.*

American Dream, 151
American Hymn, An, 178
At the Moulin Rouge: The Dance (painting), 56
Away to America, 140
De Lanterna na Mão (With a Lantern in My Hand), 344
Family (painting), 311
Gianni Schicchi (opera selections) by G. Puccini (listening), 212–215
Gypsy Rover, The, 346
Harmony, 92
Jeunes filles au piano (painting), 91
Lean on Me, 126
One, 200
Voice from a Dream, A, 375
Walk Together Children, 31
Wind Beneath My Wings, The, 385

UNIT 6 • Challenges. *A moment of decision may lead to an act of great courage.*

Accentuate the Positive, 6
Day-O, 32
Earth Kids (musical), 414
Flying Free, 64
Gianni Schicchi (opera selections) by G. Puccini (listening), 212–215
I Have a Dream, 320
John B. Sails, 347
Joshua Fit the Battle of Jericho (song and listening), 58, 76
Starlight Express (musical theater selections) by R. Stilgoe and A. Lloyd Webber (listening), 204–211
Your World (poem), 47

$\mathcal{T}$HEMATIC CORRELATIONS TO READING SERIES

Harcourt Brace & Company: *Signatures* © 1997

The following materials from Share the Music may be used with each theme in Harcourt Brace's Signatures.

THEME 1

Accentuate the Positive, 6
American Dream, 151
Day-O, 32
Earth Kids (musical), 414
Flying Free, 64
I Have a Dream, 320
Joshua Fit the Battle of Jericho (song and listening), 58, 76
Lean on Me, 126
Shall I Dream a Dream?, 380
Starlight Express (musical theater selections) by R. Stilgoe and A. Lloyd Webber (listening), 204–211
Tekanionton'néha' (listening), 171
Voice from a Dream, A, 375

THEME 2

Anasazi cliff dwelling (architecture), 175
Bo Hai Huan Ten (listening), 313
Diwali Song, 315
Eka Tala (excerpt) (listening), 216
Prologue to *Mahabharata* (excerpt) (listening), 219
Whip Man (poem), 168

See also Encore: Carmina Burana, 42–45

THEME 3

Bashana Haba'ah by N. Hirsh (Jewish New Year music) (listening), 318
Blowin' in the Wind, 259
Bo Hai Huan Ten (Traditional Chinese New Year music) (listening), 313
Dance for the Nations, 150
De Colores (Many Colors), 328
Diwali Song (Indian New Year song), 315
From a Distance, 275
Garden of the Earth (song and listening), 324, 325
Haji Firuz (Iranian New Year song), 317
I Have a Dream, 320
Montage of Performance Styles (listening), 135
Velez, Glen (recorded interview), 89
Your World (poem), 47

See also Encore: Dances of Our World, 184–187

THEME 4

American Dream, 151
Away to America, 140
Earth Kids (musical), 414
Give My Regards to Broadway, 226
Greatest Love of All, The, 271
I Have a Dream, 320
O mio babbino caro from *Gianni Schicchi* by G. Puccini (listening), 215
One, 200

One Moment in Time, 49
Our Time, 222
Trav'ler, 147
Tsing Chun U Chü (Youth Dance Song), 156
Voice from a Dream, A, 375
Whip Man (poem), 168

THEME 5

Encore: Carmina Burana, 42–45
Encore: The Story of *Carmen,* 232–235
Unit 5, Lesson 6: Opera: A Grand Tradition, 212–215
Unit 5, Lesson 7: Theatrical Traditions, 216–221

See also Alphabetical Index of Listening Selections; Fine Art Reproductions and Architecture

THEME 6

American Hymn, An, 178
Amoeba by J. Ficksman (listening), 413K
Carol from an Irish Cabin, 307
Earth Day Every Day (Celebrate), 322
Earth Kids (musical), 414
Ecce gratum (excerpt) from *Carmina Burana* by C. Orff (listening), 44
Fussreise (Tramping), 357
Garden of the Earth (song and listening), 324, 325
Look Around, 192
Spring Gardening (painting), 324
Trav'ler, 147
Your World (poem), 47

THEMATIC CORRELATIONS TO READING SERIES

Houghton Mifflin Company: *Invitations to Literacy* © **1997**

The following materials from Share the Music may be used with each theme in Houghton Mifflin's Invitations to Literacy.

THEME 1

Anasazi cliff dwelling (architecture), 175
Blowin' in the Wind, 259
Carol from an Irish Cabin, 307
Earth Kids (musical), 414
Fly Like an Eagle, 265
Flying Free, 64
Lean on Me, 126
Movin' On, 174
One Moment in Time, 49
Tekanionton'néha' (listening), 171
Your World (poem), 47

THEME 2

Accentuate the Positive, 6
Flying Free, 64
Greatest Love of All, The, 271
I Believe in Music, 54
I Have a Dream, 320
I Shall Sing, 24
Lean on Me, 126
One Moment in Time, 49
Our Time, 222
Shall I Dream a Dream?, 380
Starlight Express (musical theater selections) by R. Stilgoe and A. Lloyd Webber (listening), 204–211

Tsing Chun U Chü (Youth Dance Song), 156
Voice from a Dream, A, 375
We Are the Music Makers (poem), 1

THEME 3

Anasazi cliff dwelling (architecture), 175
Bo Hai Huan Ten (listening), 313
Taos Round Dance (listening), 166
Tekanionton'néha' (listening), 171
Whip Man (poem), 168

See also Encore: Carmina Burana, 42–45

THEME 4

Amoeba by J. Ficksman (listening), 413K
Another Op'nin', Another Show, 191
Comedy Tonight, 198
Gianni Schicchi (opera selections) by G. Puccini (listening), 212–215
Lobster Quadrille, The, 390
Music for the World, 34
One, 200
Starlight Express (musical theater selections) by R. Stilgoe and A. Lloyd Webber (listening), 204–211
Tortoises from *The Carnival of the Animals* by C. Saint-Saëns (listening), 63
We Are the Music Makers (poem), 1
Winter Poem (poem), 302

See also Encore: Performance Technology, 280–283; Encore: The Story of *Carmen*, 232–235

THEME 5

At the Moulin Rouge: The Dance (painting), 56
De colores (Many Colors), 328
Family (painting), 311
From a Distance, 275
Garden of the Earth (song and listening), 324, 325
Harmony, 92
I Have a Dream, 320
Jeunes filles au piano (painting), 91
Lean on Me, 126
Walk Together Children, 30
We Are the Music Makers (poem), 1
Wind Beneath My Wings, The, 385
You Sing for Me, 26

THEME 6

Earth Day Every Day (Celebrate), 322
Earth Kids (musical), 414
Garden of the Earth (song and listening), 324, 325
Look Around, 192

THEMATIC CORRELATIONS TO READING SERIES

Scholastic: *Literacy Place* © 1996

The following materials from Share the Music may be used with each unit in Scholastic's Literacy Place.

UNIT 1

Donegan, Dorothy (recorded interview), 133
Greatest Love of All, The, 271
Hamlisch, Marvin (recorded interview), 202
I Have a Dream, 320
I Shall Sing, 24
Jarrett, Keith (recorded interview), 135
Jeunes filles au piano (painting), 91
John B. Sails, 347
Marsalis, Ellis (recorded interview), 114
Nobody Knows the Trouble I've Seen, 334
One, 200
One Moment in Time, 49
Salerno-Sonnenberg, Nadja (recorded interview), 411
Velez, Glen (recorded interview), 89
Warner, Malcolm-Jamal (recorded interview), 278
Wind Beneath My Wings, The, 362
Zwilich, Ellen Taaffe (recorded interview), 410

See also Encore: Jazz, 132–135; Encore: The Story of *Carmen,* 232–235

UNIT 2

Accentuate the Positive, 6
American Dream, 151
Earth Kids (musical), 414
Follow the Drinkin' Gourd, 370
Gianni Schicchi (opera selections) by G. Puccini (listening), 212–215
I Have a Dream, 320

Joshua Fit the Battle of Jericho, 58
Shall I Dream a Dream?, 380
Siyahamba (We Are Marching), 309
Starlight Express (musical theater selections) by R. Stilgoe and A. Lloyd Webber (listening), 204–211

UNIT 3

Another Op'nin,' Another Show, 191
Boatman, The, 332
Comedy Tonight, 198
Drill, Ye Tarriers, 363
Earth Kids (musical), 414
El zapatero (The Shoemaker), 404
Jeunes filles au piano (painting), 91
John B. Sails, 347
Light at the End of the Tunnel, The, from *Starlight Express* by R. Stilgoe and A. Lloyd Webber (listening), 210

UNIT 4

Earth Day Every Day (Celebrate), 322
Earth Kids (musical), 414
Garden of the Earth (song and listening), 324, 325
Lobster Quadrille, The, 390
Orion, 350
Winter Poem (poem), 302

UNIT 5

Boogie Woogie Bugle Boy, 251
I Have a Dream, 320

Joshua Fit the Battle of Jericho (song and listening), 58, 76
Sound Capsule: The 1900s and 1910s, A (recorded lesson), 238
Sound Capsule: The 1920s, A (recorded lesson), 243
Sound Capsule: The 1930s, A (recorded lesson), 247
Sound Capsule: The 1940s, A (recorded lesson), 251
Sound Capsule: The 1950s, A (recorded lesson), 255
Sound Capsule: The 1960s, A (recorded lesson), 259
Sound Capsule: The 1970s, A (recorded lesson), 265
Sound Capsule: The 1980s, A (recorded lesson), 271
Sound Capsule: The 1990s, A (recorded lesson), 275

UNIT 6

America, 287
American Dream, 151
American Hymn, An, 178
Away to America, 140
Battle Hymn of the Republic, 295
Hymn to Freedom, 104
I Have a Dream, 320
Love Letter to America (poem), 137
Star-Spangled Banner, The, 292

THEMATIC CORRELATIONS TO READING SERIES

Silver Burdett Ginn: *Literature Works* © 1997

The following materials from Share the Music *may be used with each theme in Silver Burdett's* Literature Works.

TEACHER'S NOTES

TEACHER'S NOTES

TEACHER'S NOTES

 # ALPHABETICAL INDEX

See the Classified Index for recorded Assessments, Recorded Interviews, Recorded Lessons, and Performance Mixes.